SEVENTH EDITION

RISK & INSURANCE

Mark R. Greene
Distinguished Professor of Risk Management and Insurance
College of Business Administration
The University of Georgia

James S. Trieschmann
Dudley L. Moore, Jr. Professor of Insurance and Associate Dean
College of Business Administration
The University of Georgia

F55
PUBLISHED BY
SOUTH-WESTERN PUBLISHING CO.
CINCINNATI   WEST CHICAGO, IL   CARROLLTON, TX   LIVERMORE, CA

PREFACE

Since the first edition of this text appeared in 1962, many important changes have occurred in the field of risk and insurance which were reflected in subsequent editions of 1968, 1973, 1977, 1981, and 1984. This seventh edition continues the task of presenting as modern and complete a picture of risk and insurance as possible.

New Organization

The seventh edition of *Risk and Insurance* has been extensively revised and reorganized to make the book an even more flexible teaching instrument. The first three parts (Chapters 1–8) maintain the treatment of common elements of risk and insurance that characterized previous editions.

Part 4 (Chapters 9–15) covers all kinds of insurance known as "personal." This includes life and health insurance, retirement plans, and other kinds of coverages usually offered as employee benefits. Estate planning and buying life insurance are covered in Chapters 14 and 15 (buying property insurance lines is covered separately in Part 5).

Parts 5 and 6 (Chapters 16–24) are devoted to property-liability coverages (homeowners, auto, and miscellaneous personal lines) and problems in buying property-liability insurance. Part 6 treats coverages unique to business risk management such as property, liability, workers' compensation, crime, and others. Chapter 24 covers quantitative applications to risk management, a subject formerly treated earlier in the text.

Part 7 (Chapters 25–26) deals with government insurance programs, including Social Security, and regulation of insurance. Part 8 reintroduces international insurance. This subject, first included in the third and fourth editions of this text (1973 and 1977 respectively) but omitted in the fifth and sixth editions, has been reinstated as a reflection of the continued and constantly increasing involvement of the United States in world business, with attending problems in risk management and insurance. It is also a reflection of the national movement in business education sponsored by the American Assembly of Collegiate Schools of Business to provide more and better education in international business subjects in accredited schools of business across the United States.

The seventh edition of *Risk and Insurance* has been improved in a number of other ways to help make it a more teachable and useful text. Statement of new terms and learning objectives are included for each chapter. The number of end-of-chapter questions has been reduced, and there is a separation of "questions for review" and "questions for discussion" at the end of each chapter. Each chapter now contains boxed materials taken from current literature which illustrates basic principles and practices in the insurance industry and in risk management.

The Glossary has been expanded considerably, the bibliography updated, and Best's analysis of insurance companies changed to reflect Best's new format for rating insurers. Finally, the appendix contains the latest editions of policy forms being used in auto, life, and homeowners insurance.

A fundamental concept has been retained in this text: to recognize that one book in risk and insurance is the maximum that most college students will ever study. Hence, nearly all fields of insurance have been covered, and problems caused by risk in our world have been emphasized before posing solutions. In this way it is hoped that analysis of insurance will be more meaningful to the student than would be possible by factual discussion of insurance contracts without any analysis of the problems that established the need for such contracts. Emphasis has also been placed on teaching how contracts may be analyzed so that students may apply this knowledge to new policies as they are developed.

The original goals in writing the book have been preserved: (1) to cover basic ideas, problems, and principles found in all types of modern insurance and other methods of handling risk; (2) to emphasize the fundamental unifying elements of risk and insurance; and (3) to stimulate thought about the problems of risk and insurance through questions at the end of the text that often cannot be answered by short, factual statements taken directly from text material.

Supplements Two supplementary publications accompany the text to enhance its usefulness as a learning device: (1) A separate study guide for use by the student has been revised by Dr. Trieschmann. (2) The instructor's manual has also been revised and expanded. For each chapter of the text, the manual contains:

1. a complete chapter outline
2. a listing of new terms and concepts
3. answers to the end-of-chapter questions
4. several supplementary questions not found in the text
5. true-false and multiple-choice questions

Several short cases with suggested solutions are also included.

Acknowledgments There are many who should be thanked for their kind assistance and inspiration to the authors in preparing the seventh edition.

First, we are very grateful to Dr. John H. Thornton of North Texas State University for his thorough review of the sixth edition. His suggestions for changes and improvements proved invaluable.

We are also grateful to the following individuals for their assistance in reviewing the original manuscript for the seventh edition:

Dr. Thomas L. Heflin
California State University—Sacramento
Dr. William M. Howard
University of Florida
Dr. Joe H. Murrey, Jr.
University of Mississippi

In addition, we appreciate those teachers who gave generously of their time in writing letters with helpful suggestions for changes and corrections in the book. We would like to especially thank Sandra G. Gustavson and Thomas A. Aiuppa. We think incorporation of these suggestions into the manuscript has improved the book in many ways. The result should make the material more meaningful to students in the quest for a scientific study of risk and insurance.

Finally, we would like to extend special thanks to Carol Corina and Ann Clark, who contributed generously of their time and effort with proofreading and other assistance.

Mark R. Greene and James S. Trieschmann
Athens, Georgia

CONTENTS

vii

PART 1

NATURE OF RISK AND RISK MANAGEMENT

1 CONCEPTS IN RISK AND INSURANCE

After studying this chapter, you should be able to:

1. Distinguish between risk and probability of loss.
2. Describe the difference between objective and subjective risk.
3. Explain the basic concept of probability and how it is expressed.
4. Explain how the law of large numbers works in reducing risk.
5. Identify the difference between hazards and perils.
6. Explain why speculative risks are generally not insured, as contrasted with pure risks, which are usually insurable.
7. List the five basic methods used in handling objective risk.
8. Describe how subjective risk attitudes can affect decision making in handling risk.

Risk, defined as uncertainty as to loss, poses a problem to individuals in nearly every walk of life. Students, householders, business people, employees, travelers, investors, and farmers all must face risk and develop ways to handle it. If a cost or a loss is certain to occur, it may be planned for in advance and treated as a definite, known expense. It is when there is uncertainty about the occurrence of a cost or loss that risk becomes an important problem. For example, if a merchant knows for sure that a certain amount of shoplifting will occur, this loss may be recovered by marking up all goods by some percentage. There is little or no risk involved unless actual shoplifting is greater than normal. The merchant is usually more concerned about the risk of abnormal losses than about normal or expected losses.

THE BURDEN OF RISK

To some people the idea of risk bearing and risk assumption is tantalizing, an element that makes life more interesting. They probably have in mind the uncertainty of making a profit or a gain, and not the uncertainty of incurring disastrous losses. In this book we will be dealing with the latter type of uncertainty. Recognizing that risk assumption carries with it the possibility of losses as well as gains, most individuals constantly seek ways to avoid the losses in as efficient a manner as possible without destroying the possibility of gain.

How does risk create an economic burden? It does so in several ways. First, risk may necessitate the setting aside of a reserve fund to meet losses if and when they do occur. Such a reserve fund, if it were not used for this purpose, could be employed in other ways, presumably at greater advantage than is offered by demand deposit or an investment at the often low interest rates that apply to investments readily convertible into cash.

Second, the existence of risk not only raises the cost to society of certain services, but may also deprive society altogether of services "too risky" to warrant the investment of savings. There is a shortage of "risk capital" in all nations because most investors prefer a significant degree of safety. Mark Twain epitomized this attitude when he commented that he was more interested in the return *of* his money than he was in the return *on* his money. In other words, the riskier the venture, the greater the return that must be promised to investors; hence the more costly that particular service is to society. And if risk is too great, the service may be withdrawn altogether.

As an illustration of how risk might discourage investments, consider the following proposition. You are invited to invest your life savings of $9,000 into a new invention. You weigh the chances for success and failure of the invention and decide that if the business is a success, your investment will be worth $100,000; otherwise you will lose your entire $9,000. Suppose you believe that there is a 10 percent chance of success. Would you take the risk? You may reason that since you have a 10 percent chance of obtaining $100,000, the fair value of the proposition is 10 percent of $100,000, or $10,000. Since you are asked to put up only $9,000, you might make the investment if it were not for risk. However, not many individuals would trade $9,000 in cash outlay for an uncertain investment whose "expected value" is $10,000. They would probably seek better odds for success, or higher rewards. Hence, risk may hamper many new ventures whose chances for success are often lower than 10 percent.

Another example will illustrate the burden of risk in society. A member of the American Medical Society once commented that without malpractice insurance many physicians would refuse to practice medicine. The comment arose from publicity given to reports that many insurers planned to withdraw malpractice coverage from the market because of heavy losses and inadequate rates. Thus, the inability to transfer risk to others threatened the reduction of vital medical services because physicians perceived risk of loss by legal suits from patients on the medical treatment they had received.

Most people try to avoid risk as much as possible or to reduce its negative consequences. Unfortunately, not all risk can be minimized or avoided. To maximize our insulation from the adverse effects of risk, we must study the subject scientifically, learn more about the specific nature of the different types of risk, and find ways to deal with risk more effectively.

RISK DEFINED

Earlier, we defined risk as uncertainty as to loss. However, *risk* is used in many different ways. It can refer to general uncertainty, doubt, an insured object, or chance of loss. In this book risk is defined in two ways: objectively and subjectively. **Objective risk,** or **statistical risk,** applicable mainly to groups of objects exposed to loss, refers to the variation that occurs when actual losses differ from expected losses. It may be measured statistically by some concept in variation, such as the range or the standard deviation. **Subjective risk,** on the other hand, refers to the mental state of an individual who experiences doubt or worry as to the outcome of a given event. Both definitions of risk are concerned with events that may or may not produce economic loss or an involuntary parting of value.

The economic loss can take the form of loss of property by physical perils such as fire, tornado, or explosion. It can take the form of premature death of a key person in a business enterprise or of a family breadwinner. It can result from a lawsuit to recover damages for some negligent act. Whatever its form, the risk of economic loss is something most people wish to avoid. As a result, it becomes especially important to have a clear understanding of its nature.

Objective Risk

Objective risk, then, may be defined as the relative variation of actual from probable or expected loss and may be expressed as a percentage. In dealing with objective risk, we are concerned mainly with the range of variability of economic losses about some long-run average (most probable) loss in a group large enough to analyze significantly in a statistical sense. Assume, in Example I (see below), that an insurer observes that in a group of 100,000 houses there are on the average 100 losses from fire each year. The insurer is naturally concerned with the problem of whether the actual number of losses experienced will be exactly 100, or some other number, such as 95 or 105. If the insurer can be 95 percent sure that the range will not exceed the bounds of 95–105, one rate may be quoted to the insurance buyer. Now assume in Example II that another insurer is 95 percent confident that the range of losses is likely to be 80–120. Then, in Example II, a higher rate may be quoted because the objective risk is higher. The probable variation of actual losses from the average or probable loss—that is, the range—is one measure of objective risk of the insurer. It may be expressed as follows:

$$\text{Objective Risk} = \frac{\text{Probable Variations of Actual}}{\text{Probable Losses}}$$

In the preceding formula, we have used the term "probable losses." The probable losses are those that are most likely to occur—i.e., 100 losses from fire each year. The range of losses, as indicated above, is assumed to be 95–105, in Example I, and 80–120 in Example II. The objective risk in the formula then becomes

$$\text{Example I:} \quad \frac{105 - 95}{100} = 10 \text{ percent}$$

$$\text{Example II:} \quad \frac{120 - 80}{100} = 40 \text{ percent}$$

Thus, the objective risk in Example II is four times that of Example I. The insurer's premium rate will accordingly be higher in Example II than in Example I, even though in the long run the average annual losses are 100, the same in both instances. Insurers demand extra payment for bearing the risk that losses could be as high as 120 in a given year (Example II) rather than 105 (Example I).

Subjective Risk

A subjective risk is defined as a psychological uncertainty that stems from the individual's mental attitude or state of mind.[1]

The concept of subjective risk is important because it gives us a way to interpret the behavior of individuals faced with seemingly identical situations, yet arriving at different decisions. For example, one person may be ultraconservative and tend always to take the "safe way" out, even in cases which may seem quite risk-free to other decision makers. Objective risk may actually be the same in two cases, yet be viewed very differently by those examining this risk from their own perspectives. For example, one risk manager may determine that some given level of risk is "high" while another may interpret this same level as "low." These different interpretations depend on the subjective attitudes of the decision makers toward risk. Thus, it is not enough to know only the degree of objective risk; the risk attitude of the decision maker who will act on the basis of this knowledge must also be known. A person who knows that there is only one chance in a million that a loss will occur may still experience worry and doubt, and thus would buy insurance, while another would not. One can appreciate the importance of studying subjective risk by studying several examples illustrating different mental attitudes toward risk in different situations.

Banker *A* refuses a loan proposition that Banker *B* accepts easily and under equivalent conditions. Student *B* graduates and accepts a position paying a low initial salary but offering an opportunity for a large income for a few who succeed in the company; Student *A* graduates and accepts a position paying a higher and more secure salary than *B*'s position pays, but under conditions limiting the opportunities for advancement. Business *A* insures the plant against fire even though the premium may be very high, while Business *B*, a neighbor operating under similar conditions, refuses the insurance.

In these examples, *A* can be described as apparently perceiving a higher degree of risk in the given situation and behaving more conservatively than *B*.[2] *A* tends to be a risk averter, and *B* a risk taker.

Various studies have been made to learn more about the factors that influence subjective risk. The change in individual decisions regarding risk as a result of exposure to group discussion is the subject of a large body of psychological literature.[3] In general, psychologists have demonstrated that the decision maker tends to assume more risk after group discussion than before. It has been shown that age and sex influence risk attitudes, with women being more conservative than men and older people being more conservative than young people.[4] It has also been shown that there is a tendency for people to overestimate low likelihoods and underestimate high likelihoods.[5] Thus, due to mental attitude toward risk, a poker player might disregard extremely low probabilities of success and take gambles unwarranted by the size of the pot. Similarly, a person facing a substantial probability of loss of an automobile through collision might refuse insurance. Try the simple test in Figure 1–1 to learn more about your own attitudes toward risk.

DEGREE OF RISK

What is meant by a high degree of risk or a low degree of risk? The answer depends on whether we are speaking of subjective risk or objective risk. A high degree of subjective risk exists when a person experiences great mental uncertainty as to the frequency of occurrence of some event that may cause a loss, and as to the amount or severity of this possible loss. Generally, high subjective risk produces very conservative conduct and low subjective risk tends to produce less conservative conduct.

Objective risk, on the other hand, varies according to the ratio of probable variation of actual from probable loss. If a loss has already occurred, the probable variation is zero and thus objective risk is also zero. Similarly, if it is impossible for the loss to happen, the probable variation is zero and the objective risk is still zero.

Part 1   Nature of Risk and Risk Management

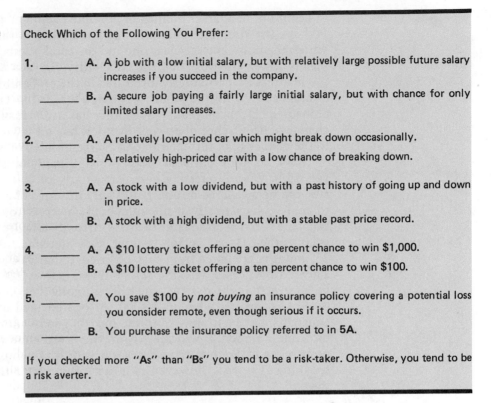

Check Which of the Following You Prefer:

1. _____ A. A job with a low initial salary, but with relatively large possible future salary increases if you succeed in the company.

_____ B. A secure job paying a fairly large initial salary, but with chance for only limited salary increases.

2. _____ A. A relatively low-priced car which might break down occasionally.

_____ B. A relatively high-priced car with a low chance of breaking down.

3. _____ A. A stock with a low dividend, but with a past history of going up and down in price.

_____ B. A stock with a high dividend, but with a stable past price record.

4. _____ A. A $10 lottery ticket offering a one percent chance to win $1,000.

_____ B. A $10 lottery ticket offering a ten percent chance to win $100.

5. _____ A. You save $100 by *not buying* an insurance policy covering a potential loss you consider remote, even though serious if it occurs.

_____ B. You purchase the insurance policy referred to in **5A.**

If you checked more "As" than "Bs" you tend to be a risk-taker. Otherwise, you tend to be a risk averter.

For example, assume that Jack Smith goes into his basement one morning and smells smoke. His house is on fire. He realizes suddenly that he has not purchased fire insurance, so right after phoning the fire department he phones his insurance agent and says, "Cover me." The agent says, "Sorry, Jack, we can't insure a burning building." Did the agent refuse because the risk was too high? Not at all. In this case there is no risk at all, for there is no uncertainty as to loss. The loss has already occurred. The agent cannot bind the insurer in such a situation. As obvious as this example may seem, there are many similar cases each year where individuals seek insurance on an event that is almost certain to cause loss. They fail to recognize that risk must be dealt with in advance of the event, when the loss is still unknown and uncertain.

RISK VERSUS PROBABILITY

It is necessary to distinguish carefully between risk and probability. Many elementary mistakes in risk management occur because of failure to recognize the difference between these two concepts. **Probability** refers to the long-run chance of occurrence, or relative frequency of some event. Probability is expressed as a ratio of the number of events which are likely to occur out of a larger number of possible events in a given group or set. Perhaps the simplest illustration of probability is that of a coin flip, in which the number of heads is one and the total number of possible events (heads or tails) is two. Thus, the probability of heads is $\frac{1}{2}$, or 50 percent.

Insurers are particularly interested in the probability or chance of loss, or more accurately, the probability that a loss will occur to one of a group of insured objects. Actually, probability has little meaning if applied to the chance of occurrence of a single event. It has meaning only when applied to the chance of occurrence among a large number of events.

Risk, as differentiated from probability, is a concept in relative variation. We are referring here particularly to objective risk. Objective risk can be measured meaningfully only in terms of a group large enough to analyze statistically. If the number of objects is too small, the range of probable variation is so large that it is virtually infinite as far as the insurer is concerned. It may be, for example, that there are 1,000,000 persons age 25, and it is predicted from past experience that 3,000 of them will die in a given time period. The *probability* of loss is thus 0.003. Mary Smith may be interested in the risk that she will be among the 3,000 who are supposed to die. An insurer who has 10,000 persons covered under life insurance contracts may be interested in the *risk* that some number other than the probable number 30 will die within the given time period. Clearly, the probability of death is the same, no matter from whose viewpoint one is speaking. The risk, however, is quite different for the insurer and the insured.

The Law of Large Numbers

The reason that the risk is different is understood, almost intuitively, by recognizing that the law of large numbers is operating in the case of the insurer, but not in the case of the individual insured. The **law of large numbers,** a basic law of mathematics, states that as the number of exposure units increases, the more certain it is that actual loss experience will equal probable loss experience. Hence, the objective risk diminishes as the number of exposure units increases. The individual seldom has a sufficient number of exposure units to reduce objective risk significantly through the operation of the law of large numbers. This individual may join with others, however, and obtain this advantage. The insurance mechanism is the device through which such grouping can be effectively accomplished.

Probability Distributions

Probability is most often studied through the concept of a **probability distribution.** Suppose a manufacturer studies loss-producing work accidents in the plant for 60 months and discovers the following:

Part 1   Nature of Risk and Risk Management

(1) Number of Losses	(2) Frequency (Months)	Amount of Loss (1) × (2)
0	10	0
1	40	40
2	10	20
Expected Value (Total)	60	60

The table reveals that 60 losses occurred, a number called the "expected value" of the loss. This number is obtained by multiplying the frequency of loss (Col. 1) by the amount of loss (Col. 2) in each category, and taking a total. The table is known as a probability distribution because it shows the likelihood of occurrence of different numbers of events (losses, in this case).

The table reveals that there were 60 accidents in 60 months, an average of one per month. But they did not occur evenly. For example, in 10 months no accidents at all occurred, and in each of 10 other months, two occurred. The data illustrate a simple probability distribution. They not only tell the total loss, but also expose the variation in losses that occurred. This variation can be measured statistically by calculating the standard deviation. (See Chapter 24 for an explanation of standard deviation.)

OBJECTIVE RISK AND THE LAW OF LARGE NUMBERS

The law of large numbers has great practical value to an insurer, who can reduce objective risk to the vanishing point in some cases by securing an ever-larger number of units in the insured group.

Effect of Numbers Exposed on Objective Risk

To illustrate the effect of the number exposed on objective risk, assume that an insurer has only 100 automobiles in an insured group and that the probability of collision loss is 0.20 per year, i.e., the insurer can expect 20 collisions per year. However, with only 100 autos, the variation from the average may be quite large. In fact, under certain mathematical assumptions, there is a chance of about 1 in 3 that the number of collisions will exceed the average by 4, and in 5 percent of the cases the number of collisions will exceed the average by 8. A variation of 8 from the average number 20 is 40 percent $(\frac{8}{20})$. The insurer may not wish to accept this much risk. However, if the number of insured autos is increased to 900, there would be only a 5 percent chance that actual losses would exceed the average losses by as much as 24. Since for 900 autos the average losses would be 180, a variation of 24 amounts to a 13.3 percent variation, or one-third of the variation experienced with 100 autos. The results may be summarized as shown on page 10.

Probability of collision loss $= 20\%$

$$\text{Objective Risk} = \frac{\begin{array}{c}\text{Probable Variation of Actual}\\ \text{from Probable Losses}\end{array}}{\text{Probable Losses}}$$

$$\underline{\text{100 autos}} \qquad \underline{\text{900 autos}}$$
$$\frac{8}{20} = 40\% \qquad \frac{24}{180} = 13\tfrac{1}{3}\%$$

By increasing the number in the insured group nine times, the risk was reduced to a third of its former level. This illustrates a fundamental point: under given mathematical assumptions, other factors remaining the same, *objective risk varies inversely with the square root of the number of exposures.* In the foregoing case, the square root of the number of exposure units increased from 10 in the first case to 30 in the second case (three times), while risk declined to one-third of its former level.

Effect of Probability on Objective Risk

In the previous example it was assumed that the underlying probability of loss did not change. We may now inquire what would happen to objective risk if the probability of loss is varied, but the number of exposure units remains the same.

At first glance it appears that the higher the probability, the higher the risk. However, this is not the case. Rather, the opposite is true because as probability increases, the *variation* of average losses from probable losses tends to decrease, assuming a constant number of insured exposure units. We know that as a loss becomes more and more certain to happen, there is less and less uncertainty (i.e., less risk), that it will not happen. If a point is finally reached where an event is bound to happen, there is no risk at all.

To illustrate, assume that employers A and B, each with 10,000 employees, desire to insure themselves against occupational injuries to workers. Employer A is in a "safe" occupation, and the probability of a disabling injury in A's plant is 0.01. Employer B is in a "dangerous" occupation, and the probability of a disabling injury in B's plant is 0.25. In the long run, Employer A may expect 100 disabling injuries per year, compared with 2,500 for Employer B. There is about a 95 percent chance that the probable variation in injuries in A's plant will not exceed 20, while in B's plant the probable variation will not exceed 87. Thus, objective risk in A's situation is $\frac{20}{100}$ or 20 percent, compared with $\frac{87}{2,500}$ or 3.5 percent for B. Although B's objective risk is only about 17 percent ($\frac{3.5}{20} = 0.175$) of A's objective risk, B's probability of loss is much larger. The principle thus emerges: *Objective risk varies inversely with the probability for any constant number of exposure units.* This law is a corollary of the law of large numbers, noted earlier.

The preceding result may be understood intuitively by taking another example. Suppose Employer A improves conditions so much that injuries are extremely infrequent, while Employer *B* lets conditions decline so much that many injuries occur almost daily. In *B*'s case, the insurer can more easily predict losses than would be true in *A*'s case, where injuries are quite infrequent. The greater the level of loss predictability, the easier it is to forecast losses and the cost of insurance. The *objective risk* for *B* would be considered quite low. For *A*, however, when a loss does occur, it may be so unusual that it produces much surprise. Here the objective risk is high.

We may now summarize the two most important applications of the law of large numbers as it affects objective risk:

1. As the number of exposure units increases in an insured group, objective risk decreases. Specifically, objective risk varies inversely with the square root of the number of exposure units, other things remaining the same.
2. Give a constant number of exposure units, as the probability of loss increases, objective risk decreases. In general, the rate of decrease in objective risk is less than proportionate to the rate of increase in probability of loss.

The Insurer's Risk

From this analysis you might erroneously conclude that an insurer would always charge a lower premium as the probability of loss rose, because of the reduced risk. Such, of course, is not the case. Basically, it is the probability of loss that governs the amount of premium charged in a given situation. However, if an insurer had so few in an insured group that it would not be possible to determine just what the losses might be—i.e., objective risk was high—the insurer would tend to assume the worst and charge for coverage based on the worst possible result. In effect, the insurer charges both for risk and for expected losses. In the event that the insurer is able to attract a sufficiently large group of insureds, thus reducing or eliminating objective risk, the charge for risk greatly diminishes.

BURDENS OF RISK

One of the burdens of risk was reported in *Inc.* magazine in 1985 as follows: "Many small businesses have been forced to 'go bare' (do without insurance) because of skyrocketing premiums or lack of capacity." The following questions then arise: How many small firms will be forced out of business due to their inability to run the risk? Why is this happening? Who is better able to run the risk, the insurer or the small business? Is uninsurable risk hurting the growth of our economy?

Frequently an insurer is asked to offer coverage on a single exposure unit. In such an event the law of large numbers is of no help to the insurer, who must rely on personal judgment and quote a rate based on subjective attitudes toward the risk. In such a situation, the risk may properly be termed subjective risk.

In practice, the insurer's risk is reduced considerably because of the operation of the **central limit theorem,** of which the law of large numbers is a special case. Under the central limit theorem, the insurer's losses of a given kind may be viewed as samples taken from a larger universe of losses. The means of these samples are distributed "normally" (see Chapter 24 for a discussion of the normal distribution). Here the variations from average may be stated with known degrees of confidence. Thus, the insurer may be able to predict losses within a known range. The relative size of the range is the insurer's measure of objective risk.

HAZARDS AND PERILS

Many persons commonly employ the terms "risky," "hazardous," and "perilous" synonymously. For clarity in thinking, however, the meanings of these words should be carefully distinguished.

A **peril** may be defined as a contingency that may cause a loss, and a **hazard** as the condition that introduces or increases the probability of loss from a peril. Both of these terms are more closely related to probability than they are to risk. For example, one of the perils that can cause loss to an auto is collision. A condition that makes the occurrence of collisions more likely is an icy street. The icy street is the hazard and the collision is the peril. In winter the *probability* of collisions is higher owing to the existence of icy streets. In such a situation, the *risk* of loss is not necessarily any higher or lower, since we have defined risk as the uncertainty that the underlying probability will work out in practice.

Our definition of hazard might also be expanded to include conditions that make the loss more severe, once the peril has been realized and has caused a loss. What are the various types of hazards that not only increase the probability of loss, but also increase the severity of loss once it occurs? There are three basic types of hazards: physical, moral, and morale.

Physical Hazard

A **physical hazard** is a condition stemming from the physical characteristics of an object that increases the probability and severity of loss from given perils. Physical hazards include such phenomena as the existence of dry forests (hazard for fire), earth faults (hazard for earthquakes), and icebergs (hazard to ocean shipping). Such hazards may or may not be within human control. For example, some hazards for fire can be controlled by placing restrictions on building camp fires in forests during the dry season. Some hazards, however, cannot be controlled—little can be done to prevent or control air masses that produce ocean storms.

Moral Hazard

A **moral hazard** stems from the mental attitude of the insured. Because of indifference to loss or owing to an outright desire for the loss to occur, the individual either brings about personal loss or intentionally does nothing to prevent its occurrence or to alleviate its severity.

Moral hazards are typified by individuals with known records of dishonesty or indifference. Moral hazards may exist in situations where excessive amounts of fire insurance are requested on "white elephant" properties (properties that are no longer profitable), where an incentive might exist to "sell the building to the fire insurance company." Every underwriter knows that fire losses are more frequent in depression periods. During the depression of the 1930s, life insurers had such a substantial rise in the frequency of claims for disability income that the coverage had to be withdrawn almost completely.

Morale Hazard

Even though an individual does not consciously want a loss, there may be a subconscious desire for a loss. The **morale hazard** includes the mental attitude that characterizes an accident-prone person. This type of individual does not appear to deliberately cause the accidents that happen, but the psychologist would probably diagnose the cause of excessive and repeated accidents as a subconscious problem of morale.

Adverse Selection

There is a tendency for those who are in a position to have a loss and who need protection against it to be the only ones in a larger group who apply for protection. Insurance underwriters are trained to recognize such situations; they refer to them as **adverse selection** or **antiselection.** Thus, those in the low areas of flood zones may be the only applicants for flood insurance. Among applicants for group health insurance, there is a tendency for those in poor health to be overly represented in the group. Those applying for life annuities are more likely to have histories of long life in their families; those whose parents died early may be more likely to seek life insurance.

Adverse selection tends to make some lines of insurance unavailable or very restrictive. An example is crime insurance (see Chapter 22), where applicants for coverage tend to be especially subject to physical hazards (high-crime neighborhoods), and to moral and morale hazards. Crime insurance is offered subject to careful scrutiny by the underwriter, and usually requires extensive loss-control measures by the insured.

STATIC VERSUS DYNAMIC RISKS

Static risks are risks stemming from a level, unchanging society that is in stable equilibrium. Examples include the uncertainties due to random events such as fire, windstorm, or death. **Dynamic risks** are risks produced because of changes in society. Examples of sources of dynamic risk include urban unrest, increasingly complex technology, concentration of property with huge values in urban industrial plants, and greater legal liability due to changing attitudes of courts. The two types of risk are not independent, for greater dynamic risks have increased the level of static risk. Insurance on static risk is expensive and often unobtainable in some neighborhoods.

PURE RISK VERSUS SPECULATIVE RISK

A distinction can be made between pure risk and speculative risk to further clarify the nature of risk.[6] In **pure risk** there is uncertainty as to whether the destruction of an object will occur; a pure risk can only produce loss, should the peril occur. Examples of pure risk include the uncertainty of loss of one's property by fire, flood, windstorm, or other peril, or the uncertainty of total disability caused by accident or illness. In **speculative risk,** there is uncertainty about an event under consideration that could produce either a profit or a loss, such as a business venture or a gambling transaction. The distinction is significant because usually the pure risk is insurable, while the speculative risk is normally handled by methods other than insurance, such as diversification or assumption of risk (see Chapter 3).

Pure risks may be further classified according to the major types of economic losses or perils they concern. Two major types of such losses exist: personal and property. **Personal losses** include all those directly affecting an individual's life or health. Examples include loss of life, hospitalization expense, loss of income due to disability, and medical expenses. **Property losses** include all those directly affecting an individual's property or monetary assets. Examples include fire, flood, windstorm, and liability for negligent conduct.

Speculative risks may be illustrated by price risks. A **price risk** is the risk that a price may decline before an inventory can be sold at a reasonable profit. If an insurer agreed to cover a merchant seeking protection against price decline, the insurer would, in effect, become a business partner with the insured and would be asked to assume serious risks at a set price, but without the corresponding opportunity to share in the profits if there should be any. Without an intimate knowledge of the business, the insurer would have little basis on which to make probability estimates of the expected gain or loss. Normally the insurer would have no opportunity to obtain the required knowledge for self-protection. For these and other reasons, specialized ways of handling speculative risks other than through insurance have been developed.

MANAGING OBJECTIVE RISK

Individuals cannot reduce their objective risk unless they control a large enough number of exposure units. Obviously most people cannot meet this condition. After all, each has but one life. Most people own just one house; and even if two or three autos are owned, this is too small a number to allow the law of large numbers to work.

14   Part 1   Nature of Risk and Risk Management

The question arises, then, "What alternatives are there for handling objective risk?" For convenience, the ways of handling risk may be grouped under the following headings:

1. Assuming the risk (risk retention)
2. Combining the objects subject to risk into a large enough group to enable accurate prediction of loss (this method includes the insurance mechanism); diversification, a method similar to combining risks, is discussed in Chapter 3.
3. Transferring or shifting the risk to some other individual
4. Utilizing loss-control activities
5. Avoidance of the risk

Risk Assumption or Retention

Risk assumption (also called **risk retention**) is perhaps the most widely used of all ways to handle risk. Risk retention may be planned or unplanned. **Planned risk retention,** often called **self-insurance,** is conscious and deliberate assumption of recognized risk. The individual or firm decides to pay losses out of currently available funds. In some cases a reserve or "rainy day" fund may be established to cover expected losses.

Some persons erroneously assume that establishing a reserve fund is equal to insurance against losses. There is an important difference. If a person saves $10,000 in the bank to pay for a hospital bill, this person has no way of knowing whether or not this fund is adequate. A single period of hospitalization could easily exhaust the savings, and a second period of hospitalization might occur before the savings could be restored. Thus, the risk of loss of savings due to illness requiring hospitalization has not actually been reduced. However, a properly drawn insurance plan, in which the risk of loss is effectively transferred to another, will take care of an indefinite number of hospitalizations.

Unplanned risk retention exists when a person does not recognize that a risk exists and unwittingly believes that no loss could occur. Such a "method" does not deserve to be called a risk management device. It stems from ignorance of risk.

Combination of Objects Subject to Risk

The method of **combination** is the system of handling risk that usually involves the use of large numbers. As pointed out previously, when sufficiently large numbers are grouped together, the actual loss experience over a period of time will closely approximate the probable loss experience. To the extent that this is true, risk has been greatly reduced or even eliminated for all concerned.

Early Chinese merchants were masters at using the combination method of reducing risk. They took periodic trips inland to gather merchantable products for sale on the coast. In travelling down the Yangtze River, the merchants would gather above the rapids and redistribute their cargoes so that each boat had a small portion of the other merchants' cargo aboard. Thus, if one boat were lost in the rapids, no one merchant would have suffered a total loss.

Commercial insurance companies utilize the combination method as the basis of their insuring operations. These companies simply persuade a large number of individuals, known as **insureds** or **assureds,** to pool their individual risks in a large group, and reduce or eliminate their risks. Under ideal conditions the insurer has little or no objective risk, due to the predictability of losses arising from the law of large numbers. When all of the individual objects are pooled into one group, the risk is no longer present, providing certain other requirements are met. This process may be compared to an alliance of a group of nations to ward off an attack. Individually, each nation may have substantial risk, but in a group the risk to each is reduced.

A commercial insurer is not the only social or economic institution that can employ the combination method of handling risk. Large business organizations often have a sufficiently large group of insurable objects so that they can accurately predict loss experience. For example, a firm may make a study of automobile collision losses to determine for a given period of time just what losses may be expected from a large fleet of autos owned by the concern. From these data the firm makes careful estimates of the funds needed to meet these losses and lays aside funds for this purpose. It does this with relative certainty that, within narrow limits, the fund so set up will actually equal the losses to be suffered. This method of handling risk is really planned retention or self-insurance, as noted above.

The method of combination also has been used to meet various types of uninsurable risks, such as the risk of losing one's markets due to product obsolescence, or of loss due to labor strikes or actions of competitors. (See Chapter 2 for further discussion.) The wave of business mergers in recent years has been attributed in part to the desire to reduce such market risk. Thus, two or more firms may combine into one for the purpose of securing a more diversified product line, so that in the event the sale of one product is unprofitable, another might compensate for it. The uncertainty of loss from one unprofitable line is thus reduced.

Risk Transfer or Shifting

In the **transfer,** or **shifting,** method, one individual pays another to assume a risk that the transferor desires to escape. The risk bearer agrees to assume the risk for a price. The risk of loss is often the same to the transferee as it was to the transferor. The risk bearer (transferee), however, may have superior knowledge concerning the probability of loss, and thus may be in a better financial position to assume the risk than the transferor. Nevertheless, the risk still exists.

It is easy to confuse the transfer method of handling risk with the combination method. The essential difference between the two lies in the fact that in the transfer method the risk is not necessarily reduced or eliminated, whereas in the combination method the risk is actually greatly reduced or perhaps completely eliminated.

Examples of risk transfer are found in many phases of business activity. A furniture retailer may not wish to stock large quanities of furniture for fear that prices may fall before the stock can be sold, or that the stock will be unsalable due to style changes. The retailer therefore buys only limited quanities of goods at a time, thus forcing a wholesaler to carry sufficient inventories to meet demand. The wholesaler in this case is the bearer of risk of loss due to price changes. The risk of loss is not necessarily reduced to the wholesaler. Such risk of loss must ultimately be charged for in the form of higher prices than would prevail if the retailer bought in large quantities. The wholesaler may in turn attempt to shift the risk to the manufacturer.

Insurance companies often operate as transferees of risk instead of using the combination method, simply because it is impossible to obtain a sufficiently large number of exposure units to allow the law of large numbers to operate. If Lloyd's of London accepts an insurance contract covering the loss of the hands of a famous pianist, it is acting in the capacity of a risk transferee, not as an agent to pool the risks of large numbers of pianists. In commercial insurance operations it is often difficult to tell just where the combination method ends and the transfer method begins, for there are many instances in which an insurance concern has an insufficient number of exposure units to obtain extremely accurate predictions of loss experience. To the extent that the loss cannot be predicted accurately, the insurance company owners act as transferees. Again, the risk is not necessarily reduced.

Other examples of the transfer method of handling risk are bankruptcy and leasing. A person or a business may voluntarily enter bankruptcy, thus shifting to creditors the losses that might otherwise be borne by the bankrupt person. A person who leases or rents property rather than owns it shifts to the lessor the ownership risk. The cost of shifting the risk is contained in the rental payments, which must be high enough to compensate the lessor for the risks as well as the costs of owning the property.

Loss Control

It is sometimes erroneously believed that loss control or loss prevention is "good insurance." Loss prevention is not insurance, but it does usually reduce the degree of subjective risk. Thus, people may worry less when they are riding in a large automobile, which is considered less susceptible to crushing during a collision. However, loss prevention may actually increase the degree of objective risk because it may reduce the probability of loss. The less probable an event is, the greater the relative dispersion of actual loss to expected loss. Even though the probable losses are reduced, risk may yet be present since there is still the possibility that there may be substantial deviations from the underlying probability. Loss control activities are discussed further in Chapter 2.

Risk Avoidance

Closely related to loss control is the method of **avoidance** of the possibility of loss in the first place, thus avoiding risk. The method of avoidance is widely used, particularly by those with a high aversion toward risk. Thus, a person may not enter a certain business at all, and avoid the risk of losing capital in that business. A person may not use airplanes and thus avoid the risk of dying in an airplane crash. Insurance companies may avoid underwriting a certain line of insurance, and thus avoid the risk of loss in that line.

MANAGING SUBJECTIVE RISK

The preceding discussion of ways of managing risk refers mainly to objective risk. What about ways of handling problems created by high levels of subjective risk? Each individual is faced with psychological uncertainty in dealing with risks (1) which can be insured or otherwise reduced or transferred by the methods outlined above, and (2) which cannot be insured or otherwise handled by formal methods. Even insurance companies are faced with underwriting decisions in which the law of large numbers is of no particular assistance, due to an inadequate number of exposed objects. In this case, the insurer must also deal with subjective risk.

There are at least three possible ways to deal with problems raised by the existence of subjective risk: through more information, group discussion, and training and education.

Search for Information

Perhaps the major way of handling subjective risk is by adding knowledge through research. A risk-averting person may be more willing to accept risk once there is a better understanding of the uncertainties, because with better knowledge one is likely to perceive less risk in the situation. A risk-taking person may be willing to assume even greater risks as his knowledge increases.

As insurers gain more experience in a given line, they very often become willing to insure risks they formerly rejected—and at reduced premiums. An example is the area of nuclear explosion, formerly uninsurable and now insurable by private insurers through pooling arrangements because of an enlarged body of knowledge and experience in the field. Lack of knowledge can produce worry and fear in the insurance buyer whose subjective risk and willingness to pay a high price for coverage are thereby heightened. At the same time, the insurer whose knowledge is greater is generally willing to accept the risk and is able to charge a higher premium because of the high subjective risk in the mind of the insurance buyer.

Part 1   Nature of Risk and Risk Management

Group Discussion

Research has established that perceived subjective risk declines after group discussion of the problem.[7] This suggests that an effective way to reduce perceived risk is to set up discussion groups, committees, or seminars to air problems, issues, and potential solutions before decisions are made. In this way, bolder and quicker action may result. Management indecision may be reduced. A practical outcome may be to relieve the burden of risk (see earlier) to a considerable extent. For example, underwriting a committee discussion may produce more liberal underwriting with less perceived risk by the insurer.

Training and Education

Closely related to the other methods discussed above is that of using training and education as a way to relieve the burden of subjective risk. Education in risk and insurance may improve the efficiency with which insurance is employed by making the user a more sophisticated buyer. For example, when the buyer really understands sound principles of insurance, premium dollars are more likely to be spent to cover serious loss exposures before minor loss exposures. However, research suggests that the opposite is often the case.

For example, in a laboratory study it was demonstrated that untrained subjects preferred to buy more insurance against events having a high probability of inflicting a relatively small loss and less against low-probability/high-loss events.[8] Thus, more subjects preferred to insure an event with a 25 percent chance of causing a loss of $1,980 than an event with a 0.2 percent chance of causing a loss of $247,000.

In conclusion, reduction of subjective risk may be at least as important as reduction of objective risk. However, much more study needs to be undertaken on such topics as the effect of risk attitudes on risk-taking behavior, how subjective risk should be measured, and better ways of handling problems created by subjective risk.[9]

SUMMARY

1. Risk is defined as the uncertainty as to the occurrence of an event.
2. Objective risk is defined as the relative variation of actual from probable loss.
3. Subjective risk is defined as that type of psychological uncertainty that stems from individual mental attitudes or states of mind.
4. Probability is the long-run chance of occurrence, or relative frequency, of some event.
5. Other things being constant, objective risk varies inversely with the square root of the number of objects in the group. Objective risk also varies inversely with the probability of loss, given a constant number of objects.
6. Risk may be classified as pure or speculative and as static or dynamic. Risk is differentiated from the concepts of perils and hazards.

7. Since risk imposes an economic burden on society and on individuals, it becomes important to develop ways of handling risk in a scientific manner.
8. Risk may be handled in several ways: by assumption, by combination, by transfer, by loss-control activities, and by avoidance. Insurance is primarily an example of the combination method, but insurance companies use the other methods as well.
9. Subjective risk perceptions may be affected by information research, group discussion, and education and training.

QUESTIONS FOR REVIEW

1. Define risk. How does it differ from probability?
2. Give an example of "the burden" of risk.
3. Differentiate between objective and subjective risk.
4. State the law of large numbers. How do insurers use this law?
5. If fire is the peril, give an example of an associated moral or physical hazard to fire.
6. Differentiate static from dynamic risk.
7. List the major ways of handling risk.
8. What type of hazard is illustrated in each of the following situations?
   (a) An accident-prone driver
   (b) A known embezzler applying for a job as cashier
   (c) The owner of several lumber mills that have burned over the years precisely when lumber prices declined sharply
   (d) A teenage driver
   (e) A tinder-dry forest
   (f) A retail liquor dealer in a high-crime neighborhood
   (g) A northern shipping route in winter
9. (a) Differentiate between pure risk and speculative risk. Why is such a distinction important? Explain.
   (b) In what way is insurance related, if at all, to speculative risk?
10. What economic institutions other than insurance companies have used the combination method of handling risk? Explain.
11. If the number of exposure units increases four times, what may be said to happen to the degree of objective risk? Explain, giving the basic principle illustrated.

QUESTIONS FOR DISCUSSION

1. What words, if any, should be substituted for *risk* in the following statements to make them accurate? Why?
   (a) When children play with fire in a dry forest, a high degree of *risk* is present.
   (b) An icy highway is a *risk* factor in driving safety.
   (c) To underwrite this *risk* (building) is dangerous.
   (d) Flood is a *risk* we won't take.
   (e) You don't have a large enough group of people to enable us to reduce the *risk* sufficiently to handle this on a group basis.
2. You are informed that you have just received an inheritance from a great uncle who was something of an eccentric. You have your choice of (a) $10,000 in cash, or (b) joining in a game of drawing marbles from an urn containing 90 black marbles and 10 white marbles. If you draw a black marble, you receive $1,000; if you draw a white marble, you receive $100,000. Which choice would you take and why? Explain how this situation illustrates the economic burden of risk.
3. *A* owns 100 buildings and averages 2 fires per year. *B* owns 1,000 buildings and averages 30 fires per year. *A* never experiences more than 3 fires a year, although in some years there are none. In some years *B* has as many as 36 fires, but never has

fewer than 24. Who is faced with the greatest objective risk? The greatest probability of loss? Explain.

4. It is stated in the text that the insurance premium varies both with probability and with risk. Which of these elements presumably becomes more important as probability of loss rises? Why? Which becomes more important as the number of exposure units declines? Why?

5. An automobile insurer decided to set auto insurance rates on youthful drivers only after scores had been taken on an "attitudes toward risk" test. Drivers with five years' experience were grouped into four classes in accordance with their test scores, and claim costs were developed based on the number of years' experience in each class.

It was found that if Group 1 costs were labelled 100 percent, then Group 2 costs were 148 percent, Group 3 costs were 199 percent, and Group 4 costs 231 percent. It was concluded that the "attitudes toward risk" test was a useful device to differentiate between drivers and to predict total claim costs of each group.

(a) In what way is the "attitudes toward risk" test similar in concept to a measurement for subjective risk? Explain.

(b) Would you prefer the use of such a test in classifying automobile drivers by a classification system that employed such variables as age, sex, geographical location, and type of vehicle? Why, or why not?

NEW TERMS AND CONCEPTS

Adverse Selection
Antiselection
Assured
Central Limit Theorem
Combination
Hazard
Insured
Law of Large Numbers
Moral Hazard
Morale Hazard
Objective Risk

Peril
Physical Hazard
Probability
Probability Distribution
Risk
Risk Retention
Shifting of Risk
Static Risk
Statistical Risk
Subjective Risk

NOTES

1 Some writers have used the word "uncertainty" to be synonymous with subjective risk as defined here.

2 It is possible, of course, for individuals to perceive high risk and still not behave in a conservative manner.

3 Russell P. Clark, III, "Risk Taking in Groups: A Social Psychological Analysis," *Journal of Risk and Insurance,* Vol. 41, No. 1 (March, 1974), pp. 75–92.

4 N. Kass, "Risk in Decision Making as a Function of Age, Sex, and Probability Preference," *Child Development,* Vol. 35 (1964), pp. 577–582.

5 M. D. Preston and P. C. Baratta, "An Experimental Study

of the Auction Value of an Uncertain Income," *American Journal of Psychology,* Vol. 161 (1948), pp. 183–193.

6 Albert H. Mowbray and Ralph H. Blanchard, *Insurance,* 5th ed., (New York, McGraw-Hill Book Company, Inc., 1961), p. 6.

7 Clark, op. cit.

8 P. Slovic, B. Fischoff, S. Lichtenstein, B. Corrigan, and B. Combs, "Preference for Insuring Against Probable Small Losses: Insurance Implications," *Journal of Risk and Insurance,* Vol. XLIV, No. 2, (June, 1977), pp. 249–250.

9 For a book-length treatment of this subject, see Mark R. Greene, *Risk, Aversion, Insurance and the Future* (Bloomington: Indiana University Press, 1971). See also Ralph O. Swalm, "Utility Insights into Risk-Taking," *Harvard Business Review* (November–December, 1966), pp. 123–138.

2 HOW INSURANCE HANDLES RISK

After studying this chapter, you should be able to:

1. Compare the size of the insurance industry relative to other financial institutions.
2. State the requirements that must exist for a healthy insurance industry.
3. Define insurance.
4. Determine what makes a risk insurable.
5. Distinguish between insurance and gambling.
6. Explain why insurance and speculation are similar, yet very different.
7. Describe the central economic and social values of insurance.
8. List some of the costs of insurance to society.

Insurance is one of the major risk-handling methods. Insurance has grown rapidly and constitutes a major social and economic force. However, there are definite limitations to its use. Not every risk is insurable, due to physical, moral, and morale hazards. Also, the cost of insurance sometimes outweighs its economic value to the user. Finally, there are certain social and economic cost considerations in determining the extent to which insurance can serve in handling risk. These and other concepts are analyzed in this chapter.

The insurance industry has enjoyed one of the most enviable records of long-term growth of any of the financial institutions. Let us look at that growth in the United States and on the international scene.

**Growth in
United States**

From humble beginnings, the insurance industry has developed into one of the major industries of the United States, and is regarded as essential to a highly industrialized nation. From 1900 to 1945, the assets of life insurance companies, for example, increased approximately 57-fold, while the assets of all banks in the United States increased about 15-fold.[1] This relative gain in the rate of growth has not been maintained in recent years, as shown in Table 2-1, where insurance firms' assets are compared with those of the major financial institutions. The table indicates the size, as measured by assets, of major financial institutions in this country in 1941 and 1985.

From the Table, we can see that the total assets of life insurance companies grew somewhat more slowly than those of mutual savings banks and commercial banks over the period 1941-1985, while property and liability insurance companies increased their assets much faster than banks. Insurance companies combined increased their assets nearly 27 times over the period, compared to a growth rate of 153 times for savings and loan associations, and 29 times for commercial banks. Although insurance companies together have more assets than savings and loan associations, it is clear that the latter institutions are growing much faster.

The importance of insurance from the standpoint of premium income may be appreciated by comparing total premiums collected by insurers to disposable personal income. It is estimated in Table 4-1 (page 82), that 23.2 percent of disposable personal income in 1985 was spent on insurance of all types. Of this amount, government insurance programs accounted for about 10.6 percent, and private insurance the remaining 12.6 percent. In 1950, private insurers collected about 7.5 percent of disposable income in

**Table 2-1
Total Assets of Major
Financial Institutions in
the United States, 1941
and 1985**

Institution	Billions of Dollars		Ratio, 1985/1941
	1941	1985	
Commercial Banks	$79.1	$2,293.0	28.9
Insurance Carriers			
Life	32.7	747.7	22.6
Property-Liability (1985)	5.3	279.9	52.8
Total Insurance	38.0	1,027.6	27.0
Savings and Loan Associations	6.0	917.0	152.8
Mutual Savings Banks	11.8	212.5	18.0

Source: *Federal Reserve Bulletin* (October 5, 1985), pp. A-18, A-26, *Insurance Facts, 1985-86* (New York: Insurance Information Institute, 1985), p. 17.

insurance premiums. Thus, insurance is gaining both absolutely and relatively to total income.

According to data collected by the American Council of Life Insurance, 86 percent of all American families are covered by life insurance. In 1983 the average amount of life insurance owned was about $63,000 per family. Sales of life insurance have been rising steadily. The sale of a new product, universal life (see Chapter 10), has been especially strong, comprising 22 percent of all policies sold in 1984.[2]

Most new life insurance is purchased by the age groups 25–34 and 35–44, which purchased 36 and 31 percent, respectively, of all new ordinary life insurance sold in 1984. These age groups are increasing rapidly in the United States' population, indicating a continuing picture of rapid growth in life insurance in the United States through the 1980s and into the 1990s.

International Insurance

International comparisons of insurance in Table 2–2 reveal that six countries write 85 percent and 82 percent of all of the world premium volume in life and nonlife insurance, respectively. The United States and Canada as an economic region clearly dominate the nonlife insurance field. The United States-Canadian region and Japan now dominate the life insurance field, together writing about two-thirds of the world's life insurance. Data reveal that insurance tends to correspond closely with gross national product, with industrialized nations spending a larger proportion of their GNP for insurance than nonindustrialized nations.

CONDITIONS FAVORING GROWTH

Insurance institutions are shaped by the nature of the economic and social environments in which they grow and mature. There are at least five basic conditions that must be met before the institution of private insurance can flourish:

1. The economic system should basically be a system of private property.
2. Society should be highly developed and industrialized.

**Table 2–2
The World's Largest
Insurance Countries
in 1983**

	Percent of Total World Premiums, 1983		Total Premiums as a Percent of GNP
	Life	Nonlife	
U.S.A.	40.20	53.91	6.90
Canada	3.14	3.54	5.08
Japan	24.43	7.59	5.90
Great Britain	8.10	4.25	6.35
West Germany	7.47	7.63	5.83
France	2.69	5.06	4.08
Rest of the World	13.97	18.02	—
Total	100.0	100.0	—

Source: Swiss Reinsurance Company, *Sigma* No. 4, April 1985, pp. 11–13.

3. Legal relationships should be well organized, known to all, and enforced fairly.
4. There must be an ethical environment for insurance.
5. Inflation should be no more than moderate.

A System of Private Property

Although insurance exists to some extent in countries where the tools of production are owned by the government and where basic economic decisions are made by some central authority, it never assumes great importance there as a separate economic device to reduce risk. The governments in such countries assume most of the risks and in a sense act as one great insurance company.

A Highly Developed, Industrialized Society

The institution of insurance does not flourish in an economy that is primarily agricultural or is industrially undeveloped. This is true because risks are not developed to the degree necessary to support a highly organized system of institutions to handle them. In an agricultural society, individuals have a tendency to be relatively independent, to be willing to assume many more risks than is true in more industrialized societies. Furthermore, people in agricultural societies are not as dependent on money, as such, as they are in more advanced economies. A large part of a farmer's needs may be supplied at home, and thus there will be little trade. A peril that destroys one crop probably will not leave the farmer entirely without food supply because other crops or help from neighbors will supply that need. If a building burns, perhaps neighbors voluntarily restore or replace it, and no dollar remuneration is felt to be necessary.

By contrast, in a highly developed, industrialized society, productive workers are dependent on money income. Their jobs are usually specialized, so that the occurrence of some peril that interrupts their income or destroys accumulated property is often a serious economic blow. Help from neighbors is usually impossible to obtain in the degree that it might have been available in earlier times, for individuals cannot take time off from their jobs at will. In the highly developed, industrialized society, standards of living are derived from trading the results of one's labor for the results of others' labor. This exchange involves the shipment of goods over long distances, which gives rise to many risks not faced in a nonmanufacturing environment. Consequently, in industrial societies, methods to meet risks must correspondingly be highly developed.

Well-Organized Legal Relationships

Insurance as an institution flourishes best within a society in which legal relationships are well organized, known to all, and enforced fairly. An impartial system of justice is an absolute essential to a sound program of insurance, for the insurance device must usually be effected by means of a legally enforceable contract. Where political influence, frequent wars or revolutions, or dishonesty of the people upset the judicial system or law enforcement, insurance does not flourish.

An Ethical Environment

Professor John D. Long has made a convincing argument that insurance cannot flourish unless the environment in which it operates is characterized by high standards of ethics and morality.[3] Ethical conduct of the people underlies a sound legal and judicial system. Ethical conduct, however, can deteriorate under a number of conditions, such as overpopulation, inflation, or too rapid advances in technology. Some degree of effective regulation of population, inflation, and technology is an additional requirement for a healthy environment for insurance.

Absence of Rapid Inflation

Rapid inflation can adversely influence insurance in many ways and reduce loss-reduction incentive. Cash value life insurance cannot be expected to flourish in rapid inflation due to loss in purchasing power of the savings contained in these policies. In property insurance, inflation is reflected in increases in the cost of settling claims above the levels anticipated when rates were established. Insurer attempts to build an adjustment for inflation into the rate structure are often only partially successful. Thus, the supply of insurance tends to diminish. Uncontrolled inflation can eliminate many types of insurance altogether, as was demonstrated in Germany after World War I, and in Japan after World War II.

All of the preceding conditions tend to characterize leading industrial countries such as those listed in Table 2-2. They help to explain the rapid growth of insurance in these nations. Absence of the aforesaid conditions helps to explain why insurance is not a major industry in China, the Soviet Union, India, and most South American countries.

INSURANCE DEFINED

Insurance may be defined in two major contexts: as an economic or social institution designed to perform certain functions, and as a legal contract between two parties. A definition that relies exclusively on either of these contexts is undesirable because each has something to offer to the person seeking a comprehensive definition. A definition that combines both approaches is needed. The following definition is offered as a basis for discussion.

Insurance is an economic institution that reduces risk by combining under one management a group of objects so situated that the aggregate accidental losses to which the group is subject become predictable within narrow limits. Insurance is usually effected by, and can be said to include, certain legal contracts under which the insurer, for consideration, promises to reimburse the insured or render services in case of certain described accidental losses suffered during the term of the agreement.

This definition stresses how the main economic function performed by insurance, namely risk reduction, is accomplished. The emphasis on the word "usually" is made because not all insurance is effected by means of a legal contract. Thus, the definition is broad enough to contemplate various types of social insurance. Furthermore, the definition will include an

Part 1   Nature of Risk and Risk Management

insurance agreement in which there is no particular reliance on the law of large numbers as a means of predicting a loss. This is so because the definition contemplates an arrangement under which risk is simply transferred by means of a legal contract.

A legal authority on insurance, W. R. Vance, states that there are five essential elements to an insurance contract: (1) The insured must have an insurable interest in the subject of insurance; (2) the insured is subjected to risk of loss of that interest by the happening of certain specified perils; (3) the insurer assumes the risk of loss; (4) this assumption is part of a general scheme to distribute the actual loss among a large group of persons bearing similar risks; and (5) as a consideration the insured pays a premium to a general insurance fund. Vance believes that when only the first three of the above elements exist, the contract is only a risk-shifting device (such as an agreement to replace defective tires). Only when the contract possesses all five elements does it become a true insurance contract, which is essentially a risk-distributing device.[4]

The earlier definition of insurance does not require that a general insurance fund be accumulated to pay losses, as stated in Vance's fifth requirement. Some insurance plans rely only on assessments of members as losses occur, and have only a very small general fund or no fund at all. Some reciprocals, insurers, and farm mutuals discussed in Chapter 4 are examples. The absence of a general loss fund is not considered desirable, since it reduces the security of the plan. Yet to specify a general loss fund as an absolute requirement before "insurance" can exist seems too stringent.

The earlier definition goes further than Vance's, since it implies that not only is insurance a risk-distributing device, but it also offers a way to predict the losses that will be distributed among the members of the insured group. The definition refers to insurance as an economic institution. The legal status of the insurer is not important, for an insurer can have the status of a chartered insurance company, a private corporation, a group of associated individuals cooperating in an insurance venture informally, or a governmental agency. The definition refers to accidental losses. Losses that are certain to occur are not insurable. The loss must be due to some chance contingency or unexpected event. An agreement to keep a television set in working order is not insurance, but a service contract. However, if a service contract covered the contingency of burglary or some other chance event, it might indeed be considered insurance.

REQUISITES OF INSURABLE RISKS

Unfortunately, not all risks are insurable. While insurance relies upon the law of large numbers as a basis for its economical operation, there are many situations that can cause loss where the law of large numbers does not operate satisfactorily; in other situations it may work reasonably well under most instances; in still other cases it works almost ideally. There are many degrees of insurability between the extremes.

In the field of life insurance, for instance, insurers have gathered reliable statistics over many years and have developed tables of mortality that have proved reliable as estimates of probable loss. Furthermore, life insurance is well accepted; it is relatively easy for the insurer to obtain a large group of exposure units. Here the law of large numbers works so well that for all practical purposes the life insurance company is able to eliminate its risk. On the other hand, insurers may not be able to predict losses nearly so well in areas such as nuclear energy liability and physical loss to ocean-based oil drilling platforms, where adequate underwriting information may be lacking.

We can classify the requisites of insurable risks under two general headings: requirements from the standpoint of the insurer, and requirements from the standpoint of the insured. These requirements should be considered not as absolute, iron rules, but rather as guides. They should be viewed as ideal standards, and not necessarily as standards actually attained in practice.

The Insurer's Standpoint

From the standpoint of the insurer, there are several requisites of insurable risks that must be met:

1. The objects must be of sufficient number and quality to allow a reasonably close calculation of probable loss.
2. The loss, should it occur, must be accidental and unintentional in nature from the viewpoint of the insured.
3. The loss, when it occurs, must be capable of being determined and measured.
4. The insured objects should not be subject to simultaneous destruction; i.e., catastrophic hazard should be minimal.

Objects to Be of Sufficient Number and Quality. The probable loss must be subject to advance estimation. If only a few objects are covered, the insurer is subject to the same uncertainties as the insured. The quality of the objects to be insured must be homogeneous so that reliable statistics of loss can be formulated. The insurer must be able to control its risk. It would be improper to group commercial buildings with private residences for purposes of fire insurance since the hazards facing these classes of buildings are entirely different. Furthermore, the physical and social environment of all objects in the group should be roughly similar so that no unusual factors are present that would cause losses to one part of the group and not to the other part. Thus, buildings located in a hurricane zone must not be grouped with buildings not found in such a zone.

Loss to Be Accidental and Unintentional. There must be some uncertainty surrounding the loss. Otherwise, there would be no risk. If the risk or uncertainty has already been eliminated, insurance serves no purpose since the main function of insurance is to reduce risk. Thus, if a person is dying from an incurable disease that will cause death within a given time, there is little uncertainty or risk concerning the payment of loss. Thus, insurance is not feasible. Theoretically, the insurer could issue a policy, but the premium would have to be large enough to cover both the expected loss and the insurer's cost of doing business. The cost of such a policy would probably be prohibitive to the insured.

Because of the requirement that the loss be accidental, insurers normally exclude in all policies any loss caused intentionally by the insured. If the insured knew that the insurer would pay for intentional losses, a moral hazard would be introduced, and there would be a tendency for losses and premiums to rise. If premiums become exceedingly high, so few would purchase insurance that the insurer would no longer have sufficiently large numbers of exposure units to be able to obtain a reliable estimate of future loss. Thus, the first requirement of an insurable risk would not be met.

It has been said that insurance is one commodity that must be purchased before it is needed. Once the fire starts, it is too late to buy fire insurance. While this statement illustrates the requirement that the loss must not be certain to happen, it ignores a basic truth about insurance. This truth is that insurance should not be purchased, as such, to recover losses, but to eliminate the adverse financial consequences that exist for each individual facing the risk of loss. Looked upon in this light, insurance performs its chief function during the period *before* any loss. The insured has the satisfaction and security of knowing that should loss occur, there will be reimbursement.

Insurance has been defined as the distribution of losses of the unfortunate few among the fortunate many, for seldom does the insurance policy fully compensate the unfortunate few for all of their losses. Even if one's insured house burns and the owner is fully insured, there is the inconvenience, possible depreciation, and perhaps the lost income resulting from the fire. Only the uninformed, or perhaps the dishonest, secretly hope for the loss to occur so they can "get something out of their insurance."

Loss to Be Determinable and Measurable. The loss must be definite in time and place. It may seem unnecessary to add this requirement, since most losses are easily recognized and most are capable of being measured with reasonable accuracy. It is a real problem to insurers, however, to be able to even recognize certain losses, let alone measure them. For example, in health insurance, the insurer may agree to pay the insured a monthly income if the individual should become so totally disabled as to be unable to perform the duties of his or her occupation. The question arises, however, as to who will determine whether or not the insured meets this condition. Often it is necessary to take the insured's word. Thus, it may be possible for a dishonest person to feign illness in order to recover under the policy. If this happens, the second requirement, that the loss is not intentional, is not met.

Even if it is clear that a loss has occurred, it may not be easy to measure it. For example, what is the loss from "pain and suffering" of an auto accident victim? Often only a jury can decide. What is the loss of a cargo on a sunken ship? It often takes a staff of adjusters many months or even years to decide. Suffice it to say that before the burden of risk can be safely assumed, the insurer must set up procedures to determine whether loss has actually occurred and, if so, its size.

Loss Not to Be Subject to Catastrophic Hazard. Conditions should not be such that all or most of the objects in the group might suffer loss at the same time and possibly from the same peril. Such simultaneous disaster to insured objects can be illustrated by reference to large fires, floods, and hurricanes that have swept major geographical areas in the past. The history of fire insurance reveals that hardly a major American city has escaped a catastrophic fire sometime in its history. In certain areas hurricanes sometimes flatten entire cities within a matter of minutes. If an insurer is unlucky enough to have on its books a great deal of property situated in such an area, it obviously suffers a loss that was not contemplated when the rates were formulated. Most insurers reduce this possibility by ample dispersion of insured objects.

The Insured's Standpoint

From the standpoint of the insured, the two main requisites of insurable risk are:

1. That the potential loss must be severe enough to cause financial hardship
2. That the probability of loss must not be too high

Large-Loss Principle. The large-loss principle states that people should insure potentially serious losses before relatively minor losses. To do otherwise is uneconomical, since small losses tend to occur frequently and are very costly to recover through insurance. If one can pay for a loss from savings or current income, it is probably too small a loss to give insurance high priority as a way of risk treatment. However, there are too many instances of individuals failing to recognize the severity of a potential loss. For example, it is not uncommon to find that a person has insured against collision an automobile valued at $1,000, and at the same time carries little or no insurance against the loss of a life, of which the value to dependents may be $100,000 or more. This is a clear violation of the large-loss principle.

Relative Cost of Transfer. One of the insured's requirements is not to insure against a highly probable loss, because the cost of transfer tends to be excessive. The more probable the loss, the more certain it is to occur. The more certain it is, the greater the premium will be. A time is ultimately reached when the loss becomes so certain that either the insurer withdraws the protection or the cost of the premium becomes prohibitive.

TYPES OF RISKS

The following outline indicates risks that are insurable risks and those that are not.

I. Risks insurable commercially
    A. Property risks—the uncertainty surrounding the occurrence of loss to property from perils that cause:
        1. Direct loss of the property
        2. Loss of property indirectly
    B. Personal risks—the uncertainty surrounding the occurrence of loss of life or income due to:
        1. Premature death
        2. Physical disability
        3. Old age
    C. Legal liability risks—the uncertainty surrounding the occurrence of loss due to negligent behavior resulting in injury to persons arising out of:
        1. The use of automobiles
        2. The occupancy of buildings
        3. Employment
        4. The manufacture of products
        5. Professional misconduct

II. Risks not insurable commercially
    A. Market risks—factors that may result in loss to property or income, such as:
        1. Price changes, seasonal or cyclical
        2. Consumer indifference
        3. Style changes
        4. Competition offered by a better product
    B. Political risks—uncertainty surrounding the occurrence of:
        1. Overthrow of the government or war
        2. Restrictions imposed on free trade
        3. Unreasonable or punitive taxation
        4. Restrictions on free exchange of currencies
    C. Production risks—uncertainties surrounding the occurrence of:
        1. Failure of machinery to function economically
        2. Failure to solve technical problems
        3. Exhaustion of raw material resources
        4. Strikes, absenteeism, labor unrest
    D. Personal risks—uncertainty surrounding the occurrence of:
        1. Unemployment
        2. Poverty from factors such as divorce, lack of education or opportunity, loss of health from military service

The several types of insurable risks that face the individual are thoroughly discussed in Parts 4, 5, and 6.

Note that some risks listed under the second section above are considered generally uninsurable from the viewpoint of the private insurer. Governmental agencies commonly insure political risks such as those arising from war (ocean marine risks during wartime) and currency restrictions (export credit insurance and investment guarantees). There is the possibility that ways and means may be found for private agencies to assume risks considered catastrophic or unpredictable in nature, or to assume speculative risks. Nevertheless, it seems likely that such a development will be slow.

Government agencies also offer protection against many types of personal risks not being met, or being met only partially, by private insurers or agencies. Thus, various social insurance and welfare programs are established to offer assistance, if needed, from risks of poverty, unemployment, and old age.

To illustrate the reason why certain risks are uninsurable, let us use market risks as the first example. Suppose a manufacturer wishes to insure that the price of a product will not fall more than 10 percent during the policy year. Such a risk is subject to catastrophic loss, since simultaneous loss from this source is possible to all the firm's products in a depression. Further, the losses are not subject to advance calculation since, in an ever-changing, free, competitive market such as ours, past experience is an inadequate guide to the future. Hence, the insurer would have no realistic basis for computing a premium. Furthermore, in times of rising prices, few would be interested in the coverage; and in times of falling prices, no insurer could afford to take on the risk. The insurer could get no "spread of risks" over which to average out good years with bad years.

Political risks are also beyond the control of the insurer for the most part, since losses from this source cannot be estimated accurately or measured. For example, many war risks are such that one cannot measure the degree to which losses stem from a war or from some other peril. Also, this peril often brings about catastrophic losses. Again, since no two wars are alike, and since their courses cannot be predicted, there is no way of scientifically calculating a premium.[5]

To the extent that risks are uninsurable, the management of a business firm, or an individual, will employ one or more of the other methods of handling risk discussed in Chapter 1. The subject of risk management is discussed more thoroughly in Chapter 3.

INSURANCE VERSUS GAMBLING

It is common to confuse insurance with gambling, for to many it is difficult to see clearly why insurance is not gambling. Even legal authorities have not always made a clear distinction between the two, classifying both insurance and gambling contracts under the category of **aleatory contracts,** under which the outcome is subject to an uncertain event.[6]

In such contracts it is possible for one party to give up a great deal more than is received in the transaction.

Aleatory contracts are contrasted with another group, called **commutative contracts,** under which each party gives up approximately equal value in exchange for the promises or acts of the other. Insurance may appear to be a contract under which there is a possibility for the insurance company to pay to a given party a great deal more than it has received in premiums; but this does not mean that insurance is thereby a gambling contract. In fact, from an economic standpoint, gambling and insurance are exact opposites.

Gambling creates a new risk where none existed before, whereas insurance is a method of eliminating or greatly reducing (to one party anyway) an already existing risk. This may be illustrated as follows: Janet said to Jack, "I'll bet you $5,000 to $50 that Dick's house will not catch fire within one year." If Jack takes the bet, a new risk has been created for each person. If the house burns, Jack wins $5,000; but if it does not burn, he loses $50. Before the gamble, neither party had any risk of losing money from this source, nor of course, of gaining any. After the gamble, each party becomes subject to a new risk of losing money.

Contrast the preceding incident with the situation in which Dick goes to the fire insurance company and insures his house for $5,000 and the insurer charges a premium of $50. Dick had the risk of loss from having his house destroyed by fire before he entered into the insurance transaction. He has an insurable interest in his house. Afterward, he has eliminated the risk of loss from this source in return for a premium of $50. He has exchanged a large *uncertain loss* for a small but *certain loss,* namely, the premium.

INSURANCE VERSUS SPECULATION

Speculation is a transaction under which one party, for a fee or other legal consideration, agrees to assume certain risks, usually in connection with a business venture. A good example of speculation is found in the practice known as **hedging.** In hedging, a flour miller, for example, may have purchased grain to grind into flour. The miller realizes, however, that before the grinding can be completed, the price of grain, and consequently that of flour, may change, causing either profit or loss. The miller prefers to avoid the price risk and to concentrate on the main business operation—flour milling. Therefore, after buying the grain, the miller enters into an equal and opposite transaction in the grain futures market whereby a speculator, in effect, assumes the price risk.

Although hedging is a complicated process, a simple illustration will clarify the central point. Let us assume that on February 1 our flour miller agrees to deliver flour on June 1, based on the February 1 price of the grain, which is $2 per bushel. Ten thousand bushels of grain will be needed to fill the order for flour. Each bushel of grain processed into flour is worth

$2.25 per bushel. Thus, the flour miller expects to earn 25 cents per bushel from the flour-milling operations.

On February 1, however, the miller has not actually purchased the grain, but expects to do so about May 1. The miller realizes that by May 1, the price of grain may rise above $2 per bushel, thus causing a reduction in the expected margin. The miller therefore contacts a speculator and buys from the speculator 10,000 bushels of grain for delivery in the future at, say, $2.10 per bushel. This is known as a futures contract. The 10-cent premium, due in part to handling costs of holding the grain until the delivery date, is known as the spread.

As May approaches, the miller decides to purchase the grain for the flour-milling operation. At this time the open market price of grain has risen by 5 cents to $2.05. However, the futures contract value would normally have also gone up 5 cents, assuming that the spread has not changed. Thus, the miller is able to sell the futures contract for $2.15, making a profit of 5 cents on this transaction, which just offsets the 5-cent loss suffered by having to pay $2.05 for grain to fill a flour contract based on a price of $2.

If the price had gone down, instead of up, the transactions described above would be reversed, with the miller losing on the futures contract, but gaining on the cash transaction. Speculators, who so willingly accommodated the miller, buy and sell futures contracts in the commodity markets just as other speculators buy and sell common stocks. They perform a valuable economic function by permitting the transfer of price risk.[7]

What is the distinction between speculation and insurance? The central purpose of the two types of transactions is very similar, but the actual contracts do not bear any obvious similarity. A speculator is a transferee of risk, and the transferor is usually a business person wishing to pass on a price risk to someone who is more willing and able to bear it. Such a business person is then using the transfer method of handling risk. Normally the risk is a type that insurers are unwilling to handle because it fails to meet the test of insurability—the risk is unpredictable or is subject to catastrophic loss. Perhaps the main difference between insurance and speculation lies in the type of risks that each is designed to handle, and in the resulting differences in contractual arrangements. The main similarity lies in the central purpose behind each transaction.

Let us follow through with the hedging example to illustrate these similarities and differences. The futures contract is one to buy or to sell grain (or some other commodity) at a given price and at a given time in the future. The futures contract does not follow the form of an insurance contract under which one party promises to reimburse another for a loss. Yet the purpose of the futures contract, from the viewpoint of the hedger, is a reimbursement for loss, if any, arising from falling prices in the future. The miller has a risk and is shifting it to the speculator by this means.

The speculator agrees to take the price risks in the hope of making a new profit out of the sum total of the transactions. In other words, the speculator hopes to "guess right" about the price trends more often than not. This position is similar to a commercial insurer who accepts risk as a transferee without the benefit of having a large number of exposure units over which to spread operations. Such a commercial insurer may be compared to an underwriter at Lloyd's who agrees to pay a given sum if rain causes a loss to the promoters of a public event.

In summary, from a legal viewpoint the purpose of the insurance contract and the speculative contract is to transfer risk. The type of contractual arrangement used in each case is entirely different because of the nature of the risk to be handled. Neither of the contracts is a gambling contract because no new risk is created that did not exist before. In most cases insurance transactions have the benefit of the law of large numbers and thus can greatly reduce the risks involved. In speculation, however, the risk is seldom eliminated, but is borne by another person who is presumably better able to handle it because of superior knowledge of the uncertainties involved, and who perceives less subjective risk than the transferor.

SOCIAL AND ECONOMIC VALUES OF INSURANCE

It has been implied in the foregoing discussion that to distinguish between insurable and uninsurable risks serves a useful purpose. Insurance has peculiar advantages as a device to handle risk and so ought to be extended as far as possible, in order to bring about the greatest economic advantage to a given society. In order to establish the validity of this point, some of the social and economic values of insurance are listed as follows:

1. The amount of accumulated funds needed by society to meet possible losses is reduced.
2. Cash reserves that insurers accumulate are freed for investment purposes, thus bringing about a better allocation of economic resources and increasing production.
3. Since the supply of investable funds is greater than it would be without insurance, capital is available at a lower cost than would otherwise be true.
4. The entrepreneur with adequate insurance coverage is a better credit risk.
5. Insurers actively engage in loss-prevention activities.
6. Insurance contributes to business and social stability and to peace of mind by protecting business firms and the family breadwinner.

Reduced Reserve Requirements

Perhaps the greatest social value, and indeed, the central economic function of insurance, is to obtain the advantages that flow from reduction of risk. One of the chief economic burdens of risk is the necessity for accumulating funds to meet possible losses. One of the great advantages of the insurance mechanism is that it greatly reduces the total of such reserves necessary for a given economy. Since the insurer can predict losses in advance, it needs to keep readily available only enough funds to meet those losses and to cover expenses. If each individual had to set aside such funds, there would be need for a far greater amount. For example, in most localities, an $80,000 residence can be insured against fire and perhaps other physical perils for about $250 a year. If insurance were not available, the individual would probably feel a need to set aside funds at a much higher rate than $250.

Capital Freed for Investment

Another aspect of the advantage just described is the fact that the cash reserves that insurers accumulate are made available for investment. Insurers as a group, and life insurance firms in particular, have become among the largest and most important institutions to collect and distribute the nation's savings. For example, in 1984 insurance companies provided about 19 percent of total funds abroad to U.S. credit markets.[8] A substantial part of the contributions of insurance companies is derived from regular savings by individuals through life insurance contracts. The provision of the life insurance mechanism, which encourages individual savings, is a most important contribution of insurance to the savings supply.

From the viewpoint of the individual, the insurance mechanism enables renting an insurer's assets to cover uncertain losses rather than providing this capital internally, much like renting a building instead of owning one. Capital thereby released frees funds for investment purposes. Thus, the insurance mechanism encourages new investment. For example, if an individual knows that his family will be protected by life insurance in the event of premature death, the insured may be more willing to invest savings in a long-desired project, such as a business venture, without feeling that the family is being robbed of its basic income security. In this way a better allocation of economic resources is achieved.

Reduced Cost of Capital

Since the supply of investable funds is greater than it would be without insurance, capital is available at lower cost than would otherwise be true. This brings about a higher standard of living because increased investment itself will raise production and cause lower prices than would otherwise be the case. Also, because insurance is an efficient device to reduce risk, investors may be willing to enter fields they would otherwise reject as too risky. Thus, society benefits by increased services and new products, the hallmarks of increased living standards.

Reduced Credit Risk

Another advantage of insurance lies in the importance of insurance to credit. Insurance has been called the basis of our credit system. It follows logically that if insurance reduces the risk of loss from certain sources, it should mean that an entrepreneur is a better credit risk if adequate insurance is carried. One of the earliest known instances of the use of insurance is in connection with credit. This took the form of what was known as a **bottomry contract,** used by the Greeks and early Romans. The bottomry contract provided that if the trader borrowed money to finance an ocean voyage, and an ocean peril caused the vessel to be lost, the money lender would forgive the debt that had been incurred. Naturally, the interest rate charged for the loan was somewhat higher than it would have been without this guarantee, the difference amounting to the premium for insurance.

IS INSURANCE NEEDED ON "SMALL" LOSSES?

A writer reports that some types of specialty insurance are relatively easy to sell, but seldom really necessary. Examples include insurance against the costs of getting cancer, insurance offering to reimburse vacation expenses if the weather turns out to be bad, insurance against loss of contact lenses, and insurance sold on rental cars. In most cases, the policyholder is already covered by other insurance, or the loss would not be large enough to justify the expense of the policy.

Today it would be nearly impossible to borrow money for many business purposes or for the purchase of a home without insurance protection that meets the requirements of the lender. One of the most significant things done to restore the confidence of people in banks following their mass closure in 1933 was the establishment of the Federal Deposit Insurance Corporation to insure deposits. Also, during the 1930s federal insurance on home loans laid the foundation for a great expansion of long-term credit for home ownership.

Loss-Control Activities

Another social and economic value of insurance lies in its loss-control or loss-prevention activities. While the main function of insurance is not to reduce loss, but merely to spread losses among members of the insured group, nevertheless, insurers are vitally interested in keeping losses at a minimum. Insurers know that if no effort is made in this regard, losses and premiums would have a tendency to rise, since it is human nature to relax vigilance when it is known that the loss will be fully paid by the insurer. Furthermore, in any given year, a rise in loss payments reduces the profit to the insurer, and so loss prevention provides a direct avenue of increased profit.

A few illustrations of the work of insurance organizations devoted mainly to loss prevention and control in the field of property and liability insurance are (1) the investigation of fraudulent insurance claims by the Insurance Crime Prevention Institute; (2) research into the causes of susceptibility to loss on highways by the Insurance Institute for Highway Safety; (3) the recovery of stolen vehicles and other auto theft prevention work by the National Theft Bureau; (4) the development of fire safety standards and public educational programs by the National Fire Protection Association; (5) the provision of leadership in the field of general safety, including public information programs on safety by the National Safety Council; (6) the provision of fire protection and engineering counsel for oil producers by the Oil Insurance Association; (7) investigation and testing of building materials by the Underwriters' Laboratories, Inc., to see that fire prevention standards are being met; and (8) appraisal, reclamation, and disposal of damaged merchandise by the Underwriters Salvage Companies of Chicago and New York.

Insurance companies support the activities of these loss-prevention agencies through an assessment on premiums. In life and health insurance, continuous support is given by private insurers to programs aimed at reducing loss by premature death, sickness, and accidents.

Business and Social Stability

Adequately protected, a business need not face the grim prospect of liquidation following a loss. A family need not break up following the death or permanent disability of the breadwinner. An unemployed worker, because of unemployment insurance, has a small income to help out until another job can be found. A business venture can be continued without interruption even though a key person or the sole proprietor dies. A family need not lose its life savings following a bank failure. Old-age dependency can be avoided. Loss of a firm's assets by theft can be reimbursed. Whole cities ruined by a hurricane can be rebuilt from the proceeds of insurance.

SEAT BELTS AND INSURANCE

Studies show that only about 15 percent of people use auto seat belts. Yet 10,000 lives would be saved annually if people would "buckle up." If people realized that in a lifetime of driving they have a one percent probability of being killed and a 33 percent chance of becoming disabled in a car accident, they might be persuaded to use seat belts more often. Television and radio messages based on a "lifetime perception" of risk would likely increase seat belt use and save lives. Auto insurance costs could be reduced correspondingly if this persuasion were successful.

SOCIAL COSTS OF INSURANCE

No institution can operate without certain costs. These are listed below so that you can obtain an impartial view of the insurance institution as a social device. The costs include:

1. Operating the insurance business
2. Losses that are intentionally caused
3. Losses that are exaggerated

Operating the Insurance Business

The main social cost of insurance lies in the use of economic resources, mainly labor, to operate the business. The average annual overhead of property insurers accounts for about 25 percent of their earned premiums, but ranges widely, depending on the type of insurance. In life insurance an average of 17 percent of the premium dollar is absorbed in expenses. The advantages of insurance are not obtained for nothing. They should be weighed against the cost of obtaining the service.

Losses That Are Intentionally Caused

A second social cost of insurance is attributed to the fact that if it were not for insurance, certain losses would not occur. These are losses that are caused intentionally by people in order to collect on their policies. While there are no reliable estimates as to the extent of such losses, it is likely they are only a small fraction of the total loss payments. Insurers are well aware of this danger and, as we shall see later, take numerous steps to keep it to a minimum, both in underwriting the risk and in effecting loss adjustments.

Losses That Are Exaggerated

Separate from, but related to the costs above, is another social cost of insurance—the tendency to exaggerate the extent of damage that results from purely unintentional loss occurrences, where the loss is insured. Several studies illustrate this point. For example, one survey noted a definite indication that loss payments to families insured for accident and sickness claims tend to be higher than the reported losses for uninsured families.[9] This is probably true because part of the extent of the loss is within control of the insured. In other words, once the accident or sickness has occurred, an individual may decide to undergo more expensive medical treatment; or the physician may prescribe it if it is known that the insurer will bear most or all of the cost.

In weighing the social costs and the social values of insurance, the advantages far exceed the disadvantages. If this were not true, in a free-market system such as ours, insurance would not be utilized to the extent that it is. Insurance is used because of the great economic services attained thereby. These services cost something, of course; but like most expenses, insurance premiums are looked upon as essential to the successful maintenance of a family or a business.

SUMMARY

1. Insurance is an economic institution that reduces risk by combining under one management a group of objects so situated that the aggregate accidental losses to which the group is subject become predictable within narrow limits. Insurance is usually effected by, and can be said to include, certain legal contracts under which the insurer, for consideration, promises to reimburse the insured or render services in case of certain described accidental losses suffered during the term of the agreement.

2. From the standpoint of the insurer, the requisites of insurable risks are four: (a) there must be a sufficient number of homogeneous exposure units to allow a reasonably close calculation of probable future losses; (b) the loss must be accidental and unintentional in nature; (c) the loss must be capable of being determined and measured; and (d) the exposure units must not be subject to simultaneous destruction.

3. From the viewpoint of the insured, the main requirements of insurability are that (a) the loss must be severe enough to warrant protection; and (b) the probability of loss should not be so high as to command a prohibitive premium when compared with the possible size of the loss.

4. Risks facing individuals may be classified into insurable and uninsurable risks. Uninsurable risks include market, political, and production risks.

5. The essential difference between insurance and gambling is that insurance transfers, eliminates, or reduces existing risk, while gambling creates new risk.

6. The main distinction between insurance and speculation is that speculation usually deals with business risk, which is not insurable, but is transferred from one party to another. In insurance, the risk concerns an insurable accidental event, and the combination method is employed to reduce it.

7. There are many social and economic values of insurance, but perhaps the greatest value lies in the reduction of risk in society. The benefits of insurance are achieved at certain social costs, the chief of which is the cost of the economic resources used to operate the insurance business.

QUESTIONS FOR REVIEW

1. How large is the insurance industry, compared to commercial banks?
2. Which of the conditions favoring the growth of insurance does not exist in some countries in Africa or South America? Explain.
3. Why is an ethical environment considered a requirement for a healthy insurance industry?
4. Define insurance. How does the definition in the text differ from the definitional requirements posed by W.R. Vance? Explain.
5. Name the four requisites of insurable risks from the standpoint of (a) the insurer, and (b) the insured?
6. Give the main distinction between insurance and gambling.
7. Why is the price risk considered uninsurable for insurance purposes, but is the central risk handled by those engaged in hedging?
8. Name the social values of insurance.

9. Give some examples of loss-control activities by insurers.
10. Which of the three "social costs" of insurance do you believe is most important? Why?
11. Two farmers agree that if either one of their barns were to burn down, the other farmer would help rebuild it. Is this an insurance arrangement? Why, or why not?

QUESTIONS FOR DISCUSSION

1. A writer on insurance states, "An adequate explanation of insurance must include either the building up of a fund or the transference of risk, but not both." Is this statement in conflict with the position taken in this text?
2. Virginia expresses disappointment that a whole year has passed and, due to no accidents, she has been unable to collect anything from her car insurance policy, for which she had laid out $300 in premiums. Is Virginia's disappointment based on sound insurance principles? Explain.
3. A firm warrants that certain parts in its used automobiles are in good running order and will function properly for a period of one year. If the parts fail, the warranty pays for the replacement. The state insurance department attempted to impose its regulations on this firm because "the company is warranting the mechanical reliability of the mechanical features of the auto, and this amounts to insuring the buyer against any defects in those parts." The firm's representatives claimed, on the other hand, that it was warranting only the fact that its inspectors had inspected a particular auto. How would you decide whether this is a proper example of insurance or not? What is your decision? Explain.
4. A text on industrial organization and management contains the statement, "Insurance should be the last resort, not the first, in meeting business risks. Insurance increases the current cost of doing business and thus narrows the profit margin and makes the product more vulnerable to competition." Evaluate this statement, indicating what elements of truth, as well as what misconceptions, underlie it.
5. It has been suggested that the following risks are uninsurable. For each risk, indicate whether you agree or disagree and why.
   (a) Risk of exorbitant demands of a union or prolonged strike.
   (b) Risk of loss through an economic depression.
   (c) Risk that trade secrets of a firm might be stolen, thus causing the firm the loss of potential profits therefrom.
   (d) Risk from loss of a market that is captured by a competitor with a better product.
   (e) Risk that a rezoning or a shift of population will reduce the value of a location owned by a firm for marketing purposes.
6. A motorist was involved in a minor accident. A shop gave her a repair estimate of $80. When the shop owner heard that the loss would be paid by insurance, however, the estimate was increased to $250. In explanation, the shop owner stated that the higher estimate involved the replacement of a bumper, rather than its repair. Should the extra cost be allowed by the insurer? If so, is anyone "the loser" other than the insurance company? Discuss.

Insurance
Requisites of Insurable
Risks
Large-Loss Principle
Aleatory Contracts

Commutative Contracts
Speculation
Hedging
Bottomry Contract

NOTES

1 Calculated from statistical tables given in *Life Insurance Fact Book 1958* (New York: Institute of Life Insurance, 1958) and *Historical Statistics of the United States 1789-1945* (Washington, D.C.: U.S. Bureau of the Census, 1949) p. 262. These data for banks do not correspond precisely with the data given in Table 2-1, since the former are derived from data from the Comptroller of the Currency, which treats branches as separate banks.

2 *Life Insurance Fact Book 1985* (Washington, D.C.: American Council of Life Insurance, 1985), p. 7.

3 John D. Long, *Ethics, Morality, and Insurance* (Bloomington: Indiana University Press, 1971).

4 W. R. Vance, *Handbook of the Law of Insurance* (St. Paul: West Publishing Co., 1951), pp. 1-2.

5 The student should examine the extent to which each of the types of risks in the outline is insurable, applying the criteria presented in this chapter.

6 See *Black's Law Dictionary*, 4th ed. (St. Paul: West Publishing Co., 1951).

7 Several other examples of speculation might have been given. Much of the stock market trading serves speculative purposes. In fact, almost any business situation in which a price risk is involved serves as a potential market for the speculator.

8 *Federal Reserve Bulletin* (October, 1985), p. A-43.

9 J. P. Newhouse, et al., "Some Interim Results from a Controlled Trial of Cost Sharing in Health Insurance," *New England Journal of Medicine*, Vol. 305, No. 25 (December, 1981), pp. 1501-1507.

3 INSURANCE AND RISK MANAGEMENT

After studying this chapter, you should be able to:

1. Define risk management and explain how it differs from insurance
2. Explain why better risk management is needed
3. Describe the functions performed by the risk manager
4. Explain how to choose risk-handling methods
5. List conditions required for effective use of self-insurance
6. Identify methods of choosing deductible levels
7. Describe a captive insurer, and explain why it is used
8. Explain what is involved in commercial insurance management
9. Determine how well risk management is being performed

The environment of modern business, particularly the large industrial unit, is becoming increasingly complex. This increased complexity creates greater need for special attention to the risks facing the enterprise. Most large corporations and many smaller ones employ specialized managers to grapple with the problems of increased risk. Called **risk managers** or **insurance managers,** these individuals are important members of the top management team in many companies. Even if a separate risk manager is not employed, someone in the firm, often the owner or chief accountant, performs risk management functions such as insurance buying or loss control.

Several factors have contributed to the increased complexity of modern enterprise and have greatly enlarged the risks faced by business. Among these factors are inflation, the growth of international operations, more complex technology, and increasing government regulation (e.g., new pension rules). Many firms experience difficulty in obtaining adequate insurance coverage at reasonable rates.

Risk managers tend to look at problems from the consumer's, not the insurer's, viewpoint. In this chapter we describe and analyze the functions of risk management in the business enterprise.

WHAT IS RISK MANAGEMENT?

The term "risk management" lacks a precise or universally accepted definition. One writer defines it as "the process for conserving the earning power and assets of the firm or individual by minimizing the financial effects of accidental losses.[1] Another defines it as "an organized method for dealing with the pure risks to which an individual, family, firm, or other organization is exposed."[2] These definitions have in common the idea that risk management is a part of a team effort to control risk and to minimize its adverse effect on assets or earning power of a business enterprise. The objectives of risk management are incorporated in the definitions. We shall define risk management, stressing the dimension of leadership in accomplishing its objectives, as follows:

> **Risk management** is the executive function of planning, organizing, and controlling those activities in the firm dealing with specified types of risk.

This definition stresses that risk management is a leadership function. Some of the "activities" referred to in the definition are frequently carried out by others in the firm, not by the risk manager *per se*. The objectives of these activities all aim at reducing the financial impact of unexpected and unintended losses. Risk management deals mainly with pure risk, but it may have an impact also on speculative risk or general business risks that are the essential responsibility of general management. For example, the risk manager usually has the main responsibility for purchasing insurance against pure risk, but he or she may also manage a self-insurance program which has considerable financial implications for the firm. The risk manager may have close dealings with, or perform functions of, the safety manager in handling programs to minimize industrial accidents. The risk manager may work with the personnel manager or the controller in developing efficient health insurance or pension plans. As another example, the risk manager may be called upon to examine the risk aspects when the firm is planning a merger with another corporation or is planning to build a new factory. The duties of the risk manager almost always include matters other than solely purchasing insurance.

THE DEVELOPMENT OF RISK MANAGEMENT

At one time business enterprises paid little attention to the problem of handling risk. Insurance policies were purchased on a haphazard basis, with considerable overlapping coverage on one hand, and wide gaps in coverage of important exposures on the other. Little control over the cost of losses and insurance premiums was exercised. Many risks were assumed when they should have been insured and vice versa. It was gradually realized that greater attention to this aspect of business management would yield great dividends. Instead of having insurance decisions handled by a busy executive whose primary responsibility lay in another area, management began to assign this responsibility first as a part-time job to an officer, perhaps the treasurer, and later as a full-time position.

As the full scope of responsibility for risk management was realized, an insurance department was established, with several people employed. At first the department manager was usually known as the insurance buyer. Later the title was changed to insurance manager or risk manager. Many different titles, including insurance buyer, are still used, but the tendency is to reflect the broader nature of the manager's duties and responsibilities. Assistants to the insurance manager often include specialists in various branches of insurance, law, statistics, and personnel relations.

Risk managers are organized into a national association called the Risk and Insurance Management Society (RIMS), formerly the American Society of Insurance Management (ASIM), with more than 1,800 member firms. ASIM was established in 1950.

Risk Manager versus Insurance Agent

It is natural to ask at this point, "Why is it desirable to have a separate risk manager in the corporation when independent agents or brokers are available to perform this function?" Is it not a waste to have two separate persons with identical or overlapping duties and responsibilities? Since the agent has to be paid the same commission whether or not a risk manager is dealt with, is not the cost of maintaining a risk management function in the enterprise an unnecessary outlay? Several answers to these questions are briefly presented here.

First, the risk manager and the insurance agent or broker do not perform identical functions, since the job of the risk manager is considerably broader in scope than merely insurance buying. Second, firms have often found from experience that it is difficult to coordinate insurance programs without having someone from inside the firm primarily responsible—an outside broker cannot have the degree of familiarity with internal business affairs necessary for a completely satisfactory performance of the insurance-buying function. Third, there is a tendency for insurance agents to sell only policies with which they are familiar or which are easily available to them. Thus, they can fail to analyze those risks for which they have no standard policies to insure. A risk manager is needed, just as a purchasing agent is needed for tangible supplies. Fourth, the responsibility for the protection of corporate property is often considered too important to place in the hands of an outsider. One of the basic duties of a corporate director is to exercise due care in protecting corporate assets against impairment. To expose these assets to loss through failure to effectively supervise their proper insurance might expose the directors to legal liability to the stockholders. If corporate officers do not directly supervise the insurance, they must delegate the authority to another—and this person is increasingly being recognized as a full-time employee, the risk manager of the company.

Figure 3–1 illustrates how the risk management function has evolved over the years. The dotted lines on the diagram show that the broker or agent plays a role by assisting and advising the risk manager, particularly in those functions involving acquiring suitable insurance.

The Need for Better Risk Management

Before examining in detail the functions and responsibilities of the risk or insurance manager, it may be helpful to consider some of the mistakes that have been observed in the business when the functions of risk management have not been carried out wisely or well. Examples of errors in insurance programs and insurance management practices include the following.

Underinsurance. Perhaps the most common error is that of failing to insure a reasonable percentage of the potential exposure to loss. If your building is worth $100,000, and you insure against fire for only $50,000, not only are you assuming a potentially serious loss of $50,000, but you may be penalized further in the event of a partial loss. (See the discussion of coinsurance clauses in Chapter 7.) Such underinsurance is in violation of a basic principle of sound risk and insurance management, "Don't risk a

**Figure 3–1
Evolution of the Risk Manager**

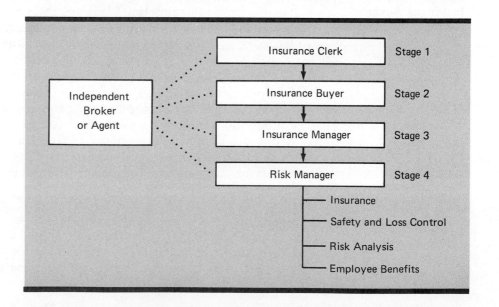

46   Part 1   Nature of Risk and Risk Management

lot for a little," because the extra $50,000 of coverage costs relatively little, and the loss, if it occurs, could be "a lot."

Coverage Errors. Many cases exist in which firms reject the use of clauses, such as coinsurance or deductibles, in which considerable savings in insurance costs would be available without significant increase in exposure to loss. An example is when you could save $500 *a year* in premiums for accepting a $500 deductible in situations where losses under $500 occur only infrequently, such as once every four or five years.

Other examples of a coverage error include failure to name on the policy all those persons who need insurance protection, failure to identify properly the location or type of property to be covered, and failure to obtain proper endorsements to the policy, such as an endorsement to extend protection to cover additional perils.

An important organizational error is failure to pinpoint responsibility for risk management. If no single person is given needed authority to coordinate all those functions relating to risk treatment, important gaps in protection may result, and unintended risks may be taken.

Failure to Review Insurance Programs. It is relatively uncommon in many firms to have their overall insurance programs reviewed periodically and brought up to date. In one case a store manager had allowed the extended coverage endorsement (providing explosion coverage) to lapse for a small savings in premium. Within five months the building was destroyed in an explosion of a dynamite truck parked near the building. In another example, it was reported that a large firm had been needlessly paying $37,000 a year in workers' compensation insurance premiums, through a misclassification of payroll expense, for work that was not being performed on that particular job.[3]

Failure to obtain competitive bids for insurance is also frequent. One small community saved $5,000 a year in its property insurance by obtaining competitive bids; the winning bidder observed that the city had been using an outdated form for its fire and extended coverage insurance and that lower rates applied to the more recently adopted form.

Failure to Adopt Loss-Prevention Techniques. Although it is well known that large savings in insurance are possible by loss-prevention techniques, many firms tend to ignore these possibilities. In one case the adoption of an automatic sprinkler system reduced fire insurance premiums from $11,000 to $1,480 annually, a saving that repaid the cost of the sprinkler system in two years. A program to cut industrial accident rates was instituted in one firm and cut the rate from 9.15 to 2.0 losses per million worker-hours, with consequent savings in workers' compensation premiums.

Authority and Responsibility of Risk Managers

In 1980 a study of risk managers whose firms were members of RIMS revealed several facts about the duties, authority, and responsibility of risk managers in industry.[4]

1. About 75 percent of the risk managers devote full time to their jobs, and 50 percent have other responsibilities as well as risk management.
2. Among full-time risk managers, 27 percent have responsibilities in the area of employee benefits as well as in property and liability insurance.
3. Between 40 and 50 percent of the full-time risk managers have relatively complete responsibility for various risk management functions. These functions include determination and evaluation of risk, buying insurance, and handling claims. These risk managers usually have shared authority for determining ways of financing risks (other than insurance), loss prevention engineering, and employee benefit design and administration.

In many corporations risk managers are asked to make recommendations for and to organize wholly owned insurance corporations called **captives** to funnel the company's insurance needs into the commercial insurance market, often on a reinsurance basis. Some corporate risk managers become presidents of these captive companies. Risk managers today are also frequently involved when a merger or consolidation takes place, since the cost of insurance and employee benefit programs may be significant factors in deciding the terms on which a merger will be negotiated.

An organization chart showing the place of the risk manager in a large company with a centralized location for risk management is given in Figure 3–2. In this organization the risk manager has responsibility for all types of commercial insurance, for self-insurance, and for loss control.

The 1983 Cost-of-Risk Survey

Approximately 800 corporate risk managers were surveyed in 1983 for information relating to the cost of risk within their firms.[5] Conclusions from the survey cast light on the nature of the risk management function and its importance in corporate financial management:

1. The average number of persons in the risk management department was 4.6. Departments of this size were responsible for an average of $1.3 billion in revenues and $2.4 billion of assets. A distribution of the risk management work force is shown in Table 3–1. Only nine percent of the firms had risk management departments of 10 or more employees in 1982.
2. The cost of risk was defined as the sum of net insurance premiums, unreimbursed losses, loss prevention measures, and administrative costs. The average cost of risk was about one-half percent of revenues. Of this amount, the cost of administering the program was .017 percent of revenues. Thus, the cost of risk management averaged about three percent of the cost of risk, as defined, a modest price to pay for handling the risk control functions.
3. The larger the organization, the less was the cost of risk financing (insurance premiums plus retained losses) as a percent of revenues. For

Figure 3–2   Organization for Risk Management

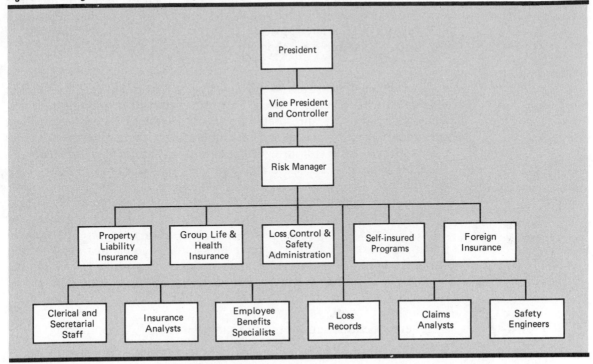

example, insurance and retained losses cost firms with $30 million of revenues an average of about 2.5 percent of revenues, compared to only .3 percent for firms with over $3 billion of revenues. Economies of scale appear to be operating in risk management.

4. Risk management budgets are divided roughly as follows: property insurance and self-insured losses, .139 percent; liability insurance and

Table 3–1
Size of Risk Management
Departments, 1982

Number of Employees	Percent of Firms*
0–1	18
1.1–2	25
2.1–5	32
5.1–10	16
10.1–20	7
Over 20	2
	100

*Based on 766 responding firms.
Source: *Cost of Risk Survey 1983* (Darien, CT: Risk Planning Group, 1983), p. 49.

self-insured losses and claims adjustment expenses, .276 percent. Thus, in 1982 liability insurance and related costs were twice that of property insurance and related costs. Total insurance costs, .415 percent of revenues, accounted for about 87 percent of the total cost of risk.

Data from the cost-of-risk survey suggest that the major tasks of risk managers are still mainly related to insurance and self-insurance programs. This should not be interpreted to mean that loss control and other activities of risk managers are not important, because the risk manager may be responsible for directing noninsurance-related activities even though the budgets for these activities may be less than the budgets for insurance.

It may be concluded that the risk management profession is gaining acceptance steadily, although a great majority of firms still do not employ a full-time risk or insurance manager or maintain a separate department for this function. Undoubtedly the profession will continue to make gains, particularly as it becomes increasingly evident that while a firm may not employ a risk manager, it must still carry out the vital functions of risk management.

FUNCTIONS OF RISK MANAGEMENT

In general, the functions of the risk manager include the following:

1. To recognize and identify exposures to loss. This is a fundamental duty that must precede all other functions. Of course, the risk manager must first of all be aware of the possibility of each type of loss.
2. To estimate the frequency and size of loss; that is, to estimate the probability of loss from various sources.
3. To decide the best and most economical method of handling the risk of loss, whether it be by assumption, avoidance, self-insurance, reduction of hazards, transfer, commercial insurance, or some combination of these methods.
4. To administer the programs of risk management, including the tasks of constant reevaluation of the programs, record keeping, and the like.
5. To review and evaluate the risk management program on a regular basis.

Identification and Appraisal of Losses

One of the risk manager's basic responsibilities is the recognition of potential losses that can be guarded against in some way. This function includes appraisal of the value of such loss.

Identification of Exposures. To recognize exposures to loss is the most difficult and complex task of all those facing the risk manager. A modern business enterprise of substantial size offers almost limitless opportunities for loss, and the risk manager (1) must be intimately familiar with all phases of the business operation in order to accomplish this task; (2) must be aware of all plans for plant expansion and for entering into new business operations;

(3) must work closely with top management and with all heads of departments in order to get a clear insight into these features; and (4) must travel extensively if the business is decentralized geographically. The risk manager must recognize that there are many types of losses other than those caused by physical perils. Examples are losses from legal liability, from lost profits and fixed charges, from dishonesty of employees, from liability assumed under contract, and from union agreements.

There are three major ways of formally approaching the task of risk identification: (1) the loss exposure checklist or survey, (2) financial statement analysis, and (3) flowcharts. Loss exposure checklists are available from various sources, such as insurers, agencies, and risk management associations. One of the best known is that prepared by the American Management Association.[6] Listed are possible sources of loss to the business firm from destruction of physical and intangible assets. Sources of loss are organized according to whether the loss is predictable or unpredictable, controllable or uncontrollable, direct or indirect, or from different types of legal liability. After each item the user can ask the question, "Is this a potential source of loss in our firm?" Use of such a list reduces the likelihood of overlooking important sources of loss.

The financial statement method of identifying loss exposures involves the analyst's going down each item on the firm's balance sheet and income statement and asking what risks exist regarding each item. For example, the risk analyst may note the existence of buildings owned by the firm and ask how the potential loss is being handled, whether insurance exists, and if so, how much, when coverage expires, and other questions. If buildings are leased, the analyst may ask whether the lease requires the tenant to carry insurance or not, what happens to the lease if the building is destroyed, and the cost of an alternative facility.

Flowcharts are often used to help the risk manager identify sources of possible loss in production processes. A simplified flowchart is presented in Figure 3–3 to illustrate the process. The risk manager may ask, "What events could disrupt the even and uninterrupted flow of parts to the final assembly floor, on which the whole production process depends?" For example, where are paints and solvents kept for the activities undertaken at stage 3 in the figure? Are appropriate steps being taken to safeguard these materials from fire? Are floors kept clean and free of grease that might cause spills? Are any particular dangers threatening the storage of finished products which may require special protection? If the finished products are fragile, are appropriate protective measures being taken in loading and unloading? The risk manager needs particularly to inspect the production processes personally.

Appraisal of Values. Once the exposure is recognized, the next step is to estimate the size and frequency of the loss. There are many losses that could be incurred, but no particular problem would arise if they were. Other

Figure 3–3   Flowchart for a Production Process

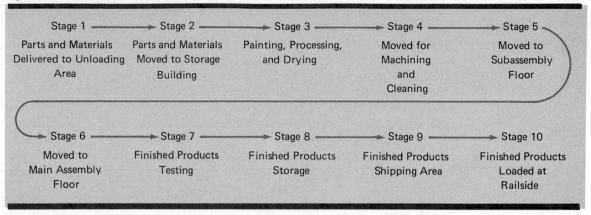

losses, however, could bankrupt the firm. The risk manager first studies the records of past losses within the firm, if any, and then consults the loss experience of other firms or a commercial insurer.

The problem of estimating values exposed to loss may best be approached by studying separately the two dimensions of frequency of loss and severity of loss. Losses which are small in amount but which occur almost daily (say, work accidents or inventory breakage) may be dealt with in one way; losses which occur infrequently but are relatively large when they do occur (accidental deaths or destruction by a large fire) may be treated entirely differently. Usually, a combination of methods is employed for the different loss exposures.

For example, the risk manager may classify and treat risk in three categories as shown in Table 3–2. What are "high" and "low" must be established individually for each company. It is desirable that written corporate policy be established to guide the risk manager in risk-handling decisions. (See the discussion below on corporate policy.)

The risk manager must keep constant surveillance over values of real estate and other property and see that up-to-date appraisals are on hand in order that the severity of loss resulting from a particular peril can be

Table 3–2
Classification of Risk of
Loss and Treatment

Frequency of Loss	Severity of Loss	Treatment*
Low	Low	Retain risk
Low	High	Transfer risk
High	Low	Loss control
High	High	Combination of methods

*In practice, firms use a combination of risk treatment methods.

accurately estimated. In one firm a study was made of fire loss in icehouses that were located on leased property with spur-track facilities and that were widely scattered geographically. The maximum original value of each house was $1,500. Since the losses suffered over a period of 15 years were almost nothing, the firm realized that the probability of loss from fire was not serious and decided to self-insure that particular risk.

Sometimes rather ingenious methods are devised to estimate the possibility of loss. One formula was developed by a risk manager to measure the exposure to dishonesty losses within a firm. This formula involved the calculation of an index made up of three elements—cash, inventory, and gross sales. For example, for small firms the amount of dishonesty insurance was calculated from a formula summing 20 percent of cash, 5 percent of inventory, and 10 percent of the annual gross sales. This system was developed after an accountant who had only $1,500 of cash at his disposal at any one time was able to steal $187,000 over a period of years.[7]

Selection of Risk-Handling Methods

Once the size of loss has been estimated, the risk manager is in a good position to decide the best method of handling the risk. For example, if the loss would cause no real hardship to the firm, the risk of loss could well be assumed.

There are five basic methods of handling risk: retention or assumption, loss prevention or control, transfer, avoidance, and combination or diversification. (See Chapter 1.)

Retention (Assumption). Many exposures to loss are so inconsequential that they may properly be ignored. For example, the risk manager may feel that the risk of collision loss to old vehicles is such that it should be entirely assumed. Or the risk manager may retain the first $250 of loss to each vehicle by using a $250-deductible policy. Such perils as pilferage, breakage of tools or windows, or robbery of vending machines are often assumed because the firm can economically absorb the occasional loss from these sources. Retention, or assumption, of small losses is justified because these losses do not cause undue financial hardship, nor do they require any particular planning activity. They may be absorbed and paid from current working capital.

Retention of larger losses may also be economical and justified. Thus, many firms retain the first $5,000 or $10,000 of loss for each accident, and obtain commercial insurance on losses in excess of these amounts. Handling of losses of this size may require specific advance planning and result from deliberate policy established by top management. For example, a reserve fund may be set up to pay such losses, or a special program of loss control may be started. (See the discussion below.)

In addition to retaining certain losses, many firms also assume responsibility for certain services necessary to the insurance device. In group health insurance, for example, the firm may handle the claims of employees for illness and accidents. It may see that proper loss forms are filled out, physicians' statements are received in satisfactory form, and other papers are filed in support of the claim. Often, the insured can perform such functions more economically than the insurer and will receive an allowance for it in the premium.

Loss Control (Prevention). The risk manager is vitally interested in loss-prevention activities. Ideally, the best way to handle risk is to eliminate the possibility of loss. While complete attainment of this goal is seldom possible, any degree to which it is achieved results in substantial savings to the insured, not only in lowered insurance premiums, but also in smoother, more efficient business operations.

Many risk managers are in direct charge of their companies' accident-prevention programs. Among their varied duties are:

1. Keeping accurate records of all accidents by number, type, cause, and total damage incurred
2. Maintaining plant safety-inspection programs
3. Devising ways and means to prevent recurrence of accidents
4. Keeping top management accident conscious
5. Seeing that proper credits are obtained in the insurance premium for loss-prevention measures
6. Minimizing losses by proper salvage techniques and other action at the time of a loss
7. Working with company engineers and architects in planning new construction to provide for maximum safety and to secure important insurance premium credits when the structure is completed and in use.

An example of what hazard-reduction activities can achieve is provided in a case drawn from aviation manufacture. A plane that was nearly finished caught fire on the assembly line. While a major catastrophe was avoided by quick action of a sprinkler system, still one life was lost, personal injuries were suffered, and property damage amounted to $500,000. Investigation showed that the fire was started when a short circuit in the electrical system ignited gasoline that was used for testing the fuel system. The testing fuel had become mixed with a "low-flash," highly flammable fuel. As a result, a new testing fuel with a "high flash point" was adopted and control procedures were tightened. Later on, a nonflammable gas that was nonhazardous and gave substantial production advantages was developed.[8] It is doubtful that these developments would have been accomplished if the firm had not had an individual—an insurance manager—to take action to see that the firm profited from past mistakes.

Transfer. Handling risk by the transfer method has been a basic tool of risk managers. Risks may be transferred (1) to an insurance company, or (2) to parties other than an insurance company. The former type is treated later in this chapter. We shall now be concerned with the latter type.

An interesting example of the transfer method to parties other than insurance companies is found in the use of lease plans. An individual firm may not have a sufficiently large number of automobiles to justify self-insurance. To minimize the administrative problems of ownership of vehicles, including the insurance details, the firm leases all its autos. Thus, it avoids the problem of auto insurance by transferring the ownership risk to the leasing firm. The firm may lease many other types of property (examples range from floor carpeting to entire buildings) for substantially similar reasons—that of transfer of the ownership risk to specialists. The lessors, of course, may use commercial insurance; but the lessee has handled the risk by transfer.

Avoidance. Avoidance is a decision not to expose the firm to a particular risk of loss if possible. Outright avoidance of hazards and risk before they are assumed in the first place is closely related to the transfer method. For example, you can decide not to manufacture certain goods so as not to expose the firm to product liability lawsuits. This may be done in the case of goods, such as untried drugs, which have the potential of causing harm to the user, even with suitable warning labels on the container. Another example of avoidance is to delay taking responsibility for goods during transportation. A customer may have a choice of terms of sale, and may have the seller assume all risks of loss until the goods arrive at the buyer's warehouse. In this way the buyer never assumes the risk during transportation and has avoided an insurance problem.

Diversification. Risk may be effectively reduced through diversification. An example lies in the use of several warehouses in different locations to store goods. If fire destroys one warehouse, the firm will have others from which to draw needed supplies. Another example is to disperse work operations in such a way that explosion or other catastrophe would not injure more than a limited number of persons. The risk manager may recommend many other types of diversification in order to minimize exposure to loss.

THE LOSS RETENTION DECISION

In recent years risk managers have increasingly relied on loss retention as a basic method of risk treatment. Losses formerly insured commercially are paid for by the corporation directly. Often a separate reserve fund is set up to pay for such losses. In other cases no reserve fund is established, but corporate financial planning is adjusted to meet the financial demands expected because of the decision to retain risk. Occasionally a commercial insurer or other outside agency, in exchange for an agreed-upon fee, is used to administer payment for such losses or to provide other services, but not to assume any risk itself. The retention decision requires careful analysis; the method is successful only under certain conditions.

There are several reasons for the substantial increase in the use of loss retention in industry. Firms have been faced with escalating costs of commercial insurance; with rate structures that fail to give sufficient credit for loss control; with unavailability of commercial insurance in some areas, such as product or professional liability insurance; and with inadequate limits of coverage available from commercial insurers. The risk manager has been under pressure to economize on insurance and to develop alternative methods of handling risk as economically as possible. Careful studies of self-insurance often show this method to be a cheaper and better way to handle risk than commercial coverage.

For example, by using self-insurance the firm avoids several expenses that must be borne by a commercial insurer, such as agents' commissions, fees paid to rating groups, premium taxes, and other items that can total 20 or 30 percent of the premium dollar. Furthermore, the self-insurer may invest the money otherwise paid to insurers and obtain interest or other investment returns on the funds until losses must be paid out. There has been increasing recognition of the expense savings, improved "cash flow," and interest gains thereby made possible.

An important reason for loss retention is the incentive it provides for minimizing losses. If a firm must pay losses directly, rather than through commercial insurance, it is likely that the direct and indirect savings through loss control are more easily and quickly recognized by management. Thus, losses themselves are likely to go down.

Requirements for Effective Self-Insurance

What are the requirements that should be met before a firm can properly retain a risk? Self-insurance will not usually be attempted unless the loss, should it occur, is severe enough to cause financial embarrassment to the insured. The following conditions are suggestive of the types of situations where self-insurance is possible and feasible:

1. The firm has a sufficient number of objects so situated that they are not subject to simultaneous destruction. The objects are also reasonably homogeneous in nature and value so that calculations as to probable losses will be accurate within a narrow range. If these conditions are present, the firm will be able to predict accurately the size of future losses.
2. Management is willing and able to meet large and unusual losses either from working capital or from a loss reserve fund.
3. The firm must have accurate records or have access to satisfactory statistics to enable it to make good estimates of the expected loss. To increase the accuracy of the calculations, it is wise to use data over as long a period as possible, not merely the last five or ten years. If outside data are used, it is necessary to exercise extreme caution to see that the data employed are applicable to the firm's own experience.

4. The general financial condition of the firm should be satisfactory. There is a tendency for business persons who are in financial difficulties to believe that loss retention is a good way to save on insurance. While it is often true that the firm can save money by self-insuring, this is only possible when all of the preceding conditions are met. If the firm cannot afford insurance premiums, it probably cannot afford the loss, should it occur.[9]

5. Loss retention requires careful administration and planning. Someone has to be in charge of managing a self-insurance fund, paying claims, inspecting exposures, preventing losses, keeping necessary records, and performing the many other duties connected with any insurance program. If the necessary specialized executive talent is not available, and if the business cannot appreciate the necessity of paying continuing attention to all the details of carry-through, self-insurance will not be a satisfactory solution.

Limitations of Loss Retention

In spite of the advantages of self-insurance, most firms continue to employ the services of the commercial insurer for one or more of the following reasons:

1. The firm may decide that even though in the long run self-insurance could result in monetary savings, there are advantages in stabilizing insurance costs and in making this cost predictable each year. The insurance premium constitutes a regular deduction for tax purposes, and also enables management to stabilize profits. Under the self-insurance plan, profits may be higher one year but drop considerably in the years in which losses occur. If one of these losses occurs in a year that has been generally unprofitable, losses are exaggerated for that year.

2. A firm may simply wish to avoid the details involved in managing what may amount to a miniature insurance company within its organization. Management may feel that to do so would result in fragmentation and diversification of executive talent.

3. The firm may want an outside, disinterested party to settle claims. In the field of credit insurance, for example, the insurer can often offer better, more efficient collection service than the insured. In workers' compensation, where personal bias may influence a claim, there are distinct advantages to having a third party, rather than the firm itself, deal with an insured employee.

4. There is always the possibility that the reserve fund could be depleted before the firm could replenish it from working capital. As mentioned earlier, the firm selecting risk retention must have financial resources to meet such contingencies.

5. The firm may want the inspection service of a commercial insurer. Let us say that a firm has steam boilers in which any loss from explosion can be virtually prevented by regular and careful inspections. However,

such inspections require a person with specialized training. It might be uneconomical for the firm to hire a full-time inspector, and an outside inspector may not be available. If, on the other hand, the firm employs the services of a commercial insurer, the insurer will furnish inspection along with the insurance policy at a reasonable cost. Even if the firm maintains an inspection department, it may wish an outside inspection as a check on its own.

6. For reasons relating to its personnel, a firm may desire outside insurance in some lines, even though self-insurance is possible. For the dishonesty peril, the fact that the employee is bonded may itself be a deterrent to wrongdoing. Also, in case of robbery, employees may feel that it is not necessary to risk their lives to save company property if the property is insured.

7. The firm may not have a sufficient number of homogeneous exposure units so situated that the potential aggregate losses can be predicted within sufficiently narrow limits; i.e., the objective risk may be too high. It usually requires a considerably large number of exposure units to reduce objective risk enough so that management may be satisfied that undue risk is not being accepted.

8. The firm may be unwilling to set up an adequate reserve for absorbing uninsured losses, believing that the money can be put to better use within the firm or invested in nonliquid securities. Commercial insurance would be used instead in order to release money that would otherwise be held in reserve funds earing a low-interest return. Analysis of this question depends mainly on the size of the reserve fund required and on the excess return available to the firm if a fund of this size is released for investment in securities or within the firm itself.

Selecting Retention Amounts

Mathematical formulas are often helpful to the risk manager in selecting appropriate retention levels, if certain conditions are met. For example, suppose the firm has a large fleet of autos (at least 59) where the probability of loss per auto is small (less than 10%) and the autos are operating under very similar conditions, meaning that each auto has about the same likelihood of being struck. The risk manager needs to "be 99 percent sure" how many collisions may be expected next year. If there are too many collisions, the firm's financial position may be hurt. Suppose the firm is willing to pay up to $20,000 a year itself as a loss retention. Then, put another way, the risk manager is willing to accept a deductible such that the chance of having to suffer a total loss of more than $20,000 a year is less than one percent.

In this example, losses may be assumed to be distributed according to the mathematical probability distribution known as the Poisson. (See the supplement to Part 6 for an explanation and illustration of the Poisson.) The Poisson distribution tells the risk manager the probability of having ten or more collisions at various probability levels, such as less than one percent. Going according to the Poisson, then, the risk manager could decide to accept a $2,000 deductible level for the fleet, because there is less than a one percent chance that total losses would exceed $20,000 ($2,000 × 10 = $20,000). A deductible of more than $2,000 per auto would not be acceptable, because in that case the risk exists of suffering more than $20,000 total loss in any one year.

Least Cost Rule

The **least cost rule,** suggested by Professors A. E. Hofflander and L. L. Schklade,[10] is a rule for selection of an automobile collision deductible which has the least cost to the insured. The rule is applicable when the risk manager is able to develop reliable estimates of the average annual number of collisions. Although the authors confined their analysis to automobile insurance problems, the rule would appear to be quite general in its application. It is based on the proposition that the cost of pure risk is equal to the premium payable plus the loss to be borne by the insured under the deductible. Of course, this latter amount will not be paid if there is no loss. The possible loss up to the amount of the deductible, therefore, needs to be estimated in order to learn the total cost.

Simply stated, the rule is to select that deductible which yields the least total expected cost (TEC), where the term TEC equals the premium payable plus the expected unindemnified loss, *i.e.,* the loss up to the amount of the deductible. In symbols,

where

$$\text{TEC} = P + qD,$$

P = the amount of the premium quoted for a given level of deductible,
q = the expected number of perils occurring in a given year, and
D = the amount of the deductible.

To illustrate this rule in auto collision insurance, suppose that an insurer provides the following data on premiums and deductibles and that the risk manager estimates the expected number of collisions as 20 percent of the average number of vehicles used. Then the TEC formula is solved as follows and shown in the rightmost column:

P	+	(q	×	D)	=	TEC
$200	+	(.2	×	$100)	=	$220
$100	+	(.2	×	$200)	=	$140
$ 70	+	(.2	×	$400)	=	$150
$ 65	+	(.2	×	$500)	=	$165

Since the TEC is lowest for a deductible of $100, this is the deductible which should be chosen, using the least cost rule.

The least cost rule may result in the selection of other deductible amounts if the preceding assumptions are changed. The risk manager can test the formula for different values of q to see what difference the rule makes in the said selection. For example, if the collision frequency in this firm is .10 instead of .20, it would pay the risk manager to select the $400 deductible, since that value would then provide the least total cost.

Use of Captive Insurers

Some corporations and associations have elected to formalize risk-retention programs by setting up captive insurers. As described earlier in this chapter, captives are wholly owned subsidiaries established to write insurance for the parent company, a noninsurance corporation. There are several advantages to setting up a captive for insuring the risks retained by the parent company instead of having the self-insurance program handled informally by the risk manager. Among these are:

1. Even though a substantial portion of a risk is retained by the firm (say, the first $5,000 or $10,000 per occurrence), the firm will usually wish to transfer the excess loss to commercial insurers. The captive offers a way to transfer such excess risks more easily, since the captive, being an insurance company, can deal directly with reinsurers, where greater flexibility in arranging coverage and setting rates exists. (Reinsurers normally deal only with other insurance companies, not with industrial companies. Thus, the captive provides the parent direct access to the reinsurance markets.)

2. The captive insurer can save and even earn money for the firm. For instance, it avoids some of the costs normally associated with dealing directly with commercial insurers, such as agents' commissions and state premium taxes. The captive may also offer insurance to outside corporations or third parties, thus enlarging its source of income. An additional source of earnings stems from investment earnings on funds that otherwise would be paid to a commercial insurer. These funds can be invested profitably until the time when they are needed to pay losses. In types of insurance losses that are not paid out for several years after they are incurred (e.g., in workers' compensation cases), the investment earnings on the reserved funds can be substantial. (See more detailed discussion following.)

3. There may be income tax and other tax advantages accruing to the parent corporation because it has set up a captive. Many captives have been set up for precisely this purpose. However, the U.S. Internal Revenue Service has ruled (Revenue Ruling 77-316, August 29, 1977), that premiums paid to captive insurers, under specific conditions, are not deductible. The reasoning behind the ruling is that no true transfer or distribution of risk exists when a parent pays a premium to its wholly owned subsidiary. Such payment constitutes only a shift of funds from "one pocket to another" or shifting funds in the same economic family, and thus is not

a deductible expense. If the captive is used principally for foreign risks (and meets certain tax requirements), an income tax advantage may exist, not only for underwriting, but also for investment earnings that may escape current taxation. Even in this case, however, the income tax of the captive is only deferred, not exempt, and must ultimately be paid when the captive is dissolved or when funds from it are repatriated to the parent organization in the form of dividends.

4. The captive can enable a parent company to obtain greater stability in reported earnings, since, in effect, losses that may occur unevenly through time are evened out by regular premium payments to a captive.

Some states, such as Colorado, Tennessee, and Vermont, have passed enabling legislation for captive insurers, exempting them from many of the regulations otherwise applicable to insurers doing business in those states. It is estimated that about 1,400 captives have been set up in other countries, such as Bermuda, the Cayman Islands, and the Grand Bahamas, where special tax advantages exist. The captive movement seems well established as a major technique in risk management.

INSURING A PARENT?

The tax status of Bluefield, Inc. of Bermuda, a wholly owned insurance captive of Mobil Corporation, was under scrutiny by the U. S. Supreme Court in 1985. The court held that insurance premiums paid by Mobil to Bluefield were not deductible for income taxes, as would have been the case for regular insurance companies. Bluefield insured (1) Mobil Corporation's risks, (2) risks of other corporations that were owned in part by Mobil, and (3) insurance or reinsurance covering property belonging to employees of Mobil or its affiliates.

An insurance expert testified that Mobil did not really purchase insurance, as defined in the field of economics. He testified that a wholly owned subsidiary cannot insure its parent because there is no transfer of risk. All risks as well as all benefits gained by Bluefield are ultimately realized by the parent corporation and are reflected on the financial statements of Mobil. The court agreed, saying that the arrangement did not result in the transfer of risk.

Mobil argued that the court had disregarded the doctrine of separate corporate entities, and that Bluefield was no different from any other insurance company from which Mobil may have purchased coverage. However, the court disagreed. The arrangement was more like changing funds from one pocket to another.

A survey of corporate risk managers in 1980 revealed that, in general, the use of self-insurance techniques is on the increase. In this study self-insurance took several forms: setting aside funds for losses, increasing the level of deductibles on insurance policies, utilizing captive insurers to a greater extent, and making greater use of retrospective rating plans.

For example, it was found that over 68 percent of the 1,429 respondents were using self-insurance for property exposures, and another 16 percent said they intended to self-insure these risks in the future. These plans were largely unfunded, but more risk managers planned to use funding in the future for property risks. Some 14 percent of the companies use captive insurers. In the field of liability insurance, 45 percent of the respondents use self-insurance to some extent. Over half of the respondents self-insured the workers' compensation risk, and an additional 28 percent said they intended to self-insure this risk in the future.[12]

**Financial
Analysis of
Loss Retention**

Two major financial factors must be considered in assessing the value of loss rentention as a way of handling risk: (1) the extent of the "cash flow" advantage, and (2) the "opportunity cost" of loss reserve funds. (See also Chapter 23.)

Cash Flow. Because losses are not always paid out in the year in which the accident producing them occurs, a company has the use of these funds for varying periods and may earn interest on them until such time as the losses are actually paid. For example, suppose it is estimated that workers' compensation payments are made to injured workers as follows: first year, 30 percent; second year, 30 percent; third year, 18 percent; fourth year, 12 percent; and fifth year, 10 percent. If investment interest is 10 percent, then a $100,000 workers' compensation fund has a present or current value of less than $100,000, due to the time value of money. Table 3–3 shows that the current worth of this loss would be $79,995.

**Table 3–3
Present Value**

Year	(1) Amount of Claim Paid	(2) Present Value of $1 Paid Out, 10% Interest Assumption	(3) Present Value of Outlay Col. (1) × Col. (2)
1	$ 30,000	$0.90909	$27,272
2	30,000	0.82645	24,794
3	18,000	0.75131	13,524
4	12,000	0.68301	8,196
5	10,000	0.62092	6,209
Total	$100,000		$79,995

If the risk manager purchased commercial insurance, the premiums would be based on an expected loss of $100,000. The true current value of that expected loss is only $79,995. The difference represents the net value of the risk retention program to the firm. The current value of the estimated interest earnings is over $20,000. The funds released may be invested or used to reduce other borrowing needs of the firm. Additional cash flow advantages may exist if the firm's actual expenses of administration are less than would be charged by a commercial insurer.

Opportunity Cost of Funds. The value of a loss-retention program is affected by the value of operating funds to the corporation. If the risk manager sets up a fund to meet losses, and if this fund is invested in a liquid form that is readily converted to cash, such as a savings account, the firm may experience some loss because the money might have been more profitably used in the business as working capital. Suppose that funds invested in the business are worth 15 percent, but that funds invested in a liquid account earn only 7 percent. The difference, 8 percent, is the **opportunity cost** of funds set aside in loss reserve accounts. For example, if the risk manager believes that a fund of $100,000 should be set aside for losses in order to guarantee a ready availability of cash needed at the time of an accident, the opportunity cost of this plan would be $8,000 annually. If funds were not kept in the loss fund, the firm's financial position would be $8,000 higher at the year's end.

Now suppose that the risk is handled through commercial insurance and the premium is $7,000. In this case, other things being equal, it would be economical to use commercial insurance rather than loss retention. With commercial insurance, a loss reserve fund would be unnecessary and the financial position of the firm at the end of the year would be $1,000 greater than if the loss fund had been established.[11] Furthermore, one loss might deplete the reserve fund; additional losses could not occur before the fund could be restored. Continuous protection is provided through commercial insurance. On the other hand, if commercial insurance costs $10,000 rather than $7,000, it might pay to use loss retention, where the net advantage is $2,000.

In general, the financial advantage of loss retention is greater when the spread is small between interest rates on liquid accounts and rates of return on capital employed within the business (if there were no difference at all between these rates, a firm could set up loss reserves at no opportunity cost); when the commercial insurance rates on the risk are relatively high compared to the opportunity cost of funds; and when the firm's perceived needs for liquid loss reserve funds are low—that is, the firm becomes more willing to accept risk. These conditions help to explain why loss retention has become more popular in recent years as commercial insurance rates have escalated along with interest rates generally.

COMMERCIAL INSURANCE MANAGEMENT

Commercial insurance is probably the most important and frequently used method of handling risk that is employed by the risk manager. Once the risk manager has analyzed exposures, determined the probability of loss, taken all loss-preventive measures, and decided which risks not to insure, which to transfer, and which to self-insure, an economical and efficient program of commercial insurance for the remaining risks must be set up.

Figure 3–4 illustrates the functions in risk management discussed so far.

Managing the insurance program involves the following steps:

1. Deciding which forms of coverage are best suited to the firm's needs
2. Selecting agents, brokers, and insurers
3. Negotiating for coverage
4. Analyzing and selecting methods of reducing insurance costs
5. Seeing that the terms of insurance contracts are complied with
6. Handling loss settlements and negotiations with adjusters
7. Designing and maintaining adequate records of coverage and other data necessary to a sound program of insurance.

Deciding on Forms of Coverage

Deciding which forms of insurance are best suited to the firm's needs presents one of the most valuable areas of creativity in which the risk manager can make a contribution. Often new contract forms, many of which have become standard offerings of the insurance companies, are initiated by the risk manager. There are literally hundreds of choices available to the risk manager, who must make a selection, usually with guidance from established agents, brokers, or insurers, to meet the firm's needs. Each program of insurance should be tailored specifically, since no two situations are exactly alike.

Before the contracts are approved, it is the duty of the risk manager to verify that the contracts actually state what is intended. Various exclusions, warranties, and conditions must be studied and any necessary changes effected. Management must also be advised of the limitations of protection. Rates, premiums, dividends, or discounts must be checked for accuracy. The risk manager submits any necessary data required under the terms of the insurance contracts. For example, many forms of coverage are submitted to an audit at the end of the year and require final data on payrolls, sales, and the like.

Selecting Agents, Brokers, and Insurers

Insurance is purchased through established agents or brokers, or sometimes directly from insurers. Wise selection of agents and brokers can make a great deal of difference in the work of the risk manager, for it is from these individuals that the risk manager obtains up-to-date information, expert advice, and skilled aid in negotiation with insurers. The risk manager cannot hope to be an expert in all lines of insurance. The help of the agent

Figure 3–4   Structure of Risk Analysis

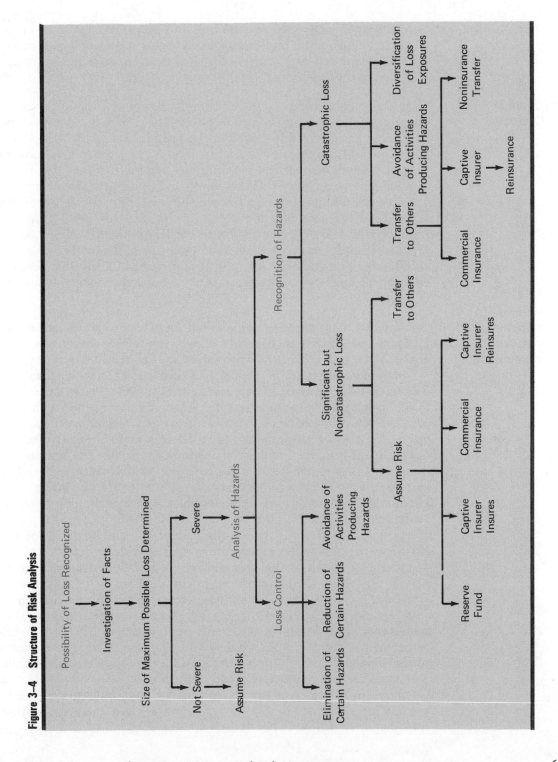

or the broker is needed in handling the many phases of work with commercial insurance. Since the quality and cost of the services of insurers, agents, and brokers vary, the risk manager must exercise great care in the selection of these persons.

Negotiating for Coverage

Negotiating for coverage is often a complicated matter that requires great ingenuity on the part of the risk manager. The firm may have specialized needs that are not readily solved in the insurance market.[13] Lengthy and complex bargaining sessions may be necessary in order to place coverage in a satisfactory manner and at a mutually agreeable price. Often it is the risk manager (frequently with help from an agent or broker) who obtains valuable concessions from insurers in the matter of satisfactory renewal of policies. The task is complicated by the fact that many times it is necessary to cover a given exposure by dealing with a dozen or more separate insurers, each of which takes a fraction of the total risk. Securing coordinated coverage of a fire exposure of perhaps $100 million, a common exposure among large corporations, is not simple when several insurers are involved.

Reducing Commercial Insurance Costs

Commercial insurance costs can be reduced in many ways, and the risk manager must analyze each method with a view toward obtaining coverage at the lowest cost compatible with safety and service considerations.

Judicious selection of deductibles can be a great cost saver. A **deductible** is an amount, expressed either in dollars or as a percentage of the loss, which is subtracted from each claim payable under the terms of the policy. While deductibles are of many types, essentially they all have one purpose—to control costs and to effect a more efficient method of handling the risk by commercial insurance. Usually the purpose of a deductible is to eliminate from the coverage small losses that are almost certain to occur and, hence, are very expensive to insure. The insurer grants a reduction in the premium for deductibles, and this reduction increases as the size of the deductible rises. However, the insurance purchaser must meet the costs of losses below the deductible, and the sum of these payments may ultimately exceed the savings expected when accepting the deductible. The job of the risk manager is to select a deductible that maximizes the net savings produced by this device.

Use of certain contractual provisions can also greatly reduce insurance costs. For example, agreements to employ certain loss-prevention methods, agreements to maintain in force sufficient coverage equal to a stated percentage of total exposed values, and agreements to assume certain administrative responsibilities will all reduce the cost of insurance if these provisions are properly analyzed and applied.

Some insurance costs can be lowered by buying in quantity and by negotiating a contract to cover a period longer than one year. Insurance costs can often be lowered by competitive bidding.

Insurance costs can also be reduced by regular reviews to eliminate duplication of coverage, needless endorsements, nonconcurrencies in the contracts, insurance on property no longer owned, insurance on personnel no longer employed, and insurance on buildings or equipment with little or no value.

Finally, insurance costs can be greatly reduced by careful attention to loss-control efforts, including recording the resulting effect of these efforts in reducing exposure to loss (e.g., installing a sprinkler system), or in reducing accident frequency. These findings must be communicated to the underwriters so that credits in insurance rates may be granted. This is especially true when insurance contracts come up for renewal or when competitive bidding takes place.

Complying with Contract Terms

The entire purpose of insurance can be defeated if the firm, knowingly or unknowingly, violates the terms of the contract and thus is unable to collect when a loss occurs. It is the job of the risk manager to know the contracts thoroughly so that the terms can be complied with before, at the time, and after the loss occurs. For example, the risk manager must see that necessary permits are granted for extrahazardous operations that might otherwise suspend coverage under the fire insurance policy. Proper methods must be followed to reduce the size of loss once the insured peril occurs. Otherwise, the firm may lose its coverage. As an illustration, a large corporation had to pay a substantial liability judgment because it had failed to notify the insurer of the accident until almost a year had passed. The terms of the policy in this case had called for immediate notification of any loss.

Handling Loss Settlements

An important and specialized task of the risk manager is to represent the firm in the negotiations with the insurer in loss settlements. Often the amount of the loss is not easily determined. If recent appraisals are not available on the value of a building now totally destroyed, it may take considerable discussion to agree on a settlement. The risk manager may have to do much research to establish the value, say, of an ocean marine loss, or of a fire loss in a warehouse of goods for which adequate records have not been maintained. The risk manager normally fills out proof-of-loss forms for employees making claims under group disability policies and sometimes is required to "go to bat" when cases are questioned. The risk manager is the one to decide whether a claim will be filed under the policies, that is, to recognize an insured loss. The terms of many policies are so complex that recoverable losses are easily overlooked. This is particularly true under the **all-risk** forms, wherein any loss that is not specifically excluded is covered.

Record Keeping

The design and maintenance of proper insurance records is itself a specialized task that may require substantial time and effort on the part of the risk manager. Typical of the records that will be kept are:

1. Insurance policy premiums and loss recoveries; termination dates by type of contract
2. List of all automobiles owned, their description, and value
3. Automobile collision losses
4. Automobile property damage and bodily injury liability cases
5. List, description, and appraisals of all real property
6. List, description, and appraisals of major classes of personal property
7. Number and type of industrial accidents and loss from them
8. Payroll summary for workers' compensation insurance
9. Status of workers' compensation claims
10. Fire loss reports, including data on cause and amount of loss

Maintaining these and other records is necessary to (1) enable the insurance manager to secure renewals of insurance coverage and avoid lapse of coverage; (2) furnish the basis for studies of self-insurance, noninsurance, and insurance proposals; (3) provide material for reports to management concerning the operation of the insurance department; (4) help control future losses and enable the risk manager to analyze the cost of losses; (5) provide data necessary for an advantageous settlement of insured loss claims; and (6) enable the accounting department to allocate insurance costs among the various divisions or locations. This list is meant not to be comprehensive, but only suggestive of the many purposes served by adequate records.

ADMINISTERING THE RISK MANAGEMENT PROGRAM

We have outlined the first three of the four major functions of risk management—recognizing the exposures, estimating the probability of loss, and deciding on the best method of handling the risk. The final function of risk management is that of administering the program. We shall consider two phases of the administration: policy formulation and organization.

Setting Corporate Policy

A **risk management policy** is a plan, procedure, or rule of action followed for the purpose of securing consistent action over a period of time. The advantage of having definite policies to guide risk management is that once the rule is adopted, executives do not have to restudy recurring problems before making decisions.

Segments from a statement of a risk management policy for a large regional bank are as follows:

It is the objective of the bank to manage, control, and minimize the risk that must be met, to the end that the financial condition of the bank and assets entrusted to it be not seriously jeopardized, that its material resources be conserved to the maximum extent possible and practicable, and that its personnel be protected from hazards . . .

It shall be the policy of the bank to purchase insurance coverage when the risk is of catastrophic nature or beyond the capacity of the company to absorb from current funds, when the expenditure for premiums is justified by services incidental to the insurance contract or other expected benefits; or when required by law.

A statement of insurance management policy for a drug manufacturer is:

It is our policy to assume the risks of property damage, legal liability, and dishonesty in all cases where the exposure is so small or dispersed that a loss would not significantly affect our operations or financial position, and to insure these risks as far as practicable whenever the occurrence of a loss would be significant.[14]

These statements of policy are expressed in general terms, and constitute *major* policies for insurance management. A firm may have hundreds of *minor* policies dealing with details of handling insurance records, purchasing procedures, and the like.

Risk Management and Other Functions

It is clear that one of the important tasks of the risk manager is to clarify relationships with other executives in the firm. Obviously these relationships will differ considerably, depending on such factors as the degree of responsibility given to the risk manager, size of the firm, personalities of the individuals involved, geographical dispersion of the firm's operations, complexity of operations, degree of centralized control, and other factors. The following discussion assumes that the firm is large enough to have assigned the risk management responsibility to one person or department and that this person will seek the assistance of other departments in coordinating the risk management function throughout the firm.

Accounting. The risk manager works very closely with the accounting department, which is usually in charge of internal systems of control and of budgeting. The accounting department is able to furnish the risk manager with estimates of property values, to maintain records of insurance policies, insurance costs, and prepaid insurance accounts, and to provide much other valuable information. For example, the internal system of accounting control is of considerable importance in designing a proper insurance system to protect the firm against employee dishonesty. Estimates of future sales and profits are necessary in order to design and install a proper system of insurance protection against business interruption from insurable perils. Finally, detailed information on payroll is necessary in order to make sure that employees are classified properly for purposes of workers' compensation insurance, and that insurance costs are therefore minimized. It should be obvious that the accounting department is indispensable to the risk manager.

Finance. Closely related to accounting as an adjunct to the insurance management function is the function of finance in the business firm. The finance manager is often the person to whom the risk manager reports. The reason for this is that the main job of the risk manager is to protect the firm's assets against loss or destruction from certain perils, a responsibility that also belongs to the finance manager. If an uninsured peril causes loss to assets, both the finance manager and the insurance manager are directly concerned with the problem of replacement of the asset. The problem of tax management is also of mutual concern to these two executives in such problems as determining the tax advisability of self-insurance, the tax treatment of lost property, and the tax treatment of programs of pensions and group insurance.

The problem of credit management is also of mutual concern to the finance and risk managers. Questions here revolve around such matters as the desirability of insuring open accounts against bad debts, the proper insurance on corporate assets pledged as security for debt, and the planning of bank credit lines to replace working capital lost from destruction of assets that are uninsured as a result of the firm's self-insurance program.

Production. Since the risk manager is concerned with accident prevention, insurance of goods in the process of manufacture, and liability exposures in the plant, a close working relationship must be maintained with the production departments in the firm. Assembly-line accidents importantly affect workers' compensation insurance costs, and faulty products expose the firm to product liability suits. Use of sprinkler systems and other loss-prevention techniques in the plant may reduce insurance costs; close communication between production and risk managers is a necessity if the firm's total profits are to be maximized.

Marketing and Transportation. Goods are exposed to serious losses during marketing and distribution, a factor that requires close cooperation between marketing and risk management. Shipping by financially irresponsible carriers unable to reimburse the firm for their negligence might affect the firm's profits in an important way unless insurance and transportation decisions are coordinated. Misleading advertising of a product might give rise to product liability suits from users of the product. Clauses found in purchase and sale orders often create liability exposures of which the risk manager should certainly be aware. For example, it is common for a manufacturer to require a retailer to hold the manufacturer harmless for the legal liability to which it would otherwise be subjected because of a faulty product. Similar requirements are often imposed on the manufacturers by their suppliers. Such clauses should be considered jointly by marketing and insurance personnel.

Personnel. Professor David Ivry conducted a survey of the extent to which risk managers are involved with programs of employee benefits, such as group insurance, pension programs, profit-sharing plans, supplemental unemployment benefit plans, and the like.[15] He discovered that risk managers are very heavily involved in these programs, an area often thought falling mainly within the purview of the personnel manager or the finance manager, or both. Thus, the risk manager and the personnel manager have need for close communication and mutual assistance.

Outside Consultants. The specialized services offered by outside consultants in risk management are often-needed adjuncts to a well-rounded program of risk management. For example, independent appraisals of real estate by appraisal firms to establish building values are often more reliable and more accurate than internal appraisals. Internal appraisals often are based on book values and historical cost rather than on replacement costs, the basis employed in insurance settlements. As another example, insurance agents and brokers can often provide specialized knowledge of insurance markets and can be of assistance in locating desirable insurers at minimum costs. University personnel, independent adjusters, attorneys, physicians, and certified public accountants are among the other types of consultants who may also be of value to corporations in reviewing risk management programs, evaluating exposures, establishing safety programs, and adjusting claims.

As we shall see, contracts of insurance are not always clear and leave much room for negotiation in their interpretation, particularly as regards claim settlement. The assistance of attorneys in this regard is often helpful. Attorneys should also be retained to review and approve the legal language used in purchase and sale agreements, leases, and other contracts so that the liability assumed by the firm will be understood and so that appropriate insurance can be secured, if necessary.

Centralization of Risk Management. When a corporation's management is decentralized, there are cogent reasons for centralizing certain functions in order to achieve uniformity and the greatest efficiency. Authority for risk and insurance management should definitely be centralized for at least three reasons: (1) to avoid duplication and overlapping of coverage with its resulting wastes; (2) to secure the economies of blanket policies, broader forms, and quantity discounts in insurance purchases; and (3) to secure the services of a full-time, specially trained insurance department that is equipped to handle all insurance questions.

When the business is large and far-flung, a carefully laid-out plan of risk management organization is even more essential. The risk manager must establish contacts with operating managers, set up machinery to process claims, devise cost allocation methods, and communicate with insurance and government officials in the various areas where the firm's operations are conducted. It is necessary to travel extensively and to secure the willing cooperation of the many executives relied upon for information.

Evaluation of Risk Management

An important function of risk management lies in its regular evaluation. Ideally, such an evaluation should be undertaken with respect to the objectives set forth for this function. Important principles to remember are that (1) the objectives should be set up in quantifiable terms, (2) the risk manager should have a role in establishing the objectives, (3) frequent reviews should be undertaken to measure progress in reaching objectives, (4) the goals should be moderately difficult to achieve, and (5) measures of progress should be made at intervals corresponding to the length of time it takes to achieve the objective.[16]

To illustrate, a major goal of risk management may be to prevent financially embarrassing losses to the firm. Achievement of this goal may be measured by determining how many large losses occurred in a certain time period, and how these losses were handled. The risk manager has served well if there is a documented record that all potentially damaging losses have been adequately covered and that protection or plans exist to continue this level of performance in the foreseeable future. Another objective of risk management may be to obtain adequate protection at less than the current total cost. The risk manager can be evaluated on the progress made in reducing transfer costs without sacrificing needed protection.

SUMMARY

1. Risk management is the executive function of directing specified risks and devising the best methods of handling such risks. Risk management has been developed most highly as a separate management science in large business enterprises because of increasingly complex problems surrounding the management of these firms. However, the risk management function should be recognized in all business enterprises as a vital part of administration.
2. The risk manager has certain specific duties: to recognize various exposures to loss, to estimate the frequency and size of these losses, to choose and implement the best of the alternative methods of handling the risk, and to administer such programs as loss prevention, record keeping, and reevaluation of exposures to loss.
3. One of the most important duties of the risk manager—supervising the insurance program—has many facets, and the job is such that specialized and concentrated attention by a full-time executive is usually justified. Use of such an officer, however, does not eliminate the need for the services of an agent or a broker.

4. There are several important ways in which a risk manager can effect savings in insurance costs without destroying the effectiveness of an insurance program. These methods include greater use of deductibles, use of certain contractual provisions, loss-prevention programs, and in some cases use of self-insurance and captive insurers. Each of these methods must be used with great care to be effective.

5. Major weaknesses are frequently observed in the performance of the risk management function, particularly when this function is not performed by professional managers. Among the weaknesses are underinsurance, errors in insurance coverage, uneconomic buying of insurance, failure to pinpoint the responsibility for the risk management function, failure to review insurance programs regularly, and failure to utilize loss prevention as a basic device to control insurance and other costs.

6. To be effective, the risk management program must be properly organized, must have realistic policies based on sound insurance principles, and must be evaluated regularly.

7. An important part of the risk manager's function is to coordinate the firm's activities as they relate to risk management. In particular, the risk manager must work closely with executives in accounting, finance, production, marketing and transportation, personnel, and other departments. Use of outside consultants such as independent appraisers, adjusters, attorneys, physicians, and certified public accountants is often justified in carrying out the risk management function.

QUESTIONS FOR REVIEW

1. Risk management is defined in the text as a "leadership function." What is the definition of risk management, and why should it be considered a leadership function?

2. Why might a company use both a risk manager and an insurance agent? Is this not a duplication of effort? Why, or why not?

3. Give three examples of the need for better risk management.

4. List the functions of risk management.

5. How large is the "cost of risk" in a typical firm? Does the modest relative size of the cost of risk imply that the function of risk management is relatively unimportant? Why, or why not?

6. List the major ways of handling risk. Give at least one example of each.

7. Explain the flowchart method of identifying sources of loss.

8. What requirements should be fulfilled before a firm should attempt self-insurance as a method of handling risk? Discuss.

9. Is the use of a "captive insurer" a method of handling risk? If so, which method does it illustrate?

10. Referring to Figure 3–4, supply some examples of each of the four types of risk, using a grocery store as a case illustration.

11. List the steps which should be carried out in managing a commercial insurance program.

12. Give examples of how risk management is affected by relationships with other major business functions, such as marketing, finance, or production.

QUESTIONS FOR DISCUSSION

1. It has been stated that risk managers should deal with property and liability risks, not group life and health insurance or other employee benefits. Do you agree? Why or why not? If you agree, who should normally supervise group life and health insurance? Why?

2. A risk manager stated, "The primary financial consideration in determining the feasibility of self-insurance versus commercial insurance is to determine which plan provides for a lower cash flow cost after considering income taxes and the cost of capital. Secondarily, which plan offers the most advantageous financing alternative?" (Cash flow cost is defined as the present value of the cash outlay after income taxes.)

(a) How would you determine the cash flow cost of a workers' compensation insurance premium of $1,000 a year for five years if income taxes are 50 percent and interest is assumed to be 7 percent? (See the interest table D-2 in Appendix D.)

(b) How would you determine the cash flow cost of the self-insurance plan for workers' compensation under the following assumptions: Gross claim outlays are $600 a year, payable at 35 percent, 30 percent, 20 percent, 10 percent, and 5 percent the first through the fifth years, respectively. Self-insurance administrative costs are $400 annually. Income taxes are 50 percent and interest assumption is 7 percent.

(c) Based on your analysis in (a) and (b) above, which plan should be selected, self-insurance or commercial insurance?

(d) In what way might the self-insurance plan considered here offer the best "financial alternative"? Explain.

(e) Why does the risk manager in this case apparently give no consideration to a requirement of a buffer fund against unusual losses? What consideration should enter into the decision other than financial? Discuss.

3. A firm earns 20 percent on its invested capital. Interest available on certificates of deposit is 10 percent. The firm is considering retaining a certain risk, but top management believes that a loss reserve fund of $75,000 is necessary. Insurance against the risk is available for a premium of $5,000. Based only on these facts, should the firm use the retention method of handling this risk, or should commercial insurance be used? Discuss.

4. A risk manager stated, "If a risk is to be properly controlled, it must be perceived, and it must be appreciated in terms of probable frequency and possible severity." The writer went on to give two examples as follows: (a) A company brings together in two airplane loads nearly all its dealers and distributors from a certain country. (b) Another company makes a special contract with the government of a foreign country for setting up a factory in that country. Special machinery is to be sent by ship, and customs duty is to be waived if the machinery arrives by a certain date. For each of these situations, indicate what losses the companies are exposed to. In your opinion, are these risks insurable? If so, what type of insurance should be purchased, if any?

5. A risk manager determines that credits for accepting deductibles are available as follows: for a deductible of $100, $500 per year savings; for a deductible of $200, $600 savings; and for $300, $700 savings. What calculations should the risk manager make in order to determine which of these deductibles to select? Explain.

NEW TERMS AND CONCEPTS

Risk Management
Risk-Handling Methods

Captive Insurers
Deductibles

NOTES

1 *The National Insurance Buyer*, Vol. XIII (September, 1966), p. 16.

2 James L. Athearn and S. Travis Pritchett, *Risk and Insurance*, 5th ed. (New York: West Publishing Company, 1984), p. 20.

3 William Guest, "Broker Saves Construction Firm $37,000 on Shea Stadium Job," *Business Insurance* (March 11, 1968), p. 15.

4 Mitchell York, "RIMS/Time Magazine Survey," *Risk Management* (June, 1981), p. 12.

5 *Cost of Risk Survey, 1983* (Darien, Conn.: Risk Planning Group, Inc., 1983).

6 *Fact Finding Techniques in Risk Analysis* (New York: American Management Association).

7 George A. Conner, "Yardstick of Dishonesty Exposure," *The National Insurance Buyer*, Vol. III, No. 6 (November, 1956), p. 42. See also William H. Rodda, James S. Trieschmann, and Bob A. Hedges, *Commercial Property Risk Management and Insurance*, Vol. II (Malvern, Pa.: American Institute for Property and Liability Underwriters, 1979), pp. 160–161.

8 George H. Connerat, "Risk Abatement," Insurance Series No. 112 (New York: American Management Association, 1956), p. 10.

9 There is an old story to illustrate the conservative approach to this problem. A young man rising in the financial world approached J. P. Morgan for advice. Wishing to impress him about his financial status, the young man asked how much it cost to own a yacht, whereupon the elder Morgan replied, "If you are worried about the cost of owing a yacht, you can't afford to own one." So it is with self-insurance. The risk manager who is in doubt should probably avoid self-insurance.

10 Alfred E. Hofflander and Lawrence L. Schklade, "A Rule for Least Cost Selection of Collision Deductibles," *Annals of the Society of Property and Liability Underwriters* (March, 1967), pp. 5–17.

11 David Houston has analyzed this problem in greater detail in "Risk, Insurance and Sampling," *Journal of Risk and Insurance* (December, 1964), p. 530.

12 Mitchell York, "RIMS/Time Magazine Survey: Where Are We Heading?" *Risk Management* (June, 1981), pp. 12–14.

13 The **insurance market** refers to the supply side of the insurance service—the sphere in which price-making forces operate between the insurance seller and the insurance buyer. When it is asked, "How is the market for fire insurance?" what is meant is, "Under what terms or conditions is fire insurance available from various sellers?"

14 James C. Cristy, "Responsibility for Risk Management," Insurance Series No. 111 (New York: American Management Association, 1956), p. 21.

15 David A. Ivry, "The Corporate Insurance Manager and Employee Benefit Plans," *Journal of Risk and Insurance* (March, 1966), pp. 1–17.

16 Mark R. Greene, "Toward Evaluation of the Risk Manager," *Risk Management* (January, 1979), pp. 41–50.

PART 2

THE INSURANCE INSTITUTION

4 THE INSURANCE INDUSTRY

After studying this chapter, you should be able to:

1. Indicate the size of the insurance industry.
2. Describe how the insurance business is divided between the private and public sectors.
3. Explain why personal insurance is larger than property insurance.
4. Identify and explain the differences between stock, mutual, Lloyds, and reciprocal insurers.
5. Indicate which types of insurance have the largest volume.
6. Explain how insurance guaranty funds operate.
7. Describe how insurance is distributed from insurers to consumers.
8. List the differences between types of agents and brokers in insurance.
9. Explain why "The American Agency System" is likely to survive.

In buying tangible goods, such as aspirin or fresh bananas, the buyer seldom inquires into the nature of the social or economic institutions that were responsible for making these products available, nor is there any compelling reason to do so. In purchasing intangibles, such as the services of a lawyer or a doctor, the qualifications of the professional are of as much importance as the needed services—and rightly so, for the two factors cannot be separated.

In buying insurance, should the buyer have a knowledge of the social institutions that provide the service? The position taken in this and the next two chapters is that the buyer should have that knowledge. The nature of the insurer and the type of distribution system employed greatly influence both the cost and the quality of the insurance service received. If the security of income and property are to be entrusted to an insurer, the buyer should certainly take a close look at the basic characteristics of that insurer.

THE FIELD OF INSURANCE

Insurance may be classified according to type of coverage— personal or property; ownership—private or public (governmental); and type of demand—voluntary or involuntary. Figure 4-1 presents the major classifications of insurance with the major types of coverage under each classification.

Personal Coverages

Personal coverages are those related directly to the individual. In personal coverage lines the risk is the possibility that some peril may interrupt the income that is earned by the individual. There are four such perils: death, accidents and sickness, unemployment, and old age. Insurance is written on each. Private insurers tend to specialize in the first two coverages in an area usually referred to as *life and health* insurance. Governmental insurers specialize in the latter two fields.

Property Coverages

Property coverages are directed against perils that may destroy property. Property insurance is distinguished from personal insurance in that personal insurance covers perils that may prevent one from earning money with which to accumulate property in the future, while property insurance covers property that is already accumulated. Property insurance as used here includes fire, marine, liability, casualty, and surety insurance. Sometimes property insurance is referred to as **general insurance,** property/liability, or property and casualty insurance. These terms are used loosely, however, and are not as comprehensive as the other names.

Private and Public Insurance

Insurance institutions in this country have taken two basic forms of ownership: private and public. (The latter is also called governmental or social insurance.)

Private insurance consists of all types of coverage written by privately organized groups, whether they consist of associations of individuals, stockholders, policyholders, or some combination of these. **Public insurance** includes all types of coverage written by governmental bodies—federal, state, and local—or operated by private agencies under governmental supervision.[1]

Figure 4–1 Major Classifications of Insurance

Figure 4–1 Major Classifications of Insurance

Insurance

Personal
Property

Governmental
Private
Governmental
Private

Governmental

Involuntary
- Social Security (Life, Old Age, and Disability)
- Unemployment Funds
- Temporary Disability Funds*
- State Industrial Accident Funds*

Voluntary
- National Service Life Insurance
- Savings Bank Life Insurance*
- Wisconsin Life Fund
- Medicare for the Aged

Private

Involuntary
- Workers' Compensation
- Temporary Disability*

Voluntary
- Life
- Health

Governmental

Involuntary
- Bank Deposit Insurance**

Voluntary
- Housing Loans Insurance
- Crop Insurance
- Export Credit Insurance
- Crime Insurance
- Flood Insurance

Private

Involuntary
- Automobile Liability*
- Transportation Insurance
- Fiduciary Bonds

Voluntary
- Fire
- Marine
- General Liability
- Automobile Collision

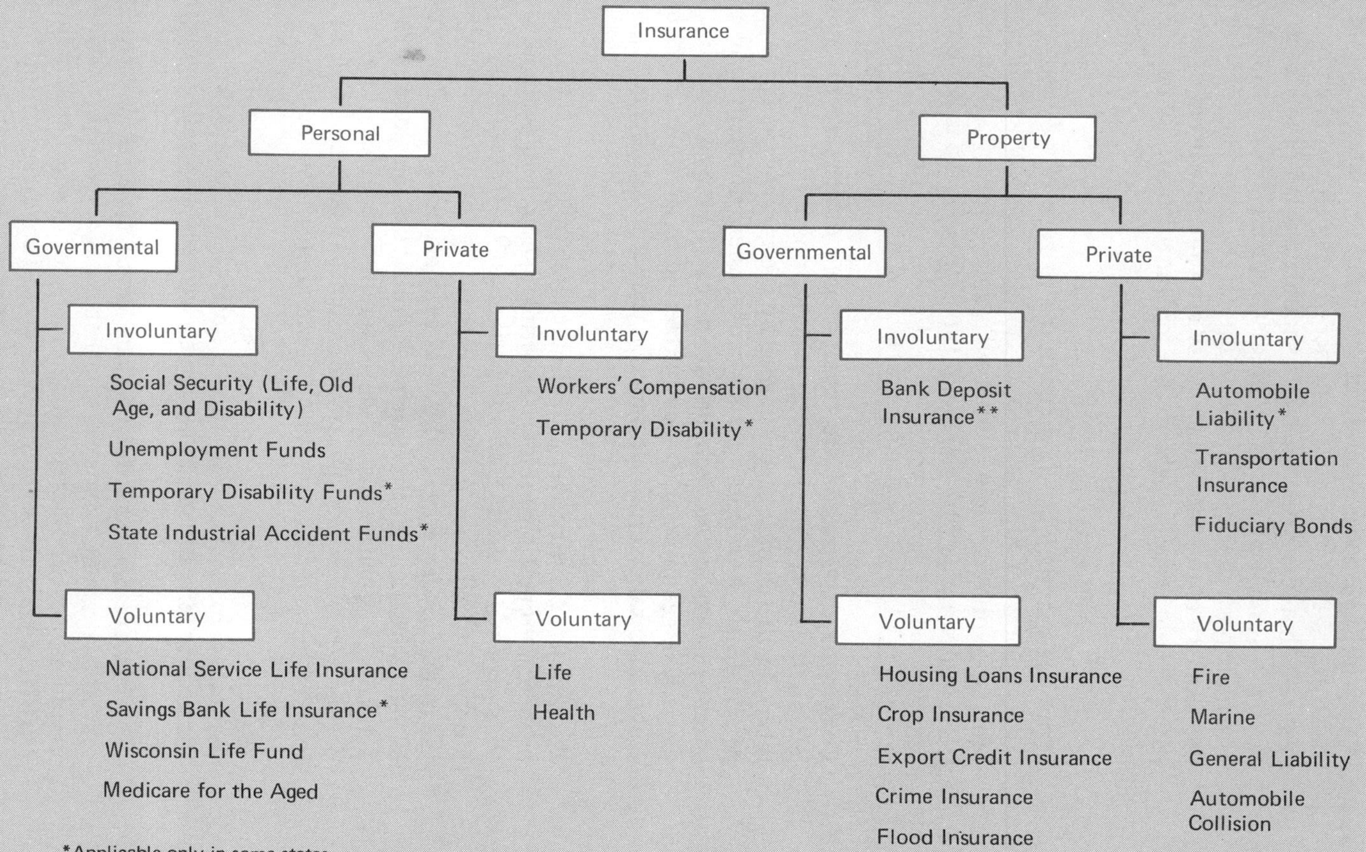

*Applicable only in some states.

**Bank deposit insurance required only in certain types of banks.

Note: In interpreting the figure, observe that the types of coverage under each heading are meant to be suggestive of each type and not a comprehensive listing. In addition, governmental insurance includes coverage offered by both state and federal agencies, and includes areas in which some governmental body merely sponsors or guarantees the coverage that is actually offered by a private agency (such as savings bank life insurance). Involuntary private insurance includes those offerings required to be purchased under certain conditions in some states.

Voluntary and Involuntary Coverages

Private and public insurance may be further classified into two subgroups: voluntary and involuntary coverages. Most private insurance is **voluntary,** although the purchase of some types of insurance is required by law. Examples include automobile liability insurance and workers' compensation insurance in many states. A major part of governmental insurance is **involuntary;** that is, it is required by law that insurance be purchased by certain groups and under certain conditions.

SIZE OF INSURANCE MARKETS

To put into perspective the relative importance of the major lines of insurance, Table 4-1 shows the estimated premiums received by each type of insurer. For example, government insurers collect about 45 percent of total insurance premiums and 53 percent of total personal insurance premiums. The data in the table are only approximate because no attempt has been made to include every conceivable type of insurance.

Note that the income from property insurance, $103 billion, is larger than the income from life insurance, $94.1 billion, among private insurers. For all insurers, however, the total of personal insurance business, 81.9 percent, is more than four times the level of property insurance, 18.1 percent, measured by premium income. There are sound reasons for this emphasis, since the greatest potential loss facing an individual is the loss of income from various perils.

The great emphasis on personal insurance by government insurers accounts for the preponderance of total premiums collected on this type of coverage. It may surprise some to observe the size of governmental personal insurance. Comparisons over a period of years show the steady growth of this insurance. The government share of total insurance premiums has grown from 27.3 percent in 1960 to 39.2 percent in 1966, 42 percent in 1971, 43 percent in 1977, 46.5 percent in 1981, and 44.6 percent in 1984.[2]

Although the government share declined slightly in 1984, it seems unlikely that the upward trend will soon be reversed. Because of the increasing number of persons covered by Social Security, particularly among the elderly population who are covered by Medicare (see Chapters 9 and 24), the premiums collected by government seem certain to rise.

Table 4-2 reveals the relative size and growth of the various types of property insurance. Automobile insurance accounts for about 48 percent of the total property insurance premiums collected by private insurers. Fire, allied fire lines, and multiple-peril insurance are second in importance, aggregating 25 percent of the total. The remaining 29 percent accounts for all other types of property insurance.

The great importance of automobile insurance in the field of property coverages is, of course, explained by the tremendous expansion of auto traffic, accompanied by steadily rising loss and premium payments. The fastest growing lines of property and liability insurance are multiple-peril

Insurance Type	Premium Income, 1984 (Billions of Dollars)	
Private Insurers		
Personal Insurance		
Life insurance and annuities[1]	$ 94.1	
Health insurance		
Group insurance policies[2]	56.5	
Individual insurance policies[3]	9.6	
Workers' compensation policies[4]	15.1	
Blue Cross-Blue Shield and other plans[5]	60.9	
Total Personal-Private	$236.2	
Property Insurance		
Property-liability policies (other than workers' compensation)[6]	$103.0	
Total Private Premiums		$339.2
Government Insurers		
Personal Insurance		
Federal civil service[7]	$ 25.42	
National Life Insurance Fund[8]	1.24	
Old-age and survivors insurance[9]	138.3	
Disability insurance[10]	18.59	
Railroad retirement[11]	2.8	
Hospital insurance for the aged[12]	38.1	
Unemployment insurance—federal and state[13]	18.63	
Medical insurance for the aged[14]	19.09	
State workers' compensation funds[15]	2.6	
Total Personal-Government	$264.77	
Property Insurance[16]		
Crime insurance (Fed. Ins. Admin.)	$ 0.012	
FAIR plans (riot reinsurance)	0.001	
Loan guaranty insurance	6.84	
Flood insurance	0.327	
Crop insurance	0.292	
State Solvency Insurance Funds	0.075	
Total Property-Government	$ 7.547	
Total Government Insurance Premiums		$272.32
Grand Total, Private and Government Insurance Receipts		$611.52

Percent Private	55.4	Ratio of insurance revenues	
Percent Government	44.6	to disposable personal	
Percent Personal	81.9	income of $2,577 billion	
Percent Property	18.1	in 1984	23.7%

(Continued)

Table 4–1
(continued)

Sources of Information for Table 4–1

Type	Source
Private Insurers	
Personal Insurance	
Life insurance and annuities	[1]*Life Insurance Fact Book, 1985.*
Group insurance policies	[2]*1985 Sourcebook on Health Insurance Data,* p. 14.
Individual insurance policies	[3]*1985 Sourcebook on Health Insurance Data,* p. 14.
Workers' compensation	[4]*1985 Insurance Facts,* p. 16.
BCBS & other plans	[5]*1985 Sourcebook on Health Insurance Data,* p. 25.
Property Insurance	
Property/liability	[6]*1985 Best's Aggregates and Averages,* p. 70.
Government Insurance	
Personal Insurance	
Federal civil service	[7]*Social Security Bulletin,* June 1984, p. 28.
National Life Insurance Fund	[8]Appendix to the *Budget of the United States.*
Old-age and survivors insurance	[9]*Social Security Bulletin,* Annual Statement, Supplement 1983.
Disability insurance	[10]*Social Security Bulletin,* June 1984, p. 28.
Railroad retirement	[11]*Social Security Bulletin,* June 1984, p. 28.
Hospital insurance for the aged	[12]*Social Security Bulletin,* July 1984.
Unemployment insurance—federal and state	[13]*Social Security Bulletin,* June 1984, p. 28.
Medical insurance for the aged	[14]*Social Security Bulletin,* July 1984, p. 35.
State workers' compensation funds computed	[15]See note 8, p. 103.
Property Insurance	
Crime insurance (Fed. Ins. Admin.)	[16]Appendix to the *Budget of the United States Government, Fiscal Year 1985.*
FAIR plans	[16]Appendix to the *Budget of the United States Government, Fiscal Year 1985.*
Loan guaranty insurance	[16]Appendix to the *Budget of the United States Government, Fiscal Year 1985.*
Flood insurance	[16]Appendix to the *Budget of the United States Government, Fiscal Year 1985.*

(Continued)

Table 4–1
(continued)

Type	Source
Crop insurance	[16]Appendix to the *Budget of the United States Government, Fiscal Year 1985.*
State solvency funds	[16]Appendix to the *Budget of the United States Government, Fiscal Year 1985.*

Table 4–2
Major Lines of Private Property and Liability Insurance, 1964 and 1984

	Net Premiums (Millions of Dollars)		Percentage Increase 1984/1964	1984 Percent of Total
	1964	1984		
Auto Liability	$ 4,886	$ 29,496		
Auto Physical Damage	2,508	21,765		
Auto Total	$ 7,394	$ 51,261	593%	48.0%
Liability, Other	1,110	6,479	484%	6.1%
Fire & Allied lines	2,211	4,852	119%	4.5%
Homeowners' Multiple-Peril	1,333	13,213	891%	12.4%
Commercial Multiple-Peril	371	8,287	2,134%	7.8%
Workers' Compensation	1,868	15,107	709%	14.1%
Inland Marine	454	3,017	565%	2.8%
Ocean Marine	248	1,155	366%	1.1%
Surety & Fidelity	391	1,995	410%	1.9%
Burglary & Theft	111	109	−2%	0.1%
Crop-Hail	112	n.a.		
Boiler & Machinery	102	439	330%	0.4%
Glass	42	28	−33%	.0%
Other Lines*	n.a.	568		0.5%
Aircraft	n.a.	393		0.4%
Total	$15,747	$106,903	579%	100.0%
Gross National Product (billions)	$685	$3,662	435%	

Source: *Best's Aggregates and Averages,* 1985, pp. 90–91. Percentages calculated.
*Other Lines includes credit, international, factory mutuals, and miscellaneous.
Gross national product data are from the U.S. Department of Commerce, *Survey of Current Business.*

Part 2   The Insurance Institution

coverages. Glass insurance is declining in volume. In spite of the growth of crime losses in the United States, burglary and theft insurance as a separate coverage is declining. Most crime insurance is now combined with multiple-peril policy forms.

It is interesting to note in the table that premium income in property-liability insurance in the U.S. increased somewhat faster than gross national product (579% vs 435%) over the period 1964–1984.

TYPES OF PRIVATE INSURERS

Private insurers are generally classified according to ownership arrangements. Four distinct types are stock companies, mutual companies, reciprocals, and Lloyds associations.

Stock Companies

A **stock company** is a corporation organized as a profit-making venture in the field of insurance. For companies organized in the United States, a minimum amount of capital and surplus is prescribed by state law to serve as a fund for the payment of losses and for the protection of policyholders' funds paid in advance as premiums. Stock companies, like all insurers, are organized with authority to conduct certain types of insurance business; and under the so-called multiple-line laws of most states, stock companies can be authorized to deal in all types of insurance, with the exception of life and health insurance. Even this limitation is not imposed in some states.

Stock companies in property insurance normally conduct their operations through the independent agency system. They usually, but not always, operate by setting a fixed rate through rate-making organizations, with the approval of the insurance commissioner of any state in which they are admitted to do business. Some stock companies pay dividends to policyholders on certain types of insurance. Stock companies never issue what are called **assessable policies,** wherein the insured can be assessed an additional premium if the company's loss experience is excessive. The stockholders are expected to bear any losses, and they also reap any profits from the enterprise.

Mutual Companies

Mutual companies are organized under the insurance code of each state as nonprofit corporations owned by the policyholders. There are no stockholders. There are no profits, as such, since any excess income is either returned to the policyholder-owners as dividends, used to reduce premiums, or retained to finance future growth. The company is managed by a board of directors elected by policyholders. The bylaws of a mutual may provide for additional assessments to policyholders in the event that funds are insufficient to meet losses and expenses. In most mutuals, however, assessments are not permitted once the company reaches a certain size. Only in very small mutuals are assessments usually provided for. Even then, the assessment is usually limited to one additional annual premium.

There are many types of mutual organizations operating under different laws and with different types of businesses. In any state it is necessary to examine the insurance code in order to determine the precise nature of the mutual.

Class Mutual. Some organizations, known as **class mutuals,** operate in only a particular class of insurance, such as farm property, lumber mills, factories, or hardware risks.

Farm Mutual. Where farm property is insured, the group is known as a **farm mutual,** and may be organized under a separate section in the insurance code. Such mutuals insure a large portion of the farm property in some states, primarily because of the specialized nature of the risks. Many farm mutuals operate on the assessment plan, and in some cases the assessments are unlimited; each policyholder is bound to a pro rata share of all losses and expenses of the company.

Factory Mutual. A class mutual specializing in insuring factories is known as a **factory mutual.** These organizations have been noted for the emphasis that they place on loss-prevention activities. Each member must meet high standards of safety before being accepted into the group. A large advance deposit premium, more than sufficient to meet expected losses of the insured, is required; any unneeded portion is returned to the insured at the end of the year. The factory mutual generally does not solicit small risks due to the relatively high cost of inspections, engineering services, surveys, and consultations that are provided by the organization in an attempt to prevent losses before they occur.

General Writing Mutual. Perhaps the most commonly known mutual in property insurance is the general writing mutual. The **general writing mutual** is one that accepts many types of insureds; it is not a specialist writing in a certain class. General writing mutuals require an advance premium calculated on about the same basis as that of a stock insurer. In contrast to specialized mutuals, general writing mutuals operate in several states or even internationally. They usually set the advance premium equal to that of the stock insurer and contemplate a dividend or a rate reduction if experience warrants it. Many mutuals insist on relatively high underwriting standards, taking only the best risks so that a dividend will more likely be paid. Some general writing mutuals reduce the initial rate below the stock company level, however, and do not plan to pay dividends. Some mutuals are both *participating* and *deviating;* that is, they plan both to cut the initial rate somewhat below stock company levels and to pay a dividend, if warranted.

Fraternal Carrier. A **fraternal** is defined as a non-profit corporation, society, order, or voluntary association, without capital stock, organized and carried on solely for the benefit of its members and their beneficiaries.

Fraternal benefit societies, which offer only life and health insurance contracts, are authorized to do business under a special section of the insurance code, provided that certain requirements are met. Fraternals have a lodge system with a ritualistic form of operation and a representative form of government that provides for the payment of benefits in accordance with definite provisions in the law. As charitable, benevolent associations, they are usually exempt from taxation.

Originally fraternals started out as pure assessment companies, charging no advance premium and assessing each member periodically for losses payable under the rules of the society. This proved to be unsound, and most fraternals now operate on a full legal reserve basis, similarly to other life insurers.

Fraternal organizations underwrite less than two percent of the total life insurance in force, and do not enjoy the rate of growth that is characteristic of the industry.

Reciprocals

A **reciprocal,** or **interinsurance exchange** as it is sometimes called, differs from a mutual in its form of legal control and capital requirements. In basic concept, both mutuals and reciprocals and formed for the purpose of making the insurance contract available to policyholders "at cost"; that is, there are no profits, as such, and no stockholders to compensate. In both cases the policyholders own the company.

In the legal control and capital requirements of reciprocals and mutuals, however, basic differences arise. In a reciprocal the owner-policyholders will appoint an individual or a corporation known as an attorney-in-fact to operate the company. A mutual is incorporated with a stated amount of capital and surplus, whereas a reciprocal is unincorporated with no capital as such. Some state laws require that a reciprocal furnish a contingent fund in the form of a deposit with the insurance commissioner for the benefit of the subscribers. Otherwise, the reciprocal organization has no capital other than the advance premiums deposited by the owners.

Reciprocals operate mainly in the field of automobile insurance. The largest is the Farmers Insurance Exchange of Los Angeles, California, one of the leading automobile insurers in the country. Most reciprocals, however, tend to be small, local associations with poor records of financial stability.

Lloyds Associations

A **Lloyds association** is an organization of individuals joined together to underwrite risks on a cooperative basis. The most important distinguishing characteristic of a Lloyds association is that each member assumes risks personally and does not bind the organization for these obligations. Each underwriter is individually liable for losses on the risks assumed to the fullest extent of personal assets, unless the liability is intentionally limited.[3]

Lloyds associations are similar to reciprocals since in both of these organizations the individual underwriter is an insurer. A Lloyds association, however, is a proprietary organization operated for profit, and the underwriter member is always an individual insurer. A reciprocal is composed of individuals seeking ways to obtain insurance "at cost," and its members are both insurers and insureds at the same time.

Lloyds associations are of two basic types: London Lloyd's and American Lloyds.

LLOYD'S OF LONDON

In 1985, articles in news media* began reporting stories about large losses suffered by underwriters at Lloyd's of London resulting from large damage awards to asbestos victims in the United States and misappropriated insurance funds. One reporter quoted an unnamed "name" as saying, "I stand to lose my home, and I have no family to turn to. It's scary."

More than 300 names (investors) refused to provide proof that they had sufficient assets to cover more than $80 million of claims which they claimed were caused by a fraudulent underwriting scheme. One article reported that an uncertainty existed in that in the future those facing large losses may argue that they also are victims of fraudulent underwriting and refuse to pay up. To guarantee that claims will be paid, the Lloyd's organization was reported to have set aside $88.4 million of its $225.7 million central contingency fund.

*For example, "Lloyd's Backers Scrambling," *Calgary Herald*, May 14, 1985, p. E-1, and "The Unthinkable Has Happened at Lloyd's," *Business Week*, August 19, 1985, p. 37.

London Lloyd's. The Lloyd's of London are among the best known insurers in the world and are, in fact, one of the earliest known types of insuring operations. Lloyd's started in 1688 in London, England, as an informal group of merchants taking marine risks. They first met at Lloyd's Coffee House. Their operations are now world-wide, and they operate extensively in the United States, largely in what is known as a surplus line market. This market consists of risks that domestic insurers have rejected for one reason or another. Lloyd's business is sold through registered brokers who are given the authority to represent them in this country. Only in Kentucky and Illinois are Lloyd's of London admitted to do business on any basis except as surplus line insurers.

There are about 26,000 underwriting members of Lloyd's of London called "names," who operate through groups known as syndicates, each with a manager who acts as a general agent to bind the individual underwriter on various risks offered. The Lloyd's corporation, it should be stressed, is not liable to the policyholder on risks assumed by its members. Nevertheless, the corporation sets up rigid standards of membership, and there has never been a reported instance in which the Lloyd's of London organization has defaulted on an obligation. There are a number of contingent funds created to back up the promises of the underwriters in the event that one of them becomes insolvent.[4]

American Lloyds. American Lloyds are authorized under the insurance laws of some states. Typically the law provides that only certain types of insurance, such as fire, ocean marine, inland transportation, and automobile insurance, may be written by Lloyds groups. The law further states that some minimum number of underwriters, such as 25, is necessary in order to start an association, each member of which must have an individual net worth of a certain amount, such as $20,000. As a protection for policy-holders, some laws provide for a minimum deposit, such as the same amount deposited by insurance. The law commonly indicates that the underwriters may not expose themselves to loss in any one risk of an amount in excess of a stated proportion of the cash and invested assets, unless proper reinsurance is effected.

American Lloyds do not enjoy the reputation for financial solvency that is attributed to Lloyd's of London. Only 37 American Lloyds organizations were listed in *Best's Key Rating Guide* for 1981. Of these, 34 are chartered in Texas, and one each in Indiana, New Mexico, and New York. Only 15 of the organizations received an A+ (excellent), from Best. In the past it has been common for members of American Lloyds associations to limit their individual liabilities and otherwise protect themselves against catastrophic claims. Reserves have been inadequate and failures not uncommon. Some states, such as New York, prohibit the formation of new associations of Lloyds.

Relative Importance of Private Insurers

In the United States there are about 3,468 property and liability (1985) and 2,082 life insurance (1984) companies. Most of the business, however, is done by relatively few insurers. It is estimated that only about 26 percent of the property and liability insurers operate in all or most states.

The leading states for property-liability insurers are Illinois (289), Texas (220), Iowa (205), and New York (202). Together, these states have a fourth of the companies of this type. It is worth noting that in 1983 U.S.-based insurers collected about 54 percent of the total world nonlife insurance premiums.[5]

Considerable concentration also exists in the field of life insurance. For example, although there are nearly 2,100 companies in the United States, 31 of these, most of them mutuals, accounted for 60 percent of the assets and 44 percent of the life insurance in force.[6]

Stock companies tend to dominate as underwriters of various lines of property-liability insurance. Stock companies write more than 80 percent of homeowners and commercial multiple-peril premiums volume, and about two-thirds of the fire and automobile/bodily-injury premiums. Mutuals enjoy their greatest markets in the fields of automobile and workers' compensation insurance. Lloyds and reciprocals account for only a small share of the total property-liability insurance market.

In the field of life and health insurance, there are far more stock companies than mutuals, but mutuals write about 43 percent of the business. For example, in 1983 stock companies constituted about 94 percent of all operating companies, but these insurers accounted for only about 57 percent of the total life insurance in force. In 1950 mutual insurers had a 70-percent share, and stock insurers 30 percent. Thus, stock insurers are gaining market share in the field of life insurance. This is due primarily to the fact that most of the new insurers that have formed in the field of life insurance since 1950 have been stock companies.

On the other hand, the mutual companies in property insurance have grown more rapidly than stock insurers, primarily because the mutuals have tended to specialize in the types of insurance (particularly automobile coverages) for which the markets have been growing most rapidly. Furthermore, mutuals have used cost-cutting methods that have made the product available at generally lower rates than those offered by stock insurers.

In summary, the data show that in the field of property insurance stock companies are most significant, while in life insurance mutual companies predominate. However, in each field the dominant type of insurer has been losing some of its share of the total market due to the growth of the other insurer group.

Insolvency of Insurers

Continuing financial solvency of the insurer with whom you deal is of obvious importance since, unless your insurer has the ability to respond to claims, the whole purpose of insurance is defeated. Insurance institutions are not backed by a federal agency in the same way bank deposits are protected. Instead, the danger of loss from insolvent property-liability insurers has been recognized by the establishment in all states of "guaranty funds." Under the terms of most laws, these funds must reimburse policyholders for any losses caused by bankrupt insurers, subject to stated deductibles and maximum loss limits which vary from state to state. The funds are supported by assessments against other insurers operating in the same state. From the inception of the funds in 1969 through 1984, 104 insolvencies have occurred among property-liability insurers, including 20 in 1984. These data do not include assessments made under New York's law,[7] which operates separately from the other funds. Guaranty funds also exist in about half of the states for life insurers, but detailed statistics on their operations are not published.

Many insurer insolvencies can be traced to the inexperience or dishonesty of management. Losses also result from poor underwriting practices, inadequate rates, investment losses, lack of attention to loss prevention, and competitive pressures. Data from Best's suggest that more life insurers than property-liability insurers are liquidated, merged, or converted from one form of organization to another. A relatively small proportion of insurers fail outright; rather, they are taken over by larger and stronger insurers without loss to policyholders.

In spite of liquidations and reorganizations of insurers, the record of longevity among U.S. insurers is very good. For example, there are 197 life insurers that have been in business for more than 50 years. Among these, 71 have been in business for more than 100 years.[8]

More than 200 property-liability insurers have operated for 100 years or more, and few have failed outright. Insurers are among the oldest companies doing business in the U.S. and include such important firms as Insurance Company of North America (chartered in 1792), Aetna Insurance (1819), New England Mutual (1835), Mutual Life of New York (1842), and Massachusetts Mutual (1851).

Employment in Insurance

The insurance industry employed about 2,000,000 persons in 1984, divided roughly as follows:

Employed by property-liability insurers	472,700
Employed by life insurance and other companies	775,100
Employed as agents, brokers, and service personnel	770,000
Total	2,017,800

Most of the jobs in insurance are salaried positions, and less than a third are in marketing or distribution. This information contradicts the frequently held opinion that most jobs in insurance are selling. Data also reveal that women constitute about 65 percent of the insurance industry work force, and women hold about 46 percent of all professional-level positions.[9]

Ownership of Insurance

A national survey conducted in 1984 revealed that the property-liability insurance industry has been able to reach most U.S. citizens who own homes or autos. The study found that about two-thirds of U.S. citizens own a home or condominium and a third rent their living space. About 93 percent of the survey-respondent homeowners indicated that they had purchased property or liability insurance on their homes and possessions, but only a third of the renters did so. Apparently, many of those who rent either do not perceive a need to insure their personal possessions or cannot afford to do so. Although most of the respondents said they believed it was important to have liability insurance, not all had this protection. Nearly

90 percent of the homeowners, but only 54 percent of the renters, said they were protected by liability coverage. It is estimated that 92 percent of the buying public has purchased automobile insurance.[10] These data reveal the industry's progress, and they expose opportunities and areas for further market penetration by those employed in insurance.

Studies by the Life Insurance Marketing and Research Association yield data showing how the life insurance industry is reaching its market. The Association reported the following: (1) The sale of life insurance is steadily increasing. For example, ordinary life insurance in 1984 gained 9 percent over 1983. (2) Two-thirds of U.S. families owned some form of life insurance, but life insurance is growing less rapidly than health insurance, which now accounts for over half of the premium income collected by life insurers. (3) Most life insurance is purchased by those in the age groups 25–34 (39 percent) and 35–44 (31 percent). These are the age groups forming new families and establishing homes. (4) The average amount of life insurance owned by insured families in 1983 was $68,300 indicating a substantial acceptance of the industry's product.[11]

CHANNELS OF DISTRIBUTION IN INSURANCE

There are many arrangements that may be made for the distribution of the insurance contract. These arrangements are comparable to the channels taken by physical goods. For example, life insurance generally takes a short, direct channel, while property insurance normally uses a long, indirect channel with one or more independent intermediaries involved. In some fields of property insurance in recent years (notably automobile coverage), increasing emphasis has been placed on the use of more direct channels. Some of the reasons for these developments will be explained here.

Direct Distribution in Life Insurance

Life insurance is distributed in two main ways: through salaried group insurance representatives and through individual insurance agents, who usually work on commission. Under each of these methods, the contact between the insurer and the customer is a direct one in which the insurer maintains a "one-on-one" relationship with the insured and in which independent intermediaries usually are not involved.

Group Insurance. Life insurers offer many of their products on a group basis, i.e., under contracts covering groups of persons rather than individuals. Examples include group life insurance, group health insurance, and group pensions. The customers for group coverage are generally business firms. Persons employed to sell and service this business usually receive a salary and bonus. Frequently the group representative works closely with commissioned agents, who may first locate a potential customer for group insurance and who receive a commission if the group representative succeeds in making the sale.

Individual Insurance. Policies sold to individuals are usually handled by life insurance employees known as agents or underwriters. The agent or underwriter contacts the ultimate consumer and reports directly to the insurer or to an intermediary, commonly called a general agent, who in turn reports to the insurer. The authority of the underwriter or agent is limited; the underwriter cannot be called an independent intermediary since he or she is actually an employee working under contract with the guidance of the insurer or the insurer's representative.

A **general agent** in life insurance is an individual employed (usually at a state or county level) to hire, train, and supervise the agents at a lower level. The general agent sometimes collects premiums and remits them to the home office of the insurer. Usually the general agent represents only one insurer and works on a salary plus commission plan, or sometimes on commission only. The general agent is not an independent intermediary in the sense that a typical wholesaler is, for the general agent does not exercise final control over the issuance and the terms of the contract. The company normally is not bound by the general agent in putting a contract in force. The general agent exercises no control over the amount of the premium, has no investment in inventory, does not own any business written, and has no legal right to exercise any control over policyholders once he or she leaves the employment of the company.

Data reveal that only about half of all persons selling life insurance obtain more than 50 percent of their incomes from this activity.[12] The remainder presumably handle, in addition, nonlife policies or perform other types of work. Thus, life insurers do not always enjoy distribution by agents exclusively devoted to their product.

The system of direct distribution has grown up in life insurance because of several basic factors:

1. The need of the insurer to maintain close control over the policy "product"
2. The need of the insurer to exercise control over sales promotion and competition
3. The infrequent purchase of life insurance
4. The ability of an agent to make a better living through specialization

Need for Close Control over Product. The insurer needs to maintain close control over the policy "product" because of its complicated nature, its long duration, and the fiduciary relationship required between the insurer and the insured. A direct channel is appropriate where such close control is desired.

Need for Control over Sales Promotion and Competition. Life insurance is very competitive. The policies of the many companies competing for business are similar in nature. Hence, extra promotion and competition on the basis of superior sales techniques of agents often represent the difference between rapid and mediocre rates of growth for a life insurer. The insurer can exercise much greater control over these factors by employing a direct channel of distribution.

Infrequent Purchase of Life Insurance. There are no compelling reasons for life insurance to be offered as one of the many contracts available from a given agent, as is true in property insurance. A buyer usually purchases life insurance infrequently, has infrequent need for claims service, and has little day-to-day contact with the agent regarding endorsements on policies, requests for information, and the like.

This is not to imply that the life insurance agent renders no service once the contract has been put in force. The agent stands ready as the local representative to the insured, answers questions, and writes letters to the insurer on behalf of the insured. But this service is not so demanding of the agent's time that a large business operation would be required to provide it. An agent's time is best spent in securing new sales.

Better Living Through Specialization. The life insurance agent who represents one insurer and deals exclusively in life insurance has usually found it possible to make a better living by specializing in one field than by taking on many different kinds of insurance. Insurance is a complex subject. Fitting life insurance to an individual's particular needs requires the professional service supplied by the agent. Advanced knowledge of the subject is needed to render the quality of sales service usually expected. An agent generally does not become an expert in all lines of insurance, but rather, concentrates in one area.

Because the agent usually finds that one company offers all the types of life insurance necessary for clients' needs, and because the agent wishes to avoid the necessity of becoming familiar with the rate manuals and procedures of many companies, the agent usually represents one company only.[13] This situation calls for a direct channel of distribution, for each life insurer can usually distribute its contracts in sufficient volume in a given area at lowest cost by hiring representatives to cover the area. There is no need for hiring any intermediary to handle the product.

Direct Writing in Property-Liability Insurance

In some lines of property insurance, intermediaries have been dispensed with and the contract is marketed directly from the insurer to the insured. Small amounts of insurance are sold directly by mail, and no agent of any kind is employed; all negotiations are made between the insurance company and the consumer. In most cases, however, the insurer employs a representative called an **exclusive agent** to handle its business, to solicit prospects, to take care of paperwork, and in general, to serve as the insurer's direct contact with the insured. Insurers who employ this type of distribution are called **direct writers.** They include some of the largest insurers in the business.[14]

Direct writers have their greatest volume in the field of automobile insurance, but are expanding into other lines such as residential fire and commercial property insurance. In general, direct writers have been able to sell insurance at lower cost to the final consumer, and this, plus a vigorous advertising campaign, has contributed greatly to their success. The lower cost has been achieved by the insurer largely through stricter underwriting and smaller allowances to the agent for the production and servicing of business. For example, stock insurers writing in New York in 1980 paid an average of 13.2 percent of premiums to agents, as commission and brokerage expense, in the area of private-passenger automobile bodily injury and auto property-damage liability. Leading direct writers, by contrast, paid commissions between 8 and 9 percent. Such differences also existed in other lines of insurance.[15]

An explanation of the growth of companies employing direct channels of distribution may be found in some observations about the nature of consumer buying habits in insurance and other fields. As noted earlier, channels of distribution tend to be fixed in a free-enterprise system according to whether or not they are as efficient as alternative methods. In the tangible-goods field, the postwar years have seen the growth of discount houses that generally concentrate on the sale of shopping goods, which are relatively high-priced items, are subject to infrequent purchase, and are substantially standardized in nature. These stores take a considerably lower markup on such goods than is traditional and still make enough profit to justify their existence. They generally offer few of the "frills" associated with the traditional department store.

In the sale of automobile insurance, a situation similar to that of the discount house exists. The product consists of a fairly standardized policy issued once or twice a year, costing a substantial sum of money and requiring little service except when a claim arises. The traditional allowance to the independent agent is about 15 percent of the premium dollar. This allowance is granted year after year, even though the agent may do little to earn it after the business is first procured. With the tremendous growth in the number of autos in the United States, a mass market in this field became possible, and some insurers saw an opportunity to capture a large amount of it by devising more efficient methods of business development. Accordingly, innovations such as continuous policies, lower agents' commissions, direct billing from the insurer to the consumer, and specialized adjusting offices to handle claims were instituted. These innovators were rewarded with a great relative growth. For example, in 1984 direct writers collected nearly 54 percent of all the automobile liability and 46.7 percent of homeowners insurance premium volume.

The gains made by direct writers were accomplished at the expense of insurers using the American Agency System, described below. For example, national and regional insurers both lost substantial market share in automobile and homeowners insurance over the period 1970–1984. (See Table 4–3.)

The channel of distribution for a majority of property insurance lines is indirect. A system of intermediaries, comparable to the wholesaler-retailer system in tangible-goods marketing, is used. This system has been termed the **American Agency System.**

In property insurance the intermediary most comparable to the wholesaler is called the **general agent,** while the retailer is called the **local agent** or **broker.** These terms are not to be confused with those that are applied in the field of life insurance.

General Agent. In property insurance the general agent usually has a great deal of authority over the distribution of the insurance product. While the general agent does not "take title" in the same sense that a wholesaler would take title to the inventory purchased from a manufacturer, nevertheless, the general agent has the incidents of ownership that accomplish almost the same purpose as would be accomplished by outright ownership. For example, the general agent can vary the terms of the contract in individual instances, has considerable authority to negotiate the price of the contract where this is permitted under state laws governing rates, and has authority over the terms of distribution agreements with local agents.

Dealings with the insurer are almost in the nature of banking. The contract of the general agent calls for producing business on the general terms agreed upon and at a given commission rate. The general agent has almost complete control over the business written and looks upon the insurer as a source to pay losses, to be responsible for policyholders' funds,

**Table 4–3
Market Shares of Major
Types of Insurers, 1970
and 1984**

	Percent Premiums Written by					
	Direct Writers		National		Regional/ Specialty	
Line of Coverage	1970	1984	1970	1984	1970	1984
Workers' Compensation	26.9	21.4	59	60.9	14.1	17.7
Automobile	43.9	53.7	38.4	29.9	17.7	16.3
Homeowners	25.4	46.7	48.9	32.2	25.7	21.1
Commercial Multiple Peril	5.8	13.3	78.7	68	15.4	18.7
Fire	10.1	20.2	67.1	49.3	22.8	30.5
General Liability		18.3		62.5		19.2
Overall P/C Mkt Prem		39.3		42.6		18.2

Sources: *Best's Review—Property and Casualty Editions,* 1970 and 1985.

to meet the requirements of insurance commissioners, to effect reinsurance agreements, and the like. The general agent, like a wholesaler, usually represents more than one company.

Local Agent or Broker. The local agent, likewise, is an independent intermediary, in the property insurance business. As the "retailer," the local agent deals with the final consumer of insurance. The local agent may represent from 10 to 20 separate insurers and has authority to bind these insurers on most of the contracts that are written. In most cases the local agent is supplied with forms, and has the authority to write a policy and deliver it to the insured. The local agent "owns" the business he or she writes; that is, the local agent has the legal right of access to customer files and to solicit renewal of policies. The insurer does not have the right to give this renewal information to another agent.

If the insurer cancels the agency contract of the local agent, usually the local agent will renew the policies of this insurer with a new insurer, and there is little that the old insurer can do about it. The agent works on a commission basis and has the responsibility of collecting premiums, and after retaining the commission, remits the balance to the general agent or to the insurer directly.

Exclusive Agent. The local agent described above may be contrasted with **exclusive agents** of direct writers, (sometimes called **captive agents**), and with brokers. Exclusive agents represent only one insurer, not several. The exclusive agent does not own the business written. Generally, the exclusive agent does not handle loss claims or collect premiums; these are billed directly to the insured from the home office of the insurer. The exclusive agent receives a commission, but as noted previously, this commission is considerably smaller than the commissions allowed independent agents. The main task of the exclusive agent is to sell new business, keep in contact with customers, and serve as a communications link between the insurer and the insured.

Brokers vs. Agents. Brokers operate in a manner similar to local agents, although legally they represent the consumer, not the insurer. Thus, if the consumer asks a broker to obtain insurance, the broker must make contact with the insurer before coverage is binding. Agents may bind coverage immediately because they are the legal representatives of the insurer. Of course, many brokers also hold agency contracts with insurers and may bind coverage immediately because of this status.

The Branch Office System. Often an insurer will not use a general agent, but will work directly through local agents or set up a branch office to work with local agents. This plan is known as the **branch office system.** It corresponds to a manufacturer's sales branch in the tangible-goods field. This system gives the insurer more control over the distribution of its contracts than when a general agent is employed.

Is the American Agency System Doomed? Naturally, those insurers and their agents committed to the traditionally long channel of distribution have become concerned over the future of their business, for the inroads of the direct writers are unmistakably clear. As shown in Table 4–3, national insurers using independent agents have lost market share in every major line of business except workers' compensation. This loss of business has occurred in commercial lines as well as personal coverages. Corresponding gains in market share have been won by direct writers, especially in homeowners' coverages. However, the market share of regional and specialty insurers using independent agents has increased in some lines, such as fire and workers' compensation and commercial multiple peril. Presumably, regional and specialty insurers offer certain advantages to the consumer in the use of independent agents.

Opinion has been expressed that the agency system is doomed, that it is only a matter of time until the direct writers take over completely and the independent agent passes from the competitive scene. Before such a radical view is taken, however, the fundamental economic basis of the independent agency system should be examined.

Advantages of the Agency System to the Consumer. The agency system grew because it was needed to distribute the product of insurance efficiently. The agency system is an efficient way for the consumer to buy insurance—especially the business consumer. A firm might be spending $50,000 a year on 100 or more policies. To place this volume of business among many insurers by direct negotiation would be a time-consuming and unrewarding task. To keep track of the many involved details, and to keep abreast of the technical knowledge needed to place this business intelligently, would be very difficult without assistance.

The independent agent, who represents many companies and receives a constant flow of information from the insurers, can effectively supply professional assistance. The consumer receives valuable aid from the agent when a loss occurs. The agent helps the insured file proofs of loss and intervenes on the insured's behalf if a controversy occurs. The agent can be instrumental in helping the insured obtain coverage for risks that might otherwise be turned down by an insurer. Finally, the independent agent helps the insured plan a well-rounded, integrated program of insurance.

Advantages of the Agency System to the Insurer. The agency system evolved also because it is economical for the insurer. Most insurers would find it uneconomical and undesirable to attempt to place a single agent or perhaps two agents in a given territory, as is done by life insurers, with the expectation that these agents would represent only this insurer for all the business that the insurer hopes to develop in the territory. There are at least two main reasons why this is true.

First, the financial capacity of many insurers is such that they cannot accept all the business offered them from one geographical or industrial location for fear of undue concentration of risks. An insurer would thus turn down business offered, its agents would lose commissions, and the consumer would have to shop around in order to obtain coverage. Matters are greatly simplified if the agent represents several insurers and can thus obtain markets for all the business developed.

Second, when an insurer enters a territory, certain minimum services to the consumer must be offered—claims must be handled, premiums collected, credit extended, and questions of policyholders answered. The insurer is expected to take care of a myriad of details that it could not handle directly. Moreover, the insurer could not afford to perform these functions through a salaried representative until the volume of business in a specific area had grown sufficiently large to justify the expense. This is usually not possible, except perhaps in metropolitan areas. Even where the volume of business does increase sufficiently, the insurer may not wish to jeopardize the good will of policyholders and agents by switching to a direct writing system.

Outlook for the Agency System and Direct Writing. Direct writing has grown fastest in lines where there is a mass market for a standardized product that requires little continuous service. As these conditions do not exist in all areas of insurance, particularly in the industrial market, it is extremely doubtful that direct writers will capture all of the market. It is perhaps true that the basic nature of a typical agency contract will be amended to reflect the changed conditions that have been brought on by direct writing. For example, insurers might take over some of the services now performed by agents and brokers, and reduce commissions accordingly. It seems unlikely, however, that the independent agency system will be replaced by direct writing unless the property insurance business should become much more greatly concentrated than it is now. As one authority stated many years ago:

> The agency companies are under pressure to cut costs, the direct writers are under pressure to give more service. The end result will probably be, not the demise of either one of the competing marketing systems, but the improvement of each.[16]

Mass Merchandising

Mass merchandising, as it has come to be known, is a method of distributing property-liability insurance directly to customers through employer payroll deduction. Underwriting is done on an individual basis. Although premiums are usually cheaper because of various economies in mass merchandising (absence of sales commissions and accounting economies), employers do not normally contribute to the premium on behalf of employees, as is common in the field of group life insurance plans. A major reason for this is the fact that such contributions are not tax deductible to the employer, and payments so made are taxable income to the employee.

In spite of their advantages, mass merchandising plans have not become extremely popular. Independent agents have generally opposed the adoption of such plans because many agents depend on individually issued personal-lines business for their livelihoods. Mass merchandising plans threaten the growth of their markets.

Another limiting factor in mass merchandising is the element of adverse selection, which has often produced poor underwriting experiences. Enrollment in plans is voluntary. For example, employees who have had poor driving records and are paying high rates on their car insurance may be attracted to a mass merchandising plan in which rates may be lower. The profit is higher than the expected losses for the mass merchandisers.

SUMMARY

1. Insurance may be classified according to type of coverage (personal or property), by ownership (private or public), and by type of demand (voluntary or involuntary).
2. There are two predominant legal forms taken by insurers: stock companies and mutual companies. Property insurance is dominated by stock companies, while life insurance is dominated by mutuals. In both lines of insurance, however, the minority forms of insurers are gaining. Lloyds and reciprocals, as types of insurers, do a negligible portion of the total insurance business in the United States.
3. As measured by premiums collected, personal insurance (coverages involving the risk of loss of a person's income) is more than three times as large as property insurance (coverages involving the risk of loss of a person's property). Governmental insurers account for about 46 percent of the total insurance premiums collected, with privately organized insurers receiving the remaining 54 percent.
4. In general, there are two basic methods of distributing the insurance service. The first method, direct distribution, used in life insurance predominantly, uses semi-independent representatives whose authority is limited. The second method, indirect distribution or the American Agency System, following the pattern of distributing tangible consumer goods, uses intermediaries who operate independent businesses.
5. While the direct writing method of distribution is gaining in prominence in lines where standardized contracts and large-scale sales are possible, the traditional American Agency System continues to dominate the insurance distribution scene because it enjoys certain basic advantages. Undoubtedly the two systems will exist side by side in the foreseeable future.

QUESTIONS FOR REVIEW

1. (a) What are two major types of insurance? Explain the basic logic behind the classification of insurance used in this chapter.
   (b) Which type of insurance is most important from the standpoint of premium income? What reasons would you suggest for the relationship observed?

2. (a) Do mutual insurers provide for assessments?

  (b) What advantages and disadvantages are there to the policyholder in being subject to assessments?

3. Suggest possible reasons why stock insurers dominate in such lines as commercial multiple-peril policies, but have a smaller share of the auto collision insurance market.

4. In both reciprocals and Lloyds associations, individuals are the underwriters. What significant differences exist between individuals in the two forms of organization?

5. What trends characterize the respective market shares of stocks and mutuals in property and life insurance? Can you suggest any reasons for these trends?

6. Why is direct writing typical in life insurance, but the exception in property insurance?

7. Does the American Agency System involve a long channel or a short channel of distribution? Is this system doomed because of the action by direct writers? Discuss.

8. What services to the buyers of insurance are rendered by the retailer?

9. The text states that survey data expose opportunities for further market penetration by the insurance industry. In what areas could additional sales efforts logically be made in insurance? Why?

10. What is the difference between direct distribution and indirect distribution in the insurance industry? Give examples of each.

11. What is meant by the term "mass merchandising" as applied to the insurance industry?

QUESTIONS FOR DISCUSSION

1. The mutual insurer has been called "communistic" in concept because there are no stockholders. Mutual advocates counter this charge with the statement that gain is the motive of the organizers of both stock and mutual companies. Evaluate both of these arguments.

2. Three items relating to insurer failures are as follows:

(a) In 1973 it was disclosed that one of the largest life insurers in the United States, the Equity Funding Life Insurance Co., had claimed assets that did not exist and had sold huge amounts of fictitious insurance policies to reinsurers. A court-appointed attorney to handle the reorganization under Chapter 10 of the bankruptcy statutes found no top executives on hand to help because they had all been fired. About 80 percent of the assets were found to be nonexistent, and so were two-thirds of its claimed policyholders. Yet in three years the company was reorganized under a new name, the Orion Capital Corp., and it continues in business today. Most of the $380 million in claims against Equity Funding were settled with notes and stock in Orion, which started with assets of about $115.

(b) A news report stated, in part, "Allied Reciprocal Insurers, formerly Peoples Inter-Insurance Exchange ... is broke. Attorney says company can't meet judgements and calls in Idaho department. . . . The underwriting exhibit of the company showed total of income of $636,777, disbursements of $677,046, incurred losses of $4,274,627, underwriting expenses of $365,482, and total net underwriting losses of $106,326 . . . the only out to pay off outstanding claims will be for the insurance department to assess the policyholders unless some other reciprocal should decide to angel its deficits."

(c) Another news report stated, in part, "The New York Insurance Department took over control of Professional Insurance Co. The department said that Professional's capacity was impaired by about $1.6 million. Professional writes primarily professional malpractice insurance. New York has . . . fund that would protect most New York policyholders."

What are the major reasons for insurer insolvencies, and which would appear to be important in the above cases?

3. In 1979 it was reported that Lloyd's of London, which had issued contracts guaranteeing against cancellation of computer leases, may lose as much as $1 billion, a potential loss greater by far than any other insured loss in history. Since Lloyd's is believed to have collected less than $50 million in premiums, some observers believe that Lloyd's may shatter precedent and refuse to pay claims in full. The huge losses were caused by wholesale cancellation of computer leases following the introduction of a new, improved, and less costly computer that gave incentive for leasing companies to replace their computers and to cancel old leases. If a lease were cancelled, the insurer was to pay the leasing company any revenues that it lost, after taking into account the proceeds from placing the computer with a new user.

(a) In your opinion, does the leasing policy meet the requirements of insurable perils? Why or why not?

(b) Do you believe Lloyd's should have refused to pay claims in full?

NEW TERMS AND CONCEPTS

Personal Coverages
Property Coverages
General Insurance
Life and Health Insurance
Private Insurance
Public Insurance
Voluntary Coverage
Involuntary Coverage
Stock Company
Mutual Company
Assessable Policy
Farm Mutual
Factory Mutual
General Writing Mutual
Fraternal Carrier

Reciprocal
Interinsurance Exchange
Attorney-in-Fact
Lloyds Association
London Lloyd's
Surplus Line Market
Underwriter
General Agent
Direct Writer
Exclusive Agent
American Agency System
Local Agent
Branch Office System
Mass Merchandising

NOTES

1 This text is devoted mostly to the field of private insurance. Some attention is given to the major types of governmentally sponsored insurance in Part 7.

2 For sources, see notes to Table 4–1 in 1962, 1968, 1973, 1977, 1981, 1984, and present editions of this text.

3 The term **underwriter** is said to have originated with Lloyd's of London. The method of assuming risk is for each member to write his or her name under the total amount of any one insurance application that the member wants to take. Thus, a member who assumes $1 million of a $10 million marine venture signs the application for $1 million and thereby assumes $1

million of liability. The member thereby becomes known as an underwriter.

4 Examples are the central guarantee fund of several million pounds held by the corporation, a trust fund deposited in New York for the benefit of American policyholders, underwriting deposits made by individual underwriters, and reserves held by underwriting agents. For a complete statement of the security provisions required by Lloyd's of London, see *Best's Insurance Guide with Key Ratings*, issued annually, D. E. W. Gibb, *Lloyd's of London* (1957), and B. Dooby, *Lloyd's of London—A Detailed Analysis of Results 1950-1977* (London, England: Lloyd's of London Press Ltd., 1985).

5 See Table 2-2.

6 *Life Insurance Fact Book 1984* (Washington, D.C.: American Council of Life Insurance, 1985), p. 89.

7 *1985-1986 Property/Casualty Fact Book*, p. 41.

8 *Life Insurance Fact Book 1984*, p. 89.

9 *1985-1986 Property/Casualty Fact Book*, p. 12. Original data were from the U.S. Bureau of Labor Statistics, the American Council of Life Insurance, and the Insurance Information Institute.

10 *1985-1986 Property/Casualty Fact Book*, p. 13.

11 *Life Insurance Fact Book 1985*, p. 4.

12 *Life Insurance Fact Book 1981* (Washington, D.C.: American Council of Life Insurance, 1981), p. 92.

13 There is a definite tendency for more and more successful agents to "broker" business through other life insurers and also to branch out into nonlife lines. However, information on the extent to which this has taken place is not available.

14 Examples are State Farm Mutual, Allstate, Nationwide Mutual, Liberty Mutual, United Service Auto, and Farmers Insurance Group.

15 *1980 Loss and Expense Ratios* (New York: New York Insurance Department, 1981).

16 Chester M. Kellogg, "Present Insurance Outlook" (an address before the conference of Mutual Casualty Companies, Lake Delton, Wisconsin, June 6, 1956).

5 FUNCTIONS AND ORGANIZATION OF INSURERS

After studying material in this chapter, you should be able to:

1. Explain why "production" in insurance is called "selling" elsewhere.
2. State the true meaning of underwriting.
3. Show how insurance premiums are calculated and adjusted.
4. Explain why some very high losses may not increase your rates significantly.
5. List the criteria a proper insurance rate must meet.
6. Differentiate between experience and retrospective rating.
7. Describe how the merger movement in insurance is affecting the business.
8. State the meaning and purpose of reinsurance.
9. Explain why "insurance exchanges" were formed in the United States.

Basic to understanding insurance is a knowledge of what functions insurers perform and how they are organized to carry out these functions. This chapter shows how the various functions and organizations are related, analyzes the influence of the merger movement in insurance, and, finally, discusses the subject of reinsurance and its techniques.

FUNCTIONS OF INSURERS

The functions performed by any insurer necessarily depend on the type of business it writes, the degree to which it has shifted certain duties to others, the financial resources available, the size of the insurer, the type of organization used, and other factors. Nevertheless, it is possible to describe the usual functions that are carried out, and it should be remembered that the specific nature and extent of each function varies somewhat from insurer to insurer. These functions are normally the responsibility of definite departments or divisions within the firm. The chief activities carried on by insurers are:

1. Production (selling)
2. Underwriting (selection of risks)
3. Rate making
4. Managing claims
5. Investing and financing
6. Accounting and other record keeping
7. Providing certain miscellaneous services, such as legal aid, marketing research, engineering services, and personnel management.

Production

One of the most vital functions of an insurance firm is securing a sufficient number of applicants for insurance to enable the company to operate. This function, usually called **production** in an insurance company, corresponds to the sales function in an industrial firm. The term is a proper one for insurance because the act of selling is production in its true sense. Insurance is an intangible item and does not exist until a policy is sold.

The production department of any insurer supervises the relationships with agents in the field. In firms such as direct writers, where a high degree of control over field activities is maintained, the production department recruits, trains, and supervises the agents or salespersons. Its responsibility runs deeper than this, however. Many insurers support marketing research departments whose job is to assist the production department in the planning of marketing activities such as determining market potentials, designing and supervising advertising, conducting surveys to ascertain consumer attitudes toward the company's services, and forecasting sales volume.[1]

In firms using independent agents as the primary channel of distribution, the extensive use of facilitating services in the production of business is not common. Special agents (or marketing representatives) are used to explain company policies and to serve as the chief point of contact between the home office and the field forces. The chief job of selling is left to the agency force.

Underwriting

Underwriting insurance includes all the activities necessary to select risks offered to the insurer in such a manner that general company objectives are fulfilled. Underwriting is performed by home office personnel who scrutinize applications for coverage and make decisions as to whether they will be accepted, and by agents who produce the applications initially in the field. The required status in the organizational structure of authority to make final underwriting decisions varies considerably among insurers and among lines of insurance. In some organizations (generally in the property-liability insurance area) agents can make binding decisions in the field, but these decisions may be subject to postunderwriting at the home office because the contracts are cancellable upon due notice to the insured. In life insurance, agents seldom have authority to make binding underwriting decisions. In all fields of insurance, however, agency personnel usually do considerable screening of risks before submitting them to home office underwriters. In some companies agents are often referred to as underwriters.

The Objective of Underwriting. The main objective of underwriting is to see that the applicant accepted will not have a loss experience that is very different from that assumed when the rates were formulated. To this end, certain standards of selection relating to physical and moral hazards are set up when rates are calculated, and the underwriter must see that these standards are observed when a risk is accepted. For example, it may have been decided that a company will accept no fire exposures situated in agricultural areas or will take no one for life insurance who has had cancer within a period of five years.

The underwriter, in reviewing an application for fire insurance where a building is located at the edge of an agricultural area, or in reviewing an application for life insurance in which the individual had cancer four and one-half years ago, asks the question, "Can I make an exception for these applications, or must I reject them because they do not come within the technical limitations of my instructions?" In answering this question, the underwriter visualizes what would happen to the company's loss experience if a very large number of identical risks were to be accepted. If the aggregate experience would be very unfavorable, the underwriter will probably reject the applications.

Sound underwriting practice recognizes that while profitable business is an important object, it is a mistake to accept only business in which it is extremely certain that no losses will occur. To do so would no doubt make the job of the producer more difficult, if not impossible, and would mean too low a volume of business to support operations. A happy medium must be sought between the extremes of very safe and very hazardous exposures on which to write insurance.

Services that Aid the Underwriter. In life insurance the underwriter is assisted by medical reports from the physician who made the examination of the applicant, by information from the agent, by an independent report (called an inspection report) on the applicant prepared by an outside agency created for that purpose, and by advice from the company's own medical advisor. In fire and liability insurance (as well as life insurance), the underwriter has the services of reinsurance facilities, mapping departments to report on the degree of concentration of exposures in any one area, and credit departments to report on the financial standing of applicants.

Company Procedures that Aid the Underwriter. The underwriter is also guided by fairly definite company procedures regarding the various physical and moral hazards that affect the probability of loss in given lines of business. In fire insurance, for example, a great deal of assistance is given by the rules that set up certain classes of buildings with definite characteristics, such as type of construction, type of occupancy, degree of protection by city services, and exposure to various physical hazards. Unless there is something unusual about the structure or its occupancy, there is very little problem of selection because most of the important underwriting decisions have already been made.

In assessing the moral hazard, however, serious problems may arise for which few rules have been promulgated. One rule that is widely observed is that if a serious moral hazard such as dishonest management is known to exist, the business is rejected outright and no attempt is made to accept it at higher than normal rates or to impose other restrictions. The difficulty lies in judging whether or not a moral hazard actually exists. The judgment of the underwriter is of paramount importance to the general success of any insurance company, and in the matter of assessing a moral hazard the quality of the underwriter's judgment is put to one of its severest tests.

Policy Writing. Part of the work of the underwriting department may be most concisely described as **policy writing.** In property and liability insurance the agent frequently issues the policy to the customer, filling out forms provided by the company. For this reason, the agent is often termed an underwriter. A check on the work of the agent to determine the accuracy of the rates charged, whether or not a prohibited risk has been taken, and other matters, is done by the **examining section** in the home office of the insurer. In life insurance the policy is usually written in a special department whose main task is to issue written contracts in accordance with instructions from the underwriting department and, since most policies are long-term in nature, to keep a register of them for future reference.

Conflict between Production and Underwriting. Because the underwriting department has often turned down business that has been previously sold by an agent, an apparent conflict of interest has arisen between these two areas. The problem is similar to that which exists between credit and sales in other firms, with a good sale ruined because credit is not approved. The conflict is, of course, only apparent. Neither the agent nor the underwriter will profit long by too strict or too loose underwriting. Too strict underwriting will choke off acceptable business and may create unnecessary expenses involved in cancelling business already bound by the agent. Too loose underwriting invites such substantial losses that the company may be forced to withdraw entirely from a given line, to the detriment of the agent.

Underwriting Associations. In 1985 there were 39 associations formed by insurers to assist in the underwriting function. These associations, or syndicates, normally specialize in certain areas, such as nuclear energy, foreign coverages, aviation risks, marine risks, grain elevator risks, and the like. Through such cooperation, the risk in these areas is spread among a large number of insurers, and specialized personnel can be hired economically to supervise loss control procedures and handle other underwriting decisions. In this way, the underwriting function can be carried out more efficiently and with less risk to individual insurers.

A prominent example of an underwriting association is the Industrial Risk Insurers (IRI), comprised of 45 large stock insurers. This organization employs nearly 600 engineers and stresses loss prevention as a key factor in its operation. It conducts research and training for its own engineers and for those of its members. Its research laboratories continuously test various materials for combustibility and reliability of operation. Field offices are maintained in large cities throughout the country. The IRI writes all types of property-liability insurance, and each member accepts a percentage of the premium and of the corresponding losses and expenses. The IRI specializes in large concentrations of value such as oil installations and industrial plants.

Another organization assisting underwriters, with special emphasis on loss control, is the National Fire Protection Association, an association of stock fire insurance companies dedicated to fire prevention. Underwriters Laboratories, originally formed for the purpose of testing combustibility of various materials at the World's Fair in Chicago in 1893, has steadily grown in influence and scope of activity; today its seal of approval is famous. This seal is looked for by most buyers of products such as electrical appliances, building materials, fireproof containers, and other products where the factor of fire safety is important. In liability insurance, the National Safety Council has had similar influence.

Rate Making

Closely allied to the function of underwriting is that of **rate making,** a function that is extremely technical in most lines of insurance. In general, rate making involves primarily the selection of classes of exposure units on which to collect statistics regarding the probability of loss. In life insurance this particular task is relatively uncomplicated, since the major task is to estimate mortality rates according to age and other factors such as sex, smoking habits, and occupational groups. In other fields, such as fire and workers' compensation, very elaborate classifications are necessary. In the latter field, for example, several hundred classes of industries are distinguished and a rate is promulgated for each. Rate making is usually supervised by specialists known as actuaries. (See Figure 5-1.)

Once the appropriate classes have been set up, the problem becomes one of developing reliable loss data for each class over a sufficiently long period of time. Converting that data into a useful form for the purpose of developing a final premium is the next step. This requires incorporating estimates of the cost of doing business into the premium structure on an equitable basis. The rate-making function uses an estimation of the cost of including certain policy benefits, or of changing policy provisions or underwriting rules, as well as the cost of writing business on which no data whatsoever have been accumulated.

Makeup of the Premium. The **insurance rate** is the amount charged per unit of exposure. The **premium** is the product of the insurance rate and the number of units of exposure. Thus, in life insurance, if the rate is $25 per $1,000 of face amount of insurance, the premium for a $10,000 policy is $250.

The premium is designed to cover two major costs: the expected loss and the cost of doing business. These are known as the **pure premium** and the **loading,** respectively The pure premium is determined by dividing the total expected loss by the number of exposures. In automobile insurance, for example, if an insurer expects to pay $100,000 of collision loss claims in a given territory, and there are 1,000 autos in the insured group, the pure premium for collision will be $100,000 ÷ 1,000, or $100 per car. The loading is made up of such items as agents' commissions, general company expenses, taxes and fees, and allowance for profit. The sum of the pure premium and loading is termed the **gross premium.** Usually the loading is expressed as a percentage of the expected gross premium. In property-liability insurance, a typical loading might be 33 percent. The general formula for the gross premium, the amount charged the consumer, is

$$\text{Gross Premium} = \frac{\text{Pure Premium}}{1 - \text{Loading Percentage}}$$

In the above example, where the pure premium was $100 per car, the gross premium would be calculated as

$$\frac{\$100}{1 - 0.333} = \$150$$

Another way to express the same concept is to divide the loss cost (pure premium) by the loss ratio (one minus the loading percentage). In the above

Figure 5-1   Organization Chart of a Large Stock Insurance Group, Handling All Lines

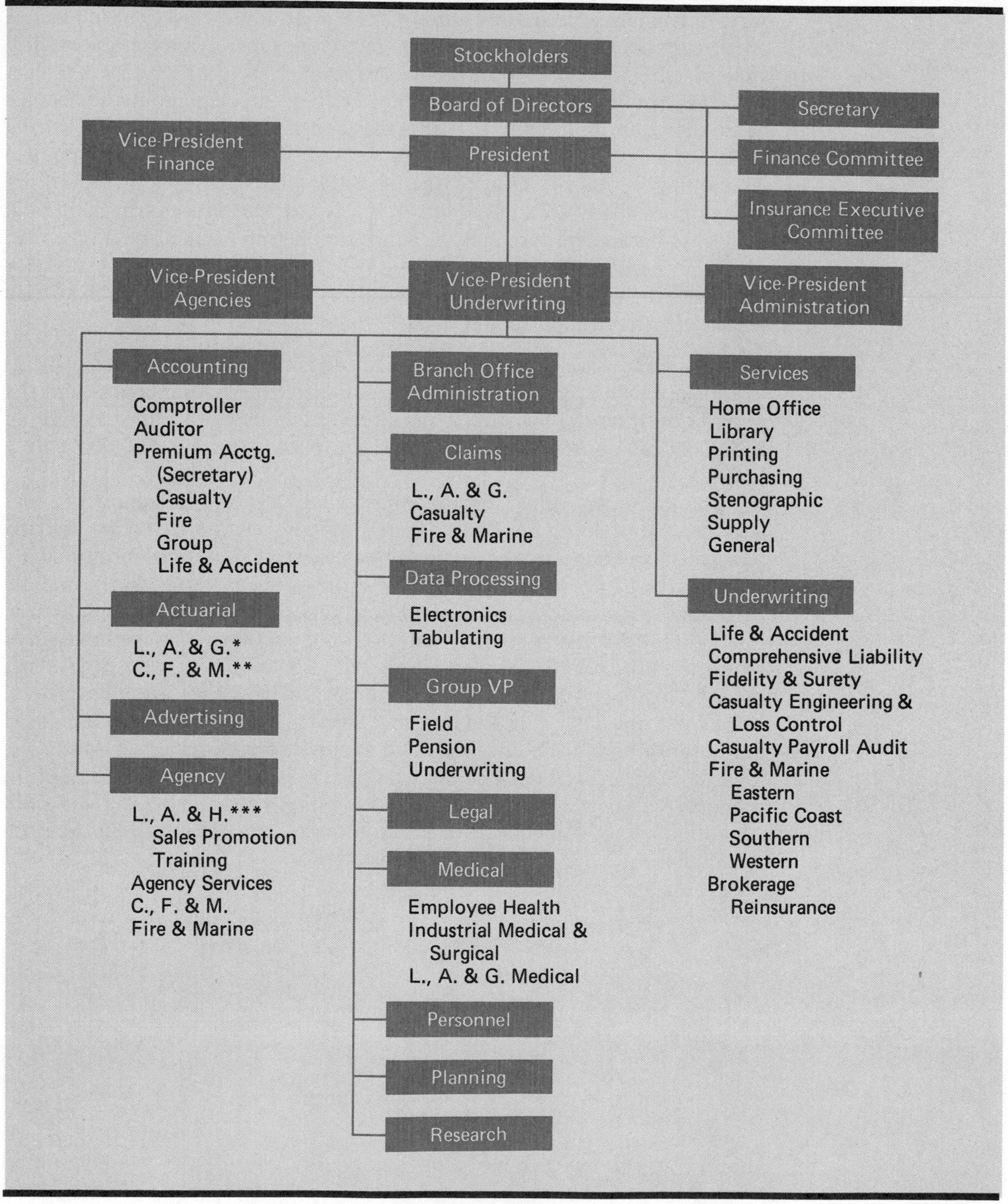

Stockholders

Board of Directors

President

Vice-President Finance

Secretary

Finance Committee

Insurance Executive Committee

Vice-President Agencies

Vice-President Underwriting

Vice-President Administration

Accounting
Comptroller
Auditor
Premium Acctg.
  (Secretary)
  Casualty
  Fire
  Group
  Life & Accident

Actuarial
L., A. & G.*
C., F. & M.**

Advertising

Agency
L., A. & H.***
  Sales Promotion
  Training
Agency Services
C., F. & M.
Fire & Marine

Branch Office Administration

Claims
L., A. & G.
Casualty
Fire & Marine

Data Processing
Electronics
Tabulating

Group VP
Field
Pension
Underwriting

Legal

Medical
Employee Health
Industrial Medical &
  Surgical
L., A. & G. Medical

Personnel

Planning

Research

Services
Home Office
Library
Printing
Purchasing
Stenographic
Supply
General

Underwriting
Life & Accident
Comprehensive Liability
Fidelity & Surety
Casualty Engineering &
  Loss Control
Casualty Payroll Audit
Fire & Marine
  Eastern
  Pacific Coast
  Southern
  Western
Brokerage
  Reinsurance

example, the loss cost of $100 would be divided by 0.667, the loss ratio, producing $150 as the gross premium.

Another way to explain rate making in insurance is by analogy with retail store pricing. If a grocer buys a loaf of bread for $1 and sells it at retail for $1.50, the grocer's gross margin (or markup) is $.50 and is expressed as a percentage of the selling price of $1.50, namely, $33\frac{1}{3}$ percent ($.50 ÷ $1.50). The grocer's cost of bread corresponds to the pure premium in insurance, ($1 in the preceding case) the expected cost of loss. The grocer's gross margin, or markup, corresponds to the loading in insurance, i.e., $33\frac{1}{3}$ percent in the case in question.

A basic difference between pricing bread and pricing insurance is that in the case of bread the grocer knows the cost of merchandise in advance, whereas in insurance the expected cost of loss, or pure premium, must be estimated. The loss, if it occurs, happens at some future time after the policy is in force. Two factors must be estimated and are subject to errors in forecasting: *frequency* of occurrence and *severity* of loss. The insurer does not know in advance exactly how often a loss will happen or what its size will be. The expected cost of loss is a function of both frequency and severity of loss.

Insurers handle forecasting errors in rate making by making estimates of both objective and subjective risk (discussed in Chapter 1). For example, the underwriters may utilize a probability distribution of loss frequency and severity. (See Chapter 4.) The underwriter may add extra margins of safety in the estimate to compensate for a large perceived subjective risk.

Interest Earnings. The basic rate-making method used in property-liability insurance does not make a direct allowance for interest to be earned on policyholders' funds held by the insurer until they must be paid out as losses. In life insurance an allowance is made for a minimum assumed rate of return on policyholders' funds. In recent years interest rates have risen to the point that policyholders are demanding that some recognition of this factor be made. Now insurers tend to adjust premiums for the interest factor, either directly or indirectly. For example, premiums may be reduced to the point that an underwriting *loss* is anticipated, in the knowledge that interest earnings can offset this loss and still produce an overall profit for the insurer.

Rate-Making Guidelines. All states set down certain criteria that insurers are expected to observe in calculating rates. Guidelines that insurers usually use specify that the rate:

1. Should be adequate to meet loss burdens, yet not be excessive
2. Should allocate cost burden among insureds on a fair basis
3. Should be revised reasonably often to reflect as current a degree of loss experience as is feasible
4. Should encourage loss-prevention efforts among insureds, if possible.

While on casual review these criteria seem simple enough, they raise many difficult problems in their application. Some of these problems, many of which will probably never be completely solved either by insurers or by regulatory authorities, are described in the following paragraphs.

Adequacy of the Rate. If a rate is to be adequate but not excessive, how wide a margin should these limits impose? From one standpoint, an underwriter may reason that to have an adequate premium it is necessary to collect an amount sufficient for all possible contingencies, while another underwriter may have a much different view of the size of these possible contingencies. This problem arises from the previously noted fact that the insurance rate must be set *before* all the costs are known. In many lines of business the entrepreneur may ascertain all or nearly all costs before setting a price. If costs cannot be determined, the entrepreneur usually will insist that the contract of sale be subject to later adjustment to reflect the actual costs or will insist on a "cost plus" type of contract. In insurance, however, a definite estimate must often be made in advance, with no possibility of a later negotiation if the estimation of loss was incorrect. Frequently an estimate is inaccurate because the underwriter uses past experience to estimate the future, while the insurance contract may involve a substantial future period during which conditions change drastically. It is easy to see that opinions as to the future of insurance costs can vary widely.

The problem of preventing rates from becoming excessive has been the subject of much legislation, yet unrestricted competition often leads to rates that are too low for the long-run solvency of insurance funds. Having rates too low is just as undesirable as, if not worse than, having them too high. Above all, the insured is seeking assurance that personal losses will be paid if and when they occur.

Fair Allocation of Cost Burden. Just how far should the underwriter go in developing a rate that completely reflects the true quality of the individual hazard, thus making the rate fair? *Theoretically,* for life insurance purposes there should be an attempt to set individual premiums on the basis of occupation, income, marital status, drug or alcohol consumption, automobile accident record, years during which cigarettes have been smoked, and longevity of parents. *In practice,* none of these factors affects the premium individually, since age and sex are almost the sole discriminants. If the criteria of fairness are carried to an extreme, it might be said that each person should receive a slightly different rate to reflect that person's particular situation. This, of course, would be impossible to administer and would make the rate-making task hopelessly complex. However, a decision must be made concerning where to draw the line and what criteria of fairness to use.

Another class of problems arising out of the criteria of fairness deals with the determination of the exposure unit to which the rate is applied. Automobile rates, for example, apply to the individual car; workers' compensation rates, to each $100 of payroll; fire insurance rates, to each $100 of building value; and life insurance rates, to each $1,000 of policy amount on an insured life. Consider workers' compensation insurance. There are two employers in the same rating class, one paying 200 workers $6 per hour, on the average, and the other paying 300 workers $4 per hour, on the average. Assuming that each has an hourly payroll of $1,200, each would pay the same workers' compensation premiums. But the first employer has an exposure of 200 workers, while the second has 300 workers. Should each employer pay the same premium? It could be argued persuasively that the first employer, aside from having fewer workers exposed to accident, probably hires more competent people who have fewer accidents. However, no one has yet instituted a superior, yet practical, base for workers' compensation insurance.

Frequent Revision to Reflect Loss Experience. Insurance rates are generally revised gradually. Often it is many years before rates can be altered to reflect higher or lower costs. Consider automobile insurance, for example. Suppose it is desired to collect all loss experience data for a given year X. Since policies are issued continuously throughout the year X and have a one-year term, the rate maker must wait until the end of year X plus one month before starting to collect loss data. It may take an additional six months to gather and interpret all data and obtain approval for a rate change. The new rate promulgated for the coming year is, on the average, one year and three months old (one-half of the period dating from the beginning of year X to the time X plus one-and-a-half). The lag is much greater for policies issued for terms longer than one year.

In life insurance new mortality tables are adopted only after periods of several years, and any errors in rate-making assumptions must be corrected, if at all, through changes in dividend schedules. Because of these lags, certain allowances are made by the rate maker for observable trends. Errors in these allowances necessarily affect the criteria of adequacy and reasonableness. However, if a method could be found to incorporate loss data into the rate structure immediately (as the losses were experienced), it would probably be undesirable, since insurance is a commodity that does not lend itself to daily changes in price. Again, some reasonable compromise between the extremes of immediate adjustment and prolonged delay must be found, even at the expense of some uncertainty and error in future rates.

Encouragement of Loss-Prevention Efforts. Although ideally the insurance rate should encourage loss prevention on the part of the insured, it is difficult to achieve this objective. Remember that losses from most insurable perils occur outside the control of the insured. In some lines of insurance, such as fire, rate credits are given for measures that tend to reduce the severity once the losses due to the peril occur. However, there is great difficulty in defending the size of these credits, since any decision as to how much a safety device is worth in reducing losses is largely an arbitrary judgment. This problem is usually handled by some form of merit rating, as is discussed below.

Rate-Making Methods. One of the most difficult problems in insurance is that of developing rate-making methods that meet the criteria analyzed above. The methods employed can seldom meet these criteria; and underwriting judgment, unsupported by statistical evidence, often plays a major role in rate making. The calculation of an insurance rate is in no sense absolute or completely scientific in nature. As in most areas of the social sciences, the scientific method in insurance makes its greatest contribution in narrowing the area within which executive judgment must operate. The basic approaches to rate making follow.

Manual or Class Rating (Pure) Method. The **manual,** or **class rating, method** sets rates that apply uniformly to each exposure unit falling within some predetermined class or group. These groups are usually set up so that loss data may be collected and organized in some logical fashion. Everyone falling within a given class is charged the same rate. Any differences in hazard attributable to individual risks are considered unmeasurable or relatively small.

The major areas of insurance that emphasize use of the manual rate-making method are life, workers' compensation, liability, automobile, health, residential fire, and surety. (Surety bonds are discussed in Chapter 22). For example, in life insurance the central classifications are by age and sex. In workers' compensation insurance a national rate-making body collects loss-experience data of more than 600 industrial groups, and these data are broken down territorially by state. In automobile insurance the loss data are broken down territorially by type of automobile, by age of driver, and by major use of automobile. In each case it is necessary only to find the appropriate page in a manual to find out what the insurance rate is to be; hence the term, "manual rate making." The central technique in manual rate making is the pure premium method, as illustrated previously.

Loss Ratio Method. It may be impractical to employ the manual rating method in developing a rate because of too many classifications and subclassifications in the manual. In other words, there may be so many categories involved that losses on only a small number of exposures occur in a given time period. This small number of losses may be deemed insufficient exposure on which to base decisions from a statistical point of view. As a consequence, the new rate is developed by comparing the **actual loss ratios** A of combined groups with the **expected loss ratios** E and using the formula

$$\frac{A}{E} = \text{Percent Change Indicated}$$

For example, suppose that the actual loss ratio is 0.70, while only 0.60 was expected when the old rate was promulgated. In this example, $A = 0.70$, $E = 0.60$, and the formula yields $\frac{0.70}{0.60}$. The new rate would be $\frac{7}{6}$ times the old, nearly 17 percent higher. The loss ratio method is actually a rate-revision method rather than a rate-making method.

Individual, or Merit Rating, Method. The **individual,** or **merit rating, method** recognizes the individual features of a specific risk and gives this a rate that reflects its particular hazard. A variety of merit-rating plans are used to give recognition to the fact that some groups of insureds, and some individual insureds, have loss records that are sufficiently credible to warrant reductions (or increases) in their rates from that of the class to which they belong.

Special Rating Classes. One generally used device is for the underwriter to set up **special rating classes** for which discounts from the manual rates are made, either beforehand in the form of a direct **deviation,** as it is called, or as a dividend payable at the end of the period. Presumably only those insureds meeting certain requirements are eligible for the special rate. For example, some direct-writing companies, such as factory mutuals, severely restrict the classes of risk they underwrite and, if warranted, pay substantial dividends as a reward for loss-prevention efforts.

In the field of life insurance, mutual insurers pay dividends that differ in amount according to the type of policy. Life insurers also grant rate deviations for special classes of insured groups, known as **preferred risks,** and charge extra premiums on other groups, called **substandard risks.** Automobile insurers have experimented with this method by distinguishing among applicants on the basis of their automobile and traffic violation records. In workers' compensation certain groups are entitled to a premium discount that varies according to the size of the annual premium.

Schedule Rating. Another widely used plan of individual rating is **schedule rating.** The best example of this is in the field of commercial fire insurance, where each individual building is considered separately and a rate established for it. The physical features of the structure are analyzed for factors that presumably affect the probability of loss, and credits in the rate are given for good features. These credits are in the form of a listing, or a schedule. In effect, the insured is rewarded in advance for features it is hoped will yield a lower loss cost for all similar structures as a group. Schedule rating is also used in burglary insurance, with the insured being given rate credits for loss-prevention devices such as burglar alarms and burglarproof safes.

Experience Rating. A third way in which an individual risk may receive special consideration by the rate maker is through **experience rating.** Experience rating is permitted in cases where the hazards affecting the insured's operation are sufficiently within the insured's control so that it is reasonable to expect a reduction of losses through special efforts. If such special efforts are made, the insured is permitted a lower insurance rate for the coming period. The experience-rating plan applies to insureds with a relatively large exposure so that the experience that is developed has some chance of being credible (see shortly). Thus, experience-rating formulas generally apply to business firms with large and diversified types of operations where the loss ratio is at least partially within the control of the insured. Unlike schedule rating, which grants a discount for safe features, experience rating requires that the insured prove the ability to keep loss ratios down before being qualified for a loss reduction. Most experience-rating formulas also impose a rate increase in case the loss ratios become higher than expected. Experience-rating plans are used in workers' compensation, general liability, group health, unemployment, and other lines of insurance.

Retrospective Rating. A final way in which attention is given to the problem of recognizing individual differences in risk is through **retrospective rating.** In contrast to experience rating, under which rate adjustments apply only to the future period, retrospective rating permits an adjustment in rates for the period just ended. The premium is determined, in whole or in part, by the actual record of losses suffered by the insured during the policy year. The contract is renegotiated, so to speak, after all the facts have been determined. Employers become partial self-insurers, but they use the commercial insurer to limit their losses.

Combination Method. In many lines of insurance a **combination** of manual and merit rating is used in different degrees. The rate maker may develop a manual rate and then proceed to set up a system whereby individual members of a group may qualify for reductions from the manual rate if certain requirements are met, or they may be subjected to rates higher than the manual rate under certain other conditions.

Credibility. A concept of basic importance in insurance-rate making is credibility. In general terms, **credibility** refers to the degree to which the rate maker can rely on the accuracy of loss experience observed in any given area. For example, assume that the rate maker is faced with the task of revising a rate for a certain type of policy issued by the company in a given geographical area. The loss ratio on these policies indicates that losses have been considerably higher than anticipated. Should future rates be based on the experience of these losses, or is there a considerable likelihood that the last year under consideration produced higher-than-average losses only by random chance? The rate maker wishes to know how many claims there would have to be before the loss experience observed should be given 100, 90, 80, 50, or 10 percent weight in preparing the rate revisions.

If upon the next renewal the rate maker raised the insurance premium of everyone who had suffered a loss, the purpose of loss spreading, which is inherent in the insurance mechanism, would be largely lost. If each small group were, in effect, required to pay for its own losses, risk transfer would not be achieved. It would not do to raise the fire rates of a small community that had a disastrous fire in only one year, because the experience for such a small class for only one year is certainly not credible. Yet the insurer, in the interest of fairness, must make reasonable classifications of insureds and perils and charge an appropriate rate for large groups falling within these classifications. It is not fair for one group to subsidize another group if each group is large enough to develop loss experience that is reasonably credible.

The Credibility Formula. The concept of credibility may be stated succinctly by the formula

$$PP = PPi(Z) + PPp(1 - Z)$$

where

PP = pure premium to be developed for a given insured i.
PPi = pure premium based on the insured's *past* loss experience.
PPp = pure premium based on the past experience of the *larger population* to which the insured belongs.
Z = the weight (credibility factor) to be applied to the insured's past experience. Z is a number ranging from 0 to 1.

Pure premium is developed by collecting all loss data falling into each class to be rated, dividing by the number of exposure units, and arriving at a number representing expected losses.

As Z increases, more weight will be applied to the insured's past experience; and if Z equals 1, the pure premium to be charged is based entirely on the insured individual's past experience. This would be the case if the insured has a very large number of homogeneous exposure units at risk and is in effect large enough to be self-rated. It should be noted, furthermore, that as Z increases, the term $1 - Z$ decreases, and with it the weight given to the loss experience of the population.

For convenience, the values given to Z are expressed as percentages. The rate maker generally develops a scale of credibility for different lines of insurance, running from 0 to 100 percent. As an example in applying the formula, let us assume that an employer's workers' compensation policy is found to produce a loss ratio of 0.70, compared with an expected loss ratio of 0.60 for employers in this occupational group. However, the number of claims on which the 0.70 loss ratio was calculated was of such size and type that only 60 percent credibility can be attached to this ratio. In the formula, $Z = 0.60$, $PPi = 0.70$ and $PPp = 0.60$. The pure premium for the employer in the forthcoming period would be based on a loss ratio of 0.66 rather than 0.70, that is, $PP = 0.70(0.60) + 0.60(1 - 0.60) = 0.42 + 0.24 =$

0.66. Because the employer's experience is not fully credible, the rate would be increased only 10 percent $\frac{0.66}{0.60}$ rather than 16.7 percent $\frac{0.70}{0.60}$.

Rate-Making Associations. **Rate-making associations,** or **rating bureaus** as they are called, are very important. Even though it might appear that such groups would be in violation of antimonopoly laws, most states specifically authorize rate-making groups. This type of cooperation is essential because many companies do not have a sufficiently large volume of business in certain lines to enable them to develop rates that are statistically sound. When the experience of many companies is pooled, however, as is done by a rate-making organization, there is a large enough body of data to permit a higher degree of credibility. The rate-making organization is usually supported financially by member companies, but in some states the government owns and operates the agency. This is common in the field of workers' compensation insurance. State regulation has general jurisdiction over insurance rating practices to see that the rate-making association does not dispense excessive or discriminatory rates. Rate-making cooperation is common in fire, automobile, bonding, inland marine, and workers' compensation insurance. In life insurance, while there are no rate-making bodies as such, a similar result is achieved by the universal adoption of certain standard mortality tables.

The influence of rate-making cooperation goes beyond the mere setting of fairly uniform rates. If companies are to charge similar rates, it follows that most of them must also plan fairly similar amounts for losses and expenses. Therefore, policy provisions must be quite uniform; otherwise the cooperating insurers will not experience loss ratios that are uniform. Thus, rate-making bodies have worked toward uniform policy provisions and standard policies in general. This has had a far-reaching influence on the insurance business and has enabled an orderly development of the coverage. As will be seen, the standardization of policies is widespread. Another influence in some lines of insurance has been the control exercised by rate-making bodies over allowances for agency commissions and other expenses. This has controlled, at least partially, competitive bidding for agents' services, and has kept the production cost of insurance at a reasonable level in most lines of insurance.

A prominent example of a rate-making association is the Insurance Services Office (ISO), which makes rates in various lines of property and liability insurance for its member companies. ISO conducts actuarial research, makes rates for some insurers, offers advice to others on rating problems, acts as a statistical agent for the submission of experience data to regulatory authorities, develops standard policies, files forms to state insurance departments, and offers management advice to its member companies. Other important rating organizations are the National Council on Compensation Insurance, which develops and administers rating plans for workers' compensation coverage, and the Surety Association of America, which makes rates for fidelity and surety bonds.

Managing Claims and Losses

Settling losses under insurance contracts and adjusting any differences that arise between the company and the policyholder are the functions of **claims management.** Claims management is often accomplished in the field through adjusters who are employed to negotiate certain types of settlements on the spot. Such adjusters may have considerable legal training. The claims department of an insurer will have the responsibility of ascertaining the validity of written proofs of loss, investigating the scene of the loss, estimating the amount of the loss, interpreting and applying the terms of the policy in loss situations, and finally approving payment of the claim. These functions are more extensive in property-liability insurance than in life insurance because of the higher frequency of losses, the predominance of partial losses, and the uncertainty of the amount of loss in individual cases.

In many cases, the adjuster is a salaried staff employee of the insurer. In territories where an insurer does not have sufficient volume of business to employ a staff adjuster, the insurer will often make use of an **independent adjuster.** This may be an adjustment bureau, such as the General Adjustment Bureau or Crawford and Company, corporations established to handle adjustment for insurers on a fee basis. There are also **public adjusters** who specialize in adjusting functions, representing policyholders in dealings with insurers. Public adjusters, who are legal agents of the policyholder (not the insurer), usually work on a contingency fee, say 10 percent, under which the insured claimant pays the adjuster according to the amount the adjuster is able to collect from the insurer on a given claim.

Careful management of claim settlements is of paramount importance to the success of an insurer. Reluctant claims settlement brings with it public ill will, which may take years to overcome.[2] Often negotiation with the claims department is the only direct contact that the insurance buyer has with the insurer. A bad impression received on that contact may result in loss of business, court action, regulatory censure, or even suspension of the right to carry on business in the jurisdiction involved. On the other hand, an overly liberal claims-settlement policy may ultimately result in higher rate levels and loss of business to competitors charging lower premiums.

Investing and Financing

When an insurance policy is written, the premium is generally paid in advance for periods varying from six months to five or more years. This advance payment of premiums gives rise to funds held for policyholders by the insurer, funds that must be invested in some manner. Every insurance company has such funds, as well as funds representing paid-in capital, accumulated surplus, and various types of loss reserves. Selecting and supervising the appropriate investment medium for these assets is the function of an **investment department.** Investment income is a vital factor to the success of any insurer. In life insurance, solvency of the insurer depends on earning a minimum guaranteed return on assets. In property and liability insurance, investment income has accounted for a very substantial portion of total profits and has served to offset frequent underwriting losses.

Since the manner in which insurance moneys are invested is the subject of somewhat intricate government regulation, the investment manager must be familiar with the laws of the various states in which the company operates. Investments must also be selected with due regard to the financial policies of the insurer. Property insurers typically have a combined capital and surplus ranging between 30 percent and 50 percent of total assets, and funds equivalent to this may be invested in common and preferred stocks. The extent to which this is done depends on the class of business written and on the need for liquidity. Life insurers, on the other hand, have few of their assets invested in common and preferred stocks, primarily because the nature of the life insurance obligation dictates that guaranteed amounts be repaid to policyholders. To accomplish this, bonds and mortgages are usually selected as the major investment mediums. Large insurers have separate departments for major classes of investments, such as real estate loans, policy loans, and city mortgages.

As shown in Table 5-1, insurers in the United States together were responsible for investing over one trillion dollars in 1984, most of it in the form of fixed obligations such as bonds and mortgages. In contrast to

Table 5-1
Where Insurers Invested Funds, 1984

	Percent of Funds Invested, by Type of Insurer	
	Property/Liability[1]	Life/Health[2]
Type of Investment		
Bonds	73%	49.6%
Common stocks	20	8.8
Preferred stocks	5	*
Mortgages and other	2	21.7
Real estate policy loans and other	—	19.9
Total Investments	100%	100.0%
Total Assets ($ billions)	$265.0	$773.0
Income from Investments ($ billions)	$17.7	$59.2
Income from Premiums ($ billions)	−$21.8	$134.8

*Not reported, or too small to be significant.
Source: [1] 1985–86 *Property/Casualty Fact Book* (New York: Insurance Information Institute, 1985), pp. 20, 23.
[2] 1985 *Life Insurance Fact Book* (Washington: American Council of Life Insurance), pp. 26, 32.

Part 2   The Insurance Institution

property-liability insurers, life insurers had substantial investments in real estate (3.6%) and policy loans (7.5%). Property-liability insurers as a group had a larger proportion of their assets invested in bonds and stocks than was true of life insurers as a group. In 1984, investment income was about 30 percent of total receipts of life insurers and accounted for the only source of gain for property-liability insurers, which lost heavily on underwriting that year.

Financing refers to the planning and controlling of all activities that are related to supplying funds to the firm. Insurance companies seldom have to raise outside funds since most of the normal financing requirements are met by reinvested profits. However, problems such as determination of dividend policies, meeting state solvency requirements, and handling the occasional negotiations for both long- and short-term capital sources fall within the province of the chief financial officer.

Accounting

The **accounting** function for insurance management has essentially the same purpose as accounting for the operating results of any firm, namely, to record, classify, and interpret financial data in such a way as to guide management in its policy making.

ARE RATE INCREASES JUSTIFIED?

Early in 1986, Ralph Nader, a prominent advocate of consumer protection, appeared on national U.S. television protesting sharp rate increases by major property-liability insurers. Mr. Nader stated that these increases were unjustified because, contrary to what insurers claimed, the insurance industry registered substantial profits in 1985 if they counted investment income, which more than offset underwriting losses they suffered that year.

Mr. Nader also argued that underwriting losses were a result of the insurance industry's own decisions to cut rates in previous years in an attempt to attract funds for investment at relatively high rates that were then available.

Spokespersons for the insurance industry countered these arguments by stating that investment income was insufficient to offset the large underwriting losses and that substantial rate increases were necessary. The property-liability insurance industry had a total net combined loss of $3.78 billion in 1984, and $3.47 billion for the first nine months of 1985. In both periods, investment income failed to offset underwriting losses. In fact, in 1985 underwriting losses were running 27 percent higher than in 1984.*

Best's Insurance Management Reports (Oldwick, NJ: A. M. Best Co., December 3, 1985).

Miscellaneous Functions

Various functions such as legal advice, marketing research, engineering services, and personnel work are often performed for an insurer by individuals or firms outside the company or by a specialized department set up within the company.

Legal Advice. The function of the legal adviser is to assist others in the company in their tasks. Underwriters receive aid in the preparation of policy contracts and endorsements so that the company's intention will be phrased in correct legal terminology. In the administration of claims, particularly disputed claims, legal aid is important; if court action is required, the legal staff must represent the company.

Legal aid is required in drawing up agency contracts, in investigating bond indentures and real estate titles, in preparing reports to the insurance commissioner, in advising on insurance legislation, and in preparing reports that are required by law. Hardly any phase of an insurer's many activities can be effectively performed without competent legal advice. Most large insurers have their own legal departments. Others use outside counsel only. All companies use outside counsel on occasion.

Marketing Research. Reference has already been made to the role of marketing research in assisting the production department. As yet, marketing research is not usually performed within the firm, except in the case of very large companies. The marketing research typically involves only selected types of research, such as testing and developing effective advertising. Such research can be a vital factor in the long-run success of any insurer. The success that direct-writing insurers have had in winning markets away from those insurers using the indirect channel of distribution has increased the interest of the latter in marketing research.

Engineering Services. Engineering services are used as valuable aids to rate making and underwriting, particularly in the field of property insurance. It is the function of the engineer to advise with respect to the conditions—that is, hazards—which make losses more likely. The services of the engineer in loss prevention and salvage operations are extremely important to the insurance mechanism.

Information concerning the physical characteristics of exposed property is necessary for intelligent underwriting. Rate-making classifications are usually developed on the basis of physical characteristics, and rate charges and credits are made on this basis. For example, the engineer provides information that will help answer the question, "How long will fireproof glass resist breaking when subjected to the heat of a burning building?" If a building has such glass, the underwriter is in a much better position to assess its importance. Again, the engineer may provide answers to the following questions: "How much will it cost to restore a burned building to its former condition? Is it economically feasible to raise this sunken oil drilling platform? For safety, in the event of an explosion, how far from buildings or vehicles should an oil tank be placed? How much do seat belts reduce injury in automobile accidents?" The usefulness of such information to the insurer is readily apparent.

Personnel Management. Personnel management normally includes selection and discharge of employees, keeping employment records, supervision of training and educational programs, administration of recreational and fringe benefit programs, and other similar functions. Most large companies and many small ones have separate personnel departments. Regardless of the size of the firm, personnel management is an essential function. Insurance, particularly life insurance, has experienced a somewhat more rapid turnover of employees than other industries. The need for giving increased attention to the problem of turnover and discovering its causes has increased the scope and importance of personnel management among insurance companies.

ORGANIZATION OF INSURERS

The organizational framework in which insurance functions are carried out varies considerably according to the size and scope of operations of the particular company. There are several ways in which organizational patterns may be classified: by function, by territory, by product line, and through groups or fleets of companies. Multiple-line and all-line organization, to be discussed, refer to the corporate structures employed to offer the insurance product. (See Figure 5–1.)

Functional Organization

Insurers frequently set up departments corresponding roughly to the various functions performed, such as underwriting, production, rate making, accounting, and financial. Each department has a supervisor or vice-president who is responsible for this function wherever it is performed throughout the organization. Functional organization is seldom used in a pure form, but is combined with other patterns.

Territorial Organization

If a company is operating over a large area, it may divide its operations according to geographical divisions. For example, in the company illustrated in Figure 5–1, the Underwriting section shows four territories established for fire and marine insurance. Many insurers organized in the eastern part of the United States have branch offices on the West Coast. Certain functions, such as investment and finance, legal, actuarial, and general accounting, are often carried out by a central office. Other functions, such as underwriting, claims, rate making, and production, are decentralized in each of the branches. Decentralization is a general practice when the size of distant markets increases to the point that it is more efficient to make certain decisions at a local level than to refer everything to a central office. An example of such a decision might be the underwriting of certain risks where frequent contact with the insured is necessary. Dealing from afar might be unwieldy and inefficient, and ultimately cause a loss of business.

Product Organization

In some insurance operations, particularly among multiple-line insurers, the problems arising from differing classes of insurance are so technical and specialized that it is inefficient to have all types of business handled by the same staff. In these cases, the business may be organized according to product divisions. As illustrated by Figure 5–1, the insurer may divide the underwriting function by line of business, such as life and accident, comprehensive liability, and fire and marine.

It is common in a life insurance company to find separate divisions handling group life insurance, group disability insurance, industrial life insurance, and group pensions. Within each group, major functions such as underwriting, accounting, claims, production, and policyholder service may be performed, with other functions carried on by the home office.

In property and liability insurance, particularly in multiple-line companies, separate divisions are commonly created for the major types of insurance, such as fire, inland marine, bonding, liability, automobile, and workers' compensation. Again, each division will perform certain major operating functions and use the centralized facilities of the insurer for the staff functions, such as actuarial, investment, legal, and general accounting. The degree of autonomy of product divisions varies with each firm, with some divisions being almost completely self-sufficient, and others being highly dependent on the centralized administration for service and for various aspects of decision making.

Group Organization

Much insurance in the world is written under the sponsorship of groups, or fleets, of insurers. A **fleet** is a group of companies operating under central holding company management. For example, in 1985 *Best* listed 296 groups operating in the United States, each of which controlled two or more companies, for a total of 1,202 insurers, both life and nonlife.[3] Groups were originally formed to enable insurers to offer a complete line of coverage because state laws restricted the types of insurance to be written by a single insurer. This restriction no longer exists because of multiple-line laws, but groups still continue to be important. The largest property-liability insurance groups in the United States in 1981 included State Farm, Allstate, Aetna Life and Casualty, Travelers, and Liberty Mutual. Group organization permits insurers to offer specialized services to clients, but at the same time consolidate functions that can best be coordinated from one central office (e.g., actuarial, financial management, and accounting). Groups also achieve other management and marketing economies, such as being able to offer a "department store" of financial services.

Multiple-Line Organization

Companies commonly described as **multiple line** are firms that underwrite many types of property and liability insurance within the administrative framework of a single organization. Only rarely may such companies handle life insurance directly; they usually must do so through a separate company. The multiple-line type of organization permits the simplification of insurance contracts. Most insurance authorities suggest that requiring a separate policy for every type of coverage is inefficient and unnecessary. Why not combine, say, fire, windstorm, automobile, residence liability, residence burglary, and a personal property floater into one "package policy" designed for the homeowner, who would then have just one company, one policy, and one agent for most insurance needs? The agent would have a much larger commission from personal lines and would be able to service each customer more satisfactorily. Furthermore, the customer would be likely to buy more coverages in a package than individually, thus enabling the insurer to obtain a wider spread of risks. The success of the homeowner's contract demonstrates the soundness of this reasoning.

Multiple-line legislation has opened up new fields to insurers. The new types of contracts that multiple-line laws have permitted have become known as **multiple-peril policies.** These are policies under which several different types of perils, formerly written under separate contracts, are now combined into one. They include both homeowners' policies and commercial multiple-peril contracts. In 1964 these contracts accounted for about 11 percent of premiums collected by major property-liability insurers, but by 1984 this percentage had risen to 19 percent. During this same period, premiums collected under fire and allied lines declined from 14 percent to 4 percent of the total.[4]

All-Line Organization

All-line organization refers to an arrangement by which an insurer may write all lines of insurance under one administrative charter. There are 13 states in which this is permitted by state law.[5] However, many insurers, through company fleets, write all lines. For all practical purposes, they seem to enjoy the same advantages as insurers who offer all-line coverages under one administrative framework.

THE MERGER MOVEMENT

Additional evidence of the interest in multiple-line and all-line underwriting among insurance company managers is the "urge to merge." Merging of insurance companies into consolidated units has been a major trend in insurance company organizational change in the post-World War II period.

Mergers in the insurance business may be classified according to the type of firm initiating the merger: insurance, financial, or industrial.

Insurance Company Initiated

The first type of merger has already been described in the discussion of multiple-line and all-line companies that have formed groups and holding companies. The major impetus to these mergers was to take advantage of legislation permitting the combination of formerly separate insurance operations into various types of insurance packages for better and cheaper distribution of insurance service to the consumer. There is also the desire of insurance companies to enter financial fields such as mutual funds, computer leasing, banking, and real estate. These companies include such giants as CNA Financial, CIGNA (a merger of two formerly independent giant insurers, INA and Connecticut General), US Life Corporation, American General, Transamerica, and Republic Financial.

Financial Company Initiated

The second type of merger occurs with the acquisition of insurance companies by concerns such as banks and finance companies. The major impetus behind these mergers appears to be the desire of financial firms to broaden their line of financial services to include insurance. Examples of firms making such acquisitions include American Credit Corporation (whose holdings include six insurance companies, both life and property), Capital Holding, Transamerica Corporation, Family Finance Corporation, Financial General Corporation, Investors Diversified Services, and CIT Financial Corporation.

Industrial Company Initiated

The third type of merger occurs when noninsurance and nonfinancial corporations begin to acquire existing insurance firms or form new ones to complement their other activities in manufacturing, retailing, or service. Examples of such mergers include International Telephone and Telegraph (which purchased Hartford Fire Insurance Co.), Leasco Data Processing (which purchased Reliance Insurance Co.), and Xerox (which merged with Crum and Forster). The captive insurer movement, described in Chapter 3, offers another example of corporate activity in the insurance arena.

Advantages to Insurers

To illustrate some of the advantages of mergers to the insurance firm, consider the case of an insurance group formerly operating in property and liability insurance, which now decides to acquire a life company. The life company has a large number of agents selling only life and health insurance. These agents have clients whose general insurance business may be solicited as well. A life agent who is not trained to handle general business or is not interested in doing so may turn over prospect lists to the insurer's local agents who specialize in this field. In return, the insurer's local agents may provide the life agent with many leads for additional sales of life and health insurance.

Acquiring a life insurer may be profitable. The life insurer may have a substantial income from investments that can bolster the earnings of the general lines insurer. Life insurance operations have had a better record of underwriting profit than general insurance, and the combined operation may thus produce higher and more stable underwriting profits. It is well known that many property-liability insurers depend on investment profits to offset underwriting losses on their general lines. The life insurance operation may lend considerable stability to an otherwise erratic profit performance among property-liability insurers.

Forming a **holding company** offers an insurer several financial advantages. For example, a holding company can raise capital through issuance of debt securities, a procedure not usually permitted an insurer. The captive insurer movement, described in Chapter 3, offers another example of corporate activity in the insurance arena. Also, holding companies, which are not subject to the investment restrictions of insurers, may compete with other financial institutions on a more equal footing.

Advantages to Financial Firms

A financial complex may acquire one or more insurers for reasons similar to those that motivate insurers to enter financial and related lines of activity. Among these reasons are:

1. The customer may be offered a "department store" of financial and related services. For example, life insurance and equities such as mutual funds often go hand in hand as an appealing plan for achieving financial security. The department store concept is especially significant in selling packages of benefits through payroll deduction, which in the future may commonly include fire and automobile insurance as well as life insurance, mutual funds, or pension plans.
2. Trained personnel are in short supply, and the merger may better utilize existing agents to handle more than one line. Very often the existence of the trained sales force of a life insurer motivates a mutual fund organization to acquire the insurer in order to obtain a ready-made sales crew.
3. Earnings may be stabilized and enlarged for the combined operation. When earnings in one type of insurance are low, they may be offset by profits elsewhere.

Advantages to Industrial Firms

An industrial concern may acquire insurance firms for several reasons:

1. The firm may be able to better utilize surplus resources of the insurer than the insurer can.
2. Many concerns, such as retailing, banks, or service companies, can sell insurance products effectively through existing distribution outlets. Thus, they can use their existing marketing position and business locations more profitably through broadened product lines. Allstate has been able to sell insurance through Sears Roebuck retail stores very effectively; similar operations have been implemented by the J. C. Penney Company. Automobile manufacturers can effectively sell their own insurer subsidiary policies through dealer outlets. Much insurance is also sold in banks. A corporation may also be able to insure its own risks effectively and economically by means of a wholly owned insurance company, a captive, as described in Chapter 3.

Disadvantages of Mergers

Merger activity has not always been advantageous to the parties involved. Insurers have sometimes entered new lines of business in which they were inexperienced and suffered unexpected losses. For example, large losses were suffered when the management of Baldwin-United, formerly known for pianos, entered the annuity field and promised interest returns to policyholders that could not be realized.

Possible Effects of Mergers on Insurance

We may speculate about the likely future effects on insurance operations as a result of the organizational changes just described, particularly the effects of the merger movement. Many of the effects to be described already are in evidence and may be expected to develop further.

Sales Effort and Compensation. Insurance salespersons may continue the trend toward becoming professional family financial counselors. The day of the part-time door-to-door insurance agent, real estate salesperson, or tax consultant appears to be passing. The straight commission compensation system in life insurance may gradually give way to the salary-bonus system. This has already occurred in group life insurance. Life insurance agents will increasingly be able to offer diverse insurance lines, particularly automobile and homeowners' coverages. Property-liability personnel will continue to offer increased services in the field of life and health insurance and pensions.

Product Lines. The tendency will continue to grow toward selling packages such as (1) insurance and mutual funds; (2) life insurance and variable annuities; (3) mortgage loans, life insurance, and property-liability insurance. The opportunities for combinations of equity products, insurance, and financial products seem limitless. Furthermore, the insurance holding company or financial holding company will be expected to offer a much broader range of services to the consumer than it does at present. Adjusting and claims handling, engineering, credit reporting, computer services, real estate services, trust services, estate planning, accounting, tax services, and many other services may be offered routinely.

Group Marketing. The new forms of business organization in insurance will reinforce the increasing tendency toward group marketing or mass merchandising. Life insurers have long been established in selling through payroll deduction systems in life and health insurance. The same systems are now being applied to property-liability insurance, equity products, and other services.

REINSURANCE

A significant part of insurance organization is **reinsurance,** a method created to divide the task of handling risk among several insurers. Often this task is accomplished through cooperative arrangements, called **treaties,** that specify the ways in which risks will be shared by members of the group. Reinsurance is also accomplished by using the services of specific companies and agents organized for that purpose. In turn, reinsurance companies also purchase reinsurance from one another on specific kinds of risks. Through reinsurance the entire industrial world is organized to share risks, so that a catastrophic loss in one part of the world may affect insurance companies and policyholders everywhere.[6]

Reinsurance may be defined as the shifting by a primary insurer, called the **ceding company,** of a part of the risk it assumes to another company, called the **reinsurer.** That portion of the risk kept by the ceding company is known as the **line,** or **retention,** and varies with the financial position of the insurer and the nature of the exposure. When a reinsurer passes on risks to another reinsurer, the process is known as **retrocession.**

Uses and Advantages of Reinsurance

Why would an insurer that has gone to all the expense and difficulty of securing business voluntarily transfer some of it to a third party? There are several reasons for this, the main one being that the primary insurer is often asked to assume liability for loss in excess of the amount that its financial capacity would permit. Instead of accepting only a portion of the risk and thus causing inconvenience and even ill will to its customer, the company accepts all the risk, knowing that it can pass on to the reinsurer the part that it does not care to bear. The policyholder is thus spared the necessity of negotiating with many companies and can place insurance with little delay. Using a single policy with a single premium also simplifies insurance management procedures. The policy coverage is not only more uniform and easier to comprehend, but the added guaranty of the reinsurer also makes it that much safer.

From the viewpoint of the insurer, reinsurance not only distributes risk; it has other uses and advantages. Stabilized profit and loss ratios are an important advantage in the use of reinsurance. It is true that good business often must be shared with others, but in return some bad business is also shared. In the long run it is usually considered more desirable to have a somewhat lower but stable level of profits and underwriting losses than it is to have a higher but unstable level.

This is not to imply that reinsurance arrangements necessarily reduce average profit levels, but they do smooth out fluctuations that would normally occur. Furthermore, reinsurance does not always mean the loss of premium volume, for one of the results of reinsurance is the procurement of new business. As a member of a group of ceding companies organized to share mutual risks, one ceding company must usually accept the business of other insurers. Some companies obtain a significant portion of their total premium volume in this manner, and others engage exclusively in the reinsurance business.

Reinsurance is also used to allow for a reduction in the level of unearned premium reserve requirements. For new, small companies especially, one of the limiting factors in the rate of growth is the legal requirement that the company set aside premiums received as unearned premium reserves for policyholders. Since no allowance is made in these requirements for expenses incurred, the insurer must pay for producers' commissions and for other expenses out of surplus. As the premiums are earned over the life of the policy, these amounts are restored to surplus.

In the meantime, however, the insurer may not be able to finance some of the business it is offered. Through reinsurance the firm can accept all the business it can obtain from its agency force and then pass on to the reinsurer part of the liability for loss, and with it the loss and unearned premium reserve requirement.

Finally, reinsurance may be used to retire from business or to terminate the underwriting on a given type of insurance. If a firm wishes to liquidate its business, it could conceivably cancel all its policies that are subject to cancellation and return the unearned premiums to the policyholders. However, this would be quite unusual in actual practice because of the necessity of sacrificing the profit that would normally be earned on such business. It would probably be impossible to recover in full the amount of expense that had been incurred in putting the business on the books.

Through reinsurance, however, the liabilities for existing insurance can be transferred and the policyholders' coverages remain undisturbed. If an insurer desires to retire its life insurance business and to cease underwriting this line, it may do so through reinsurance. Since the life insurance policy is noncancellable, the policyholder has the right to continued protection. If it were not for reinsurance, the insurer would find it difficult, if not impossible, to achieve its objective of relieving itself from the obligation of seeing that the insured's coverage is continued.

Types of Reinsurance Agreements

Organization for reinsurance is found in many forms, from individual contractual arrangements with reinsurers to pools whereby a number of primary insurers agree to accept certain types of insurance on some prearranged basis.

Facultative Reinsurance. The simplest type of reinsurance is an **informal facultative agreement,** or specific reinsurance on an optional basis. Under this arrangement a primary insurer, in considering the acceptance of a certain risk, shops around for reinsurance on it, attempting to negotiate coverage specifically on this particular contract. A life insurer, for example, may receive an application for $1 million of life insurance on a single life. Not wishing to reject this business, but still unwilling to accept the entire risk, the primary insurer communicates full details on this application to another insurer with whom it has done business in the past. The other insurer may agree to assume 40 percent of any loss for a corresponding percentage of the premium. The primary insurer then puts the contract in force.

The reinsurance agreement does not affect the insured in any way. Informal facultative reinsurance is usually satisfactory when reinsurance is of an unusual nature or when it is negotiated only occasionally. Such an arrangement becomes cumbersome and unsatisfactory, however, if reinsurance agreements must be negotiated regularly.

Occasionally an insurer will have an agreement whereby the reinsurer is bound to take certain types of risks if offered by the ceding company, but the decision of whether or not to reinsure remains with the ceding company. Such an arrangement is called a **formal facultative contract** or **obligatory facultative treaty.** It is used where the ceding company is often bound on certain types of risks by its agents before it has an opportunity to examine the applications. If the exposure is such that reinsurance is not needed or desired, the ceding company may retain the entire liability. In other cases it will submit the business to the reinsurer, who is bound to take it. Such reinsurance agreements are often unsatisfactory for the reinsurer because of the tendency for the ceding company to keep better business for itself and pass on the more questionable lines to the reinsurer.

Automatic Treaty. To protect all parties concerned from the tendency described above, to speed up transactions, and to eliminate the expense and uncertainties of individual negotiations, reinsurance may be provided whereby the ceding company is required to cede some certain amounts of business, and the reinsurer is required to accept them. Such an agreement is described as **automatic.** The amount that the ceding company keeps for its own account is known as its retention, and the amount ceded to others is known as **cession.**

Two basic types of treaties have been recognized: **pro rata treaties,** under which premiums and losses are shared in some proportion, and **excess-of-loss treaties,** under which losses are paid by the reinsurer in excess of some predetermined deductible or retention. In excess-of-loss treaties there is no directly proportional relationship between the original premium and the amount of loss assumed by the reinsurer.

There are many varieties of pro rata treaties, but perhaps the two most common are the surplus treaty and the quota share treaty. **Surplus treaties** cover only specific exposures—policies covering individuals or business firms—while **quota share treaties** cover a percentage of an insurer's business, either its entire business or some definite portion thereof. Illustrations of these agreements follow.

Under an **excess line,** or **first surplus, treaty,** the ceding company decides what its net retention will be for each class of business. The reinsurer does not participate unless the policy amount exceeds this net retention. The larger the net retention, the more the other members of the treaty will be willing to accept. Thus, if the ceding company will retain $10,000 on each dwelling fire exposure, the agreement may call for cession of up to "five lines," or $50,000, for reinsurance. The primary insurer could then take a fire risk of $60,000. On the other hand, if the primary company is willing to retain only $5,000 on a residential fire exposure, it may have only four lines acceptable for reinsurance, and could not take more than $25,000 of fire insurance on a single residence.

First surplus treaties call for the sharing of losses and premiums up to a stated limit in proportion to the liabilities assumed. Sometimes a **second surplus,** or even a **third surplus, treaty** is arranged to take over business that is beyond the limits set by the first surplus treaty. The surplus treaty is probably the most common type of reinsurance in use today.

Under the quota share treaties, each insurer takes a proportionate share of all losses and premiums of a line of business. An illustration of the quota share treaty is the **reinsurance pool** or **exchange.** Pools are usually formed to provide reinsurance in given classes of business, such as cotton, lumber, or oil, where hazards are of a special nature and where the mutual use of engineering or inspection facilities provides an economy for participating members. Each member of the pool agrees to place all described business it obtains into the pool, but it shares some agreed proportion, such as 10 percent or 16.67 percent, of the total premiums and losses. Quota share treaties are especially suitable for new small firms whose underwriting capacity is limited, and who would be unable to get started without such an arrangement because of the unearned premium reserve requirements.

It is not uncommon for a primary insurer to find that while it is willing to accept up to $10,000 on each exposure insured in a given class, it is unable to stand an accumulation of losses that exceeds $50,000. To impose a limit on such losses, the excess-of-loss treaty has been developed whereby the reinsurer agrees to be liable for all losses exceeding a certain amount on a given class of business during a specific period. Such a contract is simple to administer because the reinsurers are liable only after the ceding company has actually suffered the agreed amount of loss. Since the probability of large losses is small, premiums for this reinsurance are likewise small.

A variation of the excess-of-loss type of reinsurance is the spread-of-loss treaty under which the primary insurer decides what loss ratio it is prepared to stand on a given kind of insurance, and agrees with a reinsurer to bear any losses that would raise the loss ratio above the agreed level over a period of, say, five years. Thus, the ceding company has spread its losses over a reasonable time period and, in effect, has guaranteed an underwriting margin through reinsurance. In this way an unusually high loss ratio in a poor underwriting year is averaged in with other years.

Insurance Exchanges

In recent years a new organizational concept has evolved to facilitate the distribution of insurance through formal exchanges similar to the system employed by Lloyd's of London. Exchanges have been formed in New York, Miami, Florida, and Chicago, Illinois. The best known is in New York, which has authorized both the New York Insurance Exchange and a Free Trade Zone (FTZ).

The New York Free Trade Zone, which began operations in 1978, was formed to permit creation of insurance contracts free from New York's rate filing and other legal restrictions and taxes in given lines of coverages. To qualify for trading in the FTZ, new insurance contracts for the type of business which is already being offered by domestic or alien insurers must have first been rejected by three or more insurers. Because of the relaxation of normal controls, U.S. insurers are able to compete more effectively in world insurance markets, and in particular, to obtain business that formerly might have gone to Lloyd's of London. Examples of such business are those covering large or hard-to-place commercial exposures or special risks ($100,000 annual premium or above) in aircraft liability, oil spill insurance, satellite launches, or coverages for amusement parks.

The New York Insurance Exchange, which opened in 1980, offers insurers a trading floor where brokers may shop for coverages on behalf of clients. Coverages may include special risks, reinsurance, and foreign risks. Insurers admitted to the exchange must generally be large and experienced. Insurers work through designated "syndicates" whose broker-managers must be duly licensed by New York and must meet substantial minimum capital requirements. The advantages of the new exchange include increasing market opportunities in international insurance, enlarging world underwriting capacity, and creating new ways to invest in the insurance business.

SUMMARY

1. The major functions of an insurer are: (a) production (selling), (b) underwriting, (c) rate making, (d) claims management, (e) investing and financing, (f) accounting, and (g) miscellaneous functions, such as legal, marketing research, engineering services, and personnel management. These functions are performed both by the home office and by the agency staff in the field.

2. Underwriting is the task of selecting subjects for insurance in such a way that the assumptions underlying the rate structure are realized in practice. It is the underwrit-

ing, claims-handling, and rate-making tasks that are truly exclusive functions of insurance. The other functions, while they are necessary to carry out these basic tasks, are not exclusively insurance functions, since they are common to most business enterprises.

3. Rate making in insurance is unusual in that the price of the product must be determined before all the costs are known. The rate is composed of two elements, the loss cost, or pure premium, and loading. Various rate-making methods have been

devised to cope with the need to keep rates adequate but not excessive, fair to different classes of insureds, reasonably current, and responsive to loss-control efforts. These methods include manual or class rating, individual or merit rating, and combination rating. Insurers are assisted in the rate-making task through cooperative efforts with rating bureaus or associations.

4. Distinguishable organizational concepts are functional, territorial, product, and group organization. In general, as an insurer grows, it is more likely to use some form of territorial decentralization, and for very large insurers this is accompanied by decentralized product divisions.

5. Two central plans for organization may be identified: (a) single-line organization and (b) multiple-line organization. The former plan describes the pattern of organization typically used by insurers that write only specific lines of insurance, such as fire or life. This plan has led to what is known as group operations, or company fleets, whereby separate insurers writing one or two types of insurance merge into units under centralized control for the purpose of offering a more complete and diversified insurance service than is possible for each company operating separately. Multiple-line organization, on the other hand, describes the plan of operation used by insurers authorized to write several lines of insurance within the framework of a single administrative entity. Multiple-line organization has become legally possible in the United States only since World War II.

6. An extensive merger movement has taken place within the insurance industry. Three types of mergers are distinguished according to whether they have been initiated by insurers, financial institutions, or industrial corporations. The merger movement has had considerable effect on the insurance product, its distribution, and the financial position of the industry.

7. The insurance industry is characterized by a more extensive use of cooperative groups and associations than is true of almost any other industry. Most of these associations are formed because it is more economical to pool resources for carrying out tasks that are mutually needed than to perform them individually. Indeed, some tasks such as rate making, loss prevention, and reinsurance, can be performed in no other way.

8. Reinsurance is an important example of one task that is accomplished by external organization. The virtues of reinsurance include distribution of risk, stabilization of profits, reduction of legal reserve fund requirements, and facilitation of retirement from business. The major types of reinsurance agreements are facultative, pro rata, and excess of loss.

QUESTIONS FOR REVIEW

1. What justification is there for using the term "production" in the insurance field to refer to "selling"?

2. Distinguish between a rate and a premium in insurance.

3. An insurer develops a pure premium of $75 for residential fire insurance in Territory A. The expenses and profit allowance are calculated to be 25 percent of the gross premium. What should the gross premium be? Show your calculations.

4. (a) What criteria should a proper insurance rate meet?
   (b) Do you believe that an auto insurance rate that depends in part on the age of the driver meets these criteria? Explain why or why not.

5. Distinguish between experience rating and retrospective rating. Is the latter likely to be applied to a large firm or a small firm? Explain.

6. What major organizational difference exists between a multiple-line company and a company operating as a "group" or "fleet"?

7. What is retrocession, and how is this concept related to the internationalization of insurance?

8. What justification exists for cooperative pricing in insurance when such activity is often considered illegal "price fixing" in other industries?

9. (a) Which function has been more important to most insurers, investing or financing? Why?

(b) Are there any important differences in the functions of investing and financing among life insurers as opposed to property and liability insurers? Explain.

10. Explain the purpose of insurance exchanges. Why are they needed?

11. The text states that reinsurance allows a reduction in unearned premium reserve requirements. Explain why this is considered an advantage.

QUESTIONS FOR DISCUSSION

1. (a) How has the merger movement in insurance affected insurance organizations and functions?

(b) What advantages of mergers to the insurer seem to you to be the most important? Why? Do you see any possible disadvantages?

(c) What effects are possible as a result of the merger movement?

2. A sales manager told a group of agents that the broadened product line of the company, which through merger included variable annuities, permitted an average agent to triple commission income by combining ordinary life insurance with individual variable annuities in the same package. This was true even though the average first-year commission of ordinary life was 50 percent compared to 10 percent for the variable annuity.

(a) What might account for the phenomenon noted?

(b) What problem inherent in broadened product lines does this example illustrate? Explain.

3. A study by the New York Insurance Department found that, of 350 insurers that had ceased business in that state, the overwhelming reason for financial difficulty lay in inadequate underwriting. Explain the connection between inadequate underwriting and the financial difficulty referred to.

4. (a) Explain what is meant by the "conflict between underwriting and production" in insurance.

(b) Do you feel that such a conflict is real, or is it only apparent?

5. Insurer R has written a fire insurance policy in the amount of $2 million on A's factory. R has a net retention of $100,000 on any one fire loss, and it has a pro rata first surplus treaty of nine lines, a pro rata second surplus treaty of five lines, and facultative reinsurance of $500,000 on A's plant. It now seeks an excess-of-loss treaty that pays any loss in excess of $25,000 on any one risk.

(a) If R has a loss of $1 million from a fire at A's plant, how will the loss be distributed under the existing reinsurance treaties? Explain.

(b) If R is able to obtain the excess-of-loss treaty, how much would it be able to recover from the excess-of-loss reinsurance? Explain.

6. An actuary develops a pure premium of $200 for residential fire, based on a five-year experience period. The pure premium

in Territory *A* for last year was $400 because of a large number of grass fires which destroyed several homes. It is believed that the loss experience for Territory *A* is "25% credible." (a) Using the credibility formula given in the text, show what the new pure premium for Territory *A* should be. (b) Explain why the credibility factor is only 25%.

NEW TERMS AND CONCEPTS

Production
Underwriting
Policy Writing
Rate Making
Insurance Rate
Premium
Gross Premium
Manual Rate
Class Rating
Individual or Merit Rating
Preferred Risk
Substandard Risk
Schedule Rating
Experience Rating
Retrospective Rating
Rate-Making Associations
    or Rating Bureaus
Group Organization

Multiple-Line Company
All-Line Organization
Multiple-Peril Policies
Reinsurance
Treaties
Ceding Company
Reinsurer
Retrocession
Line or Retention
Facultative Treaty
Cession
Surplus Treaty
Quota Share Treaty
Reinsurance Pool or
    Exchange
Insurance Exchange
Credibility

NOTES

1 Examples of such studies include *A Profile of Consumer Attitudes Toward Auto and Homeowners' Insurance*, 1974, and *Businessmen's Attitudes Toward Commercial Insurance*, 1975, (Philadelphia: The Wharton School, University of Pennsylvania; Sentry Insurance; and Louis Harris and Associates, 1974 and 1975).

2 As was stated by one authority: "There is nothing quite so private as public relations. The insurance profession must handle each loss with every person in a satisfactory way. Public relations is the stone stalagmite and personal experience is the drop of water that builds the stone."

3 *Best's Aggregates and Averages, 1985*, 46th Annual Edition (Oldwick, N. J.: A. M. Best Company, 1985), pp. 210–243.

4 1964 and 1984 figures calculated from Table 4–2, p. 84.

5 Alabama, Alaska, Connecticut, Delaware, Georgia, Maine, Mississippi, North Dakota, Oregon, Rhode Island, South Carolina, Tennessee, and Wisconsin. See Hugh Harbison, "Legal Environment for All Lines Insurance," *All Lines Insurance*, edited by Dan McGill (Homewood, Ill.: Richard D. Irwin, Inc., 1960), p. 23.

6 World reinsurers include Lloyd's of London, Munich Reinsurance Co., Swiss Reinsurance Co., General Reinsurance Co., and American Reinsurance Co.

PART 3

THE LEGAL ENVIRONMENT OF INSURANCE

6 LEGAL PRINCIPLES OF INSURANCE CONTRACTS

After studying this chapter, you should be able to:

1. Explain how the principle of indemnity operates.
2. Identify situations that give rise to insurable interest.
3. Describe how the principle of insurable interest supports the principle of indemnity.
4. State how the subrogation process works and why it is desirable.
5. List the legal requirements of a contract.
6. Identify the distinguishing legal characteristics of insurance contracts.
7. Describe the legal powers and limitations of insurance agents and brokers.

Insurance is effected by legal agreements known as contracts or policies. A contract, contrary to the impressions of many, cannot be complete in itself, but must be interpreted in light of the legal and social environment of the society in which it is made. This chapter is concerned with the specific legal doctrines that underlie the insurance contract.

PRINCIPLE OF INDEMNITY

The **principle of indemnity** states that a person may not collect more than the actual loss in the event of damage caused by an insured peril. Thus, while a person may have purchased coverage in excess of the value of the property, that person cannot make a profit by collecting more than the actual loss if the property is destroyed. Many insurance practices result from this important principle.

One of the important results of the principle of indemnity is the typical inclusion in insurance contracts of clauses regarding other insurance. The purpose of such clauses is to prevent the insured from taking out duplicating policies with different insurers in the expectation of recovering more than the actual loss. Typically such clauses provide that all policies covering the same risk will share pro rata in the loss. Thus, if Jones carries $4,000 fire insurance in Company *A* and $6,000 in Company *B*, the two insurers will divide a $1,000 fire loss 40 percent and 60 percent, respectively.

There are some exceptions to the application of the principle of indemnity in property insurance. In about half the states **valued policy laws** exist whereby the insurer must pay the entire face amount of the fire insurance policy in the event of total loss of the insured object.[1] Ocean marine and some inland marine contracts are valued, and it is assumed that the insured will take out insurance equal to the full value of the object. Finally, it has become common to permit the sale of replacement insurance contracts under which there is no deduction for depreciation in the settlement of losses on depreciable property. Exceptions to the principle of indemnity will probably continue until it is felt that they begin to constitute a moral hazard, giving the insured an incentive to destroy the property in the hope of making a gain.

Though the principle of indemnity is primarily associated with property insurance, some authorities claim it applies to life insurance, too. Perhaps Robert Keeton states it best: "First, neither life insurance nor any other form of insurance is a pure indemnity contract, second, that all forms of insurance bear the marks of strong influence of the principle of indemnity, and third, that its influence is less extensive in life insurance than it is in property insurance."[2]

PRINCIPLE OF INSURABLE INTEREST

A fundamental legal principle that strongly supports the principle of indemnity is that of **insurable interest.** This principle traces its origin to an Act of Parliament in the year 1746.[3]

Under the principle, an insured must demonstrate a personal loss or the insured will be unable to collect amounts due when a loss due to the insured peril occurs. Insurable interest is always a legal requirement because to hold otherwise would mean that an insured could collect without personal loss. This would establish a moral hazard and would be deemed contrary to public policy. The doctrine of insurable interest is also necessary to prevent insurance from becoming a gambling contract. In life insurance an important reason for requiring insurable interest is to remove a possible incentive for murder.

Insurance follows the person and not the property. Thus, insurance is said to be *personal.* A policy can be written covering a certain piece of property, and an individual may be named as the one who would suffer a financial loss if the peril were to occur and cause damage. However, if at the time of the loss the individual named no longer had an interest in the property, there would be no liability under the policy. For example, suppose that *A* owns and insures an automobile. Later *A* sells the car to *B,* and shortly thereafter the auto is destroyed. *A,* who has no further financial interest in the car, cannot collect under the policy. *B* has no protection under the policy since *B* is not named as an insured or as having any interest in the auto at the time the policy was written.

What Constitutes Insurable Interest?

The legal owner of property having its value diminished by loss resulting from an insured peril has an insurable interest and can collect if able to demonstrate that a financial loss has occurred. However, in many cases a loss occurs when an individual is not a legal owner. In other words, ownership is not the only evidence of insurable interest. For instance, *C* leases a building under a long-term lease whereby the lease may be cancelled if a fire destroys a certain percentage of the value of the building. *C* has an insurable interest in the building because of the lease.

There are other rights under contract that are sufficient to establish an insurable interest in a property, and the continued existence of the right affects the contract and its value to the insured. Thus, the holder of a contract to receive oil royalties has an insurable interest in the oil property so that in the event of an insured loss indemnity can be collected, the amount of the indemnity being measured by the reduction in royalty resulting from the insured loss.[4] Likewise, legal liability growing out of contracts establishes insurable interest in property. For example, garage operators have an insurable interest in the stored automobiles for which they have assumed liability.

Secured creditors, such as mortgagees, have an insurable interest in the property on which they have lent money. Building contractors have an insurable interest in property on which they have worked because they have a mechanic's lien. In each of the two cases, loss of the building would endanger the ability to collect amounts due. However, **general creditors**—ones without specific liens on the property—are not regarded as having a sufficiently great property right to give them an insurable interest. In most states, however, a general contractor who reduces a debt to a judgment then has an insurable interest in the debtor's property. A business person has an insurable interest in the profits expected from the use of property and in the expenses incurred in managing that property.

In life insurance an insurable interest is always presumed to exist for persons who voluntarily insure their own lives. An individual may procure life insurance and may make anyone the beneficiary regardless of whether the beneficiary has an insurable interest. Of course, there are practical limits as to the amount of life insurance an individual may obtain.

Sometimes parties will attempt to avoid the insurable interest requirements in life insurance and try to use the contract as a wagering agreement. Courts will usually set aside such contracts. For example, two individuals met in a saloon and after a short acquaintance, one agreed to insure his life and then assign the policy to the other if reimbursed for the premium. The insured person died, and the insurer refused to pay when the facts surrounding the application became known. The court upheld the insurer's refusal to pay on the grounds that the transaction was conceived to use the life insurance policy as a means of effecting a wager. The intention was to avoid the requirement of insurable interest by having the *cestui que vie* (person whose life is insured) take out the policy with the sole purpose of transferring it to another who had no insurable interest.

One who purchases life insurance on another's life must have an insurable interest in that person's life. Thus, a business firm may insure the life of a key person because that person's death would cause financial loss to the firm. A wife may insure the life of her husband because his continued existence is valuable to her and she would suffer a financial loss upon his death. Likewise, a husband may insure the life of his wife because her continued existence is valuable to him and he could suffer a financial loss upon her death. The same statement may apply to almost anyone who is dependent on an individual. A father may insure the life of a minor child, but a brother may not ordinarily insure the life of his sister. In the latter case there would not usually be a financial loss to the brother upon the death of his sister, but in the former case the father would suffer financial loss upon the death of his child. A creditor has an insurable interest in the life of a debtor because the death of the debtor would subject the creditor to possible loss.

When the Insurable Interest Must Exist

In property and liability insurance it is possible to effect coverage on property in which the insured does not have an insurable interest at the time the policy is written, but in which such an interest is expected in the future. In marine insurance a shipper often obtains coverage on the cargo it has not yet purchased in anticipation of buying cargo for the return trip. As a result, the courts generally hold that in property insurance insurable interest need exist only at the time of the loss and not at the inception of the policy.

In life insurance, however, it is the general rule that insurable interest must exist at the inception of the policy, but it is not necessary at the time of the loss. The courts view life insurance as an investment contract. To illustrate, assume that a wife who owns a life insurance policy on her husband later obtains a divorce. If she continues to maintain the insurance by paying the premiums, she may collect on the subsequent death of her former husband, even though she is remarried and suffers no particular financial loss upon his death. It is sufficient that she had an insurable interest when the policy was first issued.

In a similar way, a corporation may retain in full force a life insurance policy on an employee who is no longer with the firm. A creditor may retain the policy on the life of a debtor who has repaid his or her obligation. In other words, in life insurance the general rule is that a continuing insurable interest is not necessary.[5]

PRINCIPLE OF SUBROGATION

The **principle of subrogation** grows out of the principle of indemnity. Under the principle of subrogation, one who has indemnified another's loss is entitled to recovery from any liable third parties who are responsible. Thus, if D negligently causes damage to E's property, E's insurance company will indemnify E to the extent of its liability for E's loss and then have the right to proceed against D for any amounts it has paid out under E's policy. One of the important reasons for subrogation is to reinforce the principle of indemnity—that is, to prevent the insured from collecting more than the actual cash loss. If E's insurer did not have the right of subrogation, it would be possible for E to recover from the policy and then recover again in a legal action against D. In this way E would collect twice. It would be possible for E to arrange an accident with D, collect twice, and split the profit with D. A moral hazard would exist, and the contract would tend to become an instrument of fraud.

Another reason for subrogation is that it may hold rates below what they would otherwise be. In some lines of insurance, particularly liability, recoveries from negligent parties through subrogation are substantial. While no specific provision for subrogation recoveries is made in the rate structure other than through those provisions relating to salvage, the rates would tend to be higher if such recoveries were not permitted. A final reason for subrogation is that the burden of loss is more nearly placed on the shoulders of those responsible. The negligent should not escape penalty because of the insurance mechanism.

Subrogation normally does not exist in such lines as life insurance and most types of health insurance. Also, subrogation does not give the insurance company the right to collect against the insured, even if the insured is negligent. Thus, a homeowner who negligently, but accidently, burns down the house while thawing a frozen water pipe with a blowtorch can collect under a fire policy; but the insurer cannot proceed against the owner of the policy for compensation. Otherwise, there would be little value in having insurance.

It is not uncommon for an insurer to waive rights of subrogation under certain circumstances where, by so doing, there is no violation of the principle of indemnity. Suppose that a manufacturer has agreed to hold a railroad not liable for losses arising out of the maintenance of a spur track that the railroad has placed on the manufacturer's property. In effect, the manufacturer has assumed legal liability that would otherwise be the responsibility of the railroad. Now assume that a spark from one of the railroad's engines sets fire to the manufacturer's building and the railroad is found negligent, and hence legally liable for the ensuing damage. The insurer will pay the loss, but under its right of subrogation will proceed against the railroad.

However, the manufacturer has previously agreed to assume all losses arising out of the existence of the spur track. Therefore, any amount collected becomes the ultimate liability of the manufacturer because of the hold-harmless agreement. If this were not the case, the manufacturer would have been in the position of collecting for the loss from the insurer but returning it to the railroad because of the hold-harmless agreement. Therefore, the insurer will waive the subrogation clause in the first contract because to enforce it would mean that the insured would not be compensated at all. This waiver is performed by inserting a waiver-of-subrogation clause in the manufacturer's insurance policy. Such clauses are common.

An insured who acts in such a way as to destroy or reduce the value of the insurer's right of subrogation violates the provisions of most subrogation clauses and forfeits all rights under the policy. For instance, suppose F collides with G in an automobile accident. F writes G a letter of apology and implies that F is to blame. It is later determined that G is probably negligent and, had it not been for F's statement, F's insurer would have been able to subrogate against G for amounts paid to F. The insurer may deny liability to F.

Subrogation rights of the insurer cannot be avoided by a settlement between the primary parties after the insurer has paid under the policy. In such a case the insurer is entitled to reimbursement from the insured who has received any payment from the negligent party.

The insurer is entitled to subrogation only after the insured has been fully indemnified.[6] If the insured has borne part of the loss through the application of deductibles or inadequate coverage, or because of legal costs involved in collection against third-party claims, the insurer may claim recovery only after these costs have been repaid.

The only exception to this rule is that the insurer is entitled to legal expenses incurred in pursuing the subrogation process against a negligent third party. For example, assume that Mr. Hardigree's house, valued at $80,000 and insured for $60,000, is totally destroyed through the negligence of Mr. Forehand. Hardigree's insurer subrogates against Forehand and collects $30,000 and has legal expenses of $12,000. The insurer receives $12,000 for legal expenses and Hardigree receives $18,000. If the insurer had obtained $50,000, it would have received $12,000 for legal expenses and $18,000 in subrogation benefits. Hardigree would receive $20,000 of this, which is the amount he is underinsured ($80,000 − $60,000 = $20,000).

WAIVER OF SUBROGATION

Synopsis

An insured owned property, of which a portion was leased to another individual, Polk. On a date that was within the insured's policy period, the property was destroyed by a fire. The insured made a claim to recovery for the damages from the insurer. After an investigation of the blaze, the insurer determined that the damages were caused as a direct result of the negligence of Polk, the lessee; thus, it paid off the amount of the damages to the insured. The insurer, however, started proceedings against Polk to recover (subrogate) for the damages because of Polk's alleged negligence. Polk defended on the grounds that the contract between Polk and the insured contained a waiver-of-subrogation clause.

Conclusion

Polk won. The court held that the owner's fire insurer was not entitled to subrogation against Polk for the fire loss paid to the owner. The insurer's right to subrogation could rise no higher than the subrogor's rights, and the lease agreement with its subrogation waiver excused Polk from liability for destruction of the property by fire. Since the owner had no rights against Polk, the lessee, the insurer had no subrogation rights against the lessee either.

Source: *Continental Casualty Company, et al.* v. *Polk Brothers, Inc.*, Illinois Appellate Court, November 21, 1983. *Insurance Law Reporter*, Commerce Clearing House, 1985, pp. 980–986.

PRINCIPLE OF UTMOST GOOD FAITH

Insurance is said to be a contract of *uberrimae fidei,* or **utmost good faith.** In effect, this principle imposes a higher standard of honesty on parties to an insurance agreement than is imposed in ordinary commercial contracts. The principle of utmost good faith has greatly affected insurance practices and casts a very different light on the interpretation of insurance agreements than many persons often suppose. The application of this principle may best be explained in a discussion of representations, concealments, and warranties.

Representations   A **representation** is a statement made by an applicant for insurance before the contract is effected. Although the representation need not be in writing, it is usually embodied in a written application. An example of a representation in life insurance would be "yes" or "no" to a question as to whether or not the applicant had ever been treated for any physical condition or illness by a doctor within the previous five years. If a representation is relied upon by the insurer in entering into the contract, and if it proves to be false at the time it is made or becomes false before the contract is made, there exist legal grounds for the insurer to avoid the contract.

Avoiding the contract does not follow unless the misrepresentation is *material* to the risk. That is, if the truth had been known, the contract either would not have been issued at all or would have been issued on different terms. If the misrepresentation is inconsequential, its falsity will not affect the contract. However, a misrepresentation of a material fact may make the contract voidable at the option of the insurer. The insurer may decide to affirm the contract or to avoid it. Failure to cancel a contract after first learning about the falsity of a material misrepresentation may operate to defeat the insurer's rights to cancel at a later time.

Generally, even an innocent misrepresentation of a material fact is no defense to the insured if the insurer elects to avoid the contract. The applicants for insurance speak at their own risk and if they make an innocent mistake about a fact they believe to be true, they are held for their carelessness. Thus, let us say that a person in applying for insurance on his automobile states that there is no driver under age 25 in his family. However, it turns out that his 16-year-old son has been driving the family car without his father's knowledge. Lack of this knowledge is no defense when the insurance company refuses to pay a subsequent claim on the grounds of material misrepresentation. It is not necessary for the insurer to demonstrate that a loss occurred arising out of the misrepresentation in order to exert its right to avoid the contract. Thus, in the preceding case, let us assume that *A* has the accident himself and then it is learned for the first time he has a 16-year-old son driving. Since this situation is contrary to that which *A* had previously stated, the insurer may usually legally refuse payment. However, if the court holds that a statement given in the application was one of opinion, rather than fact, and it turns out that the opinion was wrong, it is necessary for the insurer to demonstrate bad faith or fraudulent intent on the part of the insured in order to avoid the contract.[7] For example, let us say that an applicant is asked, "Have you ever had cancer?" and the applicant says "No." Later it develops that the applicant actually had cancer. The court might well find that the insured was not told the true state of his health and thought that he had some other ailment. If the question had been phrased, "Have you ever been told you had cancer?" a "yes" or "no" answer would be clearly one of fact, not opinion. An honest opinion should not be grounds for recision.[8]

Concealments

A **concealment** is defined as silence when obligated to speak. A concealment has approximately the same legal effect as a misrepresentation of a material fact. It is the failure of an applicant to reveal a fact that is material to the risk. Because insurance is a contract of utmost good faith, it is not enough that the applicant answer truthfully all questions asked by the insurer before the contract is effected. The applicant must also volunteer material facts, even if disclosure of such facts might result in rejection of the application or the payment of a higher premium.

The applicant is often in a position to know material facts about the risk that the insurer does not. To allow these facts to be concealed would be unfair to the insurer. After all, the insurer does not ask questions such as "Is your building now on fire?" or "Is your car now wrecked?" The most relentless opponent of an insurer's defense suit would not argue that an insured who obtained coverage under such circumstances would be exercising even elementary fairness.

The important, often crucial, question about concealments lies in whether or not the applicant knew the fact withheld to be material. The tests of a concealment are (1) Did the insured know of a certain fact? (2) Was this fact material? and (3) Was the insurer ignorant of the fact? The test of materiality is especially difficult because often the applicant is not an insurance expert and is not expected to know the full significance of every fact that might be of vital concern to the insurer. The final determination of materiality is the same as it is in the law of representation, namely, would the contract be issued on the same terms if the concealed fact had been known? There are two rules determining the standard of care required of the applicant: one, the stricter, applies to ocean marine risks; the other applies to insurance on land risks.

Ocean Marine Risks. In early England, ships were often insured after they had set sail. Thus, there was no way for the insurer to inspect the ship. Usually the shipper had a better knowledge of the actual conditions of the risk than did the underwriter. Furthermore, since insurance was necessary to the expanding overseas trade in England, there was a desire to do everything possible to nurture the growth of this significant activity. Accordingly, very strict rules governing disclosures were adopted. In marine insurance, intentional concealment as well as innocent concealment can void the contract.[9]

Land Risks. In land risks, the U.S. courts have been unwilling to apply the same standards of *uberrimae fidei* as they have in ocean marine risks. English courts, however, generally apply the same standards to all risks. In land risks, insurance companies generally inspect the properties they insure or have an opportunity to do so. Thus, they do not rely as heavily on the accuracy of statements by the insured, who often does not have sufficient knowledge of the facts about the risk and their significance to the insurer. Decisions have been rendered in the United States whereby failure to disclose the fact of a recent fire of incendiary origin by an unknown party or of the use of kerosene lamps in the picking room of a cotton factory did not constitute concealments.

In general, the nonmarine, or land, rule is that a policy cannot be avoided unless there is fraudulent intent to conceal material facts. Thus, in nonmarine risks, a fourth test of concealment is added. This test is: Does the insured *know* that the insurer does *not* know of a material fact? Under this test, intentional withholding of material facts with intent to deceive constitutes fraud. Assume that *H* learns that his wife *W* is going to "end it all" in the family auto by driving over a cliff. *H* immediately obtains collision insurance on the vehicle without telling all he knows. As a result, *H* is guilty of a concealment and the insurer may avoid the contract. Here *H* knows about a material fact; the insurer does not know it; and *H* knows the insurer is ignorant of it. Furthermore, *H* has no right to assume that the insurer should know of it.

In life insurance, cases of concealment are not common because of the reluctance of courts to enforce the doctrine strictly and because of the general use of a very long list of questions in the application concerning the applicant's background. An applicant's failure to disclose the fact that he or she had been threatened with murder and was carrying a gun for protection has been held not to be a concealment.[10]

In determining which facts must be disclosed if known, it has been held that facts of general knowledge or facts known by the insurer already need not be "disclosed." There is also the inference from past cases, though not a final determination, that the insurer cannot defend on the grounds of concealment those facts that are embarrassing or self-disgracing to the applicant.

Warranties

A **warranty** is a clause in an insurance contract holding that before the insurer is liable, a certain fact, condition, or circumstance affecting the risk must exist. For example, a marine insurance contract may state "warranted free of capture or seizure." This statement means that if the ship is involved in a war skirmish, the insurance is void. Or a bank may be insured on condition that a certain burglar alarm system be installed and maintained. Such a clause is condition precedent and acts as a warranty.

A warranty creates a condition of the contract, and any breach of warranty, *even if immaterial,* will void the contract. This is the central distinction between a warranty and a representation. A misrepresentation does not void the insurance unless it is material to the risk, while under common law any breach of warranty, even if held to be minor, voids the contract. The courts have been somewhat reluctant to enforce this rule, and in many jurisdictions the rule has been relaxed either by statute or by court decision.

Warranties may be express or implied. **Express warranties** are those stated in the contract, while **implied warranties** are not found in the contract, but are assumed by the parties to the contract. Implied warranties are found in ocean marine insurance. For example, a shipper purchases insurance under the implied condition that the ship is seaworthy, that the voyage is legal, and that there shall be no deviation from the intended course. Unless these conditions have been waived by the insurer (legality cannot be waived), they are binding upon the shipper.

A warranty may be promissory or affirmative. A **promissory warranty** describes a condition, fact, or circumstance to which the insured agrees to be held during the life of the contract. An **affirmative warranty** is one that must exist only at the time the contract is first put into effect. For example, an insured may warrant that a certain ship left port under convoy (affirmative warranty) and the insured may warrant that the ship will continue to sail under convoy (promissory warranty).

Insurance and the Requirements of a Contract

A contract is an agreement embodying a set of promises that are enforceable at law, i.e., for breach of which the law provides a remedy. These promises must have been made under certain conditions before they can be enforced by law. In general, there are four such conditions, or requirements, which may be stated as follows:

1. The agreement must be for a legal purpose; it must not be against public policy or be otherwise illegal.
2. The parties must have legal capacity to contract.
3. There must be evidence of agreement of the parties to the promises. In general this is shown by an *offer* by one party and *acceptance* of that offer by the other.
4. The promises must be supported by some consideration, which may take the form of money, or by some action by the parties that would not have been required had it not been for the agreement.

Insurance contracts must meet these essential requirements. The peculiar problems involved in applying the requirements to insurance are discussed in the following paragraphs.

Legality. The insurance contract must not violate the requirement of insurable interest, nor may the contract protect or encourage illegal ventures. Obtaining insurance on life or property without an insurable interest would violate antiwagering statutes and could lead to arbitrary and intentional destruction of the subject matter. In early England, private individuals were permitted to take out insurance on the lives of public figures, such as the king. The premiums for such contracts would vary daily, depending on reports from the sickbed. Such an insurance policy would be unthinkable today.

Capacity. Parties to the policy of insurance must have legal capacity to contract. There have been instances where a minor has exercised the legal right to rescind an agreement (before reaching the age of majority) and to recover the full cost of the premium without any adjustment for the value of insurance protection received.[11] This ruling follows because a minor is a legal infant and does not have the power to make binding contracts except for necessary items of support actually furnished. The courts have not yet interpreted insurance to be a necessary item in the support of an infant. Several states, however, have passed statutes granting a minor who has reached a certain age ($14\frac{1}{2}$ years in New York) the power to make binding contracts of insurance.

Other parties who have no legal capacity to contract are: (1) insane persons—those who do not have the ability to understand the nature of the agreement into which they enter; (2) intoxicated persons; and (3) corporations that act outside the scope of their authority as defined in their charters, bylaws, or articles of incorporation.

Offer and Acceptance. An insurance agreement is effected by one party making an offer and by the other party accepting that offer. Until there has been both an offer *and* an acceptance, there is no contract. To be valid, an offer must be communicated effectively to the offeree. An offer can be withdrawn at any time before it is accepted. Therefore, it becomes important to determine, in many cases, what constitutes a legal offer. If *A* goes to an agent to purchase insurance and the agent fills out an application that *A* signs, has the agent made an offer which *A* accepts by signing the application? If so, the insurance is in force. If not, when is the contract in effect? The answers to these questions are vital in determining when coverage attaches and can often spell the difference between collecting and not collecting for a loss.

It is the general rule in insurance that it is the *applicant*, not the agent, who makes the offer. The agent merely solicits an offer. When the contract goes into effect depends upon the authority of the agent to act for the principal in a given case. In property and liability insurance, it is the custom to give the local agent authority to accept offers of many lines of insurance "on the spot." In such cases, it is said that the agent "binds" the insurer. If the insurer wishes to escape from its agreement, it usually may cancel the policy upon prescribed notice. In life insurance, the agent generally does not have authority to accept the applicant's offer for insurance. The insurer reserves this right, and the policy is not bound until the insurer has passed on the application. If the insurer wishes to alter the terms of the proposed contract, it may do so, and this is construed as making a counteroffer to the applicant, who may accept or reject it.

A legal offer by an applicant for life insurance must be supported by a tender of the first premium. Usually, the agent gives the insured a **conditional receipt** that provides that acceptance takes place when the insurability of the applicant has been determined. Let us say that *B* applies for life insurance, tenders an annual premium with the application, receives a conditional receipt, passes the medical examination, and then is run over and killed by a truck, all before the insurer is even aware that an application has been made for insurance. B's beneficiaries may collect under the policy if it is determined that B was actually insurable at the time of the application and had made no false statements in the application.

An applicant for life insurance who does not pay the first annual premium in advance has not made a valid offer. In this case, the insurer's agent transmits the application to the home office, where it is acted upon and questions of insurability are determined. The insurer sends the policy back to the agent for delivery, and the agent is instructed to deliver the policy only if the insured is still in good health. This constitutes, on the part of the insurer, an offer that may be accepted by paying the annual premium at the time of delivery.

In summary, the offer in insurance can be made in either of two ways: (1) by filling out an application and rendering other considerations required of the applicant, and (2) by offering a completed policy to the applicant. Often, the offer is made by means of the first method, but occasionally, and especially in life insurance, the second method is used, depending upon the power of the agent in the circumstances.

Consideration. All contracts that are legally enforceable must be supported by a consideration, and insurance is no exception. A **consideration** is defined as a legal detriment, or more simply, as the act or promise that is bargained for. The insured's consideration is made up of monetary payment plus an agreement to abide by the conditions of the insurance contract. The insurer's consideration is its promise to pay indemnity upon the occurrence of loss due to certain perils, to defend the insured in legal actions, or to perform other activities such as inspection or collection services, as the contract may specify.

DISTINGUISHING LEGAL CHARACTERISTICS OF INSURANCE CONTRACTS

There are several legal characteristics of insurance contracts and their issuing parties that distinguish them from other contracts and contracting parties. Reference has already been made to some of these characteristics, such as the fact that insurance is a contract of indemnity, is personal in nature, and is a contract of utmost good faith. Additional characteristics follow.

It is important to distinguish insurance policies from other commercial contracts for several reasons. First of all, for tax and regulatory purposes, the insurance business is viewed quite differently from other businesses. Special statutes have been passed to give insurance firms particular tax status, some of which are especially favorable to the insurer. Insurers are exempt from federal bankruptcy statutes and are liquidated by state insurance commissioners under special regulation.

Second, the type of agreements made by firms is of value in determining whether or not a firm should be classed as an insurance company and thus whether or not is is conforming to all of the regulations under which insurance companies must operate. Issuing insurance policies may be outside the authority of the corporate charter, thus subjecting the officers to liability for *ultra vires* acts. Such acts are considered beyond the scope of, or in excess of legal power or authority of, the corporation. The Supreme Court of the United States has held that the variable annuity contract is sufficiently differentiated from insurance as to require regulation of issuing companies by the Securities and Exchange Commission as well as by insurance commissions in the various states in which they operate.[12]

Finally, whether or not an agreement is indeed an insurance contract affects the way in which it may be enforced in legal actions. A separate body of law and decisions affects the enforcement of contracts classified as insurance, as compared with contracts that are classed as ordinary commercial transactions. The question arises as to whether a given contract is in conformity with state insurance law.

For example, it has been held that certain commercial agreements that appear as though they might be insurance agreements are not insurance in a legal sense. These include contracts entitling certificate holders to medical services at free or reduced rates, a guarantee to an employee of payment for services on goods damaged or destroyed by fire, an agreement to protect an employee against other striking employees, and an agreement by a bicycle association to keep members' bicycles in repair and to replace them if stolen.

On the other hand, the following contracts have been held to constitute insurance contracts: guarantee of payment of the principal and interest of mortgage loans, contracts guaranteeing rent, contracts guaranteeing the value of corporate stock on a certain date, and comprehensive guarantee of automobile tires. It was held that a corporation that undertook for specific consideration to guarantee a revenue per acre of farming land to the owner was an insurance company.[13]

It is not always obvious whether a contract is insurance or whether the issuing party is an insurance company. Certainly the following factors are not the controlling ones in making such a determination: whether or not the term "insurance" appears in the contract or company name; a statement that the contract is not to be considered insurance; and the term or mode of payment. Rather, the courts look to the true nature of the promise or acts to be performed and the circumstances under which they will be performed.

Among the legal tests that have been used to determine whether a given transaction constitutes legally enforceable insurance are the following:

1. There must exist an insurable interest by the party seeking insurance.
2. The agreement of insurance must conform to the legal requirements of a contract offer and acceptance, consideration, legal purpose, and

capacity of parties. The agreement can include transactions that in substance are contracts although legally they may not be so. Thus, in New York a conditional sale of merchandise involving the cancellation of the debt upon death has been held to constitute a contract of insurance.[14]

3. There must exist some risk, some chance of loss, some uncertainty as to loss from designated perils.

4. The assumption of loss must be a part of a general scheme to distribute losses among a large group of persons bearing similar risks. The requirement, attributed to W. R. Vance, is also part of the statutory definition of insurance in several states.[15]

5. The insurer must assume the risk of loss. Payment to the insured may be in money or in services.

Not all state insurance laws define insurance, and those that do may have definitions that do not conform to all of the above requirements. For this reason, no single statutory definition is totally satisfactory. For example, New York's statutory definition requires that benefits of monetary value be given to the insured as a result of a fortuitous event (requirement 3 above), but the laws of Massachusetts do not require a fortuitous event. The laws of Kentucky specify that the event be a "contingency" and the laws of California specify that it be a "contingent or unknown" event.[16]

More specifically, in analyzing insurance contracts, courts are concerned with several legal characteristics, only the most important of which will be discussed in the remaining sections of this chapter. Among these characteristics are those describing (1) oral contracts of insurance, the parol evidence rule, and the effect of mistakes; (2) the classification of an insurance contract as aleatory, conditional, and one of adhesion; and (3) the legal status of the insurance agent or broker in making valid contracts.

Oral Contracts of Insurance

While most insurance contracts are written, oral agreements of insurance are very common and the courts will enforce them. Often an oral agreement for insurance is made and a written notation, called a **binder,** is issued as evidence of the oral contract until the full written policy is issued. If it were not for binders, it might be difficult to prove that an oral contract ever existed. Even if there were witnesses, it would be difficult to obtain an accurate statement of just what the agreement was. Also, in many cases the insurer's agent lacks authority to bind contracts orally. Some states have passed statutes requiring certain types of contracts, such as life or fire, to be in writing, and sometimes the provisions of the insurer's charter will not allow oral contracts.[17] For these reasons, oral contracts are discouraged.

Parol Evidence Rule

Under the **parol evidence rule,** when an oral contract is reduced to writing, the written contract is to be construed as the entire agreement; and oral testimony to change it is inadmissible except under certain circumstances. Therefore, oral agreements that are not expressed accurately in the written contract are not enforceable, and it is dangerous for the insured to rely on them.

Effect of Mistakes

When an honest mistake is made in a written contract of insurance, it can be reformed if there is proof of a mutual mistake or a mistake on one side that is known to be a mistake by the other party, where no mention was made of it at the time the agreement was made. A mistake in the sense used here does not mean an error in judgment by one party, but refers to a situation where it can be shown that the actual agreement made was not the one stated in the contract. If *A* believes himself to be the owner of certain property, and insures that property, *A* cannot later demand all of the premium back solely because he found out that, in fact, he was not the owner of the property. This was a mistake in judgment or an erroneous supposition, and the courts will not relieve that kind of mistake.

As an example of mistakes found in life insurance policies, an insured paid up a policy and through a mistake by the insurer, the endorsement stated that the value of the paid-up contract was $5,495.26, including interest. Actually the proper value was $1,994.65. The insured sued for the larger amount, and the court held that an honest mistake had been made by the company and that it was "inconceivable that a successful businessman would think that a policy which on his death paid $2,765 would at any time acquire a surrender value of $5,495.26!"[18]

In another case the insurer issued a $1,000 life policy and, by an error of one of its clerks, included an option at the end of 20 years to receive an annuity of $1,051 rather than $10.51. The mistake was discovered 18 years later. When the insurer tried to correct the error, the insured refused payment of the smaller amount. In a legal decision, the court held that the mistake was a mutual one, the error of the insurer being in misplacing a decimal point, and the error of the insured being in either not noticing the error, or if noticed, in failing to say anything, an action amounting to fraud.[19] These decisions also illustrate the fact that insurance is a contract of utmost good faith on both sides.

Aleatory and Conditional Contracts

As explained in Chapter 2, insurance is classed as an aleatory contract. Thus, the obligation of the insurer to perform is dependent on uncertainty, namely, the uncertainty that the insured peril will cause a loss. The insurance contract is conditional because the insured must perform certain acts if recovery is to be made. If the insured does not adhere to the condition of the contract, payment is not made even though an insured peril causes a loss. Typical conditions include payment of premium, providing a proof of loss statement, and giving immediate notice to the insurer of a loss. The insurer is bound to pay the insured a much larger sum of money, under some conditions, than the insured has paid the insurer in the form of premiums. Thus, the conditions are a part of the bargain. In contrast, an ordinary commercial transaction is one in which there is roughly an equal exchange of values between the parties and few, if any, conditions that must be observed to establish the bargain.

Contract of Adhesion

The insurance contract is said to be a contract of **adhesion,** meaning that any ambiguities or uncertainties in the wording of the agreement will be construed against the drafter— the insurer. The insurer has the advantage in drawing up the terms of the contract to suit its particular purposes; and, in general, the insured has no opportunity to bargain over conditions, stipulations, exclusions, and the like. Therefore, the courts place the insurance company under a legal duty to be explicit and to make its meaning absolutely clear to all parties.

For example, in the fire insurance contract, courts construe policies with conflicting loss settlement provisions covering the same property in such a way as to favor the insured, so that the insured is not deprived of recovery. In automobile insurance, a court construed an accident involving a car that left the road after being struck by a flying piece of ice to be covered under comprehensive rather than collision, an interpretation that favored the insured because no deductible applied to the comprehensive claim.[20]

In life insurance, ambiguities involving the effective date of a policy have been construed in such a way as to favor the insured. For example, some life insurance policies are antedated, that is, dated before the coverage actually begins. A majority of courts held that the one-year suicide clause runs from the earlier date of the policy and not the date the policy became effective.[21] Such an interpretation favors the beneficiary, since if the insured's suicide occurs after the one-year period stated in the suicide clause, the beneficiary may collect the full amount of the policy, whereas if suicide occurs within the one-year period, only a return of premiums results.

In interpreting the agreement, the courts will generally consider the entire contract as a whole, rather than just one part of it. In the absence of doubt as to meaning, the courts will enforce the contract as it is written. It is no excuse that the insured does not understand or has not read the policy.

Reasonable Expectations. This doctrine is an extension of the concept of adhesion. It goes further than just saying that ambiguities should be decided in favor of the insured. It makes the proposition that the insurance policy language should be interpreted as a layperson would comprehend it and not according to the interpretation of a trained underwriter.[22]

An example of this doctrine is shown in the case of an insured's policy that provided for burglary protection only when the building was open. The literature promoting the coverage and used to sell the insured referred to all-risk or comprehensive crime protection. Also, there was a picture in the material representing a burglary after a building was closed. The insured's claim resulted from a burglary loss after the building was closed and was denied by the insurer. The courts ruled that the insured had a reasonable expectation for coverage to apply and found for the insured.[23]

LEGAL POWERS OF INSURANCE AGENTS

Reference has been made frequently to the significance of the agent in insurance contracts. (See Chapter 5.) The powers of insurance agents to vary the terms of the contract, to put the insurance in force, to deal with the insured, to handle settlements, and to perform many other affairs are of vital importance to a sound knowledge of insurance. An insurance corporation, after all, is a legal entity only, and it must function through agents of various kinds.

An agent is a person given power to act for a principal, who is legally bound by the acts of authorized agents. The power of a given insurance agent cannot be determined easily by reference to whether the agent is called a general, a special, or a local agent. Unfortunately there is little uniformity in insurance terminology, and a general agent in property insurance has far different powers and functions from the general agent in life insurance. Furthermore, the sense in which insurance practitioners use the terms for various types of agents may not be comparable to the sense in which attorneys view the terms.

For example, the law recognizes two major classes of agents: general and special. A general agent is a person authorized to conduct all of the principal's business of a given kind in a particular place. A general agent is the company itself, legally speaking, in that capacity. As such, the general agent can add or detract from a printed form, waive the terms of contracts, accept or reject risks, change rates, and do almost everything the company itself could do. In life insurance, the general agent has few or none of these powers, but in property insurance the general agent often has at least some of these powers.

In the legal sense, an agent does not necessarily have to be a person serving in the channel of distribution for insurance. Any representative of the insurance corporation, such as the treasurer or the chief underwriter, who is given certain authority, is an agent. An agent may be a **special agent,** a person authorized to perform only a specific act or function and who has no general powers. If anything occurs that is outside the scope of this authority, the agent must obtain special power to handle it. An agent who handles matters outside the scope of this authority may or may not bind the principal, depending on certain circumstances.

Source of Authority

The basic source of authority for all insurance agents (using the word agent in its broad sense) comes from stockholders or policyholders and is formulated by the charter, bylaws, and custom. The agent in the channel of distribution for insurance is of greatest concern to us at this point, however, and the discussion will be confined to that agent. There are three distinct sources of authority for the agent: from the agency agreement, by ratification, and by estoppel.

Agency Agreement. Insurance agents generally obtain their authority to write insurance directly from the principal (usually an insurance company) by an instrument known as an **agency agreement.** This agreement sets forth the specific duties, rights, and obligations of both parties. Unfortunately, the agreement is often inadequate as a complete instrument; hence, the agent may do something that the principal did not intend. This situation gives rise to other methods by which an agent may receive authority from the principal.

Ratification. An agent can also obtain authority by a process known as **ratification.** That is, an individual may perform some act concerning another person without authority at all, and this act may be assented to at a later time by the person involved. Thus, A writes an insurance policy covering B's house against loss by fire. A is not authorized to do this by an insurer. However, A later persuades insurer C to accept this risk and thus becomes C's agent by ratification.

Estoppel. A third way in which an agent can obtain authority is through a process known as agency by estoppel. **Estoppel** is a legal doctrine under which a person may be required to do or to refrain from doing something that is inconsistent with previous behavior. Suppose, in the preceding example, that insurer C continues to allow A to sell insurance even though A does not have an agency agreement with C. Every time A sends in a policy, C accepts it. Gradually A becomes known as C's local agent in the community, and no attempt is made to inform the public differently. To the public, A has the power to bind C to fire insurance contracts, as is the custom with other local agents. Now A writes coverage on D's house, and before the policy is ratified by C the house burns. May C deny liability on the grounds that A had no authority to write the policy in the first place? The courts would probably say that C had led the public to believe that A had authority to bind it. To allow C to escape payment would work a hardship on an innocent party, and thus the law has provided a remedy. C is *estopped* from denying liability, and A has become an agent by estoppel.

In summary, one can obtain the authority of an agent either expressly or by implication. One can have actual authority, or if not, one can have apparent authority and may still bind the principal. Authority includes all customary and necessary powers to carry out the job of an agent. Secret limitations on authority that are not customary will not be effective as to innocent third parties. Courts have often extended an agent's authority beyond the actual authority because of these principles. For example, a company denied its liability under a policy of life insurance on the grounds of false statements in the application. It was shown that the agent had taken the responsibility of answering the questions for the insured, and that the agent had answered incorrectly even though the correct information was received. The court held that knowledge of the agent is knowledge of the company and that to deny liability would be inequitable. The insurer had to pay.[24] Of course, if the insured knew of the wrong answers recorded by the agent, the insured would be guilty of fraud and could not collect. Most courts refuse to hold that an applicant signing the application warrants the truth of everything in the application.

Estoppel versus Waiver

A **waiver** is the voluntary relinquishing of a known right. Waiver is based on consent and is similar to contract law, while estoppel is an imposed liability and is more closely associated with tort liability. Keeton describes waiver as a rare phenomenon, even though numerous court opinions use the doctrine of waiver to justify a decision.[25] Estoppel prevents one from asserting a right because of prior conduct that is inconsistent with such an assertion.

Estoppel and waiver are vital in an understanding of the law of agency. Often they are not clearly distinguished even in court actions, and sometimes they are used interchangeably. The two doctrines are of interest primarily in understanding how the acts of insurance agents may or may not be binding on insurers. To illustrate, a lower court dismissed a case involving an accidental death policy on the evidence that proofs of loss were not filed as required under the policy. A higher court found that the company's agents had told the insured that it would do no good to file a proof of loss because there was no liability for payment for accidental death. The court decided that such an action amounted to a waiver of the requirement to file a proof of loss.[26] Had it not been for the doctrine of waiver, the beneficiary would have had no chance of collecting on this policy.

Estoppel operates when there has been no voluntary relinquishing of a known right. Estoppel operates to defeat a "right" that a person technically possesses. When the enforcement of this right would work an unfair hardship on an innocent party who has been led to rely on certain conduct or actions of another person, the courts will deny the right under the doctrine of estoppel. Waiver and estoppel situations often arise when the policy is first put into force. Let us say that an agent writes a fire insurance policy with the full knowledge that some condition in the policy is breached at the time it is issued. For example, the insured might be engaged in a type of business that the insurer has instructed its agents not to write and has excluded in the policy. The agent issues the policy anyway, and there is a loss before the insurer has had an opportunity to cancel the contract. Most courts would say that the action by the agent constituted an acceptance of the breached condition, and the insurer would be liable.

Agents versus Brokers

In most areas of insurance, intermediaries known as brokers operate. (See Chapter 5.) A broker is the legal agent of the insured and does not have the same powers as a local agent, although operating at the same level. A broker is employed by the individual seeking coverage to arrange insurance on the best possible terms. The broker has contacts with many insurers, but may not have an agency agreement with them. Thus, a broker is free to deal with any insurer that will accept the business. The broker cannot bind any insurer orally to a risk because the broker has no prior arrangements such as would be described in an agency agreement. Thus, in dealing with a broker, one should not assume coverage the moment the insurance is ordered. One is covered only when the broker contacts an insurer that agrees to accept the risk. It is said that knowledge of an agent is knowledge of the insurance company. Knowledge of the broker is knowledge only of the broker.

Today the distinction between an agent and a broker is not as clear as the foregoing rule states. In many situations a person may simultaneously be an agent and a broker. Many brokers hold agency contracts with insurance companies. Typically, courts will construe the evidence in the light most favorable to the insured.

Legal Uncertainties

Although the legal principles discussed in this chapter are general rules that normally govern the settlement of disputes under insurance contracts, it should not be assumed that they apply invariably, or that settling insurance disputes is simple and routine. In many cases, courts have not upheld a certain principle because of the particular facts of a given dispute, lawyers' courtroom tactics, legal errors, or the predilections of judges.

To illustrate, ambiguities in the insurance contract may not always be construed in favor of the insured (principle of adhesion) if the insured is a large corporation that has negotiated as an equal party with the insurer in designing a particular type of contract. Influence of a state insurance commissioner may cause some insurers to grant coverage or settle claims more favorably for the insured than would otherwise by indicated by the strict terms of the policy. Difficulties experienced by lay persons in understanding insurance contracts have caused many insurers to rewrite policies in simpler, nontechnical language, but this new language may introduce further uncertainties requiring interpretations by the courts in future cases.

In spite of attempts to make the intention of the parties and the legal principles of insurance contracts clear to all, many legal uncertainties remain, requiring recourse to the courts and to legal counsel by the insured in settling insurance disputes.

SUMMARY

1. An understanding of legal principles is vital to a proper understanding of the insurance contract itself. There are several differences in the application of these legal principles to life insurance as opposed to general insurance.

2. The principles of indemnity and subrogation are closely related to the principles of insurable interest. Both are necessary to reinforce the principle of insurable interest. Insurable interest is necessary for any insurance contract to be valid.

3. Because insurance is a contract of utmost good faith, breach of warranty or a material misrepresentation on the part of the insured can void the coverage. A concealment has the same legal effect as a material misrepresentation.

4. Insurance is effected by means of a legal contract and must meet the general requirements of contracts. Thus, the insurance contract must not be against public policy, must be enacted by parties with legal capacity to contract, must be effected through a meeting of the minds, and must be supported by a monetary consideration. Oral contracts of insurance may be valid, but they should be avoided whenever possible. Insurance is a contract of adhesion, and any ambiguities are construed against the insurer. Insurance is an aleatory and conditional contract.

5. Insurance is effected through agents who have varying degrees of authority, depending upon the custom in different lines of insurance and upon the doctrines of waiver and estoppel. Brokers are agents of the insured, not the insurer, and cannot bind coverage orally.

QUESTIONS FOR REVIEW

1. Under what conditions, if any, is it necessary to prove insurable interest on the part of a beneficiary in life insurance? Explain.
2. Distinguish between the doctrine of insurable interest and the principle of indemnity.
3. D has a house valued at $150,000. D takes out insurance in two companies, each policy in the amount of $100,000. If the house is totally destroyed, can D collect in full from both companies? Why or why not?
4. In an application for life insurance, Oki Yasunari stated that she had no illness, that she went to a physician only twice a year for a checkup, and that she had no application for insurance pending with any other company. Shortly after the policy was issued, the insured died. The company denied liability when it was discovered that the insured had seen a doctor six times within ten weeks preceding her application. Furthermore, the insured had applied to another insurance company for $50,000 of life insurance at the same time.
   (a) May the insurer properly deny liability?
   (b) What legal doctrine of insurance is involved in this case?
5. What is the difference between an express and an implied warranty?
6. Can one have an insurable interest in property and still not own the property? Explain.
7. Distinguish warranty from representation.
8. What is the doctrine of reasonable expectations?
9. Name and explain the requirements of a contract and what additional features underlie contracts of insurance.
10. Explain the principle of adhesion.

QUESTIONS FOR DISCUSSION

1. Do you feel that insurance companies should be allowed to subrogate after they have paid an insured's loss? Explain.

2. Suit was filed by an insured to change the wording of a paid-up life insurance policy (*Alldredge* v. *Security Life and Trust Co.*, 92 So.2 26, Alabama, 1957). The insured claimed that the company's general agent signed an agreement that would entitle the insured to a paid-up $7,000 policy on the payment of only four annual premiums of $322.28 each. Neither the policy nor the application therefor referred to this written instrument.
   (a) Do you think the suit should be successful? Why or why not?
   (b) Upon what legal doctrines does your decision rest?

3. In *National Indemnity* vs. *Smith-Grandy* (150 Wash. 109), Smith-Grandy, an auto dealer, telephoned a general agent in Seattle to place coverage on a truck that was then in transit from Detroit to Seattle. The dealer was told that coverage would commence immediately, which was at 3:15 p.m., on June 7, 1955, the day of the conversation. But the written policy that was subsequently issued stated that the coverage was from 12:01 a.m., June 7, 1955, to June 7, 1956. It was learned later that at 2:15 p.m., the truck had been in an accident that resulted in a claim against Smith-Grandy for $200,000. The insurer refused to pay the claim because the accident occurred before 3:15 p.m. In a suit against the insurer, Smith-Grandy argued that the time stated in the written policy governed the effective time of coverage, but the insurer defended on the basis of the agent's testimony that the coverage was not placed until 3:15 p.m.
   (a) How should this case be decided?
   (b) Explain the legal doctrines involved in this case.

4. In *Liberty National Life Insurance Co.* v. *Weldon* (3 Life Cases 2 669, Alabama, 1957), the insurer issued a life insurance policy on a two-year-old girl. The applicant for the insurance was the child's aunt. The parents knew nothing about the insurance. Later the aunt poisoned the child, was found guilty, and was executed. In your opinion was the requirement of insurable interest met in this case? Why?

5. *A* is thinking of purchasing a car. *A* takes out an insurance policy on the car and orders the car delivered to another city, where *A* intends to take possession and to close the deal. Before *A* becomes the legal owner, the car is destroyed. In the meantime, the former owner has dropped the insurance coverage on the car.
   (a) Who suffers the loss?
   (b) Is there any effective insurance covering this loss?
   (c) Would your answer be different if the car had been destroyed after *A* had taken title, bearing in mind that the insurance was placed *before* title was taken?

NEW TERMS AND CONCEPTS

Adhesion	Contract
Aleatory	Estoppel
Binder	Express
Concealment	Implied

Insurable Interest
Personal
Representation
Reasonable Expectations

Subrogation
Utmost Good Faith
Waiver
Warranty

NOTES

1 Since most losses are partial, valued policy laws have relatively little actual effect in insurance. They apply usually only to real estate. Rather than appraise every piece of real estate, most insurers probably find it less expensive to pay an occasional total loss that has been insured for an amount in excess of its actual value. Valued policy laws exist in Arkansas, California, Florida, Georgia, Kansas, Louisiana, Minnesota, Mississippi, Missouri, Montana, Nebraska, New Hampshire, North Dakota, Ohio, South Carolina, South Dakota, Tennessee, Texas, and West Virginia. Several states have repealed these statutes on the grounds that the only insureds who are benefited are those desiring to defraud insurers. Georgia's law, passed in 1971, provides that if the building burns within 30 days of the date of the policy coverage, the loss is subject to settlement on an actual cash value basis.

2 Robert E. Keeton, *Insurance Law: Basic Text* (St. Paul: West Publishing Company, 1971), p. 94.

3 Ibid., p. 95.

4 See *National Filtering Oil Co.* v. *Citizens Insurance Co.*, 106 N.W. 535 (1887).

5 In Texas the rule pertaining to a continuing insurable interest has been modified by statute so that this statement is not strictly true in that state.

6 There are occasional exceptions to this rule when the contract so provides. In credit insurance, for example, the insurer and the insured would share the amounts collected from negligent third parties in the proportion that each party's loss bore to the total loss. In automobile insurance deductible settlements, it is fairly common for an insured not to recover 100 percent of the deductible, even if full recovery is made from a third party.

7 Keeton, op. cit., p. 323.

8 There are exceptions to the general rule on material misrepresentation. The primary exception comes in regard to automobile insurance in some states where there are mandatory automobile liability insurance requirements. The Supreme Courts of Georgia and Michigan have ruled in certain situations that a material misrepresentation of fact does not void automobile liability insurance in those states.

9 Keeton, op. cit., pp. 326–327.

10 *New York Life* v. *Bacalis*, 94 F. 2d 200 (C.A. Fla. 1938).

11 See *New Hampshire Mutual Fire Insurance Co.* v. *Noyes*, 32 N.H. 345. It should be added that a minor who does not rescind the contract upon reaching the age of majority is thereafter bound by it.

12 *S.E.C.* v. *Variable Annuity Life Insurance Company*, 359 U.S. 65, 75–78 (1959).

13 *American Jurisprudence* (Rochester: Lawyers Cooperative Publishing Co., 1960), 29, 440–445.

14 Harold Van B. Cleveland, "The Status of Self-insured Employee Benefit Plans," *The Journal of Insurance*, Vol. 27, No. 2 (June, 1960), pp. 7–8.

15 W. R. Vance, *Handbook of the Law of Insurance*, 3rd ed. (St. Paul: Anderson, 1951), pp. 1–2, and H. S. Denenberg, "The Legal Definition of Insurance," *Journal of Insurance*, Vol. 30 (September, 1963), p. 339. It has been held, however, that a single isolated transaction is enough to constitute insurance in some states, including New York. See New York Insurance Law, Section 41 (3) (4), and Denenberg, op. cit., p. 336.

16 Denenberg, op. cit., pp. 328–329.

17 Georgia, for example, requires that all insurance contracts be in writing to "be binding." Keeton, op. cit., p. 29.

18 *Flax* v. *Prudential Life Ins. Co.*, 3 Life Cases (2) 105, Fed. Supp. (1956).

19 *Metropolitan Life Ins. Co.* v. *Henriksen*, 126 N.E. (2d) 736 (Ill. App. Court–1955).

20 *Gruenther* v. *American Indemnity Co.*, 17 N.W. (2d) 590.

21 E. W. Patterson, *Essentials of Insurance Law*, 2nd ed. (New York: McGraw-Hill Book Company, Inc., 1957), p. 99.

22 Keeton, op. cit., pp. 350–355.

23 *Barth* v. *State Farm Fire & Cas. Co.*, 214 Pa. Super. 434, 257 A. 2d 671 (1969).

24 *Atlas Life Insurance Co.* v. *Eastman*, 320 Pac.2 397 (Okla. 1957).

25 Keeton, op. cit., pp. 343, 344.

26 *Keel* v. *Independent L. & A. Insurance Co.*, 99 So.2 225 (Fla. 1957).

7

COMMON CHARACTERISTICS OF INSURANCE CONTRACTS

After studying this chapter, you should be able to:

1. Identify and understand the basic parts of an insurance policy.
2. Explain the difference between named peril and all-risk property insurance coverage.
3. Explain why exclusions are used in insurance contracts and identify the major types of exclusions.
4. Describe how the interests of mortgagees are protected in insurance policies and why the mortgagee clause gives the best protection to the mortgagee.
5. Explain how the cancellation and assignment provisions in insurance contracts operate.
6. Distinguish between the actual cash value basis of recovery and replacement cost.
7. Describe the different types of deductibles (flat, disappearing, franchise, and participating) and why deductibles are used in insurance policies.
8. Indicate why insurance companies use insurance to value provisions and how the coinsurance clause operates.
9. Explain what apportionment clauses are and how the pro rata clause operates.

There are many similarities in insurance contracts that are best studied and analyzed at one time. For example, most contracts contain certain exclusions, such as for loss due to war, loss to property of an extremely fragile character, and loss due to the deliberate action of the named insured. Most property insurance contracts require the insured to notify the insurer of loss as soon as practicable, and usually require that the insured prove the loss. An understanding of these common elements greatly facilitates the understanding of insurance contracts generally, even when a given policy applies a different name to a certain type of provision or condition.

The basic approach used in our analysis is to examine the major parts of a policy and certain other important aspects of the policy. The major parts can be defined as (1) the declarations, (2) the insuring agreement, (3) the exclusions, and (4) the conditions. Other important aspects of a policy include its definitions, the basis of recovery, and clauses limiting the amount of recovery.

DECLARATIONS

In the declarations section of the policy, which is usually on the first page, the policy number is given as well as the address of the insured or the insured property. The insured's name, the agent's name, the name of the mortgagee, if any, and the premium are also given. There may also be some underwriting information given on the declarations page, such as the type of construction of the building or, in the case of automobile insurance, a description of the automobile. In policies where an insured has options in terms of coverages chosen, the options chosen by the insured will be shown on the declarations page.

THE INSURING AGREEMENT

One of the first things in any contract is a statement of the essence of what is agreed upon between the parties. In insurance this is found in the **insuring clause,** or **insuring agreement,** which normally states what the insurer agrees to do and the major conditions under which it so agrees. If a loss under the insured peril occurs, the insurer promises to compensate the insured if the insured meets the conditions of the contract. If the conditions are not met, the insurer has no obligation to pay.[1] The insuring agreement often starts out, "In consideration for the premiums herein paid and the conditions agreed to, the _____ Insurance Company hereby insures the above-named person . . ." The exact nature of what is promised is then set forth. The insured promises only to pay the premium and to conform to the conditions of the policy. Conforming to the conditions is a part of the consideration, so technically the insured just agrees to pay a consideration. The most crucial part of the agreement is the statement of what the insurer promises.

A common example of an insuring agreement and what it does is found in the standard fire policy.[2] The standard fire policy's insuring agreement (1) specifies the terms of the contract, (2) gives the basis of recovery, (3) limits recovery to the cost of repairing or replacing the loss with like material and labor, (4) describes perils insured against, (5) limits recovery to the insured's interest in the property, (6) provides for protection of the property while being removed after a loss, (7) requires all assignments to be in writing, and (8) stipulates that all additional provisions, conditions, and agreements attached to the contract are an inherent part of the policy. These items are examined in greater detail in Chapter 18.

The insuring agreement in the homeowners and personal automobile policy states, "We shall provide the insurance described in this policy in return for the premium and compliance with all applicable provisions of the policy." The full body of the policy follows the insuring agreement.

Within or right after the insuring agreement, one may also find a list of the perils insured against and the definition of the insured. We shall now examine these two subjects.

NAMED PERIL VERSUS ALL RISK

There are two general approaches used in framing insuring agreements. One, the traditional, is the named peril approach. The other, which is being used more and more extensively, is the all-risk approach. The **named peril** agreement, as the name suggests, lists the perils that are proposed to be covered. Perils not named are, of course, not covered. The other type, **all risk,** states that it is the insurer's intention to cover all risks of accidental loss to the described property *except* those perils specifically excluded.

A named peril policy lists and describes the various perils against which coverage may be purchased under a particular form. Such perils often include, but are not limited to, fire, lightning, explosion, riot, smoke, theft, falling objects, and collapse.

Typical of the all-risk approach is the insuring agreement of the personal articles floater, which undertakes to insure "all risks of loss of, or damage to, property covered except as hereinafter provided." The policy then goes on to impose various limitations on certain perils that are excluded (loss resulting from war, mechanical breakdown, and breakage of fragile articles).

DEFINING THE INSURED

All policies of insurance name at least one person who is to receive the benefit of the coverage provided. That person is referred to as the **named insured.** In life insurance that person is often called the **policyholder.** In addition, many contracts cover other individuals' insurable interest in the described property or cover them against losses outlined in the policy. These individuals are often called **additional interests** or **additional insureds,** and they normally receive coverage somewhat less complete than that of the named insured.

For example, the personal automobile policy not only covers the person designated on the policy as the named insured, but in addition grants exactly the same coverage to the spouse who is a resident of the same household. The policy also covers any other persons who are driving with the permission of either the named insured or the spouse, provided they are not driving the automobile in connection with any automobile business such as a service station, a garage, or a parking lot.

In the homeowners policy likewise, the policy covers not only the named insured, but also legal representatives of the named insured. Thus, if the named insured dies, the policy, by virtue of this provision, is effective in covering the estate until it is settled. In the comprehensive personal liability policy the insured includes not only the named insured, but also the spouse and the relatives of either if they are living in the same household. In addition, the policy insures any employee of the insured who is operating certain farm equipment in the scope of employment, any person under age 21 in the care of the insured, and any person or organization legally responsible for losses growing out of the use of animals or watercraft owned by an insured. Thus, if the named insured lends a horse to a neighbor, and while the neighbor is riding the horse breaks away and injures someone, the neighbor is covered under the named insured's liability policy.

EXCLUSIONS

Exclusions are used to help define and limit the coverage provided by the insurance company. Usually, the insurance company will write an insurance policy with a very broad insuring agreement and then narrow the coverage by the use of exclusions. Typically, exclusions are used to restrict coverage of given perils, losses, property, and locations.

Excluded Perils

Practically all contracts of insurance exclude from coverage certain perils among those factors that can cause losses. Normally, a separate section with all the excluded perils listed and described appears in the contract. It is vital that the exclusions be noted and understood. Providing for exclusions is the drafter's way of describing and limiting the insuring agreement to make it definite and unambiguous.

One complicating factor in the analysis of insurance contracts is the fact that most policies define and limit the peril in such a way that it is partially covered, but not completely so. Thus, in the basic fire policy fire from specific causes may be excluded, such as fire caused by order of civil authority. In the extended coverage endorsement explosion is covered, but no explosion that results from bursting of steam boilers, steam pipes, steam turbines, or other parts of rotating machinery owned or controlled by the insured. In life insurance death from war may not be covered. In accident insurance some policies restrict coverage to accidents that stem from given sources, such as travel accidents and nonoccupational accidents.

Perils may be excluded or limited in various ways for at least three different reasons:

1. Some perils are excluded because they are basically uninsurable.
2. Others are excluded because it is intended to cover them elsewhere, such as in another type of policy.

3. Still others are excluded because it is intended to charge extra for them under an endorsement that may be added to the policy at the option of the insured.

Perils That Are Basically Uninsurable. In all types of insurance it is very common to exclude loss arising out of war, warlike action, insurrection, and rebellion, because losses from such sources cannot be predicted with any degree of reliability and are often catastrophic in nature. Likewise, perils such as wear and tear, gradual deterioration, and damage by moth and vermin are excluded, because losses from these sources are not accidental and are in the nature of certainties and hence uninsurable (except at very high premium rates). For a similar reason, losses to property resulting from deliberate action by the insured, such as arson, faulty workmanship, or voluntary increase of the hazard, are excluded. In life insurance, suicide within two years of the application (one year in some policies) is an excluded peril for the same reason.

Perils to Be Covered Elsewhere. Some perils can be more easily covered in contracts that are specially designed for them. Thus, the personal automobile policy excludes losses arising out of business uses of trucks, and commercial automobile coverage excludes, under well-defined conditions, personal uses of the vehicle. The problems of insuring business and personal risks are entirely different, and policies are designed for each purpose. The exclusion serves the purpose of eliminating duplicate coverage. A similar exclusion is found in fire insurance forms, liability contracts, and inland marine policies. Another example of this type of exclusion is in the exclusion of certain water damage and flood losses from the homeowners policy. Such perils present special problems and must be insured separately.

Perils Covered under Endorsement at Extra Premium. The third type of exclusion may be illustrated by the provision in the standard fire policy that the policy shall not cover riot or explosion unless fire ensues, and in that event will provide coverage for loss by fire only. In subsequent endorsements the perils of riot and explosion are customarily added back into the policy at an extra premium. In this way the insureds who do not require additional coverage of certain perils may choose a more limited form of coverage.

Excluded Losses

Most insurance contracts contain provisions excluding certain types of losses even though the policy may cover the peril that causes these losses. For example, the fire policy covers direct loss by fire, but excludes *indirect* loss by fire. Thus, the policy will not cover loss of fixed charges or profits resulting from the fact that fire has caused an interruption in a business. Separate insurance is necessary for this protection. Neither does the policy cover losses caused by the application of any law (such as building codes) requiring that a more expensive type of construction be used in replacing a building destroyed by fire.

Similarly, in health insurance, if the policy is designed to cover hospitalization expense due to the peril of illness, it will often exclude the cost of doctor bills that result from this same peril. In automobile insurance, loss due to the peril of collision will not include losses to the property of others from this peril. Such losses must be covered under separate agreements.

Excluded Property

A contract of insurance may be written to cover certain perils and losses resulting from those perils, but it will be limited to certain types of property. For example, the fire policy excludes fire losses to money, deeds, bills, bullion, and manuscripts. Unless it is written to cover the contents, the fire policy on a building includes only integral parts of the building and excludes all contents. The automobile policy gives little or no protection to personal property carried in the vehicle. The automobile policy also gives somewhat more limited protection to nonowned vehicles than it gives to owned vehicles of the insured. The general liability policy usually excludes the property of others in the care, custody, or control of the insured.

Why are certain types of property excluded from insurance coverage? There are a variety of reasons, many of which are interrelated. First, it may be the intent of the insurer to cover certain types of property under separate contracts. A good example is the general pattern of excluding property relating to a business from policies designed primarily to insure property for personal uses. Thus, automobiles used as taxis are excluded from coverage under the personal automobile policy. Second, the property involved might be subjected to unusually severe physical or moral hazards or be especially susceptible to loss. The exclusion of bullion and manuscripts in the fire policy, for example, is made at least in part for this reason. Finally, property might be excluded because of difficulties in obtaining accurate estimates of its value at the time of loss. Special treatment of items such as works of art is often necessary, as is the insurance of intangible property, such as accounts receivable.

Excluded Locations

The policy may restrict its coverage to certain geographical locations. Relatively few property insurance contracts give complete worldwide protection. Fire insurance is often restricted to property in set locations with only a small part of the coverage applicable when some of the property is located somewhere other than on the chief premises of the insured. Automobile insurance is usually limited to cover the auto while it is in the United States, its possessions, or Canada. If the car is in Europe or Mexico, for example, coverage is not applicable.

All insurance contracts are written subject to certain conditions. Breach of these conditions is usually grounds for refusal to pay in the event of loss. Therefore, the conditions should be read with care, even though in some cases the insurer does not insist upon exact compliance. Most of the conditions have to do with such matters as loss settlements, actions required at the time of loss, valuation of property, cancellation of coverage, and suits against the insurer.

Fraud

Many contracts state that misrepresentation or fraud will void the contract. This condition may be inserted in the contract as much to serve as a warning to the insured as it is to state a condition that would be enforced by the courts even if the policy said nothing about it.

Protection for Mortgagees

The mortgagee (the person or organization holding the mortgage) requires some kind of protection by the insurance policy because if the property were destroyed, it is much less likely that the debt would ever be paid. A mortgagee can protect its interest in insured property in at least four ways:

1. Separate insurance for the mortgagee's interest
2. Assignment by the insured
3. Loss payable clause
4. Standard mortgagee clause

Separate Insurance for the Mortgagee's Interest. The mortgagee can purchase separate insurance covering its interest. This plan has the disadvantage, however, that both the mortgagee and the mortgagor will be placing coverage on the same values, since the mortgagor has an interest equal to the entire value of the property, and not just its equity. For example, if there is a house valued at $60,000 with a $40,000 mortgage on it, the interest of the mortgagee is $40,000 and the interest of the owner is $60,000. If each purchased separate coverage, there would be a total of $100,000 of insurance on the house, far more than is necessary to protect the value exposed.

Assignment by the Insured. An **assignment** is the transfer of rights of one person to another. The mortgagee could be protected by means of an assignment. The insured could simply take out a policy and then assign its benefits to the mortgagee after obtaining the permission of the insurer. The difficulty with this method is that if the owner defaults on the premium or otherwise violates a policy provision, the coverage may be cancelled and with it the protection of the mortgagee. In other words, the mortgagee receives no better protection under an assignment than is secured by the person making the assignment.

Loss Payable Clause. The mortgagee could be protected by a loss payable clause. Such a clause simply states that the benefits, if any, shall be payable to the person named. However, if the insured were to violate the policy, as by defaulting on the premium, no loss would be payable and the loss payee (the mortgagee) would receive no payment. Most jurisdictions treat the loss payable clause as an assignment of any rights to payment belonging to the insured. If the insured has no rights to collect, neither does the loss payee in these jurisdictions.

Standard Mortgagee Clause. The mortgagee may be protected by the standard mortgagee clause, which overcomes the limitations of the other methods and is now in almost universal use. Under the standard mortgagee clause, the mortgagee has certain rights and obligations, including the right to:

1. Receive any loss or damage payments as its interest may appear, regardless of any default of the property owner under the insurance contract, and regardless of any change of ownership or increase of the hazard.
2. Receive 10 days' notice of cancellation, instead of the five days given in the fire policy.
3. Sue under the policy in its own name.

The mortgagee is obligated under the standard mortgagee clause to:

1. Notify the insurer of any change of ownership or occupancy or increase of the hazard that shall come to the knowledge of the mortgagee.
2. Pay the premium if the owner or mortgagor fails to pay it. In most jurisdictions this has been interpreted to mean that the mortgagee must pay the premium only if it wishes to enjoy the protection under the policy.
3. Render proof of loss to the insurer in case the owner or mortgagor fails to do so.
4. Surrender to the insurer any claims it has against the mortgagor to the extent that it receives payment from the insurer. The insurer may under some conditions deny liability to the owner or mortgagor and therefore retain, through subrogation, all rights that the mortgagee may have had against the mortgagor. To illustrate, assume that the mortgagee, protected under the standard mortgagee clause, has a $10,000 mortgage on a $15,000 building, and that there is a $5,000 fire loss caused deliberately by the insured. The insurer denies liability to the insured, but must pay the mortgagee $5,000. The mortgagee must now surrender to the insurer $5,000 of its claim against the mortgagor. Or the insurer has the right to pay the mortgagee the entire $10,000 debt, obtain an assignment of the mortgage, and collect in full against the mortgagor. In this way, the mortgagor does not obtain any of the benefits of the insurer's payment to the mortgagee through a reduction of debt. Instead of owing the mortgagee, the mortgagor now owes the insurance company $10,000.

WHO GETS THE CHECK?

Situation

An insured's home was totally destroyed by a fire that fell within the dates of coverage for a fire insurance policy that the insured had with the insurer. Also, the insured had a mortgage on the property with a remaining balance of $140,000. The original value of the mortgage was approximately $157,000. The loss of $145,000 was paid by the insurer. The insurer paid the money jointly to the insured and the mortgagee because of their joint interests in the policy. The mortgagee wanted the entire sum, less $5,000, to settle the balance of the loan to the insured. The insured claimed that the mortgagee did not have the right to accelerate the 15-year mortgage. He wanted to take the money and rebuild, while continuing to pay off the loan as scheduled. The mortgagee claimed that it was entitled to security for the debt now and that it should not be forced to become a partner with the insured in the construction of the new premises.

Conclusion

The court held that the mortgagee of the property that had been substantially destroyed by fire was entitled to that portion of the fire insurance proceeds that would satisfy the balance remaining on the mortgage debt due. The mortgagor was not entitled to retain the proceeds to rebuild the buildings that were destroyed and thereby secure the entire mortgage security. The purpose of the mortgage clause in the policy was to satisfy the mortgage debt in the event of fire loss, and the insured mortgagor did not have the option under that clause to use the proceeds to rebuild the property.

Source: *General G.M.C. Sales, Inc.* v. *Passarella*, et al., New Jersey Superior Court, Appellate Division, August 29, 1984. *Insurance Law Reporter*, Commerce Clearing House, 1985, pp. 1131–1135.

Notice of Loss

Most contracts of insurance require the insured to give immediate written notice of any loss, if practicable. If it is not practicable to do so, the loss must be reported within a reasonable length of time. For example, if a forest fire destroys *A*'s summer cabin that is situated in a remote area, *A* may not be able to reach outside communications for several days. If *A* made an attempt to notify the insurer as soon as reasonably possible, *A* would still be able to collect on the insurance policy. The purpose of this provision is to give the insurer a reasonable opportunity to inspect the loss before

Part 3   The Legal Environment of Insurance

important evidence needed to support the claim and establish the actual amount of damage is dissipated. As another example, a person injured in an accident may be unable to give immediate notice of loss. However, failure to notify the insurer promptly would not violate the notice of loss provision in the health insurance policy.

Proof of Loss

The insured is given a certain period, usually 60 to 90 days, to render a formal proof of loss. It is not enough that the insurer be notified of the loss; it is necessary for the insured to prove the amount of the loss before being able to collect. Usually the company adjuster or agent aids the insured in preparing the proof, but the burden is on the insured to accomplish the task. In this connection, the insured must submit to examination under oath as to the accuracy of proof; must produce all books of account, bills, invoices, etc., that might help in establishing the loss; and must cooperate in any reasonable way to assist the insurer in verifying the proof.

In some cases, establishing the proof of loss is an extremely specialized and expensive task. In ocean marine insurance, for example, specialists known as **average adjusters** may spend years collecting all the proofs of loss resulting from a sunken ship, and involving hundreds of cargo owners, in order that a final settlement can be made and the loss apportioned among the various insurers that are liable. In larger fire losses, adjusters from all over the nation may spend months in the destroyed area reconciling all conflicts over claims for losses.

Appraisal

Most contracts of property insurance provide that if the two parties cannot agree on a loss settlement, each may select a competent and disinterested appraiser to determine the loss. An impartial umpire, selected and paid by each party, settles any remaining differences. Although this somewhat expensive procedure is not resorted to often, it must be complied with in many states before suit can be brought for recovery under the policy where the cause of the suit is failure to agree on the actual cash value of the loss.

Preservation of the Property

Most contracts of property insurance contain provisions requiring the insured to do everything possible to minimize losses to insured property from the insured peril. In fire insurance the insured must protect the property from further damage. This means, for example, that the insured must take all reasonable steps to cover property that has been removed from the building to protect it from rain or exposure. If the insured fails to do this, the insurer may be relieved from any further liability for loss.

Ocean and inland marine policies contain a clause known as the **sue and labor clause.** This requires the insured to "sue, labor, and travel for, in, and about the defense, safeguard, and recovery of the property insured hereunder." This means that the insured is required to hire salvors to protect a stranded ship from further loss, to hire guards to watch over a wrecked truck and its cargo, and to bring suit against a party liable for loss.

The insurer agrees to be responsible for these expenses, in addition to paying the full limits of liability under the policy for loss. Thus, if the insured pays a salvage company $5,000 to save a stranded ship, but the effort fails and the ship becomes a total loss, the insurer will indemnify the insured for full value of the ship plus the $5,000 fee for salvage.

Cancellation

All contracts of insurance specify the conditions under which the policy may or may not be terminated. In general, life insurance and certain health insurance contracts may be terminated by the insured but not by the insurer, except for a limited period named in the "contestable" clause. Property and liability contracts may usually be cancelled by either party upon specific notice.

Property and liability insurance policies usually state that the insurer may elect to end its liability for losses after 5, 10, or 30 days' notice. This gives the insured time to obtain coverage elsewhere and prevent any lapse of protection. In such cases the insurer is obligated to return any unearned premium on a pro-rata basis. Thus, if the premium has been paid in advance for one year, and the insurer cancels after one month has expired, it is obligated to return eleven-twelfths of the premium to the insured. However, if the insured cancels, the policy usually provides for a short-rate return of premium. In the above case the insured would get back about 76 percent of the premium instead of eleven-twelfths.

The reason for the difference in methods of refunding premiums lies in the fact that if the insured cancels before the end of the full term, the insurer is entitled to some compensation for the extra cost involved in short-term policies. Furthermore, if there were no penalty involved in such cancellations, there might be a tendency for better risks to drop out, leaving the insurer with the poorer risks, i.e., adverse selection would result. If the insurer cancels, however, the insured is not penalized for the short-term coverage.

Until recently, few if any restrictions were imposed on the insurer's right to cancel a property or liability insurance contract. In 1969, due to the tendency of some insurers to cancel policies without adequate explanation, the state of New York required insurers to specify the grounds for cancellation of certain nonbusiness contracts, furnish the facts on which any such cancellation is based, and show that these facts reveal some fault on the part of the insured.[3] The automobile insurance policy contains a cancellation provision that imposes certain restrictions on the rights of the insurer to cancel. (See Chapter 16.) In most contracts, however, no reason need be given when either party elects to cancel such a contract as described.

In life insurance and in certain other types of contracts, such as noncancellable disability income policies and credit insurance, there is no cancellation privilege given the insurer. If the insurer could cancel at will, the insured might be deprived of coverage at the very moment it was needed most. In these lines certain events usually become apparent that indicate the imminence of loss; thus, the insurer would be warned of impending liability.

Where a policy is not cancellable by the insurer but is subject to termination by the insured, there is no provision for return of premium as such to the insured. All premiums paid in are considered earned by the insurer. In life insurance, upon surrender of the policy, the insured is entitled to nonforfeiture values that may have accumulated under the policy. These values originate from premium payments, but they are not identified as such in the policy. Rather, they form a pool of funds that in effect are excess premiums paid in and held for the insured as savings (discussed in Chapter 11).

Assignment

As mentioned earlier, an assignment is the transfer of the rights of one person to another, usually by means of a written document. In insurance it is common to allow the insured to assign personal rights under the contract to another person. Usually such permission must be specifically granted. The person granting the right is called the **assignor** and the party to whom the right is granted is called the **assignee.** In life insurance the policy provides that if another person is to be given any rights under the contract, such as the right to receive death proceeds to the extent of a debt that existed between the assignor and the assignee, the insurance company must be notified. In the event of the death of the insured, such an assignment must be honored before any named beneficiary receives payment. This is very common when a lender requires protection before granting a loan to a borrower.

Often when a property is sold, the existing fire insurance policy is transferred to the new owner. This transfer ends the necessity of cancelling the old policy, taking a short-rate return of premium, and placing a new policy in force. Written permission of the insurer is required for such an assignment. In ocean marine insurance it is the usual practice to allow assignment of the coverage on cargo shipments without prior consent of the insurer. The assignment is accomplished by means of a document known as a **cargo certificate,** which may be endorsed somewhat in the same way as a negotiable instrument as the goods change hands in their journey from producer to final consumer.

DEFINITIONS

Many insurance policies have a definitions section in which key terms are defined. However, in other parts of the policy other words may be defined, and in some cases words used in one part of the policy may be redefined or limited in a later section of the contract. For example, in the personal automobile policy there are different definitions of "covered person" in the liability, medical payments, and uninsured motorists sections of the policy.

Smith, Appellant v. *R.B. Jones of St. Louis, Respondent.* Missouri Court of Appeals, June 5, 1984. *Insurance Law Reporter*, Commerce Clearing House, 1984, pp. 350–351.

BASIS OF RECOVERY

In property insurance contracts there are two basic methods for insureds to collect from the insurance company: actual cash value and replacement cost.

Actual Cash Value

The insuring agreement states that only the actual cash value of the property at the time of loss will be reimbursed, not to exceed the amount that it would cost to repair or to replace the property with material of like kind and quality. Some insureds might interpret this to mean that the insurer will restore all the burned property with material of like kind and quality. However, the insurer sets the actual cash value as a maximum reimbursement. **Actual cash value (ACV)** is interpreted as replacement cost at the time of loss less any depreciation. Thus, if it costs $1,500 to rebuild a 40-year-old roof that is almost worn out, the insurer normally will not rebuild the roof, but will make a cash settlement of an amount far less than $1,500 to allow for depreciation. Fire insurance is a contract of indemnity, and it is intended to put the insured in the same financial position with respect to damaged property after a loss as before the loss. Coverage that eliminates the deduction for depreciation is available, but this involves another basis of recovery.

In the case of buildings, factors such as obsolescence and a deteriorated neighborhood may be considered in arriving at the actual cash value. In a well-known case, an old brewery was totally destroyed by fire.[4] It had been insured for a substantial amount, but at the time of the fire the building was obsolete because the National Prohibition Act had made the brewing business illegal. The question was raised as to the amount of the recovery permitted under these circumstances, since the replacement cost less depreciation was substantially more than the building was worth as part of an illegal business. While no definite rule for measuring obsolescence resulted, the decision established that obsolescence could be considered in reducing the recovery below the actual replacement cost less depreciation.

The actual-cash-value basis for settling losses may not be used if the state in which the loss occurs has a valued policy law. Valued policy laws generally apply only to real property that is totally destroyed, not to partial losses.

Replacement Cost

Often the basic actual-cash-value coverage is modified to provide coverage on a **replacement cost** basis. When this endorsement is attached, recovery is on a replacement cost basis with no allowance for depreciation. However, the total reimbursement figure is limited to the cost of repairing, replacing, or rebuilding with like materials and labor. The insured cannot replace a wood frame building with a reinforced concrete one and expect the insurer to pay the additional cost. The insurer's liability is limited to the replacement cost of a wood frame building or the policy limit, whichever is less.

Replacement cost insurance may be purchased on both real and personal property. It is written more frequently on real property than it is on personal property. In order to collect on a replacement cost basis, the property must actually be replaced; the insured may not use insurance proceeds for other purposes.

CLAUSES LIMITING AMOUNTS PAYABLE

In defining the coverage of an insurance contract it is usually necessary for the insurer to limit the dollar amounts of recovery by including clauses relating to deductibles, franchises, coinsurance arrangements, time limitations, dollar limits, and apportionment clauses. A policy may contain one or more of these clauses. The clauses serve many different purposes, and it is not always possible to ascribe a single reason or even a group of reasons for the use of any one of them. In general, however, the clauses are used to reduce the costs of offering the insurance service; to prevent too many small, expensive-to-administer claims; to achieve a greater degree of fairness in the rate structure; and to place an upper limit on the insurer's obligation on any one policy. These purposes are aimed at converting the insuring agreement from a vague promise to indemnify into a definite, measurable contract that meets the requirements of insurable risks.

Deductibles

It is very common to stipulate that a definite dollar amount, say $100, will be borne by the insured before the insurer becomes liable for payment under the terms of the contract. For example, most people are familiar with the use of $100 and $250 deductibles in automobile collision insurance. More recently, $100 and $250 deductibles have been used in fire insurance contracts. The purpose of these deductibles is to eliminate small claims. Small losses are expensive to pay, sometimes causing more administrative expense than the actual amount of the payment. It is to the insured's advantage that such deductibles be available, for often the insured is able to save considerable sums in the insurance cost by their use. For example, in automobile insurance the saving in the annual premium by the use of a $100 deductible for collision claims rather than a $50 deductible might amount to $35. This is the equivalent of saying that to reduce the deductible from $100 to $50 costs $35. The insured would be paying $35 a year for $50 of added coverage, an extremely high rate compared to that charged for the entire contract.

Besides the straight deductible, there are two others of interest: the disappearing deductible used in property insurance, and the participation deductible used in health insurance.

Disappearing Deductible. When this type of deductible is chosen, the size of the deductible decreases as the size of the loss increases. Finally, at a given level of loss, the deductible completely disappears. Hence the name **disappearing deductible.** For example, in a policy with a $1,000 deductible that disappears at $26,000, all losses under $1,000 are absorbed by the insured. On a loss of $9,000 the deductible declines to $680. This reduction in the deductible results from the fact that losses are adjusted according to the formula

$$P = (L - D)1.04$$

where

P = Payment by insurer
L = Loss
D = Deductible

In the previous case, P would equal $8,320 [($9,000 − $1,000)1.04], and $9,000 − $8,320 = $680.00. If the insured desired the deductible to disappear at $10,000 rather than $26,000, then the factor for adjusting losses would change from 1.04 to 1.11. On the same $9,000 loss the insured would receive $8,880 [($9,000 − $1,000)1.11]. The larger the recapture figure, the smaller is the rate reduction received by the insured for accepting a deductible. A 1.04 factor will give an insured a larger rate credit than a 1.11 factor.

Participation Deductible. The **participation deductible** is often used in major medical health insurance, where it is frequently termed **coinsurance deductible.** Usually the participation rate is 80/20. That is, the insurance company pays 80 percent and the insured pays 20 percent of the loss. Thus, on a $5,000 hospital bill, the insurer would pay $4,000 and the insured $1,000. Since many major medical policies have $250,000 limits, it is conceivable that in a catastrophic loss situation an insured could be required to pay 20 percent of $250,000, or $50,000. This sum of money is much too large for most people to retain, so contracts are usually written so that the maximum retention amount is less than a stipulated amount, such as $6,000 for any one year. In some policies, the maximum retention amount is as low as $2,000. For example, on a $20,000 claim and a yearly retention limit of $2,000, the 80/20 participation deductible would require the insured to pay 20 percent of $20,000, or $4,000, but the yearly limit would restrict the insured's loss to $2,000, and the insurer would absorb $18,000 of the loss.

Franchises. A **franchise** is a deductible, expressed either as a percentage of value or as a dollar amount, under which there is no liability on the part of the insurer unless the loss exceeds the amount stated. Once the loss exceeds this amount, however, the insurer must pay the entire claim. Sometimes this franchise is termed "disappearing deductible," because the deductible has no effect once the loss reaches the specified amount. In ocean marine insurance it is common to use a franchise agreement expressed as a percentage. Thus, the policy might provide that there shall be no loss payable on wheat unless the loss equals or exceeds 3 percent of the total value, except for losses caused by fire, sinking, stranding, or collision. But once the loss reaches this level, the insurer is responsible for 100 percent of the claim.

There is more logic to the use of a franchise than a straight deductible if the sole purpose is to eliminate small claims. However, a straight deductible also eliminates many small claims that the insurer will never have to pay, and it eliminates a portion of large claims as well. In this way a straight deductible keeps down total loss payments. Additionally, the insured, who must pay some part of each claim, has another incentive to minimize the frequency of loss.

Coinsurance

The term **coinsurance** has different meanings in insurance. In health insurance and credit insurance the coinsurance clause is simply a straight deductible, expressed as a percentage. Its purpose in health is to make the insured bear a given proportion, say 20 percent, of every loss, because it has been found through experience that without such a control, the charges for doctors and other medical services tend to be greatly enlarged, thus increasing the premium to a prohibitive level. The insured who must personally bear a substantial share of the loss is less inclined to be extravagant in this regard.

In property insurance, the coinsurance clause is a device to make the insured bear a portion of every loss *only when underinsured.* Underinsurance is looked upon as undesirable for two reasons. First, insurance companies are supposed to restore their policyholders to their same positions before the loss. They obviously cannot accomplish this objective unless the insured is willing to protect the whole value of the property. Second, it costs relatively more to insure the businesses of individuals who are underinsured than it does to handle the businesses of individuals who purchase insurance equal to the full value of the object—that is, those who take out *full insurance to value.*

This follows because most losses are partial, and the probability of partial losses is higher than the probability of total losses. Rates depend on the probability of loss. Consequently, it follows that the rate charged for partial losses should be higher than the rate charged for total losses. No one knows whether a loss will be total or partial. Yet there is a tendency for the average person to assume that loss will be partial and therefore underinsure in order to save premium cost.

The typical coinsurance clause prorates any partial losses between the insurer and the insured in the proportion that the actual insurance carried bears to the amount required under the clause. Usually 80 or 90 percent of the value of the property is the amount required.[5] Thus, if there is a building with a value of $10,000 written with a 90 percent coinsurance clause, $9,000 of insurance is required. The insured who carries at least this amount collects in full for any partial loss. But the insured who carries half of this amount or $4,500, collects only half of any partial loss. The insured who carries $6,000 collects two-thirds of any partial loss. The amount collected in any case may be determined by the formula

$$\frac{\text{Insurance Carried}}{\text{Insurance Required}} \times \text{Loss} = \text{Recovery}$$

If the loss equals or exceeds the amount required under the clause (if the loss is nearly total), there is no penalty invoked by the coinsurance clause. Thus, if in the preceding case the loss were $9,000 at a time when the insured is carrying only $6,000 of insurance, substitution in the said formula yields

$$\frac{\$6,000}{\$9,000} \times \$9,000 = \$6,000$$

The recovery is $6,000, the amount of insurance carried, and there is no penalty other than the fact that the insured did not carry sufficient insurance to cover the entire loss. In the above case, if the loss were $1,500, the recovery would be $1,000.

By use of the coinsurance clause, the burden is placed upon the insured to keep the amount of insurance equal to or above the amount required by the clause. Failing this, the insured becomes a coinsurer and must bear part of any partial loss.

Dangers of Coinsurance. There are several factors which, by increasing the value of exposed property without corresponding adjustments in the amount of insurance coverage, might cause an insured to become a coinsurer unintentionally. If inflation increases the replacement cost of the insured's property, the insured is required to increase the amount of coverage or suffer coinsurance penalties. Other factors include unexpected or temporary increases in inventory, increases in supplier prices for replacement goods, and increased investment within the plant or store that modifies or improves the building or its equipment.

In one case, a dealer in farm machinery had decided to take on a new line of vehicles and, on the morning of an explosion that destroyed the store, had received a large shipment of parts for the new line. The dealer suffered severe coinsurance penalties in the loss settlement. In another case, a manufacturer had spent $20,000 per machine to modify them to produce at closer tolerances than had been the case when the machines were purchased for $40,000 each. This increased investment subjected the owner to sharp reductions in the effective insurance coverage through coinsurance penalties.

One solution to these problems is to maintain an appraisal program under which periodic reviews are undertaken by qualified appraisers. Such personnel may be indispensable in proving the amount of the loss, representing the insured in negotiations with loss adjusters, and alerting the insured to needed changes in insurance coverages.

Coinsurance in Residence Policies. The coinsurance clause as described above has only limited application to insurance contracts covering residences. In general, the clauses are written so that the insured will not suffer coinsurance penalties in the same way as is the case with commercial contracts. In residence policies, the coinsurance clause only has application with respect to replacement cost insurance.

Coinsurance Credits. In return for accepting a coinsurance clause in the contract, the insured is offered certain credits in rate. For example, a typical reduction in the building and/or content rate is 5 percent when one moves from an 80 percent coinsurance clause to a 90 percent clause. When an insured chooses a 100 percent coinsurance clause, the rate is reduced 10 percent from that charged when an 80 percent clause is used. By accepting the coinsurance clause, obtaining the lower rate, and buying the minimum amounts of coverage required, the insured can obtain greater insurance coverage for the same total premium than would be paid for a smaller amount of coverage written without the coinsurance clause attached. In many jurisdictions, the insured is not given the opportunity to purchase coverage without the coinsurance clause attached.

Coinsurance Rationale. The higher rates necessitated by underinsurance and the rationale of the coinsurance clause in fire policies may be illustrated by four simple hypothetical cases.

Case 1—Full Coverage. An insurer is attempting to calculate a pure premium for 10,000 uniform buildings, each valued at $10,000. (The pure premium is that number of dollars that will pay for fire losses only and is not adjusted for the cost of doing business.) It is assumed that 99 percent of the buildings have no losses; and of the remaining 100 buildings, 50 suffer a 10 percent loss during the year, 40 suffer a 50 percent loss, and 10 suffer a total loss. It is also assumed that each building's owner covers the property 100 percent to value, or $10,000. The pure premium calculation is as follows:

Insurance in Force	Losses	Fire Losses Payable
$ 99,000,000	0	0
500,000	10%	$ 50,000
400,000	50%	200,000
100,000	100%	100,000
Total $100,000,000		$350,000

$$\text{Pure Premium} = \frac{\$350,000}{\$100,000,000} = 0.0035$$
$$= \$0.35 \text{ per } \$100 \text{ of value,}$$
$$\text{or } \$35 \text{ per building}$$

In this case the insurer must charge each building owner $35 to pay for the expected fire losses. The corresponding fire rate would be $0.35 per $100 of insured value.

Case 2—50% Coverage. Assume that all facts are the same as in Case 1 except that each insured decides to insure only 50 percent to value:

	(1) Exposed Value	(2) Insurance in Force 50% of (1)
	$ 99,000,000	$49,500,000
	500,000	250,000
	400,000	200,000
	100,000	50,000
Total	$100,000,000	$50,000,000

(3) Losses	(4) Fire Losses Payable (1) × (3)
0	0
10%	$ 50,000
50%	200,000
100%	50,000*
	$300,000

*Limited by the face amount of the policy to 50% coverage.

In this case the insurer must pay out $300,000 in losses. However, if the insurer charges the $0.35 rate as developed in Case 1, it will collect only $175,000 from policyholders ($50,000,000 × 0.0035). It will therefore suffer a net deficit of $125,000 due to underinsurance.

Case 3—Charging Higher Rate. Assume that all facts are the same as Case 2 except that the insurer decides to charge a higher rate in order to prevent the deficit. Since total losses payable in Case 2 are $300,000 and there is $50 million of insurance in force, the pure premium must equal 0.006 ($300,000 ÷ $50,000,000), or $0.60 per $100. This contrasts with the situation in Case 1 where a rate of only $0.35 per $100 is needed.

Rather than charge a higher rate for coverage, the insurer may utilize the coinsurance clause, which reduces loss payments to the individual insured.

Case 4—Use of Coinsurance Clause. Assume the same facts as in Case 2, except that the insurer attaches a 100 percent coinsurance clause to each policy. The rate charged is $0.35 per $100 of value, which produces a net deficit without the use of coinsurance.

(1) Insurance in Force	(2) Insurance Required (100%)
$49,500,000	$ 99,000,000
250,000	500,000
200,000	400,000
50,000	100,000
Total $50,000,000	$100,000,000

(3) Recovery	(4) Fire Losses Incurred	(5) Amount Payable by Insurer (3) × (4)
50%	0	0
50%	$ 50,000	$ 25,000
50%	200,000	100,000
50%	100,000	50,000
	$350,000	$175,000
Premiums (0.0035 × $50,000,000)		$175,000
Deficit		0

In this case, the insurer eliminates what would be a net deficit by reducing loss recoveries by means of the coinsurance clause. Policyholders suffer $175,000 of losses through coinsurance penalties. Presumably, it is immaterial to the insurer whether a $0.60 rate is charged or the coinsurance clause is used to effect "equity" in the rate structure. The insurer might offer the insured a choice: pay the higher rate ($0.60 in the example), or allow attachment of a coinsurance clause and pay the lower rate ($0.35).

Time Limitations

Time is of the essence in most insurance policies. There are specified limits of time set forth, for example, during which the loss must be suffered, the insurer is to be notified in the event of loss, the claims are to be paid, and the proof of loss is to be submitted. We are now interested primarily in the time limits that affect the dollar amount of coverage. To illustrate, in nearly all contracts guaranteeing the payment of an income or periodic indemnification for loss, such as disability insurance contracts, there are often waiting periods before recovery begins. There are also time limitations that restrict the maximum period for which payments may be made. Thus, in a policy that pays an income to the insured who becomes permanently disabled, it is very common to provide that no income shall be payable during the first 30 or 90 days of disability.

Such a provision has the same purpose as a straight dollar deductible, namely, to eliminate small claims and to reduce the cost of coverage. In addition, the policy may provide that the income shall continue for one year, two years, ten years, or life, as the case may be. The insurer always specifies what time limit, if any, shall be imposed. This is necessary in order to meet the requirement that an insurable risk must be definite and measurable.

Time limitations are found in many kinds of insurance contracts. In business interruption insurance, the insurer promises to pay for net profits and necessary continuing expenses lost as the result of an interruption of normal business operations due to a named peril. The payment necessarily depends primarily on the length of time the business was shut down as a result of the named peril. In life insurance, the contract is often settled with the beneficiary by paying the proceeds in the form of an income, rather than in a lump sum. When this is done, the length of time the income is to continue is spelled out in the policy.

Dollar Limits

Most insurance contracts provide for maximum dollar limits on recovery for given types of losses. In addition to the limits imposed by the face amount of the policy, there are two general types: specific limits and aggregate limits.

Specific dollar limits restrict payments to a maximum amount on any one definite item of property or from a named peril, as provided in the policy. **Aggregate dollar limits** restrict payments to some maximum amount on any one group of items of property. Thus, the homeowners' policy has a specific limit of $500 on liability for loss to plant, shrub, or any one tree from any one loss. In addition, there is an aggregate limit that provides that no more than 5 percent of the amount of insurance may apply to plants, trees, and shrubs in any one loss. As it is used in liability insurance, aggregate means the policy will not pay more than the aggregate limit during the policy year. If a firm had a $100,000 per occurrence and a $1,000,000 aggregate limit, the policy would never pay more than $1,000,000 during the policy year, regardless of the number of losses.

Another example of dollar limits is found in the manner in which insurers restrict their liability for losses resulting from bodily injury liability. Usually there is a specific limit of liability for damage to any one person, and there is an aggregate limit of liability applicable to loss in any one accident. Thus, if the limits of liability are expressed as "$10,000/$20,000 BI," it means that the company will be liable for no more than $10,000 to any one person in a given accident, and in no case for more than $20,000 per accident in the event that more than one person files a claim for which the insured is liable. Unless stated otherwise, the policy could pay up to $20,000 per person per accident.

Apportionment Clauses

Practically all contracts of indemnity, and many valued contracts, contain **apportionment clauses** that limit the insurer's liability in case other insurance contracts also cover the loss.

For example, a contract may agree to pay the insured a certain income on a valued basis if the insured becomes permanently and totally disabled. It might stipulate, however, that in case the insured is collecting under other disability contracts as well, the indemnity will be reduced to the point that the insured will be prevented from collecting more than, say, three-fourths of the income received prior to the disability.

Sometimes the effect of the apportionment clauses is quite severe because one insurer may limit its liability to its proportion of all insurance covering the property regardless of whether the other insurance policies apply to a particular loss. For example, suppose A has a building valued at $10,000. A has fire policies in two companies, X and Y, in the amount of $5,000 each. The policy in company X is written to cover windstorm losses through the use of the extended coverage endorsement, but the policy in company Y does not contain this endorsement. Company X's policy contains an apportionment clause. In case of a windstorm loss of $1,000, company X pays only the proportion that its policy bears to all fire insurance on the property, or one-half. Thus, the insured collects $500 from company X and nothing from company Y because company Y's policy did not insure against windstorm. The only solution to this problem is to make sure that all policies insuring the property are identical in their coverage.

The purpose of apportionment clauses, sometimes known as **pro-rata liability clauses,** is to establish some procedure by which each insurer's liability may be determined when more than one policy covers the property. In the absence of such clauses, the insured might collect more than the actual cash loss, and a moral hazard could be created. In most property insurance lines, these clauses simply provide for an apportionment of coverage in the same proportion that the amount of each policy bears to the total insurance. In other lines, the clauses provide that with regard to certain losses, the policy will be "excess over any other applicable coverage." That is, the contract is to apply to losses only after the limits of liability of all applicable insurance contracts have been exhausted. In ocean marine insurance, it is the general rule that the limits of liability of the first policy to be written on a given exposure must be exhausted before subsequently issued contracts will have any liability. Other policies, such as the homeowners,' do not permit other insurance to be written on the described property.

Pro-Rata Clause. The pro-rata clause is a special type of apportionment clause that is found in most property insurance contracts. It typically states that if more than one policy is in force on a given piece of property, each policy will pay in the ratio of the face value of each policy divided by the total amount of insurance in force on the property. For example, if there were four policies in force on a country club for $100,000, $200,000, $300,000, and $400,000, then they would pay 10, 20, 30, and 40 percent of each loss. On a $100,000 loss the policies would pay $10,000, $20,000, $30,000, and $40,000, respectively. If the pro-rata clause did not exist, the insured would collect $400,000 on a $100,000 loss. If the latter case existed, the moral hazard would greatly increase.

A problem arises with the pro-rata clause when one of the insurers goes bankrupt or for some other reason refuses to contribute. The clause actually says the proration takes place whether all the insurance is collectible or not. Consequently, in the preceding case, if the insurer providing $400,000 in coverage went into receivership and could not pay on the loss, the other firms would still only contribute $10,000, $20,000, and $30,000 to the loss. The insured would have to absorb the $40,000 or collect from a guaranty fund of the state. Under the pro-rata clause, the risk of insurer insolvency is assumed by the insured.

It is worth noting that the pro-rata liability clause applies only to policies that cover the same legal interest. If there is more than one interest involved, such as in the case of a lessee and an owner, and there are two policies on the property, each insurer must pay to the fullest extent of its liability and the payment will not be reduced by action of the pro-rata liability clause.

Suppose a lessee spends $10,000 improving a property and insures this value. Since the value of all permanent improvements to real estate revert to the landlord upon expiration of the lease, the landlord also has an interest in the improvements, and may insure them. Since there are two interests, there may be two policies of $10,000 each. In the event that a fire destroys the entire property, both insurers would have to pay to the fullest extent of the insurable interest of each insured.

THIRD-PARTY COVERAGE

Many insurance contracts may provide coverage on individuals who are not direct parties to the contract. Such persons are known as **third parties.** The rights of third parties are outlined in each contract and vary considerably.

In life insurance, the beneficiary may be a third party who has the right to receive the death proceeds of the policy under conditions that are usually determined in advance by the named insured. The beneficiary can be changed at any time by the insured, unless this right has been formally given up—i.e., unless the insured has named the beneficiary irrevocably. The beneficiary's rights are thus contingent upon the death of the insured. Similarly, a person such as a creditor to whom a policy has been assigned has certain rights as a third party to receive death proceeds and perhaps even certain claims on the cash value of life insurance policies.

In workers' compensation insurance contracts the agreement is between two parties, an employer and an insurance company. The insurance company agrees to make payments to employees as required under the laws of the state relating to compensations of workers who suffer job-connected injuries. The insurer's obligation is directly to the injured worker, who is a third party under the contract. Depending on state law, the worker may bring legal action against the insurer for benefits even though the worker was not a direct party to the agreement.

In medical payments insurance, coverage that is granted under automobile and homeowners' policies and under various liability policies is essentially a third-party coverage. Automobile medical insurance is actually a combination of first-party and third-party protection. It will compensate the insured as well as any other individuals occupying the insured's automobile. Under third-party medical liability, individuals who are not contracting parties are covered for injuries they may suffer under certain conditions, such as while they are on the insured premises of the named insured.

In the field of property insurance, very often the third party is the one who has loaned money on property covered under the policy of the named insured. For example, in fire insurance the lender is usually covered under what is known as the standard mortgagee clause, and in automobile insurance under what is known as a loss payable clause. The lender is entitled to recover first if the property is damaged by a peril covered under the policy, with any excess going to the owner.

The lender is entitled to advance notice in case the policy is about to be cancelled for any reason and is usually permitted to pay the premium if the insured fails to do so. The lender's rights are not lost merely because the insured violates some provision of the policy and thereby loses rights under the contract. Thus, if the insured uses the vehicle as a public rental vehicle, thereby suspending coverage under the automobile policy, the lender is still entitled to the recovery of the interest in case the vehicle is destroyed. The insurer pays the lender and, through subrogation, enjoys all the rights that the lender had against the insured. In this way the insured cannot benefit from payment to a third party when the insured was not entitled to payment personally.

SUMMARY

1. There are two general approaches to insuring agreements—the named-peril and the all-risk approaches. The tendency is to expand the use of all-risk contracts.
2. It is common to cover many more than one individual as insureds under most insurance policies. These secondary interests normally do not receive as broad coverage as is given to the named insured. Policies also give certain privileges to third parties who are not direct parties to the contract. In fact, many insurance agreements are chiefly for the benefit of third parties.
3. All contracts of insurance contain exclusions. There are excluded causes of loss or excluded perils such as war, wear and tear, and intentional damage. There are often excluded losses and excluded property, so that even if a loss due to an insured peril occurs, not all the loss may be covered. Most policies exclude or limit losses caused in certain locations, such as while the goods are away from a named location, or while they are abroad.
4. The practice of limiting amounts payable is common to insurance contracts. Thus, there are various kinds of deductibles, franchises, coinsurance arrangements, time limitations, named dollar limits of liability, and apportionment clauses. These clauses serve purposes other than merely keeping down the insurer's loss payments. They may encourage the insured to take out complete insurance to value, or they may discourage this course of action. They also serve to control the moral hazard and to define the insurer's obligation more precisely than would be possible without them, thus converting what might be an uninsurable risk into one that is insurable.

QUESTIONS FOR REVIEW

1. Differentiate between excluded perils and excluded losses, giving examples of each type.
2. *A* is offered the choice of a major medical policy with a $100 deductible or with a $500 deductible. There are five members in *A*'s family, and the deductible applies on a calendar-year basis to each individual in the family. The cost of the policy with a $100 deductible is $200 a year, while the cost of the policy written with a $500 deductible is $70 a year. Which policy should *A* take? Why?
3. Explain the difference between a franchise clause and a straight deductible by use of an example.
4. A certain fire insurance policy is written with a 90-percent coinsurance clause in

the amount of $45,000. The actual replacement cost of the structure, less depreciation, is found to be $100,000.

(a) What amount may be collected under this policy in the event of the following losses? (1) $1,000, (2) $5,000, (3) $50,000, (4) $80,000, (5) $90,000. Explain.

(b) Does the clause reduce recovery below the amount insured in all of the above cases? Why?

5. Answer Question 4(a) if the amount of insurance carried had been $60,000 instead of $45,000.

6. (a) Explain the reasoning behind the use of the coinsurance clause in Question 4.

(b) Is there any way to accomplish the purpose other than through the use of coinsurance? Explain.

7. (a) Calculate the deductible on a major medical health insurance policy with an 80/20 participation deductible subject to an aggregate deductible of $5,000 if $10,000 in losses occur.

(b) What would your answer be if $35,000 in losses occurred during the year?

8. The mortgagee clause protects the lender's interest. Describe three ways the mortgagee clause aids the mortgagee.

QUESTIONS FOR DISCUSSION

1. The insuring agreement of the personal property floater reads, "Perils insured. All risks of loss of or damage to property covered except as hereinafter provided." Should one assume from this that one has all-risk coverage for the property described? Explain.

2. Explain the major reasons for excluding certain perils from insurance contracts.

3. Why are life insurance policies not cancellable by the insurer although fire insurance policies are?

4. The standard fire insurance policy provides that "this company shall not be liable for a greater proportion of any loss than the amount hereby insured shall bear to the whole insurance covering the property against the peril involved, whether collectible or not." Would the principle of indemnity be violated if this clause were not excluded? Give an illustration.

5. Y's house and its contents become a total fire loss, but Y has only a vague idea of what property actually was destroyed because there was no inventory of the household goods.

(a) How might Y go about establishing the value of the loss?

(b) Is it likely that Y will be able to collect full indemnity, assuming that Y was fully insured? Why or why not? Discuss.

6. The double indemnity provision in a life insurance policy provides that twice the face amount of the insurance will be paid for certain types of accidental death, providing death occurs within 90 days of the accident.

(a) What purpose is served by this type of time limitation?

(b) Is the time limitation in accord with sound insurance principles? Explain.

NEW TERMS AND CONCEPTS

Actual Cash Value
Aggregate Dollar Limits
All Risk
Declarations
Franchise
Insuring Agreement

Mortgagee Clause
Named Insured
Named Peril
Replacement-Cost Insurance
Specific Dollar Limits
Third Party

NOTES

1 C. Arthur Williams, George L. Head, and William G. Glendenning, *Principles of Risk Management and Insurance* (Malvern, Pa.: American Institute for Property Liability Underwriters, 1978), p. 226.

2 Ibid., p. 513.

3 *New York Insurance Code*, Chapter 189, Section 167-b.

4 *McAnarney v. Newark Fire Insurance Co.*, 159 N.E. 902.

5 The property may be insured on an ACV or replacement cost basis.

8 THE LIABILITY RISK

After studying this chapter, you should be able to:

1. Distinguish between criminal law and civil law.
2. Understand what a tort is.
3. Describe negligence and the characteristics of a negligent act.
4. Explain some of the defenses against a claim of negligence.
5. Discuss factors that are causing individuals and businesses to maintain higher standards of care.
6. Identify the basic types of liability exposures and give an explanation of them.
7. Explain what is meant by no-fault insurance.
8. Define the basic payments made by liability insurance contracts.
9. Identify some of the recent developments in the legal system that will affect one's ability to collect under a tort action.

One of the most serious financial risks covered by insurance is that of loss through legal liability for harm caused to others. Losses from this source have been so frequent and so serious in the United States that special no-fault laws have been passed in some states in the area of automobile liability. Negligence as a basis for determining liability for industrial accidents and illness has been eliminated by adoption of workers' compensation laws. Public attention has recently been focused on another area of negligence, that of medical malpractice, and legislative solutions to the handling of this risk have been proposed.

The following case is illustrative of the sometimes catastrophic losses occurring because of negligence. An 11-year-old boy was hit on the right side of the head in a schoolyard fight. He was taken to the hospital, but X-rays showed no evidence of skull fracture. He was sent home although he was pale and groggy and perspiring heavily. When he did not improve, his father took him to the hospital that night, and this time doctors decided to operate. They removed a large blood clot pressing on the brain. It was determined that had the doctors operated immediately the first time, the boy would have made a good recovery; because of the delay, however, permanent brain damage occurred. The boy was left mute and paralyzed from the neck down. The family sued the doctors, the hospital, and the school district for negligence and was awarded damages of $4,025,000, one of the largest settlements of this type on record.[1]

The DC-10 airplane crash at O'Hare International Airport on May 25, 1979, which killed 274 persons, led to millions of dollars of losses. The crash in the Canary Islands (Tenerife) killed 583 persons and had larger claims than the O'Hare accident. There is little wonder that individual major airlines carry $500 million in liability insurance to cover such accidents.[2]

TYPES OF LIABILITY DAMAGES

Individuals may be sued for numerous types of liability damages. However, insurance contracts are designed to pay only for certain types of losses. Since the primary focus of this text is the use of insurance to handle risk, it is appropriate to identify the damages that insurance contracts will cover early in the chapter, so that you will be better able to understand subsequent material in both this and following chapters. In terms of liability, insurance policies are usually restricted to pay for bodily injury, personal injury, property damage, and legal expenses.

Bodily Injury

Bodily injury liability includes liability for losses a person may incur because his or her body or mind has been harmed. Such coverage includes payments for medical bills, loss of income, rehabilitation, loss of services (household as well as marital), pain and suffering, and punitive damages.

Pain and suffering damages are designed to compensate the injured party for the pain endured due to the negligent behavior of the defendant. They are considered noneconomic damages and often are greater than economic losses, such as loss of income and medical expenses.

Punitive damages are assessed when it is deemed that the defendant acted in a grossly negligent manner and deserves to have his or her behavior made an example so as to discourage others from acting that way. Punitive damages are usually in addition to other damages and can be for very large amounts. In some states, such as New York, insurance policies are not allowed to pay punitive damages. The reasoning is that it does not punish the defendant if the insurance company pays the punitive damages.

Property Damage

Liability for damage to real and personal property is covered by insurance policies. Actual damage to the property is covered, as well as loss of use of the property. The loss of use exposure may include loss of income because the property cannot be used, or extra expenses incurred to rent property to replace the damaged property. Usually, coverage is only for tangible property.

Personal Injury

Personal injury liability losses result from libel, slander, invasion of privacy, false arrest, and the like. This coverage is often added to homeowners' policies by endorsement. It is automatically included in more modern business liability policies. In fact, in some business liability policies the term "personal injury" includes both bodily injury and libel, slander, etc.

Legal Expenses

Individuals or organizations being sued must be prepared to retain a lawyer for their defense. As the defense process can be very costly, insurance contracts are designed to cover legal expenses that result from associated losses. In some types of loss exposures, like product liability, the cost of defense may be as great or greater than damage awards.

CRIMINAL AND CIVIL LAW

People can generally be held accountable under two different types of legal proceedings: criminal and civil. **Criminal law** is directed toward wrongs against society. Examples of such wrongs would be murder, robbery, rape, and assault with a deadly weapon. Charges under criminal law are made by a governmental body such as a city, county, state, or federal prosecutor, and the guilty party is subject to fine and/or imprisonment.

Civil law is directed toward wrongs against individuals and organizations. A person may be tried for criminal and civil charges for the same action. For example, if you murder someone, the state will try you for murder, and the heirs of the murdered person may sue you in civil court for damages. Normally, in a civil action the guilty party is only required to pay a fine and/or damages, to perform a certain action, or to refrain from performing an action. Breach of contract and negligent acts are two examples of cases that would go to a civil court.

TORTS

A **tort** is a legal injury or wrong to another that arises out of actions other than breach of contract, in which courts will provide a remedy by allowing recovery in an action for damages. A legal **injury** results when a person's rights are wrongfully invaded. Examples of such rights are the right of personal privacy, the right to enjoy one's property unmolested, and the right to be free from personal injury. Examples of torts are libel, slander, assault, and negligence. We are mainly concerned here with protection against the financial consequences of civil action arising out of only one of these torts, negligence, which arises from the omission or commission of an act. Insurance against intentional torts, such as false arrest, libel, slander, trespass, battery, and assault, is also available.

BASIC LAW OF NEGLIGENCE

The basic law of negligence has many threads that are sometimes difficult for the lay person to disentangle. To see what this basic law is all about, one needs first to understand what conditions must be met before an act is considered actionable negligence. Next, one must appreciate what defenses are recognized by the courts for the protection of defendants. No matter how wrong a defendent may have been, if a suitable defense that satisfies the law can be raised, the defendant may be shielded from liability. Finally, it is necessary to appreciate how this interaction of negligence and defenses operates in the many different sets of relationships that make up our legal culture—that is, relationships that exist between employer and employee, landlord and tenant, buyer and seller, principal and agent, and driver and pedestrian. Additional standards of conduct are applied in each relationship. The law is extremely complex and is changing constantly; therefore, only a summary of highlights can be given here.

THE NEGLIGENT ACT

Negligence is the failure to exercise the degree of care required by law. What is required by law is understood to be the conduct that a reasonably prudent individual would exercise to prevent harm.

A Negative Act

A negligent act may be the failure to do something as much as it may be the positive doing of something. It arises from a breach of legal duty to another. One may drive an automobile into the rear of another car. As such, this is a positive act. A negligent act may, however, be a negative act, such as failing to signal a turn.

Negligence may be the failure to act when there is a duty to act. Thus, a gas company was held liable for a loss when it had agreed to inspect a customer's gas pipe but failed to do so.[3]

A Voluntary Act

A negligent act is one which is done *voluntarily*. If an act is done involuntarily, the act is excusable. If such were the case, the plaintiff could not collect damages. For example, it is easy to see that if one person puts a gun into the hand of another, directs the second person's aim at a target, and helps pull the trigger, the second person is hardly a free agent; and if the shot injures a person, there is doubt that the second person is necessarily negligent.

A negligent act is not excused because there was no intention to cause harm. Unintentional injury to another may give rise to both criminal and civil action at law. Negligent acts are essentially those in which the defendant may try to be excused by saying "I didn't mean to."

The law does not expect perfection to be the standard by which conduct is judged. The care expected of a trained physician who is a specialist is higher than that expected from an intern. The degree of care expected from a child is different from that expected of an adult. The care expected of an automobile driver is not interpreted in the light of what might have been had the driver been able to take full advantage of hindsight in avoiding an accident. It is interpreted in the light of the decision that any reasonable person would have made in an emergency, when there was no time to consider all the possible alternatives.

An Imputed Act

Liability for a negligent act may be **imputed** from another person. Thus, one is liable not only for one's own acts, but also for the negligent acts of servants or agents acting in the course of their employment or agency. Employers may be sued because of negligent acts of their employees. Liability for the negligence of another can rest on a contract to assume that liability. Thus, a baseball club may be held liable for accidents arising out of the use of a ball park owned by the city and leased from it, simply because the club had assumed such liability under the lease. Under so-called dramshop laws in many states, a tavern owner may be held liable for third-party damages resulting from the operation of dispensing alcoholic beverages. Thus, if a customer becomes inebriated, and because of this condition hits a pedestrian while driving home from the tavern, the tavern operator may be held liable for the loss to the pedestrian. In some states, parents may be held legally liable for the damage caused by their children who negligently drive the family automobile or who perform other torts, because the state law requires that the parents assume such liability.

Proximate Cause of the Loss

To give rise to action for damages, a negligent act must of course be the **proximate cause** of the loss. There must be an unbroken chain of events leading from the negligent act to the damage sustained. Suppose A negligently damages B's car, and as a result B is late for an important business engagement. B charges that, as a result, a sale was lost which would have netted $10,000. Can B add $10,000 to the claim for damages? Carrying the example further, suppose B claims that not only did he lose the sale, but as a result of losing it, he also lost his job. Further, because of the lost job his wife had to go to work, necessitating the expense of purchasing a second automobile and the hiring of a nurse for the children. May B also add these expenses to his claim? It is clear that the court must draw a line in determining proximate cause, or a host of sources for damage claims would open up.

DEFENSES TO NEGLIGENCE CLAIMS

Even if a person is guilty of a negligent act, certain defenses can be used to bar liability for such negligence.

Contributory Negligence

At common law, if both parties are to blame in a given accident, neither party may collect from the other for damages arising out of negligence. One must come into court with "clean hands." The one who was partially to blame was guilty of **contributory negligence** and may not collect against another, even if the other was 90 percent to blame and the plaintiff was only 10 percent to blame.

Assumed Risk

Under certain circumstances, a defendant may raise the defense that the plaintiff has no cause for action because the plaintiff assumed the risk of harm from (1) the conduct of the defendant, (2) the condition of the premises, or (3) the defendant's product. Managements of baseball parks are sometimes sued when baseballs hit members of the viewing crowds. Assuming that reasonable care has been exercised in providing appropriate wire screens, courts usually hold that a person who views a ball game is assuming the risks normally attributed to viewers and must accept the consequences as a normal result of a baseball game.

Guest-Host Statutes

An exception to the general trend toward absolute liability in our society has been the passage of what are known as **guest-host statutes.** These laws relate to the standard of care owed by an automobile driver to a passenger. The general effect of the laws is to reduce the standard of care owed to a guest in a car in such a manner that the guest, in order to prove liability for the negligence of a driver, must prove that the driver was guilty of gross negligence, or willful injury, such as might be the case if the driver were intoxicated. Under the guest-host laws, ordinary negligence will not be sufficient to sustain a case against the driver. In a number of states, guest-host statutes have been declared unconstitutional.

FACTORS LEADING TO HIGHER STANDARDS OF CARE

During the last twenty years dramatic changes have occurred in tort law. These changes have led to situations where individuals and corporations are held to a much higher standard of care. The following paragraphs examine the factors that have influenced this trend.

Expanding Application of Liability

Courts tend increasingly to impose liability in new factual settings. For example, traditionally a manufacturer might not often have been held liable for making a faulty product such as a gas tank that leaked, causing an accident. However, decisions in California held a manufacturer and a dealer liable for loss from what was defined as an unsafe gas tank design. In another case, the owner of a chimpanzee that caused ten persons to get hepatitis was held liable. Before this case, most suits involved situations in which an animal caused an injury, not an illness. In still another case, an airline was charged with undue delay in obtaining proper medical treatment for a passenger who suffered a heart attack.

Weakening of Defenses against Liability

The area of workers' compensation was the first major example of social insurance in the United States. All states have now passed this type of legislation, which represents an abandonment of the principles of negligence law in determining liability for occupational injury. Before these laws were passed (most were enacted between 1910 and 1920), the principles of negligence governed, and an employee had to seek damages at law from the employer for occupational injuries. Because this system proved inefficient, time consuming, and generally unsatisfactory, especially for the employee, it was replaced by workers' compensation laws. The employee now receives a payment for on-the-job injuries according to a schedule set up for this purpose, regardless of who, if anyone, is to blame for the injury.

Similar principles have been applied in the several states that have passed no-fault laws regarding bodily injuries in automobile accidents. (See Chapter 16.) In some of these laws, the rights of the plaintiff to bring legal action for negligence against other drivers have been restricted.

The defense of contributory negligence likewise has been weakened in various ways. In a few states statutes have been enacted that replace this principle with one termed **comparative negligence.** Under this doctrine, the liability of the defendant is reduced by the extent to which the plaintiff was contributively negligent. If the plaintiff was 20 percent negligent, the defendant is liable for only 80 percent of the plaintiff's damages. In some states, the plaintiff recovers nothing if he or she is more than 50 percent at fault.

Another way in which the defense of contributory negligence has been weakened is in the **last clear chance rule.** Under this rule, a plaintiff who was contributively negligent may still have a cause of action against the defendant if it can be shown that the defendant had a last clear chance before the accident to avoid injuring the plaintiff, but failed to do so. Thus, it is possible that a jaywalker may collect if hit by a motorist who had a chance to swerve, but failed to do so.

Res Ipsa Loquitur

Another illustration of the trend toward absolute liability lies in the more frequent use of a rule known as *res ipsa loquitur*—"the thing speaks for itself." Under this rule, a plaintiff may sometimes collect without actually proving negligence on the part of the defendant. It should be noted that under common law, before an action can be sustained against a party, negligence must be shown; that is, it must be shown that there was some failure on the part of the defendant to use the degree of care required of a reasonably prudent person in the same circumstance. Testimony of witnesses and of the injured parties must usually be brought to bear upon the case.

Res ipsa loquitur may be applied to establish a case against the defendant when (1) the defendant is in a position to know the cause of the accident and the plaintiff is not, (2) the defendant had exclusive control of the instrumentality that caused the accident, and (3) the use of the instrumentality would not normally cause injuries without the existence of negligence in its operation. As may be guessed, this doctrine has been used frequently in premises and product liability cases.

Expansion of Imputed Liability

Still more evidence of the stricter view of negligence taken by society today is the passage of what are known as **vicarious liability laws.** The effect of vicarious liability laws is to place liability on the owner of a car for the negligence of the driver, thereby expanding the common-law rule applicable to employers and principals. About 39 states have such laws. Thus, in these states, under certain circumstances, the owner of a car may be held liable simply because in good faith he or she loaned the car to someone, and that person negligently caused harm.

A major problem faced by large corporations is the **joint and several liability** situation. When an accident occurs and several different parties are negligent, the plaintiff may sue and collect from one or more of the negligent parties. Under joint and several liability the plaintiff can collect the entire judgment from a large corporation that was barely at fault, say five or ten percent. The major "tort feasor" in such cases is often an individual or small corporation with little or no insurance.

Large corporations feel this concept is unfair because they are hardly at fault; but because they have the ability to pay ("the deep pocket"), they must pay the awards. Insurers who provide them protection do not like it because it is very difficult to predict losses. The loss is a function not so much of the insured's behavior as of the insured's ability to pay.

Plaintiffs and their lawyers like it. Through its use, they are able to recover damages for injuries to the plaintiff. Several states are making a thorough review of their tort systems, and the doctrine of joint and several liability is receiving special attention. Over the next several years society will decide whether to keep joint and several liability as it is, modify it, or eliminate it.

Changing Concepts of Damage

Another factor worth noting in assessing the trend toward absolute liability is the more liberal interpretation of what types of damages may be allowed in negligence actions. Courts generally allow as damages claims for medical bills, loss of income, loss of life, property damage, and other losses for which the proximate cause was negligence. Thus, damages have usually been allowed for such things as pain and suffering, and loss of the conjugal relation by a spouse. However, more recently, damages have been awarded for such intangible losses as mental anguish, presumably under the theory that pain and suffering need not be physical to establish damages.[4]

Awards can also be used to punish defendants because their actions constituted gross negligence, or willful and wanton misconduct. In a famous case in California involving an accident in a Ford Pinto, $100,000,000 of punitive damages were awarded by the jury. On appeal, this amount was substantially reduced. Every state allows punitive damages except Louisiana, Nebraska, and Washington. As the idea of punitive damages is to punish the tort feasor, some states do not allow insurance policies to pay punitive damages. Five states (Colorado, Kansas, New York, Washington, and Wyoming) prohibit it completely. Other states may restrict it, but 32 states permit it without restrictions.[5]

Increased Damage Awards

Not only have the courts tended to widen the types of cases for which damages are awarded, but they have also tended to increase greatly the amounts of these damages.

Various reasons have been advanced for the tendency of courts to be more generous than formerly in assessing the awards given in negligence actions. The effect of inflation in reducing the purchasing power of the dollar has undoubtedly had a considerable effect. Perhaps the existence of liability insurance has caused juries to be more generous than they would be if it were known that the plaintiff would have to pay damages personally.

An organization of attorneys known as the National Association of Claimants' Compensation Attorneys (N.A.C.C.A.) has had some influence in obtaining larger judgments for claimants. This organization has been instrumental in advancing the use of ideas and methods known to be successful in obtaining larger awards than would otherwise be the case. The use of visual aids in a courtroom to illustrate vividly the scope of the damage done and the seriousness and reality of pain and suffering is an example of such methods. The N.A.C.C.A., greatly criticized by some for its activities in attempting to increase court judgments, vigorously defends its methods as only a realistic approach to what it feels is the task of raising awards that were in the past, and still are, too low for adequate compensation of injured plaintiffs.

Recent Developments

Because of unexpectedly large losses under liability insurance contracts in the mid-1980s, many insurers either began to withdraw from underwriting this coverage or raised insurance premiums to very high levels. The industry also began to support various types of tort reform to be considered by state legislatures.[6] These reforms included:

1. Imposing restrictions on the right to sue.
2. Abolishing punitive damages in civil suits.
3. Reducing the standard of care required in making products to that standard existing at the time the product was made instead of at the time the loss occurred.
4. Placing a ceiling on noneconomic damages such as pain and suffering.
5. Repealing the collateral source rule, under which courts could ignore other sources from which a plaintiff might receive indemnity for loss.

Repealing this rule would reduce the amounts awarded to liable insured parties.

It is difficult to know how far, or in what areas, tort reform will be carried out among state legislatures. Plaintiffs' attorneys usually oppose restrictions on the right to sue, while insurers', some consumer groups', and defendants' attorneys generally favor it.

TYPES OF LIABILITY EXPOSURES

In the liability area, there are numerous types of exposures. These exposures arise out of different functions performed and standards of care required of persons or organizations. The situations or relationships reviewed in the following paragraphs include contractual, employer-employee, and property owner-tenant liabilities; consumption of products; operations of a contractor; professional acts; principal-agent liability; and the ownership and operation of automobiles.

Contractual Liability

Under the concept of contractual liability, one's liability may be imputed to another by contract. For example, a city may require that a street paving contractor hold the city harmless for all negligence arising out of the operations of the contractor. In this way, suits that might otherwise be directed against the city will be directed against the street contractor. Similarly, a railroad may make a contract with the manufacturer that if there is any negligence action arising out of the operation of the railroad's locomotives or trains that have entered the manufacturer's property on a spur track in order to pick up shipments, the manufacturer will assume the liability. The railroad's liability has thus been transferred by means of a contract. Other common contracts by which liability is transferred are leases, contracts to perform services or to supply goods, and easement agreements.

Employer-Employee Liability

Employers are still subject to the law of negligence with respect to employment not covered by workers' compensation laws. In fact, workers' compensation laws do not cover many classes of employees. For example, often farm workers and workers of an employer who hires less than a specified number of people are excluded from coverage. Railroad employees and sea workers are also exempt from workers' compensation laws.

The duties owed by an employer to employees, breach of which may give rise to liability, are the following:

1. The employer must provide a safe place to work.
2. The employer must employ individuals reasonably competent to carry out their tasks.
3. The employer must warn of danger.
4. The employer must furnish appropriate and safe tools.
5. The employer must set up and enforce proper rules of conduct of employees, as they relate to safe working procedures.[7]

If a garage provides a jack to raise automobiles but does not take steps to see that it is in good working condition, and the employee using the jack is injured because the jack breaks (through no fault of the worker), the employer has probably breached a common-law duty to the employee. If an employer fails to warn a new employee of the existence of explosives in a storehouse, or hires an untrained worker to handle explosives, with resulting injury to an innocent worker, grounds exist for damage suits. An employee who disregards danger signals, or fails to use the tools provided and is injured as a result, is guilty of at least contributory negligence and under common law cannot recover. This would not affect the worker's right to workers' compensation.

The employer may use the common-law defenses in suits by employees, providing these defenses have not been lost for one reason or another. If a worker brings an action against an employer for some breach of care, the employer may argue either that the worker was partly to blame (contributory negligence defense) or that the worker should have known there were certain risks on the job and cannot complain because one of these risks materialized (assumption of risk).

Property Owner-Tenant Liability

In situations that involve the use of real property, the tenant or owner owes a certain degree of care to those who enter the premises. In most states, the degree of care is governed by the status of the person entering. The common law recognizes three classes of individuals who enter premises: invitees, licensees, and trespassers. The degree of care owed to an invitee is highest, to a trespasser lowest.

An **invitee** is an individual who is invited on the premises for his or her own benefit as well as for that of the landlord or tenant. Typical invitees are customers in a retail store and guests at a hotel or at a public meeting. It is not sufficient merely to warn an invitee of danger; in addition, positive steps must be taken to protect an invitee from a known danger and to discover unknown dangers. **Licensees** are those who are on the premises for a legitimate purpose with the permission of the occupier. Typical licensees are police officers and fire fighters; others, who may be licensees or invitees, are milk delivery drivers, messengers, and meter readers. The landlord owes the licensee the duty to warn of danger and to refrain from causing deliberate harm, but no other duty. **Trepassers** include all those other than invitees and licensees who enter on the premises.

No care is owed to a trespasser, but an owner cannot set a trap for or deliberately injure a trespasser. If the trespasser is injured by some unknown, hidden hazard, the landlord or tenant is not liable. In one case an Iowa farmer set a shotgun trap for a prowler and the prowler was shot in the leg. The injured man was able to collect damages from the farmer even though he had no right to be on the premises.

To illustrate these concepts, consider the owner of a retail store who has just polished the floors to such a high degree of slickness that they constitute a definite hazard to safe walking. A burglar enters the store at night, slips, and breaks a leg. Clearly, the owner is not required to pay any medical bills or otherwise compensate this trespasser. If a delivery driver had a similar accident, the courts would probably hold the owner innocent of negligence provided that the owner had taken reasonable steps to warn people that the floors were slick. However, if a customer slipped and broke a leg on a slick floor, the courts would award damages if the store owner could have taken reasonable steps to reduce the hazard.

There is a current trend to abolish the classifications of trespasser, licensee, and invitee, and to hold the occupier of the land liable for failure to exercise due care under most circumstances. Within this trend, the status of the plaintiff as a trespasser, a licensee, or an invitee is merely one of the circumstances, but the classification is not controlling.

During 1980–1982 several hotel accidents occurred that involved the property owner-tenant relationship. In each case the persons injured were invitees. In the MGM Grand Hotel fire in Las Vegas, 85 persons were killed and 268 others were injured. Liability awards could amount to $100,000,000 or more. Another fire at the Westchase Hilton in Houston, Texas, killed 12 persons, and a fire at the Stouffers Inn in White Plains, New York, killed 26 persons. The collapse of the skywalk at the Kansas City Hyatt Regency resulted in 200 injured persons and 114 people killed. Liability claims will probably exceed $100,000,000.[8]

Assumption of Liability by Tenant. When an individual leases a building, the question arises as to what extent the landlord is responsible for injuries to tenants. In general, when the landlord releases possession of the building, the tenant takes on whatever duty the landlord owes to members of the public. In some instances, the landlord is liable to a third person because the landlord has retained possession of the area where the third person was injured. For example, in the hallways of an apartment house occupied by several tenants, the owner has been held liable for negligence to tenants and to members of the public. In one case involving a tenant who tripped and fell over a crack in the cement slab leading to her apartment, a substantial judgment was rendered when the tenant's leg had to be amputated.[9] In another case the landlord was held liable when a tenant was injured by a loose floorboard on the front porch that had been poorly repaired.[10]

In most states it is both common and legal to require, by terms of the lease, that the tenant assume whatever liability the landlord may have had (or to reimburse the owner for liability) for injuries to members of the public or to employees of the tenant. However, there are some types of liability of an owner that cannot be so shifted. Examples are liability for the violation of a safety ordinance; failure of a subcontractor to comply with such ordinances; and failure of the contractor to exercise reasonable care in excavations, blasting, or the use of fire.

Attractive Nuisance Doctrine. Under a doctrine that has become known as the **attractive nuisance doctrine,** the liability of the occupier of land may be changed so that a trespassing child is considered, in many jurisdictions, to be an invitee. Various legal fictions have been invented to accomplish this result: that there is an implied invitation to children; and that there is an intention to harm because the landlord has placed an allurement of some kind known to attract children, who are incapable of recognizing or appreciating the danger involved. The courts, in utilizing the attractive nuisance doctrine, usually consider the age of the child in rendering judgments. The decisions in the field of attractive nuisance are contradictory among the various states. Judgments have been rendered in favor of children for injuries received when a child ventured onto a railroad track that was supposed to be fenced and when a child was lighting matches over the gas tank of an abandoned vehicle in a vacant lot.[11] In these cases it is clear that an ordinary trespasser would have no claim, but because the trespasser happened to be a child, damages were awarded.

Consumption or Use of Products

A manufacturer, wholesaler, or retailer is required to exercise reasonable care and to maintain certain standards in the handling and selection of goods in which it deals. If injury to person or property results from the use of a faulty product, there may be grounds for legal action in the courts. Such actions are generally based on grounds of breach of warranty, strict tort, or negligence.

Breach of Warranty. A warranty may be expressed or implied. Often a seller gives a written or an express warranty on goods or services sold, and it is the breach of this written contract that may give rise to a court action. However, under the Uniform Commercial Code, the seller is held to have made certain unwritten or implied warranties concerning a product. These warranties are (1) the seller warrants that the goods are reasonably fit for their intended purpose; and (2) the seller warrants that when the goods are bought by description instead of by actual inspection, the goods are salable in the hands of the buyer. Breach of implied warranty is most often used as the basis for suits for faulty products. There is an implied warranty that goods are fit for a buyer's particular purpose when the seller knows the buyer's purpose and the buyer relies on the seller's judgment in making the purchase.

Cases of liability of a manufacturer for faulty products may be brought by the injured consumer directly or by a retailer who has paid a judgment as a result of selling a faulty product, particularly in the case of food, medicine, explosives, or weapons. For example, a manufacturer paid a judgment of $111,000 when a fire resulted from the heating of some roofing primer in order to thin it.[12] The manufacturer had provided no warning that the mixture would release explosive gases when heated.

Retailers have paid losses resulting from their handling of products. In one case, a dealer sold floor stain under its own private brand. Due to faulty manufacture, the mixture exploded, causing a loss to the user; but the court held that the dealer was liable because it must answer for a product it has accepted as its own. Breach of the implied warranty of fitness has formed the basis of most suits against restaurants that serve poisoned food, and against drugstores that sell faulty medicines or cosmetics.

Strict Tort. Under strict tort liability, the manufacturer or distributor of a defective product is liable to a person who is injured by the product, regardless of whether the person injured is a purchaser, a consumer, or a third person such as a bystander. It must be shown that there was a defect in the product and that the defect caused harm. The manufacturer cannot claim as a defense that no negligence was committed or that the defect was in a component purchased from another manufacturer.

Negligence. Another basis for liability is negligence. A person injured because of the use or condition of a product may be entitled to sue for damages sustained on the theory that the defendant was negligent in the preparation or manufacture of the product or failed to provide adequate instructions or warnings. A manufacturer is held to have the knowledge of an expert with respect to the product involved and must, therefore, take reasonable steps to guard against the dangers or inadequacies apparent to an expert. A court has said:

> [A] person who sells an article which he knows is dangerous to human life, limb, or health to another person, who has no knowledge of its true character, and fails to give notice thereof to the purchaser, is liable in damages to a third person who while in the exercise of due care is injured by use of it which should have been contemplated by the seller.[13]

In a famous early case it was held that a manufacturer or a vendor had no liability for negligence unless it had a contractual relationship with the injured party.[14] Thus, an injured person could bring action only against a retailer with whom there was a contractual relationship, and not against the manufacturer. Later cases brought about a relaxation of this defense, known as lack of privity between the injured party and the manufacturer. A landmark case, *MacPherson* v. *Buick Motor Company*, which concerned the breaking of a defective wheel, established the precedent that, in the court's language, "If the nature of a thing is such that it is reasonably certain to place life and limb in peril when negligently made, it is then a thing of danger."[15] It should be emphasized, however, that a manufacturer or a seller does not guarantee the safe use of the product. For example, a court refused to indemnify damage incurred when a sparkler set fire to a child's dress.

The court reasoned that there would have been little danger if the article had been used properly.[16]

During the last several years the product liability area has been very explosive as courts have continued to expand manufacturers' liability. Large losses are occurring and are expected to continue to occur to the makers of agent orange, diethylstilbestrol (DES), and asbestos. Millions of persons have been exposed to DES and asbestos, so the magnitude of potential losses is gigantic.

LIABILITY INSURANCE: UNBORN FETUS AS A PERSON

Situation

A pregnant mother took a drug manufactured by the insured during the policy period of the insured's liability policy. At a later date that was not within the policy period, the baby was born with birth defects. It was decided that these birth defects were a result of the mother's taking the faulty drugs that were manufactured by the insured. The insured's problem was that of determining when the injury actually took place. The insured made a claim with the liability insurer that was her insurer at the time the fetus would have been originally injured or when the mother took the drug; however, the insurer refused the coverage on the basis that the fetus would not be a "person" insured under the contract.

Conclusion

The court decided that an unborn fetus later born alive after a liability insurance policy lapsed was a "person" within the meaning of the liability insurance policy under consideration. Birth defects suffered by this "person" as a result of his mother's ingestion during pregnancy of a drug manufactured by the insured constituted a bodily injury caused by an occurrence within the scope of coverage of the policy. The injury and damage to the fetus were sustained during the gestation period of the mother, and this did occur prior to the lapse of the policy. It was not the actual birth thereafter that gave rise to the injury and damage.

Endo Laboratories, Inc., et al. v. *The Hartford Insurance Group et al.*, United States Court of Appeals, November 19, 1984. *Insurance Law Reporter*, Commerce Clearing House, 1985, pp. 1254–1259.

Operations of a Contractor

A contractor who carelessly installs a water boiler or an electrical appliance that later explodes or causes a fire and resulting damage to the property or person of another may be held liable for negligence arising out of the faulty installation. This is known as **completed operations liability,** under which the damage must occur after the contractor has completed the work and the work has been accepted by the owner or abandoned by the contractor. Examples of completed operations liability include the following cases. A contractor was held liable for extensive property damage when a rubber hose connection broke in an air-conditioning system several months after the installation and admitted many gallons of water into the attic of a building.[17] In another case, a contractor was involved in litigation 17 years after he repaired an iron railing; it was alleged that faulty repair work caused injury to a person leaning on the railing.[18] An electrical contractor paid $12,000 for the death of a three-year-old child electrocuted by an improperly installed outlet on which the work had been completed 15 months prior to the accident.[19]

In May, 1979, an oil rig in the Gulf of Mexico collapsed and sank. Eight people were killed and 20 injured. Firms involved with building or replacing the oil rig will pay losses of more than $10,000,000. A survivor whose face was badly burned and disfigured received a $4.5 million award.[20]

Note that if the conduct of a contractor causes injury while the contractor is still in control of the operation, the liability is similar to that of an owner or a tenant of real property. Insurance contracts differentiate, however, between that type and the completed operations type of liability.

Professional Acts

Closely related to product liability is the area of negligence law known as professional liability. Just as a manufacturer is required to make a product reasonably fit for its intended purpose, so is the seller of services required to use reasonable care not to injure others in the performance of those services. Physicians, accountants, architects, insurance agents, lawyers, pharmacists, and beauticians are examples of those who have a professional liability exposure. In one case, a beauty parlor had to pay $15,000 in damages because a customer's hair and scalp were injured when a cold wave was applied in a negligent manner.[21]

The standard of care required of professional people is broadly interpreted to mean that these individuals must possess the degree of skill, judgment, and knowledge appropriate to their calling and conduct themselves according to recognized professional standards. These standards naturally vary from profession to profession and are changing constantly as each particular field develops. Failure to take X-rays of a patient's hip cost one physician a judgment of $38,000. The injury was diagnosed as a bruise instead of a fracture and resulted in severe complications.[22] Before it was considered standard procedure to take X-rays following accidents, the same failure would not have constituted negligence.

Damage claims for medical malpractice appear to be especially numerous and serious in recent years. In one jurisdiction it was estimated that about one in every 35 medical doctors is sued annually for malpractice. In only about one out of seven or eight cases examined by a special study group was there any substantial evidence of negligence by the practitioner, yet in about one-fourth of the suits the doctor-defendant lost.[23]

Malpractice settlements have often been large, and the physician may often be at a procedural disadvantage. For example, in a California case the physician, a specialist in vascular surgery, employed a standard diagnostic procedure to determine the specific nature of the patient's difficulty. This procedure involved the injection of certain drugs, which for unknown reasons caused the permanent paralysis of the patient from the waist down. The physician had previously performed 50 such injections with no adverse effects. The doctrine of *res ipsa loquitur* was employed, thus permitting the jury to find for the plaintiff unless the doctor could prove no negligence. An award of $250,000 was handed down, but it was later reduced to $215,000.

Use of the doctrine of *res ipsa loquitur* in medical malpractice cases appears to have had the effect of turning the doctor into an insurer, and may result in unwillingness of the doctor to try new procedures and treatment for fear of financial bankruptcy if the treatment should fail.

Insurance agents under general principles of agency law frequently have been held to be liable for negligence. For example, if an agent agrees to obtain insurance for a client and then, through neglect, fails to do so, the agent may be held liable for losses that the client incurs because of lack of appropriate coverage.[24] If the policy was obtained, but it turns out to be worthless because the insurer was insolvent, the agent can be held liable.[25] Agents have also been held liable in cases where their clients fail to comply with a warranty or condition in the policy and the insurer is thereby relieved from liability.[26] In one case, a client told his regular agent that he was about to lease a building in another state. The agent did not request to see a copy of the lease or make any other inquiry. Later the client was held liable for a $41,000 fire loss to the building, because the terms of the lease made the lessee liable. The agent was held liable for the loss for not advising the client of the potential liability in the lease or recommending appropriate insurance.[27] Fire legal liability insurance should have been purchased.

An insurance agent is also subject to damage suits by the insurers represented for failure in a common-law duty, such as loyalty or obedience that an agent owes to the principal. For example, the insurer may prohibit the agent from binding coverage on a certain class of property. The agent, in disobedience to these instructions, writes the insurance, and a loss occurs before the insurer has a chance to cancel the policy. Because the agent was the authorized representative of the insurer and had the power to bind it, and because members of the public are not bound by private instructions of a principal to an agent, the insured has a legal right to collect. The insurer may then come against the disobedient agent for indemnification.

Even attorneys have not escaped malpractice suits for negligence in the conduct of their profession. In one case an attorney was successfully sued for $100,000 for failing to perform adequate research in a divorce case. The attorney had neglected to claim the husband's military pension as community property in the property settlement, and as a result the wife was unable to share in more than $322,000 estimated pension income.

Principal-Agent Liability

Under the doctrine of **respondeat superior,** a master is liable for the acts of servants if the servants or agents are acting within the scope of their employment. An employee thus imposes liability on the employer for negligent harm to a third party even if the employee is acting contrary to instructions, as long as he or she is doing the job. If an employee is told to solicit orders for a product, and in so doing carelessly runs into the customer, the employer will probably be required to answer for the agent's act. If the employee is instructed not to call on X, but calls on and injures X, the employer cannot plead in defense that the agent acted contrary to instructions.

There is a distinction between acting as an agent or a servant and acting as an independent contractor. In the former, the employer not only controls what is to be done, but also directs the manner in which it shall be done. In the latter, the employer pays the contractor for completing a certain job, but does not exercise any control over how it is done. It is logical that the employer is not held liable for the carelessness of an independent contractor to as great a degree as for the carelessness of an agent or a servant. There are, however, exceptions to this statement. Examples include hiring contractors to perform inherently dangerous work and landlords fulfilling their duty to maintain safe premises.

Ownership and Operation of Automobiles

Under common law, an automobile owner or operator is required to exercise reasonable care in the handling of automobiles. Three situations may be distinguished in this important area of negligence:

1. Liability of the operator
2. Liability of the owner for the negligence of others operating the car
3. Liability of employers for the negligence of their servants or agents using automobiles in their employer's business, even when the employer is not the owner

Liability of the Operator. The typical damage suit in the field of automobile liability is one that charges the operator with carelessness that is the proximate cause of either bodily injury or property damage to an injured third party. As in the other areas of liability, it is impossible to lay down a comprehensive statement of what constitutes negligence in the operation of an automobile. In some states departures are made from the common law by adoption of the rule of comparative negligence and the last clear chance doctrine.[28] In certain cases guest-host statutes operate to lessen the liability of operators to passengers.

Liability of the Owner-Nonoperator. The question arises, "Under what conditions can an automobile owner be held liable for damages when not personally to blame for the alleged negligence?" If one gives a loaded gun to a child and tells the child to entertain himself or herself, and the child accidentally injures or kills someone, the owner of the gun might well be held guilty of negligence.

Does the same situation hold if one lends one's car to a person without investigating this person's qualifications to handle the car and there is a subsequent injury to another through the operator's negligence? The courts have generally agreed that the automobile is not a "dangerous instrumentality" in itself and that one is justified in assuming that the borrower of an automobile is competent to handle it unless there is obvious evidence of incapacity or known recklessness. Illustrating this is the case of an employer who successfully defended an action charging negligence in failing to examine a bus driver who, having recently returned to work from an illness, suffered a fatal heart attack and crashed the bus, causing injuries to the plaintiffs.[29]

There are, however, several exceptions to the general rule that an owner is not liable for acts of operators of automobiles. In many states,[30] vicarious liability laws have the effect of making the parent of a minor child liable for damage done by negligent operation of the car by a minor. Usually the owner-parent has signed the minor's application for a driver's license, and in so doing, is bound to be responsible for the minor's negligence. In six states,[31] any person furnishing a car to a minor is liable for the minor's negligence. In 14 jurisdictions,[32] the owner is liable for personal injuries or property damage due to the negligence of *any* driver.

In addition, there is a tendency for courts to rely more and more on the doctrine of *respondeat superior* in deciding the liability of the owner for negligence of an operator driving with the owner's permission. There is no question about the right of an injured third party to recover from the employer of an employee negligent in the course of employment, but some have questioned the propriety of making an owner liable for the acts of a borrower of a car. Yet there is a tendency for the courts to decide that the user is really the agent of the permissive owner, and hence the owner must answer for the agent's carelessness.[33] The inconsistency in this viewpoint was stated as follows:

> If I agree to take friends in my automobile to visit their relatives or am otherwise on a mission for their convenience and benefit, it is hard to see that an agency relation exists, much less that of master and servant. Any benefit accruing to me or any "business" that I may have is the purely social end of accommodating not myself but my

friends. Under these facts, then how can I suddenly become the master by relinquishing the operation of the automobile to a friend? Yet decisions so finding are almost universal, including the appellation of "gratuitous servant or agent."[34]

Another application of the agency relationship in establishing liability of an owner for negligence of an operator is the so-called **family-purpose doctrine** recognized in approximately half the states. Under this doctrine, an automobile is looked upon as an instrument to carry out the common purposes of a family. Therefore, the owner ought to be responsible for its use when any member of the family uses it because this member is actually the agent of the family head and is carrying out a family function. Yet the courts have not seen fit to extend this doctrine to any instrument or possession, such as a bicycle or a boat, in common use by a family. It would appear that the family-purpose doctrine is a legal fiction to establish the liability of the person most likely to be able to respond financially for damages incurred in the use of the automobile. Similar reasoning was applied in an Illinois case. A car owner was even held liable to a third party for the negligent driving of a thief who took a car in which the owner had left ignition keys, in violation of an ordinance to the contrary.[35]

Liability of Employers. Even those who do not own automobiles may be liable for damages through their negligent operation if by some legal construction the nonowner can be shown to be responsible. The legal construction normally employed is *respondeat superior*. The employer is liable for the negligent actions of employees whether their acts are in or out of an automobile. The ownership of the automobile is immaterial in such cases. In a famous early case, a life insurance company was held liable for a $10,000 judgment arising from the negligence of one of its salesmen driving in his own car on the way to a convention.[36] The defendant's argument that the salesman was really an independent contractor whose actions were not binding on the insurer was dismissed. In general, the courts are not sympathetic to the independent contractor argument.

MISCELLANEOUS LIABILITY

The preceding examples illustrate the major areas of negligence liability. In a similar way, legal decisions form the framework of the common law of negligence of many other types of relationships in modern society. For example, there is a body of decisions (and some statutory enactments) surrounding the areas of the liability of a parent for the negligent acts of children, of the liability of a trustee to beneficiaries for mishandling of trusts, and of the liability of owners of animals for destruction or injuries caused by these animals. Detailed inquiry into the liability law for these and other areas is beyond the scope of this text.

Because of the complexity, delays, and cost of our system of negligence law in compensating victims of accidents, much discussion has taken place of the idea of extending the no-fault principle in workers' compensation and automobile insurance to accidents in general. Courts are already tending to make negligence more and more absolute. Professor Jeffrey O'Connell has proposed a system of universal no-fault in which manufacturers, professional persons, and others would be given exemption from negligence suits.[37] Damages for pain and suffering would not be allowed, except perhaps for serious injuries. In return for such exemptions, these exempted persons would, on a voluntary or elective basis, carry insurance guaranteeing that injured persons would receive indemnity for out-of-pocket losses, regardless of whether the product or service was defective. Such insurance would be more expensive than current liability insurance because more individuals would receive benefits. Most injuries now go uncompensated because it is not feasible to bring court actions for negligence unless losses are relatively large. Even if suits are brought, they are often slow, uncertain, and expensive.

Although universal no-fault is probably a long way from adoption in the United States, it is possible that the principle may be employed on a piecemeal basis over the years ahead, as the disadvantages of the negligence system become more apparent. For example, Indiana passed a law in 1975 limiting medical malpractice claims to $500,000, and limiting any one insurer's liability under this insurance to $100,000. A patient's compensation fund was established to pay claims above the $100,000 limit up to $500,000. This fund is supported by a surcharge on premiums. Attorneys' fees are limited to 15 percent of the award. Similar bills have been introduced in other states.

SUMMARY

1. Negligence is the failure to exercise the degree of care required of a reasonably prudent individual in a given set of circumstances. Negligence that is the proximate cause of injury to the property of another may, in the absence of effective defenses, give rise to substantial court judgments against the responsible party.

2. Common law defenses that bar liability for a negligent act include contributory negligence and assumed risk. There are also statutory and contractual defenses available.

3. There is an unmistakable tendency for courts to impose liability and a trend toward "absolute" liability. Evidence of this trend includes a weakening of the common-law defenses and the recognition of new theories of liability.

4. An employer owes employees certain duties, the breach of which may give rise to damage suits against the employer. In

most cases, an employer's liability to employees is governed by workers' compensation statutes.

5. The degree of care owed by a landlord or a tenant to members of the public and others who are on private property depends, at common law, on whether the person is said to be an invitee, a licensee, or a trespasser. The highest degree of care is owed to an invitee, the lowest to a trespasser.

6. Liability of a manufacturer or a vendor for damage caused by faulty products is well established. Product liability actions are based on some failure on the part of the manufacturer to exercise reasonable care in the manufacture of a product; on the part of the vendor for breach of express or implied warranty concerning the appropriateness of a product for its intended use; or on strict tort liability.

7. Under *respondeat superior*, an employer is liable for the negligent acts of servants or agents performed while the employee is acting within the scope of the employment. This holds true even if the employee is acting contrary to instructions. It is under this doctrine that an employer is usually held liable for the negligence of an employee who is driving an automobile while performing the employer's business.

8. An automobile operator is liable for negligence in the operation of his or her car. In many cases the owner of the car, if someone other than the operator, may be held liable as well. The family-purpose, last clear chance, and *respondeat superior* doctrines and vicarious liability laws have operated to extend and to tighten the liability law applicable to owners, non-owners, and operators of automobiles.

9. Professional liability exists for individuals expected to be qualified to render a professional service but who fail to meet the standards of care or practice looked upon as necessary by other members of their profession.

QUESTIONS FOR REVIEW

1. What are the elements of a negligent act?
2. Identify and explain some of the defenses to the charge of negligence.
3. What types of losses do bodily injury liability and personal injury liability cover?
4. What are the three classes of persons giving rise to liability to a property owner?
5. What is the attractive nuisance doctrine?
6. What is *res ipsa loquitur*, and how does it relate to medical malpractice?
7. Who may be liable for the operation of an automobile?
8. Distinguish between civil and criminal law.
9. Explain the doctrine of proximate cause and how it relates to liability losses.
10. What types of tort reform is the insurance industry supporting?

QUESTIONS FOR DISCUSSION

1. Some courts have held that if the state workers' compensation board issues a safety order to regulate the conduct of employees on the job, and if a member of the public is injured as a result of the violation of this order by an employee, the employer is liable unless it can be proved that the conduct was excusable. Is this an example of the "trend toward absolute liability," or is it a normal consequence of the common-law duty of an employer to protect members of the public from harm? Discuss.
2. Look up the employers' liability statute, if any, in your state or in a nearby state. To

what extent does the statute eliminate or change the common law of the employer?

3. In a study by Dr. Hans Zeisel, 500 trial judges were asked to keep a record of personal injury cases, noting how the jury decided the case and how the judge would have decided it without a jury. The findings were as follows. (1) In 79% of the cases, judge and jury agreed—for the plaintiff in 50% of the cases, and for the defendant in 29% of the cases. (2) In 21% of the cases where they disagreed, the judge found for the plaintiff in 10% of the cases while the jury found for the defendant, and vice versa in the remaining 11%. In case of disagreement, it was found that if the defendant was a corporation, the jury tended to favor the plaintiff by a substantial margin; and if the defendant was a governmental body, the jury favored the plaintiff by an even greater margin.

(a) If you were a plaintiff in a personal injury trial, do you think it would generally be to your advantage to seek a jury trial, according to the above findings? Why or why not?

(b) Do you believe that the preceding study supports the often-heard statement that juries have a "soak-the-rich" attitude? Why or why not?

(c) What relevance, if any, does this study have to liability insurance and its influence on the outcome of jury trials? Discuss.

4. The owners of a swimming beach were sued by the parents of a boy who drowned when he swam into deep water and the lifeguard failed to reach him in time to save him. The plaintiffs argued that the defendant beach owners should have had more lifeguards. The defendants tried to prove that they had enough guards for normal needs and that the boy was guilty of contributory negligence in swimming out into deep water, which, rather than the absence of a sufficient number of lifeguards, was the cause of his death (*Spiegel* v. *Silver Beach Enterprises*, 6 CCH Neg. 2d 874).

(a) Decide who should win this case. Why?

(b) How does this case illustrate the basic requirements of a negligent act?

5. Tweed, age 59, a casketmaker from California, visited his doctor, a general practitioner, complaining about a pain in his right shoulder. The doctor diagnosed it as arthritis, ignoring a suggestion by a consulting radiologist that "a tumor must also be considered." The pain got worse in spite of 41 costly shots of a steroid drug over a three-month period. Tweed went to an orthopedic surgeon who X-rayed the shoulder and misdiagnosed the problem. Eight months later an associate of the orthopedic surgeon happened to see the X-rays and identified the illness as bone cancer. If the malignancy had been spotted in its early stages, Tweed might have been saved; instead, the illness was classified as terminal. Tweed sued both the original doctor and the surgeon; Tweed's lawyer settled out of court for $300,000. Do you think that the elements of negligence existed in the above case? Is a doctor liable for failure to cure a patient? Compare this case with one in which a mechanic fails to discover a leaking brake fluid line which later causes an accident.

6. A prominent attorney was asked why medical malpractice suits are becoming more common. The attorney responded, "Because medical malpractice is becoming more common and is increasingly being recognized by the average patient." Do you agree? Suggest other possible reasons.

NEW TERMS AND CONCEPTS

Attractive Nuisance Doctrine
Bodily Injury
Comparative Negligence
Family-Purpose Doctrine
Guest-Host Statutes
Imputed Act
Invitees
Last Clear Chance
Licensees

Negative Act
Negligence
Personal Injury
Property Damage
Proximate Cause
Tort
Trespassers
Vicarious Liability Laws
Voluntary Act

NOTES

1 *Time* (March 24, 1975), p. 60.
2 John Maes, "DC-10 Tragedy Ignites a Blaze of Big Lawsuits," *Business Insurance* (June 11, 1979), p. 110.
3 *Trimbo v. Minnesota Valley Natural Gas Company*, Minnesota Supreme Court, 110 N.W. 2d 168 (1961).
4 Harold Chase, "Changing Concepts of Legal Liability and Their Effect on Liability Insurance," *Proceedings*, 82nd Annual Meeting, Fire Underwriters Association of the Pacific (March 5–6, 1958), p. 24.
5 "Almost All States Allow Punitive Damages," *Business Insurance* (February 1, 1982), p. 14.
6 *Insurance Availability: An Industry View* (Alliance of American Insurers, the American Insurance Association, and the National Association of Independent Insurers, December 6, 1985).
7 Thomas Gaskell Shearman and A. A. Redfield, *A Treatise on the Law of Negligence*, I, 438; II, 441–442.
8 "Despite Disasters, Hotel Coverage Plentiful," *Business Insurance* (May 31, 1982), p. 3.
9 *Petrillo v. Maiuri*, 20 CCH Neg. 572.
10 *Koleshinske v. David*, 20 CCH Neg. 264.
11 However, a court refused to charge a railroad with negligence when an 11-year-old boy was injured on an overhead wire as he climbed atop one of the railroad's freight cars. The court said it would be asking too much to require the railroad to make its property "child proof" along its 275 miles of track. *Dugan v. Pennsylvania Railroad*, 6 CCH Neg. 32d 443.
12 *Panther Oil & Grease Mfg. Co. v. Segerstrom*, 224 Fed. 2d 216.
13 *Farley v. Lower Co.*, (Mass.) No. 18431 (1930).
14 *Winterbottom v. Wright*, 10 M.&.W. 109, Eng. Rep. 402 (ex. 1842).
15 217 N.Y. 382.
16 Suel O. Arnold, "Products Liability Insurance," *Insurance Law Journal* (October, 1957), p. 618, citing *Beznor v. Howell*, 203 Wis. 1. 233 N.W. 788.
17 *Saunders v. Walker*, 86 Sou. 2d 89.
18 *Hanna v. Fletcher*, 8 CCH Neg. 2d 1017.
19 *Kurdziel, v. Van Es*, 6 CCH Neg. 2d 1080.
20 "Waker Gets $4.5 Million in Ranger I Rig Collapse," *Business Insurance* (June 7, 1982), p. 2.
21 *White v. Louis Creative Hair Dressers, Inc.*, 10 CCH Neg. 2d 526.
22 *Agnew v. Larson*, 5 CCH Neg. 2d 33.
23 R. Crawford Morris, "Medical Malpractice—A Changing Picture," *Insurance Law Journal* (May, 1956), p. 319. See also G. H. Graser and P. D. Chadsey, "Informed Consent in Malpractice Cases," *Willamette Law Journal*, Vol. 6 (June, 1970), pp. 183–191, and W. A. Aitken, "Medical Malpractice: The Alleged Crisis in Perspective," *Insurance Law Journal* (February, 1976), pp. 90–97.
24 *Adkins and Ainley v. Busada*, 270 A. 2d 135 (DC App. 1970).
25 Annot., 29 ALR2d 171, 174 (1953).
26 Ibid.
27 *Hardt v. Brink*, 192 F. Supp. 879, 881 (D Wash. 1961). See also Joseph R. O'Conner, "Liability of Insurance Agents and Brokers" (Madison, Wisconsin: Defense Research Institute, 1970).
28 See page 197 for a discussion of these concepts.
29 *General Electric Company v. Rees*, 5 CCH Auto Cases 2d 330.
30 Arizona, Arkansas, California, Colorado, Connecticut, Delaware, Florida, Hawaii, Idaho, Indiana, Kentucky, Louisiana, Maryland, Mississippi, Montana, Nevada, New Mexico, North Dakota, Ohio, Oklahoma, Rhode Island, Tennessee, Texas, Utah, and Wisconsin.
31 Delaware, Idaho, Kansas, Maine, Pennsylvania (under 16), and Utah. Arizona and Virginia provide that liability exists only if the minor is not licensed.
32 California, Connecticut, District of Columbia, Florida, Idaho, Iowa, Massachusetts, Michigan, Minnesota, New York, North Carolina, Puerto Rico, Rhode Island, and Tennessee.
33 R. Parke and M. Orona, "Automobile Owner's Liability: Anomaly or Enigma?" *Insurance Law Journal* (March, 1957), p. 155.
34 Ibid., citing *Mazur v. Klewans*, 34 CCH Auto Cases 180; *Droppelman v. Willingham*, 17 CCH Auto Cases 421; *Flynn v. Kurn*, 1 CCH Auto Cases 387.
35 *Ney v. Yellow Cab Company*, 3 CCH Auto Cases 2d 888.
36 *Dillon v. Prudential Insurance Co.*, 242 Pac. 736 (1926).
37 Jeffrey O'Connell, *Ending Insult to Injury* (Urbana, Ill.: University of Illinois Press, 1975).

PART 4

PERSONAL RISK MANAGEMENT: LIFE, HEALTH, & INCOME

9 LIFE AND HEALTH LOSSES

After studying this chapter, you should be able to:

1. Explain why human life value is important and how it is measured.
2. Describe how loss of human life value can hurt business firms.
3. Identify the extent of and trends in mortality.
4. Indicate who pays for health care costs in the United States.
5. Identify the losses from sickness and accident.
6. Explain why loss due to old age is increasing.
7. Describe how well people manage to save for their old age.
8. Indicate how insurance techniques can be of value in offsetting life and health losses.

So far we have considered mainly those problems caused by the destruction of property values, and the contributions of insurance to the solution of such problems. We shall now discuss some of the problems caused by the destruction of human values. Human values, aside from being more important to us from a personal standpoint, are far greater and more significant than all the different property values combined. The true wealth of a nation lies not in its natural resources or its accumulated property, but in the inherent capabilities of its population and the way in which this population is employed. A careful study of the specific types of economic loss caused by the destruction of life or health is vital to an understanding of the insurance methods available to offset these losses.

LIFE VALUES

A human life has value for many reasons. Some of these reasons are philosophical in nature, and would lead us into the realms of religion, esthetics, sociology, psychology, and other behavioral sciences. Of greatest interest here are economic values, although it is very difficult to separate the discussion in such a way that an economic analysis would have no implications or overtones for other viewpoints.

A human life has economic value to all who depend on the earning capacity of that life, particularly to two central economic groups—the family and the employer. To the family, the economic value of a human life is probably most easily measured by the value of the earning capacity of each of its members. To the employer, the economic value of a human life is measured by the contributions of an employee to the success of the organization. If one argues that in a free competitive society a worker is paid according to worth and is not exploited, the worker's contribution again is best measured by earning capacity. It develops that earning capacity is probably the only feasible method of giving measurable economic value to human life.

There are four main perils that can destroy, wholly or partially, the economic value of a human life. These include premature death, loss of health, old age, and unemployment.

We will discuss in this chapter only the problems that arise from the first three of these perils. The peril of unemployment is analyzed in Chapter 24.

MEASURING PREMATURE DEATH LOSS

The main economic problem arising when someone in the family dies, particularly the chief breadwinner, is the loss of earnings of this person.[1] The present value of these earnings is then the measure of loss.

Capitalization-of-Income Approach

One method of determining this value is to find a sum of money which, when paid in installments representing both principal and interest over the remaining working life of the worker, will produce the same income (except for taxes and allowances for the former support of the worker) as the worker would have earned. The method is termed the **capitalization of income.** This amount, once calculated, represents the amount of life insurance that is necessary to insure the full economic value of the person and to replace the net income that was formerly produced.

To illustrate, suppose a breadwinner age 35 is expected to earn an annual fixed amount, say $25,000, over his or her remaining working years. Assuming that retirement age is 65, the remaining working years number 30, and the worker would normally be expected to earn a gross amount of $750,000. From this sum, the following deductions would be made: (1) an allowance for taxes, business expenses, etc., and (2) an allowance for the worker's own maintenance.

Assume that these items total $15,000 annually. The question is, "What sum of money now on hand would produce a payment of $10,000 a year and would last exactly 30 years?" If one assumes an 8.0 percent interest, reference to an annuity table (see Table D-4, Appendix) indicates that it would take exactly $112,577 to produce this income. This sum, when compared to the average life insurance per insured family in 1984 of $58,700, indicates to some degree the underinsurance of the human life value.[2]

Several underlying factors in the preceding calculation should be observed. First, the peril of premature death always produces a *total* loss of human life value. Second, the human life value tends to decline with age since each year that goes by means that the worker has one year less of income to earn. Third, the calculation of the human life value must assume a given value for interest, the size of the worker's contribution to the family, future income tax rates, and a given level of total earnings. Changes in these and other factors could produce substantially different results in the final figure for human life value. Finally, values should be adjusted for some assumed level of annual inflation, a factor that is omitted here for the sake of simplicity. For these reasons, the calculation produces only a rough estimate of human life value, which is a very personal matter. Life insurance designed to offset the loss of human life value must take into consideration these and many other factors and should always be tailored to fit individual needs.

Needs Approach

Another method of measuring the loss to the family in case of the death of a person is the **needs approach.** From this viewpoint, value lost is estimated in terms of the various uses to which the earnings would have been put had the individual lived to produce them. Thus, the value lost is measured by adding together sums necessary to meet certain family needs for income during various periods of life. For example, to pay last expenses such as funeral, debts, and taxes, $3,000 may be required. The sum necessary to provide a monthly income of $400 to the family during a 15-year child-raising period at 8 percent interest is about $47,860. The sum necessary to continue a monthly income of $250 to the widow for the remainder of her life, beginning after the 15-year family-raising period, would come to about $62,500 under the life income option of a typical life insurer if the widow were 50 years of age when the income payments began.

To provide a college education for two children, an additional sum of say $40,000 (depending on the school selected and the spending habits of the children) might be needed. These needs total $144,360, a minimum figure as an estimate of the value lost when a breadwinner dies.

The following are examples of needs for income and cash that the life insurance estate can fill:

Income Needs

Readjustment income to ease the family adjustment
  to a lower income level
Family income during child-raising period
Income to remaining spouse for life
Retirement income for insured

Cash Sum Needs

Death expenses (funeral, doctor bills, debts,
  cemetery lot, taxes, etc.)
Mortgage redemption
College education fund
Gift fund
Fund for emergencies

An advantage of the needs approach to an estimation of human life value is that it may focus attention on specific objectives in the purchase of life insurance. Life insurance purchased for a certain need can be arranged in the most appropriate way to provide funds for that need. Insurance bought to provide an income for children's education can be set up so that the insurer holds the funds until a given date and then pays out the income during the college period. Insurance is often purchased to offset high estate and inheritance taxes levied on the person's property after death. Without ready cash to pay these taxes, the asset might have to be sold at forced sale, thus causing unnecessary losses to dependents.

Life insurance bought for this purpose can be paid in a lump sum to the estate of the deceased, and thus be made available for taxes and other costs. Life insurance purchased to pay off a mortgage can be set up so that no matter when the property owner may die, there is a sufficient amount of life insurance to liquidate the outstanding balance of the mortgage. The needs approach thus motivates the purchase of insurance for a given objective. Since these needs arise at different times throughout life, the needs approach also provides a guide as to which need should have priority and which type of insurance should be purchased.

Naturally, this technique produces a different figure from the capitalization of income approach because of the different assumptions underlying it. The needs approach seems to be a more realistic approach to the problem of deciding upon types of life insurance to buy and when to buy them. The capitalization of income approach may be more useful in determining the total value of a human life for such purposes as justifying what loss occurred when one person was killed as a result of the negligence of another. Both methods reveal clearly that a human life is much more valuable economically than many realize, and that this value exceeds the amount for which life is commonly insured.

Loss-to-Business Approach

A business firm has a somewhat more difficult task in determining the life value of a key employee, a partner, or an important stockholder in a closely held corporation. If a key person dies, the firm may lose valuable customers whose loyalty depends on this individual. Plans on which the individual was working and in which the firm had invested money may have to be abandoned. The extra cost of training or hiring a replacement may be substantial. Key employees may quit because of the death of a partner or an officer with whom they were closely associated. Each firm must make the best estimates it can of the loss exposure and insure accordingly.

Another source of loss to a business when a partner or a stockholder dies stems from the fact that this person's ownership in the business may pass to persons unfriendly to the firm, or may even result in liquidation of the firm in order to pay estate obligations. Competitors may obtain controlling ownership of the firm by purchasing shares from families of deceased stockholders. Those who have inherited the deceased stockholder's shares may enter the business, but, because of inexperience, may cause losses or even bankruptcy. Life insurance arranged to offset or to prevent these losses is appropriately called **business continuation insurance.**

In a business continuation plan funded by life insurance, the owners of a business usually agree in advance as to what is to be done with the ownership shares in the event of a death. For example, two partners own equally a business valued at $100,000. The chief asset of the business is a factory building. Neither partner has any family member capable of stepping into management in case of death. Yet it is realized that the premature death of a partner will force the sale of the building to obtain money to retire that share of the business and to make money available for the use of the family. If the building were sold at forced sale, it is doubtful that $50,000 would be realized. To prevent this loss the partners enter into a **buy-and-sell agreement,** in which each agrees to buy the interest of the other if either dies. To fund the agreement, and to insure that money for this purpose will be available, each buys life insurance of $50,000 on the life of the other. The buy-and-sell agreement binds each partner's estate to accept a certain valuation for this share and to sell it according to the terms of the contract.

Extent of Death Loss

Aggregate death rates in the United States have been declining for many years due to advances in medical technology and improved economic status. For example, the death rate in 1920, 14.2 per 1,000, had declined to 7.1 per 1,000 by 1970. There was another 23 percent decline in the death rate in the period 1970–1983, so the aggregate rate in 1983, at 5.5 per 1,000, was the lowest in history.[3] These rates are adjusted for changing proportions in the population of people in different age groups.

What is the probability that an individual will die prematurely? Recall that for determining the economic loss of human life value we are not

Table 9–1
Commissioners Standard Ordinary (CSO) Mortality
Table (1980)

	Male		Female	
Age	Deaths Per 1,000	Expectation of Life (Years)	Deaths Per 1,000	Expectation of Life (Years)
0	4.18	70.83	2.89	75.83
1	1.07	70.13	0.87	75.04
2	0.99	69.20	0.81	74.11
3	0.98	68.27	0.79	73.17
4	0.95	67.34	0.77	72.23
5	0.90	66.40	0.76	71.28
6	0.86	65.46	0.73	70.34
7	0.80	64.52	0.72	69.39
8	0.76	63.57	0.70	68.44
9	0.74	62.62	0.69	67.48
10	0.73	61.66	0.68	66.53
11	0.77	60.71	0.69	65.58
12	0.85	59.75	0.72	64.62
13	0.99	58.80	0.75	63.67
14	1.15	57.86	0.80	62.71
15	1.33	56.93	0.85	61.76
16	1.51	56.00	0.90	60.82
17	1.67	55.09	0.95	59.87
18	1.78	54.18	0.98	58.93
19	1.86	53.27	1.02	57.98
20	1.90	52.37	1.05	57.04
21	1.91	51.47	1.07	56.10
22	1.89	50.57	1.09	55.16
23	1.86	49.66	1.11	54.22
24	1.82	48.75	1.14	53.28
25	1.77	47.84	1.16	52.34
26	1.73	46.93	1.19	51.40
27	1.71	46.01	1.22	50.46
28	1.70	45.09	1.26	49.52
29	1.71	44.16	1.30	48.59
30	1.73	43.24	1.35	47.65
31	1.78	42.31	1.40	46.71
32	1.83	41.38	1.45	45.78
33	1.91	40.46	1.50	44.84
34	2.00	39.54	1.58	43.91
35	2.11	38.61	1.65	42.98
36	2.24	37.69	1.76	42.05
37	2.40	36.78	1.89	41.12
38	2.58	35.87	2.04	40.20
39	2.79	34.96	2.22	39.28
40	3.02	34.05	2.42	38.36
41	3.29	33.16	2.64	37.46
42	3.56	32.26	2.87	36.55
43	3.87	31.38	3.09	35.66
44	4.19	30.50	3.32	34.77
45	4.55	29.62	3.56	33.88
46	4.92	28.76	3.80	33.00
47	5.32	27.90	4.05	32.12
48	5.74	27.04	4.33	31.25
49	6.21	26.20	4.63	30.39
50	6.71	25.36	4.96	29.53

Table 9-1
(Continued)

	Male		Female	
Age	Deaths Per 1,000	Expectation of Life (Years)	Deaths Per 1,000	Expectation of Life (Years)
51	7.30	24.52	5.31	28.67
52	7.96	23.70	5.70	27.82
53	8.71	22.89	6.15	26.98
54	9.56	22.08	6.61	26.14
55	10.47	21.29	7.09	25.31
56	11.46	20.51	7.57	24.49
57	12.49	19.74	8.03	23.67
58	13.59	18.99	8.47	22.86
59	14.77	18.24	8.94	22.05
60	16.08	17.51	9.47	21.25
61	17.54	16.79	10.13	20.44
62	19.19	16.08	10.96	19.65
63	21.06	15.38	12.02	18.86
64	23.14	14.70	13.25	18.08
65	25.42	14.04	14.59	17.32
66	27.85	13.39	16.00	16.57
67	30.44	12.76	17.43	15.83
68	33.19	12.14	18.84	15.10
69	36.17	11.54	20.36	14.38
70	39.51	10.96	22.11	13.67
71	43.30	10.39	24.23	12.97
72	47.65	9.84	26.87	12.28
73	52.64	9.30	30.11	11.60
74	58.19	8.79	33.93	10.95
75	64.19	8.31	38.24	10.32
76	70.53	7.84	42.97	9.71
77	77.12	7.40	48.04	9.12
78	83.90	6.97	53.45	8.55
79	91.05	6.57	59.35	8.01
80	98.84	6.18	65.99	7.48
81	107.48	5.80	73.60	6.98
82	117.25	5.44	82.40	6.49
83	128.26	5.09	92.53	6.03
84	140.25	4.77	103.81	5.59
85	152.95	4.46	116.10	5.18
86	166.09	4.18	129.29	4.80
87	179.55	3.91	143.32	4.43
88	193.27	3.66	158.18	4.09
89	207.29	3.41	173.94	3.77
90	221.77	3.18	190.75	3.45
91	236.98	2.94	208.87	3.15
92	253.45	2.70	228.81	2.85
93	272.11	2.44	251.51	2.55
94	295.90	2.17	279.31	2.24
95	329.96	1.87	317.32	1.91
96	384.55	1.54	375.74	1.56
97	480.20	1.20	474.97	1.21
98	657.98	0.84	655.85	0.84
99	1,000.00	0.50	1,000.00	0.50

interested in *whether* a person will die, but *when* this death will occur. Even life insurance company examiners, who examine a person's application for insurance with utmost care, continually accept insureds who die within a year after taking out a policy in spite of their appearance of good health. For large numbers of people, however, actuaries have developed **mortality tables** on which scientific life insurance rates may be based. These tables, which are revised periodically, state the probability of death both in terms of deaths per 1,000 and in terms of expectation of life.[4]

Table 9–1 illustrates the mortality experience in current use. It shows that a male age 20 has an expectation of living 52.37 more years. At age 20 only 190 men (105 women) in every 100,000 are expected to die before they become 21. The probability of death at age 20 is thus 0.19 percent. At age 96 the death rate is slightly over 38 percent, since 384 per 1,000 are expected to die during that year. At age 100 it is assumed that death is a certainty. The probability of death expressed in a mortality table is based on *insured* lives, and not the whole population.

Death rates as stated in the 1980 CSO mortality table are greater at ages under 35 than death rates for the general population, even though it might appear that death rates for the general population would be larger. Aggregate death statistics include people of all ages and in any state of health, whereas insured persons presumably have been subjected to medical screening before acceptance. However, insurance mortality tables are purposely "loaded" to take care of certain contingencies (such as unusual fluctuations in death rates in a given year) and to make sure that all insurers, large and small, may use the table with safety. Nevertheless, for most purposes, the mortality table is a fairly accurate representation of the death rate.

The probability that a person will live is one minus the probability of death. There is a much greater *likelihood* of a breadwinner living to retirement age than dying before that time. Current mortality tables show that out of every 1,000 persons age 20, 687 males or 833 females will live to age 65. Table 9–2 gives estimates of the expectation of life at birth in 1900 and 1983.

This table reveals the great improvements that have been made in lowering the expected mortality rates over the years. Since 1900 the expectation of life for males has increased 24.7 years, compared to a 30-year increase for females. At the present time a female can be expected to outlive a male by about 8 years, compared to two years in 1900. These data have important effects in life insurance and annuity rate-making. For example, life insurance rates for women are lower than for men. Furthermore, a woman age 20 can expect to outlive her husband by nearly eight years if they are the same age. However, since it is common for a man's age to exceed that of his wife by a few years, it appears that a considerable period of widowhood is in store for the average wife. Thus, husbands should observe that, unless some provision is made, the probabilities are that the

Table 9-2
Expectation of Life
at Birth in the
United States

Year	Total U.S. Population Expectation at Birth (in Years)		
	Male	Female	Total
1900	46.3	48.3	47.3
1940	60.8	65.2	62.9
1983	71.0	78.3	74.7
Change, 1983/1900	53.3	62.1	57.9

Source: *Life Insurance Fact Book 1985*, p. 41. Percentages calculated.

average wife will be a dependent widow for several years. The need for life insurance becomes immediately apparent, and, because women live longer than men, the amount of insurance necessary to provide a given income is greater than if the beneficiary were a man.

Improvement in longevity has taken place at a much more rapid rate at lower ages than at higher ages. For example, the life expectancy of a male age 55 has improved only 3.1 years since 1900, compared to 24.7 years additional life expectancy at birth over the same period, as shown in Table 9-2. Much of the explanation for this phenomenon lies in the fact that medical science has made its greatest strides in controlling diseases that do not primarily affect older age groups. As shown in Table 9-3, diseases affecting primarily aged persons, cardiovascular-renal diseases and cancer, accounted for 60 percent of all deaths. Although these diseases are not confined to older persons, they occur much more frequently in this group than in the young. It seems likely that until important progress is made in the control of diseases affecting primarily the aged, life expectancy in the aged will experience only a slow lengthening.

The probability of death rises rapidly with age. Figure 9-1 is a sketch of CSO 1980 death rates on a semilogarithmic scale, with age levels

Table 9-3
Causes of Death in
the United States,
1984

	Percent of Deaths
Major cardiovascular diseases	37.6
Cancer	22.2
Pneumonia and influenza	2.9
Chronic diseases of the lungs	1.3
Accidents, including motor vehicle	4.6
Suicide	1.4
Homicide	1.0
All other	29.0
All Causes	100.0

Source: National Center for Health Statistics, *Monthly Vital Statistics Report*, as reported in *1985 Life Insurance Fact Book Update*, p. 42.

Figure 9–1 The Mortality Rate, CSO 1980 Mortality Table

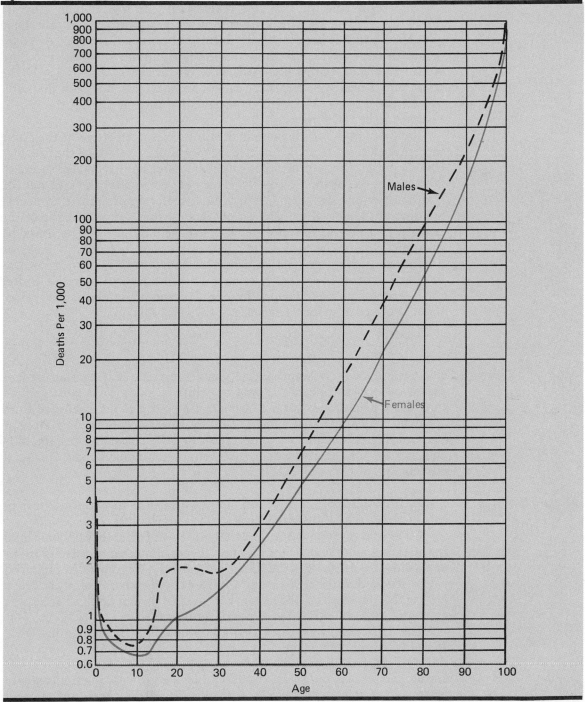

represented on the horizontal axis and death rates on the vertical axis. Death rates during the first few years of life are higher than they are following ages 9 or 10. The death rate at age 1 is approximately the same as at age 14, with lower death rates falling in between these ages. After age 30, death rates increase at an increasing rate, but are still relatively low. At age 60, the death rate is 2.4 times the rate at age 50, and by age 70 the death rate is nearly 2.5 times the rate at age 60. Thus, it is seen that after age 60 the death rates climb geometrically, until at age 99 the rate is assumed to be 100 percent.

Premium rates for life insurance follow the same pattern as the curve represented in the figure. They rise steeply after age 40 until they tend to become prohibitive for new policyholders entering the insured group at advanced ages. For this reason, very few people can afford to take out life insurance at an advanced age, and most underwriters refuse to accept applications for term insurance from persons past age 65 because of the tendency for adverse selection beyond that age. Thus, if a person seeks life insurance when it is needed the most, it is not available. It must be purchased when the probability of death is quite low. This same truth was observed in other lines. (For example, fire insurance is not available after the house catches fire.) The purchase of insurance must be arranged before the loss occurs or before it becomes highly probable.

LOSS OF HEALTH

The second major way in which human life value may be impaired or destroyed is loss of health. Loss of health is in many ways more serious than the premature loss of life because if a person is incapacitated from accident or sickness, that person's earning power is cut off completely or reduced greatly, and it becomes necessary to pay medical and hospital bills and to care for the individual. This imposes a considerable financial burden.

Income Loss

Losses from destruction of health may be measured in two ways: loss of earnings due to disability, and expenditures for medical care.

A 1972 survey[5] estimated the economic cost of disability (income loss) in the U.S. at more than 6 percent of total earned income of persons 18–64 years old. This estimate is the sum of the earnings lost entirely or reduced below levels that otherwise would have existed because of a disability lasting three months or longer. An average loss for each disabled adult was estimated at 33–45 percent of expected earnings.

The 1972 survey revealed that the probability of income loss rose sharply with age. For example, 8 percent of those under 45, 19 percent of those 45–54, and 29 percent of those 55–64 were disabled. Race, marital status, and sex also influence disability. Black persons, women, and single persons have higher disability rates than white persons, men, and married persons. Those with low educational levels also have greater disability rates than others.

In addition to direct income loss, there exists a vast amount of indirect loss from disability, such as lowered production efficiency and other additional expenses borne by employers and by families of disabled workers. The loss of services due to disability of unpaid individuals such as spouses is also significant.

Medical Costs

Estimates place the expenditures for medical care in the United States at $355 billion in 1983, or $1,459 per person. This compares with $74.7 billion in 1970, or $357 per person. Average per capita expenditures for medical care rose fourfold in just ten years, a compound annual growth rate of nearly 12 percent. Similarly, the percentage of gross national product devoted to medical care increased from 7.6 percent to 10.8 percent over the period 1970–1983. Tables 9–4 and 9–5 summarize some of the statistics relating to medical cost expenditures.

These and other data on health care costs support the following conclusions:

1. Health care costs are rising rapidly (more rapidly than national income) in the United States, some costs faster than others. For example, while the general cost of living rose 93 percent over the period 1975–1984, medical care costs rose 125 percent, hospital room costs rose 184 percent, and physicians' fees rose 122 percent.
2. The health care dollar is divided roughly as follows: hospital care, $0.41; physicians' services, $0.19; dental care, $0.06; drugs, $0.08; all other, $0.26. (See Table 9–5.)
3. The share of health care costs paid directly by individuals has been falling, and the share paid by the federal government and by private insurance has been rising over the period 1960–1984. (See Table 9–6.) Government agencies paid nearly 40 percent of health care costs in 1980, private agencies 60 percent. Individuals paid only 27 percent of their health care costs directly in 1984, compared to 55 percent in 1960.
4. The largest federal government programs are Medicare (health insurance for the aged) and Medicaid (health care for other groups). Other federal

Table 9–4
National Health
Expenditures,
1970–1983

	Amount in Billions ($)	Percentage of GNP	Amount per Capita
1970	$ 75.0	7.6	$ 350
1975	132.7	8.6	590
1980	248.0	9.4	1049
1983	355.4	10.8	1459

Source: *Health, United States, 1984* (Washington, D.C., U.S. Dept. of Health and Human Services), p. 137.

Table 9-5
The Health Care Dollar,
1983

Type of Expenditure	% of Dollar Spent
Hospital Care	41.4
Physician Services	19.4
Dentist Services	6.1
Nursing Home Care	8.1
Other Professional Care	2.3
Drugs	6.7
Eyeglasses and Appliances	1.8
Other Health Services	2.4
Expenses for Prepayment	4.4
Government Public Health Activities	3.2
Research and Construction	4.3

Source: *Health, United States, 1984*, p. 147.

programs include those offered by the Veterans Administration, by the military, and directly through publicly owned hospitals.

Distribution and Causes of Loss

The preceding data show the tremendous aggregate cost of the loss of income through illness, accident, and medical care expenditures. What is the probability that a person will be among the unfortunate individuals who are struck down annually? Again, there is no complete answer to the question because data on illnesses and accidents are not nearly as well classified as mortality data.

We know that health care costs and incidence of disability rise with age. For example, in 1978 the per capita expenditure for health care was as follows: under age 19, $258; age 19–64, $690; age 65 and over, $1,821. Thus, older persons (over 65) spent nearly seven times as much as people under 19 for health care.

Table 9-6
Distribution of
Personal Health Costs
in the United States,
1960, 1974, 1981,
and 1984

	Percent of Costs Paid			
Source of Payment	1960	1974	1980	1984
Government				
Federal	9.3	25.5	28.7	29.7
State and local	12.5	12.7	11.0	10.1
Total public	21.8	38.2	39.7	39.8
Private agencies				
Individuals	54.9	36.1	32.4	27.2
Private insurance	21.1	24.2	26.6	31.8
Philanthropy and industry	2.3	1.5	1.3	1.2
Total private	78.3	61.8	60.3	60.2

Source: *Health, United States, 1984*, p. 372.

Part 4   Life and Health Insurance

Data gathered in the 1980 *National Health Interview Survey* revealed that in 1980 the average person had 19.1 days of restricted activity as a result of chronic or acute illness or injuries. The range was 11.6 days for young people under 17 to 39.2 for adults 65 and over. Illness was a much more common cause of disability than accidents. Accidents struck down one person for each seven disabled due to illness. About 10 percent of the population was hospitalized at least once.[6]

About 14 percent of the total U.S. population suffered some activity limitation due to chronic health conditions in 1982. The amount of limitation varies directly with age. About 40 percent of those over 65 have limited activity, compared to about 9 percent for those aged 17–44, and 25 percent for those 45–64.

In 1984 permanently disabled workers drawing benefits under the Old Age, Survivors, Disability, and Health Insurance (OASDHI) program numbered about 3.8 million. To be "disabled" under OASDHI, the worker must have an impairment that prevents substantial gainful employment and is expected to last at least one year or result in death.

Accidents produce 22 percent of all conditions that become severely disabling. Males, people aged 35–44, and white people show the greatest accident rates. Most accidents occur either on the job or in a moving vehicle.

It should be noted that some major causes of acute illness (see Table 9–7) are not major causes of death (see Table 9–3). For example, infection, respiratory illnesses, and injuries are important causes of disability, but relatively minor causes of death.

The uneven distribution of health care costs represents a problem that is ideally suited to solution through insurance. The average medical bill may not be excessive, but the variation is great and an unfortunate minority will suffer an unsupportable loss each year.

LOSS DUE TO OLD AGE

Old age is a condition that often destroys earning capacity, just as does premature death or loss of health. It is certain that a young person will either die before reaching old age or reach old age. However, a male age 20

**Table 9–7
Workdays Lost Due to Acute Conditions, 1982**

Condition	Total (Millions)	Per Worker
Respiratory conditions	103	1.0
Injuries	78	.8
Infections and parasitic diseases	25	.3
Digestive conditions	13	.1
All acute conditions	271	2.7

Source: U.S. Department of Health and Human Services, reported in *Source Book of Health Insurance Data, 1984–1985*, p. 69.

has a considerably greater probability of reaching, say, age 65 than he does of not reaching age 65—he has roughly a 67 percent chance of getting "old."

For various reasons, many individuals are unable to earn much of their livelihood after reaching old age. Most must depend on personal savings of various kinds (including some forms of life insurance and annuities), private pensions, and Social Security. (See Table 9–8.)

Although people know that some day they will probably get old and be dependent unless they make provision for themselves in some manner, statistics show that all too often the arrival of retirement finds the individual with little guaranteed income and very little money or property. This situation has become a major economic interest because of the growth in the proportion of aged persons to the total population, the declining number of employment opportunities for these people, and the increasing length of life which extends the average period during which they will be dependent on others. In 1900 only 4.1 percent of the population was 65 or over. By 1981 this percentage had grown to 11.4 percent, and actuarial projections place it at 12.6 percent by the year 2000.[7] The age-65-or-over population increased from 16.6 million in 1960 to 26.3 million in 1981. The average life expectancy at age 65 in 1983 was 14.5 years for males and 18.8 years for females.

Income Status of the Aged

Annual estimates of income reveal generally low levels of income among families whose heads are 65 or over. In a study of newly retired persons under Social Security, it was shown that the average couple loses about a

**Table 9–8
Income of Social Security Beneficiaries, 1981**

| | Percent of Beneficiaries | | |
	Married Men	Married Women	Unmarried Persons
By Income Level			
Less than $10,000	15	16	55
$10,000–19,999	43	44	33
$20,000–29,999	24	25	7
$30,000 & over	18	16	5
By Source of Income			
Social Security	97.6	51.0*	97.1
Pensions			
Private	36.1	5.9*	26.8
Public	19.0	3.9	16.5
Asset income	83.8	—	69.1
Earnings	26.9	26.7*	27.1
Other sources	16.5	—	15.2

*Wives of beneficiaries
Source: *Social Security Bulletin*, January 1985, p. 9; and May 1985, p. 13.

third of their former income when they retire. At first, many retirees continue some form of paid work; retirement tends to be a gradual process. The study shows that Social Security is only one source of income; pensions, income from assets, and earnings in paid work are other sources. According to Table 9-8, about 43 percent of married men and women received between $10,000 and $19,999 in 1981, and nearly one in five beneficiaries were receiving $30,000 a year or over. Unmarried persons, however, are worse off. More than half of the unmarried beneficiaries received less than $10,000 in 1981.

From these and other data, we may draw the following conclusions about the probable economic outlook for people in the United States reaching age 65 or over: (1) About three-fourths will not keep their former jobs and will be unemployed. (2) Very few will depend exclusively on income from individually purchased insurance or annuities. (3) Nearly everyone will be able to draw Social Security, but a minority will depend on this source exclusively for income. (4) Many will be in poverty, especially single and black persons. (5) Because of the trend toward earlier retirement and increasing life expectancy, economically deprived persons will have to endure their privation for a longer period than in the past.

Recognizing the problem, the President's Commission on Pension Policy, appointed in 1979 to study the income of the elderly, recommended that Social Security be strengthened and that tax incentives be provided to encourage more individual savings for old age. The U.S. Congress adopted recommendations for the latter by allowing individuals to save up to $2,000 a year ($2,250 if a nonworking spouse exists) under tax shelter in an individual retirement account (IRA). However, the 1986 Tax Reform Act limited the number of workers eligible for new IRA plans. It is too early to judge how successful the IRA will be in improving the lot of the average elderly person.

Asset Status of the Aged

Research shows that the asset position of many elderly people is precarious and does not provide a substantial source of income to offset the drop in earnings that is typically experienced by the older citizen. In the new beneficiary study referred to above, it was found that the average net worth of couples, not counting equity in their home, was only about $20,000. (See Table 9- 9.) The average net worth of unmarried women was only $5,100. Although the chief asset of most retirees in this study was the equity in their home, this type of asset is not generally used to generate income on which to live.

In spite of the somewhat modest levels of assets and income achieved by most aged persons, their situation is improved over the last ten years according to studies by the Social Security Administration. More retired persons now have financial or property assets and greater net worth than formerly.

Table 9–9
Assets of Social
Security Beneficiaries,
1982

Asset Holding	Median Value	
	Couples	Unmarried Women
Any financial asset*	$18,000	$7,500
Home equity	$48,000	$38,000
Mortgage debt	$12,000	$10,000
Net worth	$68,000	$30,100
Net worth, excluding home equity	$20,000	$5,100

*Usually a savings, checking, or credit union account.
Source: *Social Security Bulletin*, July 1985, p. 33.

IMPLICATIONS FOR INSURANCE

Data presented in this chapter have important implications for the insurance industry: (1) Loss of income in old age can be planned for and partially offset by additional private savings, much of which can be accomplished through one or more types of insurance products. (2) Health loss is significant and growing; insurance is an ideal way in which to meet the costs of loss of income from disability, as well as hospital, physicians', and other medical expenses. (3) Loss from premature death of a breadwinner may also be offset through appropriate insurance products, so that the financial position of survivors is greatly improved over what would otherwise be the case. (4) Private insurance systems have reached only a portion of the total market potential for their products. Great opportunities and challenges exist for further development of private insurance. For example, private insurers handle only about a third of health care costs, individual policies pay a minor portion of income loss in old age, and life insurance in force is much less than estimates of human life value.

SUMMARY

1. Human life values, often overlooked in the task of obtaining adequate insurance protection against financial losses, are undoubtedly more important and far greater than all property values. Four perils cause destruction of human life values—premature death, loss of health, old age, and unemployment.

2. Premature death causes great loss to families and to employers, a loss that may be objectively measured and insured. The probability of premature death is substantial in spite of striking improvements in longevity since 1900. According to current mortality tables, approximately 33 out of every 100 people aged 20 will die before they retire at age 65. Data on the causes of illness suggest that major reductions in the

mortality rate in the future will come when medical science conquers such afflictions as heart disease and cancer.

3. Increases in longevity have brought a rise in the rate of observable loss of health, since many who formerly would have died from illness are now kept alive, but in a state of semihealth. Loss of health may actually cause more economic loss than loss of life.

4. Ill health brings two major types of losses—loss of income during the period of disability, and medical costs. While precise estimates of disability income losses are not available because of the many types of unmeasurable losses, data suggest that losses of about 6 percent of the national income are being registered in the United States annually.

5. The proportion of the gross national product being spent for health care costs is rising steadily, having reached 10.8 percent in 1983. Costs were $1,459 per capita, a 316 percent increase over 1970. Hospital and physicians' costs are rising fastest of all health care items.

6. Only 27 percent of medical expenditures are being met directly by individuals. An increasing proportion of health care costs are being met by the federal government. The proportion of health loss paid through insurance has risen from 21.1 percent to 31.9 percent over the period 1960–1983.

7. Several studies have verified the finding that while medical costs and income losses on the average do not cause an intolerable financial burden, a disproportionate amount of the burden falls on relatively few individuals. This fact has undoubtedly stimulated the use of insurance as a method of spreading the loss more evenly.

8. The probability of living to old age is nearly twice as great as the probability of premature death. The loss of income in old age suggests that not only are people failing to save sufficient amounts for their declining years, but also they have tended to rely on a combination of property income, pensions, and social insurance as methods of handling the risk of outliving their income. Relatively few old persons have annuities or life insurance proceeds on which to retire exclusively.

QUESTIONS FOR REVIEW

1. How can the economic loss of a family breadwinner be measured?

2. (a) Using the capitalization-of-income approach and a 7 percent interest assumption, calculate the present value of A's life if A earns $20,000 a year, is age 40, and expects to retire at age 65. Personal maintenance is $8,000 a year. (Use Table D–4 in the Appendix.)
   (b) If considered typical, will A have enough life insurance? Why?

3. (a) In what way does the death of a partner or a stockholder in a closely held corporation cause a loss to the business firm?
   (b) How can life insurance offset this loss?

4. Referring to Table 9–1, state the probability that
   (a) A person age 18 will live to age 19
   (b) A person age 97 will live to age 99

5. Do observable data support or weaken the statement that "a considerable period of widowhood is in store for the average wife"?

6. With the tremendous strides in medical science, longevity has increased very significantly, especially at younger age levels. What is the chief reason for this, and what implications does it have regarding life insurance?

7. Suggest possible reasons for the increase in the proportion of disposable income spent for medical care in the United States.

8. A survey by the Metropolitan Life Insurance Company revealed the following data on new long-term disability rates per 1,000 male employees: age 25–44, 1.5; age 45–54, 4.5; age 55–59, 15.5; and age 60–64, 51.0.

    (a) Compare these disability rates with the death rates shown in Table 9–1. (Use the median age in each category.)

    (b) What inferences can you draw from these comparisons as to the likelihood of disability versus the likelihood of death?

9. In the Metropolitan Life survey referred to above, a study was made of the status, after five years, of 401 men and 203 women employees who had been disabled for one year or longer. It was found that of the men, 61% were still disabled, 22% were dead, and 17% had recovered. Among women, these percentages were 56, 12, and 32, respectively. Judging from these data, which would you say is more important to have if one had to choose between them—life insurance or long-term disability insurance? Why?

10. Do data on the economic status of the aged suggest that large numbers of people are saving through life insurance for their old age? If not, what sources of income are the aged depending on? Discuss reasons for this.

QUESTIONS FOR DISCUSSION

1. It has been said that an average business person would not think of leaving a factory building uninsured, but neglects to insure the lives of important key executives who may be more valuable than the building. Do you agree? In what way might a key executive be more valuable than the building?

2. In contrast to years past, many women, both married and single, are now employed outside the home.

    (a) In your opinion, does the earning capacity of a working wife give rise to economic value for which she should be insured?

    (b) Should the life of a wife and mother not employed outside the home be insured? Why or why not?

3. The following statements were made by an investment analyst concerning a large industrial concern and the investment merit of its securities:

    ... the company shifted to a decentralized type of organization about six years ago. This move, however, did not yield the desired improvement in efficiency.... The deficiencies arising from too few centralized controls are now being corrected. A little more than a year ago a new president took office. Since then the company has come a long way in tightening up its organization.... The company is fortunate in having a well-qualified chief executive to direct its improvement program ... he combines a broad education in business with solid practical experience ... he developed a central staff of experts to provide the specialized control and knowledge that formerly were lacking....

    What are the implications of this analysis with respect to a dependence on human life values?

4. It is said that the decrease in death rates brings about an increase in disability rates.

    (a) How might this be true?

    (b) What other factors have brought about an increase in disability rates?

Capitalization of Income
Needs Approach
Business Continuation
    Insurance

Buy-and-Sell Agreement
Mortality Tables

NOTES

1 Loss to a family caused by the death of dependents is, generally speaking, not suceptible to measurement by loss of earnings. There are definite measurable losses, nevertheless, such as the loss of investment in education, the loss of unpaid-for services, and the cost of a funeral.

2 See *Life Insurance Fact Book,* published annually by the American Council of Life Insurance, for current information about this amount and for other life insurance statistics.

3 *Life Insurance Fact Book 1985* (Washington, D.C.: American Council of Life Insurance, 1985), p. 42.

4 The table in current use is the Commissioners Standard Ordinary Table (CSO), 1980, which is based on death rates recorded by insurance companies during the years 1970–1975. The CSO 1980 table replaced the CSO 1958 table, which was based on experience of the period 1950–1954. Different tables are used for other purposes, such as for annuities.

5 *Disability Survey 72, Disabled and Nondisabled Adults,* Department of Health and Human Services, Social Security Administration, Research Report No. 56 (April, 1981), pp. 4–16.

6 Susan S. Jack, "Current Estimates from the *National Health Interview Survey," Vital and Health Statistics,* Series 10, No. 139 (December, 1981), pp. 2–5.

7 U.S. Dept. of Commerce, Bureau of Census, *Current Population Reports, Population Estimates,* Series P-25, Nos. 310, 311, 519, 704, 721 (Washington, D.C.: U.S. Government Printing Office). This assumes a U.S. resident population of 229,307,000 and an age-65-and-over population of 31,451,000 by the year 2000. Current data are reported in monthly issues of the *Social Security Bulletin.*

10 LIFE INSURANCE AND ANNUITIES

After studying material in this chapter, you should be able to:

1. State the basic purpose of life insurance and annuities. Analyze the question of how much life insurance to buy. Appreciate the difference between protection and savings needs.
2. Describe the importance of the "level premium" concept.
3. Explain why term insurance is so popular, compared to whole life contracts.
4. Identify some of the newer policies such as universal and variable life.
5. List the characteristics of most life insurance buyers.
6. Demonstrate how the life insurance premium is calculated.
7. Indicate why insurers are called "legal reserve" companies.
8. Differentiate between life insurance and annuities.
9. Explain how and when to use the annuity product.

Few industries have equaled the consistent record of the long-term growth of life insurance. Yet when measured against the potential market for life insurance, sales have fallen far short of that market. Largely responsible for this is the failure of the consuming public to understand what life insurance really is, what it will do, why it is needed, and how it may be arranged. Part of the difficulty lies in the traditional methods of distribution that have been justified on the grounds that "life insurance is not bought; it is sold."

WHAT IS LIFE INSURANCE?

As a social and economic device, **life insurance** is a method by which a group of people may cooperate to ease the loss resulting from the premature death of members of the group. The insuring organization collects contributions from each member, invests these contributions, guarantees both their safety and a minimum interest return, and distributes benefits to the estates of the members who die.

Viewed from an individual standpoint, life insurance is a method of creating an estate. It is a method of seeing to it that plans for accumulating property or providing income for the benefit of others, chiefly the family, are realized regardless of whether the breadwinner dies prematurely or lives to "a ripe old age." The word "estate," unfortunately, carries a suggestion of death since the word is often employed to describe the aggregate property belonging to a deceased person. The meaning of **estate,** however, is much broader, and the term will be used here to mean an aggregate of property, including income-producing property, whether it is to be used before or after the death of a person. In the last analysis, property is accumulated for the living, not the dead, and the various plans for building an estate should recognize this fundamental precept.

It has been stated that most workers have two types of estates—the present or actual estate and the future or potential estate. The **present** or **actual estate** is the property that one has accumulated for dependents or oneself for the time when earning capacity will be cut off by premature death or old age. The **future** or **potential estate** refers to the property that one will normally accumulate to provide financial security for dependents if one lives long enough. Premature death means that the potential estate is never realized. Life insurance is a way of creating an actual estate for the benefit of dependents if the worker does not live to realize the potential estate, and it is a way of saving money for the actual estate to be used as a source of income in old age.

How Much Life Insurance to Buy?

A frequently asked question is, "How much life insurance should I buy?" There is no easy answer to this question, since everyone's needs, goals, and financial abilities vary. In general, one should buy only according to a specified need and not because "life insurance is a good thing to have," or "rates are cheaper the younger you are." The ability of life insurance to meet given types of needs is discussed below. The question is also considered in Chapters 13 and 14, where life insurance and estate planning are analyzed.

Protection versus Savings Needs

Because a clear understanding of the purposes of life insurance is of such fundamental importance in appreciating what various contracts of life insurance will accomplish, these purposes warrant special emphasis. Life insurance can accomplish two objectives: to guarantee the existence of an estate out of which one's dependents may meet debts and receive an income if the breadwinner dies; and to save money as a part of one's own living estate, which is created for future income needs. The first objective may be termed the **protection need** and the latter the **savings need.**

Life insurance policies may be purchased to reflect each of these needs in varying proportions. **Term insurance** in its various forms is wholly dedicated to the protection need. Generally, there are no cash values whatever in term insurance and hence no possibility of the savings need being met.[1] Thus, term insurance is designed entirely for death protection and to create an estate only in the event of premature death. On the other hand, **whole life insurance** is available in different forms to meet both the savings and the protection needs. These contracts may be arranged so that the savings need can receive as much emphasis as is desired, within certain limits. All whole life contracts have an element of protection that extends for the whole of the insured's life. **Endowment** and **universal life policies** emphasize the savings need, with only a small element of protection. Endowments and **retirement income contracts** are primarily savings contracts for a definite span of years with the added guarantee that if the insured does not live to complete the savings plan during this period, the insurer will complete it. These relationships are shown in Figure 10–1, which illustrates that different life insurance contracts contain varying proportions of savings and protection.

Ideally, a program of estate building should provide both savings and protection—savings if the estate builder lives, and protection if death occurs. Some individuals prefer to use the term "insurance" for protection and to emphasize other types of investments, such as stocks, bonds, savings accounts, and real estate, for the savings need. Others prefer a contract such as whole life insurance in which modest savings and protection needs can be met in one contract. Still others may be interested primarily in a savings-type insurance policy such as the endowment or universal life, in which the protection element is often small. These individuals may use separate term policies to enlarge the protection element in their estate-building plans. There is no limit, of course, to the many different combinations of insurance contracts and investment plans that can be made.

Permanent versus Temporary Needs

Another way of thinking about the uses of various contracts of insurance is to consider whether the need is temporary or permanent. Of course, what would be a temporary need to one is a permanent need to another. Generally, whole life, universal life, and retirement income contracts are

Part 4   Life and Health Insurance

Figure 10–1
**Protection Versus Savings
in Life Insurance**

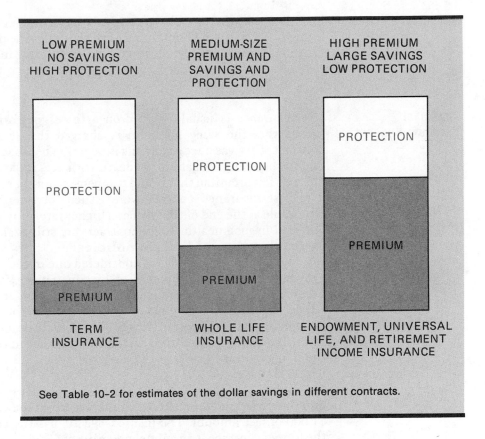

LOW PREMIUM
NO SAVINGS
HIGH PROTECTION

MEDIUM-SIZE
PREMIUM AND
SAVINGS AND
PROTECTION

HIGH PREMIUM
LARGE SAVINGS
LOW PROTECTION

PROTECTION

PROTECTION

PROTECTION

PREMIUM

PREMIUM

PREMIUM

TERM
INSURANCE

WHOLE LIFE
INSURANCE

ENDOWMENT, UNIVERSAL
LIFE, AND RETIREMENT
INCOME INSURANCE

See Table 10–2 for estimates of the dollar savings in different contracts.

considered to serve permanent needs, and term and endowment contracts are considered to serve temporary needs; hence these contracts have become known as **permanent** and **temporary** insurance, respectively.

To illustrate, examples of temporary needs would include the following: (1) Jane Roman wishes to borrow $25,000 for a period of four years for the purpose of attending medical school. Her uncle is willing to lend the money if Jane will take out a life insurance policy in favor of the uncle should Jane die before she graduates and is able to repay the loan. Jane will probably find that a five-year term policy will be the most economical form of insurance for her purpose. (2) Erik Stone, age 35, is raising a family, and his youngest child is now age five. He wishes to guarantee his family a minimum of $2,000 a month for 15 years in the event of his death. A term policy may be arranged to fill this need.

On the other hand, if Erik wishes to guarantee his wife a minimum income of $500 a month for the rest of her life in the event of his death, a term policy will not work satisfactorily because this need is continuous until Erik's death. As we have seen, Erik has a much greater probability of living to age 65 than of not living until that age. Although term insurance is available past age 65, its cost tends to be too great for most buyers above that age.

The Level Premium Concept

Life insurance is usually issued on a **level premium basis,** which means that the same premium is charged throughout the life of the contract. This was once a startling innovation because it was reasoned that due to the rising probability of death with age, it would be impossible to charge a flat premium that would compensate for the rising mortality costs. The first insurance policies were issued for one year only and were renewable at the end of this year at a higher rate, provided that the insured was still in good health. These contracts are still available and are known as **yearly renewable term policies.**[2]

The level premium idea is considered one of the most basic advances ever made in the development of life insurance. With this concept, it became possible to issue policies for longer and longer periods until finally whole life contracts were made a regular part of the business. Actuaries using refined mortality statistics could calculate exactly how much had to be charged during the early years of the contract in order to make up for the rising mortality costs of the later years. This idea is illustrated in Figure 10–2.

Figure 10–2 shows a comparison of the annual rates charged for a level premium contract, term to 65, and the five-year renewable term policy per $1,000 of face amount. The insured, age 20, has the choice of purchasing the former contract at an annual premium of $8.54 for 45 years, or of paying successively higher rates that begin at $3.73 and graduate to $29.90 at age 60. This ever-increasing rate follows the upward curve of mortality plotted on Figure 9–1, page 227. At age 40 the break-even point of these two contracts is reached. Above this age, the rate for a five-year renewable term policy rises above the rate for the level term. The overpayments in the early years of the term-to-65 policy, together with interest, represented by the shaded area to the left of the break-even point in Figure 10–2, balance the excess underpayments shown by the shaded area to the right of the break-even point.

The overpayment in the early years of a level premium life insurance policy is not really an overpayment in the sense that the insured is paying more than should be paid for protection. The insurer acts as a trustee of the premium funds, which belong to the policyholders as a group, and reduces the premium to reflect the interest earnings. The accumulation thus made is known as the **cash surrender value** or the **reserve.** If the insured desires, it is possible to borrow this value or recapture it completely upon lapsing the policy. In term policies which span many years, the size of the cash surrender value is relatively small; and for

Figure 10–2
Premium Comparisons

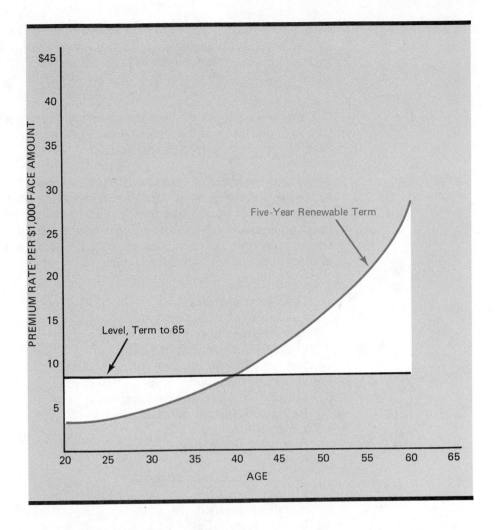

bookkeeping reasons, the insurer does not return any of these amounts to the insured, although the premium is reduced below what it would be without the interest earnings that are made. On permanent contracts the size of the cash surrender value is substantial and constitutes the savings element referred to earlier.

Thus, the reason for having a savings element in life insurance is to smooth out premium payments over a long period of years. The insurer does not accumulate reserves merely to have funds with which to engage in the investment business or to set itself up as a savings bank. The reserve has its main purpose in meeting the very substantial burden of high mortality costs in the later years of the contract. Without the reserve, it would be difficult or impossible to offer continued protection beyond a certain age, roughly age 65. There are many needs for life insurance that extend beyond this age, such as a funeral expense fund, a fund to provide income for a dependent, and a fund for estate taxes.

MAJOR TYPES OF LIFE INSURANCE

Life insurance may be divided into four major categories: ordinary (term, whole, endowment, and package contracts), industrial, group, and credit. Each of these is described in this section.

Ordinary Life Insurance

The major contracts of ordinary life insurance are of three types—term, whole life, and endowment. There are also package contracts that represent combinations of these three basic types. Countless names are applied by individual insurers to specific policies issued, but all ordinary policies are simply combinations of the three basic types. Some of the more important of these combinations are listed below.

> *Term Insurance*
>   Level-term contract
>   Decreasing-term contract
> *Whole Life Insurance*
>   Ordinary life (straight life) contract
>   Limited-payment life contract
> *Endowment Insurance*
>   Limited-term (e.g., 20 years) contract
>   Retirement income contract
> *Package Contracts*
>   Family income policy
>   Specials
>   Modified life insurance policy
>   Multiple protection insurance policy
>   Juvenile insurance
>   Family group policy
>   Variable life contract
>   Universal life policy

Term Insurance

As indicated before, term insurance contracts are issued for a specified number of years and usually contain no savings element. In this regard, they are similar to other types of insurance in property and liability lines. Term contracts therefore provide a greater amount of pure protection per premium dollar than any other type of insurance. For example, a $100 annual premium would purchase approximately $18,300 of coverage on a person age 30, on a 10-year level-term contract. The same premium spent on whole life insurance would purchase about $5,000 of coverage, slightly over a fourth as much as that provided under the term contract. For this reason, term insurance is used most often when:

1. The maximum coverage is desired, and the amount available for premiums is limited.
2. The period during which the protection is needed does not extend past age 65.

Level-Term Contract. A **level-term contract** is issued for a constant amount during its term. Examples are 5-year, 10-year, or 20-year renewable term, and term to 65. Level-term contracts are practically always renewable without evidence of insurability. Thus, an objection is removed that was formerly attributable to this type of contract in that an insured's policy could expire and leave this person without protection and uninsurable. **Uninsurability** in life insurance generally means that a person's physical condition is such that the individual cannot meet the minimum medical and other selection standards on which mortality tables are based. Other factors, such as the person's occupation and credit standing, also enter into the meaning of insurability. About 2 percent of all applications for life insurance are rejected because of uninsurability. About 3 percent of all applications are accepted at an extra premium for unusual risk.[3] The probability of uninsurability is great enough that the right of renewal without medical examination is an important feature. In the case of most insurers, however, this right expires when the insured reaches age 60 or 65.

Decreasing-Term Contract. When the amount of pure death protection gradually declines each year on a term contract, the policy is described as one of **decreasing term.** The premium payable may be constant over the term, but the insurance protection decreases. A good example of the use of decreasing-term insurance is in credit life insurance and in mortgage protection insurance. As an insured repays an obligation such as a mortgage debt, the amount of coverage decreases steadily, corresponding to the declining balance of the debt. In this way the coverage is tailored to meet the need for which the insurance was designed. Since the face amount of decreasing-term insurance is, on the average, considerably less than the face amount involved in a level-term contract, the premium is correspondingly lower. Decreasing-term insurance is also employed in the family income policy discussed later.

The relative economy of decreasing-term insurance may be shown in the following example. Suppose you purchase a new house with a $50,000, 30-year, fixed-interest mortgage loan at 12 percent interest. The amount of principal remaining on the loan after different periods, and the corresponding amounts of decreasing-term insurance provided by one prominent insurer, are as follows:

	Loan Balance	Decreasing-Term Life Insurance Provided*
Initial	$50,000	$50,000
End of 5th Year	$48,631	$49,150
End of 10th Year	$46,708	$47,250
End of 15th Year	$42,852	$43,850
End of 20th Year	$35,847	$37,600
End of 25th Year	$23,120	$26,350
End of 30th Year	$-0-	$ 5,800

*Amounts quoted are for the Connecticut Mutual Life Insurance Company in 1983.

Note that because the loan balance declines slowly at first, the required term insurance also declines slowly. Life insurers have designed mortgage protection riders to correspond to mortgage interest rates of different amounts so that the death protection will always be equal to or greater than the outstanding debt balance.

The cost of the policy illustrated for a 30-year-old male is $2.17 per $1,000 of the initial amount, about $9 a month, or approximately 1.8 percent of the monthly house payment. The cost of a regular (nondecreasing) term policy would be more than double the cost of decreasing term.

Increasing-Term Contract. Term insurance protection can be arranged to increase each year, to correspond to a need that also increases. For example, a policy can be arranged so that upon the insured's death, the beneficiaries receive the face amount plus all premiums that have been paid in. With each successive year, the sum of these premiums increases. The increasing-term protection rises correspondingly.

Convertibility. Most term insurance policies are **convertible** into a permanent form of coverage at or before the date of their expiration, without evidence of insurability. In this way persons may take out term insurance with the idea of maximizing their coverage during a period when their protection needs are at a maximum, and then convert their insurance to a permanent form of insurance for use in later years.[4]

Whole Life Insurance

As the name suggests, **whole life insurance** may be kept in force for as long as desired or until the contract expires, which is never past age 100. A cash value is built up. There are many different ways of arranging premium payments for whole life insurance, ranging from continuous installments over a person's entire life to a single installment (single-premium whole life). In other words, an insured, at age 35, may pay a single sum, say $5,000 for a $10,000 policy, and never pay another premium. At the time of death the insurer pays the insured's beneficiary $10,000. If the insured does not have $5,000 with which to pay the single premium (and few do), it may be paid by installments over whatever length of time is desired.

An **ordinary** or **straight life contract** is a contract arranged so that the premiums are payable as long as the insured lives. The contract is not paid up until one reaches age 100 or dies, whichever event comes sooner. (Sometimes additional cash payments or the use of dividends to pay up the contract will effectively convert the true ordinary life policy into a paid-up policy sooner than this.) A **limited-payment life policy** is a policy arranged so that the insured pays a higher premium than would be required on the ordinary life plan. Thus, a definite termination date can be established beyond which no further payments are due. The most common limited installment plans are 20-payment life, 30-payment life, and life paid up at age 65.

Figure 10–3 illustrates the various plans of whole life insurance. The vertical axis shows the face amount of the policy. This amount is made up of two parts, the amount at risk and the amount in the reserve fund, which is roughly equal to the cash value. For example, line SP shows that if one pays for a whole life policy in one lump sum, one has a reserve fund of approximately $500 immediately after purchase. If the insured should die the next day, the insurer would pay the beneficiary the face amount of the

**Figure 10–3
How Premium
Arrangements Affect
Reserve Values
in Common Life Insurance
Contracts**

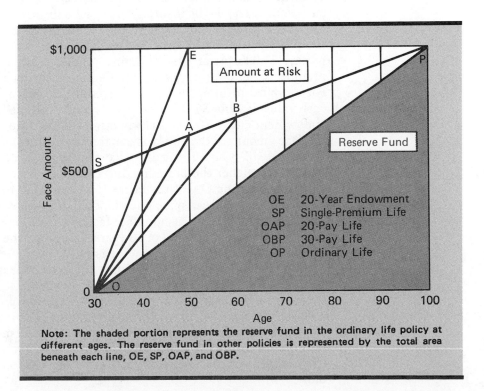

Note: The shaded portion represents the reserve fund in the ordinary life policy at different ages. The reserve fund in other policies is represented by the total area beneath each line, OE, SP, OAP, and OBP.

policy, $1,000. It may be seen then that the amount at risk to the insurer was really only $500. On the other hand, for the ordinary life policy, represented by line OP, if the insured pays one premium, there would be no reserve fund available at that time. But if the insured should die the next day, the insurer would pay the beneficiary $1,000. Thus, the amount at risk is almost the full face of the contract. As time goes on, the reserve fund grows, since the premium paid in the early years exceeds the amount needed for mortality expenses. If the insured lives to age 100, the reserve fund reaches the full face of the policy and the insurer will consider the contract to have matured and will pay the insured $1,000.

There is a difference between a policy that is paid up and one that is matured. When conditions occur to obligate the insurer to pay the face amount of the policy, the contract is said to have matured and, hence, terminated. This occurs in the event of death or when the cash values equal the face amount of the contract. Line OE in Figure 10–3 represents the reserve line of the 20-year endowment contract. This line rises steeply, so that 20 years after issuance of the contract the cash values equal the face amount and the contract is terminated by maturity. Line OAP, on the other hand, representing the 20-pay life contract, rises to a certain point (point A), after which the policy is **paid up.** This means that the cash values, together with the interest that may be earned on this amount, will be sufficient to enable the insurer to meet its obligations to all policyholders, to contribute a share of the mortality expenses each year, and to build up the principal so that at age 100 the cash values will equal the face of the policy, $1,000. After age 50 (point A) the insured need pay no more premiums, but the cash value is not equal to the face value of the policy. For a typical insurer, the 20-pay life contract with a face of $1,000 has a cash value of about $600 after it is fully paid. A whole life contract is really endowment at age 100, and is sometimes referred to in this way because the face amount of the policy is equal to its cash value at age 100.

Figure 10–3 also illustrates that the shorter the premium payment period, the higher the premium and the more rapid the buildup of cash values. Thus, line OAP rises faster than line OBP because in paying all premiums in a 20-year span, one must naturally pay more than would be necessary (and savings accumulate faster) than if one had elected to pay the premiums over a period of 30 years. Of course, the faster the premium is paid up and the faster the reserve is built up, the less is the amount at risk. In any of the plans illustrated, at the time of death the insurer must pay $1,000 to the insured's beneficiary. However, the insurer loses less with the high-premium policy than it does with the low-premium policy. That is to say, the $1,000 paid to the beneficiary may be viewed as consisting of two parts—the reserve element and the protection element. The beneficiary collects the insured's own savings and, in addition, receives a contribution from other insureds. Insureds who live to age 100 receive back their own money.

Consideration of this point shows why it is that the reserve is not entirely used up to compensate for the high mortality rate experienced by the insurer in the later years of the contract. The mortality rate at age 80 is $6\frac{1}{2}$ times as great as the rate at age 60. At age 80 the mortality cost per $1,000 might be approximately $220 or higher. Thus, the reserve would be gone in a year or two if the full $1,000 were at risk. Actually, the amount at risk declines sharply as the reserve rises, and so the mortality costs are kept within bounds. Finally, at age 100 the mortality element is extinguished entirely. This is as it should be, for at age 100 actuaries consider death a certainty. As we have learned, it is not feasible to insure against certainties. The older one becomes, the more probable death becomes each year; thus, the amount at risk in the contract declines steadily in permanent whole life contracts.

Endowment Insurance

Endowment contracts are primarily savings contracts with an element of pure protection incorporated into the policy, so that if the insured dies before the savings plan is completed the insurer completes it.

To see how an endowment contract works, assume that Adam Mosby, age 45, sets for himself the goal of saving $1,000 in 20 years. If Adam could receive 6 percent interest in a savings institution, he would have to make annual deposits of $27.18 for 20 years for a total of $543.60 in order to reach his goal. Now assume that he wishes to have a guarantee that in the event of his death before the 20 years have passed, his wife will still receive $1,000. If he purchases renewable term insurance each year for the difference between $1,000 and the amount currently on hand, the total cost of the insurance would be about $180. The total outlay to him would then be $723 ($543.60 + $180). If Adam purchases a 20-year endowment policy, he accomplishes this same goal for an annual premium of $46.50 (on a nonparticipating, or no-dividend, basis), or $930 for 20 years.[5] While the endowment contract may cost him somewhat more, there are certain features in this contract that partially offset the added cost.

Limited-Term Endowment Contract. **Limited-term endowment contracts** extend for a given period of years, usually 5, 10, 15, 20, or 30 years. A very common period is 20 years. Endowments are commonly used as savings for some specified purpose, such as education, retirement, or travel. In this way, if the saver dies before the period has expired, the purpose for which the savings plan was set up can often be accomplished by the insured's dependents.

Retirement Income Policy. **Retirement income policies** are similar to endowments, except that the former are arranged so that their cash values amount to a sum sufficient to provide $10 a month life income at retirement age, usually 65, for each $1,000 of face amount. Endowment policies are purchased for varying periods, such as a 10-year endowment, 20-year endowment, 30-year endowment, and endowment at age 65. They mature for their face value at the end of this term. At maturity, retirement income policies may have a cash value equal to about $1,400 for each $1,000 of face amount. (Some policies have different face amounts.) The reason for this is that it may require about $1,400 to purchase a life annuity of $10 a month for a male at age 65. If death occurs before retirement, the insurer will pay $1,000 or the cash value, if the latter is greater. Since cash values mount rapidly under the retirement income policy, the insurance element in the contract is relatively small.

Package Contracts

Package contracts combine or modify the basic types of life insurance to meet specialized needs. The more common packages are described in the following paragraphs.

Family Income Policy. A **family income policy** is a combination of decreasing-term insurance and ordinary life insurance. It is nearly always issued on a level-premium basis. As its name suggests, the family income policy is designed to provide a large amount of pure protection during a time when children are young and at the same time to provide some permanent insurance. The base of the contract is usually ordinary life insurance, to which is added a decreasing-term rider. The insurance under the rider is commonly expressed as so many units of income at $10 a unit. Thus, a family income policy may be composed of $10,000 ordinary life insurance plus 10 units of decreasing-term insurance, $15,000 of ordinary life insurance with 15 units of decreasing-term insurance, etc. The policy is usually arranged so that the beneficiary receives $100 (or $150) a month for a specified period, and then $10,000 (or $15,000) at the end of this period. The $10,000 ($15,000) is held by the insurer, and interest on this sum helps make the income payments.

The term rider is decreasing because the period during which the income would be payable in the event of death decreases with time. For example, let us say that Amos takes out a $10,000 family income policy with a 20-year decreasing-term rider when he is age 25 and his youngest child is age one. The income is payable to his family from a period dating from this death until the time he would have been 45, or until the youngest child is 21. If Amos dies 10 years after the policy is issued, the payments are made for 10 years. If he dies 15 years after the policy is issued, the payments are made for 5 years, after which the $10,000 payable under the ordinary life insurance portion is settled. At the end of 20 years, if Amos has survived the period, the term rider expires and this portion of the policy is terminated. The premium is usually reduced accordingly, and Amos may continue the ordinary life insurance portion as long as he wishes.

Specials. Many insurers issue **specials**—life insurance contracts with a specified minimum face amount at reduced prices. The economy rates involved in specials may stem from a number of sources. For example, it costs less to issue one policy for $50,000, or $100,000, than it does to issue five to ten policies of $5,000 each. Reductions in cost may also be made because the contracts are issued only to **preferred risks,** individuals who are nonsmokers or who pass other strict underwriting standards. Savings may also stem from a reduction of the agent's commissions on the sale of the contracts. Each of these sources of economy appears to be a legitimate method of reducing the cost of distributing life insurance. Some insurers, however, make savings in what appear to be less legitimate ways. For example, specials may contain reduced schedules of cash values, fewer or less generous settlement options, or a reduction in other services. It is not easy for the typical buyer to evaluate the differences, with the result that misleading comparisons may be made with regular contracts. Even though abuses of this kind may occur in the offering of specials, it appears desirable that insurers tailor their offerings to fit as closely as possible the varying needs of the public, particularly when reductions in distribution costs become possible.

Modified Life Insurance Contracts. Modified life insurance contracts are those in which the premiums are arranged so that they are smaller than average for the first 5 or 10 years of the policy and slightly larger than average for the remaining years of the contract. This is done by combining term insurance with some form of permanent insurance so that the insured pays more than the term policy would cost, but less than the cost of the permanent insurance. Modified life contracts thus enable the insured to obtain a permanent insurance policy at a cost that is usually one-half of what would normally be paid for the first five or ten years. The contract fits the needs of the young married person with a limited income who wants to develop a permanent insurance program but cannot afford to do so until his or her income rises. The solution could also be found in the purchase of straight convertible term insurance, but many persons would fail to convert term insurance into a permanent form because the premium increase is quite substantial. The modified life contract has the advantage that the insured need not take any positive action to convert the contract to a permanent form.

Multiple Protection Insurance Contracts. The **multiple protection insurance contract** employs term insurance to grant double, triple, or some multiple of the face amount of a permanent insurance policy for a set period, from 5 to 20 years, after which the protection is reduced to the face amount of the permanent policy. This is done by adding limited- term riders which expire after 5 to 20 years.

Juvenile Insurance. Life insurance issued on children is called **juvenile insurance.** For very young children, say between the ages of one and four, it is common to provide graded death benefits in order to limit the life insurance coverage to modest amounts, often less than $500. As the child gets older, the coverage increases automatically until it reaches some limit, say $1,000, or a multiple thereof. Normally, coverage is issued on some permanent insurance form.

Jumping Juvenile Insurance. A package contract, sometimes called **jumping juvenile,** is issued in units of, say, $1,000 at some early age. The amount automatically increases to perhaps $5,000 at age 21, without increasing the premium and without evidence of insurability. Often this insurance is sold as a savings program for college education.

Payor Clause. Insurers offer what is known as a **payor clause** on a juvenile policy, which states that if the owner (usually a parent) dies before the policy matures, all future premiums are waived until the child reaches age 21. This clause really amounts to additional insurance on the life of the parent.

Family Group Policy. One of the most successful life insurance packages introduced in recent years is the **family group policy,** in which each member of the family is insured for different amounts. The head of the family normally obtains the most coverage, and insurance on the spouse and children is limited to smaller amounts. If the owner of the policy is covered for $5,000, the spouse and the children will have perhaps $1,000 each. The $5,000 portion of the contract may be term or permanent insurance, but coverage on the spouse and children is usually convertible term insurance. One premium is charged for the entire package. This solves a common need, that of a limited amount of protection for the breadwinner's dependents, combined with insurance on the family head.

Variable Life Policy

Proposals to offer life insurance protection that varies according to inflation are relatively new. These proposals appear to be taking two general forms: policies that specify that protection levels change according to some cost-of-living index, and policies that specify that protection levels vary according to changes in some designated stock market index.

Policies using the first method, the cost-of-living index, are arrangements in which the inflation risk is assumed by the policyholder and paid for under one of several methods. For example, the insurer may offer the policyholder the right to purchase additional one-year term insurance as the cost-of-living index rises. The additional coverage is usually offered without medical examination and without heavy first-year acquisition costs. The rider permitting the additional coverage usually expires after 15 years or age 64, whichever comes earlier. The premiums to be charged and the maximum amounts of coverage that may be purchased are specified in the contract.

Variable life policies using the second method, a stock market index, are also relatively new in the United States, although forms of this policy have been used in Europe for several years.[6] The reserves of the variable life contract are invested in common stocks and other equity-type investments that fluctuate in value according to price changes in the stock market. Increases in the value of these investments are reflected in increased policy face amounts according to a formula stated in the contract. If the stock market declines, the face amount also declines, but some contracts contain a minimum death benefit equal to the original face amount.

Unfortunately, variable life insurance based on stock market values offers no guarantee that the face value or the savings element will actually offset inflation, because the stock market and the consumer price index do not by any means correspond one-to-one, particularly in the short run. However, variable life insurance is an imaginative approach to a problem for which new solutions are badly needed.

A significant advantage of the variable life policy is that in most cases the policyholder may earmark a portion of the premiums for one or more types of investment funds managed by the life insurer. Thus, the policyholder may select funds (and change them periodically, if desired), ranging from those considered very conservative to those more aggressive, from an investment point of view. Furthermore, the income from the savings element in these investment funds may be accumulated under tax shelter, as is the case with interest income in regular insurance contracts, and with universal life policies, discussed next.

Universal Life Contract

Recently, many life insurers in the United States have been offering a new contract called **universal life,** or **adjustable life.** The central idea of these policies is to combine whole life protection with a savings plan on which interest returns closely correspond to rates being paid on high-grade short-term obligations issued by the government or by corporations—so-called "money market" rates. Premiums are flexible in that they may vary according to how much money the insured wishes to save periodically. These policies have been developed to help life insurers attract funds that might otherwise be directed toward other financial institutions and media.

An example of a universal life policy is that offered by Georgia International Life Company. The main features are:

1. The premium can vary from $5 to $10 a week or from $20 to $110 a month.
2. The policy is paid up at age 95, and is issued to persons between 0 and 65.
3. The policyholder can increase or decrease the premium (and the corresponding insurance amount) at any time within the permitted ranges.
4. The death benefit is equal to the sum of some stated amount (level term) plus the cash value. (Other plans that can vary the death benefit are available as well.)
5. Each month the insurer deducts from the cash value a charge to cover the mortality costs, which in turn varies according to age and sex of the insured.
6. Each month the insurer credits interest using an index of government securities, subject to a minimum of 4 percent.
7. The cash value depends on the amounts saved, the interest earnings, expense charges, and mortality costs.
8. The insured may borrow on the cash value, paying 8 percent interest plus a $25 charge for each loan.
9. Level term insurance riders are available to cover the spouse and/or children.

An "8 percent interest" illustration of the policy showed that a male age 25, saving $40 a month, would have death protection of $71,800 as a "stated amount" and, at age 65, a cash value of $31,297, including a disability waiver of premium. An analysis of the contract reveals that the insured was being charged approximately $5 per $1,000 for the protection element and other expenses of the contract. For example, the $40 monthly is reduced to about $9 available for savings after all deductions are removed. The accumulation of $9 a month at 8 percent compound interest for 40 years will produce the estimated cash value of the policy of $31,297. In 1986, insurers were paying approximately 9–10 percent on "savings," so the universal life contract was somewhat more attractive as a savings vehicle than traditional life insurance products. The attractiveness was enhanced by the fact that if the plan met IRS requirements, interest returns could be saved under income tax shelter.[7]

An advantage of universal life contracts is that they permit the buyer to vary the amount of protection as needs change without purchasing new contracts. Thus, a buyer can simplify planning by purchasing only one contract and dealing with one insurer.

Savings Bank Life Insurance

Residents of three states, New York, Massachusetts, and Connecticut, are eligible to purchase life insurance through savings banks operating in those states. There is a maximum amount that can be issued, depending on the state of residence. Insurance is sold over the counter at inexpensive rates, reflecting the relatively low cost of distribution.

Industrial Insurance

Industrial insurance refers to a type of life insurance (usually with a cash value) sold primarily in small policies to meet burial needs. The contract is set up so that the premium charged is a given sum, say $1 or $2 a week, and the face amount varies accordingly. Ordinary life insurance is sold with the face amount specified, usually in multiples of $1,000, and the premium varies accordingly. Industrial insurance, often called **home service life insurance,** is sold by personnel known as **debit agents,** who collect premiums by calling personally at the buyer's home.

Group Life Insurance

Not to be confused with industrial insurance, **group life insurance** is commonly sold to employers of groups of workers ranging in size from ten to millions.[8] Group life insurance has shown a tremendous increase in the United States and in 1985 amounted to 38 percent of all insurance in force.

Group life insurance is almost always issued on the term plan. The employer receives a master contract that outlines the provisions of coverage, and the employee receives a certificate that evidences participation in the plan. The amount of insurance usually depends on the employee's salary or job classification and may range from $1,000 to $100,000 or more.

More than 90 percent of all groups are employer-employee groups. Union, professional society, employee association, fraternal society, and savings or investment groups constitute the remaining associations that have arranged for group life insurance. Many group plans extend coverage after retirement, although usually in reduced amounts. Many plans also cover dependents as well as employees. A recent development in group insurance is to offer benefits to survivors of workers in the form of a monthly payment continuing for life, until Social Security benefits begin, or until remarriage. Contingent benefits to children may be available if the spouse dies before the children reach majority.

Credit Life Insurance

Credit life insurance is protection offered in connection with installment sales of consumer durables such as automobiles. As in group insurance, credit life coverage is on a decreasing-term plan, arranged to expire when the installment sales contract is paid off. The cost of protection is incorporated into the regular payment made by the purchaser in connection with the purchase. If the insured dies before the loan is repaid, sufficient coverage exists to repay the balance of the debt, thus protecting the insured's dependents as well as the lender.

The Cost of Life Insurance

Life insurance prices vary according to several factors: the age and sex of the insured at the time of issue; the type and amount of the policy; the amount of dividends, if any; and in some cases, factors such as the smoking habits of the applicant and the applicant's occupation and general health history.

Although the subject is complex, some generalizations about life insurance costs can be given here. The subject is treated more fully in Chapter 14, and ratemaking methods are described later in this chapter.

1. Term insurance has a much lower premium than permanent plans such as whole life or endowments—e.g., on the order of one-fourth of the whole life premium at age 30. The lower cost of term insurance is due to the absence of any savings element in such a contract.
2. Three basic factors which affect the cost of life insurance, mortality rates, expenses (called **loading**) and interest rates, have all worked to reduce the cost of life insurance in recent years. Mortality rates and expenses have both declined, and average interest earnings of life insurers have risen steadily, reaching 9.65 percent on average assets in 1984.
3. Most life insurers offer women lower rates than men. A typical reduction is that women are offered the male rates "set back" three to six years.
4. Life insurance rates rise at an increasing rate as you get older. For example, rates at age 35 are about 50 percent higher than at age 25. Rates at age 45 are over 60 percent higher than at age 35. Rates at age 55 are about 65 percent higher than at age 45. The increase tends to follow the mortality curve shown in Figure 9–1.
5. The cost of life insurance to the consumer is importantly affected by interest earnings and income tax rules. If you purchase participating policies, (nontaxable) dividends averaging about 20 percent of your premium may be paid. Policy cash values are not subject to income tax as they accumulate, although ultimately they may become subject to taxes under some circumstances. Death proceeds of life insurance are not subject to income tax.
6. The price of life insurance varies significantly among insurers. It pays to "shop" for the most economical policy. You can compare life insurance premiums in publications such as *Best's Flitcraft Compend* (Oldwick,

N.J.: A.M. Best Co., published annually), which is available in most large libraries.

SIZE OF LIFE INSURANCE MARKETS

The types of life insurance discussed above may be studied according to how much consumer acceptance is accorded each. Ordinary insurance markets, in contrast to group, industrial, and credit markets, represent life insurance markets designed mainly for sales to individuals. Ordinary insurance includes the term, whole life, endowment, universal life, and various package contracts described earlier.

Data reveal that in 1984 each of the major markets for life insurance had the following amounts of coverage in force.[9]

	Life Insurance in Force (in Billions)	Percent of Total
Ordinary	$2,887	52.5
Group	2,392	43.5
Industrial	30	.5
Credit	190	3.5
	$5,499	100.0

Ordinary insurance is still the dominant kind of life coverage, and it is gaining relative market share. For example, over the period 1974–1984, ordinary insurance in force increased 3.4 times, group insurance increased 2.9 times, industrial insurance declined 14 percent, and credit insurance increased 1.8 times.

Group insurance has gained popularity for the following reasons: (1) It is offered as an employee benefit, with the employer paying part or all of the cost; (2) The distribution cost is minimized by issuing coverage without medical examinations, without individual policy forms, and with reduced selling commissions, and by having the premium paid in one check by the employer; (3) The premiums for group insurance usually are deductible business expenses to the employer and generally need not be reported as taxable income by the employee; (4) Group insurance growth also has been stimulated by the periodic increases in group coverage given to armed services personnel and federal employees who are covered under government-sponsored group plans.

Table 10–1 reveals that individual buyers have tended to favor term insurance over other types of contracts. During the period 1973–1983, term plans grew from 29 percent to 35 percent of the total, a 21 percent relative increase. Most other contracts declined as a percent of total. For example, investment contracts such as endowments or retirement income policies lost market share.

Their decline is due to the increasing popularity of universal life, which usually has a substantial savings element. Because of its flexibility, universal life is perhaps the most successful new life insurance product to have been offered in many years.

Table 10-1
Analysis of Ordinary
Life Purchases,
1974-1984

	Percent of Face Amount	
	1974	1984
By Type of Policy		
Straight life	25	16
Term	29	35
Endowments & retirement income	5	*
Universal life	—	22
All other	41	27
	100	100
By Age of Insured		
Under 15	5	5
15–24	24	10
25–34	39	36
35–44	20	31
45 or over	12	18
	100	100
By Size of Policy		
Under $2,000	1	*
$2,000–4,999	2	*
$5,000–9,999	7	1
$10,000–24,999	32	5
$25,000–50,000	25	11
Over $50,000	33	83
	100	100
By Sex of Insured		
Male	84	75
Female	16	25
	100	100
By Income of Insured		
Under $5,000	2	*
$5,000–7,499	12	1
$7,500–9,999	15	1
$10,000–24,999	51	34
$25,000 or over	20	64
	100	100

*Less than 0.5%.
Source: *Life Insurance Fact Book 1985* (Washington, D.C.: American Council of Life Insurance, 1985). p. 7.

Bearing in mind that most group insurance is also on a term basis, it is clear that consumers increasingly tend to favor those contracts offering pure protection, i.e., the term contract. This is not surprising in view of the increasing need for protection occasioned by rising incomes and living standards. Table 10–1 shows that 64 percent of all individual life insurance is purchased by persons earning $25,000 and over. The average face amount of the individual ordinary life insurance policy has risen steadily over the years until by 1984 it reached $42,480. In 1983 the average amount of life insurance in force per family in the United States was $63,000 about triple the level of $20,700 which was in force in 1970.[10]

Table 10–1 also shows that the largest single market for ordinary life insurance is in the age group 25–34. The age group 15–44 accounts for 77 percent of all life insurance purchased by individuals. Interestingly, the percentage of life insurance sold to women has increased 56 percent in ten years, reflecting the growing recognition that women want protection as much as men, especially if they are employed.

ANNUITIES

Life insurers sell a product called a life annuity, which, strictly speaking, is not life insurance at all. A life **annuity** is a contract under which the insurer guarantees the lifetime monthly payment of a sum called *rent*. Frequently, the death benefits of life insurance are settled as an annuity rather than as a lump sum. The person protected, called the *annuitant*, receives an income he or she cannot outlive. In life insurance, the insured is protected against "dying too soon," while in an annuity the annuitant is protected against "living too long," i.e., outliving the source of income.

Life annuities may be analyzed under several headings:

1. Number of guaranteed payments. (What happens if the annuitant dies shortly after purchasing the annuity? Do others benefit?)
2. Period when rent begins. (Now or later?)
3. Method of purchase. (Can annuities be paid for over time?)
4. Number of lives covered. (Can one arrange it so that the rent is paid to the spouse or to children after one dies? For how long?)
5. Fixed vs. variable rent. (Can rent be made payable in amounts that change with stock prices?)

We next address these issues.

Guaranteed Payments

The four major types of annuities, classified according to the type of guarantee of payments, are:

1. Straight life annuity
2. Period-certain life income annuity
3. Installment refund and cash refund annuities
4. Temporary life annuity

Straight Life Annuity. A **straight life annuity** is an annuity whose rent is paid only during the lifetime of the annuity, with no minimum number of guaranteed installments. If the insured dies the day after purchasing the annuity, there is no obligation for the insurer to return any of the purchase price. The sum paid is held for the benefit of other annuitants. In the straight life annuity, the annuity principle operates in its purest form. However, many individuals hesitate to use this form, particularly if they have heirs or dependents who would naturally like to participate in the estate upon the death of the insured. Under the straight life annuity, the rent is higher than under the period-certain life income annuity or the installment and cash refund annuities, in which some minimum number of payments must be made.

The price of annuities in recent years has been generally reduced because of rising interest rates. For example, a typical 1984 price of an immediate straight life annuity (no refund at death) was $12,000 for each $100 monthly income for a 65-year-old male. This is equivalent to approximately a 10 percent return on the cost (using both principal and interest). A price of about $15,000 was not uncommon a few years before that. Yet the price will still appear too high for many individuals who may be able to earn up to 10 percent interest on funds invested in bonds with reasonably good safety ratings. In case of death of the bond owner, the beneficiary may sell the bond for its current market value or hold it to maturity. In the case of the straight life annuity there would be no return to the beneficiary upon the death of the annuitant. The bondholder may run slightly more risk than the annuitant, but the principal can be preserved for the bondholder's heirs.

Period-Certain Life Income Annuity. When it is desired to obtain some minimum number of guaranteed payments, several different arrangements can be made. Under the **period-certain life income annuity,** the insurer agrees to guarantee 10, 15, or 20 years of payments to someone and, if the annuitant outlives this period, for the annuitant's lifetime.

Installment and Cash Refund Annuities. Other arrangements to guarantee a minimum number of payments under an annuity are the **installment refund** and the **cash refund annuities.** Under these refund annuities, the insurer subtracts from the value of the annuity at its starting date (that is, the present value) the total of all rents paid to the annuitant at the time of death. Any difference is paid to a beneficiary in cash or in installments, as the case may be. Slightly larger annuities are given for the installment refund type because the insurer will retain the funds for a longer time. If the insured spends $10,000 for a cash refund annuity at age 65 and draws $57 a month for 10 years, $6,840 would have been received in all. The beneficiary would receive a cash refund of $3,160.

Temporary Life Annuity. Assume that it is desired to guarantee an income for the life of an annuitant, but to cease payment in any case after a certain period. Thus, the annuitant receives the rent for a stated number of years, but the income stops earlier if death occurs before the period is up. This situation might arise if the annuitant has a given income at some future period, say from a trust that matures in 15 years, or from Social Security benefits. If the annuitant survives the 15 years, there will be no need for rent from the annuity. If the annuitant dies before this time, the annuity will cease at that time. Such an arrangement is known as a **temporary life annuity** and is mentioned at this point only to illustrate the many arrangements for guaranteed payments that can be worked out to fit different needs for income.

Period When the Rent Begins

The rent of an annuity can begin as soon as the annuity is purchased, in which case the transaction is called an **immediate annuity.** Alternatively, the rent can begin at some future time, in which case the annuity is called a **deferred annuity.** Often the rent begins at retirement.

Method of Purchase

An annuity can be wholly paid up in a lump-sum payment, or it can be purchased in installments over a period of years. If the annuity is paid up at once, it is called a **single-premium annuity.** If it is paid for in installments, it is known as an **annual-premium annuity.** It is possible to view a permanent life insurance policy as a deferred annual-premium life annuity because the life income option permits the insured or the beneficiary to accept the proceeds as a life annuity as one of the settlement options. A similar observation applies to the retirement income policy. Single-premium deferred annuities are common methods of funding group pension plans. The pension of the employee is made up of the rents from a series of single-premium deferred annuities bought over the working years of the employee.

Number of Lives Insured

Two major types of annuities under which more than one life is covered are the joint-and-last-survivorship annuity and the group annuity.

Joint-and-Last-Survivorship Annuity. An annuity may be issued on more than one life. For example, the agreement might be to pay a given rent during the lifetime of two individuals, as long as either shall live. A very common arrangement, this is known as a **joint-and-last-survivorship annuity,** because the rent is payable until the last survivor dies. The rent may be constant during the entire period or may be arranged to be reduced by, say, one-third upon the death of the first annuitant. Thus, a husband and wife both age 65 may elect to receive the proceeds of a pension plan on a joint-and-last-survivorship basis, with an income guaranteed as long as either shall live.

To illustrate a comparison of rents, one insurer offers the following monthly rents for male, age 65, or female, age 70, per $1,000 of proceeds:

		Index
1. Joint and $\frac{2}{3}$ to survivor for life	$5.59	100
2. Annuity 10 years certain and life	7.21	129
3. Installment refund and life	8.18	146
4. Straight life, no refund	8.79	157

Note, in this illustration, that an annuitant could get about 57 percent greater rent on a nonrefund basis, option (4), than is possible with an option of an annuity joint and $\frac{2}{3}$ to the survivor for life. Yet many annuitants hesitate to select a straight life annuity because they may wish to protect a spouse or other dependent in case the annuitant dies first. Most retired couples must decide which is best: option (4) for $8.79 per month per $1,000 as long as the husband lives, and nothing for the wife after the husband dies; or option (1) for $5.59 per month per $1,000 while both live, and two-thirds of this, or $3.73, to the survivor after either the husband or the wife dies. The advantage of option (1) lies in the protection it gives to the survivor. However, the income to the husband, if he is the survivor, is only 64 percent of the amount ($5.59/$8.79) he could have received under the straight life annuity.

If the wife is considerably younger than the husband, the rent on a joint-and-last-survivorship annuity is quite low because of the obligation of the insurer to continue payments until the wife dies. For example, if the husband is 65 and the wife 50, the joint and two-thirds to the survivor option would be only about 80 percent of the amount paid had they been of equal age.

Group Annuity. A group annuity is similar to an individual annuity, except that it is issued to an employer or some other collective entity and covers all or selected members of the group as a unit. The group annuity is the oldest and best known method of funding a private pension plan. For various reasons, including savings in administration, savings in federal income taxes, and reduction of adverse selection, the cost of issuing group annuities is less than that of issuing individual annuities.

Fixed or Variable Rent

Annuities may provide an income to the annuitant on a fixed or variable basis. **Fixed annuities** are paid in dollars, the number of which does not change during the time of the annuity. In **variable annuities** the rent can change periodically. The funds are invested by the life insurer in common stocks and other equity-type investments that change in value daily. The monthly rent is paid in units, the number of which is specified when the annuity begins. The value of the units, and hence the income, fluctuates according to variations in the value of the underlying securities.

RATE MAKING IN LIFE INSURANCE

In life insurance the pure premium method is the basis of what is essentially manual rate making. There are two basic factors that affect the pure premium: the costs of mortality and the interest rates earned by the insurer of funds deposited with it. These funds exist because of the practice of requiring payment in advance for life insurance protection, and because of the practice of issuing policies on a level premium basis. We shall see precisely how these two factors affect the calculation of the pure premium. Once the pure premium has been determined, a loading formula is applied, and the final gross premium to the policyholder is determined.

The **net single premium** is the amount the insurer must collect in advance to meet all the claims arising during the policy period. To illustrate the general method of calculating the net single premium, we shall assume that a given insurer wishes to determine the premium for a one-year term insurance contract with a face amount of $1,000 for a group of entrants age 20. Reference to the CSO 1980 table of mortality reveals that the probability of death at age 20 for a male is 0.0019. This means that out of 100,000 men living at the beginning of the year, 190 will die during the year. The rate maker in life insurance makes two assumptions in calculating the necessary premium:

1. All premiums will be collected at the *beginning* of the year, and hence it will be possible to earn interest on the advance payment for a full year.
2. Death claims are not paid until the *end* of the year in question. In practice, of course, death claims are paid whenever death occurs. Thus, the assumptions of the rate maker are inaccurate, for on the average, one-half of a year's interest will be lost on the sums so paid. However, an adjustment for this loss of interest is made in the loading formula, to be discussed later.

Calculation of the premium under these assumptions is simplified because the insurer knows that if a $1,000 policy is issued to each of the 100,000 entrants, death claims of $190,000 will be payable at the end of the year. The problem, then, is one of discounting the sum for one year at some assumed rate of interest. Thus, if the insurer is to guarantee earnings of 4.5 percent, $0.9569 must be on hand now in order to have $1 at the end of one year.[11] Therefore, to find the present value of $190,000 at the end of one year, this amount is multiplied by 0.9569, obtaining $181,811. The proportionate share of this obligation attached to each entrant is $181,811 ÷ 100,000, or $1.82. If each entrant pays $1.82, the insurer will have sufficient funds on hand to pay for death costs under the policy. The $1.82 is known as the net single premium.

The net single premium for a $1,000 term policy of, say, three years is calculated in a similar manner, except that the calculation is carried out over a three-year period instead of a one-year period. Table 10–2 illustrates the method. The net single premium is then computed: $522,331 ÷ 100,000

Table 10–2
Net Single Premium Method

Number Assumed to be Living at		Number Dying	Amount of Death Claims	Present Value of $1 at $4\frac{1}{2}$% Interest	Present Value of Death Claims
Age 20	100,000	190	$190,000	0.9569	$181,811
Age 21	99,810	191	191,000	0.9157	174,899
Age 22	99,619	189	189,000	0.8763	165,621
					$522,331

= \$5.22. It will be observed that each person must pay *in advance* the sum of \$5.22 for three years of protection.

While this calculation is a simple one, it illustrates the basic method of premium calculation in life insurance. The net single premium for a whole life policy, for example, is figured in exactly the same manner as the example above, except that the calculations are made for each year from the starting age to the end of the mortality table.

Net Level Premium

It would be impractical to attempt to collect a net single premium from each member of an insured group. Few people would have the necessary funds for an advance payment of all future obligations. Therefore, actuaries must calculate an annual premium. At first consideration, it might be assumed that the annual premium would be found by dividing the net single premium by the number of years in the premium-paying period. Such a calculation would produce a net annual premium of \$1.74 (\$5.22 ÷ 3) in the preceding example for a three-year term policy. However, this calculation would be erroneous for two reasons: (1) As the insurer will not have the entire amount of the net single premium on hand at the beginning of the period, it will not earn the amount of interest assumed in the calculation of the net single premium; (2) The individuals who die will, of course, not be able to make their annual premium payments. In calculating the net single premium, it is assumed that members of the insured group will contribute their share of total claims at the beginning of the policy period.

Actuaries find the net level premium by dividing the net single premium by an amount known as the **present value of an annuity due,** which provides for an appropriate adjustment of the two factors described above. The present value of an annuity due of \$1 a year for three years is the present value of a series of payments of \$1 each year, the first payment due immediately, adjusted for the probability of survival each year. The calculation is shown in Table 10–3. The value per entrant can then be computed: \$286,729 ÷ 100,000 = \$2.87.

The present value of an annuity due may be interpreted as follows: What is the present value of a promise of a large group of people to pay a sum of \$1 each year for three years? As the first payment is due immediately

**Table 10–3
Net Level Premium
Method**

Age	Present Value of \$1, First Payment Due Immediately, at $4\frac{1}{2}$% Interest	Number of Entrant Group Still Living	Discounted Value of Each Payment
20	\$1.00	100,000	\$100,000
21	0.9569	99,810	95,508
22	0.9157	99,619	91,221
			\$286,729

Part 4   Life and Health Insurance

(corresponding to the fact that life insurance premiums are collected in advance), its present value is $1. The second payment is due one year from now. If everyone lived to pay his or her share, the present value of the second payment would be $0.9569. Not everyone will live, however, and so the $0.9569 must be reduced to reflect this fact. The amount is therefore reduced by a factor that specifies how many may be expected to live to pay their share (i.e., the amount is multiplied by the probability of survival of the original group of entrants).

This process is continued, and we find that the present value of the promise is $2.87. If the sum is divided into the present value of the total death claims (i.e., the net single premium), the insurer knows how much must be collected annually from a specified group of insureds in order to have a sum that will enable the insurer to pay all obligations. The net level premium for the three-year term policy is thus $5.22 ÷ $2.87 = $1.82, which is, of course, greater than the quantity $5.22 ÷ 3 = $1.74 determined by a division of the net single premium by the premium-paying period.

Gross Annual Premium

The net level premium for life insurance represents the pure premium that is unadjusted for the expenses of doing business. The pure premium is actually the contribution that each insured makes to the aggregate insurance fund each year for the payment of both death and living benefits. Various formulas are used to load the pure premiums to allow for the necessary expenses of the insurer.

Examples of loading are home office clerical costs, executive salaries, rent, medical exams, agents' commissions, premium taxes, and loss of interest because premiums are not always collected in full at the beginning of a policy year but may be collected in installments. Acquisition costs are large compared to the annual premium, often amounting to more than the annual premium. To eliminate an extra charge in the first year, these costs are usually spread out over the premium-paying period. A further loading must be added to offset the fact that due to lapses, a certain portion of these costs will not be collected. The expenses of life insurers in 1984, expressed as a percentage of the premium dollar, were:[12]

Agents' commissions	5.9%
Home and field office expense	9.5
Taxes	2.7
Dividends to stockholders of stock insurers	1.7
Total	19.8%

The remaining 80.2 percent was returned to policyholders in benefit payments and reserves for future benefits.

RESERVES IN LIFE INSURANCE

Reserve liabilities are large in life insurance because of the practice of issuing life insurance contracts on a level-premium basis for long periods. This results in the collection by an insurer of amounts in excess of current mortality costs. These reserves, called **policy reserves,** are held in trust for the insured until the policy matures or is terminated, when the fund is returned to the insured. Policy reserves in life insurance are thus accumulated not because the life insurer seeks funds to invest; they are a necessary result of the level-premium concept discussed earlier.

Determination of Reserves

The amount of the reserve is determined by certain authorized assumptions as to mortality and interest, and not in terms of actual results. In other words, the reserve is expressed as a legal requirement, and indeed is a **legal reserve.** This expression is used in describing an insurer as a legal reserve life insurance company. The insurer must have actual assets equal to its required legal reserves, or it is said to be insolvent. Normally, the actuarial assumptions involved in making up rates are so conservative that the insurer will have no difficulty in meeting these legal requirements. The insurer will guarantee a lower rate of interest than it actually earns and will use a mortality table that overstates actual mortality to some extent.

The reserve in life insurance represents the amount an insurer must have on hand now in order to meet all future claims. The reserve must be equal to the present value of future benefits, less the present value of future premiums to be collected. When a life insurance policy is used, the present value of future premiums equals the present value of future benefits. Indeed, this is the way the net single premium is calculated. However, in time the present value of future benefits rises because the time is nearer when claims must be paid, and the present value of future premiums declines since fewer premiums remain to be paid. Hence, the insurer must have a reserve equal to this difference.

The reserve is an amount such that if the insurer accepted no more business, assets would be sufficient to meet all future obligations to policyholders. Thus, life insurance does not operate on a "pay-as-you-go" principle, which would mean relying on new premium dollar collection to pay current claims and expenses.

SUMMARY

1. Life insurance is a method of creating an estate of income-producing property. It is the only method of creating an immediate estate in case of premature death. It serves as a hedge against the possibility that the insured may not live to carry out property accumulation plans.
2. The chief purpose of life insurance in

estate planning is to provide for dependents in case of death of the breadwinner. A secondary purpose of life insurance is to save money for one's retirement or for other purposes. Policies are available to meet these twin purposes with many degrees of emphasis.
3. Life insurance is commonly issued on a

level premium basis. Because death rates rise substantially over a long period of years, more money must be collected in the early years to offset the higher mortality costs of the later years. For this reason, all policies except pure term insurance accumulate a cash value known as the reserve.

4. The reserve in life insurance not only serves to keep the premium level throughout the premium-paying period, but also serves many other purposes. The insured may view the reserve as a savings fund to draw on in emergencies, as a buffer against the possible lapse of the policy, as collateral for a bank loan, or as a retirement fund. The reserve makes possible the continuance of life insurance beyond age 65, a period during which there are still many needs for protection.

5. Major types of ordinary life insurance—term, whole life, and universal life—may be purchased separately or in many different combinations to meet the specific needs of insureds. Universal life and term insurance have grown most rapidly in recent years.

6. Most individuals are protected through group life insurance plans of their employers or through other groups to which they belong. The amount of protection is substantial and continues to grow steadily.

7. Industrial life insurance collected by agents through home calls, and credit life insurance to protect installment loans, represent special segments of the industry to meet specific needs of the insurance buyer.

8. There is a growing preference for term plans of life insurance among life insurance consumers.

9. Examining the life insurance premium calculation methods permits one to see clearly how life insurance operates and how contracts differ in their basic structures.

10. The policy reserve in life insurance, a measure of the security provided the policyholder, represents funds held for future benefits. As such, it is similar to the unearned premium reserve of property-liability insurers.

11. Life insurance proceeds are frequently converted to annuities, providing a life income to the beneficiary rather than a lump sum. The rent of an annuity is composed of both principal and interest. In using annuities, the buyer should compare the amount of rent to the income available from other investments which do not consume principal.

12. The price of both life insurance and annuities is not uniform among insurers. Large price variations exist among comparable products. It pays to "shop around" to obtain the best price.

QUESTIONS FOR REVIEW

1. (a) What is meant by the future estate? The present estate?
   (b) How does life insurance protect these estates?

2. It has been stated that the trouble with life insurance is that one has to die in order to collect. Is this an accurate statement? If so, why? If not, restate it more correctly.

3. "What is temporary for one person may be permanent for another." Explain, giving examples of what you consider to be permanent as opposed to temporary needs for life insurance.

4. All permanent life insurance contracts have cash values, but not all contracts with cash values are permanent. Do you agree? Why?

5. For what major purposes should term insurance be used? Whole life insurance? Endowment insurance? Defend your answers.

6. If one were to draw the appropriate line of a term-to-65 policy on Figure 10–3, where would the line be drawn? Why?

7. You are given certain data (simplified) below:

Age	Number Living	Number Dying	Present Value of $1 at 2%	
			Year	Factor
25	1,000	10	1	0.98
26	990	12	2	0.96
27	978	13	3	0.94

(a) Calculate the net single premium for a two-year term insurance policy of $1,000 issued at age 25.

(b) Calculate the net level premium for the same policy.

(c) What premium will the insured actually pay?

(d) Why cannot the level premium for the policy be properly computed by dividing the net single premium by two? Explain.

8. The formula for the prospective reserve in life insurance is calculated as the present value of future benefits less the present value of future premiums. After a policy has been in force for a few years, why is it that the present value of future benefits exceeds the present value of future premiums, thus necessitating a reserve?

9. What is the main attraction of universal life policies? Does it depend on interest rate levels? Why or why not?

10. Why is the price of life insurance trending downward?

11. Why is an annuity said to constitute insurance against "living too long"?

1. Why do life insurers issue contracts with an overcharge in the premium, while property and liability insurers do not? Explain.

2. Examine Table 10–1 and suggest possible reasons for the following changes in life insurance buying patterns:
   (a) The decline in endowment policies
   (b) The growth in purchases in the 35–44 age bracket
   (c) The increase in the sales of policies of $25,000 face amount or over
   (d) The growth of sales to women

3. Philip Ramos, age 30, has a family of five, with children aged three, five, and ten. He earns $25,000 per year and figures that he can devote $1000 a year to life insurance. He is covered by Social Security, and has a group life insurance certificate for $50,000 in connection with his employment.
   (a) For what types of life insurance would you recommend that Philip spend his insurance budget? Defend your choices.
   (b) How much death protection will your selections provide if Philip should die tomorrow?

4. Would your answer be any different in Question 3 if Philip Ramos, now age 49, earned $45,000 and his three children were aged 22, 24, and 29?

5. A certain insurer offers an ordinary life policy at age 25 at the rate of $18.56 per year per $1,000, and offers an "economy size" policy with a minimum face amount of $3,000 at the rate of $16.20 per year per $1,000. Explain the possible sources from which the savings in the premium of the latter policy might stem.

6. The text states that an investor might obtain as much income from bonds as from an annuity, since frequently the price of

annuities is not attractive. For example, if a straight life annuity costs $12,000 and offers a life income of $1,200 a year, it is better to invest the money in a bond paying 12 percent interest. Do you agree? Why or why not?

NEW TERMS AND CONCEPTS

Life Insurance
Actual Estate
Potential Estate
Protection Needs
Savings Needs
Term Insurance
Whole Life Insurance
Endowment Policies
Retirement Income
  Contracts
Level Premium Basis
Yearly Renewable Term
Cash Surrender Value
Decreasing Term
Convertible Term
Amount at Risk
Matured Policy
Paid-up Policy
Family Income Policy
Family Maintenance
Preferred Risks
Juvenile Insurance
Family Group
Variable Life
Universal Life
Home Service Insurance
Group Life
Buying Term and Investing
  the Difference
Net Single Premium

Legal Reserve Life
  Insurance Company
Policy Reserve
Multiple-Protection
  Contract
Payor Clause
Industrial Insurance
Debit Agent
Credit Life
Life Annuity
Annuitant
Rent of an Annuity
Straight Life Annuity
Period-Certain Life Income
  Annuity
Installment Refund Annuity
Cash Refund Annuity
Temporary Life Annuity
Immediate Annuity
Deferred Annuity
Single-Premium Annuity
Annual-Premium Annuity
Joint-and-Last-Survivorship
  Annuity
Group Annuity
Fixed Annuity
Variable Annuity
Net Level Premium
Present Value of an
  Annuity Due

NOTES

1 Certain long-period term insurance contracts have a small cash value, as will be explained later.
2 However, modern contracts are practically always guaranteed renewable for specified periods without evidence of continued good health.

3 *Life Insurance Fact Book 1985* (Washington, D.C.: American Council of Life Insurance, 1985), p. 43.
4 Some term policies require conversion before the protection period expires. Thus, the conversion and protection periods do not necessarily coincide.
5 The rates quoted assume 3 percent interest on reserves, CSO 1941, nonparticipating.
6 Mark R. Greene and Jacobus T. Severiens, "Variable Life

Insurance in the Netherlands—A Case Study," *Journal of Risk and Insurance*, Vol. XLI, No. 3 (September, 1979), pp. 511–521.

7 The U.S. Internal Revenue Service specifies interest and mortality assumptions to be used in determining a plan's tax status.

8 The largest single group is composed of the three million federal civil service employees.

9 *Life Insurance Fact Book 1985*, p. 10. Percentages calculated.

10 Ibid.

11 See Appendix D for an explanation of the calculation of this figure.

12 *Life Insurance Fact Book 1985*, p. 29.

11 CONTRACTUAL PROVISIONS

After studying this chapter, you should be able to:

1. State the difference between nonforfeiture options and settlement options.
2. Indicate the conditions under which using the settlement options may not be advisable.
3. Describe why it may be more advantageous to borrow on your policy rather than surrender it for the cash value.
4. State how the incontestable clause works.
5. Explain why the suicide clause is inoperative after two years.
6. Identify the spendthrift trust clause and whom it benefits.
7. List ways you can best use dividends in life insurance.
8. Differentiate group life provisions from individual life provisions.

The contractual provisions of the life insurance policy are of special significance to the insured because it is through a wise use of certain of these contract rights that some of the most valuable benefits of protection can be obtained. Furthermore, there are few contracts of insurance that contain more provisions directly bearing on the welfare of the insured than life insurance. Life insurance is usually a long-term contract effective long after the death of the insured. A clear understanding of at least the more important provisions is vital if the services of the insurer and the agent are to be employed effectively in carrying out the intentions of the insured regarding the estate.

NONFORFEITURE OPTIONS

The **nonforfeiture options** in life insurance guarantee that the savings element in the policy will not be forfeited to the insurer under any circumstances, but will always accrue to the benefit of the insured. There are three ways in which the insured may receive the cash value element: a lump sum paid in cash, extended-term insurance, and paid-up insurance of a reduced amount.[1]

Cash Value Option

The first nonforfeiture option is the **cash value option.** Under it, the policy may be surrendered for cash, a schedule of which is provided with each policy. Any indebtedness is first subtracted. The cash is usually paid immediately, but the insurer has the right to delay payment for as long as six months; after 30 days the insured is entitled to interest on the amount due.

Extended-Term Option

If the insured has not selected an option, most insurers automatically use the **extended-term option.** The cash value of the contract at the time of the lapse is used to purchase a term policy for as many months or years as are allowed by the rates in effect at the insured's age when the lapse occurred. A table in the contract states just how long this period is at various ages. Thus, for one insurer an ordinary life policy issued at age 35, in force for 20 years, has a guaranteed cash value of $371.80 per $1,000. If the insured wishes to terminate a contract, the options are to take the money in cash or to receive term insurance of $1,000 for 19 years and 317 days. (See Appendix H.)

Paid-Up Insurance Option

The insured in the above example might select the **paid-up insurance option** and thus receive a paid-up ordinary life policy of $639. This means that no further premium payments would be necessary and that the insurer would pay $639 upon the insured's death no matter when it occurred. This is almost the same as if the insured had purchased a single-premium ordinary life policy of $639 face amount for a lump-sum premium of $371.80.[2]

The nonforfeiture options are very important to the insured. The insured cannot lose savings because of the inability to continue premium payments. In addition, the insured has the right to continue insurance protection in two different ways if so desired. This exposes a fallacy often heard in reference to ordinary life insurance, namely, that you have to pay premiums all your life. Actually, one may stop paying premiums at any time and elect one of the nonforfeiture options. The extended-term option has benefited many a widow who discovered that a policy she thought had lapsed because of nonpayment of premiums was actually still in force under the extended-term option. The paid-up insurance option is especially valuable when old age reduces the ability to continue payment of premiums, and yet continued protection is needed for a dependent spouse.

SETTLEMENT OPTIONS

Settlement refers to the way in which the insurer pays the proceeds of a contract. The **settlement options** describe the different ways in which the insured may elect to receive the proceeds of a policy. The insured may choose to receive the proceeds personally or to have the proceeds paid to the beneficiaries, whether the proceeds be death proceeds or a liquidation of the cash values of the contract. There are many settlement options and combinations thereof, but the most common are lump-sum option, fixed-period option, fixed-amount option, interest option, and life income option.

Lump-Sum Option

Under the **lump-sum option,** proceeds of the life insurance are paid in a lump sum and the insurer's obligations are ended. The insurer exercises no further control over the money, and the various services offered in connection with other options are lost. For this reason, lump-sum settlements are employed most often when the insured or the beneficiary needs the money for a purpose that may best be served by a cash amount, such as for liquidation of a mortgage, for payment of last expenses, or for paying taxes. A vast majority of all life insurance policies are settled under this option.

Fixed-Period Option

Rather than being paid in a lump sum, the insured may select the **fixed-period option** under which the insurer is directed to pay the policy proceeds in installments over a set time period. Under this option, the insurer issues a supplementary contract (the old policy having been terminated) in which it agrees to pay the proceeds as directed. No extra charge is made for this service, although if a separate trust fund were set up to accomplish the same thing, a substantial cost would be involved.

As an example of a situation in which the fixed-period option would be used, consider the following case. An insured father, having provided for his family during the period when the children are young, wishes to set up an income for his wife, now age 36, to begin after their 7-year-old child is 18 and to continue until the wife is age 60. Social security income ceases during this period, and the insured observes that without at least a minimum income, the wife may be unable to meet current expenses even if she works, since help from the children is generally not likely to be substantial. The problem, then, is to provide an income to begin after a set number of years have passed and to continue for a given number of years. Using the fixed-period option, the insured instructs the insurance company that if he should die, the proceeds of the policy are to be held at interest until the wife is age 47 and then paid out to her over a 13-year period. At the end of this period the wife will be 60, and social security retirement income payments will commence.

The amount of insurance proceeds necessary to accomplish this purpose may be calculated from special programming tables designed for the purpose. Thus, at 5 percent interest, it can be calculated that it would require $6,590 of proceeds to provide $1,200 per year for 13 years, the first payment being due at the beginning of the eleventh year from the present, and the fund being exhausted at the end of the thirteenth year of payments.[3]

Fixed-Amount Option

The **fixed-amount option** is similar in purpose to the fixed-period option, except that payment of the proceeds is arranged to provide a set income, with the length of time varying with the interest assumptions and the total funds available. An insured may wish to provide a certain minimum income to the family and will instruct the insurer to pay this income for as long as the proceeds last. Interest earnings on the policy that exceed the guaranteed interest lengthen the period of payments, but do not vary the amount.

Interest Option

Under the **interest option,** the insurer holds the proceeds of the policy and pays an income consisting of interest only. The recipient may have the right to withdraw the principal. This option is often used in the following cases:

1. The proceeds of the policy may be intended to pay for last expenses, but it is not known just when these expenses will be payable. The proceeds are thus held at interest until needed and then withdrawn whenever the beneficiary wishes.
2. The proceeds of the policy are intended for use as an emergency fund for the spouse. The policy is settled under the interest option with the right of withdrawal of principal as needed.
3. Interest is needed to supplement family income, but the principal is intended to go to a child upon becoming age 21. The proceeds are left under the interest option with interest payable to the spouse, but without the right of withdrawal except by the named child upon becoming age 21.
4. It is desired to use the principal to meet income needs at a later time, but to pay out interest currently to supplement family income. The proceeds are left under the interest option until a certain time has elapsed, and then settled under the fixed-period option, the fixed-amount option, or the life income option.

Table 11-1 illustrates the amount of income from life insurance proceeds available under the preceding settlement options. When insurance is viewed in terms of the income it will provide, the need for adequate protection becomes more evident.

Table 11–1. Alternate Income Uses of Life Insurance Proceeds

Fixed-Period Option	Monthly Income Provided for Each $10,000 of Proceeds*	Time Period
	$179.10	5 years
	96.20	10 years
	55.10	20 years
	50.70	life**

Fixed-Amount Option	Insurance Proceeds	Time over Which $100 a Month Will Be Paid
	$ 5,000	4 years, 6 months
	10,000	10 years
	20,000	26 years, 11 months

Interest Option	Amount of Monthly Income Provided by $10,000 Proceeds	Interest Percentage
	$25.00	3
	33.33	4
	41.66	5
	50.00	6

*Assuming 4 percent interest
**Female beneficiary age 60, lifetime payments with 10 years certain. (See Appendix G for other options.)

Life Income Option

Under the **life income option,** the proceeds may be left in an annuity to guarantee the beneficiary a life income with or without any minimum number of guaranteed installments.

Policy Loan Value

The **loan value provision** enables the insured to remove savings from the contract without terminating the contract. If emergency cash is needed but it is not desired to terminate the policy, the cash value may be borrowed from the insurer and interest paid on this loan. Since the insurer has calculated the original premium on the assumption that interest would be earned on reserves, interest is charged to anyone, including the insured, who borrows these reserves. At the time the insured is using the reserve and paying interest on it, the insurer is crediting the insured's account with interest that it is earning on its assets. Thus, the insured may be paying 8 percent interest on an insurance loan and receiving 6 percent interest in the form of credits to the reserve account.

The loan thus costs the insured only 2 percent interest. This cost is necessary because policy loans are offered as an accommodation to the insured and are relatively expensive to administer. These arguments destroy the oft-expressed fallacy that it is inequitable for an insurer to charge an insured for the loan of the insured's own money. It is not actually the insured's money, but that of the policyholders as a group. If the insured dies with an outstanding loan on a policy, the amount of the loan is subtracted from the policy proceeds. Otherwise, there is never any obligation to repay the loan. If the entire cash value has been borrowed, it is necessary, of course, for the insured to pay the annual loan interest in cash in order to avoid a lapse.

Policy loans represent a substantial investment for insurers. In 1984 they amounted to 7.5 percent of all insurance investments.[4] Loans were up in 1984 from an average of 4–5 percent levels of the 1950s and early 1960s. One explanation for this phenomenon is that more policyholders have discovered the value of their life insurance reserves and have borrowed these values for reinvestment elsewhere at higher rates of return than the current borrowing cost of 8 percent. (Older policies usually specified 5 or 6 percent interest.)

Significance of Settlement Options

In 1981 3.7 percent of the funds most likely to be used for income purposes (death benefits, matured endowments, and cash surrender values) were set aside for future payments under income settlement options. The remaining 97.8 percent was paid in lump sums or held at interest.[5] It seems from these data that life insurance is being used primarily for lump-sum needs, and that alternative uses of insurance proceeds offer greater advantages.

By the use of settlement options, insurance can be arranged to guarantee the income security of which it is capable. It has been stated previously that the central purpose of life insurance is to replace income lost because of the premature death of the insured. If this is true, it is through income settlement options that lost income can be replaced most economically and efficiently for most people. Emphasis on settlement options furnishes a rationale for the purchase of life insurance and a guide for how much life insurance to purchase. In other words, the answer to the question "How much life insurance should I buy?" is "It depends mainly on how much income you wish to provide for yourself or your dependents." The principal sum necessary to furnish a given income level for different periods is then readily ascertainable.

Use of insurer services in managing the proceeds of the insurance costs the insured nothing extra. The proceeds are preserved from mismanagement by inexperienced beneficiaries, or from depletion by relatives or swindlers. The insured can rest in complete knowledge that fluctuations of the stock or bond market, a business depression, or other investment hazards will not interrupt the flow of income that is anticipated for beneficiaries.

Before using settlement options, however, the policyholder should compare carefully the proceeds promised by the insurer with proceeds available through alternative financial institutions. In recent years interest returns available in the open market far exceed the minimum interest guarantees, or even the interest guaranteed plus dividends, available from life insurers. To illustrate, as shown in Table D–6 (Appendix D), the policy may offer a female beneficiary age 60 lifetime monthly payments of only $50.70, with 10 years certain for each $10,000 of life insurance proceeds. This amounts to only $608.40 per year. The beneficiary could take the $10,000 in a lump sum, deposit it in an insured savings and loan association or purchase a government bond, and obtain, under today's conditions, at least a $7\frac{1}{2}$ percent return, or $750 a year, without using any principal and without significant risk. Under the life income option the payments are made up of both principal and interest, and after ten years, upon her death there would be no funds in her estate available for her beneficiaries.

CLAUSES PROTECTING THE INSURED AND THE BENEFICIARY

In addition to the inherent protective features involved in nonforfeiture and settlement options, there are other important clauses in the life insurance contract. Some of these clauses, which have as their purpose a guarantee that the life insurance contract will accomplish the purpose for which it is intended, are required by law.

Incontestability Clause

The **incontestability clause** states that if the policy has been in force for a given period, usually two years, and if the insured has not died during that time, the insurer may not afterward refuse to pay the proceeds nor may it cancel or contest the contract, even because of fraud. Thus, if an insured is found to have lied about his or her physical condition at the time application was made for life insurance, but this misrepresentation is not discovered until after the expiration of the incontestability clause, the insurer may neither cancel the policy nor refuse to pay the face amount if the insured has died from a cause not excluded under the basic terms of the policy.[6] Thus, the incontestability clause serves as a time limit within which the insurer must discover any fraud or misrepresentation in the application or be barred thereafter from asserting what would otherwise be its legal right—namely, the right to cancel the agreement. Such a statute of limitations is not typical of most insurance contracts. The legal justification for this clause in life insurance is protection of beneficiaries from doubtful claims by an insurer that the deceased had made misrepresentations, after it becomes impossible for the deceased to defend against or to deny the allegation.

Suicide Clause

The **suicide clause** partially protects the beneficiary from the financial consequences of suicide. The clause states that if the insured does not commit suicide for at least a stated period, usually two years, after issuance of the contract, the insurer may not deny liability under the policy for subsequent suicide. If suicide occurs within two years of the issuance of the policy, the insurer's only obligation is to return without interest the premiums that have been paid. A one- or two-year period is justified on the grounds that if the applicant's plans to commit suicide have motivated the purchase of life insurance, it is likely that these plans will abate after as long as one or two years.

Reinstatement and Grace Period Clauses

Under the **reinstatement clause,** contracts may be reinstated within a certain period after lapse, usually three or five years, upon evidence of insurability. The policy lapses for nonpayment of premium, but the **grace period clause** always gives the insured an extra 30 days in which to pay any premium that is due before lapse takes place. Once the policy has actually lapsed, special application must be made under the reinstatement clause to restore coverage. Sometimes a new medical examination must be taken, but usually the insured is only required to make a statement of personal good health at the time of reinstatement. All premiums in arrears plus interest must be paid. Reinstatement reopens the incontestability clause for another two years, but generally the suicide clause is held not to be reopened.

It is sometimes desirable to reinstate the old policy rather than to take out a new one, because the old policy may have certain provisions, such as more favorable settlement options, immediate eligibility for dividends, or higher interest assumptions, which are not available in the new policy. Furthermore, no new acquisition costs have to be paid on the reinstated policy, as they would on a new form. Since acquisition costs are substantial, amounting to about one year's annual premium on ordinary life policies, this is a great saving.

Automatic Premium Loan Clause

The nonpayment of a premium involves a lapse after expiration of the grace period. If the policy has a surrender value at the time of lapse, it may be surrendered for cash, changed into a different contract under extended-term insurance, or become paid-up insurance of a reduced amount. To prevent a lapse, most insurers encourage the use of an **automatic premium loan provision,** which automatically authorizes the insurer to use cash values to pay the premium and thereby to establish a loan against the policy just as though the insured had borrowed this amount for another purpose. In this way the old policy continues as before without interruption, the only change being that there is now a loan against the policy.

Misstatement-of-Age Clause

Misrepresenting one's age in life insurance is material to accepting the risk and normally would become a defense against payment of the proceeds if it were not for the incontestability clause. Without some control over this hazard, it would become possible for people to understate their age for the purpose of obtaining a lower premium for life insurance and to overstate their age for the purpose of receiving a larger or earlier retirement income. Proof of age is therefore required before proceeds are paid. Under the **misstatement-of-age clause,** if it is determined that the person's age has been misrepresented, the insurer adjusts the amount of proceeds payable rather than cancelling the agreement altogether. The actual amount payable is the amount of insurance that would have been purchased for the premium paid had the true age been stated. For example, if the premium at the true age is $30 and the premium at the stated age is $25, the insurer will pay only $\frac{5}{6}$ of the death proceeds otherwise payable.

Entire Contract Clause

The policy of life insurance generally contains an **entire contract clause** that provides that the policy, together with the application, constitutes the entire contract between the parties. This clause is desirable for the protection of the insured and the beneficiary because without the clause it might be possible to affect the rights of the respective parties through changes in the by-laws or in the charter of the insurer. With fraternal insurers, the insured's rights can be changed if the fraternal organization's charter is duly changed.

Spendthrift Trust Clause

One of the legal rights granted to the life insurance owner in most states is the exemption of death proceeds and cash values from the claims of creditors. Creditors of the insured cannot attach the cash value of life insurance for the payment of the insured's debts unless the insured has wrongfully bought or paid up a life insurance policy with money rightfully subject to creditor's claims. Neither may the insured's creditors attach the death proceeds of life insurance. This is an important right since the beneficiary is thus protected from the claims of the insured's creditors, and the indiscretions of the insured are not allowed to wreck the income security of the beneficiaries.

The question arises, however, "What about the beneficiary's creditors?" May the beneficiary incur large debts, using as security the right to receive income from life insurance proceeds? This is technically possible unless the state law has a provision to the contrary, or unless the law has permitted the attachment of what is called the **spendthrift trust clause.** If the spendthrift trust clause is attached to a life insurance policy, the beneficiary's rights to the promised income cannot be attached by creditors in any court in the state of residence. Such a clause is a valuable security measure, for without it there might be a temptation for an unscrupulous creditor to persuade a beneficiary to purchase goods beyond the ability to pay, secure in the knowledge that the life insurance trust could be attached. Thus, society grants to life insurance special status not given to other types of investments. Endorsement of the spendthrift trust clause is legal in most states. To qualify for this clause, the proceeds must usually be settled under an income option. Once the income has been paid to the beneficiary, the protection is lost when and if the money loses its identity as life insurance proceeds.

MISCELLANEOUS CONTRACTUAL PROVISIONS

Several other types of contractual provisions are common to most life insurance policies. The following paragraphs describe the most common ones.

Dividend Options

Participating policies are those under which dividends are payable to the owner of the contract. The dividend is actually a partial return of the premium payment and reflects the experience of the insurer with regard to mortality and overhead costs and net investment income. All participating life insurance contracts provide certain options in the use of dividends. In general, the insured may either take the dividends in cash, leave them with the insurer at interest, use them to buy paid-up additions or additional one-year term insurance, use them to reduce premium payments, or use them to help pay up a permanent contract sooner than it would otherwise be paid.[7]

Dividends may be substantial, so the proper choice of a dividend option is important. For example, dividends in a typical year averaged about 20 percent of the total premiums paid by policyholders.

Use as Paid-Up Additions. The use of dividends to purchase paid-up additions has four important advantages:

1. Since no acquisition charges are made in such cases, it is an economical way to buy additional life insurance.
2. Since no medical examination or other evidence of insurability is required, use of this option may enable the purchase of insurance when it is impossible to obtain coverage in any other way.
3. The paid-up additions themselves have a cash value that may be borrowed. Thus, the insured has available a large portion of the dividends if it becomes necessary to borrow the cash value of the paid-up additions. In the event of the insured's death, the beneficiary receives the additional

life insurance (less the amount borrowed) even though the insured had the use of most of the dividend payments while living.

4. For individuals in the higher income-tax brackets, paid-up additions have further advantage in that the interest earned on the dividends so employed has a tax-free status, whereas if they were left to accumulate at interest, the interest would be taxable. Dividends themselves, being considered a return of premium, are not taxable.

A limitation on using dividends to purchase paid-up additions should be mentioned. The paid-up addition represents the use of funds to purchase single-premium paid-up policies of life insurance. Most of the face amount of such policy represents cash value, and relatively little of it represents death protection. If the insured needs additional death protection more than permanent additions to the life insurance program, it might be advisable to use dividends for buying one-year term insurance additions, described next.

One-Year Term Purchase Option. Another dividend option frequently offered is that of using the dividend to purchase additional one-year term insurance for a stated amount, such as an amount equal to the cash value of the policy. The dividend will normally be more than sufficient to purchase one-year term insurance. For example, after 20 years the cash or loan value of a $10,000 ordinary life policy originally issued at age 35 in Appendix H amounted to $3,718. At this age, the cost of one-year term insurance in the amount of $3,718 will be about $75. The applicable dividend will be about $150 annually, more than enough to pay for the one-year term coverage. The balance of the dividend may be used for other purposes. In some policies, it can be used for the purchase of additional term coverage in amounts up to the face of the policy. The one-year term purchase option must be selected when the policy is first taken out, or the insured may be required to pass a physical examination to obtain this option.

The use of the one-year term purchase option is helpful in cases where the insured may wish to borrow the cash value of the policy and still maintain the full amount of the death proceeds. For example, assume you have a $50,000 policy with a cash value of $10,000. You also have the one-year term purchase dividend option in the policy. You wish to borrow $10,000, and if you do so, you realize that in the event of your death, your beneficiary would receive only $40,000 (face of the policy minus the indebtedness). You wish to avoid this, so you exercise your option to purchase one-year term insurance of $10,000, using available dividends to pay the premium.

Extensions of Coverage

For an additional premium most insurers will permit riders, which are actually in the nature of health insurance, to be attached to the life insurance policy.

Waiver-of-Premium Rider. The **waiver-of-premium rider,** which costs about 50 cents per $1,000 per year at age 30 for ordinary life policies, excuses the insured from paying any further premiums under the policy in the event of the insured's total and permanent physical disability from any cause before a certain age, usually age 60.[8] The policy will have the same cash values, death benefits, and dividends as it would have had if all premiums had been paid. Normally there is a waiting period of six months before the insurer starts to waive the premiums. The use of such a rider is recommended as a way of assuring that the life insurance estate will remain intact regardless of the insured's health.

Disability Income Rider. Carrying the waiver-of-premium idea a step further, most insurers will endorse the life insurance policy to provide a monthly income of $5 or $10 for each $1,000 of face amount in the event that the insured is totally and permanently disabled. Known as the **disability income rider,** this endorsement becomes effective after a four- or six-months' waiting period, and terminates if disability has not occurred before the insured has reached age 55 or 60, or at the maturity date of the policy if this comes sooner. The income continues as long as the insured remains totally and permanently disabled, for life in some contracts, but normally not beyond the maturity date of the policy or age 65, whichever comes sooner.

If disability continues to age 65, the policy generally becomes paid up. Often the insurer imposes certain restrictions concerning injuries that are intentionally self-inflicted or that are suffered as a result of war, while a passenger in a private aircraft, or while involved in a riot or civil commotion. The cost of disability income protection is relatively low, averaging about $3 annually for each $10 of monthly income for a person age 25. Because disability income protection is often available in separate policies on a more flexible basis than under life insurance policies, the importance of the disability income rider is diminishing.

Double-Indemnity Rider. The **double-indemnity rider** is an additional extension of coverage under which the insured's beneficiary may receive twice (and sometimes triple) the face amount of the policy if death is accidental. However, there are numerous restrictions on this benefit. For example, death from suicide, death that occurs after 120 days following an accident, death from all illnesses, death with no visible evidence of wounds or contusions, and accidental deaths due to war or aviation are excluded. While the charge for the double indemnity clause is not high, usually amounting to about $1.25 per $1,000 of face amount, coverage under the clause has the unfortunate tendency of leading the unsophisticated insured into believing that death protection has been doubled for a very small extra charge. Such could not be further from the truth. As we have seen, accidents are not the leading cause of death, and accidents that satisfy the definitions of the double-indemnity clause are an even rarer cause of death.

Another disadvantage of purchasing the double-indemnity rider is that the amount of insurance so purchased cannot be programmed for a given need, since collection of the accidental insurance proceeds is contingent upon the insured's dying in a given manner. It is probably better for the insured to use the $1.25 to buy coverage which will be available no matter what the cause of death.

Guaranteed Insurability. For an extra premium, the insured may obtain a coverage extension known as the **guaranteed insurability rider.** This rider says that the insured may purchase additional amounts of coverage in the future, if needed, without further evidence of insurability. The additional coverage may be obtained over stated periods not to exceed some aggregate amount. For example, you might be permitted to purchase added coverage during ages 25–40, not to exceed $50,000 in any three-year period, and not to exceed $100,000 in the aggregate. In this way, a young person may add to coverage as the family grows and be assured in advance that he or she will be able to obtain needed coverage regardless of current insurability.

Assignments

Rather than cash in a life insurance policy or borrow from the insurer, the insured may wish to **assign** the benefits to another, say a lender of money. This might be done because the bank may refuse to lend money to the borrower without insurance, or the borrower may have insufficient collateral to cover a loan, or the borrower is uninsurable for new coverage to protect a loan. Permission of the insurer is not necessary for the insured to assign a life insurance policy. However, the insurer must be properly notified in writing of an assignment, or the insurer is not bound by it. In the event of the insured's death, the usual procedure is for the insurer to pay to the holder of the assignment that part of the proceeds equal to the debt and the remainder to the named beneficiaries. The assignee need not have an insurable interest in the life of the insured. The insured may make a gift to someone through an assignment, for example.

Premium Payment

Most life insurers give the policyholder the right to pay premiums annually, semiannually, or quarterly. Many give the right to pay monthly. There is an extra charge, however, for paying other than annually. For example, if the annual premium is $100, the insurer may quote a semiannual premium of, say, $51. This is equivalent to charging $2 extra per year for the use of $49 for six months.[9] Reduced to simple interest terms, the cost is 4.08 percent for six months, or 8.16 percent annually. However, it may be worthwhile to the insured to pay at this rate because of the advantages of making installment payments as part of a budgeting program.

Excluded Perils

It is not common for life insurers to exclude many perils from coverage. Occasionally excluded are deaths caused by airplane accidents except for regularly scheduled flights on established airlines. Most insurers exclude only aviation deaths while on military activities. In wartime, many insurers exclude deaths caused as a result of war. There is little uniformity in the excluded perils clauses, and the practices of each insurer should be studied carefully to ascertain the coverage. If a peril is excluded in a life insurance policy, the fact that there is an incontestability clause does not prevent the insurer from denying liability, since it is held that the incontestability clause applies only to deaths from perils not excluded by the policy. Technically, the policy is not being "contested," because the insurer has simply elected not to cover certain causes of death. Fortunately, the average life insurance policy contains very few such exclusions. It is virtually a true all-risk agreement.

Beneficiary Designation

The insured may name anyone as beneficiary of a policy. The beneficiary does not have to have an insurable interest in the life of the insured. One of the great advantages of using life insurance as a method of estate creation is that the contract simultaneously provides for both the accumulation *and the distribution* of the property. The proceeds are payable directly to the beneficiary and do not pass through a probate court; hence, the proceeds are not subject to the costs and delays that probate procedures sometimes involve. However, attention should be given to the way in which the beneficiary designation is made.

Change of Beneficiary. The insured has the right to change beneficiaries without notice to those affected, provided that the insured has not named any beneficiary irrevocably. A **revocable beneficiary** has no control over the policy and has only contingent rights. Naming a beneficiary irrevocably, however, might amount to transferring all ownership rights in the contract to the person so named. It is done usually after a divorce or separation to give additional security to the beneficiary.

Divorce does not automatically affect your beneficiary designation. If you divorce and later remarry, and you wish to benefit your new spouse, you must change the beneficiary designation on your life insurance. Otherwise, your former beneficiary will receive the death proceeds.

Secondary Beneficiaries. It is common to name **secondary, or contingent, beneficiaries.** If the primary beneficiary is not alive at the time of the insured's death, the proceeds will go to the secondary beneficiary. Since secondary beneficiaries are often children, care should be taken to name a guardian to receive the funds.[10] Otherwise, the court may appoint someone who would not have been satisfactory to the insured. Also, if both the insured and spouse, who is the primary beneficiary, were to die in the same accident, and it is not determined who died first, the general rule is that the funds shall go to the secondary beneficiary.[11] However, if the spouse survives the insured, even for a little while, and then dies, the insurance proceeds go to the spouse's estate and might be inherited by the spouse's family instead of the insured's children. If the insured wishes to avoid this, it is possible to use a **common disaster clause,** which specifies that the insurance proceeds will be under the interest option for a specified time, say two months, and if the primary beneficiary is alive then, the proceeds will be distributed to this person; otherwise they will go to secondary beneficiaries or to the insured's estate.

SPECIAL PROVISIONS OF GROUP LIFE INSURANCE

Although similar to other life policies in most respects, special provisions of group life insurance, discussed in Chapter 10, merit individual attention. These provisions are summarized as follows. Many serve to prevent adverse selection and excessive claims.

1. You can obtain group life coverage without passing a medical examination or giving other evidence of insurability if you obtain coverage as soon as you are eligible—usually when you first join the employer's group. If you wait until after you have been employed for 31 days or more, you must pass a medical examination or provide evidence of insurability.
2. The group life policy contains a "facility of payment" clause, which permits the insurer to pay policy proceeds to persons not necessarily named as beneficiary, if those persons have borne the funeral or other expenses related to the insured's final illness or death.
3. The insured does not receive a policy as such, but rather obtains a certificate saying that the insured is covered under a master policy issued to the group's sponsor, usually the employer. The provisions of the master policy govern the coverage.
4. Almost all group life insurance is issued on a term plan, although permanent plans with cash value are available.
5. If you are sick or absent from work, you can usually obtain continued coverage for several months if the employer continues to pay the premium.
6. If you permanently leave your job, you can convert your group insurance to a permanent plan without evidence of insurability.
7. In case of misstatement of age, the employee's benefit is unchanged, but the employer's premium is adjusted.
8. Special conditions affecting survivors' benefits under group plans exist. These should be investigated so that their benefits can be coordinated with other insurance owned by the employee.
9. Group insurance benefits may be assigned to others, such as one's spouse. This procedure may be advantageous in estate planning.
10. Group life insurance can usually be arranged under one of the settlement options offered by the insurer under ordinary policies,

although the master contract itself often provides fewer settlement options to choose from than are available on individual contracts.

11. In the event of total and permanent disability on the part of the worker before a certain age, the usual group contract provides what amounts to a waiver-of-premium benefit.

SUMMARY

1. The nonforfeiture options in the life insurance contract refer to those provisions that grant three methods of benefiting from life insurance cash values when one no longer desires to continue the original contract or is unable financially to do so. Cash value may be (a) taken in a lump sum, (b) used to purchase extended-term insurance, or (c) used to convert the existing policy into a paid-up policy of a reduced amount. Realization of this fact ends the common fallacy that one has to "pay all my life" on a whole life policy.

2. Settlement options refer to the contractual provisions under which the insured or the beneficiary may elect to receive the death proceeds or the cash values of life insurance. The insurer will agree to act, at no extra fee, as trustee of the proceeds for the benefit of the insured's family, holding the funds at interest, or distributing them as a guaranteed life income over a fixed period or as a fixed amount for as long as the proceeds last. Thus, the insured may economically plan the distribution of the estate that has been created in such a way as to guarantee that it will serve the purpose intended and will not be lost through mismanagement, theft, or other investment hazards.

3. In the typical life insurance contract, there are many clauses designed primarily for the protection of the insured and the beneficiary and which give the life insurance contract a preferred legal status over other types of property. Among these clauses are the incontestability clause, suicide clause, reinstatement privilege, grace period, automatic premium loan clause, misstatement-of-age clause, entire contract clause, and spendthrift trust clause. These agreements reflect the basic social purpose of life insurance to provide for dependents who often would otherwise become a burden on the state.

4. Proper use of certain options can multiply the benefits to be received from the life insurance contract. The size of the insurance estate may be increased substantially through appropriate use of dividend options. The waiver-of-premium rider guarantees that the estate accumulation plans of the insured will not be interrupted because of permanent and total disability. The disability income rider replaces income lost because of permanent and total disability. The double-indemnity rider is available to multiply death protection in the event of death through accidental means.

5. Since life insurance is usually purchased for the benefit of someone else, careful attention should be paid to the naming of beneficiaries and in planning for various contingencies, so that the insurance estate will be distributed according to the wishes of the insured.

6. Group life insurance contains special

provisions that differ from those of individual life insurance. These should be given special attention by the insured in order to plan the life insurance estate to maximum advantage.

QUESTIONS FOR REVIEW

1. (a) Differentiate between nonforfeiture options and settlement options.
   (b) What are the most important advantages of using income settlement options?
2. Jack died, and the coroner estimated Jack's age as 45. There was a $10,000 life insurance policy in effect at the time of death, in which Jack's age was stated to be 35 when the policy was issued, five years prior to his death. The premium rate actually paid was $30 per $1,000, but the premium would have been $40 had the correct age been stated. The insurer offered Jack's widow a sum to reflect the requirements of the misstatement-of-age clause. The widow accepted the reduced payment.
   (a) How much did the insurer offer to pay?
   (b) What action should Jack's widow have taken before accepting the insurer's payment? Explain.
3. In a survey of insurers it was determined that about one-fourth would consent to adding a spendthrift trust clause to their policies only upon request of the insured, while the remaining insurers include such a clause automatically.
   (a) What is the purpose of the spendthrift trust clause, and why is it a good idea to include this clause?
   (b) When can the clause be used?
4. In order to join an insurance plan, the insured misstated her age to be 50 when she was actually 51. The oldest age permissible for entering the plan was 50. After the

lapse of the incontestability period, the insured died. When proofs of age were submitted, the insurance association denied liability and offered to return all premiums. The estate of the insured brought suit, complaining that both the misstatement-of-age clause and the incontestability clause prevented the insurer from denying liability. Apply your knowledge of these two clauses to decide this case. Defend your decision.
5. Using the interest tables in the Appendices, calculate how much insurance proceeds at 6 percent interest would be required to provide $1,200 a year for ten years, payment to begin after a lapse of seven years during which interest is earned. Show your work.
6. Reyes requests your advice as to whether his life insurance dividends, which amounted to $1,000 last year, are taxable under the federal income tax law. Reyes was credited with $1,000 in dividends on his policies, and, under the option he has selected, these dividends are held at interest and have earned $50 interest. Reyes is in poor health and does not wish to surrender any of his life insurance. Reyes received no cash.
   (a) Advise Reyes about the taxability of these sums.
   (b) Is Reyes making the best use of his dividends? Why?
7. Explain how and why dividends can be used to purchase additional term insurance.
8. What is the guaranteed insurability rider? Explain.

QUESTIONS FOR DISCUSSION

1. The insured had a policy with a double-indemnity rider that provided twice the payment of the face amount if the insured

were to die by drowning, directly, independently, and exclusive of all other causes, or of an external, violent, and accidental means. The insured was found dead, immersed in the bathtub. The insured was apparently in good health, and there was no evidence as to whether death resulted from an accident exclusive of all other causes.

(a) Would the question of whether or not the incontestability period had elapsed bear on this case? Why?

(b) Should the insured's beneficiary be able to collect on this claim? Why or why not?

2. An insured failed to pay a quarterly premium due on February 12. The automatic premium loan provision kept the policy in force until May 12, at which time the cash value was $4.74, insufficient to pay an additional quarterly premium. Accordingly, the policy lapsed and the insurer purchased extended-term insurance with the $4.74, thus extending the insured's coverage for 92 days. The insured died September 2. The insured's beneficiary claimed that the 92 days ran from the date of expiration of the grace period, which would have meant that the insurance was still in force at the date of death. The insurer claimed that the 92 days ran from May 12. How should this case be decided? Why?

3. A writer argued that there are many advantages to borrowing on life insurance policies as compared with borrowing from a bank or another lender, such as ease and speed of the process, cheapness of interest, and lack of any pressure to repay. On the other hand, can you think of any disadvantages?

4. An insured was divorced, and upon his remarriage he changed the beneficiary designation of his life insurance from his first to his second wife. The second marriage lasted five months, and in the divorce decree the second wife gave up all rights she might have had to any life insurance belonging to the husband. When the insured later died, it was found that he had not changed the beneficiary designation from the second wife and there was a court contest between the first wife and the second wife for the proceeds. Who should receive the proceeds? Why?

5. E. C. Mullendore, III, a Texas rancher, age 32, took out three life insurance policies for $5 million each. Most of the total premiums of about $250,000 had been financed by deferring payment to the sales agent for commissions. Just before the expiration of the grace period, and after the second annual premium came due, Mullendore was fatally shot and the killer was never apprehended. It was then discovered that two physicians had filled out the medical forms on the insured without actually giving an examination. It was also discovered that Mullendore was in deep financial difficulty and lacked the money to pay the second year's premium. The insurer, which had retained only $40,000 of the risk and had reinsured the rest, refused to pay on the grounds of fraud. Do you think the insurer should have been required to pay? Discuss.

6. Suggest reasons why no medical examination or other evidence of insurability is required in group life insurance, but is required for individual life coverage.

NEW TERMS AND CONCEPTS

Nonforfeiture Options
Cash Value Options
Extended-Term Option
Paid-Up Insurance Option
Lump-Sum Option
Fixed-Amount Option
Fixed-Period Option
Interest Option
Life Income Option
Loan Value Provision
Incontestability Clause
Suicide Clause
Reinstatement Clause
Automatic Premium
  Loan Clause

Misstatement-of-Age Clause
Entire Contract Clause
Spendthrift Trust Clause
Dividend Options
Waiver-of-Premium Rider
Disability Income Rider
Double-Indemnity Rider
Revocable Beneficiary
Irrevocable Beneficiary
Contingent Beneficiary
Common Disaster Clause
Guaranteed Insurability
  Rider
One-year Term Purchase
  Option

NOTES

1 See Appendixes D and H for illustrations of nonforfeiture options. Before the advent of nonforfeiture options (which are required by law in all states), there were cases where aged persons agreed to sell their policies to speculators when they could no longer continue the premium payments. The speculator's offer depended on the physical condition of the aged person, and a public sale often took place with the aged person present so he or she could be examined. Needless to say, the insured seldom fared well in these transactions. Elizur Wright, an early insurance commissioner in Massachusetts, was instrumental in outlawing these practices.

2 However, the insured pays no acquisition expenses for insurance purchased under dividend options or nonforteiture options, and so it might be said that this is a very economical way to acquire insurance.

3 Not all insurers will accumulate interest on death proceeds of insurance.

4 *Life Insurance Fact Book 1985* (Washington, D.C.: American Council of Life Insurance, 1985), p. 32.

5 Ibid., p. 45.

6 Sometimes the policy excludes death from war or from certain aviation accidents. Refusal to pay claims resulting from these excluded perils would not be in violation of the incontestability clause no matter when the death occurred. It has also been held that in some cases of gross fraud there was never a valid contract in the first place, and that hence the incontestability clause was never in effect. E.g., in cases where the insured has another person take a medical examination, there would not be a meeting of minds, and the contract would fail for want of a valid offer and acceptance.

7 In 1985 dividends in life insurance were used for these purposes in the following proportions: taken in cash, 18 percent; left at interest, 20 percent; used to buy additional amounts of insurance, 47 percent; used to pay premiums, 15 percent. *Life Insurance Fact Book 1986* (Washington, D.C.: American Council of Life Insurance, 1986), p. 47.

8 What constitutes total and permanent disability varies according to the interpretation by an individual insurer. A common definition is that the insured shall be considered unable to engage in a regular occupation for profit or remuneration. Total loss of eyesight, or loss of use of both hands or both feet, or one hand and one foot commonly constitutes evidence of total disability.

9 If the insured now has $51 to make the premium payment and is required to pay the rest of the $100 premium in six months, we may accurately state that if the insured were willing to pay an additional $49 now, no credit would be needed. Thus, the amount of the credit needed to take advantage of the semiannual premium payment plan is $49.

10 This is usually done in a will.

11 This result is governed by the Uniform Simultaneous Death Act, which has been passed in most states.

12 EMPLOYEE BENEFITS: GROUP LIFE AND HEALTH INSURANCE

After studying this chapter, you should be able to:

1. Explain how and why employee benefits have grown in size and scope.
2. Describe the major structure of group life and health insurance.
3. Identify major laws affecting employee benefit design.
4. List the features which distinguish group plans from individual plans of life and health insurance.
5. Explain how to maintain insurance coverage even when changing employers.
6. State the main differences in coverage of various kinds of health insurance.
7. Identify what is excluded from health insurance.
8. Explain how major medical coverage works.
9. State what to look for in selecting health insurance coverage.
10. List the advantages and disadvantages of HMOs and PPOs.
11. Describe efforts to restrict health care costs.

A substantial amount of life insurance, health insurance, and retirement income protection in the United States is provided to individuals in the form of employee benefits. **Employee benefits** are employer-sponsored plans to provide security and other services for their employees. In this chapter we describe the major types of benefits available and how they may be used effectively in one's personal financial planning.

Although issuance of policies of insurance to individuals is still an important class of business, issuance of policies to groups has become the dominant form of personal insurance in the United States. In this chapter the major provisions of group life and health insurance and of group and individual retirement plans are described and analyzed.

Individually issued health insurance contracts contain provisions which are very similar to group contracts. However, far more persons are insured under group plans than under individual plans of health insurance. Moreover, group plans account for most of the benefits paid out. Because of their numerous variations, individual policies are not described here.

MAJOR TYPES OF BENEFITS

Although the term "employee benefits" is used frequently to include a wide range of services and insurance plans offered to employees through their jobs, in this text we shall use the term narrowly to include three types of benefits:

1. Group life insurance providing death protection for families of employees.
2. Group health insurance providing medical and disability income protection.
3. Various types of retirement plans offered through one's employment, e.g., group-qualified pension plans and individual retirement plans.

Social insurance, frequently referred to as a type of employee benefit, is treated separately in this text in Chapter 24. Retirement plans are described in Chapter 13.

Scope of Benefits

The number of persons protected by employee benefits has increased since the 1930s to the point where in 1982 the following levels were reached:

	Percentage of employees covered
Group life insurance	96%
Group health insurance—employees	96%
Group health insurance—dependents	93%
Group long-term disability insurance	45%
Group accident and sickness insurance	49%
Retirement pension	82%

Source: U.S. Department of Labor, *Employee Benefits in Medium and Large Firms, 1983,* Bulletin 2213 (August, 1984), p. 16.

Data collected by the U.S. Chamber of Commerce reveal that in 1980 large employers spent the following amounts on selected benefits:

	Percent of Payroll
Group life hospital, surgical, medical, and major medical insurance premiums	5.8%
Short-term disability insurance	.4%
Long-term disability insurance	.3%
Dental insurance	.3%
Pension plan premiums	5.4%
Total	12.2%

Source: U.S. Chamber of Commerce, *Employee Benefits 1980*, p. 11.

Thus, the average worker who is covered by group plans enjoys group insurance and retirement coverage that increase his or her effective compensation by over 12 percent. Since the value of most benefits is not subject to income tax, the actual value of these benefits to the worker is enhanced considerably, depending on the income tax bracket of the employee.

Factors Causing Growth in Benefits

Several factors have accounted for the growth in employee benefits and group insurance plans. First, compared to individually issued plans, group plans are more economical to administer and install: lower costs of handling exist because of such factors as the ability to collect premiums through payroll deductions rather than having to bill individuals directly, the absence of sales commissions to agents, and the ease of handling claims.

Second, the costs of employee benefit plans are tax deductible to the employer, but the value of the benefits, with some limitations, is not currently taxable to the employee. This tax feature has greatly encouraged the growth of benefits in the United States.

Third, losses to insurers have tended to be lower for group plans than for individual plans. This phenomenon occurs because of the principle of group selection, to be explained shortly. Lower losses, in turn, mean lower costs to employers and to employees.

Fourth, from the viewpoint of the employee, benefits have been popular because their costs are subsidized by the employer, both directly and indirectly. Through various labor organizations, employees have bargained for more benefits.

Finally, several types of laws and court decisions in the United States have encouraged the growth of benefits as well as set up legal guidelines for their use. For example, tax legislation has made benefit costs deductible, and labor law has permitted unions to bargain for benefits.

Laws Affecting Employee Benefits

Although a complete description of laws affecting employee benefits is outside the scope of this text, the major legislation is as follows.

Social Security. Passed in 1935, Social Security legislation requires employers to provide basic retirement income and survivor protection for most

Part 4   Life and Health Insurance

workers in the United States. Social Security was later expanded to include long-term disability income protection and fairly complete health insurance for those 65 and over. Coverage under Social Security provides mainly a "floor of protection" and does not cover all insured losses. Privately sponsored group plans are built around Social Security to round out the protection. Their coverage is "integrated" with Social Security.

Internal Revenue Code. Also known as the tax code, the internal revenue code in the United States, supplemented by regulations of the Internal Revenue Service (IRS), provides the basic ground rule for amounts which can be deducted for various types of employee benefits and for other limitations and restrictions which apply.

Employee Retirement Income Security Act of 1974 (ERISA). ERISA governs private pension plans in the United States. Rules such as minimum standards for funding, vesting, antidiscrimination, limitations on investing, fiduciary relationships, and other items are specified. A basic purpose of ERISA was to increase the likelihood that an employee would actually receive a private pension upon reaching retirement age. A plan must meet all of the requirements of ERISA in order to obtain the status as "qualified" for favorable income treatment, including tax deductions. ERISA did not mandate private pension plans, but if a plan is not qualified, it receives no particular income tax benefits.

Age Discrimination in Employment Act of 1978 (ADEA). ADEA prohibits employers from specifying any maximum retirement age before 70 in their pension plans. ADEA also requires employers to offer equivalent benefits, or benefits of equivalent cost, to those employees who are past age 65, as is done for younger workers.

Civil Rights Act of 1974. The Civil Rights Act of 1974, as amended in 1978, prohibits employers from discriminating in their benefits program in any way based on sex, creed, or race of the employee. For example, if a health insurance plan were offered, the plan could not exclude a condition such as pregnancy, which uniquely pertains to female employees. Similarly, maternity could not be excluded as a condition prohibiting employees from drawing disability income. If a plan covers dependents, the employer must provide equal coverage for spouses of both male and female employees.

Health Maintenance Organization Act of 1973. Health maintenance organizations (HMOs) are relatively new types of firms which provide health insurance coverage to employees by supplying health care directly rather than by indemnifying employees for medical bills they have previously paid out. The 1973 federal law sets minimum standards for HMOs and decrees that if these standards are met, qualifying HMOs are eligible for financial assistance in getting started. The act also requires that employers allow employees to elect a qualified HMO if one is available in their community, as an alternative to other health care providers.

Several features of employee benefit plans distinguish them from individual insurance plans:

1. By their nature, group insurance and pension plans cover more than one person. The minimum size of a group will vary according to the insurer and state legal requirements, and by type of coverage. For example, as few as five may be enough for group life insurance, although most plans are much larger than this.

2. In group life and health insurance, evidence of insurability is not generally required. Membership in a group which has been formed for purposes other than obtaining insurance is enough evidence of insurability for the insurer. For example, if the employee is well enough to go to work, he or she is well enough to get insurance without passing a medical examination.

3. The **principles of group selection** apply to group insurance plans. Selection of risks to insure is based on groups rather than individuals. When individuals seek coverage, there is a tendency for adverse selection—those applying for coverage individually are most likely to have losses. One can minimize losses by offering coverage to groups, members of which have not been assembled primarily for the purpose of obtaining insurance. Furthermore, in groups, individuals cannot themselves decide how much coverage they are eligible for; instead, these decisions are made as a part of the plan design and are determined by such factors as the employee's salary, length of service, or position in the company. Ideally, there should be a flow of persons through the group so that younger members replace older members over time. In this way, the average age of the group is fairly constant, and loss experience tends to be stabilized. A stable age level translates into stable loss costs, since age is directly related to mortality and morbidity rates.

4. Costs of insurance are often shared by the employee and the employer. When the employee pays part of the premium, the plan is known as a **participating plan.** A typical arrangement is to have the employee pay for dependents' coverage, while the employer pays for coverage on the employee. An advantage of having the employer pay part of the cost is that the plan becomes more attractive to persons of all ages. Without such employer participation, younger members might find the costs too high and would tend to drop out, thus causing losses to rise over time, threatening the stability of the plan's premium.

5. Another important distinguishing feature of employee benefits is the way in which rates are determined. In group insurance, the losses experienced by the group influence the rates charged. Known as **experience rating,** this feature means that the group will have greater or smaller premiums in the year ahead if its losses are larger or smaller, respectively, during the preceding year. Experience rating provides employers with an incentive to keep losses of the group down

through various types of health maintenance activities, safety education, and other means of reducing health losses. These activities work toward reducing the cost of benefits paid by the employer and the employee alike.

GROUP LIFE INSURANCE

Perhaps the oldest type of employee benefit is that of group life insurance. It is also one of the most widely used kinds of benefits. As noted earlier, group life insurance covers 96 percent of the employees in medium- and large-sized firms in the United States.

There are at least four main types of group life insurance: (1) group term life, (2) group survivor insurance, (3) group accidental death and dismemberment, and (4) group credit life and health.

Group Term

Nearly all group life insurance is offered on a term plan rather than on permanent insurance forms. Group term plan benefit schedules are based either on an employee's earnings, on his or her position, or on his or her length of service. Sometimes all employees are given a flat benefit, such as $5,000 or $10,000. A typical benefit, however, is one or two times annual earnings. Thus, if you earn $20,000 annually, your group life insurance coverage might be $40,000.

To be insured, you must meet certain minimum eligibility requirements. Typically, you must be in a job that is covered, must work full time, and must be actively at work. Thus, if you obtain a job with a group plan, but you die before you actually report for work, no coverage exists since you were not actively at work.

You can name a beneficiary for your group life coverage. In general, you can name anyone beneficiary except, in many states, your own employer. Most group plans offer the same settlement options as individual policies. Thus, you can obtain an interest option, a fixed-period or fixed-amount option, and a life income or annuity option.

Group term insurance has many of the same clauses found in individual policies, such as the right to assign benefits to others, a 30-day grace period, and an incontestability clause. The misstatement-of-age clause differs, however, in that if you misstate your age, the employer is subject to an adjustment in premium; the clause does not affect the amount of insurance payable, as it does in individual policies.

The **conversion clause** in group life insurance states that if your employment is terminated, you have the right to convert your coverage to an individual plan without evidence of insurability. To take advantage of the conversion privilege, you must apply within 31 days after your termination from the group, you must purchase a permanent plan of insurance (not term insurance), and you must pay the premium applicable for the age you have attained when you apply. The face of the policy cannot exceed the amount of life insurance coverage you have under the group plan.

Survivor Income Benefit Insurance

Another major type of group term insurance, known as survivor protection, differs from regular group term insurance in that the benefit is expressed as income to specified survivors rather than a flat amount. Eligible survivors, such as a wife or children, must exist. The benefit might be 25 percent of the employee's monthly salary during the year prior to death paid to the spouse, and 10 percent of the salary for each surviving child, subject to some maximum family benefit, such as $1,000 a month for a given time period or until the youngest child reaches age 19.

Accidental Death and Dismemberment Insurance (A.D.&D.)

Accidental death benefit insurance is another common type of group life insurance, with the requirement that compensable death must have occurred by accident, as defined in the policy. Commonly excluded causes of death are suicide, disease, mental infirmity, infection, war, and travel or flight in any aircraft other than regularly scheduled commercial flights. To be covered, a death must have occurred within 90 days of the accident.

The A.D.&D. policy also covers dismemberment, paying the principal sum (face amount of coverage) for such losses as loss of both hands, both feet, both eyes, or some combination of these. One-half the principal sum might be paid for loss of one hand or one foot, or the sight of one eye.

Because A.D.&D. coverage is limited, the premium is much less than that of regular group term insurance. A typical cost might be $7 a month for each $100,000 of coverage.

Group Credit Life and Health Insurance

Credit insurance is one of the fastest growing types of group insurance. The basic purpose of this kind of life and health insurance is to protect lenders who have issued installment loans on autos, furniture, or other types of consumer commodities. If a borrower dies or becomes disabled prior to paying off a loan, the insurance proceeds are sufficient to repay the borrower's loan. The lender would be entitled to recover any outstanding debt, and the borrower's estate would receive any proceeds in excess of the outstanding loan balance.

Although credit life and health insurance is issued individually, it is still classed as group insurance, and there is no physical examination or other requirement to prove insurability. The amount of protection declines as the loan balance is reduced, and coverage expires when the loan is repaid or when the debtor dies, whichever comes first.

In contrast to most group insurance plans, group credit insurance premiums tend to be higher, not lower, than life or health insurance issued individually. Most credit insurance is sold by banks, finance companies, or savings and loan institutions, who view this type of coverage as a major source of profits.

WHAT IS HEALTH INSURANCE?

Health insurance may be defined broadly as the type of insurance that provides indemnification for expenditures and loss of income resulting from loss of health. The Committee on Health Insurance Terminology of the American Risk and Insurance Association (ARIA) has recommended the definition of health insurance as "insurance against loss by sickness or bodily injury."[1] The Committee also recommended the use of one term, "medical expense insurance," to embrace other types of health insurance.

Unfortunately, there is no sharp distinction among the various contracts as to the type of medical expenses for which indemnity is payable. For example, hospitalization policies usually pay not only for hospital services, but also for medicines used in the hospital, physicians' services rendered in the hospital, and other items. In general, however, six types of health insurance benefits may be offered on separate contracts or in combinations on a single contract: hospitalization, surgical, regular medical, major medical, disability income, and dental.

As shown in Table 12–1, group health insurance overshadows individual health insurance by a wide margin, accounting for 85 percent of total health insurance premiums in 1983. Group coverage accounts for 73 percent of disability insurance premiums and 87 percent of all hospital-medical insurance premiums.

Table 12–2 shows that, as measured by benefit payments, dental insurance is the fastest growing type of health insurance, while insurance for loss of income grew the slowest over the period 1970–1983.

Hospital-medical coverage dominates the field of health insurance, accounting for 89 percent of the total premiums and 87 percent of the total benefits in 1983.

Hospitalization

The **hospitalization contract** is intended to indemnify the insured for necessary hospitalization expenses, including room and board in the hospital, laboratory fees, nursing care, use of the operating room, and certain medicines and supplies. The agreement may set dollar allowances for the different items or may be on a service basis. Typical contracts offered by insurance companies, for example, state that the insured will be indemnified up to "X dollars per day" for necessary hospitalization, while Blue Cross arrangements may provide for "full hospital service in a semiprivate room."

**Table 12–1
Private Health
Insurance Premiums,
1983 (in Millions)**

By Type of Coverage	Total	Group Policies		Individual Policies	
		Dollars	Percent of Total	Dollars	Percent of Total
Loss of Income	$ 7,092	$ 5,099	9.0	$1,993	20.7
Hospital–Medical	59,073	51,437	91.0	7,636	79.3
Total	$66,165	$56,536	100.0	$9,629	100.0

Source: *Source Book of Health Insurance Data 1984–1985* (Washington, D.C.: Health Insurance Association of America, 1985), p. 25. Percentages calculated.

Table 12–2
Health Insurance Benefit Payments, All Insurers (billions of dollars)

	1970	1983	% Change
Medical Expense	$15.1	84.2	458
Dental Expense	0.2	7.4	3,600
Loss of Income	1.8	4.9	172
Total	$17.2	96.6	461

Source: *Source Book of Health Insurance Data 1984–1985*, p. 20.
Percentages calculated.

Surgical

The **surgical contract** provides set allowances for different surgical procedures performed by duly licensed physicians. In general, a schedule of operations is set forth together with the maximum allowance for each operation. Thus, the $300 schedule may provide $150 for an appendectomy, $25 for a tonsillectomy, $10 for the lancing of a boil, and $300 for a lobotomy. The $300 limit is the maximum allowance and applies to only a few specified surgical procedures.

Regular Medical

The **regular medical contract** refers to that contract of health insurance that covers physicians' services other than surgical procedures, and is to be sharply distinguished from the major medical contract. Generally, regular medical insurance provides allowances for physicians' visits, such as $10 per visit, regardless of whether the visits are made in the hospital, a home, or in the doctor's office. Normally, regular medical insurance is written in conjunction with other types of health insurance, and not as a separate contract.

Major Medical

The **major medical contract** is designed to meet very large medical bills on a blanket basis with few sublimitations imposed on specific expense items. The contract is issued subject to substantial deductibles of different sorts and with a high maximum limit. A major medical policy might have a $100,000 maximum limit for any one accident or illness, have a $500 deductible for any one illness, and contain an agreement to indemnify the insured for a specified percentage of the bills, such as 80 percent over and above the amount of the dollar deductible. A few insurers offer a variation of the major medical contract known as **comprehensive,** which reduces the deductible to $25 or $50.

Disability Income

Disability income insurance is a form of health insurance that provides periodic payments when the insured is unable to work as a result of illness, disease, or injury.[2] Usually there is a waiting period before the income payments commence, and the disability must be one that prevents the insured from carrying on the usual occupation. Most policies continue payment of the benefits for only a specified maximum number of years, but lifetime benefits are available on some contracts. However, under all loss-of-income policies, the benefits are terminated as soon as the disability ends.

Dental

Dental insurance is a fairly recent coverage in the U.S., developing mainly under group plans since 1968. It covers oral examinations, X-rays, cleaning, fillings, extractions, bridgework, dentures, root canal therapy, inlays, and orthodontics. Individual dental insurance policies are also available.

Group Hospital and Medical Expenses

Group hospital and medical expenses can be described under two headings: inpatient benefits and outpatient benefits.

Inpatient Benefits. The major costs in a hospital are those related to services performed while the patient is hospitalized—i.e., as an inpatient. Major services include room and board, intensive care room charges, operating room fees, laboratory services, and X-rays. Each of these may be subject to dollar limitations, although it is becoming increasingly common for group coverage to provide all of the costs of hospital confinement in a semiprivate room subject to a maximum dollar amount. Some contracts limit coverage by specifying some maximum time period, such as 365 days, for which costs will be reimbursed for any one illness.

Outpatient Benefits. Among the costs frequently covered by group hospital insurance are those applicable when the patient is not admitted to the hospital, but in which hospital services are offered on an outpatient basis. These include use of the operating room, preadmission testing, and use of the emergency room.

Exclusions. Commonly excluded from hospital expense insurance are expenses which are covered by workers' compensation or occupational disease laws; services furnished on behalf of governmental agencies, such as the Veterans Administration; cosmetic surgery which is voluntary in nature; physical examinations; convalescent, custodial, or rest care; and private duty nursing. Mental illness, alcoholism, and drug addiction care may also be excluded or limited. Deductibles do not generally apply to regular hospital expense coverage.

Surgical Expense Coverage. Coverage for the services of physicians, usually sold in connection with group hospital expense coverage, reimburses the employee for surgical procedures, including certain other procedures such as the setting of fractures, removal of foreign bodies, or suturing. The coverage provides reimbursement for physicians on one of two bases: according to a schedule of fees for different surgical procedures, and on the basis of what are found to be "usual, customary, or reasonable" (UCR) charges for given procedures in a given community.

On a fee schedule basis, the coverage may provide, say, $1,500 for an operation relating to the heart, and $150 for a tonsillectomy, with different allowances for hundreds of other procedures in between these extremes. On the UCR basis, the physician is reimbursed in full for his or her regular charges unless they exceed the reasonable and customary charges for similar treatment by other doctors in the same community.

It is becoming increasingly common to provide coverage for second surgical opinions. If the employee desires to do so, a second opinion may be obtained to see whether a given operation is necessary. If the second opinion differs from the first, the employee may decide not to have the surgical procedure. Insurance pays for the second opinion, and the second doctor knows he or she is being asked for a second opinion. Some medical insurance plans now require second opinions as a way to control the costs of medical expense, since it has been found that when a second opinion is given, many employees elect not to proceed.

Surgical coverage usually excludes dental work. Also, it does not cover doctor calls or office visits.

Other Group Medical Benefits. Group medical insurance often is written to cover additional expenses, such as treatment in an extended care facility (e.g., a convalescent nursing care facility) when full treatment in an acute care hospital is no longer needed. Some plans are extended to provide home health care benefits. These benefits may include nursing care in the patient's home, physical or speech therapy, and medical supplies and equipment. Other types of benefits sometimes offered include payment for hospice care for those who are terminally ill, birthing centers, prescription drug expenses, radiation therapy, diagnostic X-ray testing, laboratory expenses, and vision care. Figure 12–1 diagrams some of the major types of insurance available for health care expenses and income replacement.

Major Medical Insurance

Group major medical insurance plans offer reimbursement for catastrophic medical expenses up to some limit such as $1,000,000. Such plans are written either as an addition to basic medical and hospital insurance as previously described, or as a part of a total plan of coverage which includes both basic and major medical coverage.

Major medical insurance covers both hospital and doctor bills and other medical expenses on a comprehensive basis, with relatively few exclusions or limitations. Only workers' compensation, government agency work, cosmetic surgery, custodial or rest care, dental and vision care, and certain other listed expenses are excluded. Sometimes reimbursement for treatment of mental illness or alcoholism is limited to some percentage, say, 50 percent, of the actual cost.

Major medical insurance contains two main types of deductibles: a **flat-dollar deductible,** called an **initial** or **corridor deductible,** and a **coinsurance deductible,** expressed as a percentage. For ex-

Figure 12–1
Structure of Health
Insurance Coverage

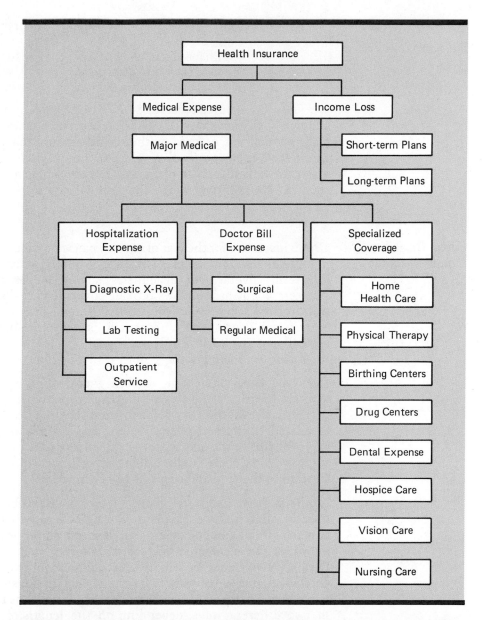

ample, if an employee had a basic medical plan plus major medical coverage with a $100 initial deductible and 80 percent coinsurance, and suffered $10,000 in expenses from a car accident, the loss might be reimbursed as follows:

Covered expenses	$10,000
Paid by basic plan	4,000

(Continued on next page)

Chapter 12   Employee Benefits: Group Life and Health Insurance   301

Difference	6,000
Less:	
Initial deductible	(100)
Balance, subject to coinsurance	5,900
Paid by major medical (80%)	4,720

Thus, the insured receives $8,720, or 87 percent of the total expense, and personally pays the $1,280 difference. Some major medical plans also place a total limit, or "cap," on the annual amount that a covered employee would have to pay personally, no matter how high the total bill runs. Most major medical insurance plans also feature a lifetime maximum benefit, such as $250,000, over which the plan will not respond. Some plans have no limit.

Group Disability Income Insurance

Group insurance for the loss of income caused by accident or illness exists in several different types of insurance plans. Social Security provides long-term coverage for disabilities lasting longer than five months. Workers' compensation laws provide coverage for a disability caused by a work-related accident or occupational illness. Sick leave plans sponsored by the employer, usually uninsured, provide for short-term disabilities typically lasting 90 days or less. Privately insured disability income plans fall under two main headings: short term and long term.

Short-Term Plans. Short-term disability protection is usually offered to workers for periods up to six months. Typically there is a short waiting period, such as seven days, before benefits begin. The amount of the benefit is related to the employee's income and usually is set equal to about three-fourths of the employee's wage, subject to some maximum amount, such as $200 weekly. In these plans, disability is defined to mean inability to perform the regular duties of one's occupation.

Long-Term Plans. Long-term plans of group disability income insurance usually offer lifetime payment, or payment up to retirement age, for covered disabilities due to accident. If the disability is due to sickness, the length of the income period is often shorter, such as five or ten years. Disability payment is usually set equal to 60 or 70 percent of the employee's income, subject to a monthly maximum such as $3,000.

The definition of disability under long-term plans is usually expressed in two different ways, depending on the length of the disability. For disabilities lasting up to somewhere between two and five years, the employee must be unable to perform the duties of his or her usual occupation. For longer disabilities, the employee must be unable to perform the duties of any occupation for which he or she is qualified by reason of education, training, or experience. Thus, a dentist who is disabled because of arthritic hands and can no longer perform dentistry may still be able to do other work, such as selling dental supplies or engaging in research. The dentist would be considered disabled for the first two to five years, depending on the terms of coverage, but not beyond this period.

Coordination of Benefits (COB). Most disability plans have a clause known as **coordination of benefits** to prevent employees from collecting more than their actual salaries under two or more plans. The employee must state whether or not he or she has other coverage; if so, the total recovery from all sources is limited to some percentage, say 66 percent, of the total income prior to disability. The plan is coordinated with other coverages, such as Social Security, workers' compensation, sick leave plans, pension plans, and other sources of disability income. Without such a clause, there exists a temptation to exaggerate or extend one's period of disability.

Dental Insurance

Group dental insurance began in the early 1970s in response to popular demand; it is one of the fastest growing employee benefits. Dental plans stress loss prevention by covering the cost of dental examinations and fillings. Plans also cover crowns, oral surgery, treatment of gums, root canal procedures, and orthodontics. The plans may limit coverage according to a fee schedule for each type of dental procedure. Exclusions exist for cosmetic treatment, duplicate dentures, and certain preexisting conditions. Some plans contain a lifetime maximum, such as $5,000.

PROVIDERS OF HEALTH CARE INSURANCE

Health insurance is provided by four main types of providers: commercial insurance companies, Blue Cross-Blue Shield associations, health maintenance organizations (HMOs), and preferred provider organizations (PPOs). Although an increasing number of health insurance plans are being handled directly by sponsoring employers through self-insurance, these plans are not discussed here. The important characteristics of the major types of providers include the following:

1. Under most state laws, Blue Cross-Blue Shield organizations receive preferential treatment as nonprofit associations. They may be taxed at lower rates, and typically they enjoy a reduced overhead expense. Originally considered to be prepaid hospital plans, the Blues, as they are called, have connections with hospitals to offer service at reduced rates.
2. The Blues traditionally offered their coverage on a *service basis*, meaning that the employee is offered service in a semiprivate room in the hospital. In contrast, commercial insurers offer coverage on an indemnity basis, meaning that the employee receives a dollar-amount indemnity for each day in the hospital. If the hospital charges more than the allowance provided, the patient pays the difference.
3. Most large commercial insurers operate on a national basis, whereas the Blues operate regionally, and if a patient is hospitalized in a region outside his or her home region, special arrangements must be made in order to obtain reimbursement.

4. The Blues traditionally charge the same rate throughout a given territory or community. This is known as "community rating." Commercial insurers, on the other hand, traditionally charge according to the loss experience of their clients. Thus, employers with better records of loss control can obtain lower rates than they get from the Blues, whose community rating system spreads losses out among all employers in the community so that everyone pays the same rate. This also tends to drive the better-than-average employer into the hands of insurers, leaving the poorer risks to the Blues. Today, many Blue Cross-Blue Shield groups have adopted experience rating in order to compete more effectively with commercial insurers.

5. Preferred provider organizations (PPOs) represent a new variation of traditional health care delivery systems in an organizational framework which offers reduced prices for health care in return for certain concessions by sponsoring employers, employees, or both. The PPO may grant a reduction of, say, 15 percent in premiums guaranteed for a set period such as one to five years. In return, the employers may agree to guarantee a minimum number of participants, to pay premiums promptly, to enroll employees in an education program designed to reduce employee claims and, hence, to reduce costs. Employees may be required to accept larger deductibles or coinsurance clauses.

   Sponsors of PPOs may include insurers, HMOs, employers, Blue Cross-Blue Shield groups, or some combination of these. The PPO movement represents a new trend in reducing the costs of health care which permits employers and other purchasers of health care to negotiate directly with the provider and in certain ways obtain direct control over some of the activities of the provider. The growth of PPOs may be restricted somewhat by legal obstacles in that some forms of PPOs have been held to have violated price-fixing rules of antitrust agencies of the government, and have thus been found to be potentially in restraint of trade.

6. Health maintenance organizations stress the maintenance of health in the first place, rather than solely indemnifying for health losses once they have occurred. These plans give employees the right to enter a clinic or a doctor's office paying only a small fee, such as $2 or $3, and receive any kind of medical service offered, such as physical examinations and minor treatment for conditions for which the employee might not seek treatment if a full charge for a doctor's office call had to be paid out. No claims forms need be filled out. If treatment by a medical specialist is needed, the HMO can refer the patient to the specialist, and no special charge is incurred by the patient. The HMO receives a set fee per month for providing all the medical service covered by the HMO plan. Two major types of HMOs exist: group practice and individual practice. In group practice HMOs, physicians work for a salary and provide complete

service to members of the HMO-covered employees. In individual practice HMOs, physicians work out of their individual offices and receive a set fee per month for each employee who is a covered member. Because of the comprehensive nature of their coverage and their emphasis on reducing health care costs, HMOs are the fastest growing type of health care provider.

CONTAINING HEALTH CARE COSTS

From 1955 to 1985, on the average, health care costs have doubled every five years. Only since 1984 has the rate of increase of health care costs slowed to approximately 11 percent. In 1985, about $425 billion was spent on health care in the United States.

Who purchases these health care services? A small portion of Americans used a disproportionate share of health care dollars. For example, almost 50 percent of the total hospital expenditures are consumed by only 2 percent of the nation's population. These high-cost users not only are typically treated for the same conditions over and over again; they also have a high probability of being heavy smokers and heavy drinkers, and having a tendency toward obesity.

Development of aggressive fitness and wellness programs for employee groups as an effort to modify the behavior of this "high health dollar consumption" group can have a major impact on the frequency of future medical claims. Programs providing preventive maintenance, such as HMOs, can also have a major impact on both the frequency and size of future medical claims.

The challenge of tomorrow is to find a way to control costs in a manner such that quality medical care is still available at a price all people, rich and poor, can afford.

Sources: Joseph Marlow, "Rationing: A Painful Process," *Best's Review*, Life/Health Ed. (December, 1985), pp. 22–24, 113–114; Pamela Loos, "If Fears Come True," *Best's Review*, Life/Health Ed. (January, 1986), pp. 14–16, 112–122.

Major advantages claimed for the HMO as a health care provider, in contrast to commercial insurers and Blue Cross-Blue Shield plans, are:

1. HMOs stress regular health care, early diagnosis and treatment, and disease prevention. Commercial group insurance plans stress indemnifying losses once sickness or accident strikes.
2. HMOs control costs through loss prevention and provision of incentives to doctors for efficient treatment. Much of the cost reduction in HMOs has been made by reducing the lengths of hospital stays. The HMO is

regularly paid a set amount for providing service. It immediately benefits financially if the costs are held down.

Commercial insurance plans control costs mainly by shifting part of the cost to the patient through deductibles and coinsurance, and by imposing maximum limits. There is little a commercial insurer can do about keeping direct costs down, because these costs are determined by doctors, hospitals, and other third parties. The burden of and risk in controlling costs is placed on the patient.

3. The HMO provides a wide variety of closely associated and interacting medical personnel to treat the patient in a single environment. Thus, services of medical specialists, mental care providers, nurses, pharmacists, hospital personnel, and others are brought to bear in a single system.

In commercial insurance, the patient seeks care from different sources separately. No single provider of service is responsible for the total health of the patient. Each is paid on a fee-for-service basis and has no particular incentive to reduce these fees.

4. Since the HMO Act of 1973 requires that the HMO be offered as an alternative to commercial insurance plans if an HMO plan is available, enrollment is voluntary by the employee. Competition between HMOs and commercial insurers tends to keep costs down. The fact that HMOs receive a fixed amount places some financial risk on them, providing further incentive to provide services as economically as possible. In commercial insurance, the employer generally seeks bids, accepts the best bid from competing insurers, and offers one plan to employees. Once the plan is installed, the employee has no choice among insurers.

Disadvantages of HMOs which have been cited include the following: (1) Some restrictions exist in the patient's freedom of choice in selecting physicians. (2) There may be a tendency for HMO physicians to economize too much on health care, since the physicians have a financial interest in the profitability of the HMO enterprise. (3) Health care may tend to become depersonalized. (4) The HMO may tend to reduce the use of second opinions and consulting expenses. These factors are usually cited by physicians who believe that the patient is better served by a fee-for-service system.

CONTROLLING HEALTH CARE COSTS

Over the period 1970–1984, national expenditures for medical care increased fivefold. Major contributing factors to the increase in costs are (1) rising prices of medical services, (2) increasing population, and (3) increasing quantity and quality of medical services developed and demanded.

Inefficiencies in the health care delivery system have also contributed to rising costs. Duplication of hospital facilities in the same community, lack of incentives to undertake economies, the increasing incidence of malpractice suits against medical personnel, provision of unnecessary services, and increasing government regulation are all cited as causes. Part of the cost escalation results from the private insurance method of paying for health care.

There is a tendency for doctors to charge more when the ability to pay, as evidenced by insurance or income level, increases. There may also be a tendency for hospitalization costs to rise because, through insurance, the ability of patients to pay for hospital services is enhanced. To combat this, the federal government has mandated a new reimbursement system for hospitalized patients covered by Medicare. Under the system referred to as diagnosis-related groups (DRGs), average costs and lengths of hospitalization for different medical conditions have been calculated. The system permits hospitals to collect only stated allowances for each admission. If a patient stays in the hospital longer than the allowed time, the hospital must absorb the extra cost or try to collect it from the patient individually. This provides an incentive for all concerned to use only as much medical service as is really required.

Insurance organizations have attempted to control losses by placing limitations of recovery in their contracts and by the use of deductibles. Further progress in reducing health care costs must come through increased cooperation between insurers, insureds, hospital administrators, physicians, and others to seek methods of increasing the efficiency of group health insurance plans, of controlling the costs of medical care, and of the administrative and acquisition-related costs of insurance.

A significant step in this direction has been the adoption of plans to set up medical boards to review claims that doctors or hospitals have charged too much or have performed unnecessary services. In this way, some outside checks exist to reduce excessive, and in some cases fraudulent, charges by medical personnel.

EVALUATION OF HEALTH INSURANCE

As mentioned earlier, private health insurance now covers a large proportion of the U.S. population for hospital and physicians' expenses. In spite of this, it is estimated that about ten percent of the general population and 16 percent of the population under 65 are without health insurance, either on a group or individual basis. This is especially true for young adults, many of whom are unemployed and who do not have group plans and cannot afford individual plans. Moreover, coverage under group long-term disability insurance is less than adequate, covering less than half the population.[3] For example, many deductions and exclusions exist, many plans do not provide the full cost of coverage in a hospital, and the maximum number of hospital days insured may be inadequate. In many cases an employee may have only basic health insurance coverage and may not be covered by major medical insurance. Even for the over-65 age group, which is covered by Medicare, so many limitations exist that private insurers are able to sell "supplementary" plans at substantial premiums to "fill in the gaps" in the federal coverage.

Because of the limitations and inadequacies of private group and individual health insurance, the U.S. Congress has considered many different plans of national health insurance. So far, however, no plan has been enacted.

GUIDELINES IN CHOOSING HEALTH INSURANCE PLANS

Several factors should be considered in choosing any plan of health insurance under which you may be covered, whether it be a group plan or an individual plan of insurance. These may be summarized as follows:

1. Individual health insurance policies should be guaranteed renewable so that they may not be terminated by the insurer or subjected to exclusions or limitations by endorsement upon renewal. Disability income policies should be purchased on a fixed premium basis to prevent the insurer from increasing the premium over time for the same benefit.
2. Policy limitations and exclusions may operate to define sickness narrowly or reduce coverage through unreasonable waiting or elimination periods. For example, some policies will pay for mental illness or alcoholic treatment, and others will not. Some will have territorial limitations so that if you become ill while on a trip abroad, coverage is suspended. Policies should not exclude preexisting conditions of which you have no knowledge at the time you are covered.
3. The policy should continue to cover the survivor if one spouse dies. Children should have the right to continue their coverage upon reaching majority. Children should be covered from birth, not after they are two weeks old.
4. In comparing medical expense health insurance policies, give special attention to surgical schedules, coinsurance requirements, maximum amounts to which coinsurance deductibles apply, ways in which the deductibles apply (annual or per disability), recurrent-disability clauses, waiting periods, preexisting condition clauses, and maximum limits. For example, major medical limits should be at least $50,000. Deductibles should apply on a calendar-year basis, not on a per-disability basis.
5. In analyzing disability income policies, favor those whose definitions of disability allow you to be eligible for coverage if you are unable to perform the regular duties of *your* occupation, not *any* occupation. Avoid contracts stating that the disability must begin within some stated period after the accidental injury. Since most disabilities result from sickness, not accidents, make sure the policy provides reasonable periods of disability from both sickness and accidents, preferably until age 65 and not for limited periods such as two or five years.
6. Make sure the policy contains a waiver-of-premium clause in the event of disability. In most policies, the premium must be paid for the first 90

or 180 days, but premiums can be refunded if the disability lasts beyond these periods.

7. If you transfer from one group plan to another, compare the coverage for which you will be eligible in the new plan. Poor coverage or absence of coverage in the new plan may influence your decision to make the transfer in the first place. Look into the possibility of converting group coverage to an individual plan if you leave the group.

SUMMARY

1. The three major types of employee benefits are group life insurance, group medical and hospital expense insurance, and group disability insurance.

2. About 90 percent of all U.S. workers are covered by group plans of life, health, and disability insurance. These plans are usually paid for mainly by the employer, although the employee may contribute toward their cost.

3. Among the reasons for the rapid growth of employee benefits, including group insurance of various types, are: (1) Group insurance plans are more economical to administer and are associated with lower costs of losses than individually purchased plans of insurance. (2) The costs of group plans are deductible for income taxes, and their benefits are not currently taxable to the employee. (3) Labor organizations have pushed hard for benefits in collective bargaining efforts. (4) Various types of laws, including Social Security, tax codes, ERISA, ADEA, Civil Rights Acts, and Health Maintenance Organizations acts, have all encouraged the growth of benefits.

4. Distinguishing features of employee benefits, as contrasted to plans which are individually purchased, include the principle of group selection and underwriting, the use of experience rating, and the shar-

ing of costs by the employer and the employee.

5. Four major types of group life insurance are commonly employed: group term, survivor income, accidental death and dismemberment, and group credit life plans. The largest class is traditional group term, although group credit insurance is the fastest growing type of group life coverage.

6. Group hospital and medical expense insurance covers hospitalization expenses, surgical expenses, and several other related expenses incurred on both an inpatient and an outpatient basis. Major medical coverage offers catastrophic-type protection for all types of health loss, subject to different types of deductibles. Dental insurance is written as a separate coverage to regular health care plans.

7. Health coverage is provided by four types of organizations: commercial insurers, Blue Cross-Blue Shield associations, health maintenance organizations (HMOs), and preferred provider organizations (PPOs). The latter are the newest type of health care provider and are growing the most rapidly.

8. Among the major problems of health care in the United States is its high cost, its inadequate and spotty coverage, and its complexity. Congress has not yet seen fit

to pass a national health insurance scheme similar to those in most other industrialized countries in the world.

QUESTIONS FOR REVIEW

1. Approximately what proportion of the work force is covered by group life and group health insurance?
2. Suggest reasons why private group long-term disability (LTD) coverage is written on less than half of the work force.
3. List the major factors which have accounted for the substantial growth of employee benefits. Which of these do you believe is the most important? Why?
4. How did the ADEA act and the Civil Rights Act of 1974 affect employee benefits?
5. What is an HMO? How does it differ from Blue Cross-Blue Shield and from commercial insurers in the way it provides for health care?
6. Name the major features of employee benefits which distinguish them from individual plans of insurance.
7. How does group term insurance differ from group survivor income benefit insurance?
8. Why does group credit life and health insurance cost more than individually issued contracts of life and health insurance?
9. List some of the major exclusions of group hospital insurance.
10. Why should "second opinion" coverage be offered in connection with group surgical coverage?
11. Jones has a $20,000 loss from hospitalization and doctor bills following an automobile accident. He is covered by a major medical plan with a $50,000 limit. His basic plan of health coverage pays $5,000 of the loss. The major medical plan has a $100 corridor deductible, and 80 percent coinsurance. How much of Jones's loss will be

paid by major medical? Show your calculations.
12. Why has the "health care cost containment" issue become so important in the field of health insurance?

QUESTIONS FOR DISCUSSION

1. A significant issue in group health insurance is how to keep costs down. Among the remedies which have been suggested is that of placing limitations on how much individuals can sue for when they are injured by hospitals or physicians in the course of their medical care. Do you believe such legislation should be passed? Discuss pros and cons as you see them.
2. Which of the advantages and disadvantages of the HMO form of health care provider do you believe are most important? For example, do you believe that the HMO might be tempted to give inadequate service because physicians have a financial interest in the profitability of the organization? Discuss.
3. Which type of disability insurance has the most value to the employee, long-term or short-term plans? Why? (Refer to data in Chapter 9.)
4. A plan of group life insurance in which an employer offers employees a choice of how much coverage they want was rejected by an insurer. The employee would have been offered a choice between $5,000, $10,000, $20,000, and $30,000 of death benefits and would have been asked to pay a correspondingly greater contribution for higher coverage. Suggest reasons why this plan was rejected.
5. The diagnosis-related groups system (DRG) has been criticized on the ground that it causes discharges of patients from hospitals "quicker and sicker" than before. Ex-

plain how and why this criticism may have arisen.

6. A study on health care cost containment showed that efforts by employers to reduce health care costs could be grouped under three headings: (1) those increasing costs to the employees by such measures as applying increased levels for deductibles, (2) those aimed at increasing the efficiency of the health care system, by covering, for example, second opinions for surgery or preadmission testing, and (3) those using measures aimed at reducing the income of physicians or hospitals. These efforts reduced health care costs by 30.5, 28.5, and 13.6 percent, respectively. Discuss the possible justification of each of the three main types of efforts to reduce the cost of health care. Are they fair? Which should be emphasized the most?

NEW TERMS AND CONCEPTS

Employee Benefits
ERISA
ADEA
Civil Rights Act of 1974
Health Maintenance
  Organization Act of 1973
Principles of Group
  Selection
Participating Plans
Experience Rating
Group Term Life Insurance
Conversion Clause
Survivor Income Benefit
  Insurance
Accidental Death and
  Dismemberment
  Insurance (A.D.&D.)
Group Credit Life and
  Health Insurance
Health Insurance
Hospitalization Contract
Surgical Expense Contract
Regular Medical Contract
Major Medical Contract

Disability Income Insurance
Dental Insurance
Inpatient Benefit
Outpatient Benefit
Major Medical Insurance
Flat-Dollar Deductible
Initial Deductible
Corridor Deductible
Coinsurance Deductible
Short-Term Disability Plan
Long-Term Disability Plan
Coordination of Benefits
  (COB)
Blue Cross-Blue Shield
Preferred Provider
  Organization (PPO)
Health Maintenance
  Organization (HMO)
Medicare
Health Care Cost
  Containment
Second-Opinion-for-Surgical-
  Expense Insurance

NOTES

1 *Bulletin of the Commission on Insurance Terminology,* American Risk and Insurance Association (May, 1965), p. 1.

2 *Bulletin of the Commission on Insurance Terminology* (October, 1965), p. 7.

3 *Source Book of Health Insurance Data 1984–1985,* p. 9.

13 EMPLOYEE BENEFITS: RETIREMENT PLANS

After studying this chapter, you should be able to:

1. Describe the role of employer-sponsored retirement plans.
2. Identify the requirements for tax-qualification of group pension plans.
3. State the differences between defined contribution and defined benefit plans.
4. List the advantages of trusteed and insured pension plans.
5. Explain how insurers compete with banks for pension business.
6. Discuss how inflation may be overcome in retirement planning.
7. State the limitations and strengths of the variable annuity.
8. Describe the value of a tax shelter in long-term savings.
9. Explain how dollar cost averaging can be used.
10. Explain the use of 401(k), Keogh, and IRAs in retirement planning.

A major class of employee benefits concerns various types of employer-sponsored plans for employee retirement. It is important to gain an appreciation of these plans to be able to coordinate their benefits with other savings programs and with the benefits provided by Social Security. In this chapter we explore two main kinds of retirement plans: employer-sponsored "qualified" pension plans, and tax-advantaged individual pension plans that are usually made available to employee groups. The second group includes such plans as tax-sheltered annuities, self-employed (Keogh) plans, individual retirement accounts (IRAs), and Section 401(k) and 403(b) plans. Also discussed are various types of insurer-sponsored retirement products for individuals.

GROWTH OF PRIVATE PENSIONS

Studies conducted by the U.S. Chamber of Commerce reveal that assets and persons covered by private pensions have increased steadily, especially since the end of World War II. In 1984 over 35 million persons (over half of the labor force) were covered by qualified pensions, and assets committed to pay pension benefits had reached the level of $932 billion. About a third of the assets were handled through insured plans and two-thirds through noninsured plans managed by banks and trust companies. As shown in Table 13-1, over the period 1974–1984, as measured by assets committed to them, insured plans experienced a growth of 409 percent. The number of persons covered by insured plans increased 148 percent.

One way to think about retirement plans and judge their relative role in enabling workers to achieve retirement goals is to consider the various sources of income typically available to employees to build a program of retirement security. Figure 13-1 presents a diagram of personal financial security in retirement. At its base is shown how nearly everyone depends on a "floor of protection" provided by Social Security benefits. On top of this lies the layer of employer-sponsored pension or retirement plans. These two are supplemented with a variety of individually planned retirement programs and funded through such means as IRAs or other tax-sheltered plans. Many basic tax-advantaged plans described earlier are augmented by personal savings or investments which have been accumulated outside a tax shelter. Finally, for about a third of the people, by choice or necessity, active work in employment will be undertaken.

Employer-Sponsored Retirement Plans

Private retirement or pension plans sponsored by employers are discussed in this section, and individual plans are discussed in the second half of the chapter. As noted, employer-sponsored plans cover over half the labor force in the United States, and the percentage is growing steadily.

Objectives. Most employer-sponsored retirement plans are set up with certain objectives in mind, such as to attract and retain valuable workers and to increase employee morale and productivity. To accomplish its goal, the plan aims at providing a reasonable living standard to employees in retirement. The plan may also be designed to restore a certain percentage of the employee's income in retirement, such as 60 or 70 percent, counting Social Security. The benefits will vary according to the employee's income and years of service. The employer plan may count other sources of income in meeting these objectives, such as income expected from Social Security. (See Chapter 25.) Usually the plan has certain eligibility standards for

Table 13-1 Major Private Pension Plans in the United States, 1984

Insured Plans	Assets (000,000's)			Number of Persons Covered (000's)		
	1974	1984	% Increase	1974	1984	% Increase
Group annuities[1]	$46,825	$229,490	397	10,555	25,390	140
Individual policy pension plans[2]	5,200	8,435	62	1,810	1,705	(6)
H.R. 10 (Keogh) plans	925	3,250	251	345	465	34
Tax-sheltered annuities	2,250	23,895	962	770	2,860	123
Individual retirement accounts (IRAs)	—	12,550	—	—	3,150	—
Terminally funded group plans	1,450	9,440	551	110	415	—
Other	4,125	—		—	—	—
Total insured	$60,775	$309,080	409	14,270	35,510	148
Trusteed Plans	n.a.	$623,348		n.a.	n.a.	

[1]Includes immediate participation guarantee and deposit administration plans.
[2]Includes group permanent and profit-sharing plans.
Source: *Life Insurance Fact Book Update 1985*, pp. 22–23; and *Life Insurance Fact Book 1975*, p. 39. Percentages calculated.

coverage, such as the requirement that the worker reach a certain age or serve a stated number of years, as a condition of earning retirement benefits.

Qualifying the Plan for Tax Deductibility

In setting objectives and other features of the plan, consideration is given to making the plan qualify for favorable income tax treatment. If the plan meets various requirements, it is said to be qualified. Advantages of having a plan qualified include the following:

1. Contributions to the plan by the employer, subject to certain limits, are deductible for income taxes.
2. The value of the benefits provided by the plan will not constitute currently taxable income to employees.

Figure 13–1
Sources of Retirement
Security

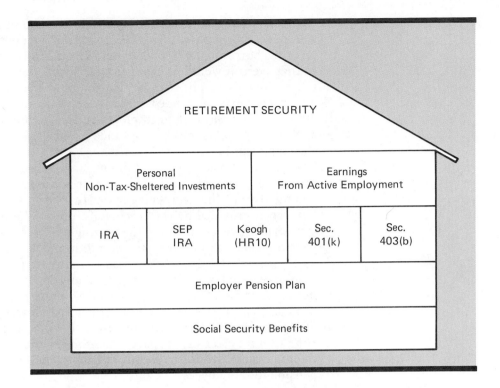

RETIREMENT SECURITY

Personal Non-Tax-Sheltered Investments			Earnings From Active Employment	
IRA	SEP IRA	Keogh (HR10)	Sec. 401(k)	Sec. 403(b)
Employer Pension Plan				
Social Security Benefits				

3. Investment earnings on funds set up to provide pension benefits are not subject to taxation as they accumulate.

The practical effect of having a plan qualified is that all of the funds contributed to the plan "go to work" in providing future benefits. If a given dollar spent for the plan were subject to prior income taxation, only a little over half would be left after taxes. Thus, the future benefits would be greatly reduced, or alternatively, a given benefit would be much more costly than would otherwise be the case. The law does not require employers to establish pension plans, but if they are to receive tax advantages, they must meet certain requirements. Because of the advantages, most private pension plans are so designed that they are tax qualified.

The main requirements specified in the law for qualification are found in ERISA and in the IRS tax codes and regulations. The chief purpose of the requirements is to assure that the proposed plan is reasonable, fair, nondiscriminatory, and so designed that the employee's chances of actually receiving a pension under its provisions are good. The major requirements are as follows:

1. The plan must be in writing and be communicated to employees. Oral statements by an employer that a pension will be provided are not sufficient to justify a tax deduction for contributions to the plan.

2. The benefits of the plan must be definitely determinable and must be exclusively for the employees. Thus, an employer may not set up a plan and then borrow back all of the plan's assets for use in the business, for in that event it would be interpreted that the plan was set up more for the employer's benefit than for the benefit of the employee.

3. The plan must be funded in advance. It is not acceptable for an employer to wait until an employee retires before setting aside funds to pay the pension; rather, the funds must be set aside in advance as the employee earns future benefits.

4. The plan must meet certain minimum standards of vesting. This means that once a worker is covered for a specific number of years (most commonly ten), that worker is entitled to the benefits of the plan which have been provided by the employer's funds. Workers who end their employment before meeting the vesting requirements will receive no pension benefits from the plan upon retirement.

5. The plan must not unfairly discriminate in favor of highly paid employees, such as officers of the company. For example, the plan may not be so structured that highly paid workers receive a much larger pension in proportion to their direct pay than lower paid workers.

6. The plan must be permanent in nature. If a plan is terminated a short time after it is started, the government may believe it was started only to obtain a tax deduction for the employer and not really to provide a pension for employees.

7. The plan may not contain a provision that requires an employee to retire before age 70. Certain other eligibility requirements must also be observed, such as those requiring coverage for older workers hired within five years of the normal retirement age.

8. The plan must contain a provision that will provide half of the pension to which an employee is entitled to the worker's surviving spouse. For example, if the employee were entitled to a pension of $1,000 a month, the plan must provide $500 a month to the surviving spouse unless a prior written request is made otherwise by the employee and the spouse.

9. Limits exist as to maximum amounts that are tax deductible.

10. Pensions paid under defined benefit plans must be insured by an agency of the federal government.

Major Pension Design Decisions

In addition to qualifying the plan for tax purposes, decisions must be made as to the type of benefit formula to be used, how much of the plan will be in the form of group plans and how much in the form of individual plans, and whether the plan will be insured or handled by a trustee.

Benefit Formulas. Two types of benefit formulas are used in qualified employer pension plans: defined benefit and defined contribution. In a **defined benefit plan,** the benefit amount upon retirement is defined, and the exact amounts needed to pay for the benefit are left undetermined. In a **defined contribution plan,** the amounts to be contributed to the plan are defined, and the exact amount of the ultimate benefit is left undetermined. For example, in a defined benefit plan, the benefit may be stated as $300 a year or some other amount, such as one percent of wages, for each year of service. Thus, if the benefit were $300 a year, an employee with 30 years' service would receive a pension of $9,000 a year (30 × 300). The sum of all the contributions on this employee's behalf would have to be enough to pay for a pension of $9,000 a year.

If the plan is a defined contribution plan, the employer may decide to contribute a given percentage of payroll, say 7 percent, to fund the plan. The ultimate benefit will depend on how much has been accumulated for employees at retirement. This in turn will depend on a number of factors, such as the investment earnings on the fund, how many years the employee works, salary levels, labor turnover, and mortality and morbidity rates.

Some employers tend to favor defined contribution plans because it is easier to budget the definite costs they involve and because certain other risks are minimized. Employees generally prefer defined benefit plans because it is easier to estimate the size of the ultimate pension to be paid. Furthermore, benefits in this type of plan are usually tied to earnings, and since earnings are usually adjusted for changes in the cost of living, the amount of the pension is more likely to maintain customary living standards when the employee retires.

Under a defined contribution plan, the risk of having sufficient funds on hand to provide an adequate pension falls on the employee. This stems from the fact that investment earnings importantly influence the ultimate size of the pension fund, and no guarantees exist as to how large this fund will be at retirement due to uncertainty about the performance of the securities markets over a long period of years.

An example will illustrate the differences described. Assume that an employee earns an average of $25,000 annually for 20 years. The goal of the plan is to restore between 25 and 30 percent of the employee's retirement income under a defined contribution approach. Suppose that the employer is willing to contribute 7 percent of payroll, or $1,750, to a fund for the employee's retirement. At an average interest return of 6 percent, the fund would grow to $64,375, and at 7 percent to $71,750. These sums would produce a monthly retirement income of approximately $536 and $598, respectively, between 26 and 29 percent of the employee's final pay. Thus, an increase in the average interest return of one percent increases the ultimate retirement income approximately 12 percent. A typical employee might not be able to make the above estimates easily and would be uncertain as to their ultimate benefit. If the plan were using a defined benefit formula of, say, 1.4 percent per year of service, the 20 years of service translates to 28 percent of the final average salary. Applying this figure to the $25,000 final salary assumed in this case produces an estimated retirement income of $7,000, or $583 monthly. The employee is more likely to understand the defined benefit method than the defined contribution method.

Group vs. Individual. Another decision in benefit planning is to decide what share of the total retirement benefit objectives will be provided through group plans and what share through individual plans. For example, the plan may be built around Social Security, which is calculated to restore, say, 30 percent of an employee's preretirement income. The employer's qualified plan might be designed to restore another 25 percent, leaving it to the employee to set up other means, such as IRAs or Section 401(k) plans, to supply any additional benefit he or she may require. Thus, if an employee wants to retire on 75 percent of the preretirement income, a "gap" of 20 percent still exists. As shown in Table 13–1, the number of families setting up IRA or Keogh plans and tax-sheltered annuities is increasing rapidly.

Insured vs. Trusteed. An important planning decision is to decide on the agency to be used to fund the pension plan. The funding agent can be a trustee or an insurance company. As already noted, advance funding is now a requirement for qualifying the plan for income tax deductibility. Table 13–1 reveals that two-thirds of all pension assets are handled by banks or trustees and one-third by insurance companies.

A trust fund plan is one in which the employer places monies to pay plan benefits with a trustee, usually a bank, which manages and invests the pension assets. The trustee pays benefits to retirees or other beneficiaries. Usually, assets are not allocated to particular employees, but rather are held and managed for the benefit of all employees as a group. If the employer becomes dissatisfied with the performance of a trustee, it is relatively simple for the employer to switch pension assets to another trustee. The main advantage of a trusteed plan is its flexibility. The trustee has a wide range of investments in which pension assets may be placed and can be given instructions regarding how the investments will be made, how the benefits will be paid out, and how eligibility and other provisions of the plan will be administered. The employer also has flexibility in making contributions to the trust fund; in a bad year contributions can be reduced, and in a good year they can be increased, subject to some limitations. However, the trustee does not guarantee investment results, safety of principal of the assets invested, or mortality rates assumed in pension calculations. In contrast, insured plans frequently guarantee a minimum interest, safety of principal, and maximum mortality costs.

At one time, trustees had an advantage over life insurance companies as pension managers because they could invest in common stocks while life insurers could not. Subsequent legislation removed this advantage, and life insurers now compete on about equal terms with trustees for pension business. Thus, life insurers now set up what are called "separate accounts" to handle pension plans. The separate account is not commingled with general insurance company assets, but rather is kept apart so that each employer's plan which is being administered can be accounted for individually.

Insured Pension Plans

One useful way of classifying insured pension plans is on the basis of whether the plan offers benefits to employees identified individually, or whether the plan covers the employee group as a whole. The first category is called **allocated,** and the second **unallocated,** pension plans.

Allocated. In allocated pension plans, a record is kept of the account of each employee. When the employee retires, the pension amount is determined by the size of the employee's account. A common example is the **deferred annuity** plan, in which a deferred annuity is purchased each year for the employee. The pension is equal to the sum of the deferred annuities purchased during the worker's career. For example, assume that an employee earns $25,000 a year and that the benefit formula is one percent of wages per year. Then the employee earns a benefit of $250 for each year, and a deferred annuity is purchased in an amount necessary to provide a pension at retirement of $250. As the worker's income increases, the amount of the pension benefit rises correspondingly. Thus, if the worker's income rises to $30,000, an annuity benefit of $300 a year at retirement is purchased. The worker's ultimate pension is the sum of all the individual annuities that have been purchased on his or her behalf.

Another example of an allocated plan is the **individual policy pension trust,** a plan often used by smaller employers. In this plan, separate insurance policies are purchased for each employee and placed in a trust for his or her benefit at retirement. Although a life insurance policy is the funding instrument in this case, the cash values are arranged so as to be enough to provide the promised pension. For example, a retirement income policy offering $10 monthly for each $1,000 of face amount may be used. If the pension is to be $250 a month, 25 units with a face value of $25,000 will be accumulated during the worker's career.

In each of the allocated funding instruments mentioned, the rights of the worker to retirement benefits are determined by the plan's vesting provisions. If the worker terminates the job before benefits are vested, all or part of the benefits are lost. In this event, the worker is often given the right to purchase the policies previously purchased for the accumulated cash value. If the termination occurs after the benefits have been vested, the trustee holds the policies until retirement and the worker receives the pension amount at that time. Figure 13–2 diagrams the major kinds of insured pension plans.

Unallocated Plans. An unallocated funding instrument is one in which no monies are accrued for individual employees during their careers; rather, the fund is kept in trust for the employees as a group, and at retirement the pension is paid from the unallocated fund. In some cases a separate

**Figure 13–2
Types of Insured
Pension Plans**

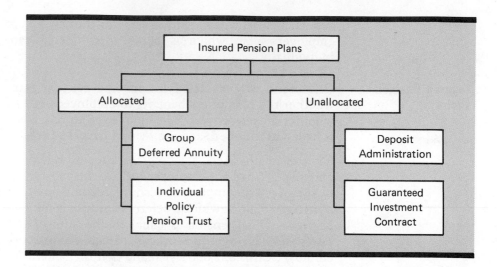

insured annuity may be purchased on behalf of the employee upon retirement. These annuities are referred to as "terminal funded group plans" in Table 13–1.

The unallocated fund is considered to be a more flexible funding instrument than allocated plans. The employer may vary the amount of contributions as business conditions vary. Since no individual policies are purchased, there is no need to cancel and rewrite policies as employees are replaced. Almost any benefit formula can be accommodated with an unallocated fund. The insurance company will guarantee some minimum annuity and interest rate to be applied once the worker retires.

The amount contributed to an unallocated fund, sometimes called **deposit administration,** depends on such factors as interest earnings, employee turnover, mortality and morbidity rates, adjustments made in the benefit formula, inflation, and salary changes. An actuary periodically examines the plan and makes recommendations regarding the adequacy of the fund to meet the future pension obligations to workers. Certification by the actuary is required for continued tax qualification.

A popular type of insured plan is called the **guaranteed investment contract** (GIC). In this unallocated plan, the insurer accepts for investment a given amount of funds at a guaranteed interest return and principal amount. Guarantees may also be extended to future contributions to the plan. If the plan is participating, workers' contributions may be placed, at the worker's option, in one or more separate investment funds, such as a mutual fund, the employer's stock, or a bond fund.

Integration. The law permits a private pension plan to be coordinated with Social Security. Legal provisions under which this is done are called **integration** rules. The general effect of integration is to permit the employer to "take credit" for the taxes paid under Social Security on behalf of employees. Since Social Security restores a larger proportion of the lower paid worker's wage at retirement than of the higher paid worker's wage, integration rules permit a private pension plan to contribute more to higher paid workers than to lower paid workers to help restore the balance. In this way, all workers can receive a total retirement benefit from both Social Security and the private pension that is aimed at restoring about the same percentage of their retirement income. Detailed explanation of integration rules, which are complex, is beyond the scope of this text.

Retirement Insurance

An employer-sponsored pension plan using defined benefit formulas must be protected by the Pension Benefit Guarantee Corporation (PBGC), an agency of the federal government. PBGC was established under the provisions of ERISA in 1974. Employers pay an annual premium for each employee. If the plan is terminated by the employer, a report must be made to PBGC, and if funds are insufficient to cover future obligations to the employee, the PBGC will take over the plan and pay the employee the promised benefit, subject to certain limitations. In this way, added retirement security is provided for tax-qualified private pension plans.

Contribution Limits

Tax laws limit the maximum amounts which can be contributed by the employer and deducted for income tax purposes. The 1982 tax act limited annual contributions to a participant's account in a defined contribution plan to the lesser of 25 percent of payroll or $30,000. If the plan uses a defined benefit formula, the employer may not promise more than 100 percent of salary in the highest three years or $90,000 a year, whichever is less. The $90,000 is reduced if the retirement benefit commences before age 65. After 1986, the $90,000 may be adjusted for inflation. Special limits exist if an employee is covered by both a defined contribution and a defined benefit plan.

INFLATION PROTECTION

The need to protect the value of a pension from being eroded due to inflation is well recognized. Even though inflation rates have been reduced to about four percent annually from levels that exceeded 15 percent in the 1970s, the problem is still severe. As shown in Table 13–2, if a pension

**Table 13–2
Effect of Inflation on Retirement Income—Real Value of a $10,000 Annuity**

	Annual Inflation Rate		
Years	4%	6%	10%
5	$8,219	$7,473	$6,209
10	6,756	5,584	3,855
15	5,552	4,173	2,394
20	4,564	3,118	1,486

Source: Calculated by the authors. See present value tables in the Appendix for other assumed rates of inflation.

starts out at $10,000 a year and inflation is four percent, the purchasing power of this pension will be reduced to $8,219 after five years, $6,756 after ten years, and $4,563 after 15 years. If the inflation rate rises to six percent, the erosion is even more severe. Since the average period during which a retiree may depend on a pension is about 15 years, it is obvious that attention needs to be directed at the problem if a lifetime of planning and saving for an adequate and comfortable retirement period is to be successful.

Several methods of planning for inflation protection are used. During the employee's active career, defined contribution-type pension plans may receive some protection through investment policies aimed at offsetting inflation. Thus, funds may be invested in common stocks selected to increase in value as the general price level increases. In the case of defined benefit plans, the worker receives some protection during working years because the pensions are linked to wages, which, in turn, are usually adjusted regularly for inflation.

The situation is different once the worker has retired. Most plans are not protected at all from inflation once the pension has begun. Some employers make periodic adjustments in pensions paid so that retirees receive the same or similar increases that are awarded to active workers. Other employers make annual adjustments to correspond to changes in the cost of living, usually with some annual limit, or "cap." That part of a worker's retirement income composed of Social Security is subject to annual adjustments for inflation if the cost of living increases by three percent or more.

Although insurance companies have developed other approaches to help solve the inflation problem, no completely satisfactory solution for handling inflation has yet been devised.

INSURANCE-SPONSORED PLANS

Conventional life insurance policies with cash value features, such as whole life, endowments, and universal life, generally do not offer long-term savers protection against inflation. To the extent that insurers earn interest in excess of levels guaranteed or assumed, policyholders may benefit through dividends, thus receiving some additional income, Still, the investment returns in life insurance are fixed in nature because assets are invested in bonds, mortgages, and other similar securities, the values of which are expressed in a fixed number of dollars with stated interest returns that usually do not change.

In recent years, however, recognizing the need for inflation protection, insurers have developed new approaches which attempt to overcome the problem. These approaches are aimed at long-term retirement planning. The following sections discuss variable annuities, mutual funds with accompanying term life insurance, and other individual tax-sheltered plans, all of which may offer some inflation protection as well as tax shelter. Most of these are offered both on a group and on an individual basis.

**The Variable
Annuity**

An ingenious scheme giving inflation protection for the retiree is the
variable annuity.[1] The objectives of the variable annuity are to offer
a method by which the long-term saver may accumulate retirement funds
in **equities**—securities the value of which are thought to follow the
fluctuations in the general price level.

The basic idea is that if the general price level rises over the
accumulation period, the value of savings will also rise, thus maintaining
their purchasing power at a fairly constant level. If the general price level
falls, the value of the savings will also fall, but their purchasing power will
still remain fairly constant. In other words, the variable annuity attempts
to provide funds for a retirement income which would have a varying dollar
value but reasonably constant purchasing power. Regular annuities
provide an income with a fixed-dollar value but varying purchasing power.
It is presumed that it is more desirable for the retired person to have an

income with a value that in real terms is fairly constant than to have an income with a fixed amount but a fluctuating real value.

Although the purchaser of a variable annuity accepts the risk that personal savings and income may decline if the stock market falls, the insurer accepts the mortality risk. The insurer guarantees some minimum rate at which the annuity will be paid, and the annuitant cannot outlive this income. Thus, the variable annuitant is assured a lifetime income that should be high enough to offset inflation and to maintain a standard of living at the level of the time of retirement.

As shown in Table 13-3, in 1984 there were nearly three million persons covered by variable annuity plans in the United States. Many of these plans were based on common stocks and fixed income securities combined; most were group plans. Individuals generally still preferred the more traditional fixed-dollar annuities, however, since the conventional annuities in force numbered 9.5 million, about three times that of variable annuities. Furthermore, annualized income from insured variable annuities was only $382 million in 1984, compared to about $19.5 billion in conventional annuities.

How the Variable Annuity Works. In practice, the details of the variable annuity are somewhat involved, but the general way in which they operate may be described by an example. Suppose that A purchased a variable annuity contract in 1950 at age 45 and that annual premium payments of $1,000 were made until A reached age 65. Each year the premiums were invested by the insurer in common stocks. Specific stocks were bought, not for A's account, but for the account of the insurer, and A now owns a small fraction of every security owned by the insurer. Thus, A owns a cross section of a broadly diversified common stock portfolio, similar to the shares in a mutual fund.

During the 20 years that A paid premiums, a total of $20,000 was deposited. If the annual premium of $1,000 had been saved at 5 percent compound interest, the value of the fund when A became 65 would be approximately $34,720. However, let us assume that due to inflation the value of the stocks is $56,600. This represents nearly perfect adjustment

Table 13-3
Insured Variable
Annuity Plans, 1984
(Dollar figures in millions)

	Group	Individual	Total
Variable			
Number of plans	38,730	—	—
Number of persons	1,802,460	1,175,040	2,997,500
Assets	$6,815	$6,471	$13,286
Annualized Income			
Variable annuities*	$338	$44	$382

*Includes income which is payable on either a variable-income basis or a fixed-income basis.
Source: *Life Insurance Fact Book Update 1985*, p. 16.

to the rise in the Consumer Price Index: the value of A's stocks, after depreciation for the declining value of the dollar, is about $35,000 in terms of 1950 purchasing power.[2]

Under the variable annuity plan, A has 63 percent more funds than would have been available at a fixed interest rate, provided that the stock market kept pace exactly with the cost of living. (The Standard and Poor's composite index of stock prices increased from 18.4 to 75.72 as of July, 1970, an increase of 311 percent.) If A had used a traditional annuity for a savings plan and had earned 5 percent on the funds, a monthly life income (straight life annuity basis) of about $300 could be expected from the $35,000 fund.

Under the variable annuity, the insurer would express the $56,600 in terms of an annuity of so many units per month for life. The initial value of these units can be any arbitrary amount, say $1. Then A would have 56,000 units credit. Assuming an annuity rate identical to that which applied to the fixed-dollar annuity in the above example, A would be entitled to about 452.8 units per month for life, with an initial monthly value of $452.80. If the stock market rose 3 percent in the second year of A's retirement, each would be worth $1.03 instead of $1.00, and A's monthly retirement income in the second year would rise 3 percent to $466.38. If in the third year the stock market should fall 10 percent, so would A's annuity. This is true regardless of what would happen to consumer prices or to living standards.[3]

Another way of contrasting a variable annuity with a fixed annuity is to consider the fixed annuity as a contract that pays a fixed number of dollars to the annuitant for life. The variable annuity, on the other hand, pays a fixed *percentage* of a fund monthly for life. For example, if the annuity costs $10,000, and the annuitant's life expectancy is such that $100 a month can be paid for life under a fixed annuity, the variable annuity might agree to pay 1 percent per month of a value of a fund which amounts to $10,000 initially, but which varies with the stock market over the retirement period. If the value of the securities rises or falls, the *amount* paid to the variable annuitant changes proportionately.

The variable annuity concept assumes that as inflation rates rise, stock prices and returns will tend to rise correspondingly on the average—although perhaps not in every year. Careful studies of the relationship of inflation and stock prices, however, cast doubt on this assumption. Frank Reilly studied five periods of inflation within the period 1941–1973 and concluded that common stock returns adjusted for price level changes actually went *down*, not up, during inflation.[4] Stock returns tended to rise only in periods when investors believed that inflation rates were stable or would decline, and that corporate earnings would not fall.

Presumably, proponents of variable annuities believe that insurers have sufficient skill to manage a stock portfolio successfully and can offset losses to investors from inflation.

Over the period 1950–1985, major stock market price indexes have not risen nearly as much as consumer prices. For example, the New York Stock Exchange Composite Index has risen from 50 to 120, with interim declines as low as 36. Over this same period, the consumer price index has increased nearly fivefold. The question arises, "How has the variable annuity worked out?" Some evidence demonstrates the potential value of the variable annuity in assisting the long-term saver in building a retirement income above that which would normally be attained using more conventional methods. Examples of such evidence are described in the following paragraphs.

College Retirement Equities Fund. The oldest variable annuity plan in operation is that offered by the College Retirement Equities Fund (CREF), a subsidiary of the Teachers Insurance and Annuity Association. This is a life insurance company chartered in 1950 in New York that distributes insurance and annuities primarily to college personnel. The 1952 value of CREF's accumulation unit was $10.52. (See Figure 13–3.)

The unit value reached a high of $53.25 in 1972. Over the period 1952–1972 the average annual rate of increase in CREF was 8.45 percent, but due to the stock market decline in 1972–1981, the average increase was reduced to 5.4 percent for the whole period 1952–1981.[5] The CREF unit dropped from $53.25 to $48.33, a loss of 9 percent in nine years, 1972–1981. This trend demonstrates the dramatic declines, as well as increases, in retirement benefits that are possible in variable annuities. By the end of 1985, CREF had recovered to $85.78, so that over the total period 1952–1985 the average annual compound rate of return was 6.57 percent.

A considerably better total average annual return is shown by CREF if, as is the usual case, the saver reinvests dividends in additional units each year. The 1985 value of an initial $10.52 unit, together with all accumulated dividends, was $254.73, equal to an annual average return of 10.10 percent. Over this same period, the average annual rate of increase in the consumer price index was 4.7 percent. (The CPI increased from 72 to 326 over that period.) Thus, the CREF variable annuity plan more than offset inflation over a 33-year period.

The CREF annuity units, reflecting actual payments to annuitants, went down in 10 of the 33 years between 1952 and 1985. The worst decline occurred during the period 1972–1977, when the saver's income dropped about 47 percent, just when consumer prices were surging ahead. After 1974 the unit increased steadily with only minor declines through 1985.

It may be concluded that on the average, the long-run saver may expect somewhere between an 8 and 10 percent return in a variable annuity, subject to considerable fluctuations from year to year. This return corresponds roughly to long-term stock market returns.[6] Yet it seems clear that the long-term saver should not rely solely upon the variable annuity, but rather should hedge investments by placing at least a portion of annual

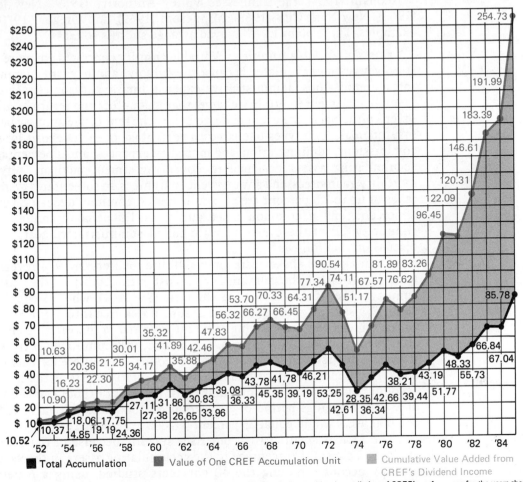

Total Accumulation   Value of One CREF Accumulation Unit   Cumulative Value Added from CREF's Dividend Income

NOTE: This graph shows CREF's past investment experience and should not be considered a prediction of CREF's performance for the years ahead.

retirement savings into fixed obligations such as bonds, mortgages, or traditional annuities.

Commercial Life Insurers. Approximately 75 life insurers have entered the variable annuity field in recent years. One of the first was the Variable Annuity Life Insurance Company (VALIC), organized in 1955, followed by leading companies such as Bankers Life of Iowa, Equitable Life Assurance Society of the U.S., Travelers, Prudential, Metropolitan Life, and Aetna. These companies have produced generally satisfactory results.[7] VALIC began writing variable annuities in 1956.

Other Variable Annuity Plans. A number of governmental agencies have established operational variable annuity plans for their retirees. Wisconsin (1957), the Tennessee Valley Authority (1959), New Jersey (1963), New York City (1968), Minnesota (1969), and Oregon (1970) are examples. These plans have enjoyed average success so far.

Costs of Variable Annuities. Variable annuity contracts are more than simply investment vehicles, because they involve annuity rent guarantees, sales commissions, administrative expense limits, and sometimes a life insurance element (mortality charge) that guarantees the return of all of a saver's principal in the event of death before the rent of the annuity begins. Insurers make two types of charges: a percentage of each deposit for sales commissions, administration, and mortality expenses; and a percentage of accumulating assets designed to cover investment advisory services, mortality guarantees, and annuity rent guarantees. In some states premium taxes of up to 2.5 percent are also collected. A common deposit charge is 6 percent, and a common asset charge is 1.0 percent annually. For simplicity, all of these expenses are called administrative costs in the discussion that follows.

An analysis of these costs among 40 life insurers in 1974 revealed a wide variation in the administrative cost ratio (ACR) of the variable annuity.[8] The ACR is defined as the ratio $(S - A)/A$, where S equals the value of a savings account at some assumed risk-free interest rate, and A is the value of the same savings amount invested in the variable annuity after the deduction of all charges. The balance is accumulated at the same interest rate assumed for the separate account. The difference between S and A represents the interest-adjusted administrative costs on the assumed account balance after varying numbers of years. For example, if the value of S after a savings period of 20 years is $20,000, and the value of A is $16,000, ACR would equal 25 percent (20,000 − 16,000)/16,000.

The ACR is small at first, but rises steadily because of the effect of applying a constant percentage to the accumulating assets in the variable annuity account. Among the 40 contracts studied, using a 6 percent interest assumption, administrative cost ratios after 10 years ranged from 7.5 to 28.1 percent; after 20 years the ACR ranged from 9.6 to 45.7 percent. The median cost among 40 insurers after 20 years was 26 percent of the account balance. In other words, if it were not for all expenses and annuity benefits charged for by insurers, a long-term saver would have approximately 26 percent more money in the savings account. Of course, with a savings account, the saver would not have enjoyed the advantages of the various services and guarantees offered under the variable annuity. It is up to the saver to determine the value of the costs. The analysis demonstrates that it is worthwhile to shop for variable annuities carefully.

Tax-Sheltered Annuities (TSAs). Many buyers of variable annuities may purchase these products without paying federal income taxes on the premiums. (See tax rules below.) Taxes are only deferred, not avoided, as the taxpayer must ultimately pay taxes when the annuity begins. The annuitant who purchases the contract under tax shelter obtains a substantial advantage that helps offset some of the rather high administrative costs that are often charged. To illustrate, if a person is in a 50 percent combined federal and state income tax bracket, $1 used for the variable annuity only costs $0.50 in current out-of-pocket expense. The taxpayer also shelters accumulating dividends and interest returns from current taxes. Tax shelter amounts to receiving an interest-free loan from the government on amounts that otherwise would be payable in current taxes.

To illustrate the value of tax shelter, suppose, using common interest assumptions, that Mr. Case is in the 25 percent tax bracket and wishes to save $100 a month for 20 years. Interest of 8 percent annually is available. Under tax shelter the entire $100 may be saved at 8 percent. The savings will amount to $58,902 in 20 years. In a taxed investment, on the other hand, only $75 will be available because Mr. Case must first pay $25 in income taxes. Furthermore, only 6 percent will be earned, since the 8 percent annual interest is also subject to income taxes of 25 percent. Accumulating $75 a month for 20 years at 6 percent yields a savings fund of $34,653, which is only 59 percent of the fund available under tax shelter.

The actual amount of the tax advantage depends on the taxpayer's wage level and consequent tax bracket, both currently and in retirement. It is influenced also by the rate of return earned on the investment (after paying administrative costs), and the inflation rate, which influences the wage level and resulting tax rate.

One study has demonstrated that under most reasonable assumptions regarding rates of investment return, wage levels, and inflation rates, the value of tax shelter is substantial when compared to a taxed investment. In one example, for a person 35, earning $30,000 a year, saving for 30 years to age 65, and receiving an average annual investment return of 8 percent with inflation averaging 5 percent, the amounts available at retirement, after paying all applicable income taxes then due, ranged from 44 to 50 percent more than a taxed investment, depending on the size of the loading factor.[9]

It should be noted that tax shelter is not an exclusive advantage of variable annuities; other investments also qualify for tax shelter. (See the discussion below.)

The Risk. It is clear that there is a significant risk to the buyer of variable annuities. As the 1972–1981 stock market experience indicates, the value of the variable annuity unit can go down more rapidly than it goes up. Furthermore, for the saver to come out ahead of a regular savings plan with a fixed rate of interest, it is necessary to have superior investment performance to offset the administrative costs.

One of the ways in which the risk of the variable annuity is reduced is through dollar cost averaging. **Dollar cost averaging** refers to a plan under which a regular and fixed amount is invested in securities at differing prices over a period of time. Using this method, the saver automatically acquires more shares when prices are low than when prices are high. Under this method the *average cost* of the purchases is always less than the average price at which purchases are made.

To illustrate dollar cost averaging, take a simple example of a person saving $1,000 regularly each year for three years in a given stock. Assume the price of the security to be $100 the first year, $50 the second year, and $100 the third year. The saver would acquire 10 shares the first year, 20 shares the second, and 10 shares the third year. At the end of the period the investor has saved $3,000 and now has 40 shares, each worth $100, for a total value of $4,000, at an average cost of $75 ($3,000 ÷ 40). The average price paid was $83.33 [($100 + $50 + $100)/3]. Dollar cost average does not guarantee the success of an investment plan, of course, since if the average price continues to decline, the investor will lose part of the savings.

Furthermore, if the stock market declines rapidly and recovers slowly, which is not unusual, there are more periods with relatively high prices than there are with low prices. A regular saver would thus not obtain new shares automatically at the lowest prices. However, if prices fluctuate and end up the period approximately the same as at the beginning, the investor will gain. As the above example shows, the saver was $1,000 ahead at the end of the three years, even though the price of the shares was $100 at both the beginning and the end. The variable annuity plan thus enables the investor to use the dollar cost averaging principle to compound the value of the investment. It also encourages regularity in the investment program, a principle that must be strictly observed if the benefits of dollar cost averaging are to be achieved.

Arguments for the Variable Annuity. We may summarize the chief arguments for the variable annuity as follows:

1. It enables the saver to obtain some protection against the long-run decline in the purchasing power of the dollar, both during the saving years and during retirement years.
2. It permits the saver to share in the economic growth of the nation to the extent that increased productivity is reflected in the stock market. In this way, the saver obtains participation in higher living standards as well as protection against lower living standards due to inflation.
3. There may be some income and other tax advantages to the variable annuity that are not available in ordinary mutual fund investments.
4. The saver may protect a long-term savings plan against adverse changes in expenses and mortality charges.

Arguments against the Variable Annuity. Opponents of the variable annuity stress the following arguments:

1. Due to an unfamiliarity with the basic assumptions of a variable annuity, savers might be misled into believing that the value of the investment will always rise. If the stock market declines, they might become discouraged and drop the plan, thus losing any possible advantages from dollar cost averaging.
2. Since it is generally recognized that the stock market is an imperfect instrument in measuring changes in purchasing power, there will be some periods when the value of the annuity may bear no resemblance to actual changes in prices. An annuitant who had relied exclusively on this method as a way of retiring would face a serious dilemma if, for example, prices rose while the stock market fell, as has happened several times in the past.
3. If the annuitant retires at the time of a severe stock market slump, not enough may be realized to retire on, and thus the annuitant would suffer loss of substantial principal.
4. The administrative costs of the variable annuity are substantial over a period of time.
5. There is no guarantee that all insurers who offer variable annuities will be able to achieve satisfactory investment results even in times when the general stock market index moves upward. Judging from the spotty record of the managers of mutual funds, who face the task of continuous investment of shareholders' funds, largely in common stocks, some variable annuity plans would not achieve results as good as those achieved by stock market averages.

In assessing these arguments, it should be observed that if one is persuaded that investing all funds in the variable annuity is too risky, one may hedge by allocating a portion of savings to fixed-dollar benefit annuities or fixed-dollar savings during the accumulation period or the distribution period, or both. Most life insurers offer both types of savings plans and permit the saver to change allocations periodically.

Mutual Funds and Term Insurance Combination

In recent years there has been considerable interest in a plan designed by some life insurance companies and mutual fund managers to combine regular investment in mutual common stock fund plans with term life insurance. The saver purchases shares in a mutual fund and at the same time buys term life insurance to meet death protection needs. This plan amounts to substituting equity-type investment for the fixed-dollar investment portion of the ordinary life insurance policy. The saver accepts the risk associated with common stock investment in the expectation that over the longer period the net gain in this combination plan will exceed that of the ordinary life plan.

The success of combination plans rests upon the assumption that in the long run stock prices will rise sufficiently to reflect both inflation and increases in national productivity, thus protecting the long-term saver against the possibility of suffering relative losses by devoting savings exclusively to fixed-dollar investments. Unfortunately, this assumption may not be justified, as noted earlier.

Other Individual Tax-Sheltered Plans

Several other individual retirement plans are available under tax shelter that may or may not employ the services of insurance companies. These include (1) individual retirement accounts (IRAs), (2) Keogh plans (H.R. 10 plan), (3) Section 403(b) plans, and (4) Section 401(k) plans. Most of these plans are designed to supplement the regular pension plan commonly provided by employers (discussed earlier). They also may be used by other persons who are self-employed or who otherwise have no basic group pension plan other than Social Security. They can be used to offset inflation because they permit equity investments on a tax-deferred basis.

Individual Retirement Accounts (IRA). The IRA is a long-term savings program under which the saver may accumulate up to $2,000 annually ($2,250 if there is a spouse without earnings). Funds may be invested with a life insurer in a fixed or variable annuity, in U.S. retirement bonds, or with another financial institution such as a mutual fund, savings and loan company, bank, or trust company. All funds deposited may be deducted for current federal and most state income taxes, and accumulating interest and investment returns also are exempt from current income taxes. IRA funds may not be invested in life insurance or endowment policies. These are specifically prohibited by law to receive current tax exemption under these plans.

The 1986 Tax Reform Act limits the amounts that can be deducted for IRAs and other tax-sheltered plans. You can still contribute to an IRA if you are not covered by an employer-qualified pension plan or if you are earning less than specified salaries ($25,000 for a single person or $40,000 for a couple filing jointly).

Certain restrictions exist for the IRA. For example, the saver must have earned income from employment and must not be over $70\frac{1}{2}$ years of age when the account is established. Funds may not be withdrawn earlier than age $59\frac{1}{2}$ or later than $70\frac{1}{2}$ without paying a 10 percent penalty on the amounts withdrawn. This penalty was built in to discourage the use of these funds for purposes other than retirement. All amounts withdrawn are subject to income taxes in the year in which they are removed. If funds are withdrawn in a lump sum after age $59\frac{1}{2}$, some income tax relief is granted under "five-year averaging" rules, designed to lessen the impact of unusual increases in one's income in a single year.

The 10 percent penalty tax does not apply if withdrawals are made because of death or disability. However, if the saver borrows money from an IRA, or uses the account as security for a loan before $59\frac{1}{2}$, the transaction is treated as a premature distribution and subjected to the 10 percent penalty tax. A similar result occurs if the IRA is invested in an unauthorized investment.

If contributions to the IRA exceed the permitted levels, a tax of 6 percent on such excess is levied. The law provides several ways by which one can handle the problems created by making an excess contribution. For example, one can contribute less than the maximum amount in the following year and apply the excess to that year's contributions. IRA contributions are subjected to Social Security taxes under current regulations. Funds in an IRA are also subject to estate and gift taxes.

IRA Rollovers. A **rollover** occurs when the owner takes funds out of one account and places them in another. Two types of IRA rollovers exist: a transfer from one type of IRA to another, and a distribution from an employer-qualified pension plan or profit-sharing plan into an IRA set up to receive such proceeds. If certain requirements are met, funds involved in rollovers escape current income taxation. For example, a saver may move funds from one mutual fund to another without tax consequence. Because of their complexity, the requirements will not be discussed in this text. However, the tax rules are not unduly burdensome, and the rollover status is valuable because otherwise the benefits of long-term savings under tax shelter might be lost.

SEP-IRAs. The simplified employee pension plan (SEP) was authorized in 1978 to make use of the machinery established by IRAs to fund an employer pension plan without the complications that typify regular employer tax-qualified pension plans. These plans have been termed SEP-IRAs. The SEP-IRA must be established by an employer under rules according to which the employer agrees to make a contribution to an IRA for each employee. All employees over 25 or who have three years of service must be covered. The contribution may not exceed $15,000 a year or 15 percent of the employee's wage, whichever is less. All employees must receive the same percentage contribution, and the plan may not discriminate to favor highly paid employees.

If the employer's contribution is less than the $2,000 permitted to an employee, the employee may contribute the difference and take a personal tax deduction for this amount. For example, suppose Helen's employer has established a 10 percent contribution to a SEP-IRA on Helen's salary of $15,000. Under the 1986 Tax Reform Act, Helen is eligible, even though she is covered by an employer plan since her salary is less than $25,000. The employer thus contributes $1,500. Helen may contribute up to an additional $500 to bring the total to $2,000. If in a later year the employer contributed only $1,000, then Helen may make up the difference by contributing $1,000 individually. Helen's employer would show the amounts contributed to the SEP-IRA, and Helen could then take an income tax deduction for these sums plus her own contributions on her individual tax return.

The SEP-IRA has no annual reporting requirements other than normal income tax reporting requirements for employees. The employer can stop making contributions at any time and resume them later without violating any tax rules. If an employer terminates the plan, the assets remain the property of that employee because the employee's account must be nonforfeitable, even if the employee quits. Many small employers find the SEP-IRA to be a simple and flexible instrument to fund retirement benefits for themselves and their employees.

Keogh (H.R. 10) Plans. Keogh plans are designed for persons with self-employment income. Frequently, people with "side jobs" shelter part of their earnings in these plans. As with IRAs, tax-sheltered contributions and accumulating investment returns are not subject to current income taxation. Under Keogh plans, the annual amounts exempted are larger—25 percent of self-employment income or $30,000, whichever is less, compared to only $2,000 for the IRA. The self-employed person must cover employees in a nondiscriminatory manner. A plan is said to be discriminatory or "top heavy" if more than 60 percent of the benefits accrue to key employees. In this case, special requirements exist, such as those requiring more rapid vesting and those providing certain minimum benefits to "non-key employees."

Funds in a Keogh plan must be withdrawn between the ages of $59\frac{1}{2}$ and $70\frac{1}{2}$ to avoid a 10 percent penalty, and a 6 percent tax is levied on any amounts contributed in excess of the limits stated in the law.

Investment flexibility in the Keogh is about the same as the IRA, with a wide variety of permitted investments. It is possible to fund a Keogh plan with an annuity or retirement income contract issued by a life insurer, provided that the life insurance element or protection is *incidental.* The test of being incidental is that the protection does not exceed 100 times the monthly retirement benefit. Thus, if a policy provides $300 in a monthly annuity, as much as $30,000 of life insurance protection may also be provided. Because a typical endowment life insurance policy provides a death benefit of about 150 times the monthly income under the policy, the endowment policy is not an acceptable investment for a Keogh plan. Other investments that are permitted include annuities, trust plans, custodial accounts, U.S. retirement bonds, and face amount certificates.

One provision of the Keogh plan is that up to $750 of annual contribution is possible, no matter what the size of the self-employment income. Thus, a person with a "side job" earning $750 a year could shelter all of it in a Keogh plan. A housewife earning $1,000 a year could shelter $750, even though 25 percent of the $1,000 is only $250.

Section 403(b) Plans. Since 1959, tax-sheltered retirement plans under Section 403(b) of the Internal Revenue Code have been permitted for employees of certain nonprofit institutions that are described in Section 501(c)(3) of the code. Employees of public schools, universities, hospitals, and the like are among those eligible. Although originally only life insurance annuities were permissible investments under these plans, the law was amended in 1974 to allow accumulations through setting up custodial accounts with mutual funds. As mutual funds offer a wide variety of investment vehicles, the 403(b) plan may serve the needs of long-term savers with many types of investment goals.

In setting up such a plan, the employee typically enters into a contract with the employer to "reduce" the contractual salary by the amount the employee wishes to save. An employee earning $20,000 who wishes to save $2,000 annually would enter into a contract with the employer to have the salary stated as $18,000. If $2,000 does not exceed the "exclusion allowance," the $2,000 reduction would not have to be reported for current income. The general exclusion allowance is 20 percent of the employee's current annual "includible" compensation, multiplied by years of service, less any amounts that were previously contributed to tax-sheltered annuities or other tax-deferred plans and were excluded from the employee's taxable income in all prior years. Some exceptions to this limitation are allowed. The value of a regular employer-sponsored retirement plan must be counted in determining the exclusion allowance. In addition, there is an overall limitation on contributions of 25 percent of salary that must not be exceeded. Users of Section 403(b) plans should follow instructions given on forms provided by the Internal Revenue Service.

Section 401(k) Plans. U.S. tax codes and regulations permit an employee of a corporation with a **thrift plan** (a savings plan offering the employee the right to save given amounts through payroll deduction and providing matching contributions by the employer) to deduct certain amounts saved for tax purposes. Restrictions on the amounts deductible are generally fewer than those applying to IRA or other individual retirement plans. Tax consequences when distributions are made from these plans are also more favorable. Technically, the employee contributions to the plan are regarded as pretax reductions in regular compensation, in a manner similar to 403(b) plans for employees of nonprofit institutions, just discussed.

Multiple Plans. It is possible to enjoy the benefits of tax deferral of retirement contributions from more than one type of individual plan simultaneously. For example, a public school teacher may set up a TSA plan to supplement a regular teachers' retirement plan offered by the school district and, in addition, may also establish an IRA and a Keogh plan for self-employment income earned from such sources as royalties, consulting, public speaking, and the like. The teacher may also be covered by Social Security and veterans' or military allowances. However, under the 1986 Tax Reform Act all tax-sheltered contributions combined may not exceed $7000 annually for 401(k) or SEP-IRAs or $9,500 annually if you use a 403(b) plan.

In summary, a basic conclusion that emerges from this discussion is that no single type of contract, savings plan, or other arrangement seems to offer the complete answer to protecting retirement savings from the inroads of inflation.[10] Variable annuities, which have much to recommend them, have enough weaknesses that they ought not be relied on as the sole vehicle for retirement. Saving under tax shelter, while obviously very beneficial in increasing the size of the savings fund available at retirement above what would otherwise be the case, is not the total answer to the problem of inflation either. Investing in mutual funds, with accompanying term insurance protection, is similar to using variable annuities as a long-term savings method during the accumulation phase, but it offers no guaranteed protection during the retirement phase of the savings period.

An analysis of the manner in which people in the United States have saved their money reveals some interesting facts. As revealed in Table 13-4, which shows the relative importance of various financial institutions in attracting funds for IRAs, the most popular place in 1984 for IRA savings was commercial banks, followed closely by savings and loan associations. Life insurers attracted only a little over 10 percent of IRA monies in 1984, down from 12.7 percent in 1981. Self-directed accounts with brokerage firms and mutual funds showed rapid growth over the period. After liberalization of tax rules under the 1982 Tax Equity and Fiscal Responsibility Act of 1982, amounts saved in these accounts ballooned over fivefold during the period 1981–1984.

Table 13–4
Investments in Individual Retirement Accounts, 1981 and 1984 (millions of dollars)

Type of Institution	Value			
	1981	%	1984	%
Commercial banks	$ 5,849	22.5	$ 37,128	28.0
Savings and loan associations	10,695	41.0	32,725	24.7
Mutual savings banks	3,405	13.1	8,504	6.4
Life insurance companies	3,320	12.7	13,942	10.5
Mutual funds	2,586	9.9	16,537	12.5
Self-directed	n.a.	—	16,000	12.0
	$26,062	100.0	$132,636	100.0

Source: *1985 Mutual Fund Fact Book* (Washington, DC: Investment Company Institute, 1985), p. 52.

SUMMARY

1. A significant employee benefit is the employer tax-qualified pension plan. More than half of the U.S. labor force is now covered by these plans, which have grown rapidly in the post-World War II period. ERISA greatly increased the security and safety of these plans.
2. Life insurers have played an important role in providing retirement security for individuals through various types of annuity contracts, both individual and group. An increasingly important role for life insurers is that of serving as a funding medium for employer-sponsored pension plans. Because of recent liberalizations in tax and other rules governing individual long-term savings vehicles, life insurers also enjoy a significant role as a funding medium for different tax-sheltered individual savings plans, including tax-sheltered annuities, Keogh plans, and IRAs.
3. There are several requirements for tax qualification of a pension plan. They include the following: plans must be nondiscriminatory, must provide definitely determinable benefits, must be in writing, must be funded, must offer vested benefits, and must meet certain eligibility standards.
4. Although pension plans are not mandatory, federal insurance applies to defined benefit plans. If an employer goes bankrupt, the covered worker will not lose all pension rights.
5. Two main approaches to benefit formula design are used: defined contribution and defined benefit. Employees generally favor the latter, while employers tend to favor the former.
6. Trusteed pension plans offer more flexibility and tend to be preferred by larger employers. Insured plans tend to offer greater services and more security. These tend to be used more by smaller employers.
7. Popular insured group pension plans include deferred annuities, deposit administration, and guaranteed investment contracts.
8. Inflation continues to present a serious threat to the adequacy of private pensions. Several approaches are used to offset inflation, including the use of equity investments, *ad hoc* adjustments, and tax shelter.
9. The variable annuity, a significant departure from traditional life insurance practice, is not a cure-all, but it holds sufficient promise to warrant careful investigation and experimentation as a way to permit the small saver to share in the long-term economic growth of the country and to obtain protection from inflation. Variable annuities should not be viewed as a substitute for, but rather as a complement to, traditional types of fixed-dollar investments.
10. Individual savings plans, and in particular the IRA, the Keogh, and the Section 403(b) and 401(k) plans, offer important ways in which a saver may supplement long-term savings programs provided by other methods. Up to $2,000 annually ($2,250 if there is a nonworking spouse) may be saved in a IRA plan, and up to 25 percent of self-employment income may be saved in a Keogh plan. Employees of nonprofit institutions may save additional sums under Section 403(b). Employees of other corporations may obtain tax deferral of retirement savings through Section 401(k) plans. These plans contain restrictions that must be carefully observed. Insurance companies offer annuity contracts through which such plans may be administered.

1. List and explain briefly the requirements for tax qualification of a private pension plan.
2. What is the main difference, from the employer's point of view, between trusteed and insured pension plans?
3. Explain each of the following: deferred group annuity, individual policy pension trust, guaranteed investment contract.
4. Differentiate between allocated and unallocated pension funding instruments.
5. A given tax-sheltered annuity has an administrative cost ratio of 25 percent. Explain the meaning of this ratio.
6. Explain why dollar cost averaging "may not always work" to solve long-term savings or investment plans from loss.
7. List the main arguments for and against the variable annuity.
8. What is an "IRA rollover"? Why is it especially advantageous?
9. Because IRAs are subject to a 10 percent penalty for early withdrawals, should IRAs be used at all if you believe you might have to take the money out before age $59\frac{1}{2}$?
10. What general class of employee is eligible for 403(b) plans? For 401(k) plans? For Keogh plans?
11. Can an employee be eligible at the same time for a 403(b), an IRA, and a Keogh plan? Explain.

QUESTIONS
FOR DISCUSSION

1. A life insurance actuary stated, "If we are willing to face the truth for ourselves, we must admit privately that life insurance and pension funds as now issued are something of a gamble insofar as the proceeds have any definite foreseeable purchasing power." Formulate a reply to this argument from the viewpoint of one strongly committed to fixed-dollar savings as an exclusive method of saving for retirement.
2. Since the CREF annuity unit went down in 10 of the 33 years of its history from 1950 to 1985, do you believe that CREF is a satisfactory retirement plan for the average employee covered by it? Why, or why not?
3. Some economists believe there is a "built-in bias" toward inflation in the United States. In your opinion, how serious is inflation as a problem to overcome in long-range retirement planning?
4. Labor economists have argued that private pension plans should not be permitted to discriminate by providing a larger relative benefit to higher paid workers than lower paid workers, now permitted under integration rules. For example, a plan can offer no benefits to workers earning less than a stated amount and still qualify for tax purposes. What is the justification for integration rules that allow such a procedure? Should integration be permitted, or should a private pension plan be required to pay on the same basis to all employees? Discuss.
5. Data reported by the U. S. Bureau of Census reveal that in 1983 the average amount of financial assets accumulated by all families was $27,365. The median income of all families was reported at $22,415, while the median income for those families headed by persons 65 and over was $12,799. In your opinion, do these data suggest a greater need for individuals to save more for their retirement? Why, or why not?
6. One of the arguments for the variable annuity is that it enables the long-term saver to share in the economic growth of the nation. If you were an opponent of the variable annuity, how might you answer this?

7. An employer pension plan provides a benefit of 1 percent of wages per year of service, wages being defined as the average highest wage of the five years preceding retirement. Vesting occurs after 10 years of service.

(a) How large a pension benefit would an employee who had worked 20 years receive if the final average wage, as defined, was $20,000 a year? How much would be received by a worker with the same salary with 9 years of service? Explain.

(b) Would the 20-year worker be better off with a "defined contribution" plan under which 10 percent of wages is set aside annually for retirement in a fund in which the interest earnings average 10 percent? Explain. (Consult interest tables at the end of this book to find out the size of the available fund after 20 years. Assume that for each $12,000 in the fund, $100 a month will be provided, and that the worker's salary is a constant $20,000 a year.)

NEW TERMS AND CONCEPTS

Funding
Vesting
ERISA
PBGC
Defined Benefit Plan
Defined Contribution Plan
Allocated Benefit Plan
Unallocated Benefit Plan
Trusteed Plan
Insured Plan
Separate Accounts
Deposit Administration
Guaranteed Investment
  Contract (GIC)
Deferred Annuity

Individual Policy Pension
  Trust
Variable Annuity
Tax-Sheltered Annuity
  (TSA)
Dollar Cost Averaging
Administrative Cost Ratio
  (ACR)
Section 401(k) Plan
Section 403(b) Plan
Individual Retirement
  Account (IRA)
SEP-IRA Plan
Rollover
Keogh (H.R. 10) Plan

NOTES

1 The Securities and Exchange Commission regulates all variable annuity contracts, which are also subject to state regulation. By 1970, most states provided for the sale of these contracts. The SEC has exempted group variable annuities from registration under conditions described in the Investment Company Act of 1940 (Rule 3(c)(3)), but individual variable annuity contracts must be sold with a full prospectus provided to each customer, as is true with new stock offerings and with mutual funds. The right of the SEC to regulate variable annuities was established, after a lengthy court battle launched by insurance companies, in *SEC* v. *VALIC*, 359 U.S. 65 (1959), and *Prudential* v. *SEC*, 326 F2 383 (1964), 377 U.S. 953.

2 Between 1959 and 1970 the dollar lost about 63 percent of its purchasing power.

3 The actual mechanics are more complicated. For example, during the period the annuity is being purchased the unit is called an **accumulation** unit. At retirement all of the accumulation units are converted into **annuity** units. The number of annuity units received depends on the age at retirement, the number of payments guaranteed, and other factors. The stated value of the annuity may be changed periodically and remains stable for a given period. If the stock market goes down during one period, the annuitant's rent is not changed until the next period, when it is reduced enough to offset the higher rent the annuitant has been paid during the period of decline.

4 Frank K. Reilly, "Common Stocks as an Inflation Hedge," in Leo Barnes and Stephen Feldman, *Handbook*

of *Wealth Management* (New York: McGraw-Hill Book Co., 1977), Ch. 5.

5 *TIAA-CREF Annual Report*, Part A., 1983.

6 Several studies on stock market returns have been made. One of the best known is Roger G. Ibbotson and Rex A. Sinquefield, "Stocks, Bonds, Bills and Inflation, Year-by-Year Historical Returns (1926–1974)," *Journal of Business*, Vol. 49, No. 1 (January, 1976).

7 Roger R. Conant, "Inflation and the Variable Annuity," *CLU Journal*, Vol. 30, No. 4 (October, 1976), pp. 12–18.

8 Mark R. Greene and Paul Copeland, "Factors in Selecting Tax-Deferred Annuities," *CLU Journal*, (October, 1975), p. 44.

9 Thomas B. Morehart and Gary L. Trennepohl, "Evaluating the Tax Sheltered Annuity vs. the Taxed Investment," *CLU Journal*, Vol. 33, No. 1 (January, 1979), p. 27.

10 Social Security benefits (see Chapter 25) represent an exception to this generalization, since under current law these benefits are adjusted automatically for cost-of-living changes.

14 LIFE INSURANCE AND ESTATE PLANNING

After studying this chapter, you should be able to:

1. Describe the meaning and methods of estate planning.
2. Explain what constitutes estate transfer costs.
3. Indicate ways to minimize estate taxes and other transfer costs.
4. State how the two-trust plan can help to distribute your estate efficiently.
5. Describe what happens to your property if you do not leave a will.
6. List the disadvantages of joint ownership of property.
7. Explain how to maximize the value of your estate through life insurance.
8. Identify business applications of life insurance.

Assuming one has been able to accumulate sufficient property, including a life insurance estate to meet foreseeable needs, an important problem lies in making effective plans to ensure that the property will be preserved and used in the manner its owner intends—e.g., to benefit family members and others. The process of accomplishing this goal is called **estate planning.** In its broad sense, estate planning includes effective means both to accumulate and manage property during one's lifetime as well as to dispose of property at one's death. In this chapter, however, emphasis will be on the latter aspect.

The objectives of estate planning include (1) reducing to a minimum the costs of transferring property to beneficiaries; (2) providing liquid funds to pay transfer costs in order to avoid unnecessary losses in values caused by the forced sale of assets; and (3) developing the best and most efficient ways to distribute property. Life and health insurance can play an important role in effective estate planning.

Estate planning is a very complex field and involves expertise in the fields of taxation, law, accounting, banking, investing, trust administration, and life insurance. Only the essential elements of estate planning are discussed in this chapter, with some emphasis on the role of insurance. The student is advised to seek technical advice for developing individual estate plans or in solving specific estate planning problems in the particular state of residence.

WHY IS ESTATE PLANNING NEEDED?

Estate planning is needed for all estates, both large and small. Without attention to estate planning, a lifetime of effort in providing for one's family's financial security could be largely wasted or at least greatly reduced in effectiveness because of excessive estate transfer costs. Dying without a will could mean that the owner's property is distributed in a way that the person would not have chosen. Failure to make tax plans could mean double estate taxation of property in the case of a married couple, once in the estate of one spouse and again in the estate of the other. Failure to "program" life insurance could mean wasting insurance proceeds through unnecessary taxation or improvident use by beneficiaries. Failure to take advantage of gift tax exemptions could mean paying far more estate taxes than necessary. An effective estate plan will help avoid these problems.

NATURE OF ESTATE TRANSFER COSTS

Since estate planning centers around reducing the costs of estate transfer upon the death of the owner, let us examine these costs in some detail. Several factors cause *estate shrinkage,* as it is called. The main factors are debts, taxes, and costs incurred by the executor and administrator of the estate.

Debts

The first instruction in a will is often that "all my just debts be paid." Debts can be sizable and typically require cash for their immediate payment before heirs can receive anything. Typical debts are mortgages, charge accounts, income taxes due, and installment obligations. They average 5 to 8 percent of the estate, depending on its size.[1]

Administrative Costs

Last expenses, such as funeral expenses, fees allowed to administrators of the estate, court costs, probate costs (costs of proving the will), bond premiums, appraisal fees, brokerage fees, and accounting charges, form a substantial block of expenses associated with estate settlements. These expenses, typically amounting to 3 to 4 percent of the estate value, must usually be paid in cash.[2] The costs are allowed as a deduction from the gross value of the estate before taxes are levied, the balance being referred to as the *adjusted gross estate.*

Taxes

A major cause of estate shrinkage is the gift and estate tax. Both federal and state laws provide for an estate tax, levied on the decedent (the deceased estate owner). For example, the federal estate and gift tax ranges from 18 to 50 percent on taxable estates with value ranges from $10,000 to $2,500,000 or over. (See Table 14-1.) The Economic Recovery Tax Act of 1981 greatly reduced the number of persons having to pay federal estate taxes. Still, even middle-income people need to be aware of estate taxes in estate planning—as we shall see.

ERTA. The **Economic Recovery Tax Act** of 1981 (ERTA) made several very significant changes in estate and income taxation:

1. Estate taxes were reduced in stages over the period 1982–1985 so that after 1985 the maximum rate at which an estate may be taxed, regardless of size, is 50 percent. Previously the maximum rate was 70 percent.
2. An allowed credit against the tax was increased in stages from $47,000, applicable in 1981, to $192,800, applicable in 1987. The credit is applied to an estate value after calculating gross taxes from the rates shown in Table 14-1. The net effect of the increased credit is to exempt gross taxable estates of up to $600,000 from estate taxation. This means that a taxable estate can reach as high as $600,000 and escape all federal estate and gift taxation after 1987.
3. ERTA made another significant change by allowing the taxpayer to leave tax exempt up to 100 percent of the estate to a spouse. Formerly the most one could leave tax exempt to a spouse, called the marital deduction, was one-half of the estate. The effect of this change is to allow one to defer *all* federal estate taxes until the death of a spouse, no matter what the size of the estate. The estate is then subject to tax when the spouse dies, unless other arrangements have been made. (See below.)
4. ERTA increased the annual gift tax exclusion to $10,000 a year per donee. Prior to 1981 the most a taxpayer could give away and still avoid paying gift taxes was $3,000 annually per donee ($6,000 annually if both spouses joined in the gift). The effect of the 1981 law is to allow gifts by two spouses of up to $20,000 a year per donee, thus reducing the estate ultimately subject to estate taxation by that amount. A couple with three children, for example, could give as much as $60,000 a year to the children, reducing the taxable estate by that amount.
5. Prior law required that all gifts made within three years of the date of death to be included (for tax purposes) in the taxpayer's gross estate at

Table 14-1   Unified Rate Schedule for Estate and Gift Taxes

If the amount with respect to which the tentative tax to be computed is:	The tentative tax is:
Not over $10,000	18% of such amount.
Over $10,000 but not over $20,000	$1,800 plus 20% of the excess of such amount over $10,000.
Over $20,000 but not over $40,000	$3,800 plus 22% of the excess of such amount over $20,000.
Over $40,000 but not over $60,000	$8,200 plus 24% of the excess of such amount over $40,000.
Over $60,000 but not over $80,000	$13,000 plus 26% of the excess of such amount over $60,000.
Over $80,000 but not over $100,000	$18,200 plus 28% of the excess of such amount over $80,000.
Over $100,000 but not over $150,000	$23,800 plus 30% of the excess of such amount over $100,000.
Over $150,000 but not over $250,000	$38,800 plus 32% of the excess of such amount over $150,000.
Over $250,000 but not over $500,000	$70,800 plus 34% of the excess of such amount over $250,000.
Over $500,000 but not over $750,000	$155,800 plus 37% of the excess of such amount over $500,000.
Over $750,000 but not over $1,000,000	$248,300 plus 39% of the excess of such amount over $750,000.
Over $1,000,000 but not over $1,250,000	$345,800 plus 41% of the excess of such amount over $1,000,000.
Over $1,250,000 but not over $1,500,000	$448,300 plus 43% of the excess of such amount over $1,250,000.
Over $1,500,000 but not over $2,000,000	$555,800 plus 45% of the excess of such amount over $1,500,000.
Over $2,000,000 but not over $2,500,000	$780,800 plus 49% of the excess of such amount over $2,000,000.
Over $2,500,000*	$1,025,800 plus 50% of the excess of such amount over $2,500,000.

*Effective as of 1985.

its value when the gift was made. This was called the "contemplation of death rule." ERTA changed this policy so that after 1981 such property generally escapes federal taxation. An exception, however, exists in the case of life insurance gifts made within three years of death.

6. ERTA provided that if one holds property in joint tenancy with a spouse, one-half of such jointly held property will be included in the estate of the first to die regardless of who furnished the original funds with which to purchase the property. Formerly, if one spouse had furnished the funds to purchase jointly held property, all of the value of this property would

be subject to estate tax in the estate of this spouse. The effect of this change is generally to reduce the size of the taxable estate of the first spouse to die.

Changes made by ERTA alter in an important way the manner in which estate planning should be carried out, including the terms of wills, the use of trusts, the arrangements to be made for life insurance settlements, and the employment of gifts made prior to death.

Table 14-2 shows effects of the changes in *average* federal estate tax burdens on estates of different sizes. The figures in the table, after giving the effects of the 1981 schedule of rates and credits, reflect the ratio of net taxes due to the net taxable estate. These figures also make allowance for normal funeral and administrative expenses, which averaged between 8.5 and 11.5 percent of the gross estate. Note that an estate of $500,000, which was reduced by about one-sixth in 1981, escapes all federal taxes in 1987. Other estate sizes enjoy substantial tax reductions. Although it is estimated that most U.S. estates will escape taxation after 1987, it is well to remember that due to inflation, the value of many estates will also rise. This increased value will put the estate into a higher tax bracket than formerly, and the estate tax saving may not be as substantial as expected. The extent to which this phenomenon of "bracket creep" occurs will depend on the rate of inflation and the nature of the assets in which estate properties are invested. Thus, for many persons, the estate planning problems created by federal estate and gift taxes are only reduced, not eliminated, by ERTA.

Figure 14-1 illustrates how an estate could be arranged to take maximum advantage of the unified tax credit if deaths took place in 1987. In the illustration, it is assumed that John Brown wills his wife, Mary,

Table 14-2
Average Federal Estate Tax Rates for Selected Taxable Estates, 1981–1987

Taxable Estate	Percentage Estate Tax (Net Estate Tax Divided by Taxable Estate)	
	1981	1987
$500,000	16.8	0
1,000,000	26.6	12.0
1,500,000	29.6	19.9
2,000,000	31.7	24.4
2,500,000	33.6	27.8
10,000,000	49.4	35.2

Source: Chris J. Prestopino, "The Progression of Federal Estate Tax Rate and Credit Reform since 1976: A Visual Summary and Critical Analysis," *The Journal of Insurance Issues and Practices*, Vol. 5, No. 2 (June, 1982), p. 82.

Figure 14–1
Federal Estate
Taxes—John and
Mary Brown—Case 1

A—Upon John's Death

Gross estate	$1,300,000
Less: Funeral costs, debts, and other administrative expenses	100,000
Adjusted gross estate	1,200,000
Less: Marital deduction (willed to Mary)	600,000
Taxable estate	600,000
Tax (from Table 14–1) $155,800 + 0.37($600,000 − $500,000)	192,800
Tax credit (available in 1987)	192,800
Federal estate tax due	$ 0

Recapitulation

Gross estate	$1,300,000
Less: Administrative expense	100,000
Amount available to heirs	$1,200,000
Estate shrinkage upon John's death ($100,000/$1,300,000)	7.7%

B—Upon Mary's Death

Gross estate	$ 600,000
Estimated general debts and administrative costs	60,000
Adjusted gross estate	$ 540,000
Estate tax (Table 14–1) $155,800 + .37($540,000 − $500,000)	$170,600
Less: Tax credit	192,800
Mary's estate tax due	$ 0

Total Estate Tax and Administrative Cost

Original estate value		$1,300,000
Administrative costs		
Upon John's death	$100,000	
Upon Mary's death	$ 60,000	
	$160,000	
Estate taxes		0
Available to children		$1,140,000
Total estate shrinkage		12.3%

enough so that the amounts remaining in his estate after taking the optimum marital deduction absorb all of the available estate tax credits. When Mary dies (also assumed to be in 1987), her estate also escapes taxation in this example. Children may inherit $600,000 upon John's death and another $540,000 upon Mary's death, and estate taxes are zero. Total estate shrinkage is a modest 12.3 percent.

It should be recalled that tax limitations usually prevent avoidance of estate taxes by removing all property in an estate through gifts made prior to death. Furthermore, all states except Nevada levy an **inheritance tax** that is charged to the heirs of the estate, not the decedent. Like estate taxes, inheritance taxes are progressive with the size of the estate. They sometimes provide larger exemptions for certain heirs such as next-of-kin, and a steeper rate progression for those of remote kinship. States also provide for estate taxes that can be used to offset part of the federal estate tax.

There may be other causes of estate shrinkage. Forced sale of certain fixed assets in the estate (buildings, business equipment) to pay costs such as required taxes may cause shrinkage in estate values. Another example is the loss in goodwill and credit when a business owner dies. A going business run by its owner is usually worth more than a business operated by an heir or an estate administrator.

Improperly drawn or outdated wills or other documents, or appointment of inexperienced executors, may cause unnecessary estate shrinkage. For example, wills that are contested may greatly enlarge administrative costs. Specific bequests that are no longer appropriate may drain assets away from primary beneficiaries. An example would be a gift by will to a charitable organization in which the decedent is no longer interested. Specific bequests must be made first before others receive their shares of estate property.

MINIMIZING TRANSFER COSTS

Various methods are available to minimize the costs of estate transfer. Perhaps the most significant single method is to plan for sufficient liquidity in the estate to avoid forced sale of assets at distress prices to pay settlement costs. Other techniques involve the proper use of wills, trusts, gifts, joint ownership, and life insurance.

Providing Liquidity

Because taxes and other settlement costs usually must be paid in cash within a year after the death of the decedent, effective estate planning requires making an estimate of these costs and providing liquid funds to pay them. In some cases involving heavy estate taxes, arrangements can be made with the government to stretch the payment out for a number of years, thus relieving the estate of the necessity of liquidating assets at forced sale for immediate cash settlement of the tax bill. However, it is possible to provide liquidity in the estate for prompt settlement through life insurance. Permanent life insurance is widely recommended for this purpose because the policies mature and are payable in cash at the time the proceeds are needed at the death of the insured, no matter how long the insured lives.

In John and Mary Brown's case, ordinary life insurance of $100,000 on John's life could be arranged to pay the needed expenses for administration. As life insurance is usually bought by installment purchase, the insured need not lay aside $100,000 in cash or liquid securities, but may pay annual insurance premiums equal to a fraction of this amount in the knowledge that the full sum will be available when it is needed. Unless the insured lives for a very long time, the sum of the premiums paid will be less than the face amount of insurance. Thus, the life insurance method of paying for estate settlement costs can be economical, as well as efficient and secure.

Wills

A **will** is a way to transfer ownership of property at death. Having a valid will is important not only to minimize estate transfer costs, but also to make sure that one's property is distributed the way one wants. Dying intestate (i.e., dying without a will) means allowing state law to decide this distribution. For example, state law may require that in the absence of a will, a surviving spouse receives one-half of the personal property (cash, stocks, bonds, personal effects) and a life interest in the real estate, with the remainder going to the children. In small estates this provision could place the surviving spouse in a very difficult financial position unless the children are willing to return their portions to the parent for his or her support, if needed. A will would have allowed the parent to receive all the property to dispose of as desired.

Without a will, it becomes difficult or impossible to take advantage of other cost-reducing devices, such as testamentary trusts, to be discussed shortly. Without a will, the decedent could lose part of the marital deduction for federal estate taxes, since the surviving spouse could get less in this situation than the marital deduction provision allows.

To be valid, a will usually must be in writing, witnessed by two persons, and signed by the **testator** (person making the will). The witness should not be a beneficiary in the will, or that witness could be disqualified from receiving the benefit to which he or she might otherwise be entitled. There are other legal requirements to be met in wills. Each state has specific laws on the subject. Therefore, the will should be reviewed each time a testator moves from one state to another. If a will is found defective, it is as though no will existed at all. Wills should be drawn up with the help of an experienced attorney.

Trusts

A **trust** is another way to transfer the ownership of property. It may be set up during one's lifetime (called an *inter vivos,* or **living trust**) or at one's death through a will (**testamentary trust**). The trust requires selecting some third party (**trustee**), usually a bank, to manage one's property for the benefit of someone else (the beneficiary). The trustee has legal ownership of the property, but the beneficiary has equitable, or beneficial, ownership. The terms of the trust give instructions as to how the property shall be managed and distributed.

The Marital Deduction Trust. A significant use of the testamentary trust is to reduce the total estate and inheritance taxes and resulting estate shrinkage upon the deaths of a husband and wife. One such trust, called the **martial deduction trust,** is established to receive part of the estate. In the John and Mary Brown example given earlier, $600,000 would be given to Mary Brown in a marital deduction trust, to be called Trust *A*. Mary would have all the incidents of ownership over Trust *A* and could draw income and principal from it as needed. Mary could dispose of Trust *A* property by will. Any funds left in it at *Mary's* death would be subject to federal estate taxes, but none of the property in Trust *A* is subject to estate taxes at *John's* death, since John effectively removed this property from his estate by establishing the marital deduction trust. The estate tax result of taking maximum tax advantage of the martial deduction is shown in Figure 14–1.

The other half of John's estate would be placed in a second trust (Trust *B*) for the ultimate benefit of the children or other heirs. During Mary Brown's lifetime she may draw income and principal as needed, but whatever is left at her death goes to the children or others in the way John has directed. There is no second federal estate tax or probate cost for Trust *B* since Trust *B* property is not part of Mary's estate.

Suppose the trust plans described above were not used and Mary receives outright the entire estate at John's death. Six months later Mary dies. What are the total estate taxes? They will be as shown in Figure 14–2.

Figure 14–2
Federal Estate Taxes—John and Mary Brown—Case 2

Upon John's Death, 1987	
Gross estate	$1,300,000
Administrative costs	100,000
Left to Mary	$1,200,000

Upon Mary's Death, 1987	
Assets in Mary's estate	$1,200,000
Administrative costs	90,000
Adjusted gross estate	$1,110,000
Estate tax (from Table 14–1)	
$155,800 + 0.37($1,100,000 − $500,000)	$ 565,000
Estate tax credit (Table 14–2)	$ 192,800
Mary's estate tax	$ 373,000

Total Estate Shrinkage	
John's administrative costs	$ 100,000
Mary's administrative costs	90,000
Estate taxes	373,000
Total	563,000
Percent shrinkage ($563,000/$1,300,000)	43.3%

Although taxes are zero upon John's death, there is a heavy tax on Mary's estate: total estate taxes are $373,000 instead of zero as shown in Figure 14–1. Total estate shrinkage is 43.3 percent in Case 2, compared to 12.3 percent in Case 1.

In addition to savings in estate taxes, the use of Trusts A and B has other advantages. Mary's property in Trust A escapes many probate costs and inheritance taxes when Mary dies because property in trust is not subject to probate. Since Mary is likely to live from Trust A first before drawing from Trust B, the amount in Trust A will likely be diminished by the time of her death. To the extent that this is true, corresponding federal estate taxes will also be reduced. Meanwhile, the property in Trust B can be distributed to heirs in accordance with John's wishes, subject always to Mary's need for income during her lifetime.

Terminable Interest Property. A change in the type of ownership possible in Trust A was made in 1981. Formerly, all property in Trust A had to be given outright to the spouse and was subject to estate tax upon the spouse's death. After 1981 it became possible to include in Trust A, under specified conditions, property that the spouse did not own outright, but had rather only a "terminable interest." In such property the spouse's interest could end at death and would not be subject to estate tax.

Property could be left to a spouse for life and then passed to a charitable institution. For example, a widow could enjoy income from the property during her lifetime, after which the property would vest in a church or charitable institution.

Gifts

Reducing one's estate through gifts is another way to minimize estate transfer costs. As noted earlier, gifts of up to $10,000 per year per donee can be made without paying gift tax. Obviously, property not in the estate is not subject to estate taxes, probate costs, or other administrative costs.

Life insurance is an effective medium for gifts because the gift is valued according to the cash value of the policy, not the death proceeds. If grandparents give a grandchild a $25,000 policy with a $10,000 cash value, there is no gift tax due in year one because the $10,000 value does not exceed the annual exemption. Subsequent premiums are exempt from gift taxes if they do not exceed $10,000. If the insured dies, the grandchild receives the $25,000 free from estate, income, and inheritance taxes and administrative expenses.

An employee may assign all interest in a company group term life insurance policy to a spouse. There is no gift tax because term coverage has no cash value. If the employee dies, the proceeds are paid directly to the spouse, with no estate, inheritance, or administrative expenses.

Joint Ownership

Property of which the title is in a form known as **joint ownership** with right of survivorship passes automatically to the survivor without delay upon the death of the joint owner. There are no probate or other administrative costs to pay. Hence, joint ownership of property such as checking accounts, the home, and a car is very common.

There are some disadvantages to joint ownership. First, joint ownership does not enable property to escape estate taxes. Second, since jointly held property does not enter the decedent's estate for probate purposes, it does not pass under a will. Thus, if all of a person's property were held this way, the purposes of a will might be defeated since there would be no property subject to the will. Third, property registered jointly may result in a gift tax liability if the joint owner has not personally contributed any part of the cost.

Finally, there may be some income tax disadvantages of joint ownership. Because jointly held property passes directly to the joint owner upon the death of the other, all of the income from the jointly held property is now taxed to the survivor, who may already be in a high income tax bracket. If the property had not been held in joint tenancy, it could have been distributed to several beneficiaries, such as children, who would probably be in lower tax brackets. Another income tax disadvantage is that jointly held property has a basis in the hands of the survivor equal to the original cost, which is often lower than the market value. Income taxes upon ultimate sale of the property will thus be larger than would have been the case otherwise. For example, if a husband owns outright $100,000 of property whose original cost is $50,000 and wills the property to the wife, the wife's cost basis is $100,000. If she sells the property for $100,000, no taxable gain exists. However, if the property is held jointly, the wife is presumed to own half, and this half would have a cost basis to her of $25,000. The half owned by the husband would have a basis of $50,000, its current market value. If the wife sells the property for $100,000, a taxable gain of $25,000 would exist.

A hypothetical case will illustrate the disadvantages of using joint ownership as an exclusive way to pass property to others at death. Suppose a husband and wife die in the same accident, the husband outliving the wife by an hour or so. By a former marriage the wife has two children who had been close to the couple and whom the couple had been helping financially. All of the property is registered in joint ownership and, because the wife dies first, the title vests in the husband, and when he dies it passes to the husband's next of kin. The only next of kin of the husband, however, is a brother with whom he has had no contact for several years. The brother receives the benefits, and the wife's children receive nothing, of the jointly held property. A will could have directed benefits to the children according to the wishes of the benefactors. Before joint ownership is used, legal and tax advice is recommended, particularly for larger estates.

Life Insurance

The use of life insurance in estate planning has been referred to several times. For example, life insurance can be arranged so as to minimize estate taxes by using it as the medium for gifts. By providing liquidity in the estate, the insurance is useful in minimizing estate shrinkage stemming from illiquidity.

Life insurance permits one to cover estate settlement expenses with "fractional dollars." For example, a person estimating that estate settlement costs will be $10,000 may maintain an ordinary nonparticipating life insurance contract, taken out at a younger age, for this need. If the policy had been taken out at age 40, the insured would have been paying in about $200 annually. It would be about 50 years ($10,000 ÷ $200) before the sum of all premiums would equal the death proceeds. If the insured dies before age 90, the insured's policy will reimburse the estate more than has been paid in the premiums. This calculation ignores the interest element that could have been earned on the premiums in a separate investment. If interest at 8 percent is considered to have been earned on the $200 premium, it would still have taken 21 years before the total would have equalled the $10,000 policy proceeds.

Life insurance proceeds are paid directly to named beneficiaries and are not subject to probate. Thus, they can escape probate costs. If paid to named beneficiaries, life insurance proceeds may also escape state inheritance taxes.

If the insured wants to avoid estate taxation of life insurance, while simultaneously making funds available to provide estate liquidity, life insurance ownership may be transferred to an irrevocable trust with instructions to purchase assets from (or lend money to) the executor of the will. The trust property ultimately is taxed in the estate of the beneficiary.

Another significant use of life insurance in estate planning is that of the settlement options. While trustees charge for managing trusts, life insurers make no extra charge for settling policy proceeds under one of the settlement options. The estate planner can use these options effectively in a process known as life insurance programming, which is explained in Chapter 15.

Income Tax Advantages. An additional advantage of life insurance in estate planning lies in its income tax treatment. Sometimes a large part of the estate debts is represented by income taxes due on gains in the value of estate property. Under the Windfall Profits Tax Act of 1980, heirs may take inherited property at its fair market value on the date of the donor's death, or six months after if the executor chooses an alternative valuation date. In the case of life insurance proceeds settled as a lump sum, no income taxes are levied, no matter how much the gain is above the amount invested.

If life insurance is settled under an installment option, the beneficiary may exclude from reportable income that portion of each installment representing the return of principal. Only the interest element is taxed. If the insured selects the life income (annuity) option, the excludible portion is found by using the formula

$$\frac{\text{Sum of Premiums Paid}}{\text{Annuity Rent} \times \text{Life Expectancy}} \times \text{Rent} = \frac{\text{Amount}}{\text{Excluded}}$$

For example, suppose John Brown has a life insurance policy of $30,000 on which he has paid an annual premium of $600 for 30 years, or $18,000. It is settled under a straight life income option paying, $2,400 a year for Mary, who is 60 when John dies. Mary's life expectancy is 20 years. Substituting in the above formula, we find

$$\frac{\$18,000}{\$2,400 \times 20} \times \$2,400 = \$900$$

The amount of return of principal excluded from Mary's taxable income is $900. The balance of $1,500 represents interest. Thus, Mary must report $1,500 of her $2,400 annuity. Had John instead settled the policy for a cash amount and invested the proceeds at, say, 10 percent interest, Mary would have received a taxable interest income of $3,000 a year ($30,000 × 0.10). By using the annuity option, John has saved substantial income tax for Mary.

Note that for income tax calculations, the *cost* of the policy is the sum of the premiums paid. Thus, the cost basis of life insurance includes the amounts paid for insurance protection, a feature that reduces the ultimate income tax due.

Dividends paid under life insurance contracts represent a return of a portion of the premium, and are not considered taxable income.

In summary, life insurance offers many features that help to minimize estate transfer costs. These features include providing liquidity, income tax advantages, and a special legal status that benefits heirs in several ways.

MAXIMIZING ESTATE VALUES WITH LIFE INSURANCE

In addition to minimizing estate transfer costs, life insurance contains several other features and uses that may serve to maximize the value of estates to heirs. The highlights of these features are discussed next.

Proper Selection of the Contract

As noted earlier, some life insurance policies are far more expensive and offer less estate protection than others, mainly because of the variation in the savings element. For example, if a male age 40 puts $1,000 annually in a nonparticipating term-to-65 contract in one insurer, he will obtain about $72,000 of estate protection in the event of his premature death. The same $1,000 placed in an ordinary life contract with the same insurer provides only about $50,000 of death protection. The difference is, of course, that at age 65 the ordinary life contract will have a considerable cash value (about $25,000), whereas the term policy will expire with no cash value.

If the insured needs estate protection after age 65, the ordinary life policy will be the obvious choice of contract because this policy may be kept in force as long as needed. The term contract is the best choice if the need for which it is purchased will end by the time the insured reaches age 65. The problem of arranging insurance to meet various needs at different ages is treated as a part of life insurance programming in Chapter 15.

Nonforfeiture Options

The nonforfeiture options in life insurance (discussed in Chapter 11) may help increase policy proceeds otherwise payable. For example, an insured may be unable to pay a premium. Instead of lapsing, the policy may remain in force for many years because the cash values are used under the extended-term option to continue the full face amount of protection.

An insured may also use cash values to pay up a policy for a reduced amount, thus enjoying some protection as long as he or she lives. In this way, premium payments can be discontinued with loss of only a part of the original protection.

Borrowing on Life Insurance

Cash values of life insurance policies can be viewed as savings, to be drawn upon as needed. These values accumulate free of current income taxation. They may be borrowed by the insured without necessity for repayment, at a stipulated interest rate of about 6 to 8 percent. (Under some conditions this charge is tax deductible so that the net after-tax cost of borrowing is minimal.)

Estate values may be enlarged in some cases by borrowing cash values and reinvesting the proceeds elsewhere for a greater return. The death proceeds of the life insurance policy are reduced by any loans against it, but the total estate values may still be greater.

Suppose John Brown has a chance to make a profitable real estate investment yielding 15 percent on a required down payment of $15,000. John's $30,000 ordinary life insurance policy has a cash value of $15,000, which John borrows at 6 percent. After 10 years, the estate values to John on the real estate investment would be $15,000 increased at 15 percent for 10 years, or $60,683. John must pay 6 percent on his life insurance loan, interest on which would amount to $11,862. His net gain is $48,821 ($60,683 − $11,862) for the 10 years. (These calculations ignore income tax considerations.) Had John died during the 10 years, his estate would have received $15,000 from life insurance (the face of $30,000 less the $15,000 loan) plus whatever the real estate investment is worth. Many policyholders borrow cash values for mutual fund purchases or other investments considered to have greater returns than life insurance and at acceptable risk levels.

Use of Dividends

Insurance dividends, which may average 20 percent of premiums, can be used economically to buy paid-up additions to life insurance protection. No agents' commissions are levied on such purchases. The paid-up additions themselves have cash values that can be borrowed, if desired.

The accumulated face value of paid-up additions over several years can appreciably increase estate values.

Protective Clauses and Optional Endorsements

Various clauses in life insurance contracts help protect estate values and may increase them over what would be the case in other types of property:

1. Cash values of life insurance may not usually be attached by the insured's creditors.
2. Provisions can also be incorporated in life insurance under the so-called **spendthrift trust** clause under which the creditors of beneficiaries may not attach the proceeds of life insurance to satisfy claims that the beneficiary may have incurred. This clause enables the insured to guarantee that no matter how indiscreet the beneficiary may be (say, due to financial inexperience), he or she will continue to receive the benefits of life insurance proceeds.
3. Under the incontestability clause, after two years insurers cannot refuse to pay death proceeds because of any misstatements made by the insured, even if these misstatements were made fraudulently.
4. Under the suicide clause, beneficiaries can still collect, even if the insured commits suicide, if the policy has been in force two years or more.
5. A double-indemnity clause is available which doubles the face amount of insurance if the insured dies by certain accidental means.
6. If the insured becomes disabled (as defined), the policy premium will be paid by the insurer under an optional waiver-of-premium clause.

Life Insurance Trusts

A frequent use of the trust device is to receive the proceeds of life insurance and to manage these funds for beneficiaries. Although, of course, the life insurer offers settlement options that accomplish a similar function, a trust can provide for greater flexibility in management of the property. For example, a trustee can be instructed to increase income to beneficiaries to adjust for inflation, something the life insurer does not offer under settlement options. The trustee often can earn a greater investment return than is paid by a typical life insurer, and with comparable safety. The creator of the trust can instruct that the trustee (usually a bank or investment company) be guided by recommendations from an outside consultant in making trust investments. In this way, the creator of the trust can designate someone he or she prefers to help make investments.

Business Applications

Another common use of life insurance is to solve certain business problems in such a way that business interests can be preserved in the insured's estate. The first example of such use is *business continuation* insurance. The problem can be outlined as follows. In many situations a business venture can produce a good income while the owner is living, but it may be of little market value upon the owner's death. Creditors may be unwilling to continue to extend credit to a firm whose owner and chief manager has just died. Much of the goodwill of the business may be lost, because it is very possible that many of the firm's best customers deal with this firm because of the personality of the owner. Potential competitors may see an opportunity to buy out the business, but may not want to pay its fair market value to the insured's estate. The owner's heirs may not be interested or able to carry on the business, or if they are, they may not be able to earn the return that has been possible in the past. In other words, there are many ways in which the death of the owner will cause a rather substantial loss to the beneficiaries unless proper plans are made. Life insurance can be of material assistance in helping to reduce these losses.

Arrangements can be made with a potential buyer (say, a key employee) to purchase the business upon the death of the owner at a price determined by some valuation formula, say 10 times average earnings in the past five years. The funds for the purchase may come from life insurance taken out on the owner by the buyer. The buyer agrees (in a separate buy-sell agreement) to use the life insurance proceeds to purchase the owner's interest from the heirs. In this way, the heirs receive cash for the business valued as a "going concern."

Since the life insurance proceeds as well as the policy itself are the property of the buyer, the beneficiaries do not have an additional amount of life insurance proceeds entering the estate for estate tax purposes. Under the federal estate tax regulations, buy-and-sell agreements funded by life insurance have been accepted in valuing the business for estate tax purposes. Thus, another uncertainty is removed in financial planning—that of the size of the estate tax.

Where the business is owned not by a single individual, but by a partnership, similar arrangements may be worked out. A partnership is legally dissolved upon the death of one partner, whose estate has a claim on the business assets representing that partner's share. Funds are needed to meet this obligation promptly and to avoid forced sale of assets to provide the necessary funds. Life insurance is the ideal way to provide the funds. For example, if there are only two or three partners, each partner may buy insurance on the life of the others in an amount sufficient to retain the same relative interest each partner owns before the death of the other. Suppose that there is a business whose value is determined to be $500,000. The business is owned equally by two partners, A and B. In a business continuation agreement, each partner takes out $250,000 of life insurance on the life of the other. In the event of either one's death, the surviving partner is bound by contract to purchase the interest of the deceased partner. In that way, the deceased partner's estate is maximized and is available immediately in the form of cash.

In the event that one partner is not insurable or is at an advanced age, when insurance becomes too expensive to purchase, other funding arrangements may be worked out. For example, the younger partner may make advance arrangements for purchasing the senior partner's interest through periodic payments, and may sign a note to that effect.

Key Employee Insurance

It is common to insure the lives of key people in such a way that the loss in value of the business (and hence of the estate) is offset. A key person may be an inventor, a star salesperson, a superb organizer, or an astute financier. The death of such a person may cause a considerable financial loss to the corporation. Many corporations insure their presidents for millions of dollars.

TIPS ON ESTATE PLANNING

1. When estate property reaches a certain size ($600,000 in 1987), a spouse should usually make a marital deduction gift to the other spouse in order to minimize federal estate taxes. Normally, this should be done by will.
2. A program of giving gifts over a period of years should be considered as a means of reducing the size of one's estate and the corresponding estate tax. Substantial savings in estate transfer taxes are made possible in this way.
3. The estate planner should maintain a complete inventory and record of property and costs to facilitate the settlement of the estate.
4. In many cases, spouses should transfer the ownership of life insurance on their lives to the other spouse. In this way, federal estate tax will be avoided on death proceeds that would otherwise be due on the estate of the first spouse to die. The spouse's will should direct the future ownership of such policies in case the uninsured spouse dies before the insured spouse. For example, the will could pass the policy ownership to another family member (other than the insured spouse) who could employ the proceeds to pay any needed estate settlement costs when the insured spouse dies.
5. Every estate planner (and spouse) should have a valid will. One should seek professional advice from attorneys, life insurance representatives, accountants, investment advisers, and trust officers in determining such matters as potential estate and inheritance tax liability, effective use of trusts, needed records, and other matters.
6. Joint ownership of property should be used sparingly to avoid estate settlement and estate tax problems. The principal residence and a checking account will normally be acceptable for joint ownership, but for other types of property, titling should be carried out with professional advice. For example, jointly owned property, such as checking accounts, are estate property, and may be tied up for weeks after a spouse's death. Some funds should be kept in each spouse's name separately to avoid such problems.
7. A testamentary trust for the benefit of a spouse and dependents should be considered not only as a tax-saving method, but also to ensure

professional management of estate assets. Trusts are especially appropriate when there are employer-provided benefits (life insurance, etc.) and when the spouse lacks expertise in managing property and money.

8. Estate plans and life insurance should be reviewed and evaluated at least every five years.

SUMMARY

1. The objectives of estate planning are to accumulate and dispose of property in such a manner as to meet the goals of the planner, to minimize estate transfer costs, and to provide sufficient liquidity to meet foreseeable needs upon the death of the planner.

2. Major types of estate transfer costs are debts, administrative costs, and taxes. The chief tools used to minimize these costs and to provide the necessary liquidity in the estate are wills, trusts, gifts, joint ownership of property, and life insurance.

3. Life insurance offers several advantages in estate planning, including provision of needed liquidity on an economical basis, flexibility in making arrangements to minimize various taxes, and security of income to estate beneficiaries through use of the settlement options. Through proper selection of life insurance contracts, estate values can be maximized and the interests of the beneficiaries made secure. This is accomplished through effective use of nonforfeiture options, dividends, and loan provisions of life insurance.

4. Business uses of life insurance are also effective in good estate planning. Business continuation plans funded with life insurance offer a way to return business interests to beneficiaries of owners in cash and without loss from forced sale of assets. Life insurance on key employees is valu-

able to offset business devaluation due to premature death of these employees.

QUESTIONS FOR REVIEW

1. What are the major costs of transferring an estate? Give examples of each.
2. Why do many estate planners avoid recommending joint ownership of property with right of survivorship?
3. Name the chief ways of transferring property at death.
4. In your opinion, should a handwritten, unwitnessed will be considered legally valid? What about an oral will given on one's deathbed in front of a witness?
5. Using the federal estate tax tables in Table 14–1, calculate the federal estate tax that would be due in 1987 on Dave Martin's estate under the following assumptions:
   (a) Gross estate value, $800,000; administrative costs and debts, $40,000. Dave dies without making any gift to Sara, his wife.
   (b) Same facts as in (a) except that Dave gives Sara one-half of his adjusted gross estate.
6. In Question 5(a),
   (a) Will an additional tax be incurred upon Sara Martin's death?
   (b) How could this problem be handled? Discuss.

7. How can use of the extended-term option in life insurance serve to maximize estate values? Explain.

8. How can estates be maximized by borrowing on cash values in a life insurance policy? Do you recommend this procedure? Explain.

9. Do you recommend the double-indemnity rider as a means of doubling the life insurance protection in an estate? Why or why not?

10. What main advantages are there in using trusts rather than life insurance settlement options as a way of handling life insurance death proceeds?

QUESTIONS FOR DISCUSSION

1. A business person had a married daughter and two sons. The sons worked with him in a business. He wished to divide his business equally among the three children without dividing the stock among them. The stock would be placed in trust, with the sons voting the stock, and would not be subject to a second estate tax when his wife ultimately died. All three children would share equally in the income. The attorney discovered that the stock was registered jointly with the owner's wife and could not be placed in the trust unless the wife died first and the husband thus would become the sole owner. How could such a situation have been prevented, and how might it be corrected? Discuss.

2. A beneficiary under an estate was receiving a regular income. The estate was protected by the spendthrift trust clause. The beneficiary was charged with a narcotics violation and fined $1,000. The federal government attempted to levy upon the beneficiary's income from the trust to pay the

fine. Do you think this action should suceed? Why or why not?

3. In a review of its life insurance policies, an insurer discovered that one of its policyholders had indicated 36 years earlier that she wished her beneficiary, her husband, to receive the proceeds of the policy under the annuity option. The husband is currently age 91. A letter was written to the insured to determine whether she wished to change the settlement option.

   (a) Why is the annuity option likely to be inappropriate in the above case? Explain.
   (b) What does this case illustrate concerning the use of life insurance settlement options?

4. A writer stated, "Many state laws provide that the estate of a childless person who dies without a will must be split between the surviving spouse and the relatives of the deceased: parents, brothers, sisters."

   (a) Why might such a result be unacceptable and undesirable to the surviving spouse?
   (b) How should this situation be prevented?

5. Two partners, Smith and Jones, own and operate a clothing factory currently valued at $600,000, mostly representing the plant, inventory, and receivables. Neither partner's family has any interest in taking an active role in the management of the factory should either partner die. Smith runs technical operations within the factory, and Jones is in charge of sales and distribution. Neither knows much about the detailed operations of the other, but they work well as a team. Neither partner has any outside business interests, and practically no other assets, other than a small amount of life insurance.

   (a) What estate planning problem apparently exists for the two partners?
   (b) Suggest a plan to solve this problem.

Adjusted Gross Estate
Economic Recovery
  Tax Act of 1981 (ERTA)
Contemplation of Death
  Rule
Will Trust
Inter Vivos Trust
Testamentary Trust
Marital Deduction

Testator
Terminable Interest
  Property
Joint Ownership
Key Employee Insurance
Probate
Federal Estate Tax
Business Continuation
  Insurance

NOTES

1 Estimated from data reported annually by the U.S. Internal Revenue Service, *Statistics of Income—Estate*   *Tax Returns* (Annual).
2 Ibid.

15 BUYING LIFE INSURANCE

After studying this chapter, you should be able to:

1. List factors which should be considered in buying life insurance.
2. Make careful comparisons of life insurance contract provisions.
3. Identify the factors that influence the cost of life insurance.
4. State and explain the fallacy of making "net cost" comparisons.
5. Discuss factors to consider in evaluating the financial strength of a life insurer.
6. Analyze the "buy term and invest the difference" strategy.
7. Explain how life insurance programming works.

Because selection of insurers and analysis of their products and services is complex, the potential buyer of life insurance should give special study to this subject. Sizeable investments in life insurance are made on the dubious assumption that "all life insurance companies and their policies are alike, so why worry?" In some cases, all that it takes to persuade the buyer is a statement by the agent that "my company is sound and has a good rating by Best." It turns out that not all companies are alike, and certainly their products and services are not all alike. Several problems face the typical person in making efficient and intelligent selections among available life insurance products and services. In this chapter we consider the main problems involved.

STATING GOALS AND PURPOSES

The first step in buying life insurance is to analyze exactly what it is that the buyer is trying to accomplish—what goals and purposes the buyer wants to achieve. The various needs for insurance were covered in previous chapters. Later in this chapter we show how, through life insurance programming, needs for life insurance can be recognized and planned for.

For example, if your goal is to provide an estate clearance fund, including payment of estate and other taxes upon your death, some form of permanent life insurance protection would be a good choice. With that choice, a whole set of implications for costs, endorsements, settlement options, and other decisions would be shaped. On the other hand, if your goal is to provide a mortgage fund to pay off the debt on your home and leave a clear title to your spouse, another set of buying decisions would be made. In this case, decreasing term insurance would be a logical choice as the type of policy to buy, and this goal would influence the way the policy is to be settled and the way the beneficiary is indicated.

Clearly, life insurance should not be purchased for reasons that are not well delineated, or because "everyone ought to have a little life insurance." To do so might well mean that the policy is inappropriate and will not do the job one needs to have done. Careless selection of insurance may also mean that contracts will be dropped after a year or so, and the high first-year costs associated with the purchase of life insurance will be repeated when a replacement contract is bought.

SETTING BUDGET LIMITS

Before buying life insurance, the buyer needs to have a general idea as to how much can be spent on the policies. That is, budget limits should be established. If only $1,000 a year can be allocated to all life and health insurance, a much different arrangement of policies will be appropriate than would be the case if $5,000 can be afforded.

COMPARING ALTERNATIVE CONTRACTS

Most buyers of life insurance "shop around" to some extent before making final buying decisions. Because prices of insurance vary widely among insurers, this is a wise procedure if the goal is to get the most for one's money. However, in making valid price comparisons, the shopper should be certain to compare "apples with apples." Although basic types of life insurance are relatively few, literally hundreds of different arrangements of these basic types are sold, and it is not easy to make sure that two policies being considered are indeed directly comparable, with equivalent provisions and conditions.

As an illustration, if you are considering two ordinary life insurance policies, you should make sure, in comparing their prices, that each has the same set of clauses, such as waiver of premium, disability income endorsement, settlement options, or double-indemnity agreements. if these endorsements are desired options. Fortunately, a certain degree of policy standardization is mandated by most state laws. This simplifies the task of policy comparisons to some extent.

An example of important differences in life insurance provisions that should be recognized is the coverage granted by the disability income or waiver-of-premium rider. One type of provision defines total disability to mean incapacity to perform any work or engage in any business or occupation for remuneration or profit. This might be interpreted to mean that if a dentist should injure a hand and be unable to carry on a practice of dentistry, disability income would be denied since the dentist would still be able to work in a retail store or perform other work. In other words, it would not be the case that the dentist would be unable to work or engage in *any* other occupation. A different type of provision may define total disability more favorably for the insured. This provision may state that for the first 24 months disability means inability to perform the duties of one's regular occupation; thereafter, it means inability to perform any type of work for which the insured is qualified by training, education, or experience. In this case, the dentist in the preceding example could draw disability income for at least the first 24 months. The second provision is worth more, and the price comparison between the two policies should recognize this fact. It is not a simple task to compare two policies with variations in wording of several types of clauses, some of which are favorable and some of which are unfavorable to the insured.

ANALYZING COST FACTORS

If two contracts are sufficiently alike to warrant a comparison of cost, the next step is to compare the gross premiums charged. At this point there is an adjustment that must be made, depending upon whether either of the insurers is offering a participating rate or a nonparticipating rate. The term **participating** refers to the common practice of making an overcharge in the premium with the idea of returning a dividend to the policyholder. Both stock and mutual insurers write participating policies, but the practice is much more common with mutuals. Stock insurers generally offer a **nonparticipating** rate, that is, a rate lower than the participating rate, but at a fixed level. The purpose of the higher participating rate is to provide a margin for contingencies. The insurer in life insurance generally guarantees for life the initial rate charged. Thus, if costs rise, the insurer has no opportunity to increase the premium. By charging a higher initial rate than is actually required, the insurer is protected so that if insurance costs rise, the costs can be passed on to the individuals involved through smaller dividends. If insurance costs fall, these same individuals can enjoy larger dividends. In the case of stock insurers writing nonparticipating insurance, it is expected that if insurance costs rise, stockholders will bear any losses, while if insurance costs fall, they will receive the resulting profits.

What are the elements of cost in life insurance? There are three: mortality, interest, and overhead or loading. The insurer with the lowest rate of mortality experience, with the highest rate of interest earned on policyholders' funds over a period of years, and with the lowest cost of doing business will be the lowest cost insurer, *other things being equal.* Unfortunately, it is seldom possible to hold other factors constant.

Mortality

The element of mortality in the cost of life insurance refers to the death rate among policyholders. Since many companies base their life insurance premiums on the same mortality table, one might expect few, if any, differences to arise from this source of cost. However, one insurer may be more restrictive in its underwriting than another and thus experience a lower rate of mortality. Unfortunately, since figures on mortality experience are not generally available, prospective buyers cannot easily obtain comparisons on this point.

Interest

Life insurers as a group earned about 9.63 percent on invested assets in 1985, excluding assets held in separate accounts.[1] However, returns vary considerably among individual insurers. An insurer earning 10 percent on its assets is very likely to be able to offer its customers higher cash values, higher dividends, or broader coverage than an insurer earning only 6 percent. The sum of $100 invested annually at 6 percent for 10 years accumulates to $1,318. At 8 percent the $100 accumulates to $1,594, a difference of $276, or nearly 21 percent more.

Even though a life insurer may earn a reasonable rate of return on its assets, the amounts paid to policyholders may be very conservative. Most studies reveal that life insurers have paid very low interest yields to policyholders on the "cash value element" of contracts that have cash values. For example, a study by the Federal Trade Commission reported a *negative* rate of return (−12.3 percent) on a $10,000 whole life participating policy issued at age 25 and held for 5 years. The same policy held for 10 years yielded less than 2 percent and for 20 years only 4.5 percent.[2] The results were even less favorable for nonparticipating policies, which were found to yield less at all ages than dividend-paying policies. A study conducted by Consumers Union comparing 40 insurers showed that the average yield on dividend-paying policies for the highest yielding insurer was only 7.28 percent for a policy held 19 years. In this study the poorest yielding insurer had a yield of only 1.22 percent on the same policy.[3]

The relatively poor yields on life insurance policies suggest that the policyholder can probably do better by saving money in media other than cash value life insurance contracts, and concentrating instead on term contracts in which only pure protection (no cash value accumulation) is offered.

For the year 1984, overhead expenses averaged 15.4 percent of premiums for all life insurance companies, made up of 5.9 percent for agents' commissions and 9.5 percent for other expenses. Variations among individual insurers are wide, although comprehensive data are not available for a thorough analysis of these variations. Some of the differences in expense can be accounted for by differences in distribution efficiency. Some insurers spend substantial sums for the specific selection, training, and supervision of their agency force. Others spend very little. It is logical that, in the long run, the insurer that has the most efficient agency plant can secure business at the lowest cost. For example, higher commissions are needed to attract agents and brokers who receive no training or other aid. Turnover among such agents and brokers is higher, thus requiring greater hiring costs. Normally, the expenses of the firm with the greatest volume of business will be lower than those of firms with relatively small volumes. This is true because the fixed costs can be spread over a larger volume. This factor favors the large insurer. Expenses of insurers employing no agents should be expected to be lower than those of companies with large agency plants. However, there are relatively few life insurers who operate without agents.

"Net Cost"
Comparisons

To aid the prospective policyholder in estimating the cost of life insurance, mutual companies usually publish scales of estimated dividends, based on past performance with respect to the three elements of cost discussed above. The total dividends for, say, 20 years, are subtracted from the total premiums to be paid in, and the difference is represented as the cost of the insurance policy. Sometimes the agent subtracts from this figure the cash value of the policy and represents any difference to be the final "net cost."

Frequently the net cost developed in this manner is negative, implying that the insured would obtain insurance for nothing and even have a gain at the end of the period. This result is illustrated in Table 15–1 for a typical policy.

It would appear from examining column 5 of the table that after 20 years a buyer is making a small gain by purchasing ordinary life or life paid-up at 65, while term insurance involves a cost of $81.20. Thus, the term policy is seen to involve the lowest gross premium outlay, but because there is no accumulation of cash value, the total cost at the end of 20 years is larger than either of the other policies illustrated. This ignores the interest that one might have earned on the difference between the term premium and the higher cost policies.

If interest is considered, a very different result is obtained. For example, the 20-year "interest-adjusted cost" (see the subsequent explanation of this term) of the ordinary life policy, given in the last column of the table, is a positive amount, $4.94 per year.

Obviously, life insurance cannot be provided free of charge. The comparisons in columns 4 and 5 of the table, although frequently used by

Table 15-1 Typical Nonparticipating Premium Rates, Male, Age 30

	[1]	Guaranteed Cash Values		[4]	[5]	5% Interest-Adjusted Cost***	
		[2]	[3]			[6]	[7]
Type of Insurance	Annual Premium	10 Years	20 Years	10-Year Cost*	20-Year Cost	10-Year	20-Year
Ten-year term	$ 2.83	0	0	$28.30	$81.20**	n.a.	n.a.
Ordinary life	$12.09	91	246	$29.90	($4.10)	$5.11	$4.94
Life paid-up 65	$14.42	105	283	$39.20	($5.40)	$5.67	$3.77

* Annual premium × 10 less cash value.
** 10-year cost + 10 × premium for the policy renewal at age 40.
*** Assuming policy is surrendered.

agents in sales presentations, are very misleading. They ignore the interest element and the time value of money. The policyholder's loss of interest on premiums paid for coverage are not counted in these calculations.

Interest-Adjusted Method

A more scientific way to estimate the true costs of life insurance is the interest-adjusted method. This method considers the time value of money. Under it, the interest earnings lost by the insurance buyer on premiums devoted to life insurance are counted as part of the cost.

One can appreciate the difference between the net cost and the interest-adjusted method of calculating life insurance costs by considering the following example of two insurers, *A* and *B*.

| Years | Cumulative Dividends Plus Cash Values | |
	Insurer *A*	Insurer *B*
1	$ 100	$ 0
5	500	300
10	1,000	600
15	1,500	1,400
20	2,000	2,000

Each policy pays the policyholder $2,000 by the end of the twentieth year, but Insurer *B* offers much lower interim values. Insurer *A* would have a lower interest-adjusted cost than Insurer *B* because of the time value of money.

The interest-adjusted method is illustrated in the following example.[4] Assume a $1,000 life insurance policy carries an annual premium of $25, with dividends of $5 a year. There is a cash value in 20 years of $350. Assume money is worth 4 percent annually. At 4 percent, $1 a year paid in advance for 20 years will accumulate to $30.969. What is the interest-adjusted cost per $1,000? The cost is developed as follows:

1. 20 years of premium accumulated at 4% (30.969 × $25)	$774.23
2. Subtract 20 years of dividends accumulated at 4% (30.969 × $5)	−154.85
	$619.38
3. Subtract cash surrender value in 20 years	−350.00
	$269.38
4. Interest-adjusted cost per year: Divide by accumulation of $1 a year for 20 years at 4% ($269.38 ÷ 30.969)	$ 8.70

The traditional net cost method would be illustrated as follows:

1. Total premiums ($25 × 20)	$500.000
2. Less dividends ($5 × 20)	−100.00
3. Less 20-year cash value	−350.00
4. Total net cost (1) − (2) −(3)	$ 50.00
5. Net cost per year ($50 ÷ 20)	$ 2.50

Note that the interest-adjusted cost per year per $1,000, if the policy is surrendered, is nearly $3\frac{1}{2}$ times the traditional net cost.

Cost Variations

Most studies support the conclusion that major variations exist in the cost of life insurance, no matter what method is used to measure costs. Belth's early studies, for example, showed a coefficient of variation of 20 percent in the price of life insurance among dividend-paying insurers.[5] The 1980 study by Consumers Union cited earlier compared surrender cost indexes of 40 cash value life nonparticipating policies with face amounts of $25,000. This study revealed a cost range of $77 to $173 for the policy. Thus, the most expensive policy costs 2.2 times as much as the least expensive policy.[6]

Table 15–2 shows the range of interest-adjusted surrender cost (IASC) indexes in a group of about 82 participating and 68 nonparticipating policies issued in 1985. Note that IASC indexes varied much more for the participating than for the nonparticipating policies. The lowest IASC index was $0.36 per $1,000 for nonparticipating policies, compared to a negative cost (i.e., *gain*) of $8.60 for the lowest cost participating policy.

Table 15–3 compares IASC indexes and historical "net costs" for ten leading life insurers for the period 1965–1985. Note that an insurer may rank fairly high on interest-adjusted cost but low on "actual" net cost and *vice versa.* For example, USAA Life ranked tenth on net cost but ranked fourth on IASC index cost. Finally, remember that the past may not be the same as the future, so insurers that have produced good results before may not do so in the future. Because of the considerable imperfections of the net cost method of making life insurance cost comparisons, it seems best not to rely on this technique.

In summary, it seems fair to conclude that although it is not easy, careful cost comparisons in life insurance are justified, especially if the contracts have cash values and if they pay dividends. It is far easier to compare the costs of term insurance contracts; these have no cash values

Table 15–2
The High-Low Range of Interest-Adjusted Cost Indexes for Selected Whole Life Policies, 1985

	Nonparticipating		Participating	
	Premium	IASC Index	Premium	IASC Index
Highest	$18.05	8.14[1]	$19.35	10.81[3]
Lowest	7.92	.36[2]	16.66	−8.60[4]

All policies are for $100,000 or more for a male, age 35, from a group of insurers operating in 25 or more states.
[1] Midcontinental Life
[2] Kansas City Life
[3] Western Farm Bureau
[4] Life of the Southwest
Source: *Best's Review*, Life & Health Ed., December 1985, pp. 76–77, and January 1986, pp. 54–55.

Part 4   Life and Health Insurance

**Table 15–3
Interest-Adjusted Cost
Surrender Indexes vs.
"Net Costs" of Leading
Life Insurers, 1965–1985**

Company*	IASC Index	Rank	Yearly Average Net Cost**	Rank
Northwestern Mutual	$2.88	1	−$8.12	1
Guardian Life	$3.52	2	−$6.83	3
Union Mutual	$3.73	3	−$7.16	2
USAA Life	$4.13	4	−$4.75	10
Central Life of Iowa	$4.21	5	−$4.98	8
Massachusetts Mutual	$4.38	6	−$6.01	6
Phoenix Mutual	$4.56	7	−$6.20	4
The Bankers Life	$4.60	8	−$5.28	7
State Farm	$4.68	9	−$6.11	5
Century Life	$4.79	10	−$4.95	9

*Participating ordinary life policies, $1,000 face amount. Rankings are from a population of 68 insurers, for a male, age 35; policies issued in 1965.
**Actual 20 years of (premium − dividends − cash surrender value)/20
Source: "20-Year Dividend Comparisons," *Best's Review*, Life & Health Ed. (December, 1985), pp. 90–98.

and tend to be fairly uniform in other respects. It is more difficult to make accurate comparisons of cash value policies because of the uncertainty as to the amount of the dividend interest assumptions and other complexities. However, at the very minimum, if the buyer is considering using interest-adjusted cost indexes, the policy with the lowest interest-adjusted cost should be preferred, other factors remaining equal or approximately so. Net cost comparisons using the traditional method should be avoided because they may be very misleading. Finally, the factors of service to the policyholder, financial stability of the insurer, and the nature of the contract provisions should all be considered.

EVALUATING FINANCIAL STRENGTH

In life insurance the two most important elements of financial strength are the safety of the investments and the relative size of the policyholders' surplus, which includes all types of reserves for contingencies and any contributed capital of the owners.

Safety of the Investments

Investment data for life insurers are reported by several rating agencies. These agencies gather information from the annual statements furnished by each insurer to the commissioners of insurance in each estate in which the insurer operates. The information is public and can be obtained directly by inquiring at the state insurance commissioner's office.

The record of investment safety in the life insurance industry is one of the best of all industries in the United States. For example, during the depression period from 1929 to 1939, only 19 life insurance companies, representing about 5 percent of all companies then operating, retired with initial losses to policyholders of $1 million or more. The initial losses totalled $130 million, 50 percent of which was later recovered as other companies took over the retired insurers' business. In the same period, 12,000 banks were reported to have failed, with losses to depositors of $3 billion.[7] The final losses to policyholders of life insurance were approximately 0.2 percent of the average assets of the companies then operating. It seems fair to state that this record of safety has reduced the risk of loss to policyholders as close to zero as is feasible for any type of saving under modern conditions. However, losses do occasionally happen, such as in the case of Baldwin United Insurance Company, which issued annuity policies in the early 1980s under promises that could not be met.

Ratings of Financial Services

The analyst of a life insurer's financial strength should consult opinions of rating agencies such as Best. These opinions encompass the quality of the investments, net cost of insurance to the buyer, significant operating ratios, and management efficiency. Best has six rating classes, A+ and A (Excellent), B+ (Very Good), B (Good), C+ (Fairly Good), and C (Fair). In addition, there are 15 insurer groups categorized according to size of the policyholders' surplus. If the rating is omitted entirely, either the insurer is not considered to be sufficiently strong, its history may be too short (less than five years), or insufficient information was available for a rating. Best does not rate fraternals or assessment associations.

For insurers with the two lowest ratings and for new, small insurers about which little information is available, the potential policyholder is advised to use caution before committing term insurance and financial planning programs to them. In all doubtful cases the policyholder should contact the state insurance commissioner.

EVALUATING SERVICE

The element of service in the selection of a life insurer has two aspects: the amount of service to be obtained from the agent, and the amount of service to be obtained from the home office of the insurer.

Service from the Agent

The agent can act merely as an order taker, or can develop and maintain over the years a comprehensive plan of insurance designed to meet the unique needs of the client. The agent can write letters on behalf of the customer, take care of details such as beneficiary changes, and handle premium collections as a convenience to the client, or the agent can ignore demands for aid or refer the client to the home office for answers. The agent can sell a policy that comes closest to meeting the real needs of the client, or one that nets the greatest agent's commission, regardless of whether the policy is appropriate.

You should ask questions about how much in the way of service can be expected of an agent. The variations in service can spell the difference between a satisfactory insurance arrangement and one that fails to accomplish many of the things that are possible, but about which the insured may not know at all. In judging the quality of service that may be received from an agent, one can get some indication from the methods employed in selling the coverage, from the length of time the agent has been in business, from references of outside impartial sources, and from evidence of professional accomplishments, such as possession of the CLU designation.[8]

Service from the Home Office

Service from the home office of the insurer is very important. The life insurance policy is often a long-term contract involving 30 or 40 years of premium payments to the company, and 20 or more years of annuity payments either to the insured or to beneficiaries. The dispatch with which these payments are handled is vital to the success of the insurance plan. Insurance companies often pride themselves on paying death claims of thousands of dollars within hours after proof of loss has been submitted. Because agents come and go, the service of the insurer as a continuing influence over the years is of greater importance than it would be if the insured could deal with one agent indefinitely.

BUY-TERM-AND-INVEST-THE-DIFFERENCE STRATEGY

Many financial planners have suggested that a good buying strategy for life insurance is to use term plans for protection needs and separate investment or savings plans for accumulating money for future use. This is called "buy term and invest the difference." To illustrate this strategy, assume Gibson is considering two policies, A and B. (See Table 15–4.) Policy A is ordinary life and Policy B is 20-year renewable term. If Gibson selects Policy B, it is with the intention of investing the "difference" in premiums (in this case $18 per $1,000) in a tax-free municipal bond fund. The value of the separate account exceeds the cash value of the ordinary life insurance by an amount that varies according to the rate of interest earned in the tax-free bond fund. The death protection under Policy B is $1,000 plus the balance in the bond fund. Thus, both the savings and death protection elements in the buy-term-and-invest-the-difference plan are superior to the ordinary life plan. For example, at the end of 20 years, Gibson would have $250 cash value in Policy A, compared to $264 in the bond fund, even if it returns only 5 percent interest. If Gibson had died during the 20 years, the beneficiary would have received $1,000 under Policy B, plus the balance in the bond fund, compared to just $1,000 in Policy A. Thus, estate values are greater using the term insurance strategy.

Of course, buying term and investing the difference has some disadvantages relative to the ordinary life plan. First, in practice, one may not faithfully "save the difference" in the separate account, whereas one is more likely to maintain the ordinary life policy premiums. Second, the ordinary life policy offers certain income tax exemption on the accumulating interest element in the policy, whereas most interest in savings accounts is fully taxable. Third, the policyholder enjoys exemption from the claims

Table 15–4 Buy-Term-and-Invest-the-Difference versus Ordinary Life Insurance

	Policy A (Ordinary Life)	Policy B (20-Year Term)	Separate Investment of the "Difference" (A − B)
Annual premium per $1,000	$ 12	$ 4	$ 8
20 years of premiums	240	80	160
20-year cash values	250	0	—
20-year value of separate savings plan at			
5% interest			264
6% interest			294
7% interest			328
8% interest			366
Amount of death protection	$1,000	$1,000 +	Balance

of creditors for the cash value of the policyholder's ordinary life policy, a condition not usually applicable to savings accounts. Fourth, the owner of ordinary life has the option of continuing this protection as long as is desired, whereas most term policies cost too much past age 65. Fifth, the ordinary life policyholder has the option of using certain settlement options that are not available to the savings account holder. For these and other reasons, those who wish to save through life insurance may consider this means a desirable one, even though they might accumulate more by separating their savings from their life insurance.

An individual wishing to take more risk in a separate investment account could purchase a common stock mutual fund in the hope that this fund would offer some protection against inflation. Such an investment, however, is usually subject to income taxes, a factor that will reduce the net return. The plan would offer the compensating advantage that at least the individual would have some opportunity for superior gains that would offset inflation, albeit at some risk of loss. The "fixed-dollar" savings plan does not offer such an opportunity.

STRATEGIES FOR BUYING: LIFE INSURANCE PROGRAMMING

An effective way to plan life insurance buying needs is integrating life insurance with other assets and resources of the planner. This is usually called life insurance programming, the essential elements of which may be expressed in the following steps:

1. Assemble the pertinent facts relating to the family and its income, assets, insurance, and other resources applicable to its financial security.
2. Develop a statement of cash and income needs to be filled in the event of the premature death of the breadwinner.
3. Compare the needs and resources determined in the first two steps; determine what deficiencies exist and how they will be met.

4. Choose methods to settle life insurance proceeds through life insurance settlement options and trusts.

The life insurance program must be revised periodically. When a plan is first drawn up, it is assumed that it will become effective immediately in case of the death of the breadwinner that night. Later the needs and resources change. For example, after a mortgage is paid off, there is no continuing need for life insurance originally purchased to meet that obligation. The revised estate plan would reflect this fact. To illustrate the foregoing steps, consider the following simplified case.

Programming for John and Mary Brown

Let us develop a simplified program of life insurance for John and Mary Brown. The following facts apply. John and Mary, ages 30 and 26, respectively, have a two-year-old son, John, Jr. John's current income is $50,000 annually, and Mary, a nurse, is not employed outside the home at present. The Browns own a home carrying a $50,000 mortgage and are covered with both individual and employer-provided life insurance and retirement plans, as well as Social Security.

It is helpful to separate programming into two segments: lump-sum needs and income needs. To simplify the discussion, we shall consider only examples of these needs.

Lump-Sum Needs and Resources

It is easiest to start with lump-sum needs and resources. In the case of John and Mary Brown, assume the following list of lump-sum needs are agreed upon in case of John's death.

Needs upon John's Death		
To retire home mortgage		$ 50,000
To provide an educational fund for John, Jr.		30,000
To pay estate clearance expenses		50,000
To provide an emergency and re-adjustment fund for Mary		30,000
Total		$160,000

Cash Resources Available to Mary		
Cash in checking account	$ 5,000	
Savings account	20,000	
Mutual fund balance	30,000	
Group life insurance John's employer	50,000	
Individual ordinary life policy on John's life	30,000	135,000
Unmet Lump-Sum Need		$ 25,000

From this comparison, it is easy to determine that there is a need for an additional life insurance coverage of $25,000 to cover the Browns' stated lump-sum requirements. Let us call this Policy *E*, for estate clearance.

Income Needs

Income needs for the Browns cause a more complicated problem in life insurance programming than lump-sum needs. This is due to varying sources of income to Mary if John dies, different interest and investment assumptions that are possible, uncertainties in future inflation rates, changes in Social Security, eligibility of Mary to receive income from employment, and other factors. Income during retirement will be assumed to be provided from sources other than life insurance, such as John's employer pension, individual savings plans, and Social Security.

To illustrate, a commonly recognized income need is to provide supplemental family income while the children are still dependent—i.e., the family income period. Assume the Browns desire $2,000 monthly until John, Jr. is 22 and has graduated from college, a period of 20 years. Assume further that $1,500 monthly is then needed until Mary is age 60. Social Security income is estimated to provide $700 monthly to the widow with one dependent child until that child is 16.[9] These income needs and resources can be charted as shown in Figure 15–1.

For simplification, assume that inflation rates are zero and that Mary does not plan to work. From the figure, John and Mary may calculate their

Figure 15–1
Income Program

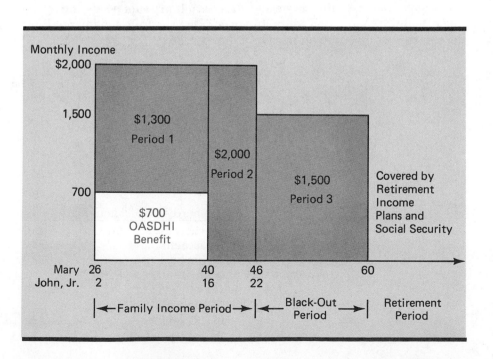

Part 4   Life and Health Insurance

income needs in three periods corresponding to varying income levels that are required.

Income Period 1	$1,300 monthly ($15,600 a year) for 14 years
Income Period 2	$2,000 monthly ($24,000 a year) for 6 years, starting after 14 years
Income Period 3	$1,500 monthly ($18,000 a year) for 14 years, starting after 20 years

The next question is to determine the amount of funds needed to produce the required income. This requires selection of an appropriate interest assumption. Assume the Browns believe 10 percent interest can be earned on the funds.

In programming problems, it is convenient to start with the latest need first, since interest income from these policies can be used to help satisfy earlier needs. Thus, starting with Period 3, we need to find how much money is needed to provide $1,500 monthly for 14 years. Referring to Table D-4, Appendix D, we learn that at 10 percent the sum of $7.36 is needed to guarantee the payment of $1 a year for 14 years. Thus, $132,480 (7.36 × $18,000) is the lump-sum equivalent of the payment of $18,000 a year for 14 years.

It should be noted that few, if any, life insurance companies currently use an interest assumption of 10 percent in fixed-period settlement options. Most guarantee only 3–4 percent, although they may pay 6–8 percent in practice. At 3 percent, it would take about $71,000 more insurance than is needed using the 10 percent assumption. However, the Browns need not use a life insurance contract settlement option, but instead may have the life insurance proceeds paid to a trustee under a life insurance trust (discussed earlier). In recent years trustees have obtained 10 percent returns or higher in long-term government bonds. Thus, the Browns should provide life insurance in the amount of about $133,000 to meet Period 3 needs. Call this Policy 3.

Before rejecting life insurance settlement options as offering an interest return that is too low, certain advantages of the life insurance method of distributing proceeds should be considered. First, some life insurers are now offering more generous interest levels than was true formerly. Second, life insurers do not levy an administration or investment fee under settlement options, as does a trustee.

On the other hand, the trust method offers much greater flexibility and frequently is preferable to life insurance settlement options, especially for larger estates.

The second income need, Period 2, to be filled is $2,000 monthly ($24,000 annually) for 6 years, to start after 14 years.

Assume that in the case of John's death, proceeds from the $133,000 policy purchased to satisfy Period 3 can be invested at 10 percent,

producing income of $13,300 a year. This leaves $10,700 a year ($24,000 −
$13,300) yet to be provided for Period 2. Using Table D-4, assuming 10
percent interest, we learn that $4.36 is required for each $1 of annual
income to be paid for 6 years. Thus, $46,652 of insurance (4.36 × $10,700)
is required for Period 2. Call this Policy 2, rounded to equal $47,000.

For Period 1, $24,000 a year, three sources of income are available:
$13,300 a year in interest from the proceeds of Policy 3, $4,700 a year
interest from the proceeds of Policy 2, and $8,400 a year from Social
Security. These total $26,700, or $2,700 more than is required for Period 1.
This extra income, $2,700 a year, can be saved to help meet other income
requirements for emergencies or to offset inflation losses, as explained
shortly.

To summarize the discussion so far, we may chart the results as follows:

Need	Income	To Be Met By	
Period 3	$18,000 14 years	Policy 3 ($133,000) Paid in Installments of	$18,000
Period 2	$24,000 6 years	1. Interest from Policy 3 2. Installments from Policy 2 ($47,000)	$13,300 10,700
			$24,000
Period 1	$24,000 14 years	1. Social Security 2. Interest from Proceeds of Policy 3 3. Interest from Proceeds of Policy 2	$ 8,400 13,300 4,700
			$26,700

**Adjustments
for Inflation**

It is unrealistic to assume a zero rate of inflation in life insurance
programming problems. Inflation causes severe losses in purchasing power
of income. Unfortunately, no investment is known that can offset these
losses with certainty. However, we may calculate the amounts needed to
make initial adjustments for inflation.

For example, assume that inflation will average 3 percent annually.
Then the $18,000 amount stated in Period 3 and the $24,000 for Period 2
in the preceding calculations will be inadequate. Using Table D-1,
Appendix D, we see that at 3 percent compound interest, $1 increases to
$1.80 in 20 years. That is, in 20 years it will take $1.80 to provide the
amount purchased by $1 today. The $133,000 fund provided by Policy 3
will have to be increased to $239,400 (1.8 × $133,000) to produce the
inflation-adjusted income that will be needed by the Browns. The $47,000
policy for Period 2 likewise will need upward adjustment to $70,970
(14-year factor of 1.51 × $47,000). (Even if these sums are available at the

start of Periods 1, 2, and 3, they will soon be inadequate if inflation continues its upward rate of 3 percent annually.)

However, the Browns can make a calculation of the *extra* sums needed to offset the assumed inflation and later make periodic adjustments as circumstances change. For example, if inflation rates decline, any insurance bought for this purpose may be conveniently dropped without restructuring the entire program.

The extra sums (rounded) needed to offset 3 percent inflation are:

Need	To Begin After	Sums Needed without Inflation	Sums Needed with 3% Inflation	Additional Sums Required
Period 3	20 years	$133,000	$240,000	$107,000
Period 2	14 years	47,000	71,000	24,000
Total		$180,000	$311,000	$131,000

The $131,000 sum needed for inflation will not be needed until the respective income periods begin. Thus, the sums can be discounted at some assumed rate, say 8 percent. The present value of $107,000 in 20 years (see Table D-2) is $59,235, and the present value of $24,000 in 14 years is $15,866. Thus, if John dies immediately (as is assumed in life insurance programming problems), the sums above would be increased through interest to the required levels in the future. The Browns may take out two policies for $60,000 and $16,000 for inflation losses. Call them Policy *3-I* and Policy *2-I* for protection against inflation in Periods 3 and 2, respectively. Insurance to cover these needs should be increased periodically as the time approaches when the sums are required. For example, the present value of $107,000 in 15 years is about $69,000. Policy *3-I* should be arranged to increase accordingly. In this case, an additional $9,000 policy could be purchased.

If Mary Works

If Mary decides to work outside the home, many of the above needs for life insurance will be reduced. Unfortunately, if Mary accepts employment, it is likely she will lose part or all of the $8,400 income from Social Security.[10] Assume that after reduction for this loss and for job and other expenses, Mary can net $9,000 a year by working. The revised income needs would be as follows:

Period 3 Income	$18,000
Less: provided by Mary's job	9,000
To be provided by Policy 3	$ 9,000
Sum required to pay $9,000 a year for 14 years at 10% interest. Rounded amount for Policy 3	$67,000

Period 2 Income	$24,000
Less: provided by Mary's job	9,000
	$13,000

To be met by:

Interest from Policy 3	$ 6,700
Installments from Policy 2	$ 6,300

Sum required to pay $6,300 a year for 6 years at 10% interest	$27,468
Rounded amount for Policy 2	$28,000

Period 1 Income	$24,000
Less: provided by Mary's job	9,000
	$13,000

To be met by:

Social Security	$ 3,120
Interest from Policy 3	6,700
Interest from Policy 2	2,800
Total provided for Period 1	$12,620
Unmet need for Period 1	$ 380

If Mary works, the size of Policy 3 is reduced to $67,000 (from $133,000), and Policy 2 is reduced to $28,000 (from $47,000), a total of $95,000 of insurance proceeds needed rather than $180,000.

It may be assumed that Mary's job pay will be adjusted for inflation, as is her income from Social Security. Only the income planned from Policies 3 and 2 will need adjustment for inflation. This may be done in the way illustrated above.

The type of life insurance that should be purchased for the program depends on the permanency of the need. For example, Policy E, covering the $25,000 estate clearance need, should probably be met with a permanent whole life policy, since estate clearance need is permanent.

Policy 3 can be on a term plan, such as level term to 65, since Period 3 is deemed to end at Mary's age 60, when other sources of income are assumed to take over.

Policy 2 can also be on a term plan, say 20-year level term, since Period 2 expires after 20 years.

Policies 3-I and 2-I, to offset inflation loss, should be on an increasing term plan. As already pointed out, the needs increase each year because less time is left to accumulate the required sums.

At John's age 30, these policies (assuming Mary does not work) would carry approximate annual premiums of:

Policy E	$25,000 whole life, non-participating	$ 375
Policy 3	$133,000 term to 60	975
Policy 2	$47,000 20-year level term	175
Policy 3-1	$60,000 term to 60 increasing 10 percent annually*	444*
Policy 2-1	$16,000 20-year term increasing 10 percent annually	60*
Total initial premium		$2,029

*Premiums and face amount of insurance rise each year.

It can be appreciated from this listing that the major insurance need and cost stems from the policies purchased to offset inflation. If inflation rates are different from those assumed, the needs and policy amounts should be adjusted accordingly. Current premiums amount to about 4 percent of John's current gross salary. If this salary is also adjusted for inflation, the total relative burden of carrying needed insurance will not change. Premiums will be less if Mary works, because total needs are less.

Using Wills and Trusts

It may be well to have all of the new life insurance for the Browns settled in cash and paid into a life insurance trust. (See Chapter 14.) If desired, arrangements can be made to set up the trust immediately as a living trust and have the trust own the policies. Trust A (the marital deduction trust discussed in Chapter 14) could be used for this purpose. In this way, the problems of managing trust property would not fall on Mary's shoulders. John could make deposits to the trust account currently to cover necessary premiums.

Obviously, a will should be drawn up covering John's estate plans. Under will, Trust B, for the benefit of John, Jr., could be established. Property in this trust would not be subject to estate taxation or probate expenses in Mary's estate because it is not a part of her estate, although she would usually be given the right to draw income from it if needed. Trustees of both trusts should be given discretion in making appropriate investments of trust property and in paying beneficiaries income which will meet their customary living standards, with due regard to inflation and other factors. In this way, the estate plan can assure that John's beneficiaries will have the lifetime income security he has planned for them. John should make use of an experienced attorney and tax advisor in drawing up his plan.

The Browns should also consider purchasing insurance on Mary's life in an amount necessary to pay extra estate taxes and administrative costs in John's estate in case Mary dies first. In this event, John will lose the marital deduction, and as a result, the entire estate will be subject to heavy estate taxes, similar to the situation for Mary, outlined in Figure 14–2. In that situation, federal estate taxes of $373,000 were due. Life insurance to cover this cost is appropriate.

At least every 5 years the Browns should review and update their life insurance program. Insurance and other needs vary constantly because of changes in the Browns' ages, income, and investment programs, and because of inflation and interest fluctuations. For example, if interest rates decrease from 10 percent to 8 percent in the above program, insurance required for Period 3, $18,000 a year for 14 years, would increase from $133,000 to about $148,000. If a house is sold and a mortgage of a different size is assumed, mortgage redemption insurance will change. Insurance that is no longer required can be dropped or reassigned to fill a different need.

SUMMARY

1. The first step in the intelligent selection of an insurer is to make sure that each insurer to be analyzed offers a comparable insurance contract. The cost of insurance, the insurer's financial strength and stability, and the quantity and quality of services offered are all interrelated. The final selection of the insurer should not be made until all factors have been studied.

2. Some notion concerning the ultimate cost of the insurance service may be obtained by an examination of the ratio of losses and expenses to premiums earned for individual insurers and resulting underwriting gains or losses.

3. The financial strength of an insurer may be judged by the relative size of policyholders' surplus, by Best's ratings, by the adequacy of reserves, and by the soundness of investments. The analyses should be compared for several consecutive years.

4. Quantity and quality of service rendered, economy, and convenience in the administration of one's insurance program are important factors in the selection of an insurer or agent. Studies reveal considerable dissatisfaction with some agents, brokers, and insurance services. The individual needs of each buyer should be weighed in selecting agents or insurers.

5. Special care should be taken to see that misleading dividend comparisons are avoided, and that interest-adjusted earnings are considered. The personal services rendered by agents differ widely in life insurance and are a significant factor in the selection of a particular insurer. Willingness of the agent to render aid in fitting life insurance to the individual needs of the buyer is also an important factor.

6. Buying life insurance wisely involves advance plans for the appropriate use of death proceeds. The life insurance buyer should ask the agent to prepare a life insurance program as a valuable guide in buying the right amount of coverage and in planning how the proceeds should be distributed.

7. Life insurance trusts may serve a valuable purpose in administering death proceeds.

QUESTIONS FOR REVIEW

1. State in your own words the main goals for purchasing life insurance.

2. In setting budget limits for buying life insurance, what percentage of income do you think is reasonable for the purpose? Should one be guided more by one's income or by one's goals in setting budget limits? Explain.

3. Why should you see that two contracts you may be comparing have the same set of

endorsements, riders, and other significant provisions?

4. Name and explain briefly the three main elements making up the cost of life insurance. Approximately how significant are each of these elements quantitatively?

5. Explain the essential difference between the "net cost" method and the "interest-adjusted" method of determining the cost of life insurance. Why is the latter method preferred?

6. By reference to *Best's Insurance Reports*, determine and interpret the financial rating given to a life insurance company doing business in your city.

7. Of what importance is "service" in the life insurance buying decision? Which service is more important in the long run—that offered by the agent or that provided by the insurer? Explain.

8. Evaluate the "buy-term-and-invest-the-difference" argument.

9. How should inflation be handled in the life insurance programming process?

10. In life insurance programming, what is the effect on the amount of life insurance needed if
    (a) the surviving spouse works outside the home?
    (b) the surviving spouse does not work outside the home? Explain.

11. How should inflation be recognized in life insurance programming?

QUESTIONS FOR DISCUSSION

1. An insurer was considering borrowing on the cash value of a life insurance policy in order to make another investment, but was reluctant to do so because of his knowledge that the loan would be subtracted from the death proceeds in the event that he died before repaying the loan.

(a) Is it necessary for a life insurance loan to be repaid at some point? Explain.

(b) Suggest a possible solution to the insured's problem, i.e., how could the insured's estate be protected from the loss due to the existence of a life insurance loan?

2. The following data on whole life insurance policies were supplied by major mutual life insurers for a male nonsmoker, age 25:

	Northwestern Mutual	Guardian Life
Premium	$17.35	$14.59
10-year premium	$173.50	$145.90
10-year dividend	$41.92	$17.54
Net payments	$131.58	$128.36
Average payment	$13.16	$12.84
Cash value	$127.09	$115.91
Net difference	$4.49	$12.45
Average difference	$0.45	$1.25
5% surrender index	$3.89	$4.24

Jane favors the lower premium Guardian Life policy, and John prefers the Northwestern Mutual. Which do you favor? Why? Give reasons. What other information would you like to have before making any final decision? Explain.

3. Make a statement of cash and lump-sum needs for yourself, and develop a "program" showing how much and what type(s) of life insurance you would purchase to supply these needs.

4. Korey, age 25, believes he can earn 8 percent on long-term savings and that it would pay him to "buy term and invest the difference." He is offered a $100,000 (nonparticipating) term policy for $372 annually. An ordinary life policy in the same company costs $749 annually. The ordinary life policy has guaranteed cash values of $15,200 in 20 years, and $45,900 at age 65. Which choice should Korey make, the term or the ordinary life plan? Give your reasons.

5. The Pennsylvania Insurance Department *Shopper's Guide* revealed that for a male, age 20, for $10,000 of nonparticipating, straight life insurance, the Travelers Insurance Company and the Surety Life Insurance Company each quoted an annual premium of $118. However, the 20-year interest-adjusted cost index for Travelers was $3.77 compared to $6.29 for Surety Life. Since neither policy pays dividends, account for the different rankings on interest-adjusted cost.

NEW TERMS AND CONCEPTS

Buy-Term-and-Invest-the-Difference

Interest-Adjusted Cost Method

Best's Rating

Loading

Life Insurance Programming

NOTES

1 *Life Insurance Fact Book 1986* (Washington, D.C.: American Council of Life Insurance, 1986), p. 64.
2 Federal Trade Commission, *Life Insurance Cost Disclosure Staff Report* (Washington, D.C.: U.S. Government Printing Office, 1979), pp. 29–30.
3 "Life Insurance—A Special Two-Part Report," *Consumer Reports*, Vol. 45, No. 3 (March, 1980), p. 176.
4 Sources such as *Best's Flitcraft Compend* (Oldwick, N.J.: A. M. Best Company), published annually, report the interest-adjusted costs of various policies of major U.S. insurers.
5 Joseph M. Belth, "Price Competition in Life Insurance," *Journal of Risk and Insurance*, Vol. 33, No. 3 (September, 1966), pp. 365–379. See also Belth's works, *The Retail Price Structures in American Life Insurance* (Bloomington: Indiana University, 1966), and *Life Insurance—A Consumer's Handbook* (Bloomington: Indiana University, 1973).

6 "Life Insurance—A Special Two-Part Report," *Consumer Reports*, Vol. 45, No. 3 (March, 1980), p. 170.
7 A. M. Best, "Rating in the Financial Structure of Insurance Companies," *Administrative Problems in Corporate Insurance Buying*, Insurance Series No. 96 (New York: American Management Association, 1952), p. 8.
8 **CLU** stands for Chartered Life Underwriter. This designation is given by the American College of Life Underwriters, Bryn Mawr, Pennsylvania, after the full-time life insurance agent has passed a series of ten comprehensive examinations in life insurance and related fields.
9 Benefits to a child may continue beyond age 16. College period benefits to a child are being phased out.
10 In 1987 she would lose $1 of benefits for each $2 earned above $6,000 (D.R. Detlief and R.J. Meyers, Guide to Social Security, 1987 [Wm. M. Mercer-Meidinger, Inc., November, 1986], p. 18). (This is an estimate for persons under age 65.) Thus, if she earned $15,000 by working, Mary might lose $\frac{1}{2}$ ($15,000 − $6,000), or $4,500, in Social Security benefits.

PART 5

PERSONAL RISK MANAGEMENT-PROPERTY LIABILITY

16 HOMEOWNERS' INSURANCE

After studying this chapter, you should be able to:

1. List the six basic coverages in a homeowners' policy and the limits of liability for each coverage.
2. Explain how the six different forms in the homeowners' program differ from each other.
3. Identify property that is excluded from the homeowners' policy and the special limits of liability for certain types of property.
4. Describe how additional living-expense losses are determined and how the settlement clause in the homeowners' policy operates.
5. Differentiate all-risk coverage from named-peril coverage.
6. Explain the doctrine of concurrent causation and its role in property insurance policies.
7. Identify the named perils insured in homeowners' policies.
8. List the coverages in the comprehensive personal liability policy (CPL) and identify the major exclusions in the CPL.
9. Discuss procedures to reduce property losses around the home.

Personal lines deal with the insurance needs of individuals rather than those of a business. We shall review some of the many contracts in the personal area, with special emphasis on the major property insurance policy, the homeowners' policy. Besides the homeowners' program discussed in this chapter, the dwelling, mobile home, and watercraft programs are examined in Chapter 18.

HOMEOWNERS' PROGRAM: DEVELOPMENT

The most comprehensive protection for owner-occupied one- or two-family residences is found in the homeowners' program. This program is an outgrowth of several attempts by the insurance industry to provide a package of protection for the average homeowner that can provide a more balanced and a more generally adequate program of insurance at a lower cost than would be available if the coverages were purchased separately. Such policies were made possible by multiple-line legislation. The homeowners' policy was developed in 1958 by the Multi-Peril Insurance Conference, an advisory and rating organization for insurance companies. It was revised in 1962 and 1968, and a major revision was made in 1976. It was again revised in 1984, and today's homeowners' policy (1) is written in easy-to-understand English; (2) is multiple-line (property and liability exposure are covered); (3) requires a minimum amount of coverage to be purchased; and (4) costs less.

Concise Language

The current version of the homeowners' policy is much easier to read than earlier policies. For instance, its insuring agreement states, "We will provide the insurance described in this policy in return for the premium and compliance with all applicable provisions of the policy." The former policy said, "In consideration of the Provisions and Stipulations Herein or Added Hereto and the Premium Above Specified, this Company, for the term shown above at noon (Standard Time) to expiration date shown above at noon (Standard Time) at location of property involved, to an amount not exceeding the limit of liability above specified, does insure the Insured named in the Declarations. . ." As you can see, today's version is 40 percent shorter and easier to read. It has 8,000 words compared to the previous edition's 12,000. Even the size of the print has been increased 25 percent so it will be easier to read. All of these changes, resulting from the consumer movement, should make a more desirable contract.

Multiple-Line

A basic objective of the homeowners' program is to provide an opportunity for the homeowner to purchase in one policy any of the many variations of coverage. Broad named-peril or all-risk protection is offered, plus such coverages as personal liability and medical payments to other persons.

Minimum Amount of Coverage

The distinguishing feature of this type of policy is that it provides a definite minimum amount of coverage acceptable to the insurer. Consequently, a single indivisible premium is charged, and the insured cannot select specific coverages.

Lower Cost

Because the insured is buying a package of coverages, costs are lower. This cost savings results from a broader range of perils being insured, which gives the insurer a better spread of loss exposures and lower administrative expenses. This arrangement allows insurers to charge up to 40 percent less for the total package than for coverages purchased separately.

While certain coverages are mandatory, there is still sufficient flexibility in the amounts required so that the form can fit the needs of most people. A brief outline of the basic coverages of the homeowners' program follows.

OUTLINE OF HOMEOWNERS' COVERAGES

Coverage	Amount
A Dwelling	Min. $15,000
B Other Structures	10% of A
C Unscheduled Personal Property	50% of A
D Additional Living Expense	20% of A
E Comprehensive Personal Liability	$25,000
F Medical Payments to Others	$500/Person

Table 16–1 summarizes the coverage offered by most of the primary homeowners' forms. Note that a dwelling must be owner occupied to qualify for the program, and minimum coverage of $15,000 must be purchased. With the average price of new homes now more than $100,000, this $15,000 limit is low. (For HO-3 the limit is $20,000.)

As used in the table, the term **limited named perils** means fire, lightning, windstorm, hail, explosion, riot, civil commotion, aircraft, vehicles, smoke, vandalism and malicious mischief, theft, and breakage of glass. However, the definitions of the same perils in the HO-1 may not be as broad as those found in HO-2, 3, 4, and 6. Also, the glass coverage in HO-1 is for only $50, while the other forms have no limit other than the appropriate policy limit. In addition to the basic six homeowners' forms, a new form, HO-8, has been issued. (There never was an HO-7 and HO-5 is not in use anymore; see pages 399–402 for discussion of 16 broad named perils.)

The HO-8 form was developed to meet a special situation in urban areas. Today many persons are moving back into older neighborhoods and remodeling the homes there. The market value of the home might be $60,000, but its replacement cost $150,000. A standard homeowners' policy would encourage the policyholder to insure to 80 percent of replacement value, or $120,000 (0.80 × $150,000 = $120,000). However, insurance companies were reluctant to insure a $60,000 home for $120,000 because of the potential moral hazard. This led to an unavailability-of-coverage problem for such older dwellings. To meet the needs of the insured and to reduce the moral hazard involved with other forms, the HO-8 was developed.

Under this form, insureds cannot collect on a replacement cost basis, but they may collect on a **cost-to-repair basis.** The cost-to-repair basis is different from actual cash value. Under the notion, there is no deduction

Table 16–1 Basic Coverages of Homeowners' Program

Provision	HO-1 Basic	HO-2 Broad	HO-3 Special	HO-4 Tenants	HO-6 Unit Owners	HO-8 Modified
Owner-Occupied 1- or 2-Family	(Not available in all states) Yes	Yes	Yes	–	–	Yes
Minimum Limits (with Exceptions)	$15,000	$15,000	$20,000	$6,000 Personal Property	$6,000 Personal Property	$15,000
Perils Insured Against	Limited Named Perils	Broad Named Perils	All-Risk Dwelling Broad Named Perils Personal Property	Broad Named Perils Personal Property	Broad Named Perils (Except Glass)	Same as HO-1
A—Dwelling	Amount Purchased	Amount Purchased	Amount Purchased	–	–	Amount Purchased
B—Other Structures	10% of A	10% of A	10% of A	Not Insured	Not Insured	10% of A
C—Unscheduled Personal Property	50% of A	50% of A	50% of A	Amount Purchased	Amount Purchased	50% of A
Unscheduled Personal Property at Secondary Residence	10% of C or $1,000, Whichever Greater	10% of C or $1,000, Whichever Greater	10% of C or $1,000, Whichever Greater	10% of C or $1,000, Whichever Greater	10% of C or $1,000, Whichever Greater	10% of C or $1,000, Whichever Greater
D—Additional Living Expense	10% of A	20% of A	20% of A	20% of C	40% of C	10% of A
E—Comprehensive Personal Liability	$100,000	$100,000	$100,000	$100,000	$100,000	$100,000
F—Medical Payment to Others	$1,000/Person	$1,000/Person	$1,000/Person	$1,000/Person	$1,000/Person	$1,000/Person

for depreciation. However, repairs may not be with like labor and material. For instance, if a slate roof is destroyed, modern roofing materials, like asphalt shingles with fiberglass backing, will be used rather than slate. Besides this restriction, only $1,000 of theft coverage is offered, and usually a $250 deductible applies to theft losses. Unscheduled personal property (Coverage *C*) is restricted to the premises rather than being worldwide. However, 10 percent of the Coverage *C* limit or $1,000, whichever is greater, may be used to cover personal property away from the premises. Also, there is no 5 percent increase in policy limits for debris removal, and recovery on plants, trees, and shrubs is limited to $250 per item. The perils insured against are the same as those in the HO-1.

Finally, the rates for the HO-8 are high. For a $15,000 to $30,000 dwelling, the HO-8 rate can be 50 percent higher than the HO-1 rate. While this represents the maximum difference between the two forms, the HO-8 is always higher. Consequently, the insured must pay more for less coverage, but at least the homeowners' approach is now available where previously it was not.

ANALYSIS OF HOMEOWNERS' POLICY

To this point we have outlined the coverages available in the homeowners' program. In the following discussion an analysis of the property coverage of one of the most popular forms, HO-3, is presented. Liability coverage is analyzed later in this chapter.

HO-3 Coverage A—Dwelling

Coverage *A* is for the residence itself, or what the policy calls residence premises. If you purchase a $60,000 homeowners' policy, Coverage *A* is for $60,000; the other property limits are a set percentage of that $60,000 and are additional amounts of insurance. A $60,000 homeowners' policy actually provides $108,000 of property-related insurance ($60,000 on the dwelling, $6,000 on other structures, $30,000 on unscheduled personal property, and $12,000 for additional living expense.)

The **dwelling** is defined by the policy as the structure on the residence premises shown in the declarations, used principally as a private residence, including structures attached to the dwelling. Examples of an item attached to the dwelling would be a patio roof, a carport, or even an attached walk-in greenhouse. If a structure is connected to the dwelling by only a fence, such a structure is protected by Coverage *B*. Besides the preceding items, the dwelling coverage also involves materials and supplies located adjacent to the residence premises for use in the construction, alteration, or repair of the dwelling or of other structures on the residence premises. This protection means that a dwelling under construction or one being repaired can be protected by a homeowners' policy. A separate builders' risk policy is not needed by the homeowner. (The builders' risk form is discussed in Chapter 20.)

In previous homeowners' editions, personal property such as building equipment and outdoor equipment pertaining to the service of the building were considered part of the dwelling; now they are not. Examples of these items are lawn mowers, garden statuary, and jungle gyms. These items must be protected under Coverage C, personal property. This modification is actually a reduction in protection, since full replacement cost coverage applies to the dwelling but not to personal property. In addition, in the HO-3 form real property has all-risk protection whereas personal property does not.

HO-3 Coverage B—Other Structures

Other structures are defined as those separated from the dwelling by clear space or connected by only a fence or utility line. A garage that is not attached to the dwelling is an example of such a structure, as is a greenhouse or a tool shed. It is usually to the insured's advantage to have a building considered an other structure if both the dwelling and the other structure are damaged, since broader limits would apply ($1.10 \times$ limit of A versus just the limit of A). However, if only the other structure is damaged, the insured may wish it had been considered part of the dwelling, since the dwelling coverage is ten times greater.

Coverage B is designed for personal use. Other structures used for business purposes or held for rental are not protected. For example, a lawyer's office in a separate structure on the residence premises would not be covered by the homeowners' policy.

HO-3 Coverage C—Unscheduled Personal Property

Coverage C is the most complex property insurance in the policy. The basic property covered is personal property owned or used by an insured while anywhere in the world subject to the exclusions discussed below. This statement means that property is protected while one is on a vacation in Europe or away at college. Types of property protected include such items as jewelry, kitchen appliances, furniture, clothes, stereos, televisions, currency, guns, and bicycles. Besides the insured's property, property of others while on the residence premises is protected if the insured requests it. Also, a person's property at any other insured residence besides the main residence premises is covered for $1,000 or 10 percent of the amount of Coverage C, whichever is greater. A vacation home is an example of such a residence.

Property that is kept year-round at the secondary residence is subject to this restriction. Personal property, such as a camera, stereo, or clothes, taken to the secondary residence is insured for the full limit of Coverage C.

While Coverage C is the coverage for personal property, certain types of property are excluded and others have dollar limitations. These dollar limitations are substantially lower than would otherwise be the case.

HO-3—Property Excluded. There are nine categories or types of property specifically excluded in Coverage C:

1. Articles separately described and specially insured in this or any other insurance, such as an expensive camera, watch, or diamond ring

2. Animals, including birds and fish
3. Motorized land vehicles, except those used to service an insured's residence which are not licensed for road use; thus, coverage for automobiles, motorcycles, golf carts, and snowmobiles is eliminated, but riding mowers used to cut the lawn and rototillers used to plow a garden are protected.
4. Sound equipment while in an automobile; no coverage exists for CB radios, tape decks, and their accessories or antennas while in an automobile. These items can be insured in an auto policy.
5. Aircraft and parts. (Older forms did not exclude aircraft parts.) Model airplanes are covered.
6. Property of roomers, boarders, and other tenants, except those related to an insured
7. Property contained in an apartment regularly rented or held for rental to others by any insured
8. Property rented or held for rental to others while away from the residence premises
9. Books of account, drawings, or other paper records; or electronic data processing tapes, wires, records, discs, or other software media containing business data. However, the costs of blank or unexposed records and media are covered.

HO-3—Special Limits of Liability. Certain types of property have special dollar limits placed on them which restrict an insured's recovery. If a person needs higher limits for the restricted items, additional coverage can be purchased through the use of an endorsement to the policy and the payment of an additional premium. The following restrictions apply:

1. $200 limit on money, bank notes, bullion, gold other than gold ware, silver other than silverware, platinum, coins, and medals
2. $1,000 on securities, deeds, manuscripts, passports, tickets, and stamps
3. $1,000 on watercraft, including their trailer furnishings, equipment, and outboard motors
4. $1,000 on trailers not used with watercraft
5. $1,000 on grave markers
6. $1,000 for loss by theft of jewelry, watches, furs, and precious and semiprecious stones
7. $2,500 for loss by theft of silverware, silver-plated ware, gold ware, gold-plated ware, and pewter
8. $2,000 for loss by theft of guns
9. $2,500 on property on the residence premises, used at any time or in any manner for any business purpose.
10. $250 on property away from the residence premises, used at any time or in any manner for any business purpose.

If an insured desires, coverage on currency can be raised to $500, but good risk control would prohibit keeping that much cash in the house anyway. If a person has a coin collection, additional insurance is most likely needed. For instance, the cost of a 1914-D Lincoln-head penny in uncirculated condition will easily exceed the $200 limit that the homeowners' policy will pay. The insured must purchase specific insurance on the collection and must remember that homeowners' insurance will not contribute one cent since it excludes coverage when items are specifically insured.

The limitation of $1,000 on securities, manuscripts, stamps, etc., is important for stamp collectors and persons who invest in stocks and bonds. Stamp collectors need to take the same precaution as coin collectors. Investors should keep their securities in safe deposit boxes or with their brokers.

The $1,000 coverage on watercraft applies to all types of watercraft and not just canoes and rowboats. However, a bass boat or a ski rig will require a separate policy since these watercraft are often worth several thousand dollars.

The coverage on grave markers is new to the homeowners' program. The major causes of loss to these items are theft, vandalism, and malicious mischief.

The theft (and only theft) limitation on jewelry, watches, furs, and precious and semiprecious stones is very important. The $1,000 limit is an aggregate limit, not a per-item one. Consequently, most people are underinsured for these items in their homeowners' coverage.

There is a $2,500 theft restriction on silverware, silver plate, and guns in the homeowners' program, and it results from increased losses in these areas. Because of the rapid increase in the cost of silverware and silver plate, these items are now prime targets for theft. Therefore, for many households the $2,500 limitation is inadequate, and the silverware and silver plate limit should be raised by endorsement. The limit on guns may not be important to most insureds, but gun collectors or hunting enthusiasts need to be aware of this limit and raise their coverage if they have more than $2,000 worth of guns.

The inclusion of $2,500 of on-premises coverage and $500 of off-premises coverage for business property gives insureds limited protection for such property. However, the business property must be of the nature of personal property, insured in the homeowners' policy, and damaged by an insured peril. This provision for business property replaces three exclusions pertaining to business in older homeowners' forms. The new provision's coverage is easier to understand, and claims are more easily adjusted on it.

HO-3 Coverage D—Additional Living Expenses

Coverage *D* is for the increased cost of living that results from an insured peril damaging the residence premises and making them uninhabitable. The insured is allowed to maintain his or her normal standard of living. If people live in a $150,000 home, they do not have to move to a motel at a

$15-per-night room charge. However, if they live in a $35,000 home, they most likely cannot move to a hotel with an $80-per-night room charge. Also, only the increased cost of living is covered. Thus, if it normally costs $250 a month to feed a family, and fire damage forces them to eat out, only the cost in excess of $250 per month is paid by the insurance company.

Besides the increase in living expenses, this provision pays for loss of rental income (less rental expenses). This lost income would arise from a situation where the insured rented a basement room to someone and a fire made it uninhabitable. If the rent was $150 per month, of which the electric bill was $20 per month, then the insurance would pay $130 per month until repairs had been completed. The repair time is limited to the shortest reasonable time required to repair the damage.

Additional Homeowners' Coverages

In the homeowners' policy there are seven additional coverages besides the basic ones. These items are (1) debris removal, (2) reasonable repairs, (3) trees, shrubs, and other plants, (4) fire department service charge, (5) removed property, (6) credit card forgery and counterfeit money, and (7) loss assessment.

Debris Removal. The cost of removing debris caused by an insured peril is covered by the policy and is included in the limit of liability. However, when the limit of liability has been exhausted, an additional 5 percent may be used to pay for debris removal. Hence, if Coverage B is for $6,000 (10 percent of $60,000), and it costs $6,000 to repair a garage, then up to $300 in addition to the $6,000 may be spent to remove debris from the premises.

Reasonable Repairs. Repairs made by the insured to protect the property from further loss, after loss from an insured peril has occurred, are covered by the policy. However, this provision does not in any way increase the insured's limit. If Coverage B is for $6,000, the repairs to protect against further damage and to fix the structure must not exceed $6,000.

Trees, Shrubs, and Other Plants. Up to 5 percent of Coverage A can be used to pay for loss to trees, shrubs, and other plants, subject to a limit of $500 for any one item. This coverage does not increase the limit of liability of Coverage A. Also, the perils insured against are limited. The policy specifies that only loss due to fire, lightning, explosion, riot or civil commotion, aircraft, vehicles not owned or not operated by a resident of the residence premises, vandalism, malicious mischief, and theft are covered. Under the vehicle coverage, if the insured drives a vehicle into some home shrubs and $200 worth of damage is done, no coverage exists. However, if the insured's neighbor drives the neighbor's car into the same shrubs, protection is provided.

The one exception to this restriction is fallen trees. If a peril covered under Coverage C causes a tree to fall and damages property covered by the policy, then there is $500 of debris removal coverage for the fallen tree. The $500 limit is an aggregate limit, not a per-tree limit.

Fire Department Service Charge. In situations where the insured lives in a rural area and a city fire department makes a charge for responding to a call, the policy will pay up to $500 for such charges. The charge must result from an insured peril, and no deductible applies to this coverage.

Removed Property. The removed-property provision is similar to the removal clause in the fire policy. It gives all-risk coverage during removal and 30 days thereafter. Of course, loss due to an insured peril must be the reason the property was removed in the first place.

Credit Card Forgery and Counterfeit Money. While a federal law limits a person's liability to $50 per lost credit card, the loss of a billfold full of cards can lead to a loss of several hundred dollars. Therefore, the $500 coverage for unauthorized use of credit cards is useful. However, if the unauthorized user is a member of the insured's household, no coverage exists. Thus, if a teenage son or daughter charges (without permission) a $500 stereo to the father, the father will have to pay.

There is also coverage for forged or altered checks, fund-transfer cards, and counterfeit money accepted in good faith. The forged-check exposure can arise when a checkbook is lost or stolen and someone writes checks on it. When the government finds counterfeit money, it retains the money and does not reimburse the citizen.

No deductible applies to any of these items, and the insurer will pay defense costs for court suits brought against the insured under the credit card or forgery coverage. But since the amount of protection under this coverage is only $500, it is doubtful that the insurer would spend much on defense costs.

Loss Assessment. A new coverage in the homeowners' policy begun in 1984 is that of loss assessment. This provision provides the insured $1,000 of coverage if he or she is assessed for damage to property that is owned by an association of property owners of which the insured is a member. The damaged property must be collectively owned by all members of the owners' association, and the peril causing the loss must be covered under Coverage A for a dwelling.

Special Conditions in Homeowners' Property Coverages

The property section of the homeowners' policy contains typical conditions pertaining to insurable interest and duties of the insured after a loss occurs. There is also an appraisal clause, a provision as to other insurance, a mortgage clause, and other normal property insurance conditions. However, three areas of the conditions section deserve special attention and will be discussed in some detail.

Loss Settlement. The loss-settlement clause determines how items will be valued for adjustment purposes. The homeowners' policy provides replacement cost coverage on the dwelling and actual cash value (ACV) coverage for personal property (within the dollar limitations). The loss-settlement clause helps classify certain items as to whether recovery is on an ACV (original cost minus depreciation) or on a replacement-cost basis. It states that personal property and structures that are not buildings shall be covered on an ACV basis. However, it then specifies certain other items as covered only on an ACV basis. All carpeting, whether wall to wall or not, domestic appliances, awnings, outdoor antennas, and outdoor equipment are covered on an ACV basis.

When recovery is made on a replacement-cost basis, an 80 percent coinsurance clause applies to the property. If one purchases a $60,000 homeowners' policy on a $100,000 home, then all dwelling losses will be paid 75 percent of their value ($100,000 × 0.80 = $80,000, 60,000/80,000 = 0.75). However, at the insured's option, ACV recovery may be made. The ACV coverage is not subject to coinsurance limitation in HO policies. Consequently, the insured is in a position to choose which option is most desirable at the time of the loss. If the dwelling mentioned earlier was worth $90,000 on an ACV basis, the ACV would equal 0.90 (90,000/100,000) instead of 75 percent of replacement cost. In the situation where only $60,000 of protection was purchased, the insured would maximize recovery by choosing to recover on an ACV basis. For instance, on a $10,000 loss, the policyholder would receive $7,500 on a replacement-cost basis and $9,000 on an ACV basis. This option available in the homeowners' policy is one of the few times an insured gets to choose the larger of two claim figures after the loss has occurred.

Pair-and-Set Clause. When part of a set or one of a pair is lost, the insurance company will pay only for the difference between the ACV of the item before and after the loss. This means that loss of one of a pair of items such as diamond earrings is not a total loss. Only the difference in value of the earrings before and after the loss is paid. However, in many cases an insurance company will take possession of the remaining item and pay a total loss or replace the item. Given insurers' familiarity with wholesale jewelers, the replacement option is often exercised.

Glass Replacement. When building codes require it, safety glazing materials (safety glass) can be used to replace ordinary glass that was damaged due to an insured peril. This clause is an example of the possibility of obtaining improved building construction at no additional cost to the insured.

PERILS COVERED IN HOMEOWNERS' INSURANCE

In the homeowners' program the various forms offer different numbers of insured perils. These differences are shown in Table 16-1. The following discussion focuses on the HO-3, which gives (1) all-risk coverage on the dwelling and other structures, and (2) broad named-peril coverage on unscheduled personal property.

All-Risk Dwelling Exclusions

As you should realize by now, the term *all risk* is a misnomer. All risk includes all physical losses except certain excluded losses. Thus, to determine what is insured, one must investigate the exclusions. Besides all the exclusions that have been previously discussed pertaining to the dwelling and other structures, there are several additional ones. These exclusions pertain to (1) freezing, (2) fences, pavement, patios (except roofs), swimming pools, foundations, etc., (3) buildings under construction, (4) vacancy, (5) seepage and leaking, and (6) general all-risk exclusions.

Loss caused by freezing of plumbing, heating, or air-conditioning systems is excluded while the dwelling is vacant, unoccupied, or during construction unless heat is maintained or the water system is shut off and the water pipes are drained. When people go on a vacation in December, they must maintain the heat in their home or drain the water pipes, or their insurance will not pay for losses due to freezing. Leaving the heat on, but with the thermostat at its lowest setting, usually meets this requirement.

When fences, pavement, patios, swimming pools, foundations, retaining walls, bulkheads, piers, wharves, or docks are damaged by freezing, thawing, or the weight of ice or snow, no coverage exists. Given the heavy snowfall in the northern section of the United States, this exclusion can be quite important.

Buildings under Construction. While a dwelling is under construction, there is no theft coverage for materials and supplies used in such activity. Coverage begins when the dwelling is completed and occupied. Notice that both conditions must be met—completion and occupancy.

Vacancy beyond Thirty Days. When a building is vacant more than 30 days, coverage for vandalism, malicious mischief, breakage of glass, and safety glazing materials is suspended. When the building is no longer vacant, coverage is restored. For the purposes of this coverage, a dwelling under construction is not considered vacant.

Leakage. Damage resulting from continuous or repeated seepage or leakage of water or steam from plumbing, heating, or air-conditioning equipment over a period of time is excluded. For instance, one could have a leak in a water pipe behind a closet where the wet wall would not be noticed easily. The continued leakage excluded from coverage could eventually cause extensive damage. However, if this water damage were sudden, the exclusion would not apply and coverage would exist.

General All-Risk Exclusion. All-risk contracts have one exclusion provision that is almost universal to such coverage. Excluded by this clause are (1) wear and tear (meaning deterioration), (2) inherent vice (natural or characteristic defect or blemish), (3) latent defect, (4) mechanical breakdown, (5) rust, mold, and wet or dry rot, (6) contamination, (7) smog, (8) smoke from agricultural smudging or industrial operation, (9) settling, cracking, shrinking, bulging, or expansion of pavements, patios, foundations, walls, floors, roofs, or ceilings, and (10) loss due to birds, vermin, rodents, insects, or domestic animals. If your pet St. Bernard knocks down a door or causes other damage to the dwelling, the loss is excluded. Likewise, termite damage is excluded.

**All-Risk
All-Property
Exclusions**

Besides the exclusions that pertain specifically to Coverages *A* and *B*, there are several general exclusions that apply to all property. These exclusions include (1) earth movement (not limited to earthquake), (2) flood and several other types of water damage, (3) war, (4) neglect by the insured to protect the insured property from loss, (5) enforcement of building laws and ordinances, and (6) spoilage. The last two items need some further explanation.

The enforcement of building ordinances or laws pertains to the situation where the building code has changed since the damaged dwelling was built. The new code might require better wiring, fire-resistant doors, a stronger foundation or basement walls, a different type of roof construction, or a number of other items. The policy will not pay for these improved building materials or specifications. It will only repair or rebuild with like material and labor. However, the replacement of regular glass with safety glass (as required by law) is the one exception.

Spoilage resulting from the interruption of power or other utility service (usually natural gas) caused by an off-premises event is not covered. However, if lightning strikes the power line pole on the premises and causes power interruption, then the policy will pay for the ensuing loss. Usually, such losses are related to frozen foods and house plants. However, in the winter, if electric power were lost the heater fan could not operate, and even with natural gas heat there would be freezing damage unless the insured drained the dwelling's water system. If the insured were away on vacation, this action would not be taken and loss to the dwelling would occur.

Concurrent Causation. During 1982 and 1983, court case law in the State of California developed a legal doctrine called "concurrent causation." This doctrine greatly expanded coverage under all-risk insurance policies. Under the all-risk policy, if a peril is not excluded, it is covered. Thus, the courts said that even if an excluded peril like flood, earthquake, or contamination occurred, coverage would exist if a concurrent event occurred and the concurrent event (peril) was not excluded.

In the California cases, the concurrent event was the improper actions of third parties. Specifically, in the Palm Desert area of California, a flood caused loss to property.[1] While the flood caused the damage to the dwelling, improper maintenance of flood structures (dikes) allowed the flood to occur. The improper maintenance was deemed to be the concurrent event, and it was not excluded from the policy. Thus, the damage by the flood was deemed covered by the all-risk policy. On appeal by the insurance company, the ninth circuit court of appeals ruled for the insured and required the insurance company to pay the loss.

Because of the court decision on concurrent causation and a similar decision on the collapse peril, today's insurance policies have a rather lengthy exclusion with respect to events that might result from concurrent causation. The collapse peril has been redefined to cover only collapse losses resulting from certain named perils.

Named-Peril Protection

In the HO-3 there is named-peril protection for personal property. The 16 different perils listed in the policy are (1) fire and lightning, (2) windstorm and hail, (3) explosion, (4) riot and civil commotion, (5) aircraft, (6) vehicles, (7) smoke, (8) vandalism or malicious mischief, (9) theft, (10) falling objects, (11) weight of ice, snow, or sleet, (12) collapse of a building or any part of a building, (13) accidental discharge or overflow of water or steam, (14) sudden and accidental tearing asunder, cracking, burning, or bulging, (15) freezing, and (16) loss from artificially generated electrical current.

The following discussion examines the meaning of these perils.

Fire and Lightning. In the named-peril tradition, fire means "hostile fire" as discussed in Chapter 18. Lightning is self-explanatory. Of course, coverage exists for loss during the act of removal of covered property to protect it from further loss.

Windstorm and Hail. The windstorm coverage is somewhat restricted because certain types of property are excluded. Watercraft and their trailers, furnishings, equipment, and outboard motors are excluded except when inside a fully enclosed building. Obviously, this coverage does the insured little good when the watercraft is on a lake or river. As mentioned before, trees, shrubs, and plants are also excluded. Wind-driven rain through an open window which damages furniture is not covered. However, if part of the roof is blown away and the furniture is damaged by wind-driven rain (or sleet, sand, or dust), coverage would exist.

Explosion. The term explosion is undefined in the policy and thus is broadly interpreted by the courts. It would include a natural gas explosion as well as a sonic boom.

Riot and Civil Commotion, Aircraft, and Vehicles. These terms are also undefined in the HO-3 form. Damage to trees, shrubs, and plants by a vehicle driven or owned by a resident of the residence premises is excluded. Aircraft includes self-propelled missiles and spacecraft. If the space shuttle falls on your home, you are covered.

Smoke. This peril only includes sudden and accidental damage from smoke. Loss caused by smoke from agricultural smudging or industrial operations is excluded. In the HO-1 form smoke from a fireplace is not covered. In the HO-3 form there is coverage for such an event.

Vandalism or Malicious Mischief. Typically, this peril involves the concept of willful intent to damage the property. However, the HO-3 does not mention this limitation, so a liberal definition of the term can be assumed.

Theft. The policy states "theft, including attempted theft, and loss of property from a known location when it is likely that the property has been stolen" is covered. In case of loss, the police must be notified if the insured expects to collect under the policy. This coverage is rather broad, and the insured is required only to show that theft of the item is a reasonable explanation of the loss. However, it is not the intent of the insurer to pay for property that the insured simply loses, and no coverage exists if any insured steals the property. Since sons, daughters, and spouses are insureds, any property stolen by them from the named or other insured is not covered. There are two special situations concerning the theft peril coverage: limitations on the premises and limitations off the premises.

Limitations on the Premises. Any materials or supplies used in the construction of a dwelling are not covered for theft until the building is completed and occupied. While this is the same exclusion that existed for the dwelling itself, it is necessary in this section too because supplies and materials, before they are attached to the dwelling, are personal property. Besides this limitation on the premises, there is no coverage for any property in that part of the residence premises rented by the insured to another. If you rent a room to a son or daughter or other relative (presumably an adult), coverage exists. However, to others (except a person under 21 in your care) who occupy that space, no theft coverage exists in the area they rent.

Off-Premises Limitations. There are four off-premises restrictions. They involve (1) trailers and campers, (2) watercraft, (3) secondary residence, and (4) student property.

No trailers or campers are insured for theft away from the premises. Watercraft and their furnishings, equipment, and outboard motors are also excluded. The third exclusion concerns property at another residence owned, rented, or occupied by any insured. No theft coverage exists on property at that type of residence unless an insured is temporarily residing there. If the insured has a summer home, there is no theft coverage on property left there except when the insured is residing in it. Therefore, during the winter months there is no theft protection on personal property at an unoccupied summer home.

There is one important exception to this exclusion, which creates the fourth limitation. It involves property of a student while at a residence away from home. If the student has been at the "away-from-home residence" any time during the 45 days immediately before the loss, coverage exists.

When a student goes home for Christmas and leaves a television at school, coverage does exist for the set if it is stolen, even though the student was not residing there at the time of the loss. However, coverage does not exist for personal property that a student leaves at school over the summer months and subsequently finds missing in the fall. No coverage exists because the student has been away for more than 45 days.

It should be noted that since 1984 homeowners' policies provide theft coverage for property left in an automobile on or off the premises, whether the automobile is locked or unlocked at the time of the theft. In prior policies the insured had to purchase an extended theft endorsement to obtain this coverage. Thus, the new homeowners' policy gives broader coverage and eliminates a temptation for the insured to break his or her own car window and claim that a thief broke into the car and stole some property therein.

Falling Objects. This peril does not pertain to property inside the building unless the roof or an exterior wall is first damaged by the falling object. Damage to the falling object itself is not covered. For instance, if a tree falls on the house, the tree is not covered by the falling object peril, but the house and any contents inside that are damaged by the tree are covered. This exclusion on the fallen object also excludes coverage for china that is dropped and broken or a picture that falls from the wall and is broken.

Weight of Ice, Snow, or Sleet. In the HO-3 this coverage applies only to contents inside the dwelling. The dwelling itself is covered on an all-risk basis. Thus, the roof would have to collapse from the weight of ice and snow, and then the contents be damaged, for coverage to exist.

Collapse of a Building or Any Part of the Building. If the contents of the dwelling are damaged by collapse, coverage exists. For example, if the ceiling collapsed and damaged a stereo, it would be insured. Falling object coverage would not apply unless exterior damage had occured.

With the rise of the doctrine of concurrent causation, the definition of collapse has been changed. Today, only certain types of collapse are covered, namely, those collapses resulting from (1) the perils insured against in Coverage C personal property; (2) hidden decay, and hidden insect or vermin damage; (3) the weight of contents, equipment, animals, or people; (4) the weight of rain which collects on the roof; and (5) the use of defective materials or methods in construction or remodeling, if the collapse occurs during remodeling. The restrictive definition of collapse applies both to the dwelling and to its contents. It is intended that collapse caused by earthquake, mudslide, or flood not be covered.

Accidental Discharge or Overflow of Water or Steam. The overflow or accident must come from within a plumbing, heating, or air-conditioning system, or from within a household appliance. No coverage exists for the appliance from which the steam or water escaped, nor for loss due to freezing, overflow, or discharge that occurs off the residence premises. In communities with little space between dwellings, it is possible for the overflow on one premises to flow to another. One usually thinks of this peril resulting from situations such as an accidental discharge from a washing machine or even a case where a child forgets to turn off the bath water. Loss due to gradual leakage over time is not covered.

Sudden and Accidental Tearing Asunder, Cracking, Burning, or Bulging of a Steam, Hot Water, or Air-Conditioning System or an Appliance for Heating Water. The obvious example of this peril is a hot water heater that explodes. It should be mentioned that no coverage for freezing is provided.

Freezing. This peril covers freezing of a plumbing, heating, or air-conditioning system, or a household appliance. No coverage exists when the dwelling is unoccupied unless the insured takes reasonable care to maintain heat in the building or shuts off the water supply and drains the system and appliances of water. When an ice storm cuts off electricity, an insured must take reasonable steps to prevent freezing of pipes and other appliances if freezing losses to plumbing systems are to be covered.

Sudden and Accidental Damage from Artificially Generated Electrical Current. A power surge that caused damage to an air conditioner would be covered by this peril. However, the policy specifically excludes loss to a tube, transistor, or similar electronic component. Stereos and televisions are the main targets of this exclusion.

Volcanic Eruption. This is a new coverage for the homeowners' program and addresses the problems that arose after the eruption of Mount St. Helens in Washington state. At the time of that explosion, it was not clear whether or not homeowners' policies covered volcanic explosions. The addition of the peril makes it clear. The policy states that one or more volcanic eruptions that occur within a 72-hour period will be considered one volcanic eruption, and that loss caused by earthquake, land shock waves, or tremors is not covered.

PROPERTY ENDORSEMENTS TO HOMEOWNERS' POLICIES

There are many property endorsements in the homeowners' program. Five of them are of particular interest: earthquake, inflation guard, replacement cost, unit owner's additions and alterations endorsements, and special personal property coverage.

Earthquake

The peril of earthquake is catastrophic in nature. However, its frequency is so low that few persons purchase the coverage even though they should. This is especially true for those persons living in the western United States where earthquakes are most likely to occur.

The actual endorsement does not define earthquake; it just states, "any earthquake shocks that occur within a 72-hour period shall constitute a single earthquake." The endorsement has a mandatory deductible of 2 percent of the appropriate limit of insurance, and it applies separately to Coverages *A*, *B*, and *C*. The minimum deductible is $250.

In the area of exclusions, the endorsement eliminates loss from flood or tidal wave caused by an earthquake and loss to exterior masonry veneer. For an additional premium the latter item can be covered, and such coverage is recommended for people living in brick houses. There are actually two earthquake endorsements, the difference between the two being the amount of the deductible. The first has a 2 percent deductible. The second one has a 5 percent deductible and is found most often in the western states. Perhaps this 5 percent deductible is why some people do not purchase earthquake insurance. On a $100,000 dwelling the deductible would be $5,000.

Related to the earthquake peril is loss from sinkhole collapse. This peril is defined as property damage caused by the sudden settlement or collapse of the earth supporting a structure. The settlement or collapse must result from subterranean voids created by the action of water on limestone or similar rock formations. The peril occurs in Florida, southern Georgia, Alabama, and other southern coastal states. This endorsement was developed specifically to meet the need of insureds living there.

Inflation Guard

When there is a rapid rate of inflation, the problem of maintaining adequate property limits has to be addressed. It has not been uncommon for construction costs to rise 10 percent per year. When replacement-cost protection is desired, an 80 percent coinsurance clause must be maintained, and policy limits need to be adjusted periodically. However, if one only adjusts once a year, problems can arise because the loss may occur right before it is time to increase the policyholder's limit. The inflation guard endorsement is a partial solution to the problem. Under this endorsement a person's limit is raised a set percentage every three months. The standard percentages are $1\frac{1}{2}$ and 2 percent. Higher percentages can be used. However, persons still need to review their policy limits annually since the inflation guard adjustments might have been inadequate. During the 1970s and early 1980s some localities had 20 percent inflation during one year for new dwellings.

Personal Property Replacement Cost

For many years homeowners have been able to purchase replacement-cost coverage on the dwelling and appurtenant structures. However, before 1980 an individual could not purchase replacement-cost coverage on an unscheduled basis on personal property in the homeowners' program. In 1980 a new endorsement was introduced; it stated that the insured could collect the least of five amounts:

1. Replacement cost at the time of loss
2. Full repair cost at the time of loss

3. Four hundred percent of the actual cash value of the property at the time of loss
4. Any special limits of liability pertaining to Coverage *C*
5. The limit of liability for unscheduled personal property Coverage *C*, which is usually 50 percent of the dwelling coverage

Certain types of property are excluded from the replacement-cost recovery. They include (1) fine arts, paintings, and antiques, (2) memorabilia and collector's items, (3) property that is not kept in working condition, and (4) obsolete property.

Usually, no payment is made until the item is actually repaired or replaced unless the loss is less than $500. Thus, for losses less than $500, one does not have to replace the item to obtain replacement-cost coverage.

There are two endorsements for this coverage. One endorsement is for HO-1, 2, and 3, and usually increases the cost of the policy by 15 percent. The second endorsement is for HO-4 and 6, and often increases the cost of the policy by 35 percent. In dollar terms these costs are nearly equal, since the HO-1, 2, and 3, policies have coverage for the dwelling and the basic premium is larger. The HO-4 and 6 forms have no dwelling coverage; thus, a higher percentage (35) is needed to produce the correct amount of premiums.

Unit Owners, Building Additions, and Alterations

An endorsement is designed to meet the special needs of condominium unit owners. In many states condominium owners hold an indivisible interest in the condominium complex and sole ownership of the air space inside their unit. This doctrine is called the **bare wall doctrine.** The unit owner owns everything inside the bare walls except for some electrical and structural items. Consequently, unit owners need to insure all their personal property as well as additions and alterations to the bare walls. The $1,000 limit for improvements in the basic HO-6 is inadequate. By endorsement, limits may be increased and coverage can be placed on an all-risk basis. Examples of items the unit owner will be insuring are paneling, wall-to-wall carpeting or hardwood floors, wallpaper, wall and ceiling fixtures, and, when carried to an extreme, nonload-bearing interior walls.

The insurance protection on the condominium itself, swimming pool, tennis courts, and other buildings associated with the condominium complex is carried by the condominium association. Thus, if one building of the complex is destroyed by fire, the association's insurance pays to rebuild it. The unit owner's insurance pays to furnish the unit and replace personal property (on an ACV basis) contained in the unit at the time of the loss.

Persons who are unit owners in a condominium may be assessed for losses paid by the condominium association. To protect against this potential loss, the HO-6 may be endorsed to cover an assessment due to a loss caused by a peril insured under the building additions and alterations coverage except earthquake. By another endorsement the peril of earthquake may be added. A second area of coverage involves losses that the liability section of the policy would pay. The endorsement has a minimum $250 deductible and a policy limit separate from the rest of the policy. Usually, $50,000 is the maximum limit available.

Special Personal Property

The special personal property endorsement provides all-risk coverage for personal property. It may be used only in conjunction with the HO-3 form. The combination of this endorsement and the HO-3 form gives the insured all-risk coverage on both the dwelling and personal property. Similar coverage used to be available under the HO-5 form that was written prior to the introduction of the Homeowners' 84 program.

Like the all-risk coverage on the HO-3, the special personal property endorsement has numerous exclusions, such as enforcement of building laws or ordinances, earthquake, flood, war, and intentional loss. In addition, there are several exclusions unique to the special property form, such as breakage of eyeglasses, glassware, statuary marble, and porcelain (these items are insured for certain specified perils like fire, extended coverage, and theft); collision; repair or refinishing of personal property; and dampness of atmosphere or extreme change in temperature.

FLOOD INSURANCE

Flood insurance for residential properties is generally administered by the Department of Housing and Urban Development. In this program HUD underwrites losses and works through private vendors and insurance agents to market and service the policies. To be eligible for the program, a community must make application with HUD and conduct extensive floodplain studies, make floodplain maps, and develop a floodplain management program. The HUD program is attractive to insureds because the federal government subsidizes the rates up to as much as 90 percent. That is, premiums only cover 10 percent of the cost of the program.

The peril of **flood** is defined in the policy as including four distinct events:

1. Overflow of inland or tidal waves
2. Unusual and rapid accumulation of run-off of surface waters
3. Mudslides
4. Excessive erosion along the shore of a lake or any other body of water

This definition covers water damage from hurricanes along the Atlantic and Gulf Coasts, flash floods in desert areas, mudslides in California, and unusual erosion around the Great Lakes.

The flood program consists of two subprograms: emergency and regular. While a community applies for the regular program, emergency status can be given. In the emergency program one can purchase $35,000 of coverage on a single-family dwelling and $10,000 on its contents. Once a community achieves regular program status, an additional $150,000 of coverage may be purchased on the dwelling and $50,000 on its contents. The two layers together allow one to purchase up to $185,000 of coverage on the dwelling and $60,000 on its contents.

COMPREHENSIVE PERSONAL LIABILITY AND MEDICAL PAYMENTS INSURANCE

Section E of the homeowners' policy provides comprehensive personal liability coverage, and Section F provides medical payments to others. The basic amount of coverage is $100,000 for personal liability and $1,000 for medical payments. If additional protection is needed, the limits may be raised. If catastrophic loss limits are desired, a personal umbrella policy should be purchased. The personal umbrella liability policy has a limit of at least $1,000,000. It will be discussed in detail in Chapter 18.

Personal Liability Coverage

Besides covering bodily injury liability and property damage liability, Section E provides standard supplementary benefits as follows:

1. Defense costs. The defense cost protection in the CPL is in addition to the policy limits, and the insurer's obligation to pay it ceases when the policy limits have been exhausted. Under this provision, the insurer agrees to defend the insured even if the law suit is groundless, false, or fraudulent. The insurance company has the right to defend the suit or to settle it without the consent of the insured. That is, as long as the insurance company is paying for the defense, it makes the decision whether to settle or defend.
2. Premiums on appeal bonds not in excess of the limit of coverage E.
3. Reasonable expenses incurred by the insured at the request of the insurer to aid in the investigation or defense of a suit. Up to $50 a day for actual loss of earnings will be paid by the insurer to the insured for assisting the insurer in the suit.
4. Interest on an entire judgment before the insurer pays or tenders payment of the judgment.
5. Prejudgment interest on any part of a judgment that the insurer must pay.

In addition to these standard liability insurance supplementary benefits, the CPL has an additional benefit: damage to the property of others. Under this provision, the insurer promises to pay up to $500 per occurrence for damage to the property of others caused by any insured. This clause provides care, custody, and control protection. It is not necessary to prove liability due to negligence. For example, if Mrs. Lenny borrowed her neighbor's power mower and hit a hidden steel stake that broke the mower, coverage would exist, even if Mrs. Lenny is not negligent. However, it is constrained by several exclusions. The insurer will not pay for the following:

1. Damage to property covered under Section One of this policy
2. Property damage caused intentionally by any insured who is 13 years of age or older

3. Damage to property owned by any insured, or owned by or rented, to any tenant of any insured, or a resident of your household
4. Property damage arising out of (a) business pursuits, (b) any act or omission in connection with premises owned, rented, or controlled by any insured, other than the insured location, or (c) the ownership, maintenance, or use of a motor vehicle, aircraft, or watercraft

Section I property is property that is insured for such perils as fire, extended coverage, etc., in the HO-2 or on an all-risk basis in the HO-3. The major significance of this exclusion is to make the property insurance primary and to make such a loss subject to the deductible on Section I losses. The damage-to-property-of-others clause has no deductible. For instance, if Mrs. Lenny had started a fire while refueling the mower, Section I would apply, so damage to property of others would not cover the loss.

This provision covers intentional acts of children under 13 years of age. If the insured's 9-year-old daughter throws a rock through a neighbor's window, coverage exists. If the daughter were 14, the loss would be excluded.

Persons Insured

In the Homeowners' 84 program the terms *you* and *your* refer to the named insured. The insurance company is identified as *we, us,* and *our.*

Given these definitions, the insurer provides protection to the following persons (*insured* means you and the following members of your household): (1) your resident relatives, and (2) any other person under the age of 21 who is in the care of any person named above. For liability coverage, *insured* means (3) with respect to animals or watercraft to which this policy applies, any person legally responsible for these animals or watercraft that are owned by you or any person included in (1) or (2). A person or organization using or having custody of these animals or watercraft in the course of any business, or without permission of the owner, is not an insured. (4) With respect to any vehicle to which this policy applies, any person while engaged in your employment or the employment of any person included in (1) or (2) is an insured. The term *resident relative* is generally considered to include a son or daughter who is away at college. A person who keeps an insured's pet while the insured is away on vacation is covered, but a veterinarian who has custody of the animal in the course of business is not. With regard to employees operating vehicles, a person employed to maintain the yard would be covered while operating a riding mower or a small garden tractor.

It should be noted that CPL applies to each insured separately. If a 15-year-old son intentionally damages a person's house, the son is not covered because it was an intentional act. However, if his father or mother were held legally responsible for his actions, the CPL insurer would defend them and pay for the loss.[2]

Insured Location

The insured location comprises several different locations.

Residence Premises. This term is defined as the one- to two-family dwelling, other structures, and grounds, or that part of any other building where you reside and which is known as the **residence premises** in the declarations. This dwelling is that which is insured under Coverages *A* and *B* in Section I of the homeowners' policy.

Other Locations. Besides the residence premises, liability in the following locations is also insured:

1. The part of any other premises, other structures, and grounds used by you as a residence and which is shown in the declarations or which is acquired by you during the policy period for your use as a residence
2. Any premises used by you in connection with the premises included in residence premises or in number 1
3. Any part of premises not owned by any insured but where any insured is temporarily residing
4. Vacant land owned or rented to any insured other than farmland
5. Land owned by or rented to any insured on which a one- or two-family dwelling is being constructed as a residence for any insured
6. Individual or family cemetery plots or burial vaults of any insured
7. Any part of premises occasionally rented to any insured for other than business purposes

Examples of the above locations that would be insured are newly acquired residence premises and secondary premises such as a mountain cabin. (The cabin would have to be specified on the declarations page.) Additional locations would include a motel room, an oceanfront apartment rented for two weeks, and even a dormitory room used by a son or daughter. The last category would include a rented lodge or hall used to give a dance or wedding reception.

Exclusions

Like all liability contracts, the CPL has exclusions. The following discussion examines several of the most important ones:

1. Intentional losses caused by the insured are excluded.
2. Loss arising out of business activities or holding property for rent or rental of such property is not insured. However, there are several exceptions to this exclusion. These items include activities which are ordinarily incidental to nonbusiness pursuits; or the rental or holding for rental of a residence of yours (a) on an occasional basis for the exclusive use as a residence; (b) in part, unless intended for use as a residence by more than two roomers or boarders; or (c) in part, as an office, school studio, or private garage.

   Examples of activities ordinarily incidental to nonbusiness pursuits are babysitting in your home, and hobbies that may produce a little outside income. The more businesslike the hobby becomes, the more likely it will be excluded. Courts have generally looked at two factors to determine whether an activity is a business pursuit: continuity and profit motive. The courts have defined **business pursuit** as a continued or regular activity for the purpose of earning a livelihood. Both elements must be present for the activity to be considered a business pursuit.[3] Commonly insured schools include those giving ballet or music lessons.

3. Loss arising out of rendering or failing to render professional services is excluded. Physicians, attorneys, insurance agents, and others must purchase professional liability insurance elsewhere. The CPL gives no such coverage.

4. Liability loss arising out of any premises owned or rented to any insured that are not insured premises under the CPL policy is not covered. This exclusion prevents any unspecified premises from being covered.

5. Liability loss is not covered when arising out of the ownership, maintenance, use, loading or unloading of an aircraft (except model airplanes), or a motor vehicle owned or operated by or rented or loaned to any insured. Also excluded is a watercraft owned by or rented to an insured at the inception of the policy, if the watercraft has inboard or inboard-outdrive motor power of more than 50 horsepower; or is a sailing vessel with or without auxiliary power, 26 feet or more in overall length; or is powered by one or more outboard motors with more than 25 total horsepower. If the insured reports in writing to the insurer (within 45 days after acquisition) an intention to insure any outboard motors acquired prior to the policy period, coverage will apply.

The exclusion relating to aircraft is quite clear. The watercraft and motor vehicle exclusions deserve more attention. While larger watercraft are excluded, the insured still receives protection on smaller ones such as sailboats under 26 feet, inboard-outdrivens with 50 or less horsepower, and outboards with 25 or less horsepower. Rental outboards are insured without any motor restrictions. If one rents a ski boat on a vacation, coverage is provided. Also, newly acquired watercraft are automatically covered until the policy is renewed.[4]

It should be noted that the definition of motor vehicle as used in the homeowners' policy is different from that of private passenger automobile used in automobile insurance policies. The homeowners' (CPL) policy defines a motor vehicle as (1) a motorized land vehicle designed for travel on public roads or subject to motor vehicle registration (a motorized land vehicle in dead storage on an insured location is not a motor vehicle); (2) a trailer or semitrailer designed for travel on public roads and subject to motor vehicle registration (a boat, camp, home, or utility trailer not being towed by or carried on a vehicle included in (1) is not a motor vehicle); (3) a motorized golf cart, snowmobile, or other motorized land vehicle owned by any insured and designed for recreational use off public roads, while off an insured location (*a motorized golf cart while used for golfing purposes is not a motor vehicle*); and (4) any vehicle while being towed by or carried on a vehicle included in (1), (2), or (3).

When the new policy was first published, category (1) required both public road travel and registration. But because mopeds are not required to be registered in some states, and since it was not the policy's intent to cover mopeds, the definition had to be changed. A recreational vehicle designed for use off public roads while on the residence premises is not considered a motor vehicle. Thus, it is covered. Also, riding mowers and garden tractors used on the residence premises are covered.

6. Liability losses due to war are excluded.

7. Loss resulting from liability assumed under unwritten contracts is excluded, as are all types of liability losses resulting from business contracts. Liability assumed under a lease of premises is insured, since it is personal in nature.

8. Damage to property owned by or rented to the insured, or in the insured's care, custody, or control is not covered. With respect to nonowned property, the perils of fire, smoke, and explosions are covered. Also, the additional coverage section provides $500 of protection that has been previously discussed.

9. Bodily injury to any person eligible to receive workers' compensation benefits is excluded. In some states, such as California, coverage may be added by endorsement.

10. Coverage is excluded for statutorily imposed vicarious parental liability for the actions of a child or minor while operating an automobile, aircraft, or watercraft. Nor is there any protection for the negligent entrustment of an automobile, watercraft, or aircraft to another person. These exposures are supposed to be covered by automobile, watercraft, and aircraft liability policies, not the homeowners' policy.

11. Lawsuits between insureds covered by the CPL are excluded. The CPL will not cover a mother sued by her son who is a resident of her household.

Medical Payments to Others

Besides the bodily injury and property damage protection provided in the CPL, there is also medical payments protection. The policy states:

> The insurer will pay the necessary medical expenses incurred or medically ascertained within three years from the date of an accident causing bodily injury. Medical expenses include reasonable charges for medical, surgical, X-ray, dental, ambulance, hospital, professional nursing, and funeral services, as well as for prosthetic devices. This coverage does not apply to you or regular residents of your household other than residence employees. As to others, the coverage applies only to:

1. A person on the insured location with the permission of any insured.
2. A person off the insured location, if the bodily injury (a) arises out of a condition in the insured location or the ways immediately adjoining; (b) is caused by the activities of any insured; (c) is caused by a residence employee in the course of the residence employee's employment by any insured; or (d) is caused by an animal owned by or in the care of any insured.

Notice that the named insured and regular residents of the insured household are not covered for medical expenses. Also, coverage is on a no-fault basis. This protection is not like liability insurance, where legal liability must exist. Since the subrogation clause does not apply to medical benefits, an injured party may collect medical payments and still sue a negligent third party. Such a party could be the insured.

Examples of situations where medical payments would cover injuries are as follows: a person falls down the insured's stairs; an insured cuts down a tree that hits a neighbor; while playing basketball, the insured's elbow accidentally hits another player's eye; a resident employee (not covered by workers' compensation) falls and is injured while taking the insured's daughter for a walk around the block; and the insured's cat scratches a friend's child.

Like liability, coverage for medical payments to others has several exclusions. The first six exclusions discussed under personal liability apply to medical payments. (See page 408). Also, injury to a resident employee is excluded if it occurs off the premises *and* is not in the course of employment. Workers'-compensation-related losses are not insured, and losses resulting from radiation or radioactive contamination are not covered.

Endorsements to the CPL

While the basic CPL gives broad coverage, certain endorsements can be used to meet specific needs. Endorsements can be added to cover watercraft liability, personal injury, business pursuits, and personal umbrella liability.

Watercraft Liability. When an insured owns a watercraft that is larger than those covered by the CPL, the policy may be endorsed to cover such boats. However, as physical damage to the vessel cannot be covered in the homeowners' policy, most people insure their watercraft exposure in a separate policy.

Personal Injury. The basic CPL only covers bodily injury and property damage. It does not insure loss resulting from slander, false arrest, malicious prosecution, defamation of character, etc. The CPL can be endorsed to cover these exposures through the use of the HO-82 (Personal Injury) endorsement.

Business Pursuits. The CPL can be endorsed to give limited business pursuits coverage. Protection is only available for the business specified on the endorsement, and the insured cannot be the owner or have financial control of the business. Teachers are likely persons to purchase this coverage, and the endorsement can be modified to cover liability resulting from corporal punishment.

Personal Umbrella Liability. In today's litigation-conscious society, certain persons, such as physicians, corporate executives, and successful business owners, need broad coverage and high limits to protect their assets. The **personal umbrella** is designed to accomplish this task. Its minimum limit is $1,000,000, and it broadens the protection of the CPL. The umbrella is designed to give protection against catastrophic losses, and it assumes that an underlying CPL exists as well as certain other coverages. The umbrella will not contribute on a loss until the limit of these policies has been exceeded. If one of these policies were allowed to lapse, the insured would have to assume any loss covered by the lapsed primary policy up to the limits of that policy. The umbrella will only pay after the required primary limits are exhausted. A more complete analysis is made of the personal umbrella in Chapter 18.

RISK MANAGEMENT— PERSONAL LINES

A reason given for not self-insuring is, "The firm may not have a sufficient number of homogenous exposure units so situated that aggregate losses to which they are subject can be predicted within sufficiently narrow limits." It is for this same reason that little self-insurance takes place in the personal lines area. However, the risk management principles of loss prevention, detection, and retention can be practiced.

In the remainder of this section, peril-detection, loss-prevention, loss-retention, and claims-settling procedures are examined. Also, the all-risk versus named-peril approach to insuring property is reviewed, as is the question of adequate limits.

Peril Detection

In the area of peril detection the purchase of a smoke detector is a wise investment. The detector should operate on its own batteries and have a signal to alert the insured when the battery is weak. It should be placed close enough to the insured's sleeping area that adequate warning time will be given. In a two-story home at least one detector should be placed on each floor. The modern detectors are quite efficient, and in several cases detectors that had been activated but not yet installed have detected fires, saving lives and property.

Television can help detect tornadoes. When a tornado is suspected, turn on the TV set and place the selector on Channel 13. Lower the brightness level until the screen is almost black. Then turn to Channel 2 and leave the setting there. Lightning will show as horizontal flashes or streaks. When the screen becomes bright or the darkened picture becomes visible and remains so, a tornado is within 20 miles of your home. Turn the set off and move to a safe place. Usually the basement is the best place to go, or if you have no basement, a closet in the center of the house is a good alternative.

Besides these peril-detection activities, one can also install a burglar alarm system. Such a system generally produces a loud sound locally and also should be connected to a central alarm switchboard so that the police are notified quickly. While such alarms are fairly expensive, they are growing in popularity. Often they are purchased by persons with large stamp, coin, or gun collections. Insurers will sometimes give a discount on insurance for such items if the alarm system is installed. In the case of fine art insurance, the insurer may require the alarm system.

Loss Prevention

The theft peril presents one area where several loss prevention steps may be taken. All doors should have dead-bolt locks. Storm windows not only conserve energy, but they also make it difficult for intruders to enter your home. Most police departments have marking tools so that residents can scribe their driver's license or Social Security number on valuable belongings. In many communities the police will periodically check homes of residents who are on vacation or away for a while. Generally, notifying the police of departure and return dates is all that is necessary. (In the case of an early return, it would be wise to inform the police of your return.) In addition, the insureds, when going on vacation, should leave with a friend or neighbor a set of house keys, a travel itinerary, and telephone numbers where they can be reached. If a loss does occur, it is important that the insured can be notified.

Besides these loss-prevention activities, people should use common sense in their daily routines. Valuable stamp and coin collections should be kept in safe deposit boxes. Minimal amounts of cash should be kept in the dwelling. Good lighting should be provided around the home. While all of these procedures will not stop a determined burglar, they will make an insured's dwelling an unattractive place to rob and encourage burglars to go elsewhere.

Loss Retention

In the personal lines area, about the only loss-retention steps a homeowner can take is the use of deductibles. Usually a $100 deductible is a must, a $250 deductible is worthwhile, and a deductible of $500 deserves attention. The problem with a $500 deductible is that sometimes one receives little premium savings.

On an HO-3 policy for a $100,000 frame dwelling in an unprotected area (no water) in Clarke County, Georgia, the premium with a $100 deductible is $691, with a $250 deductible it is $587, and with a $500 deductible it is $511. Clearly, the $250 deductible is desirable, as the insured saves $104 per year. When the deductible is raised to $500 from $250, only $66 per year is saved, and the decision is not as clear. In the first case the insured accepts a greater loss exposure per claim of $150 and saves $104 per year. In the second case the insured accepts a greater loss exposure per claim of $250 and saves $66 per year.

When the same dwelling is placed inside the City of Athens, Georgia, with a fire protection Class 3 rating, the three different deductible choices produce premiums of $381, $330, and $287. Thus, in the better protected area, the premium savings are not as nearly as great: going from a $100 deductible to a $250 deductible saves $51 per year, and going from a $250 deductible to a $500 deductible saves $43 per year. Time is well spent investigating the savings produced by deductibles.

Claims-Settling Procedure

An important precaution that should be taken by homeowners to reduce losses is to identify their possessions before a loss occurs. If one cannot remember what was lost, it is quite difficult to recover from the insurer. One should take several pictures of the items in each room in the home and put the pictures in a safe deposit box (not in the home). An inventory should be made of clothing, furniture, silverware, appliances, and jewelry, and the inventory list placed in the safe deposit box. If these precautions are taken, an insured has a much stronger case in making a claim.

A fact to remember in making a homeowners' claim is that the insurance company pays the insured on a replacement cost basis only *after* the insured replaces or repairs the damaged dwelling. The only exception to this rule is when the loss is less than $1,000 and less than 5 percent of the amount of insurance on the building. However, the contract does state that the policyholder may collect immediately on an ACV basis and later make replacement-cost recovery. By filing the ACV claim first, insureds receive their cash sooner so that they can pay the contractor or invest the money in some interest-bearing security while the house is being rebuilt. It seems logical to most people to exercise this option.

All-Risk versus Broad Named- Peril Coverage

There has been long discussion over the question of whether to purchase HO-2 or HO-3 (Table 16–1). The difference is that HO-3 gives all-risk coverage on the dwelling and other structures, while HO-2 covers only broad named perils. The following discussion gives some reasons for the use of the HO-3. Keep in mind that the HO-3 costs more, and consequently it should provide better coverage or it is a poor buy.

One of the big advantages of an all-risk form is the fact that the burden of proof is placed on the insurance company. It has to prove the loss was excluded. The insured must only prove an accidental loss occurred. Besides this conceptual advantage, there are numerous cases where HO-3 gave coverage and HO-2 would not have. The following is a list of several such instances.[5]

1. Battery acid leaked onto a hardwood floor. A large section of the floor had to be replaced.

2. A diaper bucket containing ammonia was tipped over and ruined wall-to-wall carpeting.
3. A deer jumped through a picture window and went wild, denting walls and spilling blood over the house. The HO-3 paid for the damage to the dwelling, but the broad-form named-peril coverage on contents paid nothing.
4. While working in an unfloored attic, an insured was walking on the ceiling joists and fell through the living-room ceiling.
5. While mowing the lawn with a power lawn mower, an insured cut some coil wires and piping to an air conditioner. Repair and replacement costs were paid by the HO-3.
6. One insured converted from oil to gas heat, but left the oil input pipe in place. The fuel-oil truck pumped 500 gallons of oil into the disconnected input pipe, flooding the insured's basement.
7. An insured, while driving up his driveway, hit a patch of ice and skidded into the fence.
8. A lawn sprinkler sprayed water through an open window, damaging wall-to-wall carpeting.

Most of the preceding cases are situations where falling objects (a diaper, blood, a person) damaged the dwelling without causing exterior damage. In named-peril coverage exterior damage must occur before damage by a falling object to an interior portion of the dwelling is covered. In all-risk coverage no exterior damage has to occur; consequently, if paint is spilled on wall-to-wall carpeting, the loss is covered. However, if paint is spilled on a sofa, no coverage exists because coverage on contents is on a named-peril basis and no exterior damage to the dwelling has occurred.

SUMMARY

1. The homeowners' policy is designed to give both property and liability coverage to insureds. It covers the insured's dwelling, its contents, additional living expenses resulting from an insured loss occurring to the dwelling, and personal liability claims against the insured.
2. There are six Homeowners' 84 forms. These forms are designed to meet the needs of homeowners, renters, and owners of condominiums. Coverage is available on a named-peril or all-risk basis.

3. The homeowners' policy is flexible and may be endorsed to cover earthquakes, improvements made by the unit owner of a condominium dwelling, and the problem of inflating construction costs.
4. The homeowners' policy covers direct as well as indirect losses. The indirect losses insured are additional living expense and rental value.
5. Individuals need to be aware of claims-settling procedures of insurers. Records of major purchases should be maintained and

pictures taken of personal property contained in one's home.

6. One of the big advantages of all-risk coverage versus named-peril coverage is that the burden of proof is on the insurance company. It must prove that the peril causing the loss was excluded.

7. In the homeowners' program, liability insurance is provided by comprehensive personal liability coverage (Coverage E).

8. Comprehensive personal liability (CPL) is designed to meet the needs of the typical householder for premises liability as well as for other liability arising from ordinary nonbusiness pursuits, such as sports, hobbies, and the ownership of animals.

QUESTIONS FOR REVIEW

1. Ms. Marshall owns a 30-year-old house that had a life expectancy of 60 years when it was built. Its replacement cost today is $50,000. She purchases a $25,000 fire policy with an 80-percent coinsurance clause, and a $30,000 loss occurs. How much should she receive on her loss settlement?

2. How does the HO-2 form differ from the HO-3 and HO-6?

3. A owns a residence and insures it for $35,000 on an HO-3. Show the extent to which the following losses would be covered, and give your reasons in each case:
   (a) Smoke damage from a fireplace necessitates a $250 repainting job in the living room.
   (b) A valuable antique wooden table worth $1,000 is accidentally damaged by heat when it is placed too near a hot air register.
   (c) A grass fire threatens A's house. For safety, A removes all the contents and places them in three warehouses, as follows: Warehouse X, $7,000 worth;

Warehouse Y, $4,000; and Warehouse Z, $4,000. Water damages the goods at Warehouse Z and causes a $2,000 loss two days after the goods had been stored there. Also, $500 worth of goods is stolen from Warehouse Y.
   (d) A neighbor's house burns. Firefighters' trucks gouge deep holes in A's yard.
   (e) Three teenage boys "have it in" for A and cause $25 worth of damage to the lawn hoses by slashing them with knives.

4. Ms. Vancura owns an $80,000 house insured under an HO-3 policy with a face value of $70,000. From the following data, determine how much she could recover under the HO-3 policy for additional living expenses and rental value after a fire: She rents an apartment for $450/mo., which includes utilities; her normal utilities bill is $100/mo. It now costs her $300/mo. for food; her normal cost is $200/mo. Cleaning and transportation costs are $150/mo. where normally she would pay $50/mo. for these. Restoration takes five months.

5. Mr. Vera's 12-year-old son intentionally throws several rocks through the local middle school's windows and causes $1,000 worth of damage. How will Mr. Vera's CPL respond? If his son were 15 would your answer be different?

6. C, on a business trip, rents an outboard motorboat for some pleasure fishing. Due to careless handling, the boat runs into a swimmer, causing severe injuries. Will the CPL pay the claim? Why or why not?

7. Which of the following claims, if any, would be defended under the CPL (give your reasons in each case):
   (a) A child riding a bicycle struck and injured a pedestrian. The child's parents were sued, but the supreme court found the child, and not the parents, liable.
   (b) A child struck another child and threw him down an embankment, breaking his leg. The court found the parents

liable because of their knowledge of the vicious propensities of the child.

(c) Two hunters, firing at the same time at a quail, injured a third hunter, who obtained a $10,000 judgment from each.

(d) The insured was sued when a guest tripped on steep stairs leading to the beach from an oceanfront cabin that the insured maintained as a second residence.

(e) The insured's dog bit a "trespasser" who turned out to be the meter reader.

(f) The insured's dog, a police dog, killed a smaller dog in a somewhat uneven fight.

QUESTIONS FOR DISCUSSION

1. What advantages and disadvantages are there for the average homeowner under the homeowners' program that covers multiple-peril risks?

2. Mr. Márquez leases a building from Ms. Valdez, and he causes a $10,000 fire loss. Ms. Valdez tells him not to worry because she has fire insurance and the insurance company will pay the loss. Should Mr. Márquez worry?

3. In *Providence Washington Indemnity Co. v. Varella* (8 CCH Fire and Casualty Cases 117), the insured had a CPL policy covering her residence. She also operated a hairdressing shop at another location, which she moved to her home. After this relocation of the business, a patron was injured in a stairway accident. The insurer denied liability, under the CPL. The insured claimed that the CPL applies to all activities incidental to nonbusiness pursuits. Hence, her hairdressing activities were really incidental to running a home and should be covered. Is the insurer on sound grounds in denying liability? Why?

4. In California there has been a series of losses due to the slow movement of earth that becomes loosened when water used for lawns seeps down and causes the shale to slip. When a large crack in the foundation of his house appeared, Underman submitted a claim. The insurer paid the loss and immediately cancelled the policy. A month later Underman's house fell into the bay when the entire cliff gave way. Underman made a claim for loss, but the insurer rejected the claim, arguing that the loss occurred after the policy was cancelled. Discuss the rights of the parties.

5. Tom, a married college student, visited his mother-in-law's house. A fire in the house destroyed his personal belongings. He filed a claim under his mother's homeowners' policy. At the time of the loss Tom was going to college and was entirely supported by his mother, whose address was on all his legal documents. Tom had never held a job. Under what circumstances can he collect under his mother's homeowners' policy?

6. Under what circumstances should an insured raise the deductible on a homeowners' policy?

NEW TERMS AND CONCEPTS		
	Additional Living Expenses	Cost-to-Repair Basis
	Bare Wall	Debris Removal
	Broad Named Perils	Dwelling
	Business Pursuits	Flood
	Comprehensive Personal Liability	Limited Named Perils
	Concurrent Causation	Medical Payments to Others
	Consequential Loss	Other Structures
		Pair-and-Set Clause

Personal Property
Replacement
Personal Umbrella

Unscheduled Personal
Property

NOTES

1 *SafeCo Insurance Company of America* v. *Guyton*, 692 Fed. (2d) 551 (1982).
2 Claude C. Lilly, Glenn L. Wood, and Jerry S. Rosenbloom, *Personal Risk Management and Insurance* (Malvern, Pa.: American Institute for Property and Liability Under-writers, 1978), I, p. 88.
3 *FC&S Bulletins*, Casualty and Surety Section, Public Liability, Iapt=1 (Cincinnati, Ohio: The National Under-writer Company, 1986).
4 Lilly, Wood, and Rosenbloom, op. cit., p. 91.
5 All these examples and more may be found in *PF & M Property Coverages* (Indianapolis: Rough Notes Company), p. 190.20.5.

17 PERSONAL AUTOMOBILE INSURANCE

After studying this chapter, you should be able to:

1. Define the key terms in the Personal Automobile Policy (PAP).
2. Identify the major parts of the Personal Automobile Policy.
3. State four major exclusions of the PAP.
4. Distinguish between collision and noncollision loss coverage.
5. State limitations on the insurance company's right to cancel an auto insurance policy.
6. Explain the significance of no-fault auto insurance.
7. Describe how automobile rating classes are determined and how prices compare.

Automobiles were introduced in the United States at a time when mass-production methods were just becoming technically feasible. As a result, large numbers of automobiles were produced and sold before roads could be built or before other facilities were available to cope with the traffic problem. The industry has been able to accelerate the pace of manufacture of vehicles with a degree of speed and power that has tended to outpace the skill of drivers and the capacity of highways.

These two conditions, coupled with the fact that automobiles were cheap enough for nearly everyone to own, created an ideal climate for the growth of losses from liability claims, from collision, and from bodily injuries and deaths due to accidents. Insurance premiums have grown from an insignificant amount to a level where they are among the largest costs of owning and operating a car. Measured by premium volume, automobile insurance is by far the largest single segment of all property and liability insurance business—almost as large as all other lines combined.

THE HIGH COST OF AUTOMOBILE LOSSES

The Insurance Information Institute estimates that the economic losses from automobile accidents have increased from about $58.7 billion in 1981 to $76.0 billion in 1985.[1] These costs include property damage; legal, medical, hospital, and funeral bills; loss of income; and the administrative costs of insurance. Deaths from motor vehicles, after rising sharply during the period 1961-1965, began to level off in the range of 53,000-56,000 annually after 1965. With the 55 mph restriction in 1975, deaths fell to 45,600 in 1985, but were above 51,000 in 1981. Automobile deaths account for nearly half of all accidental deaths in the United States.

It is significant that in 1985 there were 32.5 million motor vehicle accidents. Almost .14 percent of these were fatal accidents. However, a disproportionate percentage of the accident reports involved young drivers. For example, drivers under 20 made up 8.9 percent of all drivers in 1985, but they accounted for 14.5 percent of all accidents. Drivers between 20 and 24 comprise 11.3 percent of all drivers and they are involved in 19.4 percent of all accidents. Accident rates decline with age until age 75.

Death rates per 100,000 of population have remained fairly constant since 1925, ranging between 20 and 30 per 100,000 persons. Death rates per 10,000 registered vehicles, however, have declined steadily ever since automobiles came into widespread use. The death rate was 1.60 in 1985, down from 3.3 in 1975.

INSURANCE CLAIMS

Insurers have been faced with rising claims for all types of automobile insurance protection. Some statistics will illustrate the level to which claims have risen. The average paid bodily injury claim increased from $1,926 to $4,453 over the period 1972-1981, a rise of 131 percent. Average property damage claims rose from $355 to $889 over the same period, an increase of 150 percent.

In 1985, the average paid bodily injury claim had risen to $6,815, which represents an increase of 53.0 percent in four years. For paid property damage liability claims, the figure had risen to $1,217 in 1985. This represents an increase of 36.9 percent in four years. It seems that the bodily injury claim costs are continuing to rise at an even faster rate the last several years, while the property claims rate is not increasing as fast.

As one would expect, the average cost of collision claims continues to increase each year. In 1979 the loss payment for a collision claim was $1,092, and in 1984 it was $1,530. This represents an increase of 40.1

percent in five years. According to the Highway Loss Data Institute, larger models of cars tended to fare better in accidents than smaller ones. This statement is especially true concerning intermediate-size cars versus subcompacts. In addition, domestic cars were found to have lower loss payments. This result is probably due to the fact that foreign manufacturers dominate the subcompact market and most of their cars are in that category.

The federal government has begun to adopt minimum vehicle safety and antipollution standards aimed at improving the environment in which automobiles operate. For example, in 1979 bumpers were required to protect new autos from damage when they collide with concrete barriers at 5 mph. In 1980 the rule stated that only minimal damage could occur to the bumper or its fasteners. However, in May, 1982, the National Highway Traffic Safety Administration reduced bumper standards from a 5-mph no-damage standard to a 2.5-mph standard that allows unlimited bumper damage but no damage to the body of the vehicle. With these new standards, one can expect higher costs of repair in the future.

THE NEED FOR INSURANCE

In the face of the mounting costs of automobile accidents and the substantial probability of being involved in one, what should the average driver do to protect against the financial consequences of risk? For nearly everyone the answer has been insurance, in spite of its increasing cost. Insurance is a legal requirement in many states and is far superior to running the economic risks without protection (i.e., assumption of risk). Few individuals own more than three automobiles. Thus, there is an insufficient exposure to allow self-insurance. Because of the personal catastrophic loss hazard involved in the liability risk, insurance is the only feasible solution.

As part of the consumer movement designed to produce easier- to-read insurance policies, the Personal Automobile Policy (PAP) was introduced in 1977 and revised in 1986. This policy replaced the Family Automobile Policy.

Eligibility

To be eligible for the PAP, a car must be owned or leased by an individual, or jointly owned by a husband and wife for nonbusiness use. A family farm corporation may also use the PAP for cars or pickup trucks.

Definitions

You and *your*, as in the homeowners' policy, are used to refer to the named insured and spouse, if a resident of the same household.

We, us, and *our* refer to the insurance company.

No-fault, as used in this chapter, means that the insured does not have to prove another person negligent before compensation can be received from an insurer. A person whose car collides with a telephone pole would be entitled to bodily injury benefits under no-fault, even though the accident was the driver's fault. On a tort or liability basis the driver could not receive compensation. (On the liability basis one must prove another person negligent before compensation may be received.)

Only the **covered auto** is insured by your policy. This term includes four categories:

1. Any vehicle shown in the declarations
2. Any of the following types of vehicles of which you acquire ownership during the policy period, provided that you ask the company to insure the vehicle within 30 days after you become the owner: (a) a private passenger auto (PPA); and (b) a pickup, or van. If the vehicle replaces one shown in the declarations, it will have the same coverage as the one it replaces. You must ask the insurer to insure a replacement vehicle within 30 days if you wish to add or continue coverage for damage to your auto.
3. Any trailer you own
4. Any trailer or auto you do not own, while used as a temporary substitute for any other vehicle described in this definition which is out of normal use because of its breakdown, repair, servicing, loss, or destruction

With respect to replacement vehicles, one must only notify the insurer in order to obtain coverage for physical damage (damage to the replacement car). Liability protection is automatically provided for the policy term. The reason one must notify the insurer to obtain physical damage coverage is because there is a high probability that a greater exposure exists. The old auto might be a 1981 Ford and the replacement vehicle a 1987 Rolls Royce. Obviously, the insurer has a much greater exposure on the Rolls Royce and needs to decide whether or not to accept the risk.

The newly acquired car coverage can create some interesting cases. In one situation a person unknowingly purchased a stolen car and had an accident. The California District Court of Appeals ruled that no coverage existed because an insured can not acquire ownership of an auto stolen from its rightful owner.[2]

Another provision concerning automatic coverage is frequently raised: What is the status of an auto that is inoperative and not insured? The policy requires all owned autos to be insured by the same company for automatic coverage to apply to replacement or newly acquired vehicles. For a car that is inoperative and not intended to be operated, coverage should exist on other acquired or replaced vehicles. However, if the vehicle were made operative, then coverage would exist only if the vehicle had been owned less than 30 days. Thus, if you own an inoperative car and decide to repair it, you should insure it before you drive it.[3]

Trailer is defined as "a vehicle designed to be pulled by a private passenger-type auto, or a pick-up, panel truck, or van." It also includes a farm wagon or farm implement towed by one of these vehicles. The PAP also provides coverage for gooseneck or fifth-wheel trailers.

Family Member is defined by the PAP as "a person related to you by blood, marriage, or adoption, who is a resident of your household, including a ward or foster child." For example, a visiting aunt is not a family member.

Occupying is defined as "in, upon, getting in, on, out, or off." By using such a definition, the insurer provides protection for more situations than just a time when the insured is inside the vehicle.

Compared to earlier editions of the PAP, the 1986 version has four additional definitions: bodily injury, insured, business, and property damage. By defining these terms in the policy, the insurance industry is trying to guide the courts to a tighter definition of the terms.

In the PAP, bodily injury means bodily harm, sickness, or disease, including any death that results. The term insured is used in place of covered person. Business means trade, profession, or occupation. Property damage is defined as physical injury to, destruction of, or loss of use of, tangible property. These definitions are similar to ones that were used in automobile policies that existed before the PAP was introduced in 1977.

PERSONAL AUTOMOBILE POLICY COMPONENTS

The PAP has six major components: (1) liability, (2) medical payments, (3) uninsured motorist, (4) physical damage to your auto, (5) duties after an accident or loss, and (6) general provisions. The first four sections provide four different coverages, and the definitions of terms may vary between sections. In a sense, each of the first four sections is a separate policy.

Liability

Under liability coverage, the insurer promises to pay for bodily injury and property damage for which any covered person becomes legally responsible because of an auto accident. In addition, the insuring agreement states that any prejudgment interest awarded against the insured is covered. It also states that there is no duty to defend the insured in situations where the coverage is excluded, or after the limits of liability for direct damages have been reached. Many courts have held that an insurance company has a duty to defend that is greater than the duty to pay claims. By making statements about their duty to defend, insurance companies are trying to narrow the difference between the duty to defend and the duty to pay claims.

The limit of liability is a single amount. The policy does not have a per-person limitation, and it applies to both bodily injury and property-damage liability. With respect to the liability section, the policy defines the **insured** as:

1. For the ownership, maintenance, or use of any auto or trailer, you or any family member
2. Any person using your covered auto
3. For your covered auto, any person or organization, but only with respect to legal responsibility for acts or omissions of a person for whom coverage is afforded under liability coverage

4. For any auto or trailer, other than your covered auto, any person or organization, but only with respect to legal responsibility for acts or omissions of you or any family member for whom coverage is afforded under liability coverage. This provision applies only if the person or organization does not own or hire the auto or trailer.

In the PAP there is no requirement that the named insured or a family member have permission to operate the vehicle. The same situation applies to other persons using your covered auto. However, the policy excludes coverage if any person uses a vehicle without reasonable belief that he or she is entitled to do so.

The preceding items 3 and 4 refer to two situations. The first occurs when a fellow employee drives your car. In this situation your employer is covered. The second situation occurs when you drive a fellow employee's car. Again the employer is covered. Of course, employment situations are not the only ones covered by these two provisions. Activities involving an individual's church, fraternity, or sorority are also covered.

Supplementary Benefits. Standard supplementary benefits are provided by the PAP. Defense costs are covered under the liability section and are in addition to the policy limits. When the policy limits of the contract have been exhausted, the insurer's duty to defend terminates. Bail bonds up to $250 are covered for an accident resulting in bodily injury (BI) or property damage (PD). Because of the BI or PD requirement, a bail bond posted for a speeding violation or driving while intoxicated (DWI) is not covered unless either BI or PD occurs. Besides bail bond costs, premiums on appeal bonds and bonds to release attachments are insured. Interest that accrues after a judgment and reasonable expenses incurred at the insurer's request are also included. Up to $50 a day is available for loss of earnings resulting from attending trials or hearings at the insurer's request. There are no emergency-first-aid benefits, as are contained in many liability insurance contracts.

Limit of Liability. The limit of liability is a single limit that applies to both BI and PD. There is no per-person limitation coverage, and coverage is on a per-accident basis. The use of the word *accident* is designed to make the contract easier to read and not to reduce coverage. As is common in automobile contracts, coverage applies to each covered person separately. However, regardless of the number of insureds, the limit of liability is not increased.

Exclusions. In the PAP liability section there are 13 exclusions, of which we shall examine only a portion. No protection exists for persons who intentionally cause a loss. Damage to property owned or being transported by an insured is excluded, as is property rented to, used by, or in the care of an insured. However, damage to a nonowned residence or private garage is protected. Thus, if you drive your neighbor's auto and cause damage to it, there is no property damage liability coverage because that auto was in your care, custody, and control. However, if you have purchased physical damage coverage in the PAP, there is coverage on borrowed cars for such loss, over and above any collision insurance carried by the car's owner.

Vehicles operated to carry persons or property for a fee are not covered. Share-the-expense car pools are not affected by this exclusion. Courts have generally held that coverage exists in this area if the car is not held out indiscriminately to the general public for carrying of passengers for hire. In one case a man used an auto to carry domestic workers to their place of employment. He charged the employer the same fee whether the car owner provided the transportation or not. There was no explicit fee for the transportation service.[4] Vehicles with fewer than four wheels are excluded. Therefore, motorcycles are not covered.

Several exclusions pertain to business use of automobiles. If an employee of the insured is injured, the PAP will not pay. However, if a domestic employee is injured and workers' compensation is not required, coverage exists. This provision eliminates business-related accidents but protects the insured's personal exposure.

No protection is given to someone in the automobile business unless the insured's covered auto is being driven by (1) the insured; (2) a family member; (3) any partner, agent, or employee of the insured; or (4) an employee of a family member. This exclusion eliminates coverage for a service station mechanic who drives your car and has an accident. As the insured, you are protected, but the service station is not. Consequently, your insurance company can subrogate against the service station for any loss caused by an attendant while driving the insured's car.

No insurance is provided for a person operating any business automobile except a private passenger automobile. This exclusion eliminates coverage for commercial vehicles and trailers, such as a large truck. However, an owned pickup or van is insured. If you use your own pick-up in a business situation, coverage exists. When you use a friend's pickup for business purposes, no coverage exists under your PAP unless you are a farmer.

Another exclusion that is important to many people is the one that excludes an auto owned by you (other than the covered auto) or furnished or made available for your regular use. For example, if an employer provides you with an automobile, your PAP will not cover it. You need an extended liability endorsement to give protection for such an exposure. This exclusion prevents an insured from obtaining double protection from a single premium: the PAP will not cover both the employee's personal automobile and the vehicle furnished by the employer.

Not all situations are as clear-cut as an employer-furnished car. Courts are not always consistent in applying either of the terms *furnished* and *available*. In at least two cases insureds used another car three to nine times and had to ask permission to obtain the keys, and the courts said coverage existed. The fact that permission had to be obtained to get the keys seemed to be a critical point.[5]

Related to the preceding exclusion is the one that excludes any vehicle, other than the covered vehicle, which is owned by, furnished, or available for the regular use of any family member. An exception to this exclusion exists when such a vehicle is driven by the named insured or spouse. For example, if Mr. Lilly used his son's car (son owns the car, lives at home, and insures his auto separately from Mr. Lilly's), Mr. Lilly is covered on an excess basis by his own PAP. While Mr. Lilly is driving the son's car, assuming permission exists, the son's policy is primary. If the son has no insurance or his limits are exhausted, there is no coverage for the son under Mr. Lilly's policy while Mr. Lilly is driving the son's auto. Mr. Lilly's insurance company could subrogate against his son. For instance, if Mr. Lilly drove the vehicle and, because of faulty brakes, caused injury to a third party, his insurer could subrogate against the son if the son were held responsible for the faulty brakes.

Other Liability Conditions. Another provision in the PAP is the out-of-state coverage, including coverage in a Canadian province. This clause states that if you have an accident in a state with higher required liability limits than your state, the policy will pay up to the higher limits. For instance, if you live in Illinois, the required minimum limits of liability are 15,000/30,000/10,000. In Minnesota they are 30,000/60,000/10,000. When you are driving in Minnesota, your policy will pay on the basis of 30,000/60,000/10,000 if you have an accident in that state. With respect to when your PAP liability coverage is primary or excess, the general rule is that when your owned auto is involved, your policy is primary. When your policy applies to a nonowned vehicle, it is excess. When there is other insurance that will also pay for a loss on an excess basis, the PAP and the other policy will pay on a pro-rata basis.

Medical Payments

The PAP will pay on a no-fault basis for reasonable and necessary medical expenses caused by an accident and sustained by an insured. Such expenses must be incurred within three years of the accident. This three-year limitation means costs must be paid. If more treatment is needed but has not been paid, the policy will not cover it. Consequently, one father whose nine-year-old child was injured in a car accident prepaid the medical expenses. The services involved dental work which, because of the child's young age, could not be done for several years. The court allowed him to recover his expenses because they met the time limitations and were a direct result of a covered accident.[6]

For medical payments, insured means (1) you or any family member when occupying or, as a pedestrian, when struck by, a motor vehicle designed for use mainly on public roads, or by a trailer of any type, and (2) any other person while occupying your covered auto.

If you are struck by a bulldozer, coverage will not exist because such a vehicle is not designed for use on public roads. When you are driving a nonowned motor vehicle, your medical payments will protect you, but no passengers in the vehicle. (To be covered yourself, you must have a reasonable belief that you are entitled to operate the automobile.) Passengers must turn to their own medical payments coverage or to that of the owner of the vehicle.

Exclusions. The medical payments coverage does not pay for injury sustained while riding a motorcycle, but if a motorcycle collides with you or your vehicle, you are insured. There is no protection while your vehicle is used to carry people or property for a fee. As in liability insurance, share-the-expense car pools are exempted from this restriction. Any bodily injury received while occupying a vehicle located for use as a residence or premises is also excluded. This clause eliminates medical payments for losses associated with a mobile home.

As in the liability section, there is no coverage if workers' compensation is supposed to provide benefits. No protection exists while occupying an owned auto (other than your covered auto) or one furnished or available for your regular use. Also, business use is excluded except for (1) a private passenger auto, (2) an owned pickup, van, or panel truck, and (3) a trailer used with a vehicle described in (1) or (2). Besides these exclusions, losses due to war, discharge of a nuclear weapon, and radioactive contamination are not insured.

Other Conditions. The policy limits are on a per-person basis, such as $2,000 per person. If six people were in an auto at the time of the accident, all six could collect $2,000 each. The PAP specifically states that the maximum amount receivable is the per-person limit stated on the declarations page. This limit is the maximum, regardless of the number of autos insured. For example, if Ms. Epstein had three autos insured, she could only collect $2,000 for medical payments. She could not stack the individual limits ($2,000 + $2,000 + $2,000) to obtain $6,000 of protection. The PAP pays on a pro-rata basis in cases where other insurance applies on an equal basis. However, with respect to nonowned automobiles, it is always excess.

Uninsured Motorist

Uninsured motorist insurance pays for your bodily injuries that result from an accident with another vehicle if the other driver is negligent and does not have any insurance (or insurance less than that required by law). Insured persons include the named insured and family members, any person occupying your covered auto, and other persons who are entitled to recovery because of injury in the first two categories. For example, a man could be injured in an accident and his wife might seek to recover for loss of consortium in addition to any claims her spouse made.

Uninsured Motor Vehicles. The policy defines an **uninsured motor vehicle** as a land motor vehicle or trailer of any type with the following specifications:

1. One to which no bodily injury liability bond or policy applies at the time of the accident
2. One to which a bodily injury liability bond or policy applies at the time of the accident, but with a limit for liability less than the minimum limit specified by the financial responsibility law of the state in which your covered auto is principally garaged
3. One which is a hit-and-run vehicle whose operator or owner cannot be identified, and which hits you or any family member, a vehicle occupied by you or any family member, or your covered auto
4. One to which a bodily-injury liability bond or policy applies at the time of the accident, but which is covered by a bonding or insuring company that denies coverage or becomes insolvent

However, none of the following is considered an uninsured motor vehicle:

1. One owned by, furnished to, or available for the regular use of you or any family member
2. One owned or operated by a self-insurer under any applicable motor vehicle law
3. One owned by any governmental unit or agency
4. One operated on rails or crawler treads
5. One designed mainly for use off public roads while not on public roads
6. One located for use as a residence or premises

Most of the definition is clear; however, one interesting court decision is worth noting. A Michigan court ruled that a bulldozer was an uninsured vehicle.

Exclusions. In addition to the exclusions under uninsured motor vehicle, the uninsured motorist coverage has five exclusions for bodily injury:

1. If the injury is sustained while occupying, or when struck by, any motor vehicle or trailer of any type owned by you or any family member which is not insured for this coverage under this policy
2. If the claim is settled by the injured or legal representative without consent of the insurer
3. If the injury is sustained while occupying your covered auto when it is being used to carry people or property for a fee (does not apply to a share-the-expense car pool)
4. If the injury is sustained while using a vehicle without reasonable belief that you are entitled to do so
5. If the coverage directly or indirectly benefits any insurer or self-insurer under any workers' compensation, disability benefits, or similar law.

This exclusion is designed to prevent a workers' compensation insurer or a self-insured employer from collecting funds from the uninsured motorist coverage of the insurance company. Uninsured motorist insurance is not intended to pay for workers' compensation claims.

Other Conditions. The maximum limit of liability is the amount shown on the declarations page. The number of persons or vehicles insured does not affect this limit. As in the case of medical payments, no stacking is allowed. Coverage is excess on nonowned vehicles. When a dispute develops between the insured and the insurer on a claim, the policy gives either party the right to ask for binding arbitration. Unlike previous policies, local rules of law as to procedure and evidence apply. (The rules of the American Arbitration Association were used in previous policies.)

Physical Damage to Autos

In this section the insurer provides protection for direct accidental loss to the covered auto or to a nonowned auto. A **nonowned auto** is defined as any private passenger auto, pickup, van, or trailer not owned by or furnished for the regular use of you or any family member while in the custody of or being operated by you or any family member. However, the term *nonowned auto* is defined differently than is a "temporary substitute vehicle." Such a vehicle is protected under coverage D, physical damage, as a covered auto. Coverage for a nonowned auto is equal to the broadest protection provided for a covered auto. Note that nonowned trucks are not covered under the definition of nonowned autos.

Coverage is separated into two sections: *collision* and *loss other than collision*. **Collision** is defined as upset of your covered auto or its impact with another vehicle or object. This definition is new to the PAP, and it clarifies what some persons thought was awkward in the old definition. The old definition used the word collide to define the term collision. Using another form of the same word does not clarify the meaning of the word. By definition, the following are considered losses other than those due to collision: losses to an auto caused by missiles, falling objects, fire, theft or larceny, explosion, earthquake, windstorm, hail, water, flood, malicious mischief or vandalism, riot or civil commotion, contact with a bird or animal, or breakage of glass. If breakage of glass is caused by a collision, you may elect to have it considered a loss caused by collision. (This qualification about damage to glass is made so only one deductible is applied. A car could collide with a telephone pole and have glass damage. Without this alternative approach on glass, a deductible could be required for the collision loss and another deductible, on loss other than collision, for the glass.) The advantage to the insured for not having the preceding perils considered collisions is that loss other than collision usually has a lower deductible than collision, or it has no deductible. In addition, loss-other-than-collision claims often will not raise an insured's rates, while a collision claim will.

Much discussion has occurred over whether certain accidents were loss-other-than-collision or collision claims. Usually the insured desires the claim to be considered loss other than collision. The following examples provide a series of interesting cases on the subject:

1. A moving car caught fire and wrecked. The court called it loss other than collision.[7]
2. A bulldozer struck a valve of a liquid propane pipeline. No damage on striking occurred, but gas escaped and froze when exposed to air. It also froze the bulldozer. The court called it collision.[8] The insured had only collision.
3. A truck backed close to the edge of an excavation site, the dirt gave way and the truck fell in. The court called it loss other than collision, and the insurer paid for damage and the cost of pulling out the truck.[9]
4. The insured parked a car in a carport. He said the wind blew the car down the driveway. The insured did not carry collision. The court ruled it was collision since the wind on the day of the accident was 18 to 25 mph.[10] In cases where an insured was driving a vehicle in wind and rain, lost control, and had an accident, courts have ruled it loss other than collision since the storm was the primary cause and it could be proven that the windstorm occurred.
5. In the area of water damage, flood losses are usually considered loss other than collision. However, when a car plunges off a bridge or highway into a river, lake, or ocean, it is collision.[11]
6. In an old case, but one that may occur more often today (especially in Florida), the court held that when a car sank in a roadbed (sinkhole effect), its damage was loss other than collision. There was no colliding with an object since the car never moved.[12]

Exclusions. The physical damage section excludes loss resulting from the operation of a vehicle used to carry persons or property for a fee (share-the-expense car pools excepted). Damage resulting from war, radioactive contamination, and discharge of any nuclear weapon is excluded.

The PAP physical damage section has a series of exclusions pertaining to auto accessories. All of the following items are excluded:

1. Loss to equipment designed for the reproduction of sound, unless the equipment is permanently installed in your covered auto. The question frequently arises about what is permanently installed. The New York State Supreme Court has ruled that an item is permanently installed if it is bolted to brackets that in turn are bolted to the underside of the insured's vehicle.[13]
2. Loss to tapes, records, or other devices for use with equipment designed for the reproduction of sound
3. Loss to a camper body or trailer not shown in the declarations. (This exclusion does not apply to a camper body or trailer of which you acquire

ownership during the policy period if you ask the company to insure it within 30 days after you become the owner.)

4. Loss to TV antennas, awnings, cabanas, or equipment designed to create additional living facilities

5. Loss to any custom furnishings or equipment in or upon any pickup, panel truck, or van. Custom furnishings or equipment include but are not limited to (a) special carpeting and insulation, furniture, bars, or television receivers; (b) facilities for cooking or sleeping; (c) height-extending roofs; and (d) custom murals, paintings, or other decals or graphics. If insureds desire coverage for custom items, they may be added by endorsement.

6. Loss to any of the following or their accessories: (a) citizens band radio, (b) two-way mobile radio, (c) telephone, and (d) scanning monitor receiver. This exclusion does not apply if the equipment is permanently installed in the opening of the dash or console of your covered auto or any nonowned auto. The opening must normally be used by the auto manufacturer for the installation of a radio.

7. There is no coverage for a nonowned or temporary substitute vehicle used by you or a family member without a reasonable belief that such a person is entitled to do so. If you steal a car and wreck it, there is no coverage on that auto.

Finally, the policy excludes damage from wear and tear, freezing, and mechanical or electrical breakdown or failures, and road damage to tires. The PAP does not pay for flat tires. If you fail to put enough antifreeze in your car in the winter, and the engine block freezes and cracks, no coverage applies. However, if someone steals the car and the engine block freezes, coverage is provided because the proximate cause of the loss is presumed to be theft. All coverage for a nonowned auto or a temporary substitute vehicle is excess over any other collectible insurance.

Transportation and Towing. The PAP will pay up to $10 per day (maximum $300) for transportation expenses incurred by you because someone stole your car. Coverage does not begin until 48 hours after the theft occurs. Also, the condition section of the contract requires you to notify the police promptly. The transportation expenses incurred may be for car rental, bus fare, a taxi, or a commuter train. However, such expenses must be used to provide substitute transportation for the stolen covered automobile. The coverage is automatically provided in the PAP.

For an additional premium (about $4), towing and labor cost coverage may be added. The insurer's limit of liability is $25, and all labor must be performed at the site of the disablement. If you go on a picnic and your car will not start, this coverage will pay up to $25 to have someone tow you into a garage or a service station. If you have an accident due to collision or loss other than collision, any towing charges will be covered by these two coverages. Towing and labor cost coverage is only needed when collision or loss other than collision does not occur. Consequently, most persons really do not need it, but because the premium is so low, many persons purchase it.

Other Provisions. The insurer limits its liability to the actual cash value of the loss or the amount necessary to repair or replace the property, whichever is less. The policy states that the term actual cash value includes an adjustment for depreciation and the physical condition of the auto. By making this statement, insurers are trying both to avoid having to pay for the replacement cost of the auto and to reduce misunderstandings about the basis of recovery to which the insured is entitled. In the case of antique or customized automobiles, a stated-amount endorsement may be used. This endorsement sets a specific policy limit, such as $5,000. The stated amount is the maximum the insurer will pay.

The insurer reserves the right to pay for the loss in money, repair, or replacement of the damaged or stolen property. If the car is stolen, the insurer will pay for the cost of returning the vehicle to the owner. If the cost of repair or replacement is greater than the value of the property, the insurer may declare the loss a total loss and pay the ACV of the vehicle. Sometimes it may cost $3,000 to repair a vehicle worth $1,500. In such situations the insurer will generally pay only $1,500 (less the deductible, if any).

Another policy provision states that the insurance shall not directly or indirectly benefit any carrier or bailee. Such persons include a railroad or shipping line that transports your vehicle as well as a parking lot operation. This provision allows the insurer to subrogate against the bailee when the bailee is negligent.

Duties after an Accident or Loss

When an accident or loss occurs, the insured must promptly notify the insurance company of how, when, and where the accident or loss happened. Typically, reporting such information to your agent is considered reporting it to the company.

Besides this requirement, any person seeking coverage under the PAP must be willing

1. To cooperate with the company in the investigation, settlement, or defense of any claim or suit
2. To send the company copies promptly of any notices or legal papers received in connection with the accident or loss
3. To submit, at the company's expense and as often as reasonably required, to physical examinations by physicians selected by the company, and to examination under oath
4. To authorize the company to obtain medical reports and other pertinent records
5. To submit a proof of loss when required by the company

A person seeking uninsured motorist coverage must also be willing to (1) notify the police promptly if a hit-and-run driver is involved, and (2) send copies of the legal papers to the company if a suit is brought. The requirement under uninsured motorist coverage with respect to hit-and-run accidents is introduced so that insureds will be discouraged from making a claim that a hit-and-run driver forced them off the road when in reality they fell asleep. Insurers believe that the requirement to notify the police promptly will reduce the moral hazard.

When a claim is made under the coverage for damage to your auto, you must meet three conditions:

1. Take reasonable steps after a loss, at company expense, to protect your covered auto and its equipment from further damage
2. Notify the police promptly if your covered auto is stolen
3. Permit the company to inspect and appraise the damaged property before its repair or disposal

If you have an accident, the insurer will pay towing expenses. If the disabled vehicle were left at the scene of the accident, there is a good chance that someone would strip it of its salable parts. Promptly notifying the police when theft occurs increases the probability of recovery. It also reduces the moral hazard of an insured's selling the vehicle and then reporting it as stolen to the insurer. The third item allows the insurer to make its own claims adjustment if it desires. In some locations insureds and repair mechanics have filed inflated claims in order to collect excess monies. This provision helps the insurer prevent such activities.

General Provisions

The policy states that its territorial limits are the United States, its territories or possessions, and Canada. Transportation of the auto between any of these points is also covered. Technically, a commonwealth, Puerto Rico, is also within the territorial limits. It should be noted that Mexico is not a covered territory. One should purchase auto insurance from a Mexican insurer before operating an automobile in Mexico.

Other conditions include a policy change provision that says all policy modifications must be in writing. When a policy is changed to give greater coverage without additional charge, the insured's policy is automatically modified. The insured cannot start legal proceedings until full compliance with all policy terms have been met. The policy cannot be assigned without the permission of the insurer. Bankruptcy of the insured does not relieve the insurer of its obligations.

The PAP policy has a rather lengthy termination (cancellation) provision. The insured can cancel at any time by returning the policy or giving written notice of the time when the insured intends to cancel. Termination by the company is more complex.

During the first 60 days of the policy the insurer may cancel for any reason, and it may cancel for nonpayment of premium at any time. The insurer has 60 days to investigate the insured and make its underwriting decision. During the first 60 days the insurer must give 10 days' notice before cancelling. After the policy has been in effect for 60 days, the insurer can cancel only (1) for nonpayment of premium, (2) if the insured or a resident of the household, or someone who regularly uses the auto, has his or her license suspended or revoked, or (3) if the policy was obtained through material misrepresentation. When cancellation is made after the first 60 days, 20 days' notice must be given. If the insurer decides not to renew your policy on its anniversay date, it must give you 20 days' notice.

For example, if you purchase your insurance on February 1, 1988, pay your premium, and do not have your license revoked, after 60 days the insurer cannot cancel your policy. Thus, after April 1, 1988, the insurer must wait until policy renewal time to take action. On or before January 11, 1989 (20 days before the anniversary date), the insurer would have to decide not to renew your policy. The effect of this cancellation clause is to give insureds some assurance that coverage will be provided until the policy's anniversary date.

If your state requires longer notice than the PAP gives, then your state law will determine the notification period. The insurance company is obligated to give you a refund of premium if one is due. However, it is not required to tender the refund when it cancels. You may have to ask for it.

Endorsements to the PAP. The PAP may be endorsed to give physical damage coverage to owned trailers. This endorsement is made on a schedule basis. When nonowned autos are furnished for your regular use, the extended nonowned liability endorsement is needed. This endorsement gives coverage for nonowned autos furnished for your regular use, business use (except auto business) of commercial vehicles (trucks), and the operation of a vehicle to carry persons for a fee.

In the case of a custom van, the insured needs to add a covered property endorsement. If this action is not taken, all the custom work on the van will be excluded.

The underinsured motorists endorsement is a recent development. It provides the insured protection when another person causes the insured injury but the negligent party's insurance is inadequate. For example, the negligent third party might carry limits of $50,000, but the insured suffered injuries of $150,000. Uninsured motorist protection will not pay, since the $50,000 coverage meets the financial responsibility law. However, if underinsured motorist protection of $100,000 had been purchased, the insured could collect $50,000 from the negligent third party and $100,000 from the insurance company.

Motorcycles and Other Vehicles

Because of changing life styles and the fact that people own more than just one type of motor vehicle, insurance companies have developed coverages to meet the needs of the public. Through the use of the "Miscellaneous

Type Vehicle Endorsement," a person can insure under the PAP motorcycles, motor homes, golf carts, or other similar types of vehicles. In addition, a private passenger auto owned jointly by two or more resident relatives other than a husband and wife may be insured. An example would be a father and a daughter. Through this endorsement almost any vehicle may be insured. (A notable exception is a snowmobile.) Coverages available include liability, medical payments, uninsured motorists, collision, and loss other than collision.

When this endorsement is used, the definition of your covered auto is modified to fit the description of the miscellaneous-type vehicle. All the provisions of the PAP are retained and apply to the miscellaneous vehicle.

While very similar in coverage to the PAP, this endorsement creates some changes:

1. Newly acquired miscellaneous vehicles are covered if they are like the insured vehicle. Thus, if a motorcycle is insured, then an additional motorcycle would be covered, but a motor home would not.
2. Temporary substitute autos of any kind are covered. However, other than for a temporary substitute auto, there is no coverage for nonowned vehicles.
3. There is no coverage for property damage to a nonowned auto.
4. Exclusion with respect to vehicles with fewer than four wheels is changed when a motorcycle is insured.

Snowmobiles

Snowmobiles may be insured by endorsement to the PAP. This approach has advantages over purchasing snowmobile insurance through the homeowners' program. When the PAP is used, one can purchase uninsured motorist and physical damage insurance in addition to liability insurance, snowmobiles subject to motor vehicle registrations can be covered, and the named insured and family members may be covered under medical payments.

AUTOMOBILE INSURANCE AND THE LAW

In every state and in all the provinces of Canada, legislatures have passed some form of automobile insurance law designed to solve the problem of the uncompensated victim of financially irresponsible automobile drivers. In other words, the law has stepped in because without some system of financial guarantees, motorists are forced into assumption of risk whether they are financially able to or not. Most often they are not. Accordingly, legislatures have attempted various methods to cope with the problem. Laws have taken the following forms:

1. Financial responsibility laws
2. Compulsory liability insurance laws
3. Unsatisfied judgment fund
4. Uninsured motorist endorsement
5. No-fault and compensation laws

Financial Responsibility Laws

Financial responsibility laws represent a common approach to the general problem of the uncompensated victim of the financially irresponsible motorist. There are two basic requirements of most such laws:

1. Motorists without liability insurance who are involved in an automobile accident must obtain and maintain liability insurance or other proof of financial responsibility (say, a surety bond) of a specified character for a given period, usually three years, as a condition of continued licensing of the operator and registration of the vehicle.
2. Motorists without liability insurance who are involved in an automobile accident must pay for the damages they have caused, or give evidence that they were not to blame, as a condition for the continued operation of their vehicle.

In their early development, financial responsibility laws often contained only the first requirement, but gradually the second requirement, called **security provisions,** was added. Financial responsibility laws have no penalty other than the suspension of driving privileges, and hence are not guarantees that the uncompensated victim will actually be paid. The effectiveness of the laws in this regard rests on the hope that most drivers will be led to purchase insurance rather than face possible loss of their driving privileges.

Although financial responsibility laws are better than nothing, they have serious drawbacks as solutions to the problem of compensating victims of uninsured or financially irresponsible motorists. Major weaknesses include:

1. There is no assurance that all drivers will have liability insurance. The laws aim only at assuring financial responsibility for the irresponsible motorist's second and subsequent victims, not the first victim.
2. The penalty for not complying with the law is weak; the motorist is subject only to the loss of driving privileges.
3. There is no protection against hit-and-run, stolen car, or motorists driving illegally. Enforcement procedures against these drivers is difficult and relatively unsuccessful.

Those in favor of financial responsibility statutes are usually opposed to any further strengthening that probably would lead to either compulsory insurance or a compensation system similar to workers' compensation laws. The proponents point out that these laws, where they have been enforced effectively and are doing a good job of meeting the problem, have generally resulted in a very high percentage of insured drivers.

General dissatisfaction with financial responsibility laws has resulted in a national movement to strengthen and extend them. Compulsory liability statutes and no-fault laws are being adopted rapidly in many states to solve the problem of compensating the victims of uninsured motorists.

Compulsory Liability Insurance Laws

During the last several years there has been a distinct movement by many states to require automobile owners to purchase liability insurance; included are Alaska, Arizona, California, Colorado, Connecticut, Delaware, the District of Columbia, Georgia, Hawaii, Idaho, Indiana, Kansas, Kentucky, Louisiana, Maryland, Massachusetts, Michigan, Minnesota, Montana, Nevada, New Jersey, New Mexico, New York, North Carolina, North Dakota, Ohio, Oklahoma, Oregon, Pennsylvania, South Carolina, Texas, Utah, West Virginia, and Wyoming. The strictness of these laws varies, but in theory, liability insurance is required of all registered car owners. (See Table 17–1.)

Unsatisfied Judgment Fund

The **unsatisfied judgment fund (UJF)** is a fund set up by a state to pay automobile accident settlements that cannot be collected by other means. If the negligent motorist is insolvent, does not carry liability insurance, or has voided insurance through violation of a policy provision, or if the insurer is insolvent, the innocent victim may collect from the UJF after every other means of collection is exhausted. The UJF is actually broader than compulsory insurance, as it covers cases in which insurance was carried but the damage is still uncollectible. However, the UJF is based on the principle of negligence; hence, if there is no legal liability, there can be no payment from the fund. Furthermore, the UJF has the right of subrogation; that is, it must be paid back by the negligent motorist if he or she obtains property on which liens may be obtained. In any case, the negligent motorist loses driving privileges until the fund is repaid.

Uninsured Motorist Endorsement

The solution to the problem of the uncompensated victim of the uninsured motorist has been proposed and supported by private insurance companies in the form of an endorsement to the automobile policy known as the **uninsured motorist protection,** also known as the **uninsured motorist endorsement (UME).** Under the terms of this endorsement, which usually applies only to bodily injury claims (property damage is covered in some states), if it is determined that an insured driver is injured by a driver who is uninsured, the insured driver's company will act as the insurer of the negligent motorist and pay any legal liability that the negligent uninsured motorist would be obligated to pay. The insurer naturally has the right to collect from the negligent uninsured motorist for any damages paid to the insured motorist.

The UME does not go as far as the UJF or compulsory liability insurance in solving the problem of compensating innocent victims of uninsured motorists, but it does overcome an important weakness in the typical financial responsibility law. For a small charge, an individual may be protected against bodily injury damage caused by uninsured motorists. While the individual does not always receive similar protection for property damage, physical damage insurance can always be purchased for protection against property loss.

Table 17-1   Automobile Plans: Summary of Insurance Plans and Required Limits of Liability, 1985

State	Compulsory	Required Limits	No-Fault	Some Tort Restrictions	Financial Responsibility	Mandatory Liability Insurance
Ala.	N	20/40/10	N	N/A	Y	N
Alaska	Y	50/100/25	N	N/A	Y	Y
Ariz.	Y	15/30/10	N	N/A	Y	Y
Ark.	N	25/50/15	Y	N	Y	N
Cal.	Y	15/30/5	N	N/A	Y	Y
Colo.	Y	25/50/15	Y	Y	Y	Y
Conn.	Y	20/40/10	Y	Y	Y	Y
Del.	Y	15/30/10	Y	N	Y	Y
D.C.	Y	10/20/5	Y	Y	Y	Y
Fla.	N	10/20/5	Y	Y	Y	N
Ga.	Y	15/30/10	Y	Y	Y	Y
Hawaii	Y	25/unlimited/10	Y	Y	Y	Y
Ida.	Y	25/50/15	N	N/A	Y	Y
Ill.	N	15/30/10	N	N/A	Y	N
Ind.	Y	25/50/10	N	N/A	Y	Y
Iowa	N	20/40/15	N	N/A	Y	N
Kans.	Y	25/50/10	Y	Y	Y	Y
Ky.	Y	25/50/10	Y	Y	Y	Y
La.	Y	10/20/10	N	N/A	Y	N
Maine	N	20/40/10	N	N/A	Y	N
Md.	Y	20/40/10	Y	N	Y	Y
Mass.	Y	10/20/5	Y	Y	Y	Y
Mich.	Y	20/40/10	Y	Y	Y	Y
Minn.	Y	30/60/10	Y	Y	Y	Y
Miss.	N	10/20/5	N	N/A	Y	N
Mo.	N	25/50/10	N	N/A	Y	N
Mont.	Y	25/50/5	N	N/A	Y	Y
Nebr.	N	25/50/25	N	N/A	Y	N
Nev.	Y	15/30/5	N	N/A	Y	Y
N.H.	N	25/50/25	Y	N	Y	N
N.J.	Y	15/30/5	Y	Y	Y	Y
N.M.	Y	25/50/10	N	N/A	Y	Y
N.Y.	Y	10/20/5	Y	Y	Y	Y
N.C.	Y	25/50/10	N	N/A	Y	Y
N.D.	Y	25/50/10	Y	Y	Y	Y
Oh.	Y	12.5/25/7.5	N	N/A	Y	Y
Okla.	Y	10/20/10	N	N/A	Y	Y
Ore.	Y	25/50/10	Y	N	Y	Y
Penn.	Y	15/30/5	Y	N	Y	Y
R.I.	N	25/50/10	N	N/A	Y	N
S.C.	Y	15/30/5	Y	N	Y	Y
S.D.	N	25/50/25	Y	N	Y	N
Tenn.	N	20/40/10	N	N/A	Y	N

(Continued)

Table 17–1 Automobile Plans: Summary of Insurance Plans and Required Limits of Liability, 1985 (*Continued*)

State	Compulsory	Required Limits	No-Fault	Some Tort Restrictions	Financial Responsibility	Mandatory Liability Insurance
Texas	Y	20/40/15	Y	N	Y	Y
Utah	Y	20/40/10	Y	Y	Y	Y
Vt.	N	20/40/10	N	N/A	Y	N
Va.	N	25/50/10	Y	N	Y	N
Wash.	N	25/50/10	N	N/A	Y	N
W.V.	Y	20/40/10	N	N/A	Y	Y
Wisc.	N	25/50/10	N	N/A	Y	N
Wyo.	Y	25/50/20	N	N/A	Y	Y

N = No Y = Yes
NA = Not Applicable
Sources: *Insurance Facts 1985–1986* (New York: Insurance Information Institute, 1985), pp. 103–105; *P.F. & M. Fire Casualty and Surety Analyses, Analysis of U. S. Automobile Insurance Laws* (Indianapolis: The Rough Notes Company, 1986), Section 224.3, pp. 1–11.

A summary of the uninsured motorist insurance available in the various states is included in Table 17-1. Information is given on whether coverage is mandatory, bodily injury liability as well as property damage limits, and deductibles that apply to property damage.

No-Fault and Compensation Laws

There has been a growing body of opinion that the economic importance of automobile accidents is such that we can no longer trust the legal liability system with the task of solving the problem of compensating the victims. It is argued that it is impossible to determine the precise degree of negligence in a given accident, even if any exists, and that too often the automobile accident victim is without any means to meet the cost involved. It is said that it is the person with the best lawyer and the most cooperative witness who is compensated, and the absence of scientific method is conspicuous. The concept of fault in a society on wheels is not workable. In recognition of this argument, a number of states have passed no-fault laws under which injured victims in automobile accidents may recover loss (up to a stated amount) under their own automobile policies rather than under tort liability policies of other parties.

Background of No-Fault. The problem of uncompensated victims of uninsured motorists has been studied intensively. Perhaps the best known work was written by Keeton and O'Connell, whose book was a major influence in initiating a national movement toward no-fault laws.[14] This movement was further encouraged by the U.S. Department of Transportation in an extensive study of the automobile accident problem. The DOT study was published in 28 volumes in 1970–1971. In 1971, the National Association of Insurance Commissioners, an advisory committee to the U.S. Department of Transportation, recommended that individual state legislatures pass no-fault laws. As of this writing, 25 states and Puerto Rico have passed such laws, which, although not uniform in their provisions, are all aimed at overcoming some of the weaknesses in the tort liability system. In some ways the laws are similar in concept to workers' compensation statutes, which provide reimbursement for occupational injuries without regard to fault.

Summary of No-Fault Statutes. The no-fault statutes of every state are given in Table 17–1. Notice that some state laws do not restrict any tort action. One of the basic foundations of a no-fault system is some restriction on a person's ability to sue. The present tort system uses a large portion of insurance premiums to pay for insurance company operations and litigation costs. The no-fault approach was supposed to eliminate litigation costs and overpayment of small claims. The DOT study estimated that under the tort system, claims under $500 recovered 4.5 times their actual amount in reparations. However, persons with losses of $25,000 and over collected only 30 percent of their losses. People supporting no-fault felt monies could be moved from the overpaid group to the undercompensated group by restricting one's right to sue in situations where losses were low. Keeton and O'Connell recommended a threshold of $10,000 in 1966. Most laws placed the threshold at a much lower level. Consequently, many states do not have a plan that will significantly redistribute payments from persons with small losses to those with larger losses.

Effects of No-Fault. In an insurance industry study that investigated automobile injuries and compensation, some interesting results were found.[15] About 77 percent of all auto injury claims were paid in the 16 no-fault states surveyed. In states that do not have no-fault, 34 percent of the auto injury claims were paid.

While no-fault threshold figures are low in many states, they do seem to have some effect. In the 16 states restricting tort liability, the researchers felt the thresholds had eliminated about 42 percent of the potential liability claims among injured persons who were paid on a no-fault basis. These results show that no-fault potentially reduces liability costs. However, the study also indicated that under no-fault more persons collect than under tort liability systems. Approximately 50 percent more persons involved in single-car accidents collected insurance benefits in the no-fault states than those in tort liability states. Also, the distribution of benefits to different age groups varied between no-fault and tort liability states. In the no-fault states drivers 16 through 24 and those over 65 were able to collect more than before. The study implied that these people were less likely to receive funds under a tort system.

One of the original arguments for no-fault was that it would pay more for real economic loss and less for general damages (pain and suffering). The study confirmed this belief. In no-fault states, 52 cents of the premium dollar went for economic losses and 48 cents went for general damage. In the tort liability states, 43 cents went for economic losses and 57 cents went for general damages. As might be expected, attorneys were involved more frequently in tort liability states than in no-fault states.

RISK MANAGEMENT AND PERSONAL AUTOMOBILE RATING

Before an informed risk-management decision concerning personal automobile insurance can be made, an understanding of automobile insurance rating is needed. In this section an explanation of some rating fundamentals is presented, as well as the cost of choosing higher deductibles and limits of liability.

Rating Principles

While rating plans have state-by-state variations, there is a common basis. This review will look at that basis. The rating system analyzed is the 161-class plan used by a majority of states. Two other plans exist: the nine-class plan, which seven jurisdictions use, and the 270-class plan used by four states.[16]

161-Class Plan. Under this plan there are two rate factors, primary and secondary. The primary factor involves an insured's age, sex, marital status, and use of automobile. The secondary factor includes the type of vehicle, the number of vehicles insured, and an insured's driving record. The two factors added together determine an insured's rate factor.

The primary system assumes that a male driver between the ages of 30 and 64 who uses the auto only for pleasure purposes has a rating of 1.00.[17] Deviations from this basic index number require either additions or subtractions to be made. For instance, a female driver between 30 and 64 would have a primary rating index of 0.90. A 17-year-old male who is a principal operator and has no driver education or student discount would have a primary rating factor of 3.5. In this rating plan, rate credits are given for driver education until a person is 21. Credits are also given for being a good student until age 24.[18]

Youthful Driver. A special subset of the primary rating factor is the **youthful driver** or underage driver category. A person is considered a youthful driver until age 25 if a female and age 30 if a male. In Table 17–2 the primary rating factor for several groups of people in this category is given. (The age-18 group was deleted from the table in order to conserve space.)

Notice that marriage has a definite effect on rating. An unmarried male is considered a youthful driver until 30, but if he is married the category is terminated at 25. The same effect is seen with respect to females. They are rated underage until 25 if not married, but if they are married the youthful rate ceases at 21.

Marriage, a good-student discount, and driver education credits are important rating factors.[19] A 17-year-old unmarried male who is a principal operator without any of the three credits has a 3.3 rating factor. With these

Table 17–2 Primary Rating Factors for Underage Drivers

	Rating Factors				Rating Factors		
Male Operator under 25 Unmarried—Not Owner or Principal Operator				Male Operator under 30 Unmarried—Owner or Principal Operator			
Age	Driver Education	Good Student	Primary Rating Factor	Age	Driver Education	Good Student	Primary Rating Factor
17	N	N	2.30	17	N	N	3.30
	Y	N	2.10		Y	N	2.95
	N	Y	1.90		N	Y	2.65
	Y	Y	1.75		Y	Y	2.40
19	N	N	2.30	19	N	N	3.30
	Y	N	2.10		Y	N	2.95
	N	Y	1.90		N	Y	2.65
	Y	Y	1.75		Y	Y	2.40
20	N	N	2.30	20	N	N	3.30
	Y	N	2.10		Y	N	2.95
	N	Y	1.90		N	Y	2.65
	Y	Y	1.75		Y	Y	2.40
21–24	NA	N	1.40	21–24	NA	N	2.10
					NA	Y	1.75
				25–29	NA	NA	1.50

Male Operator under 25, Married				Female Operator under 25, Unmarried			
Age	Driver Education	Good Student	Primary Rating Factor	Age	Driver Education	Good Student	Primary Rating Factor
17	N	N	1.90	17	N	N	1.65
	Y	N	1.75		Y	N	1.55
	N	Y	1.65		N	Y	1.45
	Y	Y	1.55		Y	Y	1.40
19	N	N	1.90	18	N	N	1.65
	Y	N	1.75		Y	N	1.65
	N	Y	1.65		N	Y	1.45
	Y	Y	1.55		Y	Y	1.40
20	N	N	1.90	20	N	N	1.65
	Y	N	1.75		Y	N	1.55
	N	Y	1.65		N	Y	1.45
	Y	Y	1.55		Y	Y	1.40
21–24	NA	N	1.30	21–24	NA	N	1.25
	NA	Y	1.20		NA	Y	1.15

Assumes pleasure use, subclass 0 on safe-driver plan; single car, standard performance; N = No; Y = Yes; NA = Not Applicable

Source: Insurance Service Office, June, 1984

credits, he has a 2.4 rating factor. The credits reduce his insurance cost by 27.3 percent ($\frac{0.9}{3.3}$). As he grows older, the effect of the credit is reduced. At age 21 there is no driver education discount, and the good student discount only reduces his rate by 27 percent ($\frac{0.65}{2.40}$). After age 24 the good student credit is discontinued.

The secondary rating classification uses four categories of vehicle performance: standard, intermediate, sports, and high. The standard category has the lowest rate, and the high category has the highest rate. Besides the vehicle performance categories, there are five driving experience categories for the safe-driver plan: 0, 1, 2, 3, and 4. Points are assigned for certain types of convictions. For example, a driving-while-intoxicated (DWI) conviction is worth three points. Each point places the insured in a new category range. The DWI conviction would place you in class 3. If you have no chargeable points, you are in class 0. The third factor in the secondary rating classification is the number of cars insured. When more than one car is insured, a multiple-car discount is given.

When one combines the two systems of rating (primary and secondary), it is found that the lowest rating factor is 0.75. Such a person is an unmarried female between the ages of 30 and 64. She lives on a farm, her auto is rated for farm use, she receives a multicar discount, and she has had no points assigned under the safe-driver plan. The highest rating factor is 5.95. The "lucky" person to receive this rating is a 17-year-old unmarried male who is the owner or principal operator of one vehicle. He is driving a high-performance car to work or to school 15 or more miles (one way) each day. He has had 4 points assigned in the safe-driver plan, which places him in category 4.

Once an individual's rating factor is determined, it is multiplied by a specific company's base rate for the coverage desired. If the insurer's basic liability rate were $200 for the just-described 17-year-old male, he would pay $1,190 per year for liability insurance. If his "coverage for damage to your car" rate were $100, he would pay $595 for that item. For the two coverages, he would pay $1,785. When people start to pay higher rates, they look for ways to reduce costs. The following analysis of deductibles will help insureds make such a decision.

Deductibles for Damage to Your Auto

In the PAP there are deductibles for collision and for loss other than collision (comprehensive) discussed earlier. The schedules in Table 17–3 show, in relative terms, the premium discount one can receive for accepting a higher deductible.

A person having a rate credit of 0.75 will not find large deductibles an attractive alternative. However, someone with a rating of 5.95 may find deductibles to be a necessity. For instance, if the 17-year-old male described earlier had a Corvette with a collision base rate of $200 with a $200 deductible, higher deductibles would be attractive. The base rate would convert to $1,190 ($200 × 5.95). By increasing the deductible from $200 to

Table 17–3   Credits for Deductibles

Deductible	Collision	Deductible	Comprehensive
$ 250	95% of $200 deductible rate	$ 200	85% of $50 deductible rate
500	80% of $200 deductible rate	250	80% of $50 deductible rate
1,000	55% of $200 deductible rate	1,000	50% of $50 deductible rate

Source: Insurance Services Office, February, 1985.

Table 17–4
Liability Rate Factor for
Personal Auto Policy

Limit	Factor
$ 25,000	1.00
50,000	1.20
100,000	1.33
500,000	1.69
1,000,000	1.89

Source: *Personal Auto Manual,* 1978, GAE-4.

$500, he could save $238 ($1,190 − 0.80 × $937.50). A $1,000 deductible would save an additional $297.50 for an increased deductible of $500. Consequently, the $500 deductible seems to make good economic sense, but the $1,000 deductible is not as attractive.

Selection of Liability Limits

When people are choosing their liability limits, they should *think big*. Each year awards increase as both economic inflation and social inflation occur. If liability rate schedules are examined, it can be shown that on a relative basis, higher liability limits are not overly expensive. Table 17–4 shows a typical schedule.

From the table, it can be seen that you can raise your liability limits from $25,000 to $50,000 for only a 20 percent increase in premium, and you can go from limits of $50,000 to $500,000 for an additional 41 percent increase in premiums $\left(\frac{1.69}{1.20}\right)$. Such a rating schedule makes higher liability limits an attractive purchase.

SUMMARY

1. The cost of automobile accidents, in both absolute and relative terms, has been rising steadily in the United States for many years, posing a serious problem as to the most efficient and equitable manner in which the economic burden can be borne.

   If the real causes of accidents were known, steps might be taken to handle the risk by placing greater emphasis on reduction of hazard. Less emphasis would have to be laid on the reduction of risk to the individual through private insurance, a state fund of some sort, or assumption of risk by a person unable to bear it. One example of the significance of this point is the relationship of age to the probability of having an automobile accident. At present, insurers seem to assign higher rates to certain classes of youthful drivers without any real knowledge as to what causal factors result in higher accident rates in youthful drivers.

2. Because a single automobile accident may be catastrophically expensive to the victim, and because of the relatively high probability of loss, insurance is the only feasible method to protect against the risk involved.

3. The provisions of the personal automobile policy (PAP) are representative of those found in most contracts covering the use of automobiles. The PAP is one of the most comprehensive contracts, insuring against losses due to legal liability for negligence, medical payments, and physical damage to the vehicle. Under the terms of the PAP, the words *insured* and *automobile* are defined broadly enough to protect the typical car owner and to give nearly the same protection to anyone else driving the automobile with the owner's permission.

4. Liability coverage under the PAP covers against loss due to legal liability for damage to the person or property of others arising out of the ownership, maintenance, and use of the automobile. Medical payments coverage insures the loss due to accidental bodily injuries of occupants of a vehicle regardless of negligence of the insured driver. Physical damage insurance reimburses the owner for physical loss of a vehicle from almost any peril, whether or not the insured caused the accident.

Uninsured motorists endorsements protect insureds when they have an accident with a negligent uninsured motorist. This coverage is mandatory in 19 states.

5. Because the definitions, exclusions, and conditions are as important as they are basic to an understanding of the PAP, they must be studied carefully to ascertain the scope of coverage. In general, coverage granted when the insured is driving non-owned cars is less comprehensive than when the insured is driving his or her own car.

6. Among the approaches that have been tried to improve the effectiveness of the tort-liability system are financial responsibility laws, compulsory liability insurance, unsatisfied judgment funds, and no-fault insurance laws. The latter are the most recent measures. No-fault laws represent a basic reform in that, subject to certain limits, the negligence principle is abandoned and benefits are paid to victims by their own insurers on a first-party basis. No-fault laws are still experimental, but they offer considerable promise in improving the system. No-fault laws do not eliminate the need for liability insurance, which is still necessary to protect the motorist against loss due to liability for accident costs that exceed the exemptions specified in no-fault laws.

7. Most states use a 161-class auto rating plan that combines a primary rate and a secondary rate to determine an insured's rating factor. Auto rates are affected by an insured's age, driving record, marital status, type of vehicle driven, sex, and number of vehicles insured.

QUESTIONS FOR REVIEW

1. Since Y's car is broken down, Y borrows his son's car to run an errand. The son, who

lives with *Y* in the same household, does not have his car insured. If *Y* had an accident, would his PAP cover him? Explain why or why not.

2. *G*'s daughter gives permission for a neighbor to borrow her father's car, thinking it will be all right because the neighbor is a good friend of her family. Under the terms of the PAP, will the neighbor be covered while driving *G*'s car? Why?

3. *S* pulls a large house trailer behind his vehicle each year on a winter vacation that lasts four months.
   (a) Assuming limits of $10,000 property damage, what coverage is granted to *S* under the PAP if the trailer sideswipes another car, causing a $1,000 loss to the trailer and a $2,000 loss to the other car?
   (b) Would your answer be different if the trailer had been a small two-wheel camping trailer with sleeping accommodations for two? Why?

4. An insured's mentally deranged son, after becoming intoxicated, broke into the insured's locked vehicle and, while driving it at high speed, wrecked the vehicle. If the insured had loss-other-than-collision insurance but not collision insurance, what line of reasoning might lead to the conclusion that the damage was covered under the PAP? Discuss.

5. Josephine has a $100 deductible collision on her car, while Ellen carries a $200 deductible. If Josephine borrows Ellen's car and has a collision in which $200 damage is done, which policy must respond and in what amount? Why?

6. In the case of *Farm Bureau Mutual Automobile Insurance Company* v. *Boecher* (48 N.E. 2d 895) the insured was involved in an accident while driving a car made available to employees by his employer, an auto dealer. The insured, who had never driven this particular vehicle before, applied for coverage under his private automobile policy and was denied protection on the grounds that the policy excluded coverage on nonowned cars. With reference to the provisions of the PAP, discuss the correctness or incorrectness of the position taken by the insurer.

7. How may motorcycles be insured under the PAP?

8. Under automobile rating schedules, what factors reduce a person's rates and what factors contribute to rate increases?

9. If you are riding in a school bus and there is an accident, how will the medical payments section of your PAP respond with respect to your injuries and the injuries of others on the bus? Explain.

10. If you do not tell the truth on your automobile insurance application, what recourse does the insurance company have? Explain.

QUESTIONS FOR DISCUSSION

1. "About one in four drivers is expected to have an accident in a typical driving year, but some drivers have a much higher probability of loss than others." Explain.

2. Suggest possible reasons why auto manufacturers do not make cars safer than they do, thus reducing insurance costs of operating them.

3. Discuss the basic reason for the exclusion in the PAP of injury to employees of the insured.

4. What are the major weaknesses of the tort-liability system as a way to compensate injured victims for automobile accidents? What major group do you believe would vehemently resist the idea that the tort-liability system should be done away with? Discuss.

5. Analyze the arguments against no-fault

laws. For example, do you believe that these laws will result in drivers becoming less careful in their driving? What about the other arguments? Discuss.

NEW TERMS AND CONCEPTS

Collision

Department of
  Transportation

Financial Responsibility
  Laws

Loss Other than Collision

Medical Payments Insurance

No-Fault Insurance

Personal Automobile Policy

Underinsured Motorist

Uninsured Motorist
  Endorsement

Unsatisfied Judgment Fund

NOTES

1 *Insurance Fact Book 1986–1987* (New York: Insurance Information Institute, 1986), p. 75.

2 *Napacate, Inc., v. United National Indemnity Co.*, 336 Pac. (2d) 984 (1959).

3 *Storkberger v. Meridian Mutual Insurance Company*, 395 N.E. (2d) 1272 (1979).

4 *American Fidelity Insurance Company v. Parko*, 299 N.Y.S. (2d) 521 (1969).

5 *Hughes v. State Farm*, 1976 CCH (Automobile) 9020; *Waggoner v. Wilson*, 1973 CCH (Automobile) 7695.

6 *Maryland Casualty Company v. Thomas*, 289 S.W. (2d) 652 (1958).

7 *American Indemnity Company v. Haley*, 25 S.W. (2d) 911 (1930).

8 *New Hampshire Insurance Co. v. Frisby*, 522 S.W. (2d) 418 (1975).

9 *City Coal and Supply Co. v. American Automobile Insurance Company*, 133 N.E. (2d) 415 (1954).

10 *McClelland v. Northwestern Fire and Marine Insurance Co.*, 86 S.E. (2d) 729 (1955).

11 *Triten v. First Georgia Insurance Company*, 160 S.E. (2d) 903 (1968).

12 *Aetna Casualty and Surety Company v. Cartmel*, 100 Sou. 802 (1924).

13 *Troncillito v. Farm Family Mutual Insurance Co.*, 406 N.Y. (2d) 143.

14 Robert E. Keeton and Jeffrey O'Connell, *Basic Protection for the Traffic Victim* (Boston: Little, Brown and Co., 1966).

15 Alliance of American Insurers, "Automobile Injuries and Compensation," The AIRAC study, *Journal of American Insurance* (Winter, 1978–79), pp. 6–10.

16 Nine-class plan—Arkansas, Connecticut, Kansas, North and South Carolina, Virginia, and Puerto Rico; 270-class plan—Alabama, Maryland, Oklahoma, Rhode Island; 161-class plan—the remaining states.

17 Pleasure purposes means not used in business (does not include clergy); not driven to work or school more than three miles one way; or driven to work or school three or more, but less than 15, road miles one way, if such usage is not more than two days per week or two weeks per five-week period.

18 A good student is one who has at least a 3.0 on a 4.0 scale or ranks in the top 20 percent of the class, or is on the dean's list or honor roll, or has a B average.

19 At present, the traditional rating system is being investigated by the National Association of Insurance Commissioners. During the next decade the traditional factors of age, sex, and marital status may be discontinued or at least modified.

18 MISCELLANEOUS PERSONAL LINES

After studying this chapter, you should be able to:

1. Explain why policies other than the homeowners' are needed for some dwellings.
2. Describe how mobile homes are insured.
3. Identify the special property-liability insurance needs of farmowners-ranchowners.
4. Discuss the history, use, and content of the Standard Fire Policy.
5. Explain how watercraft should be insured, and why the homeowners' policy is not an appropriate way to insure watercraft.
6. Explain how to insure expensive personal items like jewelry, paintings, antiques, and cameras.
7. Describe an umbrella liability policy and its purpose.

This chapter will examine several different types of property-liability insurance coverages that individuals might need to purchase. For the most part, these coverages are bought only when the homeowners' or the personal auto policy cannot be used.

A brief overview of these policies is as follows:

1. *Dwelling policy.* Can be used for dwellings that are not owner occupied, have up to five rooms for boarders, and are ineligible for a homeowners' policy.
2. *Mobile home policy.* Used to insure mobile homes, which are not eligible for dwelling or standard homeowners' policies.
3. *Farmowners'-ranchowners' policy.* Policy that covers the farm dwelling and farm operations.
4. *Fire policy.* Used extensively in most property contracts for many years. It is usually used today in personal lines to cover property not eligible for the homeowners', dwelling, or mobile home policies.
5. *Watercraft policy.* Provides property and liability insurance on personal watercraft. The homeowners' policy is really not adequate for watercraft exposure.
6. *Personal property floater.* Provides all-risk coverage on unscheduled personal property.
7. *Personal articles floater.* Provides all-risk coverage on scheduled personal property.
8. *Personal umbrella policy.* A liability insurance policy that broadens coverage for comprehensive personal liability as well as personal auto liability. It also provides limits of liability of one million dollars or more.

DWELLING PROGRAM (NOT HOMEOWNERS')

The dwelling policy program is a monoline program (property only) designed to give coverage to properties that cannot be insured under the homeowners' program or where the insured does not want to purchase a homeowners' policy. Like the homeowners' program, new sets of policies were developed in 1976–1978. The provisions of the standard fire contract are in the policy, but the fire contract itself is not.

Underwriting Eligibility

As a general rule, the following criteria are used to determine whether property is eligible for a dwelling policy. The property must be one of the following:

1. A dwelling used exclusively for dwelling purposes; not excluded are incidental occupancies such as offices, private schools, music or photography studios, and small service occupancies such as barber shops, beauty salons, and shoe repair shops with not more than two persons at work at any one time. The dwelling should not have more than five rooms for boarders in total. Included are trailer homes or mobile homes used exclusively for dwelling purposes at a fixed location, and floating unpowered houseboats located at a specified location.
2. A one- to four-family dwelling in a town house or row house structure
3. Household and personal property in an apartment or private living quarters of the insured
4. A dwelling while in the course of construction

As you can see, more kinds of structures are eligible for the dwelling program than for the homeowners'. The structure need no longer be owner occupied, it may have four families living in it, and it may be a trailer, mobile home, or even a houseboat.

Property Insured

The dwelling program and homeowners' program are similar in that the dwelling program contains many of the same property coverages (A = dwelling, B = other structure, C = unscheduled personal property). Coverage D in the dwelling program is called rental value and includes the rent the building could have earned at the time of the loss, whether or not it actually was rented. Additional living expense may be added by endorsement to Dwelling Form 1 (DF-1), and is in forms DF-2 and 3 under Coverage E.

Form	Building	Contents	Perils
Basic DF-1	yes	yes	Fire, EC, V & MM
Broad DF-2	yes	yes	Broad Named Perils
Special DF-3	yes	yes	Special All-Risk

Dwelling Perils Forms

The basic form (DF-1) is quite limited in its perils coverage. Unendorsed, this form insures against fire, lightning, removal, and inherent explosion. However, coverage may be modified to cover windstorm, hail, explosion, riot, civil commotion, aircraft, vehicles, and smoke. This collection of perils is often written together and is called extended coverage (EC). It represents one of the very first multiple-peril endorsements developed in the insurance industry. Besides extended coverage, vandalism and malicious mischief (V&MM) can also be added. Actually, all these perils are included in the DF-1 and DF-2 forms, but an additional premium must be paid to make each (EC and V&MM) active. Neither form provides any theft or glass breakage, as do the HO-1 and other homeowners' forms.

DF-1 is rather limited in its coverage, and for mobile home, trailer, and houseboat dwellers, knowledge of these restrictions is important because this basic form is the only dwelling form they can use. The broad and special forms are not used with these three types of dwellings.

With respect to perils insured against, the broad form (DF-2) and the special form (DF-3) are much like their homeowners' counterparts, HO-2 and HO-3.

MOBILE HOME ENDORSEMENT TO HOMEOWNERS' POLICY

Since the dwelling program offers only limited coverage to persons living in mobile homes, and because there are millions of year-round mobile-home units in the United States, a special endorsement has been developed to serve the market. Not only has the number of units increased significantly, but the quality of their construction has also increased. Construction codes are more demanding, units are often permanently attached to a foundation, and mobile home parks have been upgraded.

Mobile Home Eligibility

The endorsement is designed for a mobile home that is a portable unit, built to be towed on its own chassis, comprised of frame and wheels, at least 10 feet wide and 40 feet long, and designed for year-round living (but seasonal occupancies are allowed). The unit is supposed to be owner occupied and used for private residential purposes, though the typical incidental occupancies are allowed.

Mobile Home Coverage

As used in the endorsement, the term *mobile home* (written there as one word, incidentally) includes the unit itself, equipment originally built into it, steps, and oil or gas tanks connected to it for the purpose of furnishing heating or cooking.

In prior years there was a mobile home program similar to the homeowners'. Today, mobile home coverage has been made a part of the homeowners' approach. By endorsement (MH-200), mobile homes are insured under an HO-2 or HO-3 policy. This endorsement changes the definition of the insured residence to fit a mobile home. The coverage parts are similar to the homeowners' policy.

Coverage A is for the mobile home unit and must be for at least $10,000. Recovery is on a replacement cost basis, and carpeting and appliances are considered part of the coverage.

Coverage B is for separate structures and is 10 percent of coverage A, subject to a minimum of $2,000. A tool shed would be an example of a separate structure.

Coverage C is unscheduled personal property and is 40 percent of A, subject to a $4,000 minimum. The percentage may be raised or lowered.

Coverage D is for additional living expense and is 20 percent of coverage A.

Mobile Home Endorsements

There are several additional endorsements that may be employed with the MH-200 endorsement.

The transportation endorsement (MH-82) may be used to give coverage for up to 30 days during which the mobile home is transported. The perils insured against include collision, upset, stranding, and sinking. The territorial limits are the continental United States and Canada.

If the insured does not want replacement cost on the mobile home (because it is too expensive), or if the insurer does not want to offer it (because loss exposure is too high), the basis of recovery may be changed from replacement cost to actual cash value. Endorsement MH-202 is used to make this change.

FARMOWNERS'-RANCHOWNERS' POLICY

The farmowners'-ranchowners' policy is designed to cover (1) the dwelling and commercial structures on the farm, and (2) the personal and commercial liability that might arise from living and working on the farm.

To be eligible for the farmowners'-ranchowners' program, the main farm dwelling must be a one- or two-family dwelling used exclusively for residential purposes. The standard incidental office, professional and private schools, and studio activities are excepted. The farm dwelling does not have to be owner occupied, but it must not be vacant. The farm owner may occupy the dwelling and not operate the farm.

When the farm is incorporated, the insured (the farmer) as well as the interest of the corporation is covered. A major function of the farmowners'-ranchowners' policy is to cover personal and business interest in the same policy.

Farmowners'-Ranchowners' Forms

There are numerous forms for the farmowners'-ranchowners' program. These forms are designed to insure the dwelling and its contents, as well as farm structures and equipment. One can insure property on a basic named perils, broad named perils, or all-risk basis. The personal and commercial liability of the farmer may be covered, and by endorsement, the liability of a corporate farm.

THE FIRE POLICY

The most commonly used fire insurance policy is the Standard Fire Policy adopted by the State of New York in 1943. This policy is given in Appendix E.

Prior to 1976 the Standard Fire Policy was included in almost all homeowners' and major multiline insurance policies. Today, it is used much less frequently. Its major use in personal lines is as a policy that is selected when nothing else can be used or in states where its inclusion in a property insurance contract is still mandatory. However, because the fire peril is so important in property insurance, and various provisions of the fire policy are used in many insurance contracts, the content of the 165-line Standard Fire Policy will be examined in detail.

Conditions and Stipulations—165 Lines

The New York Standard Fire Policy (1943) contains 165 lines of provisions and stipulations that form the basis of the insurance coverage. Some of the provisions may be amended when various property forms are added, but by and large the 165 lines set the pattern. The line references in the following material refer to some important lines of the standard fire policy shown in Appendix E.

Concealment and Fraud. The first six lines concern misrepresentations of material fact, concealment, and fraud. If the insured willfully commits any of these acts before or after the loss, the policy is void.

For instance, a Virginia man moved into a new community, requested an agent to find coverage on some vending machines, and gave his son's name as the insured. During the term of the binder a fire loss occurred. Investigation after the loss showed that the man had 20 unsatisfied claims against him, and if the insurer had known this fact no insurance binder would have been given. In litigation, a lower court held for the insured, but the Virginia Supreme Court overturned the decision and held for the insurer.[1]

Excluded Property. Lines 7–10 refer to excluded property, which is divided into two classes: property that may not be covered at all under the Standard Fire Policy, and property that may be insured by specific endorsement. Separate coverage is provided for property such as money and securities, because the special underwriting problems that arise make it desirable to give that class of property special attention. Bullion and manuscripts need to be described carefully before insurance can be granted.

Excluded Perils. Lines 11–24 name the perils that are excluded from coverage. For example, if there is an invasion or a war that results in a fire, and this fire destroys the insured property, it is the position of the insurer that the proximate cause of loss is war, not fire. (War is a peril that is almost universally excluded in private insurance contracts.) Likewise, if the insured deliberately fails to call the fire department until after the fire has a good start, coverage will probably be denied because the proximate cause of loss was the willful neglect of the insured to use all reasonable means to save the property.

Excluded Losses. Lines 28–37 exclude three types of losses:

1. Those occurring while the hazard is increased by any means within the control or knowledge of the insured.
2. Those occurring while the building is vacant for a period beyond 60 consecutive days. (This period is often extended in some territories.) The term vacant generally means that no person is using the premises and there are no contents inside the structure.
3. Those occurring as a result of explosion or riot, unless fire ensues, and then for the fire loss only.

The first type of loss involves situations in which the insured may change the basic character of the risk by some action, such as switching the use of the building from a garage to a manufacturing establishment. The insurer is entitled to be told of this situation, and if it is not, the coverage is suspended. Often this exclusion is waived for residential property.

Cancellation. The provisions within lines 56–67 specifically set forth the terms under which the policy may be cancelled by the insurer or by the insured. Termination by the insurer is effective five days after the written notice of cancellation is communicated to the policyholder. The policy remains in force during the five days, which are counted from midnight on the day in which the notice is received to midnight five days later. The notice must either be accompanied by a return of the unearned premium or contain a statement that the pro-rata unearned premium will be returned to the insured. The purpose of the five-day notice is to give the insured an opportunity to place the coverage elsewhere. In the case of cancellation by the insured, refund will be made of the excess of paid premiums above the customary short rates for the expired time, upon surrender of the policy. Neither party to the contract is required to give a reason for the cancellation.

Mortgagee Interest and Obligations. Lines 68–85 contain the standard mortgagee clause that was explained in Chapter 7.

Pro-Rata Liability. The pro-rata distribution clause discussed in Chapter 7 is contained in lines 86–89, and it provides a way to distribute loss payments when more than one policy is used to insure a piece of property. Without such a provision, a person could insure a home with two insurers and collect $10,000 from each insurer on a $10,000 total loss. Obviously, if this arrangement were allowed, the moral hazard would increase substantially.

Requirements when Loss Occurs, and Appraisal. Lines 90–161 of the standard fire policy spell out the procedures that are to be followed when a loss occurs, in order that disagreements and expensive court litigation may be avoided. These procedures must be followed before suit can be filed under the policy.

In case loss occurs, there are several obligations that must be met by the insured. Violation of any of these obligations may jeopardize the protection. They include (1) giving immediate written notice to the company or its agent, (2) protecting the property from further damage, (3) separating damaged from undamaged property and furnishing an inventory of all property, (4) filing detailed proof of loss within 60 days of the loss, and (5) submitting all evidence available to the insurer's adjuster to aid in determination of the amount of the loss as may be reasonably required.

The fire policy requires the insured to sign and swear to the proof-of-loss statement as well as to submit to examinations under oath. Even constitutional protections against self-incrimination may not protect the insured. In *Dyno-Bite, Inc.* v. *Travelers Companies*, one corporate officer refused to appear at a hearing and another one gave incomplete testimony. A New York Supreme Court ruled that while the Constitution protected them from having to answer the insurer's questions concerning the fire, it did not relieve them of the policy provisions concerning requirements in case of loss. Therefore, the court upheld the insurer's denial of coverage.[2]

If the adjusters and the insured cannot agree on the amount of the loss, the policy details the procedures that must be followed before any legal action can be taken. It provides that each party, upon the written demand of the other, must select an impartial appraiser, who will then select an umpire to arbitrate any disagreements that still exist after the appraisers have rendered their separate judgments as to the amount of the loss. The insurer reserves the right to take over the damaged property and to pay the insured its sound value, to repair or rebuild it, or to make a cash settlement for the amount of the loss. Normally the last method is used. These are company options, not those of the insured. The insured may not elect to abandon the property that has been partially or totally destroyed and demand payment therefor.

Once the proof of loss is agreed upon by all parties, payment is due within 60 days. This gives the insurer time to investigate further, if it wishes, or to raise the money for payment in the event the loss is so large as to require liquidation of securities or collection from reinsurers. Finally, the policy provides that any legal suit must be commenced within 12 months of the loss. This provision places a sort of statute of limitations on all disputes and prevents indefinite prolongation of uncertainty about them.

Subrogation. Lines 162–165 provide for subrogation rights of the insurer in case the insured has legal rights against liable third parties for any loss.

Insurers value this provision, as evidenced by the case where a pastor's wife, while cooking in the parsonage, caused a grease fire that caused $25,000 in damages. The insurers involved paid the church that owned the parsonage and then took legal action against the pastor's wife. They won and collected from her. Fortunately for the woman, her liability policy paid the $25,000 judgment.[3]

Contract Components and Insuring Agreement

The fire policy by itself does not make up the entire insurance contract. First, there is normally a declaration page that provides information such as the insured's name, the location of the property, the amount of insurance, the premium, the type of construction, and the insuring agreement. Second, the basic conditions of the fire policy are then added to this page. Finally, to these items is added some type of policy amendment or endorsement the most common being the general property form that is discussed in Chapter 20. The insuring agreement on the declaration page is of particular importance because it explains several important concepts and conditions, and the perils insured against.

Consideration. The consideration for a contract consists of both a specified premium and an agreement to the provisions and stipulations that follow. Failure to pay the premium or to abide by these provisions means failure of the consideration, and may lead to a failure of the contract itself if the insurer gives notice of cancellation.

Policy Term. Traditionally, the fire policy has started at 12 noon. However, in 1977 the major insurance rating bureau, the Insurance Services Office (ISO), changed the time of inception of the fire policy to 12 midnight. Several states have a statutory requirement that the fire policy start at noon, but the policy now starts at midnight in all other states. Besides giving the inception and expiration point, the policy term provision states that standard time at the location of the property governs the time. The policy may be written in New York for a client living in Texas for property located in Oregon. In this case midnight Pacific Standard (Oregon) time is the determining point. If a fire begins at 11:55 p.m. on the day the policy expires and most of the loss occurs after 12 midnight, the policy still pays the whole claim.

Actual Cash Value. The insuring agreement states that only the actual cash value (replacement cost minus depreciation) of the property at the time of the loss will be reimbursed, not to exceed the amount it would have cost to repair or to replace the property with material of like kind and quality.

Interest of Insured. Recovery is limited to the extent of the insured's legal financial interest in the property described. Insurable interest exists, for example, when the insured owns the property, is a mortgagee, has beneficial use of the property, or is responsible under contract for damage to the property. All of these situations favor the purchase of insurance to protect the insured's insurable interest.

Direct Loss. The words, "direct loss by fire, lightning, and by removal from premises . . ." are of great importance. By **direct loss** is meant loss of which the proximate cause is one or more of the three sources listed in the insuring agreement. The **doctrine of proximate cause** says that a peril may be said to cause a loss if there is an unbroken chain of events leading from the peril to the ultimate loss. No indirect loss, such as loss resulting from interruption of business or manufacture, is covered. Separate coverages are provided for these exposures and are examined in Chapter 20.

There have been many controversies in insurance over the meaning of the words, "direct loss by fire." In the 1918 Standard Fire Policy the peril, lightning, was not automatically covered and had to be added by endorsement to the basic contract. Many fires were caused by lightning, and without the endorsement it became necessary to differentiate that part of the loss caused by lightning from that caused by fire because the policy covered only direct loss by fire. Thus, if a building were struck by lightning, split in two, and then burned to the ground, the policy would restore the value of a building that had been split in half.

To avoid such difficulties, the 1943 Standard Fire Policy added lightning to the basic coverage, but the problem still exists with regard to other physical perils (such as windstorm), for which protection must be added by endorsement. Suppose a building burns and leaves one wall standing. A week later this wall falls down during a windstorm and damages the insured's building next door. Is this a fire loss or a windstorm loss? It can be argued that if it had not been for the fire, the windstorm would not have had an opportunity to blow down the wall; therefore, the fire is the proximate cause of loss. On the other hand, it might be argued that the wall might have stood indefinitely had it not been for the windstorm; therefore, the windstorm was the proximate cause of loss. Adjusters and sometimes ultimately the courts have the responsibility of interpreting each case in the light of this doctrine in order to ascertain the real meaning of "direct loss by fire."

Sometimes the question is raised as to what constitutes fire. A **fire** may be defined as combustion in which oxidation takes place so rapidly that a flame or glow is produced. Rust is a form of oxidation but, of course, is not a fire. Scorching or heat is not fire. Furthermore, the fire must be **hostile;** that is, it must be of such a character that it is outside its normal confines. Fires intentionally kindled in a stove are not covered in the policy, nor are articles accidentally thrown into the stove. Such fires are said to be **friendly.** However, once the fire escapes its confines, it becomes hostile and all loss resulting from it is covered. For instance, the New Hampshire Supreme Court ruled that scorching caused by a lighted cigarette falling onto a rug was due to a hostile fire. The court reasoned that the lighted cigarette was friendly while in the ashtray but was outside its intended place (hostile), when it reached the rug.[4]

Direct loss by fire also includes such losses as damage from water or chemicals used to fight the fire, and broken windows or holes chopped into the roof by fire fighters, since these are often an inevitable result of the fire itself.

In addition to the perils of fire and lightning, the fire policy also covers loss resulting from removal of property from the insured's location in order to protect it from one of the perils insured against. If the policy covered only fire and lightning, and the insured moved the property in order to avoid a water-damage loss, no removal coverage would exist since water damage was not insured. This coverage for removal is very broad and basically all-risk with few limitations. If property is damaged while being transported to a new location, the insurer pays. If the insured drops an item while carrying it from the endangered location and it breaks, coverage exists. Courts have even held that theft resulting from the removal process is covered, even though theft is specifically excluded from the fire policy.

Location. The insuring agreement makes it clear that the coverage applies only while the insured property is at a location specified in the declarations, unless, as stated above, a fire threatens and the goods are moved to a safe place for the sake of preserving them from destruction. The danger of fire varies greatly depending on the location of the property, and the insurers wish to restrict their coverage to areas that they have had an opportunity to inspect and approve. However, permission is granted to remove the goods to another place for a limited time, set at five days, for safety. Extensions of this period to 30 days are typical in endorsements that modify the basic agreement.

The insuring agreement also provides that it may be amended by later endorsements. Without such permission a question might be raised as to which provision holds, the basic agreement or later stipulations? Later amendments govern the coverage, even if they directly contradict earlier provisions, unless the basic agreement specifically prohibits such amendments.

Assignment. Because the insurer wishes to reserve the right to choose the ones with whom it will deal, the contract provides that assignment of the policy rights will not be valid without the written consent of the insurer. The personal element in insurance is an important underwriting characteristic, and without this provision the original insured might assign the policy to someone who is a poor moral risk.

Several courts have considered the change-in-risk factor to be more important than strict policy interpretation. Their position is that the intent of the assignment provision is to prevent an increase in hazard without the insurer's knowledge. The Iowa Supreme Court ruled that coverage existed when one partner sold his share of the business to the other partner. The original partnership was the insured.

The court felt that no increase in hazard had occurred, and the new owner was no stranger to the insurance company since he had been a partner in the old partnership. If a change in ownership had involved totally different parties, it is more likely that the assignment provision would have been upheld by the court.[5]

WATERCRAFT PROGRAM

In the homeowners' program there is only $1,000 coverage on watercraft, and theft is excluded. In the dwelling policy only rowboats and canoes are insured, and in the mobile home form no watercraft coverage is provided. Therefore, if one owns an outboard motor and boat or an inboard watercraft, additional property insurance is needed.

Inboard Watercraft

Inboard watercraft and sailboats are generally classified for insurance purposes as yachts. Consequently, they are insured on an ocean marine policy appropriately called a yacht policy. This is a package policy giving coverage on the hull (the boat) and liability arising from colliding with other vessels. By endorsement one can add general watercraft liability (called protection and indemnity coverage), medical payments, and Longshoremen's and Harbor Workers' Compensation. Perils insured against with respect to the hull include, but are not limited to, collision, windstorm, fire, and theft. However, for most people it is the outboard motor and boat policy that is of interest, and that is the policy that we now examine.

Outboard Watercraft

The outboard motor and boat policy is not uniform, so the description provided here will summarize what one generally finds in such policies. Typically, the policy covers outboard motors and outboard motor boats used for personal pleasure purposes. The insured must warrant that the watercraft is not held for hire or charter purposes. Coverage applies while on the water and on shore. Perils insured against may be on an all-risk approach or broad named-peril basis. The all-risk approach is the most popular, and under this form the boat, its motor or motors, its equipment, and the boat trailer are covered. Recovery is on an ACV basis, and often market value is used in place of ACV. However, depreciation charts do exist and depreciation rates of 10 to 15 percent are common. No replacement-cost protection is available. The premium rate for all-risk protection ranges from 3 percent to as high as 8 percent of the value of the watercraft, but deductibles of $100 or more may be used to help lower the cost to the insured.

Personal-Property Floater (PPF)

The PPF policy is designed to give all-risk protection to an individual's personal property. Its territorial limits are virtually worldwide, and property is covered on both a scheduled and an unscheduled basis. Scheduled property is usually limited to valuable items such as jewelry and furs that have a combined value of over $500. Because several of the homeowners' forms insure personal property on a broad named-peril basis, the personal-property floater is not used very often today. If people live in their own home and desire all-risk coverage, the HO-3 can be so endorsed. If they do not live in their own home, or live in a condominium, a personal property floater can be used to give all-risk coverage. Typically, the policy is considered a luxury policy and is purchased only by affluent individuals.

Personal-Articles Floater (PAF)

The PAF contract is an all-risk contract designed to give broad coverage to valuable personal possessions. Included in this category are such items as personal jewelry, furs, fine arts, cameras, golfer's equipment, musical instruments, silverware, and stamp and coin collections. Typically, it is added to the homeowners' form when an insured has property in these categories that needs protection. For instance, a person may have a $5,000 diamond ring that is kept in the home. The HO-3 policy only provides $1,000 theft insurance on the ring, and loss of the stone from its setting is not covered.

The PAF provides coverage for a stone lost from its setting and has limits on jewelry on a scheduled basis. If the insured schedules the stone for $5,000, then there is $5,000 worth of protection. Except for fine arts, coverage is on a worldwide basis.

For most insureds it is more sensible to purchase an HO-2 or HO-3 and to also purchase a PAF to cover high-value items such as jewelry and furs, rather than to purchase a personal property floater that covers all their property on an all-risk basis.

PERSONAL UMBRELLA POLICY

In this section we shall explore in greater depth the personal umbrella policy described in Chapter 16. The umbrella policy is a liability policy designed to give greater breadth of coverage than the comprehensive personal liability (CPL) policy. It is purchased in addition to CPL, and its limits are in addition to the limits of CPL. Desirable contract provisions are examined, as well as eligible persons.

Personal umbrellas are not a standard contract such as the homeowners'. Significant variations occur between the policies of the various companies that offer them. For this reason, it is important that prospective insureds examine the specific contract they intend to purchase.

Availability of Umbrella Policies

Not everyone should purchase an umbrella. Such policies are purchased by people who need to protect large accumulations of assets and/or high incomes. However, insurers will not sell the policy to all such people. Certain occupations have been deemed unattractive for the purpose of selling personal umbrellas, and people in those occupations may have difficulty in obtaining coverage. Among such occupations are assigned-risk drivers; professional politicians; professional entertainers; newspaper reporters, editors, and publishers; labor leaders; and athletes.

Limits of Liability and Self-Retained Limits

The minimum limit for an umbrella is $1 million above the self-retained limit (deductible) or the required primary coverage. Policies may be purchased with higher limits. For instance, a $5 million policy may be purchased for a premium 2.35 times more than the cost of $1 million policy. The $1 million policy has a premium in the range from $65 to $200. The premium is a function of the location and operation of the insured, as well as the insurance company's desire to write the business.

With respect to self-retained limits, $250 is the most frequently chosen one. This deductible is applied when there is no underlying primary coverage. If the primary coverage applies, then the deductible is not employed. Certain states and insurers require a deductible greater than $250. This situation is undesirable to the insured because usually there is little rate credit given for higher deductibles. Under most circumstances a deductible greater than $250 is not a wise decision, since the premium savings are only minimal.

Underlying Limits

Umbrellas require certain types and amounts of underlying insurance. Table 18–1 shows the normal underlying limit requirements. Over the last 10 years these limits have risen 100 percent or more.

Umbrella Contract Provisions

There are many provisions in the umbrella contract that should be examined before the policy is purchased. The following paragraphs review several of the more important clauses and describe some coverage that is desirable from the viewpoint of the consumer. Insureds need to determine

Table 18–1
Umbrella Limits

Policy	Limit (1986)
Automobile	$500,000
Comprehensive Personal Liability	$100,000–$300,000
Watercraft	$100,000–$500,000
Business	$100,000–$500,000
Recreational Vehicle	$500,000

which provisions are important to them and to purchase their umbrella policies accordingly.

Personal Injury. The personal injury definition used in umbrellas has a much broader meaning than that used in primary coverages. As used in the umbrella, personal injury includes bodily injury, property damage, libel, slander, defamation of character, invasion of privacy, humiliation, wrongful eviction, wrongful entry, malicious persecution, false imprisonment, wrongful detention, and false arrest.

Property in the Insured's Care, Custody, or Control. Property owned by or rented to the insured is excluded. Also, when the insured agrees to assume liability under a contract for property damage, such losses are excluded. However, with respect to other nonowned property, the umbrella is designed to provide some protection. For example, if you borrow your neighbor's videotape recorder and break it, the umbrella will cover the loss. Loss from the operation of nonowned watercraft up to 26 feet long is insured. With regard to automobiles, if the primary insurance covers the loss, the umbrella will too.

Incidental Business Pursuits. Typically, insureds' umbrellas will provide coverage for incidental business pursuits, but often it is no broader than the underlying primary coverage. This limitation is important in automobile coverage. Somewhat related to the business pursuits coverage is that of board-of-directors' liability. If an insured is on the board of directors of a religious, charitable, or civic nonprofit corporation, coverage is often given. No coverage exists if the board of directors is for business purposes.

Automobiles. Some umbrellas give broader coverage than underlying auto policies; however, many do not. Therefore, it is important to have as broad a primary policy as feasible. The one area in which some umbrellas give broader coverage than the primary is the business auto section. In these broader policies, there is some bodily injury liability coverage for the operation of trucks in a business situation.

SUMMARY

1. The dwelling policy is used for properties that do not qualify for the homeowners' program, and up to five boarders may be in the dwelling. Mobile home coverage is provided by using a special endorsement to the HO-2 or HO-3 policy.
2. The farmowners'-ranchowners' policy is designed to cover the personal and commercial property liability loss exposures of farmers and ranchers. It is unusual in that it combines both personal and business coverages in the same policy.
3. The fire policy contains many important contract provisions, such as the pro-rata, cancellation, appraisal, and subrogation clauses, and requirements in case of loss.
4. Watercraft insurance covers physical damage to an individual's boat and may be arranged so that bodily injury as well as property damage liability from the operation of the watercraft are covered.
5. The personal umbrella gives broad-range liability insurance to individuals as well as providing catastrophic limits of liability. The standard minimum policy limit is $1,000,000. Underlying liability insurance for such loss exposures as the operation of an auto or watercraft and personal activities are often required.

QUESTIONS FOR REVIEW

1. How is the dwelling program similar to the homeowners' program?
2. Why do some people need to purchase a personal articles floater?
3. What does the term "personal injury" mean in the context of the personal umbrella policy?
4. In the Standard Fire Policy, what steps must an insured follow after a fire occurs?
5. How are disputes over the value of a loss determined between the insured and the insurer in the Standard Fire Policy?
6. What are the characteristics of a hostile fire?
7. Who should buy a personal umbrella liability policy? Explain your answer.
8. Why don't farmers or ranchers purchase a homeowners' policy rather a farmowners'-ranchowners' policy?
9. How should a boat owner insure his or her boat for property-liability loss exposures?

QUESTIONS FOR DISCUSSION

1. Discuss how the eligibility requirements of the dwelling, mobile home, and farmowners'-ranchowners' policies differ. Why don't insurance companies just have one policy for everyone?
2. Explain why insurance companies have such legal distinctions as hostile and friendly fires.
3. The personal umbrella provides broad coverage with high limits for liability insurance. How would you design a property insurance contract to provide similar coverage for the property loss exposure of individuals?
4. Explain why insurance companies do not just sell one liability policy with high limits, broad coverage, and first-dollar protection rather than having consumers purchase primary coverage and then buy an umbrella liability policy.
5. Insurance companies support various organizations, such as the National Board of Fire Underwriters and the National Fire

Protection Association, which attempt to reduce the losses from fires that occur in the United States.

(a) A certain agent suggests that this activity, if completely successful, would put insurance companies out of business. Comment.

(b) Is it in the best interest of insurance companies to attempt to eliminate loss from fire or other perils? Discuss.

NEW TERMS AND CONCEPTS

Consideration
Direct Loss
Dwelling Policy
Farmowners'-Ranchowners' Policy
Friendly Fire
Hostile Fire
Form
Indirect Loss

Mobile Home Policy
Personal Articles Floater
Personal Property Floater
Personal Umbrella
Proximate Cause
Outboard Watercraft
Self-Retained Limit
Standard Fire Policy
Underlying Limits

NOTES

1 *FC&S Bulletins*, Fire and Marine Section, Fire-Csfc-2 (Cincinnati, Ohio: The National Underwriter Company, 1982).

2 *FC&S Bulletins*, Fire and Marine Section, Fire-Lsfe-1 (Cincinnati, Ohio: The National Underwriter Company, 1982).

3 *FC&S Bulletins*, Fire and Marine Section, Fire-Csfe-5 (Cincinnati, Ohio: The National Underwriter Company, 1982).

4 *FC&S Bulletins*, Fire and Marine Section, Fire-Ff-4 (Cincinnati, Ohio: The National Underwriter Company, 1982).

5 *FC&S Bulletins*, Fire and Marine Section, Fire-Csfb-3 (Cincinnati, Ohio: The National Underwriter Company, 1982).

19 BUYING PERSONAL INSURANCE

After studying this chapter, you should be able to:

1. List the factors to examine in determining the financial stability of an insurance company.
2. Discuss the importance of cost comparisons in buying property-liability insurance.
3. Describe the role that availability of coverage plays in the decision to purchase.
4. Identify problems associated with insurance company solvency.
5. Explain the relationship between the level of underwriting profits and the underwriting cycle.
6. Discuss how the quantity and quality of insurer services may affect the decision to purchase.
7. List factors to consider in selecting an agent.

In Chapters 15 through 18, major property-liability coverages that an individual might wish to purchase were discussed. This chapter examines those factors that a consumer should consider before deciding which insurance company and agent to buy the insurance from. Consumers should not take insurance-buying decisions lightly. In terms of personal expenditures, property-liability insurance expenses are significant. Nationwide, consumers spent over $73 billion on homeowners' and auto insurance in 1985.

Many consumers own two or more autos. It may well cost over $2,000 a year to insure these vehicles, especially if there are youthful drivers in the household. Homeowners' insurance premiums can easily reach $600 per year. Add to these costs the expense of insuring second homes, motorcycles, and recreational vehicles, together with a personal umbrella policy, and a family can easily spend $3,000 to $4,000 per year on property-liability insurance.

BUYING WISELY

In making an informed buying decision, the consumer should examine (1) the availability of coverage, (2) the cost of coverage, (3) the financial strength of the insurer and the quality of its services, and (4) the agent. Let us examine each of these in turn.

Availability of Coverage

The first step in making an intelligent selection of an insurer is to find a group of insurers that is willing to offer comparable contracts to the applicant on terms that are satisfactory. Not all companies offer every insurance facility or every type of insurance contract.[1] If there are only one or two available insurers, the problem is considerably simplified. Furthermore, some insurers refuse, even for an additional premium, to delete or to add certain features that the insured may desire. This may further narrow the field of choice. Finally, contrary to the understanding of most lay persons, some insurers may not be interested in accepting the insured's application at the rate that they are allowed to charge because the insured may not meet minimum underwriting standards or because the particular class of business is not profitable to the underwriter. Thus, drivers under a certain age may not be considered a profitable class of risk and are rejected by some companies.

Cost of Coverage

Because insurance contracts and services vary so widely among insurers, it is generally difficult to make precise comparisons of insurance costs. Insurance is a service in which the cost must be estimated in advance by the insurer. Considerable variation among underwriters in these estimates should be expected. In some cases, excess charges for contingency reserves are returned to the insured in dividends or under various types of pricing methods. In other cases, the initial premium is fixed and no dividend or premium adjustment is anticipated. It is very difficult to quantify the many nonprice aspects of insurance. Nevertheless, it is worthwhile to examine several methods of comparing costs and analyzing their limitations. These include:

1. Direct comparison of gross premiums
2. Comparison of gross premiums less estimated dividends
3. Comparison of operational efficiency

In the following discussion we assume that no major differences exist in contractual provisions, the quality of agency services, the financial strength of the insurer, or other factors of importance to the insurance buyer in making a decision.

Direct Price Comparisons. If there are no dividends or other later premium adjustments to be considered, and all other matters of importance surrounding the insurance transaction are approximately equal, it seems clear that the insured should select the insurance policy with the lowest price. Because of the complexities involved, it often takes courage to accept the lowest price. It is easy for an experienced insurance sales agent to attempt to confuse the price issue by pointing out the many ways in which his particular policy or company differs from that of a competitor. There is no substitute for a careful analysis of the facts by the insured.

One factor that can mislead an insured on the price issue is that of the "loss leader." For example, one insurer might offer the lowest premium in the first year in an attempt to "buy" business, in the same manner as a retailer advertises a loss leader in order to attract people into the store. Then, in later years, after the policyholder is a customer, the premium may be raised, certain services eliminated, claims settled inadequately, contractual provisions restricted upon renewal, or other methods used to make the business more profitable.

Premiums Less Dividends. As mentioned earlier, some insurers deliberately charge a higher premium to allow for contingencies. Thus, they anticipate returning any excess to the insured group in the form of a dividend or a premium reduction for the renewal policy. In selecting insurers of this type, the insured must consider estimated dividend schedules, including the timing and the form of the dividend, in deciding whose price is the lowest.

As a general rule, dividends are not nearly as common in personal line property and liability coverages as they are in life insurance.

Operational Efficiency. One method of judging insurance costs is to compare insurers on the basis of their internal operating efficiency, in the belief that the most efficient insurer will, in the long run, be the cheapest and best. Internal operating efficiency may be difficult to judge, but some indications may be observed in the loss and expense ratios. In published statistics, the **loss ratio** is defined as the ratio of losses incurred to premiums earned.[2] **Expense ratio** is defined as the ratio of expenses incurred to premiums written. The sum of these ratios is known as the **combined ratio.** If the combined ratio exceeds 100 percent, the insurer has incurred a loss on its underwriting. This may happen if expenses get out of control or if losses are greater than expected due to such factors as poor underwriting practices, unexpected catastrophes, inadequate rates, or rapid inflation in repair costs. Consistent underwriting losses cast doubt upon the insurer's operational efficiency. Rising combined ratios often predict increased rates to be charged to the insured on renewal of the policy.

Some insurers in property-liability fields set rates low so as to break even on underwriting and attempt to register most of their profits as investment gains. In such a case, loss and expense ratios may appear artificially high because premiums are low. This may not necessarily be all bad, because investment profits can be substantial. This is possible since all insurance premiums are collected in advance from the policyholder. Losses are not paid unless and until they are incurred. In the meantime, the insurer may invest the premium funds, receiving interest, dividends, or capital gains thereon. It may be several years before losses are actually paid out, such as in the case of prolonged court trials to establish the extent of liability to which an insurer must respond on behalf of a policyholder.

It may not necessarily be wrong for an insured to take advantage of a rate that is set low, as long as the financial ability and willingness of the insurer to pay losses and render other services remains unimpaired. Investment gains may offset underwriting losses to such an extent that insurer finances are actually improved.

Stocks versus Mutuals. One may inquire whether an insured is better off financially with a mutual company or a stock company. The main argument for mutuals is that they operate at cost since they are owned by policyholders, while stocks operate at a profit. In spite of the theoretical advantage of mutuals in this regard, an examination of past loss and expense ratios reveals little consistent difference between stocks and mutuals in most lines of insurance.

A fair conclusion seems to be that the particular form or organization does not appear to guarantee to the insured group any major cost advantage or gain in long-run efficiency.

Financial Solvency and Stability of the Insurer

To obtain insurance at a lower cost at the expense of financial strength in an insurer is obviously foolish. If bad financial policies, inadequate premiums, or poor underwriting standards endanger the fund that is set aside for losses, the insured may find that insurance has been carried for many years to no avail. The loss occurs, but the insurer is bankrupt.

It is often assumed that, because of the system of state regulation over insurance, financial solvency of the insurer is more or less guaranteed and that the average policyholder has little to fear. While this assumption is no doubt justified in most cases, there have been and *will continue to be* failures, with consequent losses to policyholders.

Insolvency Funds. The danger of loss from insolvent insurers has been recognized by the recent adoption of laws in all states. These laws established state insolvency funds. Subject to $100 deductibles and maximum limits of liability, these funds promise to reimburse policyholders for any losses caused by bankrupt insurers. The funds are supported by other insurers operating in the same state.[3] In spite of such protection, careful attention to the financial condition of an insurer is warranted for the thoughtful insurance buyer.

Over the period 1969–1985, state insurance guaranty funds have assessed domestic property-liability insurers a total of $871 million for 125 insolvencies. Total assessments have been a small percentage of the total premiums collected, typically ranging between 0.1 and 0.2 percent of premiums collected by solvent insurers.[4]

Financial Statement Analysis. Analysis of the financial solidity of an insurer follows the same basic principles as analysis of any corporate entity. Conventional financial statement analysis applies, but certain adjustments, to be explained presently, are necessary in order to fit technical insurance concepts into conventional financial analytical molds.

In any corporate balance sheet, the analyst who seeks a guide to financial solvency usually directs attention first to the amount of debt shown in relation to the net worth of the enterprise. Too much debt indicates a possible inability to pay interest and to repay principal in times of stress, with resulting bankruptcy. Thus, the **net-worth-to-debt-ratio** is a common tool of financial statement analysis. Such a ratio is usually calculated over a period of years in order to discover any adverse trends, and it is usually compared with that of similar business concerns in order to discover any deviation from the average.

Net-Worth-to-Debt Ratio. For property and liability insurance companies, the net-worth-to-debt ratio is one of the most widely used ratios. On insurance company balance sheets, the term "net worth" is usually called "policyholders' surplus" and the "debt" becomes the sum of various miscellaneous liabilities. The largest single item of debt on a property insurer's balance sheet, for example, is called the "unearned premium reserve." One authority, Roger Kenney, insisted that for satisfactory strength, the ratio of the policyholders' surplus to the unearned premium reserve should be at least 1:1, unless extenuating circumstances exist that would permit a lower ratio.[5] The 1:1 ratio means a margin of safety of 100 percent of the unearned premium reserve.

What light does the net-worth-to-debt ratio throw upon the financial stability of property and liability insurers? The rationale of the ratio may be explained as follows. Items of debt on the insurer's balance sheet represent amounts that must be returned to policyholders. The two most important items are unearned premium reserves and loss reserves. As the name suggests, unearned premium reserves represent advance premiums paid in for protection and not yet earned by the insurer. If the policy is cancelled, these advance premium payments must be returned to the policyholder in cash. Since the policy may be cancelled at any time by the insurer or the insured, the funds must be kept in fairly liquid form. They are typically invested by the insurer in bonds or other negotiable securities, or kept in cash. Loss reserves represent amounts that must be paid out in losses once the precise amounts are reported to the insurer, and the reserves are liquidated by actual payment of the loss.

The main items of debt on an insurer's balance sheet represent amounts due to policyholders on a potentially short-term basis. They do not represent long-term debt, such as bonds. The assets protecting these obligations must be sufficient at all times and ideally should exceed the obligations by some margin. The 1:1 ratio of net worth to debt suggests that a suitable margin is 100 percent; that is, for each $1 of debt, there is also $1 of surplus. Thus, there should be $2 of assets protecting the debt. Then, in case of business depression, or other disruption that reduces the value of the assets, there will be a cushion to meet the insurer's obligations to its policyholders.

Some analysts believe that a 1:1 margin is too conservative, since the assets typically are invested in liquid securities and may be converted to cash quickly. Furthermore, the insurer may use current income to liquidate debt. Finally, an insurer whose underwriting is conservative and whose losses are low and stable has less need for a large surplus to absorb unusual losses. Thus, the ratio of surplus to debt may safely fall below 1:1 without endangering the position of policyholders. With such a conservative ratio, the capacity of the insurance industry to accept new business is below what it would otherwise be, and this tends to hinder the industry in meeting its expanding obligations to the public in offering coverage.

What is the ratio of net worth to debt currently for the property and liability insurance industry? As of 1985 the industry in the United States had about $311 billion of assets, $75.5 billion of surplus, and $235.5 billion of obligations to policyholders. Hence, the ratio for the industry as a whole was 75.5:235.5, or roughly 0.32:1 instead of 1:1. Apparently, insurance industry standards are less conservative than traditional standards of financial solvency as measured by net worth to debt.

Premium-to-Surplus Ratio. Another standard of financial solvency is that the ratio of premiums written to policyholders' surplus should not exceed 3:1[6]. That is, property and liability insurers should not accept more than $3 in new premium volume for each $1 of policyholders' surplus. The rationale is that new premium volume represents potential liability to policyholders for loss payments and for premium refunds in the event the policies are cancelled. Hence, premium volume becomes a substitute measure for debt. The property and liability insurance industry in the United States wrote $144.2 billion of premiums in 1985. Since the surplus for the industry as a whole was $75.5 billion, the premium-to-surplus ratio of 1.91:1 was slightly more conservative than the preceding standard of 2:1. In 1974 the U.S. stock market declined sharply, reducing the value of assets held by insurers. This caused the ratio of premiums to surplus to rise to about 2.5:1, producing a ratio above the standard.

The practical implication of adverse ratios may be shown by a simple example. Suppose an insurer writes $10 million of premiums, but has only a $2 million surplus cushion. The ratio of premiums to surplus is thus 5:1. Now assume that loss experience is somewhat heavy in a given year, and the combined ratio rises to 110 (not an unusual experience). This means that underwriting losses are 10 percent of premium written, or $1 million. This sum is equal to 50 percent of the insurer's surplus of $2 million. In a single year the company has lost half of its surplus, and if this adverse experience continues into the second year, the company is approaching insolvency.

In the same case, if the company had written only $4 million of premiums, its ratio of premiums to surplus would have been a more conservative 2:1. In this event, the single year's loss of 10 percent would have been only $400,000, equal to only 20 percent of the available surplus instead of 50 percent. The ratio of premiums to surplus is a measure of financial leverage for insurers. The greater this ratio, the greater the financial leverage. A ratio of 5:1 magnifies profits or losses fivefold. A ratio of 2:1 magnifies profits or losses twofold, and so on.

An examination of ratios reported in *Best's Key Rating Guide* (Table 19–1) is a simple way to get a general perspective of the financial health of a prospective insurer. For example, the ratios of two insurers, *S* and *V*, are

Table 19–1
Ratio Analysis in Selecting Insurers

Year	Policyholders' Surplus / Debt		Premiums Written / Policyholders' Surplus		Combined Loss and Expense (Ratios)	
	S	V	S	V	S	V
1	0.37	0.36	2.8	2.2	88.4	100.7
2	0.34	0.34	2.9	2.6	94.5	105.6
3	0.32	0.28	3.1	2.7	93.0	110.5
4	0.41	0.33	2.3	2.6	99.2	110.4
5	0.44	0.26	2.2	3.4	93.0	120.3
Total					93.6	109.5

	S	V
5-year underwriting gain (loss) in millions	$29.7	($12.3)
5-year investment net income (loss) in millions	$30.0	$8.5
Policyholders' surplus in millions	$47.0	$7.3

Source: *Best's Key Rating Guide 1977* (Oldwick, N. J.: A. M. Best Company, 1977), pp. 160 and 184.
Note: Insurer S is the Southern Farm Bureau Casualty Insurance Company of Mississippi, and V is the Volkswagen Insurance Company of St. Louis, Mo.

Part 5   Personal Risk Management—Property Liability

presented in the table. Insurer *S* has made both underwriting and investment profit for each of the five years. It accepts only a modest amount of business. The ratio of premium to surplus falls between 2:1 and 3:1, which is conservative. Its combined ratio has always been less than 100. Although *S*'s surplus is relatively small compared to its debt, less than 50 percent, the stability of its underwriting and investment profits helps to offset this weakness. Also, the ratio of surplus to debt is rising, a favorable factor.

Insurer *V*, a smaller company, shows much greater financial weakness than Insurer *S*. *V* lost money (about 10 percent of premiums written) on underwriting in the last five years. Underwriting losses exceeded net investment income by a factor of 1.5:1. These losses, which were in a rising trend, totalled $12,326,000 in five years, of which $4,880,000 occurred in year 5. They exceed the surplus of $7,373,000. At the current rate of loss, *V* will be insolvent in about two more years. *V*'s ratio of premium to surplus is quite high (3.4:1 in year 5), implying that *V* is using substantial financial leverage. This leverage is working against *V*, since the business it accepts produces an underwriting loss rather than a gain. Insurer *V*'s surplus cushion, which is in an adverse trend, is considerably less than that of *S*. *V* has only $0.26 in surplus for each $1 of debt, compared to $0.44 per $1 of debt for *S*.

In view of this analysis, the potential policyholder should seek additional information before accepting coverage from Insurer *V*. The analysis does not establish that *V* should be rejected outright, but the "red flags are up." Best rated Insurer *S* as "Excellent" (A) and Insurer *V* as "Fairly Good" (C+). (See the discussion of Best's ratios next and in Appendix B.)

Ratio analysis should be used in conjunction with other factors. If the ratio characterizing a given insurer is far out of line with industry averages, the insurance buyer should examine that particular insurer in greater detail to seek the reasons for the deviation; if reasons are not apparent, that insurer may be viewed with suspicion as far as its potential solvency is concerned. For example, an insurer with nonconservative ratios may be protected by favorable reinsurance arrangements or by guarantees of a parent company. Hence, it might be acceptable in spite of these ratios.

Best's Ratings. One approach to judging the financial strength of an insurer is illustrated by the financial ratings given by Best.[7] The ratings attempt to measure the following factors that affect the financial stability of an insurer:

1. Underwriting results
2. Economy of management
3. Adequacy of reserves for undischarged liabilities of all kinds
4. Adequacy of policyholders' surplus to absorb unusual shocks
5. Soundness of investments

Best's ratings would consider, for example, that although an insurer had a high ratio of policyholders' surplus to unearned premium reserves, careless underwriting, extravagant management practices, or unsound investment policies with asset losses could, within a short time, completely offset its good surplus position.

The great majority of insurers meet Best's high standards of financial safety.[8] The public has further protection in that the insurance commissioner in most states must examine each insurer for financial solvency at least once every three years.

NAIC Early Warning System. In 1973 the National Association of Insurance Commissioners (NAIC) developed a system of 12 financial ratios to warn regulators of possible impending insurer failure. A normal range for each ratio is stated. An insurer having four or more ratios outside the normal range is designated as a "priority" company for further observation and close supervision. The system is expected to "flag" between 15 and 20 percent of the insurers and to correctly predict 96 percent of all company failures within one year of the prediction and 82 percent within three years of the prediction.

In a study of the effectiveness of the NAIC early warning system, Hershbarger found that the system falls somewhat short of predictability expectations.[9] Thus, the system is not perfect. The ratios found to be best in predicting insurer failures included the ratios of premiums to surplus, various ratios of underwriting profitability, and various ratios of surplus to liabilities.

Other financial ratios also have been found to be significant in predicting insurer failures. Ratios measuring the quality of accounts receivable from agents and the profitability of investments have been found to be effective in discriminating sound from unsound companies.[10]

The NAIC has worked hard on its early warning system and its watch list of troubled insurers. However, problems do exist. One of the biggest problems is the ability of regulators (and Best's) to determine the adequacy of the loss reserve account. Best's does not go on site to audit loss reserves, and insurance regulators usually do so only every three years. If loss reserves are consistently understated for several years, a firm with relatively strong financial statements can become insolvent very quickly when all the losses must be paid. In time periods like 1984–1986, several insurers went bankrupt with little warning as their liability loss reserves proved to be inadequate.

Financial Stability and Profits

It should now be clear that the financial stability of insurers is directly related to their underwriting and investment profits. Underwriting profits in turn are intimately connected to loss and unearned premium reserves. Let us consider these reserves in more detail.

Part 5   Personal Risk Management—Property Liability

Loss Reserves. Loss reserves are set up by the insurer when notice of loss is first received. In most cases these loss reserves are based on subjective judgment. They are revised periodically as more information about the loss is received. It is possible for the estimates of loss to be either excessive or inadequate. If an insurer's management wishes to dress up a balance sheet or an income statement, it can direct underwriters to understate loss reserves, thus maximizing apparent profit and minimizing apparent debt. These acts could overstate profit ratios and ratios of net worth to debt. The financial analyst should judge the adequacy of loss reserves in a company only after studying trends over a period of years to see if the insurer's data are reported consistently.

Unearned Premium Reserves. Unearned premium reserves must usually be adjusted to obtain a true notion of the profits of an insurer. As noted previously, these reserves are established to represent the unearned portion of an advance premium. These sums would have to be returned to policyholders if the coverage is cancelled, and are taken into earnings pro rata as the policy runs its course. However, the expenses incurred in connection with new business must be written off as soon as the policy is sold (a statutory requirement). A policy with an expense allowance of, say, 40 percent, and an expected loss ratio of 60 percent, running for three years, would show a statutory loss for the first year.

Consider Table 19-2. Suppose a three-year fire insurance policy is written on July 1. It carries a premium of $1,200. The law requires that all of the expense be written off in year 1. Assume that losses are incurred exactly as expected (at 60 percent of premiums), and are paid out evenly throughout the policy period. This would mean that $\frac{1}{6}$ of the expected loss is paid out in year 1, $\frac{1}{3}$ in year 2, $\frac{1}{3}$ in year 3, and $\frac{1}{6}$ in year 4. Assume that the premium quoted has no built-in profit allowance. The financial results from this policy would be as shown in the table.

The insurer reports a $400 statutory loss the first year, which it must advance from its surplus. This charge is recovered in the remaining years of the policy. It is called the **equity in the unearned premium reserve.** Was the first year's loss real?

Table 19-2
Hypothetical Financial Results—Statutory Profits and Losses

	Year 1	Year 2	Year 3	Year 4	Total
(1) Premium Written	$1,200	0	0	0	$1,200
(2) Earned Premiums	200	400	400	200	1,200
(3) Unearned Premiums	1,000	600	200	0	0
(4) Losses	120	240	240	120	(720)(60%)
(5) Expenses	480	—	—	—	(480)(40%)
(6) Statutory Profit					0
(7) (2) − (4) − (5) =	(400)	160	160	80	0

No, it resulted from a regulatory requirement that expenses must be written off immediately and that corresponding premiums may be recognized only pro rata over the policy period.

From a financial analyst's viewpoint, the loss in year 1 will be adjusted by adding back in 40 percent of the increase in the unearned premium reserve in order to find the true profit for year 1 (i.e., adjusting for the equity in the unearned premium reserve). If this adjustment is made, $400 (0.40 × $1,000) will be added, producing zero profit for the year, as expected. In year 2, unearned premiums fell $400, so 40 percent of this will be subtracted from statutory profit, again producing a zero profit, etc.

Note that a rapidly growing insurer will show growing statutory losses, due to the peculiar accounting requirements of the insurance industry. The reverse holds true for an insurer that is writing a smaller amount of insurance each year. Without the adjustments, it would appear that the growing insurer is unprofitable and that the declining insurer is profitable, when in fact the opposite is true. Note also that a growing insurer must have a surplus from which to draw for meeting unearned premium reserve requirements generated by the new business it writes. This is an additional reason for examining closely the net worth of an insurer to see if it is adequate to finance the insurer's growth.

In summary, there are no simple methods to determine the financial strength of an insurer. No single test of financial strength should be relied on in evaluating an insurer. Instead, several tests over a period of years should be employed. Sufficient study of this subject has been conducted to demonstrate the seriousness of the problem of insurer failures, the value of financial ratios in predicting failures, and the need for consumers to be concerned and to make appropriate investigation before committing their financial future to an insurer.

Level and Stability of Profits in Insurance

The level and stability of profits in nonlife insurance as a whole have been of considerable public interest because of the importance of profits and their measurement to the regulatory process. Regulators have been concerned with the rising consumer costs of insurance, particularly liability insurance, and have been under pressure to give more weight to insurers' investment profits as well as to underwriting profits. It is claimed by some that industry profits have been reported at unrealistically low levels in order to justify higher insurance rates, and that if investment profits were considered, the returns in insurance would be highly adequate and would permit premium reductions. Regulators have also been concerned with such questions as the relative monopolistic position of insurers and the economies of scale in insurance. For example, if large insurers operate more efficiently than small insurers, would the consumers' interest be served by regulations that encourage greater industry concentration?

In 1971 a study was made of risk-adjusted rates of return among 40

Part 5   Personal Risk Management—Property Liability

large insurers, 40 medium-sized insurers, and 40 small insurers. In this study, risk-adjusted return was defined as the rate of return (defined in several different ways) divided by the standard deviation of these returns (defined in two separate ways).[11] It was discovered that over the period 1955–1968 the average risk-adjusted rate of return in property-liability insurance was significantly lower than comparable measures in other industries, regardless of the method of measuring risk. The data showed that rates of return in nonlife insurance, as defined, were not generally below those of other industries if the data were unadjusted for risk; but once risk was taken into consideration, the returns became relatively unattractive to the investor.

This study also revealed that large-sized firms had lower unadjusted rates of return than medium- or small-sized firms, but when adjusted for risk, the returns were larger than those of either medium- or small-sized firms. This finding shows that large firms are not necessarily more profitable than smaller firms in insurance unless the risk factor is considered. Large firms have been able to reduce their risk considerably through diversification techniques. However, large firms evidently do not enjoy monopoly positions, or their unadjusted rates of return would be much higher than they are.

Total rates of return in the property-liability insurance industry began to improve after 1970. For the period 1971–1980, the aggregate rate of return averaged about 13 percent on net worth, about the same as several other comparable industries.[12] In property and liability insurance, investment income is a major source of profit. Not only are investment income and capital gains usually larger than underwriting gains, they are also generally more stable. In a tabulation by Best covering the 59-year period 1918–1977, in all but 14 years investment results were superior to underwriting results for a group of stock insurers whose assets in 1977 totalled $100 billion.

After 1980, the rate of return on net worth for property liability insurers deteriorated. The average rate of return for the years 1981 through 1984 was 7.67 percent, about half the rate of the previous ten years. Based on price increases after 1984, one would expect the industry's rate of return on net worth to increase in the latter half of the 1980s.

The Underwriting Cycle. Profits and losses in the underwriting of property-liability insurance tend to run in three- to eight-year cycles. Table 19–3 shows the ratio of underwriting profits or losses to premiums earned for a large group of stock insurers over the period 1945–1984.

Note that the longest period of consecutive underwriting profits, 1948–1955, was eight years, while the underwriting losses seemed to run three years each, except for the 1946–1947 period of two years. However, beginning in 1979, the property liability insurance industry began its longest series of consecutive years of underwriting losses (1979–1985). Intense price competition in commercial lines was a major reason for this

Table 19–3
Ratio of Underwriting
Profits or Losses to
Premiums Earned, U.S.
Stock Insurers,
1945–1984

1945	1.44	1959	0.74	1972	3.44
1946	(5.78)	1960	0.64	1973	0.78
1947	(1.44)	1961	0.28	1974	(5.60)
1948	4.99	1962	0.02	1975	(8.34)
1949	9.51	1963	(1.89)	1976	(3.43)
1950	4.00	1964	(2.81)	1977	1.65
1951	0.24	1965	(3.19)	1978	2.41
1952	3.08	1966	0.70	1979	(0.60)
1953	5.00	1967	0.07	1980	(2.98)
1954	5.50	1968	(1.17)	1981	(5.41)
1955	3.49	1969	(2.07)	1982	(7.70)
1956	(1.75)	1970	(0.72)	1983	(9.90)
1957	(4.33)	1971	2.85	1984	(16.1)
1958	(1.05)	1972	3.44	1985	(16.3)

Source: *Best's Aggregates and Averages*, 1986, p. 154.

low level of profitability. Records show that in all but four of the years in the 1945–1985 period in which underwriting losses occurred, investment gains offset the underwriting losses recorded. Without investment income, the insurers clearly would have had to charge higher rates or to have been more selective in underwriting or both.

The underwriting cycle appears to be caused by several factors: (1) Insurance managers compete with each other to attract premiums for investment purposes, especially when interest rates are high. Underwriting standards are relaxed, rates are cut, and underwriting losses and expenses may later exceed the premiums collected. Managers hope that interest and investment returns will offset these losses by a sufficient margin so that total operations will be conducted at a profit. Known as "cash flow underwriting," this process may backfire if everyone tries it at once, because increased competition for business and for the investment dollar drives returns down. (2) When underwriters believe that rates have become too low and underwriting standards too relaxed, they attempt to reverse themselves, but this process takes time. In some states regulators may be slow to allow rate increases. It is difficult to stop a battleship quickly, even when the propellors are reversed. (3) Inflation rates may be such that losses are higher than anticipated because of the higher costs of making claim settlements. Even though underwriters attempt to adjust for anticipated inflation when making rates, these adjustments may be inadequate. Although insurance managers recognize the danger of the underwriting cycle, they appear to be powerless to stop it, short of collective actions that may not be allowed under current state and federal regulations.

Insurance consumers can take advantage of the underwriting cycle by studying the changes in underwriting profits of insurers with whom they are dealing. Consumers can bargain more successfully for reduced rates or easier underwriting standards, or both, after periods of rising insurer profits. When profits are falling, consumers can anticipate the reverse situation—higher rates and tougher underwriting standards.

Conclusion. The level and stability of profits in the property and liability insurance industry have been relatively low. This poor profitability has had at least two unfortunate results:

1. Managers have tried to tighten underwriting requirements and raise insurance rates to stem losses. This has caused shortages of insurance. As a result, the government has entered the insurance business to supply coverage.
2. It has been difficult for the insurance industry to attract new capital. Most growth is internally financed. This makes it difficult for the industry to meet the needs of a growing economy.

It is anomalous that an industry whose purpose is to reduce risk has been unable to achieve a level of profits that is considered adequate and stable. There are, however, several sources of potential improvement. The wave of mergers in the industries is expected to increase diversification among insurance companies, with an improvement in the stability and level of profits. Increased attention to expense control may help, particularly in the distribution of insurance through greater use of group plans. Greater attention to the causes and prevention of losses could also have a major beneficial effect. Finally, advancing computer technology may be of major assistance to underwriters in the development of more sensitive and accurate rating systems by predicting losses more accurately.

Quantity and Quality of Service Offered

Given insurers with comparable contracts and equivalent degrees of financial strength, the applicant for insurance is faced essentially with the question, "Do the insurers competing for my business offer coverage at lower cost, and if so, what in the way of service, if anything, is given up in obtaining this lower cost?" The question of service is a vital one in determining whether any saving in insurance cost is actually a net saving or merely a symptom of the fact that certain functions are not being performed by the insurer.

Various studies have suggested that the quality and quantity of services provided by insurers and their agents often do not live up to expectations. One study of consumer attitudes toward automobile and homeowners' insurance, for example, revealed that some type of unfair treatment toward the policyholder was the reason most often given for a change in insurer. Respondents complained that agents failed in updating coverage and in presentation of coverage alternatives.[13]

Each insured should carefully consider the quantity and quality of services expected and, through careful inquiry, attempt to select the agent who will meet these expectations. If the insured has little need for agency services, the other factors in selecting an insurer, such as savings in premiums, may be stressed more highly. A firm with international operations may find that only a few brokerage firms, those with overseas offices, are suitable for its contracts.[14] An industrial firm may find only one or two agencies in its locale large enough to provide sufficient contacts with the insurance market, as well as loss-prevention service.

Selection of the Agent

When an individual is making the decision to buy an auto or a homeowners' policy, an agent must be chosen to complete the transaction. In choosing this agent, the following qualities should be examined:

1. Training and education
2. Experience
3. Professional reputation

In order to serve the consumer properly, the insurance agent must know and understand the policies that the consumer needs to purchase. He or she must also know how the various policies fit together so that duplicate coverages will not be purchased. An agent with good training and education will know these facts. To determine an agent's background, the consumer should inquire about the agent's training and education. An agent with a college degree in insurance and who is a Chartered Property Casualty Underwriter (CPCU) is well qualified to help a buyer. Such persons have a high level of academic and professional education.

The student may ask, "What is a Chartered Property Casualty Underwriter?" A CPCU is an insurance person with at least three years' experience in the insurance field and who has passed ten rigorous examinations. These examinations cover risk management, over 50 insurance policies, loss control, insurance company operations, law, finance, accounting, economics, and ethics. He or she has also agreed to accept a Code of Professional Ethics.

In the agent selection process, the consumer should look for an agent with experience. An agent with at least three to five years' experience has seen many different insurance problems and had the opportunity to solve them. The experienced agent should have a good understanding of the marketplace and how an individual consumer fits into the marketplace. If the agent represents several companies, he or she can rely on experience with these companies to choose the best one for the insured.

Agents may have excellent training and experience, but if their professional reputation is poor, the consumer should avoid them. Consumers must have confidence in their agents. Agents must act in good faith toward consumers, and be willing to put the consumers' needs above their own desires to make a commission on a sale.

SUMMARY

1. The first step in the intelligent selection of an insurer is to make sure that each insurer to be analyzed offers a comparable insurance contract. The cost of insurance, the financial strength and stability of the insurer, and the quantity and quality of services offered are all interrelated. The final selection of the insurer should not be made until all these factors have been studied.

2. Some notion concerning the ultimate cost of the insurance service may be obtained by an examination of the ratio of losses and expenses to premiums earned for individual insurers and resulting underwriting gains or losses.

3. The financial strength of an insurer may be judged by the ratio of policyholders' surplus to liabilities, by Best's ratings, by the adequacy of reserves for contingencies, by the soundness of investments, and by the trends in loss and expense ratios. The analyses should be compared for several continuous years.

4. Quantity and quality of service rendered, economy, and convenience in the administration of one's insurance program are important factors in the selection of an insurer or agent. Studies reveal considerable dissatisfaction with some agents, brokers, and insurance services. The individual needs of each buyer should be weighed in selecting agents or insurers.

5. In selecting an agent, the consumer should investigate the agent's training and education, experience, and professional reputation.

QUESTIONS FOR REVIEW

1. Explain the terms:
   (a) Loss ratio
   (b) Expense ratio
   (c) Net underwriting profit

2. On July 1, the Shifting Sands Insurance Company writes a one-year insurance policy with an advance premium of $100,000. All expenses are incurred in the first month. The expense ratio is 35 percent and the anticipated loss ratio is 65 percent.
   (a) What must the insurer show as the unearned premium reserve on this policy on December 31?
   (b) What will be the "statutory loss" if losses on the policy as of December 31 are exactly half of those expected when the policy was written?
   (c) What will be the equity in the unearned premium reserve effective December 31?

3. Explain why a 1:1 ratio of policyholders' surplus to total liabilities means $2 of assets behind each $1 of liabilities.

4. Jack is seeking automobile insurance for a fleet of cars, and his agent recommends the policies of the Maine Insurance Co., Portland, Me., whose financial data Jack immediately looks up in *Best's Key Rating Guide.* He discovers the following facts:

Total assets	$4,301,000
Policyholders' surplus	1,723,000
Loss reserves	1,226,000
Unearned premium reserves	1,168,000
Net premiums written	4,289,000
Underwriting losses, last 5 years	(832,000)
Underwriting loss, latest year	(555,000)
Investment gains, last 5 years	362,000
Investment gains, latest year	138,000

(a) Calculate the ratio of net worth to debt. Explain the meaning of this ratio. How does it compare with industry averages?

(b) Calculate the ratio of premiums to net worth. Explain the meaning of this ratio.

(c) Assess the significance of the underwriting results of this insurer to Jack.

(d) On the basis of your analysis, would you recommend that Jack accept his agent's recommendation? Under what conditions? Discuss.

5. What is a CPCU? How does a person who is a CPCU meet the desired characteristics of a good agent?

QUESTIONS FOR DISCUSSION

1. Insurance company insolvencies have caused a clamor for some method under which claimants against insolvent companies can be paid for their losses. The number of insurance companies that have failed in recent years has increased, as well as the number of policyholders affected.

(a) Look up the statute in your state to determine the nature of the insurance company insolvency law, if any, and report on its provisions.

(b) Do you believe insolvency statutes should apply to insurers only, or should they relieve any creditors, such as creditors of a retail store, of loss from insolvency of the debtor? Discuss.

(c) Should insolvency plans be financed by all insurance buyers, through higher premiums, or by general tax revenues? Discuss.

2. What is the NAIC early warning system? In your opinion, does this system eliminate the need for rigorous attention to the problem of insurer insolvency by the insurance buyer? Why or why not?

3. *A* argues that the insurer with a high loss ratio is actually more desirable than one with a low loss ratio because a high loss ratio is the best evidence that management is returning to the policyholder group a larger proportion of the premium dollar than the company with a low loss ratio. Criticize this argument.

4. The text states, "Insurance is a service in which the cost must be estimated in advance by the insurer." Explain the significance of this statement with regard to the problem of selecting insurers on the basis of prices quoted for coverage.

5. Of the three factors to consider in selecting an insurance agent, which do you think is the most important? Why?

NEW TERMS AND CONCEPTS

Best's Ratings
Chartered Property Casualty Underwriter (CPCU)
Combined Ratio
Equity in Unearned Premium Reserve
Expense Ratio

Insolvency Funds
Loss Ratio
Loss Reserve
Net-Worth-to-Debt Ratio
Premium-to-Surplus Ratio
Underwriting Cycle
Unearned Premium Reserve

NOTES

1 For example, only a few insurers were accepting medical malpractice liability insurance in the period 1985–1986.

2 See *Best's Key Rating Guide, Property-Casualty*, and *Best's Insurance Reports* (Oldwick, N.J.: A. M. Best Company), published annually.

3 Harold Krogh, "Insurer Post-Insolvency Guaranty Funds," *Journal of Risk and Insurance*, Vol. 39, No. 3 (September, 1972), pp. 431–450.

4 *Insurance Facts 1986–87* (New York: Insurance Information Institute, 1986), p. 41.

5 See Terrie E. Troxel and Cormick L. Breslin, *Property-Liability Insurance Accounting and Finance,* 2nd ed. (Malvern, Pa.: American Institute of Property and Liability Underwriters, 1983), pp. 201–222.

6 Ibid., pp. 234–236.

7 See *Best's Insurance Reports* (Oldwick, N.J.: A. M. Best Company) or a summary of various types of financial data found in *Best's Key Rating Guide.* Each of these annual publications covers more than 1,100 property-liability insurance carriers in the United States. Fairly complete financial information about any carrier is available.

8 Appendixes B and C explain the methods used in compiling Best's ratings.

9 Robert A. Hershbarger, "The Effectiveness of the NAIC Early Warning System for Predicting Failures among Property-Liability Companies" (Paper given at the ARIA Risk Theory Seminar, Athens, Georgia, April, 1979).

10 J. S. Trieschmann and George E. Pinches, "A Multi-variate Model for Predicting Financially Distressed P-L Insurers," *Journal of Risk and Insurance,* Vol. 40, No. 3 (September, 1973), pp. 327–338.

11 James S. Trieschmann, "Property-Liability Profits: A Comparative Study," *Journal of Risk and Insurance,* Vol. 38, No. 3 (September, 1971), pp. 437–453. The two ways of measuring risk were spatial and temporal. Spatial risk measures variation in rates of return among a group of companies each year, and the separate measures are then averaged for the number of years studied. Temporal risk is the variation of a single firm's rate of return throughout the time period to be studied. The industry temporal risk is the weighted average of the average risk-adjusted rates of return for all firms comprising the industry.

12 *Insurance Facts 1981–82,* p. 18.

13 J. D. Cummins, D. M. McGill, H. E. Winklevoss, and R. A. Zelten, *Consumer Attitudes Toward Auto and Homeowners Insurance* (Philadelphia: The Wharton School, University of Pennsylvania, 1974), p. 223. See also Robert E. Osborn, Jr., *The Need for Consumer Orientation in Insurance Marketing* (Eugene: University of Oregon, 1969).

14 Large international brokerage firms include Marsh and McLennan, Johnson and Higgins, Alexander and Alexander, Fred S. James, and Frank B. Hall.

PART 6

BUSINESS RISK MANAGEMENT

20 BUSINESS PROPERTY INSURANCE

After studying this chapter, you should be able to:

1. Explain how the Simplified Commercial Lines Portfolio policy meets the property loss exposures of consumers.
2. Describe how insurance contracts can be designed to insure consumers' property that fluctuates in value.
3. List the different types of consequential loss exposures and types of insurance coverages available for such loss exposures.
4. Explain how floater insurance policies help meet the insurance needs of businesses whose property is moved from one location to another.
5. Identify the perils of transportation and the carrier's liability on the land and sea.
6. List the major types of property insurance available for ocean and inland marine loss exposures.
7. State the difference between general and particular average losses.
8. Describe expressed and implied warranties as they are used in ocean marine insurance.

In this and the folowing four chapters our emphasis will be on the insurance needs of business organizations. We shall examine the property liability loss exposures of business firms and the insurance coverages available to insure them. In Chapter 24 several risk-management tools and techniques are applied to the insurance needs of the business enterprise. Let us begin by examining several of the property insurance contracts that business persons use to protect their property:

1. The Simplified Commercial Lines Portfolio policy (SCLP)
   a. Business and Personal Property Coverage Form (BPPCF)
   b. Liability (see Chapter 21)
   c. Crime
   d. Boiler and machinery
2. The Special Multiple policy (SMP)
3. The Business Owners' policy
4. Builders' risk and reporting forms
5. Consequential loss exposures and insurance policies
6. Business floater insurance policies
7. Ocean marine insurance
8. Inland marine transportation insurance

THE SIMPLIFIED COMMERCIAL LINES PORTFOLIO POLICY

In January, 1986, a new simplified approach to commercial insurance coverages was introduced by the insurance industry. Under the **Simplified Commercial Lines Portfolio policy** (SCLP), the insured can obtain almost all insurance coverages. Not only is there a wide variety of coverages, but there are also broader contract provisions in the SCLP.

The Simplified Commercial Lines policy has four separate sets of coverages: commercial property, liability, crime, and boiler and machinery. As each of these topics is discussed in the next four chapters, reference will be given to how the SCLP gives coverage for these loss exposures.

Building and Personal Property Coverage Form (BPPCF)

Basic protection for buildings and personal property in the SCLP is provided under the building and personal property coverage form (BPPCF). In this form the definitions of all the property insured are given, as well as any limitations or extensions of coverage. The perils insured against are determined by one of three causes-of-loss forms. Property coverage is divided into three major categories: owned buildings, owned business personal property, and nonowned business personal property.

Owned Buildings. Owned buildings includes the building(s) described on the declarations page and any additions, extensions, fixtures, and machinery and equipment constituting a permanent part of it as well as service equipment. In rental properties appliances provided by the owner are also considered a part of the building. This inclusion as a part of the building is important to the insured because the building rate is normally less than the contents rate. Thus, any item declared a part of the building saves the insured money.

Owned Business Personal Property. Personal property includes business personal property owned by the insured and usual to the occupancy of the insured. Of course, there are limitations and exclusions like that found in the homeowners' policy. For instance, motor vehicles, aircraft, and watercraft are subject to such limitations or exclusions.

Nonowned Business Personal Property. The third type of property insured, nonowned business personal property, consists of two parts: improvements and betterments, and personal property of others in the insured's control. Improvements and betterments represent alterations made to a leased building by the insured that the insured cannot legally remove when the lease is terminated. Examples include modification of a storefront, decorations, partitions, paneling, and wall-to-wall carpeting. The personal-property-of-others exposure develops in situations where the insured repairs property of others. Radio, shoe, auto, boat, and watch repair businesses all have this exposure.

Extensions of Coverage. In addition to the basic coverage that exists when the appropriate premium is paid, the BPPCF has extensions of coverage that expand protection to six other categories of property. These extensions are meant to supplement the basic coverage, and if any major exposures exist in any of the six areas, the insured needs to purchase additional insurance. The six extensions are as follows:

1. *Newly acquired buildings or additions.* Twenty-five percent of the building limit, subject to a maximum of $250,000 per building. The insured must report additions or newly acquired buildings within 30 days.
2. *Business personal property located at newly acquired premises.* Ten percent of the business personal property limit, subject to $100,000 maximum per building. Coverage expires 30 days after acquiring the property.
3. *Personal effects and property of others.* $2,500 of coverage for the personal effects of the named insured, officers, and employees and personal property of others in the insured's care, custody, or control.
4. *Valuable papers and records.* $1,000 limit, covering the cost of researching, replacing, or restoring the lost information on lost or damaged valuable papers and records.
5. *Off-premises property.* $5,000 limit, covering property while it is temporarily at a location the insured does not own, lease, or operate. Only insured perils are covered, and property in a vehicle is excluded.
6. *Outdoor property.* $1,000 limit, but not more than $250 per tree, shrub, or plant. Coverage applies to outdoor fences, radio and television antennas, signs, trees, shrubs, and plants. Perils insured against are limited to fire, lightning, explosion, riot, and aircraft.

All of these extensions of coverage are an additional amount of insurance, and they apply only if the policy has an 80 percent or higher coinsurance clause.

Scheduled versus Blanket Coverage. Under the general form, coverage may be on one of two bases: scheduled or blanket. Under **scheduled coverage,** property at two or more locations is listed and specifically insured. Under **blanket coverage,** property at several locations may be insured under a single item. For example, the policy could provide $87,500 of insurance on all contents at plants in five different cities. Or under blanket coverage, classes of property usually insured separately might be lumped together and be insured as a single item, such as $10,000 on stock, furniture, fixtures, and machinery.

While blanket coverage performs a useful function, it does not do so without a certain cost. This cost comes in the form of a mandatory 90 percent coinsurance clause and a premium based on the 80 percent coinsurance rate. Normally, when one goes from 80 percent coinsurance to 90 percent, the premium rate is reduced 5 percent. For example, if the 80 percent coinsurance rate were $10 per thousand, the 90 percent coinsurance rate would be $9.50 per thousand. Thus, if the insured had $1,000,000 of property to insure on a blanket basis, $900,000 of coverage would have to be purchased at the $10 per-thousand rate. The $900,000 of insurance would cost $9,000 (900 × 10) on a blanket basis, and $8,550 (900 × 9.50) on a specific basis.

Common Clauses in the BPPCF. Some of the common clauses found in the BPPCF involve coinsurance, subrogation, electrical apparatus, power failure, operation-of-building laws, and alterations and repairs. The power failure clause says spoilage due to power failure from an insured peril is not covered unless the loss of power is from an on-premises insured peril. If a windstorm blows down a transmission line next door, there is no coverage. The alteration-and-repair provision allows the insured to make these types of modifications without its being considered an increase in hazard which would cause the coverage to be suspended. The building law clause says that no loss will be paid that results from the operation of building codes. This clause, which requires three endorsements (contingent liability from the operation of building codes, demolition, and increased cost of construction), is included in the endorsements discussion. The electrical apparatus clause states that no loss to electrical items will be covered if caused by artificially generated electrical currents, unless fire ensues, and then loss is covered only for the fire damage.

Perils Insured Against. In the BPPCF there are three options with respect to perils insured against: basic, broad, and special causes-of-loss forms.

The basic form covers fire, lightning, explosion, windstorm, hail, smoke, riot or civil commotion, vandalism, sprinkler linkage, sinkhole collapse, and volcanic action. If an insured does not have automatic sprinklers, no charge is made for that peril.

The broad form includes the basic perils plus breakage of glass ($500 maximum); falling objects (exterior damage must occur before interior damage is covered); the weight of ice, sleet, and snow; and accidental discharge of water or steam from a system or appliance containing steam or water other than an automatic sprinkler system.

The special cause-of-loss form covers all direct accidental losses except those that are excluded. Examples of excluded perils are earth movement, flood, war, enforcement of building ordinance, smog, insect damage, and wear and tear.

Endorsements Used with the BPPCF. There are numerous endorsements available for an insured to use with the BPPCF. An insured can add earthquake, volcanic eruption, and radioactive contamination to the list of perils insured against. The limits of recovery on such property as outdoor signs, trees, shrubs, plants, and radio and television antennas may be increased. Special market value endorsements are available for distilled spirits and wines.

Some other endorsements that modify the BPPCF include replacement cost, increased cost of construction, contingent liability from operation of building codes, and demolition cost. The replacement-cost endorsement is like that found in the homeowners' policy and changes the basis of recovery from actual cash value to replacement cost. The increased-cost-of construction endorsement is used when an older building must be repaired according to a more stringent building code. This form usually is used only when replacement-cost coverage exists.

The contingent liability from operation of building codes covers the situation where more than a set percentage (40 or 50 percent) of the building is damaged by an insured peril (say, fire) and the building law requires the remaining portion of the building to be torn down. The fire policy pays the fire damage, and the contingent-liability-from-operation-of-building-laws (CLOBL) endorsement pays for the remaining part of the building. But who pays for the demolition of the undamaged portion? The fire policy does not, because it excludes loss resulting from building codes; the CLOBL does not, because it just pays to rebuild. Therefore, another endorsement is needed, the demolition-cost endorsement. This form covers the cost of tearing down the undamaged portion of the building because the building code requires it. The demolition form can be used only if the CLOBL is also purchased.

SPECIAL MULTIPERIL POLICY (SMP)

One of the first comprehensive coverages in multiple-line insurance was the special multiperil policy (SMP) for given types of commercial and institutional organizations. Introduced in 1960 as a special form for motel risks, the special multiperil policy was expanded gradually, until by 1966 it was revised to meet the needs of retail and wholesale establishments, apartment houses, offices, and institutional, service, manufacturing, and processing exposures. After 1966 the program was substantially revised, so that a set of general rules applies to the various coverages issued under the SMP program. Endorsements to tailor the coverage to particular needs were revised and reissued.

In 1977–1978 the SMP again went through a major revision and expanded the underwriting categories to eight: apartment house, contractors, motel/hotel, industrial and processing, institutional, mercantile, office, and service. The SMP is currently a good, versatile multiline program and one of the best buys for insureds. Packaging the coverages and making certain ones mandatory allows the insured to receive a 10 to 25 percent discount. This discount makes the SMP attractive to insureds, but it also makes insurers more stringent underwriters when a person applies for an SMP policy.

Areas of Coverage

The SMP policy is divided into five major sections. The first section is a six-page section giving many of the conditions and definitions used in the policy. The remaining four sections describe the coverage provided, and include property, liability, crime, and boiler/machinery. Of these four coverages, only property and liability are mandatory.

Perils Insured Against

Under the property coverage (building and personal property), an individual can obtain basic named-peril coverage for fire, extended coverage, and coverage for vandalism/malicious mischief. To this required protection an insured may add coverage for sprinkler leakage and earthquake, and the optional perils form that includes limited glass breakage, falling objects, weight of ice and snow, water damage, and collapse. For those desiring even broader coverage, all-risk protection can be purchased on either the buildings, its contents, or both.

Forms Used in SMP Program

In the special multiperil policy, unlike many other insurance policies, different forms are used to insure buildings and unscheduled personal property. To insure both categories of property, an insured must make sure that both forms are attached to the policy. However, if the insured is leasing property to others, only the building form is used. If the insured is the lessee, only the personal property form is employed.

Besides extending the insured perils, the SMP has a full range of indirect loss coverages, as well as coverage for loss due to theft. Property may be insured on a specific or blanket basis, and several scheduled personal property forms are available. About the only major types of coverage that cannot be written on an SMP policy are automobile, workers' compensation, surety bonds, and life or health insurance.

As the Simplified Commercial Lines Portfolio policy is more widely distributed, the use of the SMP should decline. By the early 1990s it may not be used at all. The insurance industry is trying to make the SCLP policy its primary insurance contract for commercial lines. With its hundreds of endorsements, the SCLP can be designed to meet almost any commercial customer's insurance needs.

BUSINESS OWNERS' PROGRAM

The business owners' program is designed for certain small- to medium-sized businesses. The underwriting manual defines "small to medium" to mean apartments of less than seven stories and no more than 60 units, and office buildings of less than four stories with no more than 60 units and with a total area of less than 100,000 square feet. Retail establishments must have a floor space less than 7,500 square feet, whether the insured owns the building or leases. Other types of leased occupancies may have up to 10,000 square feet per building. Besides these size guidelines, a list of noneligible occupancies are also given, including contractors, bars, places of amusement, lending institutions, manufacturers, and automobile businesses.

Property Forms Used

Only two property forms are used: named peril and all risk. Options are limited, but basic coverage is quite broad. There is mandatory coverage for both direct and indirect loss to property, liability (bodily injury, property damage, and personal injury), and medical payments. Options include boiler and machinery, glass breakage, earthquake, crime, and employee dishonesty.

Recovery Basis

The underwriting manual for this program assumes that the insured will insure 100 percent to value, and the recovery basis to all types of property is replacement cost. Interestingly, while the manual emphasizes the 100 percent insurance-to-value concept, there is no coinsurance clause in the contract. If the insured does not insure 100 percent to value, there is no coinsurance penalty.

OTHER COMMERCIAL PROPERTY FORMS

There are two additional commercial property programs and forms with which you should be familiar: the difference in conditions and the builders' risk. The difference-in-conditions form is used to give all-risk coverage, and the builders' risk form insures buildings under construction.

Difference-in-Conditions Insurance (DIC)

The DIC is written with the insured's basic contract since the DIC excludes fire, extended coverage, vandalism/malicious mischief, and sprinkler leakage. However, it can be written to insure almost any other peril, even earthquake and flood. It has no coinsurance or pro-rata clause but usually has a sizable deductible. As a general rule, only large firms purchase the coverage, but its use is becoming more popular and smaller businesses are starting to use it. (See Chapter 27.)

Builders' Risk

The builders' risk form is used to insure buildings under construction. The usual approach is to use a completed value form that requires the insured to purchase an amount of insurance equal to the finished value of the building. However, since the exposure is equal to that value only when the structure is finished, the rate charge is usually 55 percent of the standard rate. Using this approach, the insured has full coverage during the construction period and does not have to be concerned with filing reporting forms and making updates with the insurer. The policy may be written so that the insurable interests of the building owner, the general contractor, and the subcontractor are covered.

The BPPCF has several builders' risks available for insureds to use.

REPORTING FORMS

Reporting forms are designed to adjust insurable coverage on contents to changing property values at one location or in different locations. Reporting forms have several advantages: (1) the amount of insurance protection is automatically adjusted to changes in values of property at different locations; (2) new locations are automatically covered; (3) the insured does not have to pay premiums on limits of liability in the policy, but rather pays premiums according to the actual values at risk; (4) the possibility of having gaps in coverage or duplication of insurance is virtually eliminated; and (5) the insured avoids being short-rated when coverage is reduced.

An important purpose of this type of form is to adjust insurance protection to business firms that have many plants located in different geographical areas or that wish protection to be adjusted automatically to constantly changing values at these plants. It would be cumbersome, indeed, if a business enterprise carrying on a nationwide operation involving 10 manufacturing or processing plants and 20 warehouses and other distribution centers had to purchase a separate policy for each location. For example, there would undoubtedly be much duplication of coverage when goods were shipped from one location to another (being insured by both the sender and the receiver) and many instances of omission of insurance protection altogether (each party believing the other to have taken care of the insurance).

Coverage may be written in the SMP program, on a reporting-form basis as well as with the BPPCF. In addition, reporting forms are used with multiple-location forms that are used to cover one insured's property at numerous locations. Either buildings, contents, or both may be insured on a multiple-location form.

Each month the insured is required to report to the company what the actual values were at each location on a specific date. If the insured understates the actual value and later suffers a loss, there is a penalty in the recovery, and only that portion of the loss that the amount reported bears to the actual values at risk can be recovered. Thus, if the insured reported $50,000 of inventory at location *C*, and it was determined that the true value was $60,000, only five-sixths of any subsequent partial loss could be recovered. Also, if the insured fails to make a report on the required date, recovery is limited to the values reported on the last date a report was made. Thus, the insured is denied automatic protection when values rise between reporting dates. For example, if on January 1 the insured reports correctly $10,000 of values at location *D*, and on January 15 there is a loss of $15,000 (made possible because incoming shipments of goods raised the values exposed), the entire loss is paid if it falls within the limitation of liability at location *D*. However, if the loss occurs on February 15, and no report had been made on February 1, when it was due, the limit of liability is $10,000.

CONSEQUENTIAL LOSS COVERAGE

The nature of consequential losses can best be understood by use of an example. Suppose a small manufacturer suffers a serious fire that shuts down its plant for two months while repairs are being made. The manufacturer is fully insured against direct loss by fire, but carries no consequential loss coverage. The fire policy pays for the cost of lost raw materials, goods in process, and finished goods, as well as repairs to machinery and buildings. However, the manufacturer finds that it is necessary to keep certain key employees, such as plant managers and salespeople, on the payroll to help with the reorganization and to render service to customers. In addition, there are expenses such as taxes, insurance premiums, interest, heat, light, power, and depreciation, that are incurred regardless of the volume of operation. Finally, the manufacturer has not been able to earn any profit on the unsold finished goods or on the volume of goods that would normally have been produced during this period. The sum of such losses may be so severe that the manufacturer is unable to continue in business. Consequential damage contracts have been devised to indemnify for this type of loss.

The importance of consequential losses has long been recognized in personal insurance lines. Life insurance, for example, is intended to replace lost income due to the premature death of the breadwinner. Disability income insurance is designed to restore income lost as a result of total disability. In property insurance, however, consequential losses have not generally been recognized for the serious exposure that they really are. In a study of 21 losses of steel manufacturers it was found that in 15 cases the consequential loss exceeded the direct physical loss.[1] The physical loss was placed at about $381,000, while the consequential losses were estimated to be $2,654,000, or about seven times as great. The largest single direct loss was $86,800, while five of the consequential losses exceeded $400,000, the largest amounting to $675,973.

While comprehensive data on the premium volume from consequential business are not available, there is little question that such premium volume accounts for a small portion of the total fire insurance written. The central reason for the failure to insure such an important exposure appears to lie in the somewhat complicated techniques employed to put the coverage into effect. Furthermore, agents have found consequential loss coverage difficult to understand completely and have thus not been able to educate their clients to the need. In addition, loss settlements are involved because it is difficult to determine precisely the true amount of dollar losses.

A consequential loss contract is usually written as an endorsement to the BPPCF or is listed on the form. The perils insured against usually include the basic cause-of-loss perils in the BPPCF. Also, the indirect-loss situation may be insured under an all-risk endorsement. Thus, if an interruption of business income or other consequential loss results from damage to property by any of the perils in the contracts, the insured is indemnified. Consequential loss contracts may be divided into time- and nontime-element contracts.

TIME-ELEMENT CONTRACTS

Business Consequential Losses

Time-element contracts measure the indirect loss in terms of so many dollars per unit of time that passes until the subject matter can be restored.

Businesses face indirect losses of a much greater magnitude than do individuals. This statement is true not only because businesses handle larger amounts of wealth, but also because the restoration can take much longer. It may take one or two years to rebuild a factory, while most houses can be rebuilt within three to six months. In this section we shall examine the following types of time-element business consequential losses: business income, extra expense, leasehold, and excess rental value.

Business Income Insurance

Business income insurance undertakes to reimburse the insured for profits and fixed expenses lost as a result of damage to the property from an insured peril. It is generally a contract of indemnity.[2] Thus, one of the important problems in this line of insurance is to acquire a firm understanding of methods of determining losses which, by their very nature, depend on future events. Because the future is an unknown quantity, this problem is sometimes complicated.

Basic Characteristics. The business income contract has certain fundamental provisions that are frequently a source of much misunderstanding. The policy will indemnify the insured subject to the following conditions:

1. There must be physical damage to property by a fire or other insured peril.
2. There must be a reduction in business, and this reduction must result from the physical damage caused by the named peril and not from some other cause such as a strike or a shortage of supplies.
3. During the period of restoration, it must be established that the business would have continued to operate had it not been for the occurrence of loss from the insured peril.

4. The loss must occur during the policy term at the described location.
5. If the insured loss had not occurred, the business would have earned a profit or a portion of fixed costs.

If the business had only been breaking even at the time of occurrence of the insured loss, there would be a question raised as to whether any profits would have been earned. If it were found that no profits would have been made even if the business had not been shut down, no real loss from this source would have been incurred, and hence no indemnity for lost profits would be paid. Of course, if the business had been earning its fixed charges, these would be reimbursed. Thus, even though a business is losing money, there is an insurable value to the extent that it was earning its fixed charges. As might be surmised, it might be a considerable source of conflict to resolve the question as to what profits might be in the future.

Business Income Value. Business income value is sometimes referred to as use-and-occupancy value, because all value is supposed to result from the use and occupancy of the damaged building. The value of the possible loss may be measured by different methods, but the central idea is to examine the income statement of the firm and derive from this statement the various items of income and expense that are to be insured. An example of such a technique is as follows:

Total gross earnings from all sources derived from the use and occupancy of the described building less returns and allowances		$400,000
Less:		
Cost of materials consumed in the manufacturing process, or the cost of goods sold in a mercantile business	240,000	
Cost of supplies	40,000	
Sales taxes	20,000	
Bad debts	4,000	
Total		304,000
Remainder—Profits and all other expenses		$ 96,000

In other words, the process of isolating the insurable value is to deduct from total gross earnings the expenses and costs that are variable—that is, those that may be discontinued if a fire or other peril were to cause a shutdown of the business. The amount so obtained is the **insurable value** and forms the basis of the loss settlement. The BPPCF gives it the name "business income."

Coinsurance. The importance of determining business income value becomes even more evident when it is realized that most business income forms contain a coinsurance clause. Coinsurance requirements vary from 50 percent upward, depending on the amount of coverage desired. If the business concern elects to take the 50 percent form, it is required to carry at least 50 percent of its annual insurable value. Failing to carry this amount, it becomes a coinsurer.

To illustrate, assume that the sum of the annual fixed charges and profits during the prior year is $96,000. When the policy was originally issued, the insurable value was $80,000; the firm now carries $40,000 of business income insurance. In the event of a shutdown for three months, and assuming an even rate of operations and earnings, the firm will have lost $\frac{3}{12}$ of its year's profits and fixed charges, or $24,000. Does the firm collect this amount? No, because it has not been carrying the amount of insurance required by the coinsurance clause. Since it carries $40,000 and is required to carry $48,000 (one-half of its annual insurable value of $96,000), it collects only $\frac{40}{48}$ of the loss, or $20,000. Methods that may be employed to avoid the coinsurance penalty are discussed at the end of the chapter.

How Much Insurance to Carry? The question frequently arises, "How much business income insurance should be carried?" The answer depends on what the firm believes the maximum loss might be. Coinsurance forms are available that allow the insured to carry as little as one-half of its annual insurable value. However, if the firm has reason to believe it might take as much as a year to restore the business to regular operations, it should, of course, carry insurance equal to its full insurable value. Generally, insurance on more than one year's insurable value is not available.

It should be remembered that some firms operate on a seasonal basis, and a few months' operations might account for an entire year's profits. If the loss occurs just before an operating season that lasts only three months, a whole year's profits might be lost and probably a good part of the year's expenditures for fixed charges would not be earned. Such a situation would, of course, justify carrying insurance on the profits and fixed charges of a whole year. The policy does not require that the lost profits or charges be incurred in any particular time period, as long as they do not exceed the time that it reasonably takes to restore the building and to resume operations.

On the other hand, the loss may be only partial; that is, if the business is only partially shut down, indemnity can be collected for the partial loss. If it takes an entire year to make repairs and restore normal operations, and the firm is forced to reduce operations by one-fourth of its normal level, the indemnity would be one-fourth of the annual insurable value, assuming the operations to be level throughout the year.

Special Provisions. The basic business income policy limits payments to the length of time it reasonably takes to restore the property physically to normal operating conditions so that the same level of operation exists as existed before the loss. The insured is given additional time to process raw stock to the same stage of manufacture as existed at the time of loss, but no such indemnity is available for finished stock. If a civil authority, such as a local government, prohibits access to the insured's premises because of other damage in the area arising during the insured period, the policy provides up to two weeks' indemnity for loss from this source. However, no indemnity is payable in case a building ordinance, on-premises strike, or lease agreement results in a delay in rebuilding. Electrical power failure is excluded as a source of loss unless fire ensues, and then coverage pertains only to the resulting fire. If a larger building replaces the destroyed structure, indemnity is adjusted for the length of time it would have taken to rebuild a comparable building of the same size as the one destroyed.

An endorsement is available to alter some of the basic requirements just noted. Under the terms of the **extended-period-of-indemnity endorsement,** the period of loss is defined to mean that period necessary to return to normal business operations, and not just the period necessary to reopen business physically. For example, a small manufacturing company may suffer a fire that stops physical operations for three months. At the start of business, however, its chief customers have found new suppliers, and it may take several more months to obtain new customers and to achieve the same level of operation it enjoyed prior to the fire. The extended-period endorsement is offered in units of 30 days, so that the above manufacturer could purchase three units of coverage, or as much as needed. If the manufacturer is able to resume normal operations in less than 90 days, it can recover only for the shorter period, as the contract is on an indemnity basis.

The BPPCF automatically gives the insured 30 days of extended-period-of-indemnity protection, and additional time may be added by endorsement with the payment of an additional premium.

Insurance-to-Value Requirements. In the BPPCF the insured can choose coverage with or without an insurance-to-value requirement. The basic business income coverage has a minimum 50 percent coinsurance clause. However, an insured can choose the **earnings form,** which does not contain a coinsurance clause.

In the standard approach the insurance-to-value requirement is based on the estimated business income that is expected during the 12 months following the date of purchase of the insurance policy. If the policy were purchased on March 15, 1988, then the 12-month period would end on March 14, 1989. This approach is a decided improvement over older forms that used the 12-month period immediately following the loss. The new approach reduces some of the uncertainty associated with estimating the required amount of insurance, as the insured knows exactly which 12 months will be used in making the calculation.

There is usually a 50 percent minimum coinsurance clause in the business income form. For persons with a restoration period (the reasonable time necessary to repair or rebuild the damaged property) greater than six months, this requirement does not pose a problem. But since a 50 percent coinsurance clause implicitly assumes a six-month restoration period, those firms with a maximum restoration period of less than six months may have to purchase more insurance than they can collect. To address this problem, the BPPCF has two optional coverages from which to choose: maximum period of indemnity and monthly limit of indemnity.

Maximum Period of Indemnity. This option replaces the insurance-to-value requirement with a maximum restoration period of 120 days. If the maximum restoration period for an insured is less than 120 days, this is an excellent option. However, if the insured underestimates the restoration period and it goes beyond 120 days, the insurance will not pay the loss even if the policy limits have not been exhausted.

Monthly Limit of Indemnity. This option is the BPPCF's version of the earnings form. It is designed for small businesses and does not have a coinsurance clause. The rate is higher under this form than for the gross earnings form, and recoveries are limited to $16\frac{2}{3}$, 25, or $33\frac{1}{3}$ percent of the total amount of coverage in any one month.

To assure full recovery for any loss, the insured must carry sufficient limits so that the selected limit will cover the total earnings for any one month.

As an example, suppose a retail store obtains one-fourth of its year's earnings, as defined, in the month of December, not an uncommon occurrence. To recover in full for a shutdown during the month of December, the firm must carry policy limits equal to four times its December earnings. This limit is not cumulative, but applies monthly. There is no prorating of coverage for loss periods of less than one month. Suppose the firm has $20,000 of coverage with a 25 percent monthly limitation, and is shut down for 40 days. It is established that the loss during the first 30 days is $6,000, and the loss for the remaining 10 days is $2,000. The recovery is limited to $5,000 for the first 30 days (one-fourth of $20,000), plus $2,000 (and not one-third of $5,000) for the remaining 10 days. Thus, if the firm believes that the maximum period of shutdown is three months and that the maximum loss in any one month is $5,000, it should take $15,000 of coverage with a one-third monthly limitation.

Business Income Rates. Rates for business income insurance are usually based on the 80 percent coinsurance fire rate applicable to the building. In New York they are based on the contents rate. A typical charge is 90 percent of the rate applicable to the building if the business income policy has a 50 percent coinsurance clause, or 70 percent of the building rate if the business income policy has an 80 percent coinsurance clause.

For the earnings form, rates vary according to the monthly limitation percentage and are somewhat higher than the regular gross earnings form. Rates in most territories vary from 85 to 110 percent of the 80 percent coinsurance building rate. Thus, insureds must pay a rate that is 20 to 50 percent higher than that of the standard form in order to escape the coinsurance clause. This price may be worth it, however, in view of the severe loss-recovery penalties sometimes imposed under the gross earnings form.

Criticisms. Business income insurance has been criticized for its complexity, uncertainty of loss adjustments, and operation of the coinsurance clause. The insured often cannot understand being required to purchase a minimum of 50 percent of annual gross earnings, even though being shut down 50 percent of a year is extremely unlikely. The effect of this requirement is to force the insured to pay for more insurance than could be collected in most circumstances.

Even the insured who carries, say, an amount equal to 50 percent of annual gross earnings is not assured of full recovery for losses during shutdowns of periods of less than six months, because of coinsurance. For example, if business had been 50 percent higher during a given year and the policy was not properly written, recovery for any one month would be reduced to two-thirds of that month's actual loss. To illustrate, if the gross earnings were estimated at $120,000 annually but were actually running at the rate of $180,000, and if the coinsurance requirement were 50 percent, the insured could collect only six-ninths of any partial loss.

To solve this problem, the insured may choose to purchase the agreed value option in the BPPCF. This option substitutes an agreed dollar figure for the coinsurance percentage. If the insured buys that amount of insurance, then no matter what his or her business income is for the next 12 months, there is no coinsurance penalty. However, this option does require the payment of an additional premium.

Contingent Business Income. It sometimes happens that a firm is forced to shut down, not because an exposure to a peril occurred and damaged its plant, but because an insured peril forced the shutdown of the plant belonging to a supplier or to an important customer on whom the firm depends. Thus, a manufacturer of air conditioners may find that its plant is shut down because the supplier of compressors has suffered a fire. The consequential loss is just as severe, perhaps, as if the fire had occurred at the firm's own plant, because it may require several months to obtain another supplier. Similarly, a firm may find that its chief customer has cancelled orders because of a fire or other disaster at its plant.

To meet such situations, **contingent business income insurance** has been devised. The regular business income policy will not cover the losses described above because the insured peril did not cause any damage at the firm's own plant. Insurable value for contingent business income insurance is calculated in the same manner as it is for business income insurance.

Extra-Expense Insurance

Certain types of business firms do not find it possible or expedient to close down following the destruction of their physical plants. Such firms as laundries, newspapers, dairies, public utilities, banks, and oil dealers will often continue their businesses using alternative facilities. The closing of these firms would deprive the public of a vital service or would involve a complete loss of goodwill or of business to competitors.

Since these firms will continue to operate if a loss occurs, business income insurance is not attractive. If business income insurance were purchased, they could not collect it or could collect only a very small part of it since they would be maintaining full or partial operations. Such firms need extra-expense insurance that covers expenses beyond the normal cost of conducting business. Examples of extra expenditures include rental of quarters, purchase of extra transportation facilities, leasing of substitute equipment, overtime payments to employees, the cost of moving to temporary facilities, and the cost of additional advertising to inform the public you are still operational.

It should be mentioned that the business income form contains both business income and extra-expense coverage. However, for insureds who must maintain operations, only the extra-expense option is more economical, because under the business income form they would have to pay for business income protection that they would never collect on.

Leasehold-Interest Insurance

A **leasehold** may be defined as an interest in real property that is created by an agreement (a lease) that gives the lessee (the tenant) the right of enjoyment and use of the property for a period of time. A leasehold may become very valuable to the lessee because changing business conditions, improvements in the property, and good management may increase the rental value of real estate considerably above the rental due under the lease. For example, the Y Department Store may negotiate a 20-year lease on its store building, calling for a rental payment of $12,000 a year. Due to a growing business community, comparable property might rent for $15,000 within five years after the lease has been signed. This increase in value creates what is known as **leasehold interest,** or **leasehold value.**

Given the situation described above, what insurance problems are raised? If the lease is lost because of the occurrence of a fire or other physical damage to the building, the Y Department Store might be forced to sign a new lease calling for an increased rental of $15,000. It is very common in leases to provide that the agreement is void or voidable if the premises are destroyed by fire, or if a certain percentage of the sound value of the premises is destroyed by fire, or if the premises are so damaged that they cannot be restored within a given number of days. It is this source of loss that is insurable under a form of coverage known simply as **leasehold-interest insurance.**

In the preceding illustration, such a policy would provide indemnity for the loss of $15,000 a year for the unexpired term of the lease, which is 15 years. The policy, giving consideration to the interest factor, defines the loss as the present value of a sum of payments of $15,000 compounded annually at 4 percent. The form provides a table that enables the insured to see what the indemnity will be for each dollar of leasehold-interest value. When the policy is written, the value of the lease at that time is estimated and this amount is named as the face amount of the policy. The amount for which the insurer may become liable is diminished over time because the remaining period of lease grows shorter each year. The premium, therefore, is computed on the average leasehold value over the life of the lease.

Excess Rental Value

The question arises, "Suppose the rental value of the property has *fallen* since the lease was signed, and it is the landlord, not the lessee, who loses by cancellation of the lease in the event of fire or other insured peril?" In this case, a policy known as **excess rental value** may be written to cover the landlord's loss. Coverage under this policy parallels that given the lessee under the leasehold-interest form.

Rental-Income or Rental-Value Insurance

Rental-income or rental-value insurance can be purchased for business concerns. **Rental income** relates to rents collected from others who occupy property owned by the insured. **Rental value** refers to rent that could be collected from others if the insured did not occupy the premises or that the insured would not collect if the premises became uninhabitable. Rental-income insurance is usually purchased by owners of motels, apartment houses, or duplexes, but almost any business person could need rental-value insurance. It is expected that the BPPCF for business income will replace the need for separate rental-value forms.

CONTRACTS WITHOUT TIME ELEMENT

Contracts without time element are used to insure losses that result from fire, but where the loss cannot be measured either by direct damage by fire or in terms of elapsed time.

Profits Insurance

Profits insurance differs from business income insurance in that the latter covers profits that would have been earned in the future had the fire or other insured peril not damaged the firm's plant. **Profits insurance** covers the loss of the profit element in goods already manufactured, but destroyed before they could be sold. Suppose that a plant is manufacturing refrigerators and is disabled by fire. Among the lost property, stored in a warehouse, are finished refrigerators with a sales value of $10,000. This figure includes an expected profit of $2,000. The standard fire policy indemnifies the insured only for the replacement cost, which would be $8,000. The business income policy would not cover the $2,000 loss of expected profit because the policy applies only to refrigerators that would have been produced during the period of interruption by fire, and not to those already produced. To receive full indemnity for its $2,000 loss, the manufacturer would have to be covered by profits insurance.

Accounts receivable insurance attempts to indemnify an insured for the loss brought about because of the inability to collect from open-account (unsecured) debtors after a fire destroyed accounts-receivable records. If a catastrophe such as fire makes it impossible to prove the existence of a debt because there are no records of the transaction, some debtors may refuse to honor their obligations. Most debtors are honest and will pay, but a loss from unscrupulous debtors may result as a consequential loss from fire or other peril.

Accounts receivable insurance is written as an all-risk cover, with the only exclusions being war and infidelity of the insured's main partners or officers. The coverage applies only while the accounts receivable records are on the premises, but for an additional premium the records may be covered while at another temporary location. It may be required that the records be stored in a vault or a safe when the business is closed.

Indemnity under accounts receivable insurance is made for (1) uncollectible accounts, the sole reason for which is the damage or loss of records, less an allowance for normal bad debts, less any debts that can be reestablished or proven by other methods or records; (2) interest on loans made necessary by the loss; and (3) excess collection expense or the reasonable cost of reestablishing proof of an account. To establish the amount of the loss in the absence of accounts receivable records, projections from accounting data for prior years are made, with adjustments for seasonal or cyclical fluctuations. The rate for this coverage, as is true of most consequential loss contracts, is based on the fire rate in the territory served.

Rain, as such, seldom causes any direct damage to property. The accumulation of water due to extended rainfall, of course, does cause much loss to property in the form of flood or rising water, but such coverage is generally not available from private insurers. Rain itself, however, may be a source of considerable *indirect* loss because its occurrence may greatly reduce the expected profits of promoters of an outdoor or public event. **Rain insurance** is designed to cover the loss of profits and fixed charges or extra expenses due to rain, hail, snow, or sleet of anyone having a financial interest in an event that is dependent on good weather for its success.

The advisability of purchasing rain insurance depends on the promoter's estimate of the actual effect of rainfall on anticipated attendance and the resulting profit. In some areas rain is so common that it does not discourage attendance substantially, while in other locations even a light rainfall will ruin attendance. If an event is very popular and is sold out by advance ticket sales that are nonrefundable, the profit is assured in advance and there is no reason for rain insurance. Among the possible users of rain insurance are sponsors of auction sales, sporting events, boat excursions, carnivals, fairs, conventions, and dances.

FLOATER CONTRACTS

The practice of insuring property at a fixed location or while it is being transported by a common carrier is well established. The need for coverage is universally recognized, and owners of such goods rely on fairly standard contracts to protect them. A more difficult insurance problem is the risk of loss associated with property that is either not at a fixed location or not being transported by a common carrier.

For example, Contractor Brown owns $100,000 worth of equipment that is used in building bridges and roads. This equipment includes such items as cranes, tractors, diggers, winches, hoists, small tools, cement mixers, and cable. The equipment is being moved constantly from job to job and is exposed to losses from many types of perils such as landslide, theft, flood, fire, windstorm, collision, explosion, and vandalism. Since the equipment is seldom located at any one place very long, coverage under traditional property insurance forms is not suitable. Because the equipment neither is being moved by, nor is in the custody of, common carriers, the usual transportation insurance forms are not applicable. Clearly, there is a need for giving specialized attention to Brown's problem. The answer is found in a floater policy—more particularly in the contractors' equipment floater.

The term **floater policy** has never been satisfactorily defined, but it is generally understood to be a contract of property insurance that satisfies three requirements:

1. Under its terms, the property may be moved at any time.
2. The property is subject to being moved; that is, the property is not at some location where it is expected to remain permanently.
3. The contract insures the goods while they are being moved from one location to another, that is, while they are in transit, as well as insuring them at a fixed location.

Bailed Property

A **bailment** exists when one has entrusted personal property to another, such as occurs in the case of laundries, repair establishments, and garages. Special forms of insurance are available to bailees, the owners of such establishments, to cover loss to bailed goods for which they might be liable. Homeowners' forms also cover such losses, but only with respect to the bailor's (the individual's) interest.

Business Floater Policies

The nature of business property makes necessary more complex types of floaters, including block policies, scheduled property floaters, and miscellaneous business floaters.

Block Policies. The term **block** in insurance language, while having no precise meaning, connotes the general idea of a contract that is somewhat broader than the traditional forms of inland marine or fire insurance. A **block policy** covers *en bloc*, on an all-risk basis, the stock in trade or the equipment belonging to a business firm, no matter where the property happens to be located. In Chapter 12 the coverages known as the commercial property program (a development in multiple-line underwriting) were described. That program comes very close to providing for wholesalers and retailers generally what block forms provide for specific types of business firms. Since block policies on jewelers, furriers, camera and musical instrument dealers, and agriculture and construction equipment dealers have been issued for many years by inland marine insurers, these and a few other types of firms are not eligible for the commercial property coverage program.

Jewelers' Block Policy. One of the oldest and broadest of all block contracts, the **jewelers' block policy,** is written to insure all the stock in the trade of a typical jeweler on an all-risk basis. Thus, such property as jewels, watches, precious metals, glassware, and gift items are covered whether they belong to the jeweler or to a customer, or whether they belong to another firm and are in the store on consignment, so that the jeweler is legally liable for their safety or has a financial interest in them.

The jewelers' block policy covers not only property belonging to the jeweler as an owner, but also property of the customer bailor. Thus, the jewelers' block policy is another example of bailee liability insurance. Its coverage may be extended to insure property anywhere in the world, and while in transit to or from the jeweler's place of business, such as while the property is in the hands of messengers, salespersons, customers (on approval), common carriers, other jewelers, repairers, the post office, or an express agency.

Camera and Musical Instrument Dealers' Policy. Another significant example of the block idea in inland marine insurance is the **camera and musical instrument dealers' form.** An all-risk policy, it covers all goods typically stocked by camera and musical instrument dealers while the goods are in transit or at any location in the United States or Canada. Like the jewelers' block policy, it covers both owned property and goods of others in the insured's custody for repair, delivery, or storage.

Equipment Dealers' Policy. A third example of an all-risk block form is the **equipment dealers' policy,** designed for retailers and wholesalers of heavy agricultural and construction equipment, such as road scrapers, bulldozers, pneumatic tools, compressors, harvesters, tractors, binders, reapers, plows, and harrows. The policy covers property belonging to others that is in the insured's control, but excludes automobiles, trucks, motorcycles, aircraft, or watercraft, which are insured under automobile forms.

Scheduled Property Floater Risks. Many types of movable business property are insurable under a form known as the **scheduled property floater,** a general or skeleton form to which is attached an endorsement describing specific types of property and the conditions under which they are insured. The basic form contains fairly standard provisions such as subrogation, appraisal, loss adjustment, cancellation, misrepresentation, and fraud clauses. Losses are settled on an actual cash value basis. The policy provides that it is to be excess over any other collectible insurance on covered property. Some of the scheduled floaters are all risk, but a majority are on a named-peril basis.

Included among the various types of property insured under the scheduled property floater are contractors' equipment, mobile agricultural equipment, office machinery, salespersons' samples, theatrical equipment, railroad rolling stock, oil-well drilling equipment, patterns and dies, goods on exhibition, neon and mechanical electric signs, radium, livestock, and instrumentalities of transportation and communication. Because inland marine floater forms covering these types of property are similar in nature, only two commonly used floaters—the contractors' equipment floater and the livestock floater—will be discussed here.

Contractors' Equipment Floater. One of the most important classes of property insured under the scheduled property floater form is contractors' equipment. The **contractors' equipment floater** is typical of most floaters on scheduled property. Contractors have a special need for protection against the many perils that can cause loss to movable equipment. Very large sums are often invested in a single piece of equipment that is used under basically dangerous conditions.

The contractors' equipment floater insures such items as tractors, steam shovels, cement mixers, scaffolding, pumps, engines, generators, hoists, drilling machinery, hand tools, cable, winches, and wagons.

The floater covers property whether it is owned, leased, or borrowed. Insurance attaches no matter where the property is located. However, property permanently situated at a given location is not eligible for coverage under this floater. Property such as designs, plans, surveying equipment, and underground cable is usually excluded.

Not all contractors' equipment floaters are the same, but in general the following perils are covered: fire, lightning, collision or overturning of a vehicle on which the equipment is being transported, explosion, collapse of bridges, windstorm, earthquake, landslide, flood, and theft. Sometimes deductibles are applied to certain types of perils, such as theft and collision. The form usually contains the following perils exclusions: wear and tear, war, riot, strike, civil commotion, infidelity of employees, overloading of lifting equipment, and damage to electrical apparatus unless caused by fire.

Livestock Floater. Illustrating the flexibility of coverage that is possible in inland marine floaters on scheduled property is the **livestock floater,** available to owners of cattle, horses, hogs, sheep, and mules, whether these animals are kept for farming purposes or otherwise. This floater, which is on a named-peril basis, gives worldwide insurance to the owner against loss by death or destruction of the animal due to such perils as fire, lightning, windstorm, hail, explosion, riot and civil commotion, smoke, aircraft, collision with vehicles, theft, overturn of conveyances, earthquake, flood, and sinking or stranding of vessels while the animals are being transported.

Miscellaneous Business Floaters. There is a wide variety of miscellaneous business floaters, each designed to meet a specific need for insuring property in a given situation. While no attempt will be made to list them all, or even to classify them, two will be discussed as examples of the wide range of risk management problems that can be at least partially solved by the use of inland marine floaters.

The Conditional Sales Floater. The **conditional sales floater** insures goods against loss from named perils, and may be written to insure (1) only the seller's interest in the goods, in which case the floater is known as a **single interest form;** (2) both the seller's and the buyer's interest under what is called a **double interest form;** or (3) on a **contingent basis,** where indemnity is paid to the creditor only if the debtor cannot be made to pay.

If a loss occurs under a single interest form, the customer's debt is cancelled and the seller recovers the amount of the unpaid balance. There is no insurance on the customer's equity in the goods, as is true in the double interest form. In the double interest form, if goods are destroyed by an insured peril, both the equity of the buyer in the goods and the unpaid debt are covered. The policy is considered excess over any other insurance that covers building contents; there is no collection from the conditional sales floater. Once the full purchase price has been paid, the conditional sales floater coverage is terminated.

Under the contingent form, the customer's debt is not cancelled, nor is the customer's equity in the goods covered. The seller is obligated to make full effort to collect the unpaid balance due. If the unpaid balance proves uncollectible, the insurer reimburses the seller for this loss.

Shipments by Mail. The United States Postal Service is not a common carrier and has no liability for the loss of goods entrusted to it unless they are insured by the post office. Therefore, anyone using the mails, and especially those sending a considerable volume of shipments annually by the mails, is in need of obtaining protection for the shipments. The insurance industry has designed forms to meet the needs of almost everyone, from the person sending only a relatively small volume of mail, to the shippers of very large values of securities and currency. The following list summarizes the major policies of this nature:

1. Parcel-post policy—covers merchandise shipments only
2. First-class mail floater—three forms are available for different classes of customers sending securities, coupons, stamps, and other papers of value by first-class or certified mail

3. Registered-mail floater—covers bonds, stocks, currency, bullion, precious metals, warehouse receipts, and other valuable shipments by registered mail or express

Policies issued by private insurers generally offer the advantages of greater convenience, broader coverage, lower cost, and faster claims service than post office coverage. These advantages are more apparent to the large shipper than to the occasional shipper. For example, shipments under a registered-mail policy are covered from the moment they leave the premises of the sender until they arrive at the premises of the addressee, and not only during the time they are in the hands of the post office or the express company. Under the first-class mail floater, it is not necessary to wait in line at the post office to purchase insurance each time a shipment is mailed, or to trust a messenger to make proper arrangements each time. Each of the policies discussed below is all risk, with the chief exclusion being for the peril of war.

Parcel-Post Policy. Covering shipments on an all-risk basis from the time they are in the custody of the post office until final delivery, the **parcel-post policy** is available for merchandise but not for money or securities. Perishable merchandise, packages not labeled "return postage guaranteed," packages bearing descriptive labels on the outside, and shipments not made in accordance with the General Parcel Post Act of 1912 are among the excluded items of property. There is a limit of liability of $100 on unregistered mail.

First-Class Mail Floater. Users of the **first-class mail floater** enjoy all-risk coverage on incoming or outgoing shipments by first-class or certified mail. While the rates are somewhat higher than those charged for the registered-mail policy, considerable savings and added conveniences are effected for certain types of shipments by the use of first-class mail instead of registered mail.

Registered-Mail Floater. The **registered-mail floater,** one of the oldest of inland marine floater policies, gives all-risk protection to a wide variety of shipments, including currency and precious metals, by either registered mail or express. Depending on the rate charged, coverage may be worldwide or restricted territorially. Except for currency, there are no stated limits of insurance; the coverage is equal to the values reported by the insured.

TRANSPORTATION INSURANCE

Insurance on the risks of transportation of goods is one of the oldest and most vital forms of insurance. All types of trade depend heavily upon the availability of insurance for successful and expeditious handling. If it were not possible to trade with others, it would not be feasible to manufacture goods on a mass-production basis. Without mass production, life would be entirely different and probably not as comfortable and easy.

Insurance played a vital part in stimulating early commerce. In Roman times, and earlier, contracts known as **bottomry** and **respondentia** governed the terms under which money was borrowed to finance ocean commerce. Under these contracts, the lender of money took as security for a loan either the ship itself, in the case of bottomry bonds, or the cargo in the case of respondentia bonds. However, if the ship or cargo was lost as a result of ocean perils, the loan was cancelled. If the voyage was successful, the loan was repaid and substantial interest was charged mainly because the interest included an allowance for the possibility of loss of the security; this extra charge was essentially an insurance premium.

THE PERILS OF TRANSPORTATION

The perils that may cause a loss to goods being transported may be appreciated by realizing the inability to control adequately or completely the forces of nature, or to prevent human failure as it affects the safe movement of goods. For example, in spite of the gyroscope, the compass, radar, sonar, and all the other modern safety devices, ocean tragedies still occur. Storms can capsize even the largest ocean vessels. Huge waves driven by hurricane winds often dump tons of sea water onto a vessel and damage cargo stowed inside. Engine failure may subject a ship to the mercy of a storm, driving the ship aground, where it quickly breaks up by the pressure of waves grinding it against rocks and sand. Poor visibility still causes collisions, and fires occur frequently. Goods are sometimes lost as a result of basic dishonesty, negligence, or incompetence of the crew handling them, or through faults in the management of the vessel. Likewise, loss of goods shipped on land comes from sources such as overturn of the vehicle, collision, fire, theft, flood, rough or careless handling, and unusual delays that result in spoilage.

THE LIABILITY OF THE CARRIER

The question arises, "Is not the carrier of the goods responsible for their safe movement?" The answer is, "Yes, to some extent." The common-law liability of the carrier differs depending upon the country in which the transportation conveyances are chartered, the applicable statutes, custom, the type of shipping, and other factors.

The Carrier's Liability in Ocean Transportation

In the field of ocean shipping, the carrier, or shipowner, is responsible only for failure to exercise due diligence. The responsibility of the carrier, which is spelled out by the Carriage of Goods by Sea Act, passed in the United States in 1936, is to make the ship seaworthy; to employ proper crew; to equip and supply the ship; and to make all holds and other carrying compartments safe and fit for the goods stored there. In addition, the carrier must exercise due care in loading, handling, and stowing cargoes, etc.

The act lists specific causes for which the carrier is definitely *not* liable. For example, the carrier is not liable for loss resulting from:

1. Errors in navigation or management of the vessel
2. Strikes or lockouts

3. Acts of God
4. Acts of war or public enemies
5. Seizure of the goods under legal process
6. Quarantine
7. Inherent vice of the goods
8. Failure of the shipper to exercise due care in the handling or packing of the goods
9. Fire
10. Perils of the seas
11. Latent defects in the hull or machinery
12. Other losses where the carrier is not at fault

Even though the carrier must prove that it was not to blame, the shipper of the goods has little claim against the carrier for loss of goods by some force outside the control of the carrier, such as windstorm or other perils of the sea.

The Carrier's Liability in Land Transportation

The common-law liability of the land carrier is considerably greater than that of the ocean carrier, but it is still not absolute. In addition to being responsible for failure to exercise due diligence, the land carrier is responsible for *all loss* to the goods *except* for acts of God, acts of public enemies or public authority, acts or negligence of the shipper, or inherent vice or quality of the goods.

Acts of God have been interpreted to mean perils such as earthquakes, storms, and floods which could not have been reasonably guarded against. Fire is not an act of God, and hence the carrier is liable for damage caused by this peril to goods in its custody.

The term **public enemy** has been interpreted to mean the action by forces at war with a domestic government, not acts of gangsters, mobs, or rioters. Thus, the carrier is liable for losses of goods by organized criminals as well as by a single thief. However, the carrier is not liable for loss when the goods are taken by legal process against the owner, such as confiscation or contraband.

Under the heading **acts or negligence of the shipper** come such causes of loss as improper loading or packing, and instances where the nature of the goods is concealed. Thus, if packages contain glassware but are not clearly marked "fragile," the carrier may be excused from loss due to breakage. Loss from poor packing that was visible to the carrier when the goods were accepted for shipment falls upon the carrier.

A loss from the **inherent nature of the goods** may be illustrated by losses due to decay, heating, rusting, drying, or fermentation. In one case the shipper sent a car of Christmas trees from Vermont to Florida. When the trees arrived, it was found that they had sustained damage by mold and rot. Investigation revealed that the trees had been shipped with excessive moisture and were locked in a steel car. As the train proceeded south, temperatures rose and the heat ruined the shipment. The carrier was held not liable because the loss stemmed from the inherent nature of the goods.[3]

Need for Transportation Insurance

The preceding discussion reveals that many types of transportation losses fall outside the responsibility of the common carrier. Furthermore, common carriers have been slow to settle losses for which they are legally liable. In land transportation the shipper usually sends goods under what is known as a **released bill of lading.** The effect of shipping goods under a released bill of lading is to limit the dollar liability of the carrier for any loss to the goods. In return, the shipper obtains a lower freight rate. In effect, the difference in freight rates is intended to compensate the shipper for the added risk of loss that must be assumed. Thus, a shipper may use outside insurance in order to achieve a prudent level of security and safety.

It is possible, of course, to shift the risk of transportation losses to the consignee of the goods. For example, goods may be shipped under terms such as FOB (Free on Board) mill or FOB factory. These terms mean that the selling price does not include the cost of freight or insurance and that the title to the goods is transferred to the buyer when the goods are laid down for shipment at the railway siding or at the pier.

OCEAN TRANSPORTATION INSURANCE

Insurance has been developed and has attained a high degree of refinement in modern-day commerce. As world trade grew and values at risk became larger, the need for coverage became more apparent. Larger ships and more refined instruments of navigation made long voyages possible, and with this development insurance protection was looked upon as almost a necessity. The major source of underwriting capacity was in England, probably because England was among the first to develop a refined system of admiralty law, a very necessary adjunct to successful insurance underwriting.

Major Types of Coverage

The four chief interests to be insured in an ocean voyage are:

1. The vessel, or the hull
2. The cargo
3. The shipping revenue or freight received by the shipowners
4. Legal liability for proved negligence

If a peril of the sea causes the sinking of a ship in deep water, one or more of these losses can result. However, each of these potential losses can be covered under various insurance policies.

Hull Policies. Policies covering the vessel itself, or **hull insurance,** are written in several different ways. The policy may cover the ship only during a given period of time, usually not to exceed one year. The insurance is commonly subject to geographical limits. If the ship is laid up in port for an extended period of time, the contract may be written at a reduced premium under the condition that the ship remain in port. The contract may cover a builder's risk while the vessel is constructed.

Cargo Policies. Contracts insuring cargo against various types of loss may be written to cover such losses only during a specified voyage, as in the case of a hull contract, or on an open basis. The latter is probably the most common type of contract. Under the **open contract,** there is no termination date, but either party may cancel upon giving notice, usually 30 days. All shipments, both incoming and outgoing, are automatically covered. The shipper reports to the insurer at regular intervals as to the values shipped or received during the previous period. The shipper declares the classes of goods and the ports between which these goods move. There is usually a limit of values that may be insured on a single vessel and a limit on the goods stowed on deck.

Freight Coverage. The money paid for the transportation of the goods, known as **freight,** is an insurable interest because in the event that freight charges are not paid, someone has lost income with which to reimburse expenses incurred in preparation for a voyage. Under the laws of the United States the earning of freight by the hull owner is dependent on the delivery of cargo, unless this relation is altered by contractual arrangements between the parties. If a ship sinks, the freight is lost and the vessel owner loses the expenses incurred plus the expected profit on the venture. The carrier's right to earn freight may be defeated by the occurrence of losses due to perils ordinarily insured against in an ocean marine insurance policy. The hull may be damaged so that it is uneconomical to complete the voyage, or the cargo may be destroyed, in which case, of course, it cannot be delivered. Also, the owner of cargo has an interest in freight arising from the obligation to pay transportation charges. Freight insurance is normally made a part of the regular hull or cargo coverage instead of being written as a separate contract.

Legal Liability for Proved Negligence. In the **running down clause (R.D.C.)** in ocean marine insurance policies covering the hull, the hull owner is protected against third-party liability claims that arise from collisions. Collision loss to the hull itself is included in the perils clause as one of the perils of the sea. The R.D.C. clause is intended to give protection in case the shipowner is held liable for negligent operation of the vessel which is the proximate cause of damage to certain property of others. The vessel owner or agent of that owner who fails to exercise the proper degree of care in the operation of the ship may be legally liable for damage to the other ship and for loss of freight revenues. The R.D.C. clause normally excludes liability for damage to cargo, harbors, wharves, or piers, and for loss of lives or personal injuries.

To provide liability coverage for personal injuries, loss of life, or damage to property other than vessels, the **protection and indemnity (P. & I.) clause** is usually added to the hull policy. This clause is intended to provide liability insurance for all events not covered by the more limited R.D.C. clause, except liability assumed under contract. Similarly, the policy may be extended to insure the shipowner's liability under the Federal Longshoremen's and Harbor Worker's Compensation Act.

Perils Clause

In 1779, Lloyd's of London developed a more or less standard ocean marine policy containing an insuring clause, the wording of which has been retained almost in its original form in policies issued today. The wording, which has been the subject of repeated court decisions interpreting almost every phrase, is as follows:

> Touching the adventures and perils which we the assurers are contented to bear and to take upon us in this voyage; they are of the seas, men of war, fire, enemies, pirates, rovers, thieves, jettisons, letters of mart and countermart, surprises, takings at sea, arrests, restraints, and detainments of all kings, princes, and people, of what nation, condition, or quality soever, barratry of the master and the mariners, and of all other perils, losses, and misfortunes, that have or shall come to the hurt, detriment, or damage of the said goods and merchandise, and ship, etc., or any part thereof.

This clause might be interpreted as an all-risk contract, since it makes reference to certain named perils "and *all other* perils, losses, and misfortunes." However, the courts have interpreted the quoted phrase as "all other *like* perils." Hence, it cannot be said that the policy is an all-risk contract, although it is very broad in its coverage. Essentially, the insuring clause covers perils *of* the sea and not all perils. Perils *on* the sea, i.e., those not finding their inherent cause arising out of the sea, are not insured unless they are specifically mentioned. Fire, for example, is a peril on the sea and is insured by specific mention. Examples of perils of the sea are action of wind and waves, stranding, and sinking. Gradual wear and tear caused by the ocean is not considered a covered peril.

The insuring clause does not specifically exclude the perils of war. However, most modern policies contain a **free-of-capture-and-seizure (F.C.&S.) clause** which excludes all loss arising out of war. In 1982 a normal war risk premium for a ship was two cents per $100. In the area around Lebanon, it was twenty-five cents per $100. In the Iraq and Iran area, rates were $1.25 per $100, or five times higher.[4] In the ocean marine policy, losses from pirates, assailing thieves, or overt dishonest actions by the ship's master or crew (barratry) are considered similar to burglary and robbery protection on land and are not losses from war. Typically, pilferage is not covered, but it may be added by endorsement.

Deductibles

Ocean marine insurance policies have two chief types of deductible clauses: memorandum and free of particular average. Attached to cargo policies, the **memorandum clause** lists various types of goods with varying percentages of deductibles that apply on a franchise basis. Thus, the memorandum clause may specify that there will be no loss payment for loss to tobacco under 20 percent, nor to sugar under 7 percent, nor to any partial loss to cheese or certain other perishables.

Some policies covering the cargo and the hull may obtain a type of deductible known as the **free-of-particular-average clause (F.P.A.).** In ocean marine insurance terminology, the word average, stemming from the French word *avarie*, means loss or damage to a ship or a cargo. Particular average means a partial loss to an interest that must be borne entirely by that interest. Particular average is contrasted to general average, which will be explained shortly. The free-of-particular-average clause usually provides that no partial loss will be paid to a single cargo interest unless the loss is caused by certain perils such as stranding, sinking, burning, or collision. Often the F.P.A. clause is limited to those losses under a certain percentage, such as 3 percent.

General Average Clause

The **general average clause** refers to losses that must be partly borne by someone other than the owner of the goods that were damaged or lost. General average losses may be total or partial, while particular average losses, by definition, are always partial. To illustrate, suppose that a certain cargo of lumber, wrapped in a large bundle, is stored on deck. To lighten the ship during a heavy storm that is threatening the safety of the whole voyage, the captain orders the lumber, worth $5,000, to be jettisoned. The action of the captain is successful in saving the ship and all the other interests. Such a sacrifice would be termed a general average, and the interests that were saved would be required to share a pro-rata part of the loss. Thus, if the ship and freight interests were valued at $100,000, and the other cargo interests at $95,000, the shipowner would have to pay one-half $\left(\frac{100}{200}\right)$ of the value of the lumber. The other cargo interests would share $\frac{95}{200}$ of the loss, and the owner of the lumber would bear $\frac{5}{200}$ of the loss. All ocean marine policies provide coverage for general average claims that may be made against the insured.

General average claims must meet certain requirements before they can be properly described as general average. The sacrifice must have been voluntary; it must have been reasonably necessary; and it must have been successful. If in the preceding case the lumber had washed overboard just before the captain ordered it jettisoned, the loss would not be termed a general average because it was not a voluntary sacrifice. This is true even though the result of the loss saves the other interests. Likewise, if the ship sinks, even though the sacrifice was voluntary, there will be no general average contributions because the sacrifice was not successful in saving the other interests.

Sue-and-Labor Clause

A clause of basic importance to the ocean marine insurance policy is known as the **sue-and-labor clause.** Under this clause, the insured is required to do everything possible to save and preserve the goods in case of loss. The insured who fails to do this has violated a policy condition and loses the rights of recovery. This means that the insured must incur reasonable expenses such as salvage fees, attorney's fees, or storage, which may be reimbursed by the insurer even if such expenses fail to recover the goods. It is possible to recover for a total loss plus sue-and-labor charges even if the face amount of the policy proceeds is exhausted.

Abandonment

In ocean marine insurance, two types of total losses are recognized: actual and constructive. **Actual total loss** occurs when the property is completely destroyed. **Constructive total loss** occurs when, even though the ship or other subject matter of insurance is not totally destroyed, it would cost more to restore it than it is worth. Under American law, before constructive total loss is said to have occurred, the damage must equal 50 percent or more of the ship's value in an undamaged condition, while under English law, damages must exceed 100 percent of the ship's sound value. In most hull policies, the English rule is stated as a policy provision. Such a provision says that if it costs more to repair the ship than its agreed-on value as stated in the policy, the ship may be abandoned to the insurer and the insured collects the full amount of the policy. The salvage then belongs to the insurer, who is usually in a better position to dispose of it than the insured, since the insurer deals with salvors all over the world and is experienced in such matters.

Warehouse-to-Warehouse Clause

Under the terms of the **warehouse-to-warehouse clause,** such protection as is afforded under the insuring agreement extends from the time the goods leave the warehouse of the shipper, even if it is located far inland, until they reach the warehouse of the consignee.

Other Insurance Clause

Unlike other forms of insurance, the ocean marine contract specifies that if there shall be more than one insurer covering a given interest, each policy shall contribute to the loss in the order of the date of its attachment. Where two or more policies attached on the same date, each would contribute in the proportion that the face amount of each policy bears to the total insurance.

Coinsurance

While there is no coinsurance clause as such in ocean marine policy, losses are settled as though each contract contained a 100 percent coinsurance clause. Ocean marine contracts are usually valued. Total losses result in an enforceable claim for the entire limit of liability as stated in the policy, and partial losses are determined, insofar as possible, by sale of the damaged article or by independent appraisal.

Warranties in Ocean Marine Insurance

There are two types of warranties in marine insurance: express and implied. **Express warranties** are written into the contract and become a condition of the coverage relating to potential causes of an insured event. **Implied warranties** are important, too. However, they are not written into the policy, but become a part of it by custom. Breach of warranty in marine insurance voids the coverage, even if the breach is immaterial to the risk.

Express Warranties. Express warranties are often used to effect certain exclusions. The following discussion reviews several of these warranties.

F. C. & S. Warranty. Under the **F. C. & S. warranty,** both parties agree that there shall be no coverage in case of loss from such perils as capture, seizure, confiscations, weapons of war, revolution, insurrection, civil war, or piracy.

S. R. & C. C. Warranty. Under the **S. R. & C. C. warranty,** it is agreed that the insurer will pay no loss due to strikes, lockouts, riots, or other labor disturbances.

Delay Warranty. Under the **delay warranty,** the insurer excludes loss traceable to delay of the voyage for any reason, unless such liability is assumed in writing.

Trading Warranty. A class of express warranties known as **trading warranties** is important in ocean marine insurance. Examples of trading warranties are warranties restricting the operation of the ship to a given area, such as a certain coastal route; warranties specifying that the insurance issued represents the true value of the ship or other interests; and warranties restricting the time during which the ship may operate, such as only during the open season on the Great Lakes.

Implied Warranties. There are three implied warranties in marine insurance. These relate to seaworthiness, deviation, and legality.

Seaworthiness. If a ship leaves port without being in safe condition, the implied warranty as to seaworthiness has been breached and the entire coverage is immediately void. If the ship were seaworthy when it left port but became unseaworthy later on, the warranty is not breached. Seaworthiness involves such factors as having a sound hull, engines in good running order, a qualified captain and crew, proper supplies for the voyage to be undertaken, and sufficient fuel.

Deviation. The warranty as to deviation is breached when a vessel, without good and sufficient reason, departs from the prescribed course of the voyage, but without the intention of abandoning the voyage originally contemplated. The liability of the insurer ceases the moment that the ship departs from its course; but mere intention to deviate, not accompanied by an actual change of course, does not relieve the insurer of liability. Undue delay may constitute a deviation. The deviation or delay does not have to increase the hazard of the voyage in order to release the insurer, because any breach of warranty, regardless of whether or not the warranty was material to the risk, voids the contract. Even if the ship later resumes course and then suffers a loss, there is no coverage unless later negotiations with the insurer have restored the insurance.

There are certain causes that will excuse a deviation that has not been authorized by contract. These fall into two main groups: unavoidable necessity and aiding in saving human life. **Unavoidable necessity** may be proved when a ship is blown off course, puts into a port of distress, deviates to escape capture, is taken over by mutineers, or is carried off course by a warship. **Aiding in saving human life** is illustrated by a ship's deviating to help a vessel in distress. It is to be noted, however, that deviation to save *property only* is not permitted.

Legality. The implied warranty of legality is one that is never waived. If the voyage is illegal under the laws of the country under whose dominion the ship operates, the insurance is void. Under the laws of the United States, insurance on a ship engaged in running marijuana would be void, but such a purpose might not be illegal under the laws of another country, and in that country the insurance contract would be enforceable. To provide insurance against illegal enterprise is obviously against public policy, and this accounts for the fact that the warranty of legality cannot be waived.

LAND TRANSPORTATION INSURANCE

In the early period of industrial development, buyers of goods generally took delivery at an ocean port and conducted most of their business from that port. With the growth of inland centers of commerce, inland shipments of ocean cargo by way of railroad or canal became common, and pressure grew for an extension of the ocean marine contract to cover the perils of land transportation. The warehouse-to-warehouse clause was developed to meet this need. But the ocean marine contract was not suited to the needs of land transportation insurance, and so there developed a branch of insurance known as inland marine.

The Marine Definition

Inland marine insurance is defined by criteria known as the nationwide marine definition of the National Association of Insurance Commissioners. This definition, first formulated in 1933 and completely revised in 1953, serves as a guide for regulatory authorities in governing rating procedures, underwriting methods, contract provisions, and other matters. The five subjects of insurance that are recognized include contracts covering imports, exports, domestic shipments, instrumentalities of transportation and communication, and floaters, which are policies on movable property.

The nationwide marine definition does not distinguish between inland or ocean marine insurance. It permits insurance on certain classes of goods and contains a section of prohibited risks. In general, the basis for differentiating permitted from prohibited risks is mobility.

Imports and Exports. Imports and exports may be covered under marine contracts as long as the perils of transportation are included. When goods lose their identity as shipments, they are no longer eligible for coverage under a marine policy. Thus, an import loses its characteristics as an import when it is sold and delivered by the importer, removed from storage and placed on sale as part of the importer's stock in trade, or delivered for manufacturing or processing.

Domestic Shipments. Domestic shipments may be insured under a marine contract as long as the policy covers the perils of transportation. Goods qualify for coverage while they are in a fixed location of a customer who has them on consignment, or in a warehouse of a carrier where storage is incidental to their transportation. However, such goods may not be covered under a marine contract while they are at the factory or warehouse location of the owner.

Instrumentalities of Transportation and Communication. Bridges, tunnels, piers, wharves, docks, pipelines, power transmission and telephone lines, radio and television towers, outdoor cranes, and loading bridges are among the so-called instrumentalities of transportation and communication that may be insured under a marine insurance contract.

Inland Transit Policy

A basic contract covering domestic shipments primarily by land transportation systems is known as the **inland transit policy.** Sometimes called the **annual transit floater,** this form of insurance is designed for manufacturers, retailers, wholesalers, and others who ship or receive a substantial volume of goods. The contract usually covers shipments by rail and railway express, and by public truckers, and may cover coastal shipments by ship between ports on the eastern coast of the United States and the Gulf of Mexico. It covers goods in the hands of other transportation agencies when in connection with rail, railway express, or steamer shipments. Shipments by mail or by aircraft are not usually covered unless they are specifically named in the policy.

Perils. There is no standard form for the inland transit policy, but all contracts follow a similar pattern. The contracts are typically written on a named-peril basis, covering the perils of transportation, which include collision, derailment, overturning of the vehicle, rising water, tornado, fire, lightning, and windstorm. Sometimes the policy covers theft of an entire shipping package, but it seldom covers pilferage except when the goods are shipped by express. In general, the policies exclude loss due to strike, riot, civil commotion, war, delay of shipment, loss of market, illegal trade, inherent vice of the goods, leakage, or breakage, unless caused by one of the basic perils insured against.

Among the types of property excluded are accounts, bills, deeds, evidences of debt, money, notes, securities, and exports after arrival at seaboard. Variations in these provisions are frequently negotiated between the parties. For example, an all-risk form for the inland transit policy is available for certain types of shippers, with the insuring clause reading, "This policy insures against all risks of loss or damage to the insured property from an external cause (including general average and/or salvage charges and expresses) except as herein excluded."

Loss Limits. The inland transit policy normally has several types of liability limits. For example, there will be a limit of loss of a given amount, often 5 percent of the annual estimated shipments, while the goods are in the custody of any one shipping agency. There will be a limit of 10 percent of the annual estimated shipments in any one casualty. For purposes of loss settlement, goods are valued at invoice cost plus any prepaid or advanced freight or other costs due on the goods.

Rates. If the common carrier assumes the liability for loss of goods at their full valuation, the rates are considerably higher than if the goods are shipped under a released bill of lading, whereby someone else assumes liability for losses above a certain amount. The express agency, for example, charges 10 cents per $100 for any declared valuation in excess of $50, whereas the insurance rate will probably be about half of that amount, depending on the individual circumstances of the shipper's business. Furthermore, the insurance coverage is broader than the protection given by the express company, which insures only for the amounts for which it is legally liable. This liability is less than complete or absolute. A deposit premium is required by the insurer, and the final premium is determined by audit.

Trip Transit Insurance

For the individual or business firm that makes only an occasional shipment, the trip transit policy is especially applicable. This policy covers on a named-peril basis and is written for a specific shipment of goods between named locations. The type of conveyance may be either a common carrier or a private carrier of some type, such as a horse-drawn vehicle, a public trucker, or a trailer. It is common to insure household furniture, merchandise, machinery, or livestock under trip transit insurance contracts. The perils insured, conditions, and exclusions are similar to the inland transit and blanket motor cargo contracts. For example, leaking, marring, scratching, and breaking are excluded unless caused by certain named perils. This limitation is of special interest to shippers of household goods that are susceptible to damage by freight car movement.

SUMMARY

1. The building and personal property coverage form (BPPCF) provides coverage for owned real property, owned personal property, and nonowned personal property.

2. Coverage under the BPPCF may be scheduled (the property insured is specifically listed) or blanket (multiple properties are insured under a single item).

3. The special multiple policy (SMP) is designed to meet the needs of business people. Fire and extended coverage on the building is mandatory, as is liability insurance. Crime insurance and boiler/machinery policies may be purchased on an optional basis. The program is attractive to business people because rate discounts are given.

4. The major contracts of insurance covering indirect or consequential losses are classified under two headings: contracts with and without a time element. Time-element policies measure the loss in terms of given time periods, while those without a time element use some other basis in measuring loss.

5. Consequential losses are often greater than the loss of property destroyed directly by fire or some other peril. Yet they are often overlooked in an otherwise complete insurance program.

6. The most important single type of time-element contract is called business income insurance, which is designed to indemnify the insured for loss of profits and fixed charges that are occasioned by stoppage of business due to some named peril.

7. Other time-element contracts of insurance are (a) contingent business income insurance, which indemnifies for losses due to interruption of the business of a major supplier or customer; (b) extra-expense insurance, which indemnifies for the extra cost caused when a named peril, while not causing a business shutdown, necessitates a higher cost of operation than normal; (c) rental-value insurance, which indemnifies for loss of rents when fire renders a building unlivable; (d) leasehold-interest insurance, which indemnifies the tenant for loss of a valuable lease cancelled before its usual termination due to fire or some other named peril; and (e) excess-rental value insurance, which indemnifies a landlord who loses a favorable lease due to fire or some other named peril.

8. Examples of contracts of insurance without a time element are (a) profits insurance, which indemnifies the insured for loss of profits expected from the sale of finished goods; (b) accounts receivable insurance, which indemnifies for accounts rendered uncollectible because a fire or other named peril destroys the records that give evidence of the debts; and (c) rain insurance, which indemnifies for the loss of profits and for expenses incurred when rain or other type of precipitation decreases expected attendance at some public event.

9. Reporting forms are used to insure property that fluctuates in value from one period to the next.

10. Two of the factors that increase the demand for transportation insurance are the seriousness and frequency of losses from transportation perils and the fact that the legal liability of the common carrier for safe shipment of the goods is neither absolute nor complete.

11. The major types of policies in ocean marine insurance are contracts covering the hull, the cargo, the freight, and the legal liability of the carrier for proved negligence. The

coverage is broad, but it is still on a named-peril basis.

12. Warranties in ocean marine insurance are of extreme importance, and any breach, no matter how slight, voids the contract. Express warranties are typified by trading warranties of various kinds. The implied warranties are those of seaworthiness, deviation, and legality.

13. Insurance on the perils of land transportation grew out of contracts of ocean marine insurance. The marine definition delineates five types of insurance to be allowed as marine insurance, with no distinction now being made between ocean and inland marine. The five groups are contracts covering imports, exports, domestic shipments, instrumentalities of communication and transportation, and floater risks. The one element common to all these contracts is that the subject of insurance is essentially mobile, either actually or constructively.

14. The inland policy, the blanket motor cargo policy, and the trip transit policy are three basic contracts covering the perils of land transportation. In general, it is cheaper and better to use these policies than to rely on insurance covering the interest of the common carrier or on the common-law liability of the common carrier for safe carriage of the goods.

15. Block policies, issued on an all-risk basis to specific types of retail and wholesale concerns by inland marine insurers, are significant because they have tended to set the pattern for all-risk insurance on floating business property, issued under the commercial property policy program. Common block policies are the jewelers' block, the camera and musical instrument dealers' block, and the equipment dealers' block.

16. In contrast to block forms, scheduled property floaters, generally issued on a named-peril basis, cover an extremely wide variety of floating business property. Examples of the different needs met by these forms are the contractor's equipment floater and the livestock floater.

17. Because of the increasing importance of credit sales in the United States, the conditional sales floater, covering unpaid-for property in the hands of buyers, has assumed some significance as a tool of risk management in retail stores, in sales finance institutions, and for others who take installment sales risks. The conditional sales floater insures the goods against loss from named perils and may cover the interest of the buyer and seller.

The parcel-post policy, the first-class mail floater, and the registered-mail floater, used by those who ship valuables by mail, may be arranged in an economical and convenient manner to meet the widely varying needs of these individuals.

QUESTIONS FOR REVIEW

1. The Bond Company takes out $100,000 of business income insurance with 50 percent coinsurance. It is estimated that business income is $200,000. The Perez Company also estimates business income at $200,000, but takes out $150,000 coverage on the gross earnings form with 50 percent coinsurance and with the agreed amount endorsement. In each case actual business income turns out to be $400,000.

   (a) Contrast the coverage coinsurance effects.

   (b) If Perez's gross earnings had increased to $500,000, would it have been subject to coinsurance penalties? Why or why not?

   (c) Could Perez have collected as much as $150,000 if its business income had been $250,000? Why or why not?

2. What are the extensions of coverage in the building and personal property form? Why are they included in the contract?

3. How does the building and personal property form provide coverage for perils insured against? Explain the different options available for perils insured against.

4. Why do insureds need reporting forms? Explain what happens when there are late or incorrect reports under a reporting form.

5. What are some of the problems associated with business income insurance policies?

6. Under accounts receivable insurance, what three indemnities are made by the insurer?

7. What is the difference between rental-value and rental-income insurance?

8. What perils are insured against in an ocean marine insurance policy?

9. Identify and explain the major ocean marine coverages available.

10. How does the liability of the carrier differ between land and ocean transportation?

QUESTIONS FOR DISCUSSION

1. "In a sense, life insurance may be properly termed a consequential-loss contract." Explain.

2. Distinguish between time-element coverage and contracts without a time element.

3. If business improves considerably during the year, the individual purchaser of business income insurance may fail to collect in full for a partial loss under the policy. How is this possible? Explain.

4. How should a firm go about determining how much business income insurance to carry? Discuss.

5. A dairy asks its agent to look into a business income insurance policy, but the agent, upon inquiry, recommends that this type of insurance would not be suitable for the dairy. The agent recommends another policy. Why might business income insurance not be appropriate for the dairy, and what other policy would the agent probably recommend?

6. In a recent case (*Bolta Rubber Company* v. *Lowell Trucking Corporation*, 37 N.E.2d 873) a trucking company insured under a motor cargo policy to protect its legal liability as a common carrier. The policy contained a warranty that each insured truck would be equipped with a burglar alarm in good working order. A truck was held up. It was determined that the burglar alarm system had been turned off at the time of the holdup. The trucker was held liable for $1,000. Discuss the liability and rights of the insurer and the trucker.

7. The antiquated wording in the 1779 Lloyd's ocean perils clause is retained in its essential outline in modern-day policies. Suggest reasons for this.

8. The S. S. *Victory* runs aground as it enters the harbor at Honolulu. Due to various contingencies, it is impossible to refloat the vessel before a storm strikes. Considerable damage is done to the vessel and the cargo, especially to the Number 3 hold in which the Smith Company's merchandise (pens and pencils) is packed. The pens and pencils are so badly battered that in order to save the shipment from being a total loss, it is necessary that $2,000 be spent on reconditioning them. The Smith Company seeks recovery from the insurer for the entire $5,000 for which the shipment is insured, on the grounds that there is actually a total loss. Do you agree? Why or why not?

(a) Explain in your own words the meaning of general average.

(b) Why should the various interests be required to pay such claims?

NEW TERMS AND CONCEPTS

Acts of God
Acts or Negligence
    of Shipper
Agreed Amount
    Endorsement
Bailee
Bailor
Block Policy
Bottomry Contracts
Building and Personal
    Property Coverage Form
Business Income
    Insurance
Consequential Losses
    Earnings Form
Contractors' Equipment
    Floater
Extended Period of
    Indemnity
Extra Expense

Free of Capture and Seizure
Freight
General Average
Inherent Nature of Goods
Jewelers' Block Policy
Memorandum Clause
Nontime-Element Contracts
Parcel-Post Policy
Profits Insurance
Protection-and-Indemnity
    Clause
Public Enemy
Released Bill of Lading
Rental Income
Rental Value
Running-Down Clause
Scheduled Property Floater
Simplified Commercial
    Lines Portfolio Policy
Time-Element Contracts

NOTES

1 R. E. Lauterbach, "Business Interruption," Insurance Series No. 115 (New York: American Management Association), pp. 43–44.

2 Occasionally, valued policies are written in the London market.

3 *Austin* v. *Seaboard Air Line Railway Co.*, 188 Fed. (2d) 239 (1951).

4 *Business Insurance* (July 19, 1982), p. 46.

21 BUSINESS LIABILITY INSURANCE

After studying this chapter, you should be able to:

1. Describe the content of insuring clauses in commercial general liability policies and the supplementary benefits of such policies.
2. Explain how limits of liability are determined in commercial liability policies.
3. Differentiate between claims-made coverage and occurrence coverage.
4. Identify the different parts of the commercial general liability policy, the policy's exclusions, and several endorsements that can be used with it.
5. State the difference between professional liability insurance and regular liability insurance.
6. Indicate how businesses use commercial umbrella policies.

Liability insurance is an outgrowth, and in fact is an inevitable result, of the legal relationships in society that can produce successful lawsuits against individuals for negligence. This is a key factor in understanding the scope of and the reasons for the liability contracts to be discussed in this chapter.

As it became recognized that negligence formed the basis for a damage suit, a demand arose for protection against the financial consequences of such suits. At first the courts frowned upon liability insurance in the belief that contracts of this nature would tend to encourage reckless conduct and thus result in more injuries to persons and property. Later it was recognized that there was a true need for financial protection and that the existence of insurance did not cause an unwarranted degree of irresponsible conduct. Today the law takes the attitude that *failure* to obtain liability insurance against consequences of negligence in itself constitutes irresponsible financial behavior. The prime example is that all states have enacted legislation imposing penalties for failure to provide some sort of financial protection against negligence in the operation of automobiles.

COMMON LIABILITY CONTRACT PROVISIONS

No matter what type of liability a policy insures against, there are certain provisions that appear in all liability insurance contracts. They include the insuring clause, supplementary payments clause, definition of the insured, exclusions, limits of liability, subrogation, and notice.

The Insuring Clause

Some insuring agreements contain separate clauses for bodily injury and property damage, and sometimes the two are combined into one clause such as the following:

> To pay, on behalf of the insured, all sums that the insured shall become legally obligated to pay as damages because of bodily injury, sickness or disease, including death at any time resulting therefrom, or because of injury to or destruction of property, including loss of use thereof, sustained by any person and caused by accident.

The following points apply to the interpretation of this typical agreement:

1. The policy of liability insurance almost invariably states that the insurer is bound to pay only the sums that the insured is legally obligated to pay. Unless specifically insured, voluntary payments are not covered, even if made in good faith because of what is felt to be a moral obligation to the injured party. This, of course, does not mean that every case must be brought into court to determine legal obligation—it is estimated that more than 95 percent of all cases are settled out of court.
2. The act causing the injury must be accidental. However, the insured can be covered for torts other than negligence, such as libel, slander, and assault and battery, which are not accidental. It will be recalled that a basic requirement of an insurable peril is that it be fortuitous in nature. In spite of this, most liability policies now appear without the "caused by accident" clause. Instead, wording is substituted under which the insurer is liable for any "occurrence" giving rise to legal liability. Even though these policies declare that injuries caused intentionally by the insured are excluded, there is the probability that the use of "occurrence"

gives more coverage than the "caused by accident" wording. The word "accident" suggests a sudden, unexpected, abnormal event, while the word "occurrence," when modified to exclude intentional acts, connotes unexpected and abnormal events, but not necessarily sudden events. For example, suppose a contractor is blasting an excavation for a new building and, while there is no immediate damage observable to a neighboring property, over a period of days the earth is so shaken that the foundations of nearby buildings are damaged. Under the "caused by accident" wording, there may be some doubt that this injury is covered since the contractor should know the probable consequences of his actions and there is no sudden damage due to the blasting. Under the "occurrence" wording, unless it is demonstrated that the contractor deliberately continued actions known to be destructive, the liability for the damage would be recovered.

Supplementary Payments

Supplementary benefits are an important portion of any liability insurance contract. These benefits are paid in addition to any benefits paid by the basic liability policy. The insurance company promises to provide coverage for bodily injury and property damage liability and also supplementary benefits. Typically, the insurer states that it will:

1. Defend any suit against the insured alleging an injury, sickness, disease, or destruction and seeking damages on account thereof, even if such suit is groundless, false, or fraudulent; but the company may make such investigation, negotiation, and settlement of any claim or suit as it deems expedient.
2. Pay all premiums on bonds to release attachments for an amount not in excess of the applicable limit of liability of this policy, and all premiums on appeal bonds required in any such defended suit, but without obligation to apply for or furnish such bonds.
3. Pay all expenses incurred by the company, all costs taxed against the insured in any such suit, and all interest accruing after entry of judgment until the company has paid or tendered or deposited in court such part of such judgment as does not exceed the limit of the company's liability thereon.
4. Pay expenses incurred by the insured for such immediate medical and surgical relief to others as shall be imperative at the time of the accident.
5. Reimburse the insured for all reasonable expenses, including loss of earnings up to some limit (usually a specified dollars-per-day limit that varies by contract) incurred at the company's request; and the amounts so incurred, except settlements of claims and suits, are payable by the company in addition to the applicable limit of liability of this policy.

In other words, all contracts of liability insurance provide in the insuring agreement to pay for the legal defense of the insured and other related costs. Liability insurance has sometimes been termed defense insurance because in a majority of cases liability suits are settled out of court by negotiation between attorneys. The insured knows that the worry and care of negotiations are assumed by the insurer. The following points concerning the supplementary payments provisions are worth noting:

1. The fact that the insurer agrees to defend any suit, even if it is groundless, false, or fraudulent, relieves the insured of the worry and expense of nuisance cases. In such cases the plaintiff is relying on the fact that a reputable business house will sometimes settle a small but groundless claim rather than go to the expense of defending itself in court. The insurer already has a legal staff, the cost of which is distributed over many similar claims in a given year and can thus handle each case economically. Without insurance, a defendant might wish to retain counsel even if the amount involved were small. It should be noted that the term *any suit* does not mean that the insurer will defend a court action falling outside the scope of a negligence action.

2. Sometimes courts require that the alleged wrongdoer post a bond to guarantee that, pending the outcome of a negligence action, he or she will not dispose of property subject to confiscation if the case is lost. In cases where a decision has been lost in the lower court and is appealed to a higher court, a bond must be posted to guarantee that if the defendant loses in the higher court, the judgment will be paid. The insurer agrees to pay the premium on these bonds, plus any accrued interest after the date of the judgment.

3. Under the other terms of the liability policy, the insurer has the right to require the insured to appear in court personally in legal actions arising under the policy.

Definition of the Insured

All contracts of liability insurance specifically set forth the party who is to be considered the insured. The concept of the insured individual in liability policies is generally very broad, and the wording differs for each type of policy. In the case of a business firm, the intent is to include all partners, officers, directors, and proprietors in their capacities as representatives of the particular business. It is not uncommon to write liability contracts, for payment of an extra premium, naming other parties as additional insureds.

Exclusions

Among the various liability insurance contracts, certain exclusions appear almost universally. Among these are the following:

1. In the case of business policies, all nonbusiness activities giving rise to damage suits are excluded. In personal contracts, all business pursuits giving rise to damage suits are excluded.

2. There is an attempt in each policy to exclude all sources of liability intended to be covered in other contracts, or intended to be covered by a special provision for an extra premium. Thus, in the commercial

general liability policy, liability from pollution is excluded.

3. Nearly all liability contracts exclude damage to property belonging to or rented to the insured, or property in the care, custody, or control of the insured, under the general theory that a person cannot be liable to one's self for one's own negligence. The insured is expected to obtain physical damage insurance, such as fire or lightning insurance, to cover the accidental loss of property that he or she owns or is otherwise legally liable for.

The question sometimes arises as to the conditions under which property is in the care, custody, or control of the insured. For example, if a mechanic is working on the fan belt of an engine in a customer's car, and the fan blade accidentally breaks off and puts a hole in the radiator, is the damage covered under the garage liability policy, or is it excluded under the construction that the car is in the care and custody of the insured and hence damage to any part of the car is excluded? A liberal policy interpretation would hold that the damage is covered and that only damage to property actually being worked on is excluded. Thus, in one case a contractor installed a heat exchange unit. While it was being tested, but before the job was abandoned, damage resulted. The court held that the damage was covered.[1] In another case, however, the court held that damage to a concrete retaining wall by a bulldozer was excluded because the wall was "in the care, custody, and control" of the contractor at the time of the damage.[2] There seems to be no general rule applicable to such cases, except the general rule that always applies—ambiguities in contractual language will be construed against the insurer.

Some insurers offer broadened policies under which the "care, custody, and control" exclusion is liberalized. Of special interest to contractors, the **broad form property damage liability program,** as it is called, spells out in considerable detail just what property is covered and under what terms.

Limits of Liability

Under all policies of liability insurance, there are limits of liability of various sorts. For example, in the Business Auto Policy contract, the limits might be $100,000 for bodily injury liability for any one person, and $300,000 for each accident. For property damage liability, there might be a limitation of $50,000 for each accident. This means that if three or more of the insured's customers are injured in a single accident, there is an aggregate limitation of $300,000, with no coverage for each individual claim to be in excess of $100,000. If there is more than one insured named in the policy, the question arises, are these limits of liability applicable to each insured, thus doubling or tripling the stated limits? The answer is no.

In some policies, such as the comprehensive personal liability policy (CPL), there is only a single limit of liability. Both bodily injury and property damage liability are insured under this limit. As there are no per-person restrictions with respect to bodily injury, the entire policy limit may be paid to one person.

Aggregate limits are also used in liability policies. They are most often applied to product liability and property damage liability policies. Under the aggregate limit approach the policy limit is placed on an annual basis rather than on an occurrence basis. If the product liability limit were set at $500,000, regardless of the number of claims or their severity, the insurance company would only pay up to $500,000 on the insured's behalf during the year. Under an occurrence limit it is theoretically possible that an insurer could pay several $500,000 claims during the contract year.

Another important aspect of the policy limit is the time period covered. The policy obviously has an inception and termination date, but does it cover a loss when a person is exposed (**exposure doctrine**) to a product or a dangerous substance, or should coverage apply only when the claimant's disease (injury) is discovered (**manifestation doctrine**)? Still a third approach would be to say that all policies in force during the exposure and manifestation period would apply. This last approach is called the **triple-trigger approach** and provides the greatest amount of coverage for the insured. These doctrines were very important in the DES drug and asbestos trials.[3]

In October, 1981, the District of Columbia Court of Appeals ruled in *Keene* v. *INA* that the triple-trigger rule was more appropriate, and in March, 1982, the Supreme Court of the United States declined to review the case when INA appealed. Now drug manufacturers are asking the courts to apply the triple-trigger rule to the DES cases.

While the triple-trigger approach is very attractive to insureds, it causes some problems for insurers. For instance, a firm could self-insure for three years and then purchase insurance for a large amount in the fourth year. Since either the exposure or the manifestation approach would apply, the insurance would cover the three years when the insured did not purchase insurance. This entire area of policy limits in the product liability line is very complex. With the courts constantly expanding insurer liability, the future is very uncertain regarding the cost and availability of product liability insurance.

To address some of the problems presented by courts' liberal interpretations of policy limits, insurance companies have established a new set of limits in the Simplified Commercial Lines Portfolio policy (SCLP). The liability coverage in the SCLP policy is called the Commercial General Liability form. Its initials, CGL, are the same as an older policy called the Comprehensive General Liability policy. In our discussions CGL means Commercial General Liability.

The SCLP has separate limits of liability for general liability, products and completed operations, advertising and personal liability, medical payments, and fire legal liability. In addition, there is an annual aggregate limit of liability that applies to all general, advertising, personal injury, medical payments, and fire legal liability claims. Once the total amount claimed from these four exposures exceeds the annual aggregate, the insurance company will not pay any more claims under that policy. An aggregate limit means that the policy will only pay up to a predetermined amount per year regardless of the number of claims or defense costs. The products and completed operations limit is separate from the overall aggregate liability limit. However, it also has an aggregate limit that represents the maximum amount that the insurer will pay in one year.

Claims-made versus Occurrence Coverage

Due to the tremendously high dollar amount of claims and awards associated with asbestos and other "long tail" liability exposures, the insurance industry is attempting to reduce its uncertainty concerning the payment of future claims. By a liability line's having a "long tail" it is meant that that line will take a long time (four to ten years) to develop claims from a given event. Product liability and professional liability are examples of "long tail" liability lines.

Under the traditional occurrence policy, any event in 1988 that led to a claim in 1988 or any future year would be covered by the 1988 policy. Thus, if a member of the public was exposed to some harmful substance in 1988 and it took ten years for the injury to manifest itself, the 1988 insurer was expected to defend and settle the claim in 1998 and beyond. This approach gave the insured great certainty, but left the insurer in a situation where it did not know the cost of its product (1988 losses) for five, ten, or fifteen years.

Prior to the 1970s the occurrence approach worked in a reasonable manner. However, the combination of social pressure and rapid economic inflation led to a situation where insurers felt they could no longer accurately price their products under an occurrence policy. As a result, the claims-made policy was developed.

Under the original claims-made policy, a 1988 policy pays only for those claims that are made during 1988. The event that caused the claim to be made can occur in 1988 or any prior year. Once the year 1988 is over, the insurer can determine the total amounts of claims paid and of claims outstanding, and can have more current data to price its product for the following year. The only major uncertainty to the insurer for the 1988 policy year is whether the loss reserves on reported claims is accurate. However, the insured is not in such a secure position. The certainty gained by the insurer is offset by greater uncertainty on the part of the insured.

Under the claims-made approach, the insured has protection for 1988 events only if insurance is purchased every year after 1988. If for some reason insurance is not purchased in 1990 (say, coverage is not available or is priced too high), and a claim from a 1988 event is filed in 1990, the insured does not have any protection.

When an insured first changes from an occurrence to a claims-made policy in a given year, there are few problems. The old occurrence policies pay for claims from events occurring before year x, and the claims-made policy pays for claims made in year x arising from events in year x. However, in subsequent years problems can arise. If in year x + 5 a major loss occurs, and the insurance company does not renew the policy, the insured must find another insurer. The new insurer will most likely choose a retroactive date that starts on January 1, year x + 6. The retroactive date determines the time on which the policy becomes effective for prior events that lead to claims made in year x + 6. In the present case it is possible for the retroactive date to be year x, but most likely it would be the beginning of year x + 6. Any claim from year x + 5 will not be paid by the new policy. Thus, since the claims for the new policy were not made in year x + 5, the policy will not pay. Accordingly, the insured, lacking coverage, must carry the burden of maintaining continuous coverage.

To ease the burden placed on the insured by the claims-made policy, the insurance industry has instituted the following special provisions for such policies.

Basic Extended Reporting Period. This provision has two parts. The first gives the insured an extra 60 days of coverage for a claim to be made for an event (unknown to the insured) that occurred before the policy expired. For example, an event could have happened on December 24, year x + 5, and a claim not made until February 15, year x + 6. The policy would still cover the loss. If the claim had been made on March 15, year x + 6, no coverage would be available on the policy.

The second provision provides an **extended period of indemnity** of five years for known events, but where claims were not filed during the policy year. Again, assume a loss on December 24, year x + 5, that is known to the insured and the insurer. In year x + 9 a claim resulting from that event is filed. In this situation the claims-made policy covering year x + 5 will pay the claim. However, if the claim was made in year x + 12, the policy would not pay because the claim was made after five years had elapsed.

These two provisions provide some added protection for the insured; but even when combined, they are not as good as the traditional occurrence policy. To match the coverage of the traditional occurrence coverage, the insured must purchase the supplemental tail.

Supplemental Tail. This endorsement must be requested in writing within 60 days of the end of the policy term. If the policy ends on December 31, the endorsement must be requested by March 1. The supplemental tail has its own aggregate limit equal to the original policy's limit, and the insurer cannot charge more than 200 percent of the original policy's premium. While the supplement can be expensive, it does offer an alternative for an insured with a severe liability loss exposure.

Subrogation

Practically all contracts of liability insurance are subject to the right of subrogation by the insurer against any liable third party. This right is very important. It may turn out, for example, that while the insured is held legally liable for some act of negligence, someone else has agreed to assume this liability by contract or is held liable because the insured is the agent or servant of a third party. If the insurer pays the claim, it has a right to any such claims that the insured may have had against others.

Notice

Like all insurance policies, liability contracts require immediate notice of accident and claim or suit. It is especially important that this condition be complied with, since otherwise available witnesses may be dispersed and evidence dissipated so as to make it difficult or impossible to determine later what actually happened. Such information is vital to the successful defense of the insured, and without prompt notice the insurer is greatly handicapped.

COMMERCIAL LIABILITY INSURANCE

Various types of business liability policies are available for business concerns. Our investigation will focus on the commercial general liability, business auto, professional liability, and commercial umbrella policies.

COMMERCIAL GENERAL LIABILITY (CGL)

The commercial general liability policy is designed to give the insured considerable flexibility. It consists of a policy jacket that contains a declarations page and a series of definitions of important terms used in the policies that are attached to the policy jacket.

The CGL covers, on an occurrence or claims-made basis, bodily injury and property damage losses resulting from (1) conditions of the premises, (2) business operations, (3) products liability, (4) completed operations, and (5) operations of independent contractors.

Loss arising from the conditions of the premises include customers slipping on a wet spot on the floor, falling down unsafe stairs, or being exposed to caustic chemicals on the insured's premises. Business operations liability losses could result from performing activities at a customer's home: while installing drapes the insured's employee could damage property at the customer's home, or a furniture store's delivery people could drop a piece of furniture and damage a customer's floor.

Products liability is different from (1) and (2) in that the loss must occur away from the premises and after the business person has relinquished control. An exception is a situation where the product is consumed on the premises, as in a restaurant.

Situations where product-liability claims have arisen are numerous. In one case a five-year-old boy was awarded $193,000 because the suit his parents purchased was considered highly ignitable by the court. The boy had burns covering 80 percent of his body.[4] In another case a kitchen stove was held to be defective, and the manufacturer had to pay $85,000 for damages to a home. The stove was supposed to be one equipped with "a burner with a brain." Unfortunately the brain didn't work very well and the stove created a fire that destroyed the house.[5]

Completed operations losses are most often associated with contractors or maintenance people. These losses are said to occur after a person has finished the job and given control of it to the customer. (If the loss occurs while the contractor is working on the item, the loss is considered a business operations loss.) Examples of completed operations losses are as follows. (1) A steel bin was built by a contractor, and after the bin collapsed it was found that certain welds were not made. Extensive damage to buildings and machinery occurred, and one person was killed. The court awarded a judgment of $199,650.[6] (2) A plumbing firm was held liable for $5,000 of water damage to a home when a pipe connected to a washbowl became disconnected. The court ruled that the plumber had been negligent in installing the pipe.[7] (3) A thermostatic fan system was installed by a furnace company and was not operating properly. The furnace company was called several times to fix it, but before the firm did so the system caused $5,500 of damage for which the furnace company was held responsible.[8]

Losses resulting from operations of independent contractors are automatically insured in the CGL. In other business-liability contracts the protection may be added by the protective liability endorsement. This coverage provides protection to the insured from (1) a loss caused by an independent contractor hired by the insured, and (2) an act or an omission of the insured in supervising the activities of an independent contractor.[9] In one case an oil company contracted with a construction firm to build a pipeline. While blasting, the construction firm caused damage to a third party's property. The court held the oil company liable even though the oil company and the contractor signed an agreement making the contractor liable for the blasting.[10]

All newly acquired premises are automatically covered for the duration of the policy. After the policy's term expires, the insurer will audit the exposure and collect an additional premium if any new premises have been acquired or if unforeseen exposures have developed. Likewise, it would refund some premium if the deposit premium had been in excess.

Exclusions in the CGL

While the CGL provides very broad coverage, it does have numerous exclusions. Excluded business liability exposures include owned watercraft away from the premises; aircraft; property in the insured's care, custody, and control; transportation of mobile equipment; failure of an insured's product to perform; injury to work performed by the insured; war; nuclear exposures; and workers' compensation. Besides these exclusions, there are several others that deserve special attention.

Automobile. The automobile exposure is excluded except for the parking of nonowned automobiles on the premises. This exception is beneficial to restaurants and hotels whose employees park their customers' automobiles.

Product Recall. The act of recalling (withdrawing) defective products from the marketplace is excluded in the CGL. This exclusion is called the **sistership exclusion.** A manufacturer can purchase recall insurance to cover this exposure. Protection is available in nonstandard markets under specialty forms containing detailed provisions requiring the insured to (1) take all reasonable steps to prevent further loss once a defective product is identified, and (2) repair faulty work.

Liquor Liability. Finally, liability arising from the responsibility imposed by a liquor law is excluded. Known as the **dramshop exclusion,** this provision appears in most liability contracts because in some states the dramshop laws make the seller or distributor of alcoholic beverages liable for losses that can be traced to the use of alcohol sold or distributed by him or her. Thus, an intoxicated person may leave an establishment that dispenses liquor and injure someone or destroy property. Under the state's dramshop law, the liability might be traced back to the insured establishment. This liability may be covered by payment of an additional premium.

Pollution. In the commercial general liability policy liability for pollution loss is excluded. In the old comprehensive general liability policy accidental pollution was covered, but courts were so liberal in their interpretation of what an accident was, that insurers felt that they had to exclude the pollution peril altogether.

Endorsements

There is no need for as many endorsements as in the past, since the commercial general liability form is designed to give coverage for medical payments, advertising and personal liability (libel and slander), contractual and host liquor liability, (but not liquor liability), limited worldwide coverage, and limited nonowned watercraft and fire legal liability. However, for an additional premium, insurance companies are willing to add endorsements that give broader coverage. Examples of such endorsements would be product recall insurance, pollution insurance, and full worldwide coverage.

A new endorsement, **exclusion of specific accident(s), products, work, or location(s),** in the commercial general liability policy gives the insurance company the ability to exclude losses from a specific product or accident, a batch of a product, and a given location or locations of the insured. Through the use of this endorsement, the insured may be able to obtain an earlier retroactive date than if the specific items were not excluded. Also, the endorsement can be used where the insured wants to self-insure some products or locations but buy insurance on all the others.

Vendor's Endorsement. Because of the importance of the products liability hazard, many retailers refuse to handle the goods of a manufacturer or a wholesaler unless they are provided with evidence that the distributor has protected them with products liability insurance. This is usually accomplished by naming the retailer in a **vendor's endorsement** as an additional insured on the wholesaler's or the manufacturer's products liability policy. This endorsement covers not only claims based on breach of the manufacturer's warranty, but also those claims based on the retailer's negligence, or upon the retailer's own warranty of the goods. Of course, an extra premium is charged for the endorsement. Since the retailer often carries products liability insurance as well, the effect of the vendors' endorsement is to provide higher limits of liability for products hazard claims.

BUSINESS AUTO COVERAGE

As the PAP is designed to insure private passenger and similar autos owned by individuals, corporations and the owners of large trucks need separate coverage. This protection is obtained through the use of the Business Automobile Policy (BAP). With this policy, insureds can purchase the same coverages as found in the PAP. The term automobile in the policy means a land motor vehicle except mobile equipment. Mobile equipment is insured under the CGL for liability exposures. With such a simple definition, most business motor vehicles can be insured under a BAP. For instance, motorcycles, dump trucks, tractor-trailers, and buses may be insured. Insureds can choose from a variety of coverages that are indicated by a series of symbols numbered 1 to 9.

1. Any auto
2. Owned auto only
3. Owned private passenger autos only
4. Owned autos other than private passenger autos only
5. Owned autos subject to no-fault
6. Owned autos subject to compulsory uninsured motorist laws
7. Specifically listed autos
8. Hired autos only
9. Nonowned autos only

By choosing only those coverages needed, an insured can minimize the firm's automobile insurance costs. For instance, a firm may cover private passenger autos under symbol 1 for liability but use symbol 4 for collision and loss other than collision. Such a firm would be fully covered for liability but be a self-insurer with respect to private passenger auto physical damage. High-cost vehicles such as dump trucks and tractor-trailers would be insured for physical damage.

PROFESSIONAL LIABILITY INSURANCE

Because general liability policies usually contain exclusions for all claims arising out of error or mistake of a professional person in the performance of the duties of the profession, separate policies covering this important form of legal liability have been developed. These contracts are sometimes referred to as **malpractice** and sometimes as **errors-and-omissions**

policies, depending on the type of professional person utilizing them. Essentially, the two contracts are similar and have many provisions in common. Three examples of these policies follow, with the peculiar characteristics of each analyzed.

Professional versus Other Liability Contracts

Important differences between professional liability and other liability insurance contracts are as follows:

1. In professional liability insurance the insurer often needs the permission of the insured to settle claims out of court by tendering sums in return for releases of liability by the plaintiff. The practice of out-of-court settlement is very common in other liability claims, but it is easy to see that to allow this in the case of professional liability would tend to damage the reputation of, say, a doctor who admits malpractice by settling claims in this manner. Therefore, even though it might be less expensive for the insurer to pay a claim regardless of its validity, the professional person has the right to insist that the insurer defend him or her in the courts.

2. The professional liability policy is usually written with only one major insuring clause, with no distinction made between bodily injury or property damage liability, and with no limit *per occurrence.* Usually there is a limit of liability *per claim* stated. Thus, if the policy has a $25,000 limit of liability per claim and a $100,000 aggregate limit, and two damage suits arise out of a single error, say one by the patient and another by the patient's spouse, the limits of liability would be $50,000 ($25,000 per claim). Other liability policies, on the other hand, invariably state the limits of liability in terms of so much per accident or per occurrence.

3. The professional liability policy does not restrict its coverage to events that are "caused by accident," because usually the act that gives rise to a claim is deliberate. The event has an unintended result, but may not always be described as accidental. For example, a druggist may sell a patent medicine for the relief of itching. If this medicine causes a severe allergic reaction in the customer, certainly the result is unintended, but the act of selling the drug was deliberate. Medical malpractice insurance would cover such a loss. However, the policy always excludes illegal or criminal acts from its coverage.

4. The professional liability policy usually does not exclude damage to property in the care, custody, or control of the insured, as do general liability contracts. Normally this type of loss will be at a minimum since, for the most part, the contracts cover personal injuries.

5. Unlike other liability policies, and products liability in particular, professional liability contracts protect the insured against all claims that had their basis in the service or the acts performed during the policy term. It is not necessary for the claim itself to be made during the policy

term, but the professional error must have been committed during the policy period.

6. The products liability policy insures against claims arising out of a breach of warranty of the vendor regarding the goods. If a retailer says a product is good for a certain purpose, and it turns out to be definitely wrong for this purpose, "an action lies" for which the policy must respond. In the professional liability policy, however, there is generally an exclusion for any agreement guaranteeing the result of any treatment. A suit by a patient, irritated because the treatment failed when the doctor promised it would succeed, is thus not covered. The policy responds to suits based on a physician's error, mistake, or malpractice in rendering the service, but not to any warranty for successful results; these cannot be guaranteed. Similar clauses are found in other types of professional liability contracts.

Medical Malpractice Insurance

One of the major professional liability contracts is the physicians', surgeons', and dentists' liability policy. In it the insurer agrees to pay

> ... all sums which the insured shall become legally obligated to pay as damages because of injury arising out of malpractice, error, or mistake in rendering or failing to render professional services in the practice of the insured's profession described in the declarations, committed during the policy period by the insured or by any person for whose acts or omissions the insured is legally responsible.

The insuring clause refers to "injury," not bodily injury. Thus, the clause covers a broad range of claims, such as mental anguish, false imprisonment, slander, and libel, based on professional acts. The insuring agreement refers to acts arising in the "practice of the insured's profession." If a patient slips on a wet doormat while entering the premises, however, the malpractice policy would not cover any damages, since this is not part of a professional service. The professional person thus needs premises liability insurance as well as professional liability coverage.

The insuring agreement covers the insured's liability for the act of a nurse, assistant, technician, etc., but does not cover the personal liability that might attach to such a person. The nurse, assistant, or technician is expected to provide professional coverage separately. Often the insurer permits this coverage to be endorsed on the employer's policy.

Because of the increasing frequency and severity of medical malpractice claims, some contracts now limit the time during which coverage exists under a policy, or its renewal after termination, to some period such as three years. Thus, coverage would have to be renewed periodically for a retired physician wishing coverage for acts performed during the time of active practice. Under traditional contracts, coverage exists even if the claim is presented years after the alleged malpractice. Thus, a person age 21 might sue for a malpractice committed during childbirth.

Lawyers' Professional Liability

Another example of malpractice insurance is found in a more or less standardized contract that covers the professional liability of lawyers. This contract is now offered by most liability insurers on a form developed by the National Bureau of Casualty Underwriters. The contract is similar in wording to other professional liability contracts, with adaptations to fit the particular needs of lawyers. The insuring agreement is very broad, covering liability "because of any act or omission of the insured, or of any other person for whose acts or omissions the insured is legally responsible, and arising out of the performance of professional services for others in the insured's capacity as a lawyer." Like other professional liability contracts, it makes no reference to "accidents," and the insurer may not settle a claim without the permission of the insured. The contract covers claims arising out of any act or failure to perform, if the act or failure occurred during the policy term, with no time limit as to when the claim must be presented.

Insurance Agents' and Brokers' Errors and Omissions Liability

The agents' and brokers' errors and omissions policy insures the agent against all losses that the agent must pay because of negligent acts, errors, or omissions of employees in dealing with clientele. While these contracts are not standardized, most insurers give the agent the option of protection against similar claims from the insurance companies represented. Usually the contract is written with a substantial deductible amount, say $500 or $1,000. The policy pays only if legal liability on the part of the agent can be proved, and does not respond to payments made to customers voluntarily in order to preserve goodwill. Like other professional liability contracts, errors and omissions insurance covers only professional mistakes.

To collect, the agent need only show that the claim was brought during the policy term, regardless of when the professional mistake occurred. However, for the protection of the agent, the contract requires that if the insurer refuses to renew, the coverage is extended for one year against claims arising from mistakes occurring during the policy term. It might happen, for example, that an agent realized on December 28 that an error was committed for which the agent is liable, there having occurred a loss left uninsured because of the agent's mistake. The professional liability insurer, learning of this, might refuse to renew the errors and omissions policy in the knowledge that a claim would not be submitted before the expiration of the policy on December 31. The provision granting the extension of coverage on such claims thus protects the agent from being unjustly denied recovery on the errors and omissions contract.

Commercial Umbrella

To purchase liability limits great enough to pay for catastrophic losses, companies purchase commercial umbrella policies. These policies, or combinations of them, are used to give limits of liability of $100,000,000 or more. Commercial umbrella liability policies are not uniform, and there is a good deal of variation of policy wording among insurers. Thus, the following discussion provides only an overview of the topic.

As in personal umbrellas, the commercial umbrella insurer will require primary insurance in the form of a general liability policy (probably the CGL), a business auto policy, workers' compensation and employer's liability, and insurance for any owned watercraft. Often the commercial umbrella will not cover owned aircraft liability even if there is primary insurance. For the most part, the insured must have $500,000 to $1,000,000 limits under the primary coverage.

Coverage under the umbrella is quite broad. Property in the insured's care, custody, and control may be covered, worldwide products coverage is available, and employer's liability is insured, as is liquor liability. In fact, umbrellas are frequently written with few exclusions, and endorsements are used to limit coverage. This approach is the opposite of the one used in primary insurance policies, where endorsements usually broaden coverage.

To obtain high limits of liability coverage, insureds also buy excess umbrella policies. These policies pay only after the underlying umbrella pays, and the excess umbrella policy usually "follows form." That is, it provides coverage on conditions identical to those of the underlying layers of coverage.

SUMMARY

1. All liability contracts have certain elements in common. The insuring agreements are fairly well standardized. The major differences lie in whether the event giving rise to a legal claim is interpreted to be an "occurrence" or an "accident." The occurrence basis, being broader than the accident basis, is a preferred wording from the viewpoint of the insured. Liability contracts vary in the definition of who or what is insured. All liability contracts guarantee that the insurer will bear the cost of defense in addition to paying any judgments up to the limits of liability.

2. Common exclusions peculiar to liability contracts include (a) nonbusiness activities

in the case of business liability policies, and business activities in the case of nonbusiness liability contracts, and (b) damage to property in the care, custody, and control of the insured. Because of its inherent ambiguity, the latter exclusion has resulted in much litigation.

3. Most business liability insurance is now written on the CGL form as a part of the simplified commercial lines portfolio policy. One can insure general liability, products and completed operations, personal injury, advertising liability, medical payments, and fire legal liability in this contract. The form has two options for events that "trigger" coverage: claims made

and occurrence. Claims-made coverage is not as desirable as occurrence coverage.

4. Products and completed operations liability insurance, which may be written with the CGL, is distinguished from general liability insurance in several ways, the major distinctions being that the occurrence giving rise to the claim must take place away from the main premises of the business and must arise out of a faulty product sold or a service rendered by the insured after the insured has completed work. Products liability insurance covers the loss no matter when the deficient product was sold or the faulty service was performed. It never covers loss to the product itself, but only damage caused by its faulty manufacture.

5. Professional liability (malpractice) insurance covering liability for claims arising from professional errors is distinguished from other liability contracts in a number of ways. Generally, professional liability contracts do not permit out-of-court settlements without the permission of the insured. They can be issued on a per-claim basis instead of a per-accident basis, and do not restrict their coverage to accidental occurrences. Professional liability policies will neither cover dishonest or criminal acts nor insure any claim arising out of any guarantee that professional services rendered will accomplish a specified result.

QUESTIONS FOR REVIEW

1. Define legal liability insurance.
2. Explain the difference between single limits of liability and split limits of liability.
3. Identify the exclusions that are almost universal to liability insurance contracts.

4. Explain the difference between claims-made and occurrence coverage.
5. What are the coverages provided by the commercial general liability policy?
6. What are the differences between professional liability insurance and other liability insurance policies?
7. Why do businesses purchase commercial umbrella policies, and what are the general characteristics of such policies?
8. How does the definition of an automobile differ between the BAP and the PAP?

QUESTIONS FOR DISCUSSION

1. Do you feel that the claims-made policy with the supplemental tail endorsement is as good as the occurrence policy? Explain your answer.
2. What effect, if any, will the new aggregate limit in the CGL have on the level of liability limits purchased by risk managers? Explain your answer.
3. Mr. Wood purchases a furnace to install in a mobile home that he sells to Ms. Hampson. Mr. Wood is in the business of selling mobile homes. If the furnace explodes and Ms. Hampson brings suit against Mr. Wood, how would his CGL respond, since he did not make the furnace?
4. A department store has a CGL policy with products liability covered. A woman came into the store to look at an automatic washer. After she purchased the washer, she asked to see once again how the bleach dispenser operated. During the demonstration of the machine, a metal strap snapped out and bruised her hand. Medical attention was necessary, and a claim for damages resulted.
   (a) Under which portion, if any, of the CGL policy would this claim be paid, if negligence is found?

(b) How, if at all, would your answer have changed if the accident had occurred after the washer had been delivered to the home of the buyer?

5. In *Meiser* v. *Aetna Casualty & Surety Co.*, 98 N.W. (2d) 919, the insured, a plastering subcontractor, spilled plaster on some expensive windows. In attempting to remove the plaster at the request of the owner, the windows were damaged. The plasterer was sued by the owner of the windows, and the liability insurer under the CGL denied liability on grounds that the windows were "in his care, custody, and control," and therefore were excluded from coverage. Decide this case, stating your reasons.

6. In *Marks* v. *Minneosta Mining and Manufacturing Co.*, San Francisco, CA, County Superior Court #78976, November, 1983, a 34-year-old housewife underwent insertion of silicone breast implants manufactured by Defendant, a division of 3M Corp. On three occasions, the implants spontaneously ruptured. The defendant disclaimed liability.

(a) Decide whether the defendant is liable or not? Explain your answer.

(b) What type of business liability coverage would the defendant need for insurance protection? Explain.

NEW TERMS AND CONCEPTS

Aggregate Limit
Broad Form Property Damage Program
Business Auto Policy
Claims Made
Commercial General Liability
Commercial Umbrella
Dramshop Liability

Extended Reporting Period
Errors and Omissions Liability
Medical Malpractice
Occurrence
Professional Liability
Sistership Exclusion
Supplemental Tail
Vendor's Endorsement

NOTES

1 *Boswell* v. *Travelers Indemnity Company*, 8 CCH Fire and Casualty Cases 936.
2 *Jarrell Construction Company* v. *Columbia Casualty Company*, 8 CCH Fire and Casualty Cases 642.
3 Rhonda L. Rundle, "Keene Jackpot: $300 Million in Coverage," *Business Insurance* (October 26, 1981), pp. 1 and 47.
4 *LaCorga* v. *Kroger Co.*, 275 Fed. Supp. 373.
5 *Travelers Indemnity Co.* v. *Sears Roebuck and Co.*, 1972 CCH.

6 *F.C.&S. Bulletins*, Sales Section, Losses, Pro-3 (Cincinnati, Ohio: The National Underwriter Company, 1986).
7 *Rinkle* v. *Lees Plumbing and Heating Co.*, 10 CCH (Negligence 2d) 347.
8 *Handy* v. *Holland Furnace Co.*, H CCH (Negligence 2d) 988.
9 Donald S. Malecki, James H. Donaldson, and Ronald C. Horn, *Commercial Liability Risk Management and Insurance* (Malvern, Pa.: American Institute of Property and Liability Underwriters, 1978), p. 347.
10 Ibid., p. 348.

22

WORKERS' COMPENSATION AND SERVICE GUARANTEES

After studying this chapter, you should be able to:

1. Describe how workers' compensation developed and identify recent trends in the field.
2. State the different alternatives available to fund workers' compensation losses and the relative importance of each alternative.
3. List coverages provided in a workers' compensation policy.
4. Identify the different rating plans available for workers' compensation.
5. List the kinds of credit insurance and explain why businesses use credit insurance.
6. Explain the need for and use of title insurance.
7. Identify property and perils covered by boiler and machinery insurance.

In this chapter we examine workers' compensation insurance and types of insurance that involve a high level of services: credit, title, boiler and machinery, and plate glass insurance. In these four contracts the services provided by the insurer are nearly as important as the indemnification itself.

WORKERS' COMPENSATION INSURANCE

Workers' compensation insurance covers the loss of income and medical and rehabilitation expenses that result from work-related accidents and occupational disease. It is the single largest line of commercial insurance, with premium volume of $16.8 billion in 1985, second only to private passenger auto ($48.9 billion) among all lines of insurance.[1] During the 1970s workers' compensation premium growth was very high, but it has slowed during the 1980s. Part of this reduction was due to the deep recession in 1982 which reduced the number of persons employed and led to intense price competition among insurers.

Workers' compensation developed in the latter half of the 1800s in Europe and in the early 1900s in the United States. It resulted because of hardships placed on workers by common law. Under common law it was difficult for a worker to collect from employers for job-related injuries. Under workers' compensation a worker receives a guarantee of compensation, and the employer is protected from employees seeking damages in tort for work-related injuries.

Recent Changes

Because of various weaknesses observed in workers' compensation, The National Commission on State Workmen's Compensation Laws was created under the authority of the Occupational Safety and Health Act of 1970 to determine the extent to which state laws provided adequate, prompt, and equitable compensation to injured workers. About 40 studies were commissioned and later published in three volumes.[2] In general, the studies raised doubts about the effectiveness of workers' compensation as it operated in the United States at the time the studies were made.

Since the studies were published and the 1972 final report of the Commission rendered, state legislatures have passed numerous reforms to comply with some 19 "essential" recommendations of the Commission. These recommendations included objectives calling for (1) full coverage for medical care and rehabilitation, (2) adequate income replacement, (3) coverage of all workers, (4) cost-of-living adjustments, and (5) improved data systems.

Because of the Commission's recommendations, tremendous change has occurred. By 1979 all states had unlimited medical care, and coverage was mandatory in 50 jurisdictions. In 1983 86 percent of all wage and salary workers were covered by workers' compensation. In 42 states the maximum weekly benefit equaled or exceeded $66\frac{2}{3}$ percent of the average weekly wage, and it was 100 percent or more in 31 states. By comparison, in 1972 only 43 jurisdictions had compulsory programs, while in 1974 only 32 states paid $66\frac{2}{3}$ percent of the average weekly wage, and only 9 states paid 100 percent or more.[3]

Insurance Methods

There are three methods by which an employer can provide employees with the coverage required by law:

1. Purchase a workers' compensation and employers' liability policy from a private commercial insurer.
2. Purchase insurance through a state fund or a federal agency set up for this purpose.
3. Self-insure.

All states require selection of one of these methods by employers subject to the law.

Private Insurance. The standard workers' compensation and employers' liability policy has two major insuring agreements: (1) coverage *A*, to pay all claims required under the workers' compensation law in the state where the injury occurred, including occupational disease benefits, penalties assessable to the employer under law, and other obligations; and (2) coverage *B*, to defend all employee suits against the employer and pay any judgments resulting from these suits. Coverage *B* is separate and distinct from Coverage *A*. While it was not anticipated that there would be many employee suits, such claims are surprisingly frequent because methods are constantly being found to bring an action against the employer in spite of the intention of the statutes to discourage such suits. Under Coverage *B* there is a separate limit for bodily injury by accident and by disease. Coverage *B* is similar to that given in general liability policies. There is no specific limitation for coverage *A*; any limits are outlined by the state compensation law.

While the private insurance method involves a contract between the employer and the insurer, the insurer deals directly with the employee and is primarily responsible to the employee for benefits. Thus, even if the employer should go out of business, the injured employee's security is not jeopardized.

State Funds and Federal Agencies. In 13 states[4] an employer has the choice of using a private insurer or a state fund as the insurer of workers' compensation. In six states[5] the employer does not have this choice, but must insure in an exclusive state fund or, in two of the states, may self-insure. Five of the compulsory state funds were established during the period 1913–1915 when compensation laws were new and the success of private insurers in handling the business was uncertain. Most of the Canadian provinces established exclusive state funds. Oregon had an exclusive state fund until 1966, when the law of the state was amended to permit self-insurance and private insurance as alternatives to the state fund.

In addition to state funds, federal agencies provide for workers' compensation coverage. For example, the federal Longshoremen's and Harbor Workers' Compensation Act provides for coverage for certain classes of dock and maritime workers. In 1969 the federal government created an agency to provide coverage for coal miners afflicted with black lung disease. Since 1908 the federal government has operated a workers' compensation system for its civilian employees.

Self-Insurance. In most states, under specified conditions, an employer is permitted to self-insure the workers' compensation coverage.[6] Self-insurance is generally not permitted in Canada. Self-insurers are generally large concerns with adequate diversification of risks in order to qualify under the law.

Evaluation of Insurance Methods. Data from the Social Security Administration show that in 1982 losses paid by private insurers were 52.8 percent of the total amount of losses; losses paid by state and federal funds were 28.7 percent of the total; and losses paid by qualified self-insurers were 18.5 percent of the total.[7] It seems clear that private insurers are preferred by most employers in states where they are permitted to operate. Some of the major reasons for this are:

1. Private insurers offer the employer an opportunity to insure in one contract all the liability likely for damages arising from work-connected injuries, whether these damages stem from employee suits, statutory benefit requirements, or other sources.
2. Private insurers offer more certainty in handling out-of-state risks. Most compensation laws are extraterritorial, and there are many complexities to consider in making sure of coverage if the employer has widespread interests. Most state funds do not automatically cover such risks.
3. While the expenses of state funds—at least exclusive state funds—are somewhat lower than those of private insurers, this difference is not as great as rough comparisons often lead one to believe. After adjustment for differences in the quantity and the quality of services rendered, many would argue that the supposed cost advantage of exclusive state funds is of insufficient size to warrant giving up the convenience and certainty involved in the private contract, including the ready availability of agents who provide services not usually supplied by the state fund.
4. Self-insurance has the handicap that it is necessary for the insured to enter into the insurance business, which is essentially unrelated to the insured's main operations. Also, contributions to a self-insurance fund are often not tax deductible, a factor that may add materially to the cost and risk involved in self-insurance.
5. Experience rating and retrospective rate plans enable the large firm to use a private insurer's facilities in transferring as much or as little of the risk as is desired at a very modest cost.

Major Features of State Laws

The provisions of workers' compensation laws are subject to constant change, but a pattern exists even though details of the provisions may vary with each meeting of the state legislature. The features necessary for a general understanding of the coverage provided by these laws are described in the following paragraphs.

Employment Covered. Compensation laws do not cover all workers. For example, domestic labor and farm labor are often excluded. Employers with just a few employees are excluded under compulsory laws. Because of various exclusions, only about 86.0 percent of all workers are covered. One result of this condition is that liability suits are necessary if an excluded worker is to recover anything, even though a basic purpose of compensation legislation was to eliminate this condition as a prerequisite for employee recoveries. It is the small employer who is excluded from compensation laws and who is most likely to be the object of such suits. This smallness often could mean that either (1) a successful suit will bankrupt the employer, or (2) if the employer is more or less judgment-proof, the injured worker will recover nothing.

Income Provisions. Compensation laws recognize four types of disability for which income benefits may be paid. These are permanent and temporary total disability, and permanent and temporary partial disability. The laws generally limit payments by specifying the maximum duration of benefits and the maximum weekly and aggregate amounts payable.

For permanent total disability benefits, most states permit lifetime payments to the injured worker who is unable to perform the duties of any suitable occupation. In the remaining states a typical limitation is between 400 and 500 weeks of payments, and there is also usually a limitation on the aggregate amount payable.

There is a common limitation that income benefits cannot exceed about two-thirds of the worker's average weekly wage or some dollar amount. A few states make extra allowances for dependents. Because average weekly wages have risen faster than legislative adjustments, the limiting factor is usually the dollar maximum.

Weekly benefits for temporary total disability are usually the same as for permanent total disability, except that often there is a lower maximum aggregate limitation and a shorter time duration for such payments.

In addition to income benefits, most workers' compensation laws specify that lump sums may be paid to a worker as **liquidating damages** for a disability, such as the loss of a leg or an eye, that is permanent but which does not totally incapacitate the worker. The worker may usually draw income benefits during the time that the permanent partial disability prevents the worker from doing anything, and then the worker may receive a lump sum that varies with the seriousness of the injury.

Survivor Benefits. In case of fatal injuries, the widow or widower and children of the worker are entitled to funeral and income benefits, subject to various limitations. The maximum benefits to the widow or widower alone are generally less than they would have been to the disabled worker, but if the survivor has children, these benefits are comparable to what the worker would have received for permanent total disability.

Medical Benefits. Most workers' compensation laws provide relatively complete medical services to an injured worker, including allowances for certain occupational diseases. In all jurisdictions there is unlimited medical care for accidental work injuries, and broad coverage on occupational disease is provided.

Rehabilitation. Benefits for rehabilitation, both physical and occupational, are provided by most states, but it is generally recognized that the quantity and quality of these services are subject to wide variation. Some states still provide no automatic rehabilitation benefits. For example, Georgia and Maryland provide for vocational rehabilitation, but no physical rehabilitation, which is apparently considered a part of the worker's medical benefits. Absence of or restrictions on maintenance benefits during rehabilitation are especially common. The general area of rehabilitation of the injured worker is one that needs much closer attention than it has received in the past. Examples of the potential savings in medical costs, community aid, and lower compensation premiums made possible through rehabilitation demonstrate that from an economic standpoint alone, the effort is extremely worthwhile.

Costs. The cost of workers' compensation as a percentage of payroll averaged 0.89 percent in 1957, 0.96 percent in 1962, 1.48 percent in 1976, and 1.903 percent in 1979, but declined to 1.67 percent in 1983. In most states employees are exempt from sharing workers' compensation premiums. For individual employers the premium ranges widely, depending on the hazards attached to the line of business. The rate for clerical help, for example, may be 0.1 percent of payroll, and that for metal bridge painters 24.5 percent. The rate also varies by geographical area. Then, too, costs depend on the type of insurer chosen, the type of rating plan used, and other factors.

Experience Rating

Experience rating plans are widely used in workers' compensation insurance. The general theory is that an employer has some control over loss ratio and is entitled to a credit for a good loss-prevention record, or, on the other hand, should pay a higher rate if the loss record is poorer than the average.

In the experience rating plan adopted by private insurers and administered by the National Council on Compensation Insurance, a national rate-making agency, each employer must have some minimum premium, such as $1,500, that would be payable if standard manual rates were charged. The details of the plan are very complex, but the general procedure is to determine, for each occupational class, some expected loss ratio against which the insured's actual loss ratio is compared. If the actual loss ratio is 90 percent of the expected loss ratio, the insured's rate for the coming year is 90 percent of the manual rate. If the actual loss ratio is 130 percent of the expected loss ratio, the insured must pay 130 percent of the manual rate during the coming year.

Under experience rating plans not all losses suffered by an insured are counted. The plan uses a stabilizing factor so that unusually large losses cannot operate to increase the small employer's rate unreasonably.

However, for the large employer, the employer's loss experience becomes more important as its expected losses become greater. For example, for the state of Georgia in 1986, when a corporation's three-year expected losses are $890,000 or greater, there is no sharing of losses with other organizations. The effect of this modification factor is that the large employer is basically self-rated.

Medium-sized and small employers receive a credit less than they would receive if they were self-rated in years in which losses are low. In those years following a period of high losses, the medium-sized and small employers pay a penalty that is not as large as it would be if they were self-rated. Over a period of years, if the loss experience in a given category of industry is consistently bad, the manual rate and expected losses for that class will be adjusted so that in any given period a certain rating class of risks will tend to bear its total loss burden. But experience rating deals with rate adjustments for individual insureds within a given class on a year-to-year basis.

Experience rating in workers' compensation gives employers an incentive to do whatever is within their control to prevent accidents, a very desirable objective of any rating system. It rewards the safety efforts of employers by the test of "what effect did it have?" not "what effect should it have had?" as is the practice in fire insurance. Employers may spend a great deal of money on safety efforts, but if these efforts fail, no rate credit will be forthcoming.

Retrospective Rating

In workers' compensation insurance, experience rating is applied automatically, but retrospective rating is entirely a voluntary agreement between the insured and the insurer. If the employer's payroll is such that a standard premium of $1,000 or more is incurred, it is considered that the firm is large enough to develop experience that is partially credible. (A **standard premium** is defined as what the employer would have paid at manual rates after adjustment for experience rating, but before any adjustment for retrospective rating.) In practice, an employer likely to use retrospective rating is generally considerably larger than this, since a standard premium of only $1,000 means that the payroll approximates $100,000, and the number of employees is therefore only about 10 (assuming an average wage of $10,000 a year). Even one accident could easily cause a loss in excess of $1,000. This might cause a very substantial increase in the employer's retrospective premium, depending on the nature of the plan selected.

There are various plans of retrospective rating, and the employer must choose one. Assuming that the employer is large enough and that both parties are agreeable to retrospective rating, which plan should the employer use? Essentially, this question reduces to one of how much risk the employer is willing to assume, i.e., how great a loss the employer is willing to accept if the experience turns out to be bad, in return for a reduced premium if the experience is good.

The basic retrospective rating formula is given by the expression:

$$R = [BP + (L)(LCF)]TM$$

where

R = Retrospective premium payable for the year in question
BP = A basic premium (in dollars) designed to cover fixed costs of the insurer in handling the business
L = Losses (in dollars) actually suffered by the employer
LCF = Loss conversion factor, a multiplying factor designed to cover the variable costs of the insurer (such as claim adjustment expenses)
TM = Tax multiplier, a factor designed to reflect the premium tax levied by the state on the insurer's business[8]

The basic premium declines as the size of the employer increases, and differs with the type of plan used. The loss conversion factor is a constant percentage, as is the tax multiplier, regardless of the size of the employer. The formula is subject to the operation of certain minimums and maximums, both of which decline as the size of the employer increases, except for the plan in which the maximum amount paid by the employer is the standard premium.

The operation of the formula is such that the larger the employer, the less risk there is associated with the use of retrospective rating. (The maximum and minimum premiums decline.) Yet, a relatively small employer who is accepted for retrospective rating has an opportunity to lower the premium if the losses can be kept within bounds and still obtain protection against paying more than would be the case in the absence of the retrospective plan.

RISK MANAGEMENT AND WORKERS' COMPENSATION

Workers' compensation is one of the most frequently self-insured coverages in the risk management area. It is characterized by relatively high-frequency and low-severity losses. In recent years, the motivation to self-insure a portion or all of this exposure has increased because of rapidly rising benefit levels and high interest rates. When interest rates are high, the cash flow benefits of self-insurance are greater and self-insurance becomes more attractive.

Factors Favoring Self-Insurance

The basic factors that lead a firm to self-insure revolve around lower costs. These cost savings take the form of lower administrative expenses, cash flow benefits, and a more claims-conscious management.

Lower Administrative Expenses. When a firm establishes a self-insured workers' compensation program, it eliminates most of the premium paid to an insurer. (Some premium is still paid to purchase excess insurance.) In the standard premium, there is a loading (charge) for acquisition costs. These costs include the agent's commission, as well as the cost of inspection and underwriting. In addition, there is the insurer's profit. However, in recent years the underwriting profit on workers' compensation has been very small or nonexistent.

Cash-Flow Benefits. Besides cost savings, the self-insurer also receives substantial cash-flow benefits. Actually, the cash-flow benefits are probably greater than the cost-savings aspect of self-insuring workers' compensation.

Under a traditional insured plan the insured pays the premium, and at some later date the insurer pays all the claims. In the aggregate, this arrangement provides the insurance company with a large amount of money that can be invested in income-producing securities until the claims are paid. As the insured pays a premium each year, the insurer can always have funds invested in income-producing securities. When a firm self-insures, it holds the money until the claims are paid. As it takes several years (five or more) to pay all the claims from a given year's loss experience, the self-insurer has the use of some of the funds for a fairly long time. Of course, the process is repeated from one year to the next, so there is a perpetual sum of money available for investment in securities or in the self-insured's own operations. The cash-flow benefits can be a significant portion of the original premium. If a firm held an amount equal to half a given year's premium for three years at 12 percent interest, it would earn an amount equal to 20 percent of the original premium:

$$0.5p \times [(1.12)^3 - 1] = 0.20p$$

Claims-Conscious Management. Another benefit of self-insurance is that management often becomes more claims conscious when it is paying directly for workers' compensation losses. When *insurers* are paying the claims, there is only an indirect effect seen by operating managers. They pay their insurance premiums, losses occur, and in two or three years premiums may be increased. When firms self-insure, they pay the claims as they occur. There is little or no delay in increased costs when accident rates start to increase. Managers tend to react to these increased costs and become more loss conscious. As a consequence, workers' compensation losses often decline when a firm initiates a self-insured program.

Factors against Self-Insurance

Self-insurance is not desirable for many firms. Factors that can influence the self-insurance decision include the size of the firm, stability of the work force, tax consequences, availability of services, and rate of benefit increases.

Size of Firm. A company must be financially capable of retaining self-insured losses. If it cannot absorb those losses, it should not self-insure. Also, it must have a large enough exposure so that it can predict much of its losses. Unless it has numerous losses, it will have a difficult time predicting future experience.

Generally, a firm with an annual premium of less than $100,000 will not self-insure. However, because benefit levels vary between the states, a firm might self-insure in one state when its premium volume is $200,000 and purchase insurance in another state when its premium volume is $400,000. For instance, $215,000 in three-year losses in Georgia is comparable to $479,000 in three-year losses in New York, because New York's rates and payrolls are higher. Each situation must be judged on its own merits.

Stability of Work Force. By stability of work force is meant "how much turnover does the firm have, and how rapidly is it expanding?" (Newly employed people as well as younger employees have higher accident rates than more mature workers.) New plants tend to have higher accident rates than established ones. If a firm is planning to open a new manufacturing plant, it may wish to postpone starting a self-insurance program until the new workers are trained and have become accustomed to their new work environment. This adjustment period is often 12 to 24 months.

Likewise, if major plant closings are to occur, self-insurance may be avoided. Often when a firm closes a plant, a much greater number of employees file claims. In one General Motors plant that was closed, more than 50 percent of the employees filed workers' compensation claims.

Tax Consequences. An often-stated advantage of an insured workers' compensation program is that premiums are tax deductible when paid. Under a self-insured program, one cannot take a tax deduction until the funds are actually paid. For instance, a worker may become disabled and the self-insurer knows it has a liability over the expected life of the employee of $400,000. However, no tax deduction is allowed for this liability. Only as dollars are paid to the employee can deductions be made. This rule discourages self-insurers from establishing loss reserves, since any reserve would have to be funded with after-tax dollars.

Availability of Services. When a firm decides to self-insure, it must provide or purchase services that were formerly provided by the insurance company. These services include loss-prevention activities, claims adjusting, data processing, and program administration. Today, a firm can usually buy these services from companies that specialize in such activities, even insurance companies. However, the purchase of these services adds to the cost of self-insurance and may lead to a greater administrative burden on the risk manager than if insurance coverage were bought. Besides the administrative burden, the desired services may not be available or may be available only at an unattractive price. In such a case, insurance may be the only solution.

Rate of Benefit Increase. Another factor that can influence the decision not to self-insure is the rate of benefit increases. In the 1970s costs soared due to inflation and increased benefit levels. Under a self-insured program, these costs are quickly reflected in workers' compensation claims. In an insured plan, there is some lag between the time when benefits are increased and the time when insurance rates are increased. While this factor may not be as important as the others, it can affect the timing of a self-insured plan.

Excess Insurance

Most firms do not completely self-insure the workers' compensation exposure. The reason is the catastrophic nature of certain types of worker compensation losses. Such claims as long-term disability or death may add up to hundreds of thousands of dollars. For instance, if a 25-year-old worker in the state of Oregon were disabled for 40 years, this payment could total $465,920. Such a loss truly is catastrophic, and most businesses would not desire to retain it. To prevent such circumstances, self-insurers purchase excess insurance.

There are two basic types of excess insurance: specific and aggregate. Under specific excess insurance, the self-insurer absorbs the first x dollars on any loss. This is similar to the flat deductible found in homeowners' insurance, except the size of the deductible is much greater ($25,000 to $100,000). If a firm had a policy with a specific excess limit of $50,000, and all per-accident losses for the year were below $50,000, the specific excess insurance would not pay, even if the sum of all such losses were $200,000.

Under aggregate excess, the policy operates like an aggregate deductible. Typically, the aggregate limit is at least the level of what the workers' compensation premiums would have been if insurance had been purchased. If the premium were $200,000, then the excess insurer would not pay for any claims until $200,000 of losses and associated expenses had been retained by the self-insurer.

Unlike workers' compensation policies, excess policies have dollar limits. So even when a self-insurer purchases excess insurance there is still some exposure to catastrophic losses.

CREDIT INSURANCE

The use of credit in modern economic societies is universally recognized as a key factor in facilitating growth.[9] Without credit, it is very doubtful that the modern industrial economy could have developed at all. However, the use of credit has created many complex problems, not the least of which is the risk that debts will not be paid because of the occurrence of some peril that is often outside the control of the debtor.

Kinds of Credit Insurance

There are many types of credit insurance. Several of the major ones offered by private insurers and through governmental programs are discussed below.

Insurance of Bonds. A development related to loan insurance is the practice of issuing insurance against the default of credit instruments such as municipal bonds in order to improve the instruments' investment quality and reduce interest costs. The American Municipal Bond Assurance Corporation (AMBAC), which issues such policies, estimates that a municipality may realize savings in bond interest ranging from $20,000 to $118,000 over the life of a $1,000,000 bond depending on the quality of the bond and the length of the period of amortization. The insurance premium absorbs from 28 percent to 39 percent of the interest cost savings.[10] The insurance guarantee may reduce the risk enough to enable the sale of bonds by small municipalities that might not otherwise be able to issue their bonds at reasonable cost. AMBAC specializes in small and medium-sized issues that receive medium-grade ratings by agencies such as Standard and Poors.

Credit Life and Credit Accident/Sickness. Insurance against failure to pay a debt because of death of the borrower is known as **credit life insurance.** This contract is basically the same as any contract of life insurance except for the manner in which it is arranged and marketed. Suffice it to say that credit life insurance should not be confused with other forms of credit insurance. A similar comment applies to credit accident and sickness insurance that is arranged to liquidate payments on an installment debt during the time the debtor is disabled because of accident or sickness.

Accounts Receivable Insurance. Insurance protecting the creditor against inability to collect a bad debt because accounting records have been destroyed by certain listed perils is known as **accounts receivable insurance** and was analyzed in Chapter 20.

Domestic Merchandise Credit Insurance. In the United States, Canada, Mexico, and most European countries, sellers may obtain insurance, called **domestic merchandise credit insurance,** against the insolvency of domestic debtors on credits arising out of the sale of merchandise on an unsecured basis. Such coverage has been sold in the United States since 1890. Insurance against failure to repay a cash loan is generally not available in the United States, except as it is applied for through a government agency.

In most countries credit insurers give only limited coverage in that only certain business customers, such as manufacturers and wholesalers, are eligible. Not all types of transactions are insured, not all perils are covered, and losses are not indemnified 100 percent. In the United States there are two main private insurers, the American Credit Indemnity Company and the London Guarantee Company.

The American Credit Indemnity Company writes three-fourths of all the merchandise credit insurance in the United States. Its contracts, which are very similar to those of the London Guarantee Company, are analyzed in the section entitled "Types of Domestic Merchandise Credit Insurance" to follow.

Governmental Credit Insurance. There are several types of governmental credit insurance programs. Probably the most well known is the **deposit insurance program.** The Federal Deposit Insurance Corporation (FDIC) and the Federal Savings and Loan Insurance Corporation (FSLIC) insure accounts held in insured institutions. The maximum amount of liability per account is $100,000.

Another federal program is **cash loan credit insurance.** Government agencies (the Veterans Administration and Small Business Administration) sponsor programs to insure cash loans made by banks to individuals and certain business enterprises that cannot obtain credit from other sources.

A very popular government credit program is the one that insures long-term loans made to property owners. The Federal Housing Administration and the Veterans Administration are the two best-known agencies in this area of credit insurance.

A less well-known type of government credit insurance is one in the international area. Through export credit insurance and foreign investment guarantees, the federal government has attempted to stimulate international business.

Types of Domestic Merchandise Credit Insurance

Credit insurance contracts, as written in the United States by the American Credit Indemnity Company, may be classified into two categories: (1) back coverage and forward coverage, and (2) general coverage and restricted coverage.

Back-Coverage Contract. Credit insurance contracts termed **back coverage** apply only to losses incurred during the policy term (one year). Under these policies claims can arise from sales made during the year prior to the commencement date of the policy. Back-coverage contracts account for the major portion of all credit insurance in force.

Forward-Coverage Contract. Under the terms of **forward-coverage** contracts, the policy indemnifies the insured for losses stemming only from accounts created by sales made during the policy term. Accounts already on the books when the policy is purchased are not insured. However, if on the last day of the policy term a credit sale is made that ultimately becomes a bad debt, the contract is applicable, even if it is not renewed.

General Coverage Form. Under **general coverage** policies, insurance covers all debtors falling into given classes of credit ratings on a blanket basis. Thus, the policy may specify that $100,000 of coverage applies to the bad debts of any debtor who has a 3A1 Dun and Bradstreet credit rating. However, the insurer often is willing to name specific customers of the insured for coverage in excess of the blanket limit. The blanket coverage is scaled down for firms with lower credit ratings. All back-coverage policies are of the general coverage type.

Restricted Coverage Form. Under **restricted coverage,** only debtors named specifically are insured. The amount of coverage is not based on credit agency ratings and remains fixed for the full term of the policy, unless cancelled by the insurer or the insured.

Establishing a Loss

To establish a loss, the insured must first show what credit rating the debtor had at the time the goods were shipped. It is this rating that determines the limit of coverage under the credit insurance policy, unless the particular debtor has been specifically named beforehand for additional coverage. The policyholder must show that a legal obligation exists and that the debt arose because of bona fide sales of merchandise or services normally dealt in by the seller. Under the terms of the contract, a loss is said to have occurred under two general situations: (1) a debtor simply does not pay the account by the due date but is not insolvent, and (2) a debtor becomes legally insolvent as determined by specific events listed in the contract.

Deductibles

Loss settlements under the credit insurance contract can be subject to one or both of two kinds of deductibles: a stated dollar amount, and a percentage (10 or 20 percent) of the individual loss. The dollar deductible, called the **primary loss,** is intended to represent the normal credit losses of the firm. Since these losses are expected and are in the nature of a certainty, they are excluded from coverage. The amount of normal loss varies with the industry and is adjusted according to the experience of the individual insured. It is applied to the total of the insured's losses in a given policy term.

The percentage deductible, called **coinsurance,** is a deductible that applies to each individual loss. It is intended to control the moral hazard, the tendency for the insured to be careless in granting credit in the knowledge that if the debtor does not pay the insurer will. The reasoning is that if the insured knows that at best only 90 percent of a given account can be collected from the credit insurer, the insured will be less tempted to sell to marginal credit risks. Collection of only 90 percent of an account from the insurer will usually not leave any profit. The coinsurance for poorly rated or nonrated accounts is increased to 20 percent from the usual 10 percent.

Collection Service

Studies of credit insurance have concluded that many insureds look upon the collection services of the credit insurer as a very important part of the benefits secured under the contract. Part of the efficiency of the efforts of insurers in this regard is due to the fact that failure to collect accounts placed with them by policyholders will normally result in a loss under the policy. Hence, the credit insurer has a greater stake in a given account than does a typical collection agency. The insurer will make strong efforts not only to collect the account, but also to preserve the customer's goodwill. If goodwill is sacrificed in the process of collection, the insured and the insurer may lose a good customer.

TITLE INSURANCE

Title insurance is a device by which the purchaser of real estate may be protected against losses in case it develops that the title obtained is not legitimate or can be made legitimate only after certain payments are made. Defects in titles may stem from sources such as forgery of public records, forgery of titles, invalid or undiscovered wills, defective probate procedures, and faulty real estate transfers. Thus, a person may occupy real property for years only to find that the one who conveyed title was not the rightful owner. True ownership may lie in the possession of another, say a former spouse who had been wrongfully deprived of property rights.

Usually all rights in real property, such as encumbrances, liens, and easements, must be duly recorded in the courthouse of the county or parish in which the property lies. Before title insurance became common, the real property buyer usually retained an attorney to search these records and render an opinion on the validity of the title. The attorney based this opinion in large part on an **abstract,** which is a brief history of title to the land. The purpose of the abstract is to reveal the nature of any legal obstacle that may cloud the title or leave a way open for someone else to make a legal claim against the land.

After examining the abstract and perhaps other matters that may not appear as a matter of public record, the attorney rendered an opinion. The attorney, however, could be held liable only for negligence in the title search. If it turned out that there was some unusual defect in title not discoverable by a reasonable and diligent search, there was no remedy for the unfortunate "owner" of the land. Thus, the need for a formal guarantee of the completeness and accuracy of the title search arose. Note that if the title is defective, title insurance does not guarantee possession of the property.

Special Characteristics of Title Insurance

Some of the differences between title insurance and other contracts of property and liability insurance may be summarized as follows:

1. The premium for title insurance is almost entirely intended to cover the necessary services in investigating possible sources of loss of title marketability, and not an expected loss. The title insurance company, in fact, expects no losses, feeling that if an adequate job of investigation

is performed before the policy is issued, there will be no loss to pay on the policy.

2. Title insurance covers title defects that have occurred before, but are discovered after, the effective date of the policy.
3. Title insurance contracts are not cancellable by either party, and the premium is fully earned once it is paid; that is, there is no refund of premium under any conditions.
4. Title insurance has no expiration date; the coverage is effective indefinitely.

The Title Insurance Contract

There is no standard title insurance contract, but the general form of the insuring clause is fairly uniform. The insurer agrees to indemnify the owner against any loss suffered "by reason of unmarketability of the title of the insured to or in said premises, or . . . from all loss and damage by reason of liens, encumbrances, defects, objections, estates, and interests, except those listed in Schedule B." Schedule B is a separate endorsement on which is listed all title defects or rights in the property found during the title search.

Defense. Under the typical policy the insurer agrees to defend the insured in any legal proceedings brought against the insured concerning the title, assuming that the action involves a source of loss not excluded under the contract. The insured is required to notify the insurer of any such proceedings and to cooperate in any legal action by the insurer.

Premium. The premium in title insurance is paid only once, and it keeps the policy in force for the named insured for an indefinite period. If the property is transferred, a new premium must be paid for the protection of the new purchaser. The old policy is not assignable to the new buyer. Usually there is no reduction in premium, even if the property is transferred a short time after the prior purchase. Thus, if a residence is built in one year and is resold five times in the next five years, a title insurance premium might be charged five times.

BOILER AND MACHINERY INSURANCE

Explosions caused by steam boilers, compressors, engines, electrical equipment, flywheels, air tanks, and furnaces constitute a serious source of loss which the layperson often does not recognize. Since the causes of boiler and machinery explosions are technical in nature, the danger is usually minimized by the would-be insured.

Special Characteristics

Boiler and machinery insurance has been developed along somewhat different lines from the usual insurance contract. First, recognizing that prevention of losses is even more important than indemnification of loss, insurers have taken on the service of inspection and servicing of boiler operations and technical machinery. Approximately one-fourth of the total premium collected is used for the service function. The insurer typically sends an inspector to the insured plant two or more times each year, depending on the size of the firm. In many states these inspections substitute for an inspection required by law. Technical specialists examine boilers and pressure vessels both internally and externally, using special equipment to detect minute cracks, crystallization, deterioration of insulation, vibration, and general wear. Failure of a vessel to pass an inspection may mean imminent danger of continued operation. As a result, the insurer reserves the right to suspend coverage immediately if recommended repairs or replacements are not made.

Second, because of the technical nature and diversity of boilers, tanks, furnaces, and electrical equipment in use, the boiler and machinery policy specifies by endorsement the exact definition of "accident" applicable to each insurable object. The insurer requires a series of separate endorsements describing in detail the nature of the insured object and what will constitute an accident. An insured may have ten types of objects with a different definition of accident for each one.

Third, because the damage caused by an exploding boiler may result in legal liability for damage to the property or persons of others, direct loss to the property of the insured, and substantial indirect loss due to shutdown of the plant, the single boiler and machinery contract provides coverage against different types of losses.

The policy also contains a unique feature in that an aggregate limit of loss is stated for the first four coverages.[11] All payments are to be satisfied out of this aggregate limit in numerical order. Thus, if a policy has a $50,000 limit, and $40,000 is paid out under the first coverage, $10,000 remains for the second. If no liability exists for this, the $10,000 is available to satisfy any liability for the third coverage, and so on, until the $50,000 is used up, after which the limits are exhausted for that particular accident.

Insuring Agreements

The following comments describe the coverages commonly found in boiler and machinery policies and endorsements that may be added. The first five coverages are part of the basic contract. The remaining ones are added by endorsement.

Loss of Property of the Insured. Perhaps the chief reason for the purchase of boiler and machinery insurance is to replace damaged property belonging to the insured in the event of sudden or accidental loss, or to prevent the occurrence of such a loss. The insuring clause excludes loss when the proximate cause is fire, because fire losses are paid under the standard fire policy. Indirect losses are excluded but may be insured separately by endorsement. The insurer reserves the right to replace or repair the property or to indemnify for its actual cash value.

Expediting Expenses. The insurer agrees to pay for the reasonable extra cost of expediting repair of the machinery, including overtime costs and the extra costs of express and other rapid means of transportation. Payments under this section may not exceed $5,000 or the amount payable under the section for loss of property of the insured, whichever is less.

Property Damage Liability. The property damage liability protection in the boiler and machinery policy is restricted to property in the insured's care, custody, and control. The CGL will cover other property damage liability. Bodily injury liability is also provided by the CGL.

Defense, Settlement, and Supplementary Payments. As in the typical agreement in general liability insurance coverages, the insurer assumes all legal defense of liability suits caused by the occurrence of an accident, as defined in the policy. This cost is paid above any amounts payable under other agreements.

Automatic Coverage. Under the **automatic coverage** endorsement, the insurer agrees to cover accidents from all machinery of the same type as those specifically listed in the endorsement. (The coverage does not extend to just any additional equipment purchased.) The insured is required to apply for coverage on any additional equipment thus acquired within 90 days and to pay an additional premium thereon.

Business Income Insurance. One of the important types of loss stemming from the failure of a steam boiler or from other vital machinery is the shutdown of an entire plant. Thus, business income insurance, often called **use and occupancy** in this line of insurance, is commonly added by endorsement to the boiler and machinery contract. The contract is similar to business income insurance as written in connection with fire insurance. It is available on the valued form or on an actual-loss-sustained basis. On the valued form a daily indemnity is stated, say $1,000 per day, with an aggregate limit, say $50,000. This amount is paid without proof of loss in case the plant is totally shut down. Proportionate parts of this amount are paid for partial shutdowns.

Extra Expense. This coverage was formerly called outage insurance. However, it does differ from the old outage coverage. Losses are paid on an actual-loss-sustained basis rather than on a valued basis, and only the increase in expenses is insured. Because of the valued-policy nature of outage, there was some coverage for loss of income.

A need for extra expense coverage could arise from the failure of a heating plant boiler, forcing a business to install temporary alternative methods of heating at considerable expense. A power plant failure may force the firm to purchase standby power from another source at extra cost. Extra expense insurance is especially appropriate for office or apartment buildings, schools, and stores, where failure of an insured object would not usually stop operations, but would cause considerable extra cost in keeping everything running.

Power Interruption Insurance. The **power interruption endorsement** is available on a boiler and machinery contract to provide coverage for two types of losses stemming from interruption of electricity, gas, heat, or other energy from public utilities: (1) loss from interruption of operations, and (2) loss from damage through spoilage to property of the insured. The first type of loss is paid on a valued basis, and it is not necessary to prove any losses. All that must be shown is that the outside power source failed for a period of longer than five minutes. Indemnity is paid according to the length of time of the interruption.

The second type of power interruption loss is on an actual-loss-sustained basis. If the power or energy source is cut off for longer than a five-minute period, the insured may claim any amount of indemnity up to the policy limits, assuming it can be proved that spoilage of goods actually occurred. Thus, if a high wind destroys the power company's distribution facilities and electricity is cut off for ten hours, the insured may lose an entire cold-storage warehouse of perishable foodstuffs and may collect the entire amount of the policy.

Consequential Damage. Coverage similar to the second type of power interruption loss just described is provided on the **consequential damage endorsement.** In this case, however, the interruption is due to failure of an insured object within the insured's own premises. In the case where the insured has a cold-storage warehouse filled with perishable foodstuffs and the refrigeration system is inoperative due to failure of the compressor system within the insured's plant, indemnity would be payable under a consequential damage endorsement. Firms such as cold-storage warehouses, breweries, creameries, florists, ice plants, and hothouses are among the more likely candidates for consequential damage and power interruption coverage.

Boiler and Machinery and the SCLP

The simplified commercial lines portfolio policy (SCLP) has a separate and simpler coverage for boiler and machinery. Fourteen different object groups are reduced to four: pressure and refrigeration, mechanical, electrical, and turbine.

Covered property is property owned by the insured or in the insured's care, custody, or control. Expediting expenses, automatic coverage, defense cost, and supplementary benefits are covered in the extensions-of-coverage section. This reorganization of the policy means that expediting expenses are paid *after* payment for damage to property of others rather than before. The basic limit for expediting expenses remains $5,000.

PLATE GLASS INSURANCE

Plate glass has assumed great significance in modern architecture, not only as physical protection against the elements, but also because of its advertising value. Use of plate glass in show windows is of great importance in successful merchandising. There are many uses of glass objects, other than for plate glass windows, in which large investments are made and for which insurance is sought. Examples include glass signs, motion picture screens, halftone screens and lenses, stained glass windows, glass bricks, glass doors, neon signs, showcases, counter tops, and insulated glass panels.

The comprehensive glass policy provides a place in the declarations for a detailed description of each plate of glass, the value of lettering and ornamentation, the position of the plate in the building, and its size. The insuring clause indicates that the insurer agrees:

1. To pay for damage to the glass and its lettering or ornamentation by breakage of the glass or by chemicals accidentally or maliciously applied[12]
2. To pay for the repair or replacement of frames when necessary
3. To pay for the installation of temporary plates or boarding up of windows when necessary
4. To pay for the removal or replacement of any obstructions made necessary in replacing the glass

Each of the last three agreements is subject to a loss limitation of $75 per occurrence. There is no dollar amount of liability stated. Unlike fire insurance loss settlement procedures, it is the practice of insurers to replace the glass insured under the policy, and to do so immediately after the loss. Insurance on the replacement glass continues as before without extra premium.

SUMMARY

1. The basic purpose of workers' compensation insurance is to replace the negligence system as a method of meeting the costs of occupational injuries. All states now have workers' compensation laws, under which benefits include lifetime payments, if necessary, for permanent disabilities; income benefits for dependents; death benefits; lump-sum benefits for permanent partial disabilities; and medical and rehabilitation benefits.

2. Experience rating affects the individual rate an insured must pay after an actual loss experience in a given period has been analyzed. The revisions, if any, affect the future premium rate. Retrospective rating allows the insured to determine the premium, in whole or in part, for the period under consideration; i.e., the final premium for a period is determined by the loss.

3. Credit, title, boiler and machinery, and plate glass insurance have the common element that the insurer renders certain collateral services in addition to the indemnification and risk-reduction function.

4. Credit insurance seems useful when a firm has a few large accounts, the failure of any one of which would cause a severe and crippling loss, or when it is desired to use the credit and collection services of the insurer. A careful analysis must be made of the firm's exposure to loss, and the policy

must be tailored to fit these specific needs.

5. Title insurance is purchased largely for the title investigation that accompanies it. Also important, of course, is the protection it gives against losses caused by discovery of defects that impair the marketability of the insured title.

6. Boiler and machinery insurance exists because of the severe and crippling losses that can stem from an exploding boiler or broken machinery. Not only direct losses, but also many types of indirect losses, are so caused. Inspection of boilers and other insured machinery is an important feature of the boiler contract and accounts for a substantial element of cost in the premium.

7. The comprehensive glass insurance contract is a type of coverage that seems to find its justification more in the convenience it provides in the replacement of broken glass and in the comprehensive nature of its coverage than in the risk-reduction function. It generally duplicates, at least to some extent, glass coverage granted on other contracts.

QUESTIONS FOR REVIEW

1. What coverages are provided by the boiler and machinery insurance policy?

2. What is the basic distinction between experience rating and retrospective rating? What is the basic similarity?

3. It has been argued that retrospective rating eliminates the need for self-insurance in the lines of insurance where it is used. Do you agree? Why or why not?

4. Discuss the factors that favor self-insuring workers' compensation.

5. Why should not everyone self-insure workers' compensation loss?

6. Why do persons need plate glass insurance?

7. What are the types of domestic merchandise credit insurance?

QUESTIONS FOR DISCUSSION

1. A writer stated that credit risk cannot be transferred entirely to an external agency; some residual risk must always rest on the shoulders of the independent businessperson as a necessary consequence of engaging in business. Explain why this is true or untrue.

2. Since workers' compensation is generally required of employers by law, do you feel it should be sold only by the government? Explain your answer.

3. A writer reported the following incident. A department store in a small city had, within a fairly short period, three explosions of fuel oil vapor in the furnace of its boiler. In one of these accidents $25,000 of damage was caused, including the loss of plate glass windows. Many people, frightened by these explosions, stopped trading at the store and even crossed to the opposite side of the street to avoid passing near the store. What moral do you see in this incident for the insurance manager of the department store?

4. Of what benefit is title insurance if the insurer excludes all title defects occurring after the policy is issued and, in addition, all defects known to exist before the policy is issued? Explain.

5. (a) It is claimed that the premium for title insurance is unfairly high when the property is transferred frequently. Do you agree?

   (b) What justification could the title insurer have for not reducing the premium when the property is transferred frequently?

NEW TERMS AND CONCEPTS

Abstract
Boiler and Machinery
   Insurance
Cash Loan Credit Insurance
Consequential Damage
   Endorsement
Credit Insurance
Deposit Insurance
Domestic Merchandise
   Credit Insurance
Excess Insurance
Expediting Expense
Experience Rating
Forward Coverage

General Coverage Insurance
Liquidating Damages
Outage
Plate Glass Insurance
Power Interruption
   Endorsement
Primary Loss
Rehabilitation Benefit
Retrospective Premium
Standard Premium
Title Insurance
Use and Occupancy
Workers' Compensation
   Insurance

NOTES

1 "Review and Preview," *Best's Review: Property/Casualty Insurance Edition* (Oldwick, N.J.: A. M. Best Company, January, 1986), pp. 87 and 91.

2 National Commission of State Workmen's Compensation Laws, *Vol. I, Principles of Workmen's Compensation; Vol. II, Income Maintenance Objective; Vol. III, The Safety Objective* (Washington, D.C.: U.S. Government Printing Office, 1973).

3 Ibid.

4 Arizona, California, Colorado, Idaho, Maryland, Michigan, Minnesota, Montana, New York, Oklahoma, Oregon, Pennsylvania, and Utah.

5 Nevada, North Dakota, Ohio, Washington, West Virginia, and Wyoming. In Nevada, Oregon, and West Virginia, the laws are elective so that under certain conditions the employer may purchase voluntary compensation from a private insurer, the employer may not insure, or the employer may purchase employers' liability insurance for protection against possible employee suits.

6 Self-insurers must usually post bond.

7 David N. Price, "Workers' Compensation: Coverage, Benefits, and Costs, 1983," *Social Security Bulletin* (February, 1986), pp. 5–11.

8 There are other elements in retrospective rating formulas, such as adjustments for individual loss limitations, but for simplicity they will be ignored in the present discussion.

9 One of the earliest works on credit insurance was published in 1848 by Robert Watt, and was entitled *Principles of Insurance Applied to Mercantile Debt.*

10 American Municipal Bond Assurance Corporation, *Questions and Answers* (New York, 1971), p. 8. This company is a subsidiary of the Mortgage Guarantee Insurance Corporation, a private firm that issues loan insurance on some conventional mortgages issued by banks and savings and loan associations on home loans when the loans are not subject to insurance by the Federal Housing Administration.

11 These coverages are property of the insured, expediting expenses, property damage liability, and bodily injury liability.

12 Scratching or defacing is not the same as breakage and is not insured.

23 CRIME INSURANCE AND BONDING

After reading this chapter, you should be able to:

1. Explain the differences between insurance and bonding.
2. Describe how individuals and businesses use bonds.
3. Identify the differences among burglary, robbery, and theft.
4. Explain the nature of crime insurance policies.
5. Explain why we have a federal crime insurance program and how it operates.
6. List ways in which crime losses can be reduced.

Crime against property in the United States is one of the most serious and most underinsured perils. It is estimated that less than 10 percent of loss to property from ordinary crime is insured. In addition, although statistics on losses are not available, facts suggest that loss from organized crime is tremendous. The crime loss problem has become so serious in recent years that the federal government has entered the field of burglary and robbery insurance.

LOSS DUE TO STEALING

During the 1960s and 1970s, there was a dramatic increase in acts of stealing in the United States. However, in the mid-1980s these statistics began to change. Much of this decrease in stealing was due to a decline in the number of young persons. The 15- and 19-year-old age group made up 7.0 percent of the population in 1984 and committed over 30 percent of the acts of stealing. This decline in the number of youths should continue for several more years.

Table 23-1 shows that since 1981 the crime loss per 100,000 people declined. This decline is due to both an increase in population and an absolute decrease in the number of crimes against property. While these statistics are encouraging, crime is still higher than any time in history except the peak years of 1980-1983. The stealing rate is declining, but the absolute level remains high.

Crimes rates against property are about three times as high in cities over 250,000 as in rural areas. Forty-eight percent of all arrests for larceny were of persons under age 21. Females comprised 30 percent of all arrests for larceny.[1] A small percentage of property crimes is solved. The following percentages of property crimes were cleared in 1984: robbery, 26 percent; burglary, 14 percent; larceny, 20 percent; and auto theft, 15 percent.[2]

The Small Business Administration (SBA) made a study of the incidence and type of crime losses from a sample of 5,200 business firms representing the United States business population of 8 million firms in 1967-1968. The results represent the first available information of this type. Total crime losses were estimated to be more than $3 billion in 1967-1968, of which burglary represented 31 percent and vandalism 27 percent. Other types of crime, in order of relative size, were shoplifting, employee theft, passing bad checks, and robbery.[3]

Embezzlement

According to the SBA study, employee theft was estimated to have caused $381 million of losses in 1967-1968, or about 13 percent of the total loss from crime. It is very likely, however, that the total losses from employee stealing are much greater than this figure suggests, as swindled employers are reluctant to admit that they have been cheated by their own employees, and some losses remain undiscovered.

**Table 23-1
Property Loss from Crime, 1984**

Crime	1984 Rate Per 100,000 Population	Percent Change 1984 v. 1981
Robbery	205.4	−22.0
Burglary	1,263.7	−29.2
Larceny-theft	2,799.1	−11.5
Motor vehicle theft	437.1	−7.5

Source: Federal Bureau of Investigation, 1984 Uniform Crime Reports, *Crime in the United States* (Washington, D.C.: U.S. Government Printing Office, 1986), p. 36.

Forgery losses involving the passing of bad checks are among the most common types of dishonesty losses and yet are among the easiest to prevent. Most of such losses are caused by amateurs; it is estimated that only one-third of the total check losses are caused by professionals. Forgery most commonly involves the issuance of entirely fictitious checks, although alteration of, and false signatures upon, legitimate checks are frequent.

CRIME INSURANCE AND BONDS

There are two basic types of financial protection against the catastrophic losses that can be caused by crime: surety bonds and fidelity bonds; and burglary, robbery, and theft insurance. **Surety bonds** and **fidelity bonds** provide guarantees against loss through the dishonesty or incapacity of individuals who are trusted with money or other property and who violate this trust. **Theft insurance,** on the other hand, provides coverage against loss through stealing by individuals who are not in a position of trust.

Insurance versus Bonding

A **bond** is a legal instrument whereby one party (the **surety**) agrees to reimburse another party (the **obligee**), should this person suffer loss because of some failure by the person bonded (the **principal** or **obligor**). Thus, if a contractor furnishes a bond to the owner of a building, the surety will reimburse the owner if the contractor fails to perform as agreed upon and thereby causes a loss to the owner.

A bond may appear to be a contract of insurance, but there are some important differences to be considered:

1. In bonding, the surety sees as its basic function the lending of its credit for a premium. It expects no losses, and reserves the legal right to collect from the defaulting principal. The insurance contract is set up with the presumption that there will be losses, and is viewed by its managers as a device to spread these losses among the insured group.
2. The nature of the risk is different. Usually a bond guarantees the honesty of an individual, as well as the capacity and ability of that individual to perform. These are matters within the control of the individual. The insurance contract, ideally, covers losses outside the control of the individual.
3. In bonding, if the principal defaults and the surety makes good to the obligee, the surety enjoys the legal right to attempt to collect for its loss from the principal. In insurance, the insurer does not have the right to recover losses from the insured; this would defeat the purpose of the contract.
4. The bonding contract involves three primary parties, while the insurance contract normally involves only two.
5. Finally, in insurance, the contract is usually cancellable by either party, and nonpayment of premium or breach of warranty by the insured is

usually a good defense on the part of the insurer to obviate its liability. In a bond the surety is often liable on the bond to the beneficiary regardless of breach of warranty or fraud on the part of the principal. In addition, the bond often cannot be cancelled until it has been determined that all the obligations of the principal have been fulfilled.

Fidelity and Surety Bonds

Strictly speaking, all bonds are surety bonds, but it is convenient to classify them into fidelity bonds and surety bonds.

Fidelity bonds indemnify an employer for any loss suffered at the hands of dishonest employees. As such, the bonds are hardly distinguishable from insurance as far as the employer is concerned. While technically there are three parties to a fidelity bond—the employer (obligee), the employee (obligor), and the insurer (surety)—in practice the main parties are only two, the employer and the surety.

Surety bonds, sometimes known as **financial guaranty bonds,** are contracts between three parties: the principal (obligor), the person protected (obligee), and the insurer (surety). Under the contract the surety agrees to make good any default on the part of the principal in the principal's duties toward the obligee. For example, the principal might be a contractor who has agreed with the obligee for a given consideration to construct a building meeting certain specifications. The owner-obligee requires the contractor to post a bond to the effect that this contract will be faithfully performed. If the contractor fails in some way, the surety must "make good" to the owner and then has the right to recover any losses from the contractor.

Requirement of Collateral

As an outgrowth of the fundamental nature of a surety bond, the surety often requires collateral before it will issue the bond. The surety bond is an instrument for lending the superior credit of the surety to the obligor in return for a premium payment. The surety may decide that the credit position of the obligor is strong enough so that definite collateral in the form of cash, securities, or property is not needed. But in many cases such collateral is required as a matter of routine to protect the surety against losses, particularly in risky ventures. It may be questioned why an obligee requires a bond at all. If the obligee wants security, why does it not accept the collateral of the obligor directly? The answer lies basically in the fact that the obligee is usually in no position to assess the value of the many varieties of collateral that might be offered, or to attend to the details involved in obtaining legal security. The bonding company can perform the function much more economically and more efficiently than the typical obligee. Furthermore, many surety bonds are required by statute, and collateral may not be acceptable under the statute.

Types of Fidelity Bonds

Fidelity bonds may be classified into two groups: (1) bonds in which an individual is specifically bonded, either by name or by position held in the firm, and (2) bonds that cover all employees of a given class, called **blanket bonds.** Blanket bonds may also cover perils other than infidelity.

Bonds in Which an Individual Is Specifically Bonded. Bonds in which an individual is specifically bonded are of two types. **Individual bonds** name a certain person for coverage. If the employer suffers any loss through any dishonest or criminal act of the employee, either alone or in collusion with others, while the employee holds a position with the employer, the surety will be good for the loss up to the limit of liability, called the **penalty** of the bond. **Schedule bonds** may list many employees by name and bond them for specified amounts, in which case the bonds are known as **name schedule bonds.** Additional names may be added or old names deleted upon written notice to the surety.

Blanket Bonds. Blanket bonds have several advantages over individual or schedule bonds, making the use of blanket bonds heavily favored among most business firms:

1. Automatic coverage of a uniform amount is given on all employees, thus eliminating the possibility that the employer may select the wrong employee for bonding.
2. New employees are automatically covered without need of notifying the surety.
3. If a loss occurs, it is not necessary to identify the employees who are involved in the conspiracy in order to collect, as is required on individual or schedule bonds. It need only be shown that the loss was due to employee infidelity.
4. Because blanket bonds are subject to rate credits for large accounts, the cost may be no more than that of schedule bonds.

There are two major types of blanket bonds: the blanket position bond and the commercial blanket bond. These two bonds, whose terms are standardized by the Surety Association of America, differ primarily in the manner in which the penalty of the bond is stated. The **blanket position bond** has a penalty, ranging in amounts from $2,500 to $100,000, that applies to each employee. The **commercial blanket bond** has a penalty, ranging upward from $10,000, that applies to any one loss.

Important Provisions of Fidelity Bonds. All fidelity bonds are characterized by certain standard provisions.

Continuity of Coverage. Most fidelity bonds are continuous until cancelled by either party. They have no expiration date, only an anniversary date. Coverage on any one employee is automatically cancelled once an employer learns of any dishonest or fraudulent act committed by the employee either before or after the employee was hired. Thus, if an employer learns of a theft committed by an employee five years before being hired but decides to forgive the employee and give him or her a second chance, the employer must take the risk for any later stealing.

Noncumulative Penalty. The penalty of the bond is the maximum amount payable for any one loss for any one employee. The employee may steal $5,000 each year over a long period of time under a bond where the penalty, is, say, $5,000, but the total amount payable for losses traceable to the employee remains at $5,000.

Losses and Perils. Fidelity bonds generally cover losses occurring while the bonds are in force or when discovered within a certain period, known as the **discovery period** (usually of two years' length), after the bonds have been discontinued.

Most fidelity bonds cover any dishonest act or any criminal act of covered employees, but some bonds are restricted to certain crimes, such as larceny and embezzlement.

Salvage. Recoveries of stolen property from employees, after the surety has fully indemnified the employer, are, of course, returned to the surety. If the surety has not fully indemnified the employer, say because the loss exceeded the penalty of the bond, some bonds require that any recoveries go to the employer until he or she is fully restored for the loss.

Property Covered. Bonds covering employee dishonesty do not restrict the type of property for which indemnification is payable. Stealing of cash, inventory, equipment, securities, or any other property is covered. The property does not have to be owned by the insured, but may be merely held in trust for others to whom the insured may or may not be legally responsible. Sometimes there are territorial limits as to where the stealing may be insured.

Restoration. When a loss is incurred, the question arises as to what happens to the amount of bond penalty available for other losses. In blanket bonds there is an automatic reinstatement of bond limits (or restoration clause) immediately after the payment of any loss. For example, under the commercial blanket bond written with a $50,000 limit, payment of $30,000 for one loss from one employee does not reduce the $50,000 penalty applicable to thefts by other employees. As to the employee who stole the $30,000, however, only $20,000 remains as coverage for other stealing, no matter when it is discovered. Of course, all coverage in the future for this employee is cancelled. Since the blanket position bond limits apply separately to each employee, there is no need for a restoration clause.

Excess Insurance. Under bonds written with limits that apply to individual employees, it may sometimes be desirable to place larger limits on certain employees on an excess basis. Such coverage can be arranged without disturbing the primary bond and, therefore, without increasing the limits of the primary bond for all employees. While it may be more economical than increasing the limits of the primary bond, use of excess insurance on certain employees means that the employer must single out certain employees for higher coverage, an uncertain process at best since it cannot be predicted in advance which employee(s) will steal.

Inventory Shortages. One of the most common types of loss from employee dishonesty is that of stealing various items of inventory. Yet, the existence of an inventory shortage does not necessarily mean that an employee is to blame; shoplifting, sneak thievery, or natural evaporation or spoilage may account for the loss. In individual and schedule bonds there is no recovery under the bond for any loss unless the defaulting employee can be identified positively, including, of course, cases where the accounting system reveals an inventory shortage. In blanket bonds, where identification of the individual employee causing the loss is not a requirement, a question arises as to whether the bond will pay for a loss where an abnormal inventory shortage exists and where no explanation other than employee dishonesty could account for it. The bond provisions state that there must be conclusive proof that employees, though unidentified, have been responsible for the shortage.

Types of Surety Bonds

Surety bonds may be classified into three categories: construction bonds, court bonds, and miscellaneous surety bonds. A brief description of each type follows.

Construction Bonds. A commonly used surety bond is the construction bond. Construction bonds are classified as contract, bid, completion, and owners' protective bonds.

Contract Construction Bond. From the standpoint of premium volume, probably the most important type of surety bond is the **contract construction bond** (sometimes call a **final,** or **performance bond**). The contract construction bond guarantees that the principals (contractors) involved in construction activities will complete their work in accordance with the terms of construction contracts and will deliver the work to the owner free of any liens or other debts or encumbrances. To the owner, particularly in the case of corporate or municipal owners who let contracts for large projects to the lowest bidder, the construction bond is an indispensable financial security mechanism. Only through use of a third-party guarantee, namely the guarantee of the surety company, can the owner realistically give a contract to the lowest bidder.

Bid Bond. A **bid bond,** in contrast to a contract construction bond, guarantees that if the bidder is awarded the contract at the bid price and under the terms outlined, the bidder will sign the contract and post a construction bond. The bid bond thus involves the same risk as the contract construction bond.

Completion Bond. Bid and contract construction bonds are required for the protection of the owner. The **completion bond,** on the other hand, is required by the lender or the mortgagee, who also may have an interest in the property because of financing arrangements. The completion bond guarantees that the person who borrows the money for the project (who may be either the contractor or the owner) will use the money only for the project and will ultimately turn over to the lender the completed building or project, free of any liens, as security for the loan.

Owners' Protective Bond. A form of the contract construction bond known as the **owners' protective bond** is issued for private construction only. The owners' protective bond provides that if the principal defaults, the surety has a direct obligation to take over and to complete the contract or to pay the loss to the owner in cash. This bond differs from the usual form of contract bond, in which the owner has to take over and complete the work in order to determine the loss.

Court and Miscellaneous Bonds. There are many types of surety bonds used in connection with court proceedings. Examples are **fiduciary bonds,** insuring that persons appointed by the court to manage the property of others will carry out their trust; **litigation bonds,** insuring certain conduct by both defendants and plaintiffs; **license and permit bonds,** which are often used to guarantee the payment of taxes and fees; **lost instrument bonds,** which are required when individuals seek replacement of lost securities or other valuable papers; and **public official bonds,** which offer guarantees that public officials will perform their duties according to the law.

BURGLARY, ROBBERY, AND THEFT INSURANCE

As used in insurance contracts, the meaning of the terms burglary, robbery, and theft are important in understanding the extent of coverage. These terms always refer to crimes by persons other than the insured, officers or directors of the insured, or employees of the insured, coverage on which is provided by fidelity bonds.

Burglary is defined somewhat narrowly to mean the unlawful taking of property from within premises closed for business, entry to which has been obtained by force. There must be visible marks of the forcible entry. Thus, if a customer hides in a store until after closing hours or enters by an unlocked door, steals some goods, and leaves without having to force a door or a window, the definition of burglary is not met under a burglary policy.

Robbery is defined to mean the unlawful taking of property from another person by force, by threat of force, or by violence. Personal contact is the key to understanding the basic characteristic of the robbery peril. However, if a burglar enters a premises and steals the wallet of a sleeping night guard, this crime is not one of robbery because there was no violence or threat thereof. The person robbed must be cognizant of this fact. On the other hand, if the thief knocks out or kills the guard and then robs the guard or the owner, the crime would be classed as robbery. Robbery thus means the forcible taking of property from a messenger or a custodian.

Theft is a broad term which includes all crimes of stealing, robbery, or burglary. Theft is a catch-all term and is usually not distinguished from larceny. Thus, any stealing crime not meeting the definition of burglary or robbery is theft. Confidence games or other forms of swindles are thefts, not robberies or burglaries.

Business Coverages

There are a variety of coverages for the stealing crime peril for businesses. The following paragraphs describe a few examples, ranging from the least comprehensive to the most comprehensive coverage.

Safe Burglary Policy. As one of the oldest business crime policies, the **safe burglary policy** restricts its coverage to loss of property taken by forcible entry from a safe or a vault described in the declarations as the insured safe. Visible marks, such as those made by tools, explosives, electricity, or chemicals, must evidence the entry. If the safe combination is used or the lock is manipulated, there is no coverage. If the property owner is forced to give the combination, there is no coverage; such a loss is covered under a robbery policy.

Damage to the safe or vault, to the building or its furniture, fixtures, equipment, or to other property on the premises but outside the safe or vault is covered under the safe burglary policy, provided, of course, that there has been evidence of an actual safe burglary. Any type of property (except books and records) stolen from a safe burglary is covered, not just money or securities; but if the burglar takes other property outside the safe, there is no coverage.

Mercantile Open Stock Burglary Policy (MOS). Demand for crime insurance against the loss of stock on merchants' shelves as well as property contained in a safe gave rise to the **mercantile open stock burglary policy (MOS).** The MOS covers loss by burglary (as usually defined) or by robbery of a night guard while the premises are not open for business, of merchandise, furniture, fixtures, and equipment within the premises or within a showcase or show window. (The showcase may be outside the main premises, but must be within the building line of the premises.) Money and securities are not insured, nor are books, records, manuscripts, or furs taken from a showcase that was broken into from the outside.

The MOS is written with a coinsurance arrangement requiring the insured to purchase coverage equal to the lesser of the following: (1) a certain percentage, ranging from 40 to 80 percent, of the value of the exposed property, or (2) a dollar amount, called the **coinsurance limit,** which varies with the type of merchandise and its location. Failing to carry this amount, the insured may collect only that proportion of the loss as the amount of insurance carried bears to the amount required. This provision, which is designed to prevent underinsurance, may be illustrated as follows. A hardware store owner with $20,000 of stock may decide that thieves could never carry away more than $5,000 worth of merchandise at one time, and so this is the limit of coverage purchased. However, the MOS contract has a coinsurance percentage of 40 percent and a $10,000 coinsurance limit. Since 40 percent of the value of the stock is $8,000, and this is less than $10,000, the merchant would collect from the insurer only $5,000/$8,000, or $\frac{5}{8}$ of any loss. To avoid coinsurance penalties, the merchant must carry at least $8,000 insurance in this case. The merchant may obtain rate reductions by accepting higher coinsurance percentages or limits.

For an additional premium the retail merchant may, by endorsement, broaden the coverage under the MOS to include any kind of theft, not just burglary or robbery of a night guard. The theft coverage is subject to a $50 deductible and is written to exclude normal inventory shortages.

Storekeepers' Burglary and Robbery Policy. The **storekeepers' burglary and robbery policy** is a package policy designed to fit the typical requirements of the small retail establishment. It covers seven perils in one policy: (1) burglary of a safe; (2) mercantile open stock burglary; (3) damage to money, securities, merchandise, furniture, fixtures, and equipment caused by burglary or robbery; (4) theft of money or securities from a residence or night depository of a bank; (5) kidnapping, meaning compelling a messenger or custodian to give the thief access to the premises for purpose of taking money, securities, merchandise, or equipment; (6) robbery, outside the premises, of the insured or a messenger of the insured; and (7) robbery inside the premises.

For each of these perils, the policy contains a limit ranging from $250 or multiples thereof up to $1,000. There is a loss limit of $50 applicable to burglary of money or securities outside a safe, such as from a cash drawer or cash register.

Money and Securities Broad Form Policy. The storekeepers' burglary and robbery policy gives protection against one of the chief crime perils facing a business enterprise: theft of money or securities. The **money and securities broad form policy** is designed to meet the needs of any business enterprise for money and security protection in any limits desired. Furthermore, the peril under this form is broader than just theft, and includes loss of money or securities due to destruction of any kind, including fire, and almost any type of disappearance or wrongful abstraction. Thus, if paper money blows out a window while it is being counted, if fire or flood ruins securities and paper money, or if money mysteriously disappears, the policy will cover. If money is taken from a cash drawer or a safe by manipulating the lock, the safe burglary policy does not apply since this is not a burglary under the definitions; but the money and securities broad form policy would cover the loss. In addition, coverage is given for damage to the premises or to furniture or equipment caused by burglary or robbery, and for loss of merchandise due to interior robbery. Notice that loss of merchandise due to burglary is not insured, and therefore there is still the need for the MOS burglary policy that insures this loss.

The money and securities broad form policy is divided into two parts: loss inside the premises and loss outside the premises. Coverage outside the premises is limited to actual destruction, disappearance, or wrongful abstraction of money or securities from a messenger or armored car company, or from the home of a messenger.

Dishonesty, Destruction, and Disappearance (3D) Policy. The **dishonesty, destruction, and disappearance policy,** often called a **3D policy,** is a package contract with five basic parts: employee dishonesty coverage; money and securities broad form, inside the premises; money and securities broad form, outside the premises; money orders and counterfeit paper currency coverage; and depositors' forgery coverage.

The first three parts of this comprehensive contract are forms already analyzed in this chapter. The fourth coverage indemnifies the insured for loss in case counterfeit money or illegal or counterfeit money orders are accepted.

The fifth coverage, **depositors' forgery,** also known as **outgoing forgery,** covers the insured for losses suffered when checks are endorsed, when a check is issued to a person posing as a legitimate payee and the legitimate payee's signature is forged on the instrument, or when a check legally issued by the insured to a legitimate payee is endorsed and cashed by someone else without the authority of the legitimate payee. Court and legal costs involved in any suit over an allegedly forged instrument are also covered under the policy.

For an additional premium, an endorsement may be added to the 3D policy giving the insured protection in case of *incoming* check forgery. For example, losses incurred when the insured accepts a forged check in payment of merchandise or services may be insured.

In addition to incoming check forgery, mercantile open stock burglary, mercantile open stock theft, and certain other crime coverages may be endorsed on the 3D policy. Thus, the insured is provided a means of covering practically all crime exposures in one contract.

CRIME COVERAGE IN THE SCLP

In the Simplified Commercial Lines Portfolio (SCLP) policy, the insured may choose from any of the coverages available in the new commercial crime program. This new program has 14 basic coverage forms plus numerous endorsements. The insured may use one or more of the basic forms to obtain the coverage desired. Some of the coverages contained in the program are as follows:

1. Employee dishonesty
2. Forgery
3. Theft, disappearance, and destruction
4. Robbery and burglary of a safe
5. Burglary of premises
6. Computer fraud
7. Extortion
8. Liability of guests' property
9. Safe deposit liability

It is expected that this commercial crime program will become the dominant means of insuring businesses against loss due to an act of stealing.

Personal Coverage

The **broad form personal theft policy** is a form of theft insurance written for the individual. Defining theft as *any act of stealing,* the policy covers against loss by either theft or mysterious disappearance of any property from a private home, or from another depository such as another private dwelling, a public warehouse, a bank, or a trust company. The policy provides for limits of liability under two categories: loss on the premises, and loss off the premises. Today, most personal theft coverage is provided in the homeowners' program and not in a separate policy.

Federal Crime Insurance

Because of difficulties in securing private insurance, particularly in some large city areas, the federal government began to offer crime insurance to the public in 1971 in certain states on a subsidized basis. Coverages are noncancellable and include burglary, robbery, and theft. Premiums are quoted so that the cost of crime coverage appears affordable to the average buyer. Although private insurers and their agents administer and market the coverage, the federal government, through the Federal Insurance Administration (FIA), is the bearer of the risk under the policies issued. About 9,975 businesses and 28,499 residences in 23 states, the District of Columbia, Puerto Rico, and the Virgin Islands participate in this program.

To be eligible for federal crime insurance, the insured must (1) live in a state deemed eligible for the crime coverage; (2) meet certain protective device standards; (3) agree to permit inspections of the premises at reasonable times; (4) agree to report to the insurer all crime losses, whether or not a claim is filed; and (5) accept the form of coverage prescribed by the FIA.

Residence Policy. The residential crime policy covers burglary, robbery, observed theft, or attempted theft of insured property, including damage caused by attempted theft. The coverage includes vandalism and malicious mischief on owned property. It may be written on one-, two-, three-, or four-family residences in multiples of coverage from $1,000 to $10,000.

The policy carries a deductible of $75 or 5 percent of the gross amount of loss, whichever is greater. The deductible is applied against the total loss, and not the policy limit. Thus, if an insured had a $3,000 loss, but only $2,000 of coverage, the deductible of 5 percent ($150) would apply against $3,000 and the insured's recovery would be the full $2,000, the policy limit. The policy applies as excess coverage if the insured has other insurance. Thirty days' notice of cancellation is required, and the insurer has a limited right to cancel only for specified reasons.

Commercial Policy. Coverage under the commercial crime insurance policy is issued in amounts ranging from $1,000 to $15,000. There is a deductible between $50 and $200 per loss or 5 percent of the loss, whichever is greater. Businesses are assigned one of three ratings according to the degree of hazard for that line of business. Premiums vary according to the class of business, territory of operation, sales volume, and amount of insurance.

The rating structure of commercial policies assumes that larger firms are more hazardous to insure than smaller firms. Only a modest quantity discount for larger policy amounts is justified, and a different concept of an affordable rate exists in businesses as distinguished from residential policies. For example, while the owner of a residence with $5,000 of contents may pay $60 annually for coverage, a business firm with a $5,000 coverage and $100,000 of annual sales would pay more than ten times that amount, presumably because of greater ability to pay and greater exposure to loss. The business policy, for example, covers the following perils: theft inside or outside the premises, kidnapping, safe burglary, theft from a night depository, and burglary or robbery from a night guard. Excluded from the business policy are the perils of embezzlement, war, revolution or rebellion, fire, nuclear reaction, and loss of manuscripts, records, or accounts.

RISK MANAGEMENT OF THE CRIME PERIL

Management may attempt to handle the crime risk through several methods, including assumption, loss prevention, and insurance. Each of these methods is deficient in some respect. The method of assumption may invite ruin. Loss-prevention efforts tend to be haphazard and are often ineffective. Insurance methods suffer from adverse selection, high costs, and gaps in protection because of narrow definitions of perils.

Assumption

Evidence suggests that the method of assumption of risks has had serious negative consequences for many business firms. The SBA study reported that in three cities characterized by high crime rates, Boston, Chicago, and Washington, D.C., 20 percent of the businesses surveyed in 1966 were out of business by 1968, and 5 percent had moved to a new location. Survival rates were significantly higher in the areas with the lowest crime rates. Retailers were least likely to survive.[4] While these data do not prove that crime was the major cause of the business mortality noted, the association between the two factors seems apparent. Even though crime loss is still a relatively small 0.23 percent of total receipts, the losses can be catastrophic for some firms. Yet assumption remains perhaps the most generally used method of handling the crime peril.

Loss Prevention

Efforts to prevent losses due to crime appear to be the best solution to the problem, but total effectiveness, even in the long run, seems doubtful. Loss prevention can be considered in two perspectives: efforts that seek to reform society to eliminate basic causes of crime, and efforts that attack the symptoms of crime.

Sociological, economic, political, and legal reforms appear to be crucial in obtaining any permanent success in preventing the most serious losses from crime. As examples, these measures would include efforts to eliminate poverty, to reform prisons and the judicial system, to speed justice, and to help the criminal to adjust to society; medical research to cure mental and emotional disorders; improved community planning to eliminate crowding; and programs to improve education.

Efforts to control the crime problem by relieving its symptoms are also important. Among these efforts are providing police protection, private guards, burglar alarms, locks and shields, surveillance mechanisms, and sensing devices. All of these play a role in detecting and deterring crime once the criminal has initiated the act or has determined to do so. However, the three-city survey by Aldrich and Reiss reported little evidence that the presence of protective devices in areas previously without them had the effect of reducing the rate of burglaries in the two-year period.[5]

The conclusion is suggested that protection and loss-prevention measures attacking symptoms alone have their limitations as a way to meet the crime risk. Also potentially valuable are such measures as community programs to show citizens how to cope with crime and to report observed crime, reducing the exposure to loss (for example, making more frequent bank deposits of cash receipts), installation of protective materials such as specialized glass to lengthen the time it takes to enter the premises, and use of devices to alert police.

Insurance

Even with rapid detection of crime, effective systems of court action, and rehabilitation efforts applied to the criminal, it appears that crime is a problem that will always characterize society. Insurance remains as a potentially effective device to spread the inevitable crime losses among insureds.

Unfortunately, insurance as a way of handling the crime risk suffers from serious weaknesses. Crime insurance is used sparingly and, as noted above, covers less than 10 percent of the total crime loss in the United States. Adverse selection is present due to the tendency of those applicants who are most likely to suffer loss (such as pawn shops and jewelry and liquor stores) to apply for the most coverage. A moral hazard exists in the temptation of those who are insured to take advantage of opportunities to arrange a robbery or burglary with an accomplice in order to collect illegally from the insurance company. Also, it is often difficult to establish the amount of the loss when it occurs because of inadequate inventory control methods or lack of adequate records. For example, a burglary to a retailer might occur, evidence of which is obvious. But the insured may try to include in the loss claim some shortages of inventory that are in reality due to shoplifting or employee theft. It may be difficult for the claims adjuster to prove otherwise.

Among the solutions that have been proposed for the problems that characterize crime insurance are the following:

1. Offer crime insurance through the federal government. This method was tried, but has not been an outstanding success. (See Chapter 25.)
2. Reduce what have been termed excessive agency commissions, which reduce the profitability to insurers and discourage them from making crime coverage more readily available.
3. Permit group crime coverage to be made available through trade associations.
4. Use deductibles and package policies to obtain greater spread of risk and hence less risk to the insurer.
5. Require more attention to loss prevention as a prerequisite to offering insurance.
6. Alter the premium structure by making the rate-making base the standard metropolitan area rather than the county. This would tend to produce lower rates for suburban businesses and would make firms in the urban area share more fairly in the cost of crime.[6]

Even though insurance is not a total solution to the problem of managing the crime risk, it is one of the most immediately practical methods by which the business firm may obtain financial protection against crime. If understood thoroughly, insurance and bonds can play effective roles in the war against crime.

SUMMARY

1. Crime statistics show that the perils of dishonesty and human failure cause more total losses than other major perils. Yet the crime peril is greatly underinsured. Prominent among the reasons for this underinsurance are the tendency for business firms to refuse to recognize that trusted employees can and do steal, and the lack of publicity that attends these crimes.
2. The two major types of crime protection are (a) bonds, and (b) burglary, robbery, and theft insurance. Bonds give protection against losses due to defalcations by persons in a position of trust, while theft

insurance gives protection against crimes of so-called outsiders.

3. There are some important differences between bonds and insurance. Basic is the fact that bonds provide the surety's financial guarantee of the principal's honesty and ability, with the understanding that the surety can attempt to recover from the principal. In an insurance contract the insurer pays on behalf of the insured and has no recourse against the insured.

4. Fidelity bonds, which are similar to an insurance contract in their operation, appear in many forms that may be adapted to the needs of a particular business firm. They cover against loss due to dishonesty of employees, while surety bonds provide financial guarantees of both the honesty and the ability of the principal to perform according to a given agreement.

5. Three major types of losses due to crime from outsiders are burglary, robbery, and theft. These perils are usually defined carefully in insurance contracts, and their meanings differ from the meanings commonly ascribed to them by the lay person, who may make no differentiation among them. Crime policies have certain major underwriting characteristics that help to explain the insurance practices involving their use. Chief among these characteristics are the existence of underinsurance, a high degree of moral hazard, and a tendency toward adverse selection.

6. Contracts of insurance against each of the three major crime perils are available, both for personal and business use. In addition, all-risk coverage against loss of money and securities is available. The best known comprehensive crime policy for business is the 3D—dishonesty, destruction, and disappearance—contract which covers in one scheduled form fidelity insurance, broad form money and securities destruction insurance, and forgery and counterfeit money insurance.

QUESTIONS FOR REVIEW

1. An employer has a blanket position bond with a $10,000 penalty. Three employees are caught in a scheme whereby fictitious employees are kept on the payroll and their names are forged on paychecks by the group. The total amount of theft is $36,000, of which $12,000 is finally recovered by the surety.
   (a) What is the amount payable to the employer under the bond? Explain your answer.
   (b) How would the salvage be divided under a bond with (1) a full salvage clause? (2) a pro-rata salvage clause? Explain all calculations involved.

2. A burglar enters a jewelry store at night by forcing a window. Just as the burglar begins forcing open the safe, a night guard arrives on the scene. There is a struggle, the guard is knocked unconscious, and the burglar escapes with gems taken from the safe. Is this crime compensable under the usual burglary policy? Why or why not?

3. The manager of a clothing store maintains an average inventory of $15,000. The manager purchases an MOS policy of $6,000 with a coinsurance percentage of 60 percent and a coinsurance limit of $10,000.
   (a) How much may the manager collect in the event of a $1,000 loss caused by robbery? Why? For a $2,100 loss caused by burglary? Why?
   (b) How could the manager have made sure that it would be possible to collect in full for these losses? Explain.

4. A certain dairy bonded all its financial personnel as well as its driver-collectors on a position schedule bond. A laborer in the

yard made arrangements to purchase empty wooden butter cartons at five cents each for his "hobby." It turned out some months later that the laborer had systematically stolen several thousand dollars' worth of butter in the "empty" boxes. How could the dairy automatically have protected itself against such a loss?

5. "Federal crime insurance is not aimed at 'taking over' crime insurance from private insurers. In fact, the number of policies decreased 15 percent in 1981."

   (a) What is the aim of federal crime insurance?

   (b) Why has the number of policies failed to grow or shown slow growth since 1971?

QUESTIONS FOR DISCUSSION

1. Suggest reasons for the relative lack of acceptance of insurance against crime, in spite of the constant reminder of the danger of losses due to crime in the public media.

2. Writing on the subject of the tendency of management to ignore danger signals from losses due to dishonesty, an author stated: "Besides overlooking obvious danger signals, management often places undue confidence in its alarm systems. The principal alarms for embezzlement are the accounting system and the auditor. Both, for this purpose, are overrated. Most large embezzlements are hidden in accounting systems, remaining hidden through one audit after another. The internal accounting systems are not primarily established to detect fraud, and auditors can't audit what they can't find. More embezzlements are discovered by good luck than by good accounting." Comment. Does this imply that audits are completely useless? If not, what value might they have?

3. Judge Louis D. Brandeis was reported to have called fidelity insurance "an abomination," stating that it is ridiculous "to think of insuring management against the consequences of its own failure to know and supervise its trusted employees!"

   (a) Discuss arguments for and against this position.

   (b) Do the facts support Brandeis's opinion?

   (c) What relationship does this argument have to the increasing dominance of professional managers in business as opposed to the former eminence of individual entrepreneur-owners?

4. Professor John D. Long writes: "Unless most persons in society are honest in most little matters and unless virtually everyone is scrupulously and compulsively honest in big matters, insurance will not function . . . (yet) some types of insurance, particularly dishonesty insurance, require instances of nonconformity to the law." Reconcile this apparent contradiction.

5. In an address to local agents, a bond underwriter stressed the following: "In looking over an application for a bond, the underwriter's first question is, 'Who is going to pay if the principal does not?'" Does this statement imply that the surety is not going to meet its obligations under the bond if a loss develops? If not, explain what steps the surety takes to insure that a loss to it will not occur.

NEW TERMS AND CONCEPTS		
	Blanket Position Bond	Completion Bond
	Bid Bond	Contract Construction Bond
	Burglary	Depositors' Forgery
	Commercial Blanket Bond	Discovery Period

Dishonesty, Destruction,
and Disappearance Policy
Fidelity Bond
Fiduciary Bonds
Individual Bond
Mercantile Open Stock
Insurance Policy
Money and Securities Policy
Obligee

Obligor
Principal
Penalty
Robbery
Schedule Bond
Storekeepers' Burglary and
Robbery Policy
Surety Bond
Theft

NOTES

1 Federal Bureau of Investigation, 1984 Uniform Crime Reports, *Crime in the United States* (Washington, D.C.: U.S. Government Printing Office, 1985), pp. 13–35.

2 Ibid., p. 153.

3 Small Business Administration, *Crime Against Small Business*, Senate Document 91-14 (Washington, D.C.: U.S. Government Printing Office, 1969), p. 25.

4 Howard Aldrich and Albert J. Reiss, Jr., "A 1968 Followup Study of Crime and Insurance Problems of Businesses Surveyed in 1966 in Three Cities," Appendix B to Small Business Administration, *Crime Against Small Business*, Senate Document 91-14 (Washington, D.C.: U.S. Government Printing Office, 1969), p. 146.

5 Ibid.

6 Herbert S. Denenberg, "Insurance Study," Appendix F to Small Business Administration, *Crime Against Small Business*, Senate Document 91-14 (Washington, D.C.: U.S. Government Printing Office, 1969).

24 SPECIAL PROBLEMS IN RISK MANAGEMENT

After studying this chapter, you should be able to:

1. State the meaning of several statistical terms that are used in making quantitative applications in risk management and insurance.
2. Explain how one can determine the number of observations necessary to have a given degree of accuracy in making predictions of losses.
3. Measure utility.
4. Use utility analysis to explain why people purchase insurance even though it has a negative expected value.
5. Use quantitative techniques to choose an insurance deductible.

Quantitative techniques can be very useful in risk management and insurance. This chapter examines several of these techniques.

STATISTICAL TERMS

In order to analyze risk scientifically, one needs a clear understanding of basic statistical terms. In this section the concepts of probability distribution, measures of central tendency, and standard deviation are reviewed.

Probability

As defined earlier, the probability of an event refers to the long-run frequency of occurrence of the event. All events have a probability between zero and one. To calculate the probability of an event, we divide the number of times a given event occurs by all possible events of that type. For example, if we observe 1,000 automobiles in operation and determine that 150 accidents occur, then we could say there was a 0.15 probability of an accident $\left(\frac{150}{1,000}\right)$. If we throw a six-sided die, the probability of one particular side coming up is one-sixth. The sum of the probabilities $\left(\frac{1}{6}+\frac{1}{6}+\frac{1}{6}+\frac{1}{6}+\frac{1}{6}+\frac{1}{6}\right)$ in such a distribution equals 1. The probabilities may be obtained from a formula, table, graph, or chart.

Probability Distributions

A **probability distribution** is a mutually exclusive and collectively exhaustive list of all events (losses) that can result from a chance process and contains the probability associated with each event (loss).[1] Probability distributions are also called **relative frequency distributions.** They can be used to describe how often a given event will occur. In risk management at least two types of probability distributions can be used: empirical and theoretical.

To form an **empirical distribution,** one actually observes the events that occur. A firm may monitor the losses that occur to its automobiles. It can then determine how often certain-size losses occur. If the number of similar-sized losses observed is large enough, the firm can use that distribution to predict future losses. If the number of observed events is not large enough to predict future losses, the firm may choose a theoretical or mathematical distribution that is similar to the firm's own past distribution of losses. To create a **theoretical probability distribution,** we use a formula. By changing the values of the variables in the formula, we create the probability distribution. The advantage of using a theoretical distribution is that we can determine with some degree of accuracy how often a given event will occur without having a large number of loss exposures. However, the risk manager must be reasonably confident that the firm's loss distribution is similar to the theoretical distribution chosen.

Measures of Central Tendency

When people discuss **measures of central tendency,** they are concerned with one number that most closely resembles an *average* measure. In terms of a probability distribution, they are concerned with a measure of the center of the distribution.[2] Several types of such measures exist: the mean, median, and mode. The most widely used is the arithmetic mean.

The Arithmetic Mean. The **arithmetic mean,** which is the mean usually signified by the symbol x (x bar), can be defined as the sum of a set of n measurements $x_1, x_2, x_3, \ldots, x_n$ divided by n. That is,

$$\overline{x} = \frac{x_1 + x_2 + x_3 + \cdots + x_n}{n}$$

where

$$\bar{x} = \text{arithmetic mean}$$
$$x = \text{measurement}$$
$$n = \text{total number of measurements}$$

In calculating the mean, equal weight is given to each observation (measurement). For example, the mean of the five numbers 0, 1, 2, 3, and 4 is $0 + 1 + 2 + 3 + 4)/5 = 10 \div 5 = 2$. Each observation counts only once and so has equal weight. If some numbers are to receive more weight than others, the concept of expected value is useful.

Expected Value. A special case of the arithmetic mean, and similar to it, **expected value** is obtained by multiplying each item or event by the probability of its occurrence. For instance, assume the following hypothetical distribution of loss from fire to a group of buildings.

Event	Amount of Loss if Event Occurs		Probability of Loss		
A	$ 1,000	×	0.40	=	$ 400
B	2,000	×	0.30	=	600
C	5,000	×	0.20	=	1,000
D	10,000	×	0.10	=	1,000
Total	$18,000		1.00		$3,000
					Expected value

To determine the expected value of losses, multiply each loss amount by its probability, and then sum. The expected value is $3,000. The arithmetic mean would be $4,500 ($18,000 ÷ 4), because it places an equal weight on each event. In effect, the expected value figure is a weighted average and reflects the best estimate of long-run average loss for a given loss distribution.

The Median. The **median** is the midpoint in a range of measurements. It is the point such that half of the items are larger and half are smaller than it. For instance, in a series of five losses of $1,000, $3,000, $5,000, $6,000, and $30,000, the median loss would be $5,000. Half of the losses are greater than that value, and half are smaller than that value. (The mean of the series is $9,000.) One of the advantages of the median is that it is not affected greatly by extreme values, as the mean is affected. In the preceding loss situation, $5,000 does a much better job of describing the average loss than $9,000, because the extreme loss of $30,000 distorts the mean.

The Mode. The **mode** is the value of the variable that occurs most often in a frequency distribution. If a firm experienced eight losses of $25, $30, $30, $40, $40, $40, $50, and $60, the mode would be $40. The mode is not as widely utilized as the mean or median.

Standard Deviation and Variance	The **standard deviation,** usually signified by the greek letter σ (sigma), is a number that measures how close a group of individual measurements is to its average value. For example, assume a manufacturer has 100 employees who are injured during a year. The dollar loss from these injuries ranges from $500 to $25,000, with a mean of $12,500. The range of the individual losses is rather great, from $500 to $25,000. To say that the average injury loss is $12,500 is not very descriptive of the magnitude of the average loss, especially if one is comparing it with another group of 100 losses that have a range in severity from $11,000 to $14,000, but where the average loss is also $12,500. It is helpful to state precisely just how the two groups differ. This can be accomplished by use of the standard deviation. By comparing the standard deviation of the magnitude of two sets of injuries, the precise variation in injuries becomes clear.

To calculate the standard deviation of a group of measures, first determine the arithmetic mean. Then subtract each individual value from the mean and square the resulting figure. Add these squared differences and divide the result by the total number of measurements. You then have the mean of the squared deviation, which is known as the **variance.** The square root of the variance is the standard deviation. For example, the standard deviation of the five numbers 0, 1, 2, 3, and 4 is calculated as follows. The mean is $(0 + 1 + 2 + 3 + 4)/5 = 10 \div 5 = 2$. Deviations from the mean are $-2, -1, 0, 1, 2$. The sum of the squares of these numbers is $4 + 1 + 0 + 1 + 4 = 10$. The mean of these squares is $10 \div 5 = 2$, which is the variance. The standard deviation is $\sqrt{2}$, or 1.41.

Suppose there are two factories with the same average loss. However, the dollar loss of all injuries in one factory falls within one standard deviation of the mean loss, while in the other factory only 10 percent of the injuries fall within one standard deviation of the mean loss. With such a statement, we have a much better understanding of the average injury loss in these two factories. The dispersion of losses in the first factory is much less than in the second. Thus, the standard deviation is a gauge of the dispersion of measurements about the mean. That is its statistical use.

Coefficient of Variation	When the standard deviation is expressed as a percent of the mean, the result is termed the **coefficient of variation,** which is one way to characterize the concept of mathematical risk to the insurer. It is the same as the method used in Chapter 1 to measure objective risk. If losses from a group of exposure units have a low coefficient of variation, there is less risk (less variation) associated with this group of exposures than with another group with a high coefficient of variation.

Theoretical Probability Distributions	There are three theoretical probability distributions used widely in risk management: the binomial, the normal, and the Poisson. In each of these distributions it is assumed that events occur randomly (the probability that any one event will occur is equal to the probability that any other event

will occur) and independently (when one event occurs, the probability that a second event will occur is not changed).

The Binomial Distribution. Suppose we know that the probability that an event will occur in a single trial is p.[3] Then the probability q that the event will not happen can be stated by the equation $q = 1 - p$. We can calculate how often an event will happen by means of the **binomial formula.**[4] Suppose we need to estimate the probability of certain numbers of losses in an insured group. If there are 10,000 automobiles being insured, the binomial formula (or other approximating formulas) may be used to calculate the chance of 10 losses, 100 losses, 200 losses, or any other number of losses, providing we know both p and q. Similarly, if there are 100 exposure units, such as houses, and we know from past experience that the separate probability of loss of any one house by fire each year is 0.01, reference to a binomial table tells us that the probability is

0.37 that 0 houses will burn
0.37 that 1 house will burn
0.19 that 2 houses will burn
0.06 that 3 houses will burn
<u>0.01</u> that 4 or more houses will burn
Total 1.00

The probability q that one (or more) houses will burn is $1 - 0.37 = 0.63$.

The Normal Distribution. As the number of observations increases, the binomial distribution may be used to approximate another distribution called the normal distribution. The **normal distribution** is a very useful type of mathematical distribution. Shown graphically in Figure 24–1, it is perfectly bell shaped. When one knows its mean and standard deviation, the distribution is said to be completely defined. For instance, the loss distribution in Figure 24–1 is a normal distribution of 500 losses with a mean value of $500 and a standard deviation of $150. When risk managers have this information, they can assume that about 68 percent of all losses will be within ± 1 standard deviation of the mean. The figure shows that 340 losses (75 + 95 + 95 + 75) are between $350 and $650, which is the range of ± 1 standard deviation. Likewise, about 95 percent, or 470, of all losses should occur within ± 2 standard deviations of the mean. These losses would be within the $200 to $800 range.

About 99 percent of all observations should be within ± 3 standard deviations of the mean. If risk managers know that their loss distributions are normal, they can assume that these relationships hold and they can predict the probability of a given loss level occurring or the probability of losses being within a certain range of the mean.

It should be noted that the binomial distribution requires variables to be discrete (loss or no loss). Thus, in the earlier example using the binomial table, it is assumed that either 1, 2, or 3 houses will burn, but not $1\frac{1}{2}$ houses.

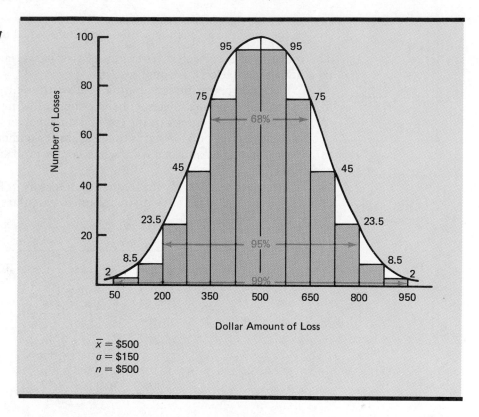

**Figure 24–1
Normal Probability
Distribution of
500 Losses**

$\bar{x} = \$500$
$\sigma = \$150$
$n = \$500$

In the normal distribution, variables may be continuous, having a value of any number from zero to infinity. As a result, the normal distribution can be employed in more situations and is more versatile and more realistic than the binomial.

The Poisson Probability Distribution. The **Poisson probability distribution** is another theoretical probability distribution that is useful in insurance situations.[5] For example, auto accidents, fires, and other losses tend to fall in a manner approximately according to the Poisson distribution.

One determines the probability of an event under the Poisson distribution using the formula

$$p = \frac{m^r e^{-m}}{r!}$$

where

p = the probability that an event n occurs
r = the number of events for which the probability estimate is needed
$r!$ = r factorial. If r is 5, for example, $r!$ is $5 \times 4 \times 3 \times 2 \times 1 = 120.0$

m = mean = expected loss frequency
e = a constant, the base of the natural logarithms, equal to 2.71828

The mean m of a Poisson distribution is also its variance. Consequently, its standard deviation σ is equal to $\sqrt{m}$.

To obtain a better understanding of how the Poisson distribution is used to calculate probabilities, consider the following example. Suppose Mr. Marshall has 10 trucks to insure, and on the average a total of 1 loss occurs each year ($p = 0.1$). What is the probability of more than 2 accidents in a year? Or stated another way, what is the probability of 3 or more accidents?

To calculate m, multiply the frequency of loss by n. Thus, $0.1 \times 10 = 1.0$, and $m = 1.0$. The probabilty distribution is calculated in the following manner:

Losses	Probability		
0	$\dfrac{(1.0)^0 e^{-1}}{0!}$	$= \dfrac{1 \times 0.3679}{1}$	$= 0.3679$
		$0! = 1$	
1	$\dfrac{(1.0)^1 e^{-1}}{1!}$	$= \dfrac{1 \times 0.3679}{1}$	$= 0.3679$
2	$\dfrac{(1.0)^2 e^{-1}}{2!}$	$= \dfrac{1 \times 0.3679}{2 \times 1}$	$= 0.1839$
3	$\dfrac{(1.0)^3 e^{-1}}{3!}$	$= \dfrac{1 \times 0.3679}{3 \times 2 \times 1}$	$= 0.0613$
4	$\dfrac{(1.0)^4 e^{-1}}{4!}$	$= \dfrac{1 \times 0.3679}{4 \times 3 \times 2 \times 1}$	$= 0.0153$

To determine the probability of 3 or more losses, add the appropriate probabilities and subtract them from 1. Consequently, to find the probability of 3 or more, subtract the sum of the probabilities of 0, 1, and 2 from 1. In this case, there is a probability of 0.0833 ($1 - 0.9167$) for 3 or more losses.

Note that the preceding probabilities are similar to those found for the binomial distribution, where the mean loss was also equal to 1. When the probabilities of loss are greater, the difference between the two distributions is greater. However, it should be noted that as n increases and the probability of loss decreases, the binomial distribution approaches the Poisson distribution as a limit.

From a risk-management viewpoint, the Poisson distribution is most desirable when more than 50 independent exposure units exist and the probability that any one item will suffer a loss is one-tenth or less.[6] However, when one has fewer than 50 exposures, but each one can suffer multiple losses during the year, a common situation, the Poisson distribution can still be used. Given these characteristics, the Poisson can be a very useful probability distribution for risk managers.

In Chapter 1 the law of large numbers was examined, and it was found that as the number of insured items increases the more predictable is the loss experience. In this section an application of the concept of the law of large numbers is made. A statistical technique to determine the number of observations needed to make accurate predictions is presented. Note that the term *credibility* is often used by the insurance industry when using data to make predictions. The more credible the data, the more likely it is that the predictions (forecast) will be accurate.

**Number of
Exposures
Required
for a Given
Accuracy**

A question of considerable interest, both to the commercial insurer and the would-be self-insurer, is how large an exposure (that is, what number of individual exposure units) is necessary before a given degree of accuracy can be achieved in obtaining an *actual* loss frequency that is sufficiently close to the *expected* loss frequency. As the number of exposure units becomes infinitely large, the actual loss frequency will approach the expected true loss frequency. But it is never possible for a single insurer, whether a commercial insurer or a self-insurer, to group together an infinitely large number of exposures. Undoubtedly, many individuals are under the mistaken assumption that they are in a position to self-insure if they have under their own control, say, 10 automobiles. These individuals think that certainly it would be unusual for more than one or two automobiles to be lost in a given time period, or that more than one damage suit would befall them. This position is a dangerous one.

The question arises, How much error is introduced when the insured group is not sufficiently large? More precisely, an insurer might wish to ask, "How many exposure units must be grouped together in order to be 95 percent sure that the number of actual losses will differ from expected losses by no more than 5 percent?" It is assumed that the expected losses for a very large population of exposures either are known, or can be estimated from industry-wide data, or can be determined subjectively. Essentially, the insurer wishes to know how stable its loss experience will be, i.e., how much objective risk must be accepted for a given number of exposure units. Certain mathematical and statistical laws help provide an answer to this question. While the assumptions required by these laws may not always hold in the real world, they enable the insurer to make an approximation that will be of considerable help in making a sound decision. The required assumption is that the losses occur in the manner assumed by the binomial theorem. In other words, each loss occurs independently of each other loss, and the probability of loss is constant from occurrence to occurrence.

A simple mathematical formula is available that enables insurers to estimate the number of exposures required for a given degree of accuracy. However, unless mathematical tools such as the one to be given are used with great caution and are interpreted by experienced persons, wrong conclusions may be reached. The formula is given only as an illustration of how such tools can be of help in guiding an insurer to reduce risk. The formula is based on the assumption that losses in an insured population are distributed normally.[7] The formula concerns only the occurrence of a loss, and not the evaluation of the *size* of the loss, which is an entirely different problem and beyond the scope of this book.

The formula is based on the knowledge that the normal distribution is an approximation of the binomial distribution, and that known percentages of losses will fall within 1, 2, 3, or more standard deviations from the mean. The formula is[8]

$$N = \frac{S^2 p(1 - p)}{E^2}$$

where

N = the number of exposure units sufficient for a given degree of accuracy
E = the degree of accuracy required, expressed as a ratio of actual losses to the total number in the sample
S = the number of standard deviations of the distribution. The value of S tells us with what level of confidence we can state our results. Thus, if S is 1, we know with 68% confidence that losses will be as predicted by the formula; if S is 2, we have 95% confidence, etc.

As an example, suppose that in the preceding case our probability of loss is 0.30 (not an unusual probability in certain areas for collision of automobiles), and that we want to be 95 percent confident that the actual loss ratio (number of losses divided by total number of insured units) will not differ from the expected loss ratio of 0.30 by more than 2 percentage points, that is, 0.02. In other words, we want to know how many units there must be in our insured group in order to be 95 percent confident that the number of losses out of each 100 units will fall in the range 28–32. Substitution in the formula

$$N = \frac{S^2 p(1 - p)}{E^2}$$

yields

$$N = \frac{2^2 (0.30)(0.70)}{(0.02)^2}$$

or 2,100 exposure units. The value of S is 2 in this case because of our requirement of a 95 percent confidence interval statement—we know that 95 percent of all losses will fall within a range of 2 standard deviations of the mean.

In the preceding illustration the probability of loss was very large. In many fields of insurance it is somewhat unusual to experience such large probabilities. It is much more common for the probability of loss to be about 5 percent or less. If the probability of loss is only 5 percent, the insurer will undoubtedly wish to insist on a higher standard of accuracy than was true in the preceding case. Thus, 0.03 might be satisfactory when the expected loss ratio is 0.30, because a deviation of 0.03 from a mean of 0.30 represents only a 10 percent error $(0.03 = 0.10/0.30)$. If the expected loss ratio is only 0.05, however, an error of 0.03 in the above formula becomes a deviation of 60 percent away from the expected loss ratio $(0.03/0.05 = 0.60)$. Hence, the insurer may say that if the expected loss ratio is 0.05, the standard of accuracy will be 0.005, or 10 percent away from the expected loss ratio. Substitution of 0.005 for E in the foregoing general formula yields, at a 95 percent confidence level,

$$N = \frac{2^2(0.05)(0.95)}{(0.005)^2}$$

or 7,600 exposure units as the minimum number necessary.

In life insurance it is interesting to observe that at a young age, such as 20, the probability of loss is less than 0.002. If a life insurer is to be 95 percent confident that its actual number of deaths among all insured lives that are age 20 is to be within 0.0002 (again, 10 percent away from the expected loss ratio) of its expected death rate, it must insure

$$N = \frac{2^2(0.002)(0.998)}{(0.0002)^2}$$

or 199,600 lives.

The formula produces a very large number of lives required for the degree of risk acceptable, but the example illustrates a fundamental truth about insurer risk: when the probability of loss is small, the insurer needs a larger number of exposure units for an acceptable degree of risk than is commonly recognized. Mathematical formulas such as the ones used in these examples can assist the insurer considerably in making estimates of the degree of risk assumed with given numbers in an exposure group.

Formulas such as those given offer a way for an insurer to consider simultaneously the relationships among numbers of exposure units, probabilities of loss, errors in prediction, and confidence levels of future estimates of loss. Once any three of these variables are ascertained, the fourth may be found. Using the formulas, a commercial insurer may discover, for example, that a much larger penetration of an insurance market is necessary to reduce the risk to acceptable levels. A decision to withdraw from a given market or to spend additional sums in promotional efforts may thus be made with greater intelligence.

RISKS OF THE INDIVIDUAL

The basic risk to an individual is the uncertainty as to whether the loss will be a personal one. An insured may know that the probability of loss is small, but there is no way of knowing where or on whom the lightning may strike. If the *possibility* of a serious loss exists, even though its *probability* is small, the individual will generally seek some way of avoiding this possibility.

As mentioned earlier, rarely will a private individual have a sufficient number of exposure units to achieve a high degree of accuracy in statistical predictions of loss. We may say that for the individual, risk is very high indeed. Hence, to avoid this risk, insurance may be purchased or other methods of transfer or avoidance may be sought. Of course, an individual may not really care whether a loss occurs or not, since the amount of money involved may be very small in relation to existing wealth. An individual may be unwilling to buy insurance against the occurrence of a small loss, such as fire insurance on a woodshed, even if the coverage is very inexpensive. Yet the insured may be willing to buy insurance on a new automobile, even if the mathematical expectation of loss is less than the premium to be paid, simply because there is unwillingness to expose to loss an investment that is relatively large when compared with total wealth.

For example, suppose that there is a 2 percent probability that a collision will completely destroy a person's automobile, that is, a 98 percent probability of a partial loss. The owner of a $10,000 auto may realize that the expected value of the loss is $0.02 \times \$10,000$, or $200. Yet the owner may find that collision insurance would cost $400 because the insurer must charge enough to pay for all expected losses plus the costs of doing business. Should the owner insure? If a $10,000 auto represents a large portion of this person's total wealth, insurance will likely be purchased. If, however, the person is wealthy and has several other vehicles more valuable than this one, insurance may not be purchased. This situation suggests a very important fundamental principle of insurance: *due to the element of risk, an individual may be willing to pay more to avoid a loss than the true expected value of this loss.* In fact, if it were not for this phenomenon, insurance could not exist. The insurer must always charge more for service than the expected value of the loss. If an individual acted solely according to the criterion of expected loss, insurance might never be bought, assuming, of course, that the expected value of the loss is known. In many cases, however, the expected value of the loss is not known. Nevertheless, risk is a burden on society, and most individuals are willing to pay money to avoid it.

UTILITY ANALYSIS OF INSURANCE CONSUMPTION

Subjective risk stems from mental attitudes toward uncertainty. If people tend to act according to their mental attitudes, and if we could measure these mental attitudes, presumably we would have a valuable tool with which to predict human behavior in given situations. In particular, we might be able to predict risk behavior such as insurance buying by knowing more about mental attitudes toward risk. One concept that has been employed to measure mental attitudes toward risk is that of utility.

Utility is the subjective value an individual ascribes to commodities, services, or other things of personal worth. Such utility value summarizes all psychological, economic, and sociological factors into one net figure.

Economists have long used the concept of utility to explain price and demand in the market. If a basket of groceries and a table radio each have the same total utility to the buyer, presumably the prices of these two commodities will be equal in a free market, and the buyer is indifferent as to which commodity to choose. In the same way, if the probability of winning a certain sum of money is equated in the mind of the consumer with the price of a lottery ticket, presumably the consumer is indifferent about buying or not buying a ticket. If the price of the ticket is reduced slightly, perhaps the consumer will decide to gamble and will purchase the ticket. The utility of goods and services is not necessarily related to their cost of production. Hence, the seller can get a profit over cost by raising the value of a commodity in the mind of the consumer through such techniques as advertising.

In order to explain the fact that increasing the quantities of goods available for sale tends to depress price, economists have relied heavily on the concept of diminishing marginal utility.

Marginal Utility

Marginal utility refers to the subjective value to the consumer of the last unit of a commodity purchased. It is presumed that the value of each additional unit of a good has less value to the consumer (although the price is the same) than the unit immediately preceding it. As more and more goods are purchased, a point is reached where the price of the article will not be worth its cost to the user. Thus, the consumer will buy no more goods at that price. Following this reasoning, the loss of a marginal unit of a good is considered less serious to a rich person than to a poor person, who will therefore have a greater reason to insure against loss than a rich person.

Graphically, a person with decreasing marginal utility will have a utility curve that looks like curve A in Figure 24-2. On this line, the utility of a person with $2,000 of wealth is two, but for three times this level of wealth, $6,000, the utility does not increase proportionately. In fact, curve A shows that $6,000 of wealth corresponds to only four units of utility, twice the previous level.

A person with **linear utility** would have a utility graph like line B in Figure 24-2. Persons with linear utility place the same unit value on each additional dollar of wealth. Thus, $2,000 would have two units of utility and $6,000 would have six units of utility.

In summary, the concept of diminishing marginal utility explains why a person would often be willing to pay more for insurance to avoid loss than the true expected value of the loss.

Some support for the utility hypothesis in explaining insurance-buying behavior is found in certain psychological experiments where it has been shown that people tend to overestimate small probabilities, and to underestimate large probabilities, of loss or gain. A dividing line of approximately 0.20 was established in one experiment conducted by Preston and Baratta as being the point below which subjects tended to

Figure 24–2
Graphical Utility Analysis

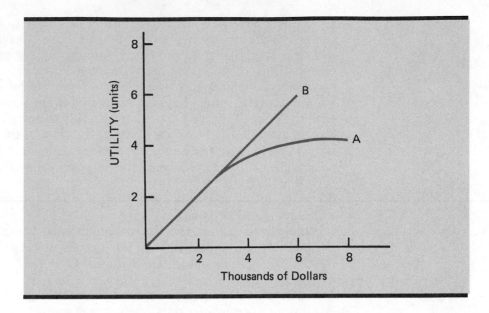

overestimate the true probability of loss.[9] Since most probabilities involving insurance are quite small, it can be seen that there may be a tendency for individuals to believe that the true probability of loss (and consequent loss in expected utility) is larger than it really is. Hence, the cost of insurance appears relatively small to such persons.

Friedman and Savage noted that some persons will purchase insurance, and yet, in a seemingly inconsistent manner, will also enter into gambles.[10] If a person's utility curve were shaped like curve A in Figure 24–2, that person would not gamble, since the expected marginal utility of the gain would be less than the marginal utility of the stake. Accordingly, Friedman and Savage hypothesized that it is possible for a person's utility curve to appear as an elongated *S*, first increasing at a decreasing rate, then at an increasing rate, and finally again increasing at a decreasing rate as wealth or income rises. If a person's income or wealth is at one of the points at which the *rate of change* in utility begins to increase, presumably this person would be willing to gamble, since above this level of wealth the expected gain in utility from winning would be worth more personally than the utility lost by paying the stake.

Measuring Utility

There are several ways to measure utility.[11] The approach taken here is called the **reference contract** method. It allows one to measure risk attitudes as well as gain (loss) in satisfaction when certain increases (decreases) in wealth occur.[12]

In using the reference contract technique, an arbitrary utility value, say 100, is placed on a loss amount. The number 0 is assigned to the situation in which no loss occurs. Consequently, the range of utility is from 0 to 100 for situations varying from no loss to the worst possible loss.[13]

Assume that Donna Jones is the risk manager of the XCU Company and that you are asked to determine a utility curve for her. The first step is to determine what is the worst possible loss, say $1,000,000, and assign an arbitrary utility value to it, say 100 points. (See column B in Table 24–1.)

Ask Ms. Jones how much she would pay to eliminate a loss situation where there was a 0.50 probability of a $1,000,000 loss and a 0.50 probability of no loss. If she responds that she would pay $650,000 for such a trade-off, we can determine the utility of the $650,000, using the following formula:

$$\text{Utility of } \$650,000 = 0.50 \text{ (utility of } \$1,000,000 \text{ loss)} + 0.50 \text{ (utility of } \$0 \text{ loss)}$$

Substituting assigned numbers in this expression, we have:

$$\text{Utility of } \$650,000 = 0.50 \ (100) + 0.50(0)$$
$$\text{Utility of } \$650,000 = 50 + 0$$
$$\text{Utility of } \$650,000 = 50$$

Ms. Jones places a value of 50 units on the sum of $650,000. In this example, it may be said that the $650,000 amount is the maximum insurance premium Ms. Jones would pay to avoid a loss situation where there is a 50 percent chance of a loss of $1,000,000 and a 50 percent chance of no loss. At this premium level she is indifferent between self-insuring and purchasing insurance. A higher insurance premium would lead her to self-insure. A lower premium would cause her to purchase insurance.

Finally, you must determine the maximum premium she would pay to avoid a situation where there is a 50 percent chance of losing $650,000 and a 50 percent chance of losing $0. Again, you are trying to find the point where she is indifferent to the two choices. She should be just as satisfied with paying the premium as accepting the risk-of-loss situation. Referring to the table, one sees that Ms. Jones said she is indifferent as to the choice between paying a premium of $400,000 and running a risk in which there is a 50 percent chance of losing $650,000 and a 50 percent chance of losing $0. Using the utility formula, one finds a value of 25 utility points for the dollar amount of $400,000:

$$\text{Utility of } \$400,000 = 0.50 \text{ (utility of } \$650,000\text{)} + 0.50 \text{ (utility of } \$0\text{)}$$
$$= (0.5) \ (50) + (0.5) \ (0)$$
$$= 25$$

This procedure is repeated for each value shown in the table.

Now, if Ms. Jones is faced with a loss situation with a long-run expected value of $212,700, what insurance premium should she be willing to pay to transfer risk to others? This question may be answered by finding what sum of dollars is equivalent to a loss of utility associated with a risk in which the expected loss is $212,700. Table 24–1 shows that the expected loss in utility associated with a loss of $212,700 is 8.28. Examine the table to discover how much money actually paid out would be associated with the utility of 8.28. Since the number 8.28 does not appear (in column B) precisely, we may find the answer by linear interpolation between the two nearest numbers. The number 8.28 lies above 6.25, which is the utility lost by paying $200,000. Thus, letting X equal the utility value 8.28, we have:

$$\frac{\$300,000 - \$200,000}{12.5 - 6.25} = \frac{X - \$200,000}{8.28 - 6.25}$$
$$X = \$232,480$$

Thus, Ms. Jones would find herself indifferent between assuming a risk where the expected loss is $212,700 (depicted in the table) and paying an insurance premium of $232,480. If she paid a premium greater than $232,480, she would be sacrificing more utility than she would lose by assuming the risk. Note that she is willing to pay a transfer premium greater than the expected loss because of her utility preferences.

In reality, most insurers would probably not offer to insure the risk for only $232,480, since this premium does not allow enough margin for expenses. Dividing losses by the premiums, a loss ratio of 0.915 and an expense and profit allowance of 0.085 percent is determined. The latter allowance equals one minus the loss ratio (in this example, $1 - 0.915 = 0.085$). Typically, an insurer desires an expense allowance of 25 to 35 percent and a 2 to 5 percent underwriting profit goal.

The preceding procedure for determining utility values is numerically precise, but has serious limitations in practice. Persons' responses to hypothetical questions may differ considerably from their behavior in real life. Also, utility preferences may not be constant through time: an

Table 24–1 Expected Utility of XCU Corporation's Losses

(A) Possible Loss	(B) Utility Units	(C) Probability of Loss	(D) Expected Utility of Loss (B) × (C)	(E) Expected Monetary Value of the Loss (A) × (C)
1,000,000	100.00	0.002	0.20	$ 2,000
650,000	50.00	0.010	0.50	6,500
400,000	25.00	0.048	1.20	19,200
300,000	12.50	0.250	3.13	75,000
200,000	6.25	0.400	2.50	80,000
125,000	3.12	0.200	0.62	25,000
62,500	1.56	0.070	0.11	4,375
31,250	0.78	0.020	0.02	625
Total		1.000	8.28	$212,700

individual may have one set of utility preferences one month and another set the next month. The analyses demonstrates, however, that people will pay more than the expected value of a loss to transfer it, due to risk aversion. Utility analysis is thus a significant, although imperfect, measure of risk aversion.

Utility and Insurance-Premium Calculation

Insurance pricing may be affected by utility analysis. In developing the premium rate, an insurer first develops the pure premium.

For automobile insurance, as an example, suppose the pure premium in collision insurance ($50 deductible) for low-priced passenger cars in five counties of a certain state, with class 1A drivers (no male operator less than 25 years of age, and car not used in business or to drive to and from work) is $65 for a certain time period. This means that *on the average* the insurer had to pay $65 per car for collision losses falling into the classification named.

The rate maker must then allow for **loading,** which is the amount of the insurer's expenses and profits, if any. Since loading is usually expressed as a percentage of the final gross premium, the pure premium is divided by 1 minus the loading percentage. In the foregoing case, loading may be 35 percent of the final premium. The gross premium is found by dividing $65 by 0.65, thereby obtaining a figure of $100. Although methods are more refined in practice, this formula is the basis of any such method.

From the preceding discussion, it can be seen that the price of insurance on the average must be greater than expected losses by a margin sufficient to cover the insurer's expenses. However, if the consumer's perceived risk is low, the loss of utility by running the risk may also be low, and insurance will not be purchased unless premiums are held to low levels. In some lines of insurance losses are highly predictable, and unless the cost of transfer is low, the business consumer with a large number of exposure units may elect to self-insure the risk because of its low perceived risk.

On the other hand, if the perceived risk is high, the loss of utility by running the risk may be so high that the consumer is willing to pay a high premium to transfer it. Insurers' pricing may reflect the consumer's risk aversion and may in some cases be higher than normal expense allowances would indicate. An example might be in cancer policies, where loss ratios are relatively low and expenses and profit margins are high.

THE DEDUCTIBLE DECISION

In this section some of the statistical techniques and terms examined in the chapter will be illustrated to show how the risk manager should select the proper deductible level.

Need for Deductibles

A deductible is useful in risk management because, as discussed in Chapter 3, it helps lower the cost of insurance and increase its availability. Also, it makes management more loss conscious, since within the deductible level a firm must absorb the loss itself. However, as a general rule, one does not accept a deductible unless it offers a sufficient premium savings and one can afford to bear the potential loss involved by accepting it. A given deductible may offer a very attractive premium reduction, but if numerous losses occur, the combined effect of several deductibles could cause financial embarrassment to the insured.

Types of Deductibles

One type of deductible, a **per-occurrence deductible,** applies to each loss. A $100 deductible on automobile collision is an example. Another type is called an **aggregate deductible,** under which the deductible applies for the year. A firm absorbs perhaps the first $20,000 in losses during the year, and the insurer pays for all losses over that amount.

Quite often the two deductibles are used together. A firm may have a $1,000 per occurrence deductible subject to an aggregate deductible of $20,000. Under this approach, the firm would never pay more than $1,000 on any one loss and would not absorb more than $20,000 in losses during the year. If only a per-occurrence deductible of $1,000 were used, the firm would have a potential liability much greater than $20,000, if numerous losses less than $1,000 occur and total more than $20,000. In the following examples, the concepts of per-occurrence and aggregate deductibles will be demonstrated.

Sample Problem

Mr. King is the risk manager of the Hall Shoe Corporation, which operates 100 shoe stores in 100 different cities. All stores are located in suburban shopping centers, have similar construction characteristics, and have the same fire rating. Each store has a value of $150,000. Table 24–2 shows the firm's losses for the past 12 months, which are typical of its loss experience over the last several years.

From the table, one can determine that the mean loss was $8,000 ($40,000 ÷ 5) and that the median loss was $2,500. The standard deviation is about $11,000. The loss frequency is 5 fires per year per 100 stores.

The firm is willing to retain no more than $10,000 in fire losses during the year. In effect, it wants to have an aggregate deductible equal to $10,000. The risk manager must determine the size of the per-occurrence deductible that should be selected in order to absorb no more than $10,000 in losses during the year.

**Table 24–2
Fire Losses of the Hall Shoe Corporation**

198X	Amount
January 30	$ 2,000
March 17	30,000
May 30	1,000
July 4	2,500
October 12	4,500
	$40,000

Solution

This problem can be solved by employing some of the statistical techniques discussed in the initial part of this chapter. Mr. King's firm has more than 50 loss exposures, and the probability of loss is less than 10 percent $\left(\frac{5}{100} = 5\%\right)$. These two characteristics indicate that the Poisson distribution may be suitable to use in simulating losses.

Because the mean is distorted by the $30,000 loss, the median is a better measure of central tendency in this case. Consequently, the figure of $2,500 will be used to represent the average loss.

Using the Poisson distribution, Mr. King knows that with an average loss frequency of 5 per year, the probability of losses will be as shown in Table 24–3.

For the example, using equation

$$p = \frac{m^r e^{-m}}{r!}$$

the probability of no loss at all would be

$$\frac{5^0 e^{-5}}{1} = 0.0067$$

Therefore, the probability of 1 or more losses is $1 - 0.0067$, or 0.9933.

Table 24–3 may be interpreted as follows. There is a 0.0318 chance that 10 or more losses will occur when only 5 losses are "expected" on the average. There is a 0.0681 chance that 9 or more will occur, etc. Thus, if King chooses a deductible of $1,000 per occurrence, there is a 0.0318 chance that his losses will equal or be greater than $10,000 ($10 \times \$1,000$), a 0.0681 chance that his losses will equal or be greater than $9,000 ($9 \times \$1,000$), etc.

These probabilities may also be interpreted as yearly frequencies, with 0.0318 being equivalent to 31.45 years ($1.00 \div 0.0318$), 0.0681 being equivalent to 14.68 years ($1.00 \div 0.0681$), etc. Thus, King can assess risk by realizing that if he chooses a $1,000 deductible, an aggregate loss of

Table 24–3
Probability of Losses
Using a Poisson
Distribution with $m = 5$

Number of Losses	Probability of Losses
0 or more	1.0000
1 or more	0.9933
2 or more	0.9596
3 or more	0.8753
4 or more	0.7350
5 or more	0.5595
6 or more	0.3840
7 or more	0.2378
8 or more	0.1334
9 or more	0.0681
10 or more	0.0318

$10,000 will be exceeded each 31.45 years, an aggregate loss of $9,000 will be exceeded each 14.68 years, and so on.

If King raises the deductible to $2,000, an aggregate loss of $10,000 could be exceeded after five losses. The table shows that the probability of five more losses is 0.5595, or once each 1.79 years (1.00 ÷ 0.5595). This frequency may be unacceptable due to King's subjective risk level, and the analysis would indicate that the deductible should be reduced. By continuing this process, some number may be chosen that represents the maximum acceptable deductible, given King's utility schedule for money, i.e., his subjective risk level.

Once an appropriate maximum per-occurrence deductible is selected, Mr. King should then compare premium savings available for deductibles less than the maximum. For example, suppose King can save $500 by taking a $1,000 deductible (versus no deductible at all) and can save $450 by taking a $500 deductible. He may choose a $500 deductible even though his utility preferences would show that a $1,000 deductible would be acceptable. This follows because King may reason that a saving of only $50 does not justify an extra $500 loss retention per occurrence. Table 24–3 shows about a 56 percent probability of having five or more losses. Thus, there is a 56 percent chance that losses would aggregate to $2,500 or more by accepting an extra $500 deductible.

The $50 saving would be viewed as the price of a risk where the average expected loss is $1,400 (0.56 × $2,500), a rather unfavorable trade-off for King. Stated in utility terms, this is equivalent to asking, "Is the utility gained by saving $50 more than offset by the utility lost by running the risk of an expected loss of $1,400?" The chances are that King would view the gain of $50 too small to offset a possible loss of $2,500 whose probability is 0.56.

CAPITAL BUDGETING AND RISK MANAGEMENT

The techniques used in making capital budgeting decisions in finance and accounting can be applied to risk management. The following example makes an analysis of the decision of whether or not to install a sprinkler system. The present value of the after-tax cash flows from the installation of the system are compared to the present value of the cash outlay and maintenance cost. In this case the loss reduction and premium savings are treated as income.

The Factory Company wants to determine whether the installation of a sprinkler system is desirable in its plant. It is estimated that the system will cost $600,000 and have a useful life of 15 years with no salvage value. The firm's insurer has stated that with the sprinkler system Factory's insurance premiums will be reduced by $63,000 per year. Factory's risk manager estimates that uninsured losses will be reduced $80,000 a year. These losses include direct and indirect property losses as well as workers' compensation losses. It is also estimated that maintenance and repair cost to the system will be $3,000 a year. The firm's cost of capital is 10 percent and its tax rate is 40 percent.

The cost of the sprinkler system represents a cash outlay of $600,000 for the firm. The premium savings and loss reduction represent a cash inflow of $143,000 per year ($63,000 + $80,000). The annual maintenance cost of $3,000 will be a $3,000 cash outflow each year. To determine whether the system is desirable from a financial viewpoint, one should calculate the present value of the cash flow. If the net present value is positive, the system should be purchased. If the net present value is negative, it should not be purchased. The net present value is equal to the present value of the cash inflow minus the present value of the cash outflow.

From Table 24–4 it can be seen that there is a cash outflow of $600,000 in year 0 and a net after-tax cash inflow of $100,000. The cash inflow consists of $143,000 of savings minus $3,000 for maintenance and $40,000 a year in income taxes. Since depreciation is a noncash expense, it is deducted to determine the firm's tax liability but is added back to the firm's cash flow in order to determine the cash inflow of the project. Consequently, the $100,000 of cash flow represents $60,000 of after-tax cash savings and $40,000 of depreciation.

In this example the cash flows are the same for each of the 15 years. So one can multiply the $100,000 by the present value of one dollar per year for 15 years at 10 percent (7.6060, see Table E-4). This figure represents the present value of a dollar received at the end of each year for 15 years. By multiplying 7.6060 by $100,000, one determines the present value of the cash inflows, or $760,600. When $600,000 (the cost of installation) is subtracted from $760,600, a net present value of $160,600 is obtained. From

Table 24–4 **Net Present Value** **Analysis of Installation of** **Automatic Sprinkler** **System**	Year	0	1 . . . 15
	Installation Costs	$600,000	
	Loss Reduction		$ 80,000
	Premium Savings		63,000
	Maintenance		−3,000
	Before-Tax Cash Flow		$140,000
	Depreciation		40,000
	Taxable Savings		$100,000
	Taxes (0.4 × $100,000)		40,000
	Income after Taxes		$ 60,000
	Depreciation		40,000
	After-Tax Cash Flow		$100,000

Present value of the cash flow = $100,000 × 7.6060 = $760,600
Net Present Value (NPV) of the investment = $760,600 − $600,000 = $160,600
Decision: Since the NPV is positive, make the investment.

this analysis, one can state that the installation of the sprinkler system is desirable if a 10 percent cost of capital is used.

Note that premium savings alone would not justify the purchase of the sprinkler system. In loss prevention analysis, the reduction in insurance premiums is only one part of the analysis, and often that reduction by itself will not justify the investment being considered. Other factors, such as loss of income from destruction of the building, damage to personal property, and loss of income due to injuries to the public and employees, must be considered.

SUMMARY

1. The basic theorems of probability are of great importance in insurance, especially in rate making, financial management, and contractual provision formulation. They are of crucial importance in protecting the solvency of the insurer by enabling more accurate predictions of losses, especially when empirical data are scanty and educated guesses must be made as to the course of future events. They give guidance to the risk manager in determining what constitutes an adequate number of exposure units in order to achieve financial stability. Probability theory is also an important guide to the would-be self-insurer in assessing the nature of a risk.

2. The concept of expected value is basic to probability calculations. The expected value of an event or a series of events is calculated by preparing a schedule of possible outcomes, multiplying each outcome by its probability, and adding.

3. The statistical tools of theoretical frequency distributions and measures of central tendency can help risk managers make financial decisions.

4. The chief risks of the risk manager are (a) the uncertainties involved in estimating the probability of an event, (b) the uncertainties involved in determining whether the events to be insured are independent

and random, or whether they conform to other mathematical assumptions, and (c) the fact that the insurer may not have a sufficient number of exposures to predict losses with a required degree of certainty. The coefficient of variation is one way to characterize the objective risk in obtaining a sufficient number of exposure units for mathematical accuracy.

5. The concept of utility is an important tool in explaining the economic growth of the insurance mechanism as a way of handling risk. Without the idea of utility, it is difficult to explain why anyone would pay $20 for insurance against a loss of $10,000 whose expected value is $10. The answer lies in the fact that to most people the potential loss of $10,000 is so great that they are willing to pay far more than $10 to avoid the possibility of losing this much.

QUESTIONS FOR REVIEW

1. If y has a loss distribution that is Poisson distributed:
   (a) What is the probability of 1, 2, 3, 4, and 5 losses if

$$m = 2$$
$$e^{-2} = 0.13534$$

(Use the formula for the Poisson on page 585.)

(b) What is the probability of 2 or more losses?

2. Assume that a loss-prevention program would cost $100,000 per year in education and inspection, that it had first-year start-up costs of $1,000,000, and that it was to be used for 10 years. What would be the net present value of the program if it reduced losses $300,000 per year? Assume a 10-percent discount rate and a 40-percent tax rate. Would you make the investment? Explain.

3. A firm is considering the advisability of self-insuring bodily injury liability from the operation of automobiles. In this field, the firm's expected loss frequency is only 0.04; but the severity of losses, once they occur, is such that the average amount of claim is $10,000. The firm is insistent that before self-insurance can be attempted, there must be a 95-percent probability that the actual loss frequency will not differ from the expected losses by more than 0.004. How many automobiles must the firm have to self-insure its bodily injury liability risk?

4. Jones has two factories, A and B. In factory A, the mean loss from industrial injuries is $100,000 with a standard deviation of $5,000. In factory B, the mean loss is $50,000 with a standard deviation of $5,000.

(a) In which factory, A or B, is Jones's risk greater?

(b) On what measure of risk are you basing your answer?

5. In terms of probability of loss, when are the binomial and Poisson distributions similar? When are the binomial and the normal distributions similar?

6. Smith's losses over the last ten years are as follows: 6 years, zero; 3 years, $1,000 each; 1 year, $5,000.

(a) Set up an empirical probability distribution for Smith.

(b) What is Smith's expected loss?

QUESTIONS FOR DISCUSSION

1. You are given an opportunity to purchase a ticket on a horse whose probability of winning is 50 percent.

(a) How much would you pay for the ticket? How much would you pay if the winning ticket (whose probability of payoff is still 50 percent) paid $10? $1,000? $10,000? $1,000,000? In each case, assume it is your own money you are paying and that you have this amount of money plus a 10-percent margin in your bank account.

(b) What has this experiment to do with risk?

2. Why is determining utility values of limited use in a business environment?

3. The text states that "If an individual acted solely according to the criterion of expected loss, insurance might never be bought." Why is this true?

4. "Uncertainty is a form of disutility that no one will voluntarily incur unless something is to be gained by so doing." Do you agree? Explain.

5. An insurer is asked to insure under a group policy the lives of the passengers on a large ship, but refuses on the grounds that the events are not distributed randomly. Explain the insurer's attitude. Is it logical?

6. How would your answer to the problem presented in Table 24–4 change if the sprinkler system could be depreciated over 5 years and the before-tax cash flow were $120,000? The present value of a dollar a year for 5 years at 10 percent is 3.7908, and for years 6 through 15 it is 3.8153. Explain the difference in the two answers.

NEW TERMS AND CONCEPTS

Aggregate Deductible
Coefficient of Variation
Expected Value
Independent Event
Linear Utility
Loading
Marginal Utility

Median
Mode
Per-Occurrence Deductible
Probability
Probability Distribution
Random

NOTES

1 Samuel B. Richmond, *Statistical Analysis*, 2nd ed. (New York: The Ronald Press Company, 1964), p. 119.

2 William Mendenhall and James E. Reinmuth, *Statistics for Management and Economics*, 2nd ed. (N. Scituate, Mass.: Duxbury Press, 1974), p. 36.

3 The events in the binomial process are called Bernoulli trials, after Jacob Bernoulli, who was one of the first mathematicians to formalize this theorem.

4 The binomial formula says that the probability of r successes in n trials equals

$$\frac{n!}{r!\,(n-r)!}\, p^r q^{n-r}$$

The expression $n!$ is read "n factorial." The word "factorial" refers to a successive multiplication of the numbers $n, n, -1, n-2, \ldots, 1$. Thus, 4! means $4 \times 3 \times 2 \times 1$, or 24. (0! is conventionally defined to be 1.) Tables of binomial probabilities are generally available for obtaining the values in the above formula for small values of n (150 or less). For larger values of n, other formulas, such as the normal density function, are used as an approximation.

5 Mendenhall and Reinmuth, op. cit., p. 125.

6 Arthur Williams and Richard M. Heins, *Risk Management and Insurance*, 3rd ed. (New York: McGraw-Hill, 1976), p. 72.

7 Of course, there is no guarantee that losses will be distributed normally. Statistical tests can establish the existence or nonexistence of a normal distribution of past loss histories, on which assumptions can be made concerning a future expectation for a loss experience. If the tests of a binomial distribution are met, however, losses will be approximately normally distributed.

8 E. Parzen, *Modern Probability Theory and Its Application* (New York: John Wiley & Sons, Inc., 1960), pp. 228–232.

9 M. G. Preston and P. Baratta, "An Experimental Study of the Auction Value of an Uncertain Outcome," *American Journal of Psychology*, Vol. 61 (1948), pp. 183–193.

10 Milton Friedman and L. J. Savage, "The Utility Analysis of Choices Involving Risk," *Journal of Political Economy*, Vol. LVI (1948), pp. 279–304.

11 Mark R. Greene and Oscar N. Serbein, *Risk Management: Text and Cases*, (Reston, Va.: Reston Publishing Company, 1978), pp. 58–66.

12 Williams and Heins, op. cit., pp. 657–662.

13 Since losses are the subject being analyzed, the values discussed represent **disutility.**

PART 7

GOVERNMENT AND INSURANCE

25 GOVERNMENT INSURANCE PROGRAMS

After studying this chapter, you should be able to:

1. Explain how social insurance, public assistance, and private insurance principles differ.
2. Identify the essential features of OASDHI.
3. Describe the financial soundness of the OASDHI program.
4. State why and in what areas the government has entered the insurance business.

So far we have been concerned primarily with private approaches to the problem of economic insecurity. Public agencies also concern themselves with the problems of premature death, health loss, old-age dependency, and unemployment—the four major perils that threaten personal financial security. Public bodies use several methods to handle these problems, but this chapter will explain the insurance method.

There is an implicit assumption that the insurance institution accumulates an advance fund for payment of losses. Not all government plans to meet personal security problems meet the requirements of this assumption; the state simply meets costs as they occur out of general tax revenues. On the other hand, a state plan to finance unemployment benefits by charging each employer a premium that bears some relationship to the risk involved generally falls within the definition of insurance.

Government insurance may be discussed under two general headings: (1) social insurance, and (2) all other. Social insurance includes Social Security (OASDHI), workers' compensation insurance, unemployment insurance, and temporary disability insurance. Other government programs include veterans' life insurance, various property-liability insurance programs such as crime and flood insurance, and different insured-loan programs. The differences between government and private insurance are discussed in this chapter, and the major government programs are analyzed. Workers' compensation insurance is analyzed in Chapter 22.

BACKGROUND OF SOCIAL INSURANCE

Social insurance is that type of government insurance, usually compulsory, that is designed to benefit persons whose incomes are interrupted by an economic or social problem or condition, or who are faced with personal losses from these conditions.

Social insurance plans are usually introduced when a social problem exists that requires governmental action for solution and where the insurance method is deemed most appropriate as a solution. A social problem is a condition or set of circumstances that society as a whole finds undesirable, and for which the solution is generally beyond the control of the individual. Examples are the problems of crime, poverty, unemployment, mental disease, ill health, dependency of children or aged persons, drug addiction, industrial accidents, divorce, and economic privation of a certain class, such as agricultural workers. Insurance is not an appropriate method of solution for many of these problems because the peril is not accidental, fortuitous, or predictable. In other instances insurance is perhaps feasible, but due to the catastrophic nature of the event (as in unemployment), private insurers cannot undertake the underwriting task because of lack of financial capacity. This means that if the insurance method is to be used as a solution to certain problems, governmental agencies must either administer or finance the insurance plan.

The justification for social insurance, then, lies in the fact that some insurance tasks either cannot be or are not accomplished by private insurers without assistance from a government. These tasks concern social problems that are deemed too important to ignore. The economic problems involved in social insurance are such that governmental action is necessary to solve legal difficulties, to supplement financing, to introduce compulsion, to give organization, and to supply other ingredients in a successful insurance formula.

U.S. Programs

The United States, slow to get started in the field of social insurance,[1] has developed the field rapidly since the passage of federal Social Security legislation in 1935. As revealed in Table 4–1, on page 82, the premium income of all governmental insurers is only slightly less than the premium income from all private insurers. From another viewpoint, the importance of social insurance can be seen by the fact that in 1985 under OASDHI there were 25.7 million retirement, 7 million survivorship, 3.8 million disability, and 2 million unemployment beneficiaries. In addition, there were 1.7 million federal civil service and railroad retirees, and about 3 million veterans drawing cash benefits. Thus, over 43 million persons, about 18 percent of the population of 238 million, were drawing income benefits from the government in 1985.[2]

Table 25-1 shows the relative growth of expenditures for social insurance and public welfare during the 35-year period ending in 1985. Several conclusions may be inferred from the table. First, there has been a steady growth in the relative amounts of personal income devoted to social insurance and welfare payments in the United States. The total now constitutes 13.3 percent of personal income.

Second, the relative payments for public assistance have remained quite level over the 35-year period, and constitute only 1.2 percent of personal income.

Third, there is an apparent tendency for the method of social insurance to be preferred to other methods as a device for transferring payments from taxpayers as a whole to certain elements of the population. In 1950 social insurance accounted for only 3.0 percent of personal income, compared with 12.1 percent in 1985. Other items of public welfare have shown very little relative growth.

Fourth, without the relative growth of social insurance programs, which provide formal ways for society to meet certain social costs, other techniques, such as public aid, would have been substituted. It is a tribute to the insurance device that its use is preferred. The certainty of benefits may be viewed by the majority as outweighing the costs of administration of the insurance system. Without social insurance, society would still seek to prevent or alleviate social hardships through private or public charity or through placing the burden on the relatives of those affected. Society

Table 25-1
Growth of Social Insurance and Public Assistance Payments from 1950 to 1985

Year	Percent of Personal Income	
	Social Insurance	Public Assistance
1950	3.0	1.0
1955	4.2	0.8
1960	5.9	0.8
1965	6.3	0.8
1970	8.0	1.2
1975	11.3	1.7
1980	11.7	1.2
1985	12.1	1.2

Source: *Social Security Bulletin* (January 1986), p. 91.

Part 7   Government and Insurance

has elected to bear these burdens through the more formal insurance system.

Thus, social insurance has a basic purpose of providing protection against risks that tend to be beyond the control of the individual or a group of individuals organized by a private insurance company. In an industrialized economy such problems as old-age dependency, ill health, and unemployment are essentially beyond the power of any individual to solve. It is no longer accepted reasoning, for example, that individuals are solely to blame for their unemployment and should personally bear the entire cost. It also may be beyond the power of the individual to provide completely for old age because of inflation and other factors.

Table 25-2 displays the relative importance of the major types of social insurance in the U.S. in 1985. Note that OASDHI accounted for more than 71 percent of the benefits. Public employee retirement benefits were second in importance, with 18.7 percent of the total.

International Programs

Social insurance has been accepted throughout the world as a universally adaptable device to meet various economic and social problems, particularly in industrialized societies. The tabulations shown in Table 25-3, reported by the U.S. Social Security Administration, reveal the major types of programs around the world and their growth. As of 1983, 140 nations reported one or more programs, the total number of which has more than doubled in the past 43 years.

It may be observed that old-age, disability, and survivor programs are growing faster than any other type, with family allowances next. A work injury compensation program existed in every country. Unemployment insurance, the type of program least popular, existed in only half the countries. National health insurance existed in some form in 85 countries, about 60 percent of the total reporting.

Most of the new growth in social insurance programs since the late 1970s has been in developing nations. Among existing plans, there has been

Table 25-2 Size of Social Insurance Benefits in the United States, 1985

Type of Social Insurance	Cash Benefits (Billions)	Percent of Total
OASDHI, including lump-sum benefits	$175.6	71.3
Railroad retirement	6.1	2.5
Public employee retirement*	21.5	8.7
Veterans' compensation	13.9	5.6
Unemployment	13.6	5.5
Temporary disability	1.8	0.7
Workers' compensation (for 1979)	13.7	5.5
	$246.2	100.0

*Federal civil service plus state and local (estimated).
Source: *Social Security Bulletin* (March 1986), p. 24. Percentages calculated.

Table 25–3
International Social
Insurance Programs

Type of Program	Number of Countries			Percent Increase
	1940	1958	1983	1983/1958
Any type	57	80	140	75
Old-age, disability, and survivor	33	58	130	124
Sickness and maternity	24	59	85	44
Work injury	57	77	136	77
Unemployment	21	26	40	54
Family allowance	7	38	67	76

Source: U.S. Social Security Administration, *Social Security throughout the World, 1983* (Washington, D.C.: U.S. Government Printing Office, 1984). Percentages calculated.

a general trend toward liberalization of benefits, such as increased benefits, broader coverage, lower retirement age, and expanded health care.

Social Insurance versus Private Insurance

An understanding of social insurance coverages can be facilitated by an appreciation of the basic differences between these and privately sponsored insurance devices.

Compulsion. Most social insurance plans are characterized by an element of compulsion. Because social insurance plans are designed to solve some social problem, it is necessary that everyone involved cooperate. Thus, if an employer qualifies under the law, this employer and all employees must be covered by workers' compensation and unemployment insurance.

Set Level of Benefits. In social insurance plans little if any choice is usually given as to what level of benefits is provided. Thus, even if so desired, an employee cannot purchase more or less unemployment insurance than is offered under the plan. Further, all persons covered under the plan are subject to the same benefit schedules, which may vary according to the amount of average wage, length of service, or job status. In private, individual insurance, of course, one may usually buy any amount of coverage desired.

Floor-of-Protection Concept. A basic principle of social insurance in a system of private enterprise is that it aims to provide a minimum level of economic security against perils that may interrupt income. This principle, known as the **floor-of-protection concept,** is not always strictly observed, but it is still a fundamental theme of most social insurance coverages in the United States. In workers' compensation insurance, for example, an injured worker is usually given complete medical care, but under most state laws, during the time of disability, less than half of the former income is received.

In 1985 the average benefit for a retired worker under Social Security was only $463 per month, and the average benefit for a surviving widow was $228 per month.[3] This may be compared to the average monthly wage of about $1,200 in 1985 for nonfarm workers. The worker is expected to have made other arrangements through private insurance plans if a higher level of benefits than that provided by Social Security is needed. The purpose of social insurance plans is to give all qualified persons a certain minimum protection, with the idea that more adequate protection can and should be provided through individual initiative. The incentive to help oneself, a vital element of the free-enterprise system, is thus preserved.

Subsidy Concepts. All insurance devices have an element of subsidy in that the losses of the unfortunate few are shared with the fortunate many who escape loss. In social insurance it is anticipated that an insured group may not pay its own way, but will be subsidized either by other insured groups or by the taxpayers generally. Thus, when retirement benefits were introduced into Social Security legislation, many individuals who worked only a minimum of one-and-one-half years were able to draw a lifetime pension that had a value far in excess of the premiums paid by them and their employers. The younger workers, of course, were subsidizing the old, and still are. Some social insurance plans have access to general tax revenues if the contributions from covered workers are inadequate.

Unpredictability of Loss. For several reasons, the cost of benefits under social insurance cannot usually be predicted with great accuracy. Therefore, the cost of some types of social insurance is unstable. For example, in a general depression unemployment may rise to unusual heights, causing tremendous outlays in unemployment benefits that may threaten the solvency of the unemployment compensation fund. Old-age benefits under Social Security depend on such unpredictable matters as future fertility rates in the population, the general level of employment opportunities for the aged, the proportion of widows who will elect to work rather than to receive benefits, the average wage level of the worker over the earning years, and price changes.

Attaching conditions to the right to receive payments is not a feature of private insurance, as it is in social insurance. In a life insurance contract the worker may elect to use cash values at retirement to purchase a life annuity of a definite promised amount, regardless of employment status or whether the worker meets a retirement test. In a private loss-of-income contract, a worker receives a definite benefit in the event of disability. In workers' compensation, however, the benefit may depend on what the worker's average earnings were, what the number of dependents is, or whether permission is given to bring legal action against a third party who was the cause of the loss.

One might argue that it is wrong to attach conditions to recovery in social insurance under the theory that one should receive benefits as a matter of right. However, an insured worker has no particular inalienable right except the right given by the social insurance law under which the worker is protected. The employee's right can and probably should be conditional. To have it otherwise would mean that some would be receiving payments not really needed, and either the costs would rise or others would be deprived of income that is their sole source of support. One of the basic advantages of social insurance is this very flexibility that permits those most in need to receive a greater relative share of income payments than others whose economic status is such that they do not require as much.

Contributions Required. In order to qualify as social insurance, a public program should require a contribution, directly or indirectly, from the person covered or the employer or both. Thus, social insurance does not include public assistance programs wherein the needy person receives outright gifts and must generally prove inability to pay for the costs involved. This does not mean that the beneficiary in social insurance must pay *all* of the costs, but the beneficiary must make some contribution or the program is not really an insurance program, but rather a form of public charity. For example, welfare payments to dependent children under the Social Security Act is not seen as a form of social insurance, as the term is normally understood, although such payments are undoubtedly made to solve a social problem that could have been met by insurance.

Attachment to Labor Force. While it is not a necessary principle of social insurance, most social insurance plans cover only groups that are or have been attached to the labor force. The basic reason for this is that nearly all social insurance plans are directed at those perils that interrupt income. Private insurance contracts, of course, are issued to individuals regardless of employment status.

The requirement of attachment to the labor force has been a subject of frequent criticism by those who want a greater expansion of social insurance. Among the questions asked are (1) What about the family man who is unemployed but is not eligible for unemployment insurance benefits because he has not worked long enough or has not worked in covered employment? and (2) What about the unemployed person who is injured while looking for a job but is not eligible for workers' compensation because of the existing unemployment status and the consequent fact that the injury was not work inflicted? These represent problem areas that have not been answered by social insurance, but may be handled by other means, either private or public in nature.

OLD-AGE, SURVIVORS', DISABILITY, AND HEALTH INSURANCE

The Old-Age, Survivors, Disability, and Health Insurance program (OASDHI) is the only major plan of social insurance that is federally financed and administered.[4] OASDHI is one of the basic parts of the Social Security Act originally passed in 1935. The other programs are (1) a grant-in-aid plan to states for medical assistance to dependent children and the poor (Medicaid), (2) a grant-in-aid plan to states for services provided for maternal and child welfare, (3) a grant-in-aid plan to states for administration of state unemployment compensation funds, (4) hospital and medical insurance for the aged, and (5) income for needy aged, blind, or disabled persons. The first two grant-in-aid plans mentioned are usually referred to as public welfare plans, the third as simply the unemployment insurance program, the fourth as Medicare, and the fifth as Supplemental Security Income (SSI).

OASDHI Benefits

While the levels and types of benefits have changed frequently under OASDHI, it is instructive to examine the main features of current benefit provisions as a basis for understanding the law itself. The following discussion is based on the Social Security Act, as amended in 1985 and thereafter.

Retirement Benefits. The basis on which all OASDHI benefits are paid is the primary insurance amount of an insured worker. The monthly benefit in 1986, based on the age-65 worker's average indexed monthly earnings (AIME), is subject to a maximum of $788.20. Since 1981, there has been no statutory minimum benefit for newly eligible workers. The average earner retiring in 1986 received monthly benefits of $602, and the minimum wage earner received $400. (The actual benefit is determined from the statutory table.) The average retirement benefit in 1985 for different types of beneficiaries is given in Table 25–4. According to this table, for example, an average retired couple both drawing benefits receives $692 monthly.

The formula used in calculating the monthly benefit is such that it gives more weight to income of low-wage workers than it does to that of high-wage workers. For example, the formula provides 90 percent of the first $297 of AIME, 32 percent of the amount between $297 and $1,790 and 15 percent of amounts in excess of $1,790. Thus, the low-income earner is

Table 25–4
Average Amount of Monthly Benefits, OASDHI, by Type of Beneficiary, 1985

TO RETIRED WORKERS AND DEPENDENTS	
Retired Workers	$463.68
Wives and Husbands	228.59
Children	191.13
TO SURVIVORS OF DECEASED PERSONS	
Children	320.05
Widows and Widowers	419.03
Parents	321.52
TO DISABLED WORKERS AND DEPENDENTS	
Workers	469.51
Wives and Husbands	228.59
Children	137.71

Source: *Social Security Bulletin* (January, 1986), p. 16.

treated more favorably than the high-income earner. In 1985 the retirement program was restoring about the following percentages of wages:

	Worker	Worker and Spouse
Low-income worker (earning the minimum wage)	57%	84%
Medium-income worker	41%	62%
High-income worker	27%	41%

Thus, the benefits represent a fairly substantial proportion of preretirement income, especially for low- and medium-income workers. Because many expenses in retirement are reduced (for example, OASDHI taxes, work expense, and retirement savings), a benefit equal to 40 percent of gross income before retirement may be equal to two-thirds of net take-home pay. Furthermore, the current procedure used in calculating average wages, i.e., developing the AIME, is designed to adjust the initial retirement benefit to reflect current prices and living standards. During retirement, as noted before, the benefit is adjusted annually for cost-of-living changes.

In any year during which living costs increase by 3 percent or more, benefits are increased by the same percentage. Inflation protection is a major benefit to anyone on a fixed income. The OASDHI retirement benefit, although designed to provide a "floor of protection," actually accomplishes much more than this: it provides much of the total retirement income of the average worker.

The Retirement Test. Before one may receive a retirement benefit, it is necessary to meet a retirement test. The test is expressed in terms of income earned in any employment or from self-employment after retirement. In 1987 one is permitted to earn income up to $8,000 each year (less if the retiree is under 65) and receive all benefits for the year. If earnings exceed this exempt amount, benefits are reduced. The sum of $1 in benefits is withheld for each $2 earned. Full benefits are paid after reaching age 70, regardless of earnings. Income from dividends, interest, pensions, annuities, and certain other sources do not affect the retirement test.

To illustrate the retirement test, assume that Arnold Smith earns $18,000 in a year he would otherwise be getting $8,000 in OASDHI retirement benefits. Smith's reduction in benefits is $5,000 [$\frac{1}{2} \times$ ($18,000 − $8,000)]. If Smith delays retirement, his initial benefit is increased by $\frac{1}{4}$ percent for each month of delay. This adjustment is made until age 70. Smith's benefit could be increased up to 15 percent in this manner.

Disability Benefits. In 1956 Congress amended the Social Security Act to provide disability income to an insured worker who became disabled between the ages of 50 and 64. Dependents of the disabled worker became eligible for benefits in 1958. In 1960, Congress amended the act to provide for the payment of disability benefits to workers regardless of age and to their eligible dependents. The disability income is equal to the individual's primary insurance amount, and the benefits are increased if the worker has dependents. The dependents each receive one-half of the primary benefit, subject to a family maximum.

A dependent spouse must be 62 or older (or be any age if there are dependent children under 16) to receive disability benefits as a dependent spouse. A spouse who is disabled may receive benefits based on his or her own work record, even if the other spouse is active and working.

To be eligible for disability, workers must have a specified minimum work record. For example, one test is that the worker must have worked at least half the time between a twenty-first birthday and the time of disablement.

In order to prove disability, there must be medical evidence that the insured is unable to engage in substantial gainful activity. There is a waiting period of 5 months, and the impairment must be such that it is expected to continue at least 12 months. Thus, an illness that is expected to be disabling for a period longer than 5 months but less than 12 months is not compensable under the law. This illustrates the fact that social insurance does not replace private insurance, but merely supplements it. A disability that is fully compensable under a commercial disability income policy may not be compensable at all under OASDHI because of a different definition of disability or a different standard of claims adjustment.

Survivors' Benefits. Dependents of covered workers who die are entitled to survivors' benefits. For example, a widow may receive income benefits as long as she has dependent children under 16, and again, upon reaching age 60. These benefits are about three-fourths of the worker's benefit. Children also receive survivors' benefits until they are age 18. A husband can draw survivors' benefits based on earnings of a deceased wife, regardless of whether or not the husband was dependent upon the wife during her life.

OASDHI provides for substantial amounts of life insurance under the survivors' provisions. Suppose a widow aged 40 is entitled to $500 a month for ten years, until her children are 16 or over. At age 60, ten years later, assume she is eligible for a retirement benefit of $250 monthly for life. The life insurance needed now to replace these incomes, assuming 6 percent interest (see Appendix D) would be about $44,000 for the child-raising period and about $17,000 for the retirement period.[5]

The survivorship and retirement benefit programs of OASDHI compete directly with programs offered by private life insurers. In 1985 OASDHI paid out about $180 billion in lump-sum and monthly amounts to nearly 37 million persons. That year all life insurers combined paid out $60 billion, less than a third of the OASDHI payments.[6] The OASDHI program obviously has grown to the point where it overshadows the private life insurance business.

Health Insurance for the Aged (Medicare). Under the 1965 amendments to the Social Security Act, Congress took a far-reaching step in expanding the scope of the social insurance system in the United States. For the first time a program designed to meet the growing needs for health insurance on persons past age 65 was created. Two basic plans were formulated: a compulsory hospital plan and a voluntary medical plan.

Hospital Insurance. Effective in 1985, the hospital insurance plan provides the following benefits for persons age 65 and over: (1) Inpatient hospital services for a maximum of 90 days for each benefit period. The patient must bear a deductible of $492 for the first 60 days, and must pay $51 a day for each day in the hospital between the sixtieth and ninetieth day of care. (2) Extended care for a maximum of 100 days in a qualified institution. After 20 days of such care, the patient will pay $61.50 a day for the remaining 80 days. (3) Posthospital home health services for as many as 100 visits after discharge from a hospital or an extended care facility. (4) An extra 60 days of hospital coverage, known as reserve days, available only once, subject to cost sharing by the patient of $246 a day. A benefit period is considered to begin when the individual enters a hospital or extended care facility for 60 consecutive days. The deductible amounts applying to the above coverages are geared to hospital costs and will be increased as hospital costs rise.

Financing of the new hospital insurance program is accomplished by contribution of employers and employees, based on annual earnings of up to $42,000 in 1986, at a rate of 1.45 percent of earnings.

Medical Insurance. The medical insurance plan covers physicians' services, home health services, and several other medical and health services in and out of medical institutions. Coverage is voluntary, with each person age 65 and over being eligible to enroll during a seven-month period, beginning three months before reaching age 65. (Later enrollment is also permitted.) The premium in 1986 was $15.50 a month, an amount that is supplemented by the federal government from general funds. The plan pays 80 percent of the patient's allowable medical bills above a $75 annual deductible amount. Covered expenses include office and home calls, diagnostic X-ray and laboratory tests, ambulance service, surgical dressing and splints, rental of medical equipment, and prosthetic devices. Coverage on mental or psychiatric treatment is limited to $250 or 50 percent of the expense in any calendar year, whichever is smaller. As of July, 1972, Medicare and hospital insurance protection are available to persons who have been disabled (and are receiving OASDHI benefits) for 24 or more consecutive months.

The administration of the medical insurance plan is carried out by private insurers under government contract. The administering bodies are charged with determining whether medical charges are reasonable.

Expenses not covered under the plans of medical and hospital insurance for the aged include the following: routine physical checkups, eyeglasses, hearing aids, private duty nurses, custodial care, extras such as telephone or television service in a hospital room, and drugs not administered by a physician. It can be seen that the combination of hospital and medical insurance under the program reduces, but does not eliminate, the need for private insurance on the losses due to ill health of aged persons.

Supplemental Security Income. In January, 1974, the Social Security Administration began to administer the public assistance programs formerly operated by states for needy, blind, aged, and disabled persons. Under this program, called **Supplemental Security Income (SSI),** cash benefits are paid to eligible persons without the requirement that these benefits be earned by that person's having been attached to the labor force or paying taxes. Financing is by general revenues of the federal government. SSI appears to be a step in the direction of ultimate takeover by the federal government of public welfare programs administered by states. It may also be a forerunner of a move to partially finance all Social Security programs from general revenues as well as from payroll taxes.

To be eligible for SSI, the individual or couple must be over 65, or blind, or disabled under the same definition currently used for OASDHI recipients. An individual must also be in need, with less than a specified amount in countable income and less than a given amount of countable resources. In determining resources, a person need not count a home, car of reasonable value, personal effects, or life insurance of $1,500 face value or less. The first $20 of income earned is excluded from these amounts. In 1986 an individual could receive a maximum of $336 under SSI ($504 for a couple), plus state health benefits (Medicaid).

Insured Status

The benefit provisions apply only if the worker is fully insured or currently insured under the law. A worker becomes fully insured upon meeting certain tests, and once this status is reached, the worker and all dependents are entitled to certain benefits. If a deceased worker fails to meet the test of being fully insured, but meets the test of being currently insured, monthly benefits may be payable to the minor children and the widow or widower for as long as the survivor is caring for the minor children. A person becomes **fully insured** after meeting either of two tests: (1) Having worked in covered employment for 40 quarters (10 years); (2) Subject to a minimum of six calendar quarters, having worked in covered employment at least one-fourth of the number of calendar quarters elapsing from the starting date (1951 or the year of attaining age 22, if later) until age 62 is attained, or disability or death occurs, whichever happens first. Quarters of coverage can be earned earlier than the "starting date."

Generally, workers are credited with a quarter of coverage if they are paid at least $440 (as of 1986) in any calendar year. (The amount is adjusted for inflation.) Thus, if the workers' starting date is January 1, 1967, they become fully insured under OASDHI if they work continuously in covered employment for at least one-fourth of the elapsed quarters until death or retirement. Once they have worked 10 years, they are fully insured no matter how much longer they work. It should be observed that being insured has nothing to do with the calculation of benefits. Insured status is simply a prerequisite to being eligible for *any* benefits.

Workers are **currently insured** if they have worked in covered employment at least 6 of the last 13 quarters, including the quarter in which death occurs or in which they become entitled to benefits. Thus, workers could enter the covered labor market 30 years after their starting date, work for 6 quarters, and if death occurs, they are currently insured and have certain rights under the law.

OASDI: INFLATION ADJUSTMENT

Old age, survivors', and disability insurance (OASDI) benefits are adjusted every year for inflation. For example, the benefits were adjusted 3.1 percent in December, 1985, to reflect the amount of inflation in the economy in 1985. Beneficiaries have received a wide range of increases over the last 10 years, ranging from 14.3 percent in 1980 to 3.5 percent in 1983.

The inflation adjustments are based on increases in the consumer price index for urban wage earners and clerical workers. Benefits are adjusted whenever the CPI for the third calendar quarter is 3 percent or more above the level of the previous year's third quarter. A "stabilizer" provision allows the benefit adjustment to be based on the CPI or the increase in average wages, whichever is lower. The stabilizer takes effect whenever the ratio of OASDI trust funds to expenditures is below a certain amount; in effect, this allows a lower adjustment when OASDI funds are low.

Source: Joseph Bordar, "Effects of the OASDI Benefit Increase, December 1985," *Social Security Bulletin* (March, 1986), p. 14.

Financing the OASDHI Program

OASDHI is financed by a tax on the employee and the employer in equal amounts. At first, an employee paid a 1 percent tax on the first $3,000 of annual income earned in covered employment, but this base has been

Table 25–5
OASDHI Taxes,
1980–1990

Year	Tax Rate Paid by Employer and Employee as a Percent of Taxable Wage	Self-Employed
1980	6.13%	8.10%
1981	6.65	9.30
1982–1983	6.70	9.35
1984	7.0	14.0
1985	7.05	14.1
1986–1987	7.15	14.3
1988–1989	7.51	15.02
1990 and after	7.65	15.3

increased gradually until by 1986 it had reached $42,000. It will be increased automatically thereafter as earnings levels rise.

Table 25–5 shows the tax rate paid by employers and employees for OASDHI. Table 25–6 shows the amount of tax paid by a worker earning the maximum taxable wage for the period 1976–1986. OASDHI taxes have increased 235 percent in 11 years, and many workers are paying as much or more for Social Security as they are for federal income taxes. Most workers will have all of their wages subject to OASDHI taxes. The rapid increase in OASDHI taxes was mandated by Congress to preserve the actuarial soundness of the program. After 1981 taxable wages are subject to annual adjustment, depending on changes in living costs. In 1986 all wages up to $42,000 were subject to taxation.

In spite of the rapid increase, the average worker will be entitled to benefits of which the average value is probably much greater than the total

Table 25–6
OASDHI Taxes in Dollars
(1976–1988)

Year	Taxable Wage Maximums	Amount of Tax
1976	$15,300	$ 895.05
1977	14,100	824.85
1978	15,300	895.05
1979	22,900	1,403.77
1980	25,900	1,587.67
1981	29,700	1,975.05
1982	32,400	2,170.80
1986	42,000	3,003.00
1987 (est.)	43,800	3,131.70
1988 (est.)	45,600	3,260.40

amount of taxes paid in by the worker. In addition, under OASDHI the worker will be eligible for health insurance and other benefits. Thus, the value of OASDHI is still relatively high for present workers, in comparison to the taxes paid in. For younger workers today, however, the present taxes more nearly represent the true present value of the OASDHI benefits they will receive in the future.

Actuarial Soundness of OASDHI. Social Security is essentially a "pay-as-you-go" system, with current taxes nearly matching current outlays. Social Security fund balances are minimal, approximating only six months' benefits, enough to provide for a smooth flow of checks to beneficiaries. Being dependent on tax revenues, Social Security does not need large reserves, as might be true of private insurers. In fact, to accumulate "actuarial reserves" in a manner similar to a life insurer would be a practical impossibility for a system as large as OASDHI. The agency can be expected to continue indefinitely and has as its essential security the power of taxation of the federal government. OASDHI is said to be in actuarial balance if the present value of future benefits is equal to the present value of expected taxes.

Prior to the 1977 amendment there was serious doubt that OASDHI was in actuarial balance, because future benefits exceeded the present value of anticipated taxation to pay these benefits. In fact, it was anticipated that unless changes were made in the law, total outgo would be about 75 percent greater than scheduled tax income.[7] This resulted from, among other things, inflation, unemployment rates higher than expected (which reduced expected tax income), and higher-than-expected disability insurance expenditures. In addition, there was a technical flaw in the 1972 automatic inflation adjustments that would have caused a majority of OASDHI beneficiaries to receive more in retirement benefits than they were receiving in wages prior to retirement. Another problem was created by the fact that due to a slowdown in population gain, the proportion of active workers to retired workers was expected to change from three-to-one in 1980 to about two-to-one by the year 2000. Thus, fewer workers will have to support more and more retirees.

The 1977 amendments went a long way toward overcoming these problems by increasing the rate of taxation, increasing the wages subject to taxation, and indexing wages on which benefits are based to produce the AIME factor described previously.

The revised method of calculating benefits was expected to eliminate about half of the actuarial deficit that would have otherwise occurred over the next 75 years. The increased tax and wage bases are expected to eliminate much of the other half. However, the amendments in 1977 did not address either the problems created by escalating costs of providing medical and hospital insurance for the aged or the problems arising out of anticipated changes in the ratio of active to retired workers.

OASDHI amendments made in 1983 further reduced benefits and accelerated taxes, bringing the program more nearly into actuarial balance. Among these measures were the following:

1. The tax base was enlarged by requiring coverage for groups previously excluded from Social Security, such as federal employees and employees of nonprofit organizations. Employees of state and local government that previously could terminate their coverage could no longer do so.
2. The **cost-of-living adjustment** (COLA) mechanism was modified so as to reduce the cost of these adjustments under certain conditions.
3. Greater incentives were added for persons to continue to work past age 65 (and thus reduce the cost of paying benefits to this group). For example, after 1990 the worker will be given a greater benefit than at present for each year he or she delays filing for benefits and continues to work. This is known as the **delayed retirement credit,** which is scheduled to rise from 3 to 8 percent per year, over the period 1990 to 2008.
4. The normal retirement age will be increased from 65 to 67 in stages, beginning in the year 2000. A person retiring at age 62 now receives 80 percent of the benefit payable at age 65. Ultimately, the person retiring at age 62 will receive only 65 percent of the benefit available at age 65.
5. The "retirement test" was eased so as to encourage workers to continue to work past 65. Now, a worker loses $1 in Social Security benefits for each $2 earned above a certain amount. Starting in 1990, the worker will lose $1 for each $3 earned above a certain amount. This change will reduce the "penalty" for working and earning money past age 65.
6. Beginning in 1988, the tax on self-employment income will be raised, as will be the tax schedule on employees and employers.
7. Beginning in 1984, a portion of Social Security benefits became subject to federal income taxes for certain workers. If income from all sources, including tax-exempt bonds, exceeds $25,000 ($32,000 for couples filing jointly), up to one-half of OASDHI benefits becomes subject to federal income taxes.

With these changes, it seems likely that the financial soundness of Social Security has been assured, at least for the foreseeable future.

THE UNEMPLOYMENT PROBLEM AND INSURANCE

The problem of unemployment is perhaps the most serious single economic problem faced by modern industrial societies under the free-enterprise system. The economic reasons for unemployment in a capitalistic society and the proposed solutions have occupied the attention of economists for centuries. In the United States a typical peacetime year finds from 4 to 7 percent of the civilian labor force unemployed, and during depression years this figure is often much higher, having reached nearly 25 percent in 1933. The problem is considered so serious that, in the Full Employment Act of

1946, Congress expressed its intention to do whatever possible to prevent unemployment.

Unemployment insurance is designed to alleviate certain types of unemployment, but not all unemployment. Unemployment problems are more serious for some industries, occupations, and age and racial groups than for others, but unemployment insurance makes no distinction among them. In keeping with the basic purpose of a social coverage, unemployment insurance tends to offer only a floor of protection, leaving the remaining loss to be handled by private solutions. To offer full wage restoration might tend to reduce initiative, to remove incentive for personal saving, to cause unwarranted work stoppages, to discourage efforts on the part of private industry to stabilize employment, and to have other undesirable economic side effects.

Unemployment insurance is provided under four major programs: (1) state unemployment insurance laws operating under federal guidelines, (2) coverage for veterans, (3) coverage for federal civilian workers, and (4) coverage for railroad workers. The first program is by far the largest.

Employment Covered

The unemployment insurance laws of all states, conforming to minimum federal requirements, cover firms employing four or more workers. Twenty-one state laws cover employers with one or more workers. Most states also specify that the worker must have been with the employer for some minimum period, often 20 weeks, before the employer must pay a tax on the worker's wages. The laws do not cover all types of employments. Among employments or employees usually excluded are railroad workers (covered under a separate federal law), agricultural labor, domestic service in private homes or in fraternity and sorority houses, service rendered by a child under 21 for a parent, employees of nonprofit organizations, state and local government employees (although many states provide some form of coverage for their own workers), commissioned agents, maritime workers, and self-employed persons.

In 1978 Congress required that states cover agricultural and domestic workers of certain larger employers, as well as certain state and local government employees. In most states, employers may elect, on a voluntary basis, coverage of services that are excluded from the definition of employment under their laws. The effect of these exclusions and other limitations is that only about two-thirds of the total number unemployed are insured.[8]

Benefits

The various states have developed somewhat complicated and diverse formulas for defining the benefits under their unemployment insurance acts. There is general agreement on the main features, but it is necessary to examine the law of a particular state to determine the rights of an insured worker.

In most states the worker must either have worked for some minimum period during a base year, as defined, or have earned some minimum amount of wages, such as $400, or both. Most states require some waiting period, usually one week of total or partial unemployment, before benefit payments begin. The amount of benefit is some fraction of the wages earned during the base year or during some part of the base year. The base year is usually defined as the year preceding the date the claim is filed, with some lag ranging from a week to six months. Once a claim is filed and the weekly income payments begin, a benefit year commences and payments typically continue for a period not to exceed 26 weeks. However, a few states have extended this period to as many as 39 weeks, and benefits beyond these limits have been authorized under federal legislation. The benefit formula is so arranged that if a worker has been fully employed during the base period, the worker may, subject to a minimum and maximum amount, expect to receive benefits equal to about one-half of the normal wage. In many states the worker may receive up to two-thirds of the average weekly covered wage within the state. For March, 1985, the average weekly benefit amount in the U.S. was $129, which represented 43 percent of the average weekly wage of about $300.[9]

The worker would receive nothing if there were no earnings during the base year. If the worker was employed only part time or earned very little, the benefits would be reduced accordingly, subject to a minimum weekly amount. A few states allow additional benefits for dependents. States are prohibited from paying unemployment benefits to retirees to the extent that such a benefit would exceed the worker's pension allowance.[10]

State laws usually permit some unemployment benefits if the worker is not totally unemployed but is able to earn something, say through odd jobs, which is less than the worker's usual wage. In most states the amount of the benefit is the regular benefit less actual earnings or other payments. If actual earnings are less than some allowances, say one-half or one-third of the weekly benefit, there is no reduction in payment. These provisions reduce the temptation for a worker to cease all attempts at earning something for fear of losing the unemployment check. In some states, workers' compensation benefits disqualify the worker.

Eligibility Requirements

In order to receive benefits, unemployed workers must usually demonstrate not only that they are unemployed but also that they are actively seeking work, that they are able and willing to work, that they are not out of work because they voluntarily quit their jobs without good cause or were discharged for misconduct, and that they have not refused suitable work or are disqualified for other causes. The enforcement of these conditions is different in each state, not only because of legal provisions but because the administrative agency may choose to enforce them differently.

Ability to Work. All states require that a claimant be able to work if work is offered. Except in a few states, physical illness would therefore cause a worker to be ineligible for benefits. A worker can usually satisfy the ability-to-work requirement by registering for work at a public employment office. Six jurisdictions have enacted special legislation to care for workers who are unemployed and unable to work because of physical disability. States may not automatically deny benefits to pregnant women because they are pregnant.

Eleven states have added a provision in their laws that illness or disability will not disqualify an unemployed worker for benefits under the ability-to-work requirements if this disability is the only reason for refusing to accept a job that is offered.

Availability for Work. While each state law specifies that the worker must be available (and in most states, actively looking) for work, if offered, as a condition for drawing benefits, the enforcement of these provisions varies widely. In a few states the law says that the worker need only be available for suitable or usual work or work for which the applicant is reasonably fitted by training or experience. In other states it is suspected that administrative officials enforce the available-for-work provisions with some latitude. Often the law may make an exception for certain types of workers. Thus, in Connecticut and New Hampshire, workers are not required to be available for work between the hours of 1:00 a.m. and 6:00 a.m.; and in Alaska a worker does not lose a benefit check when hunting or fishing for survival (and hence not available), provided that no suitable work is offered.

Disqualification. The unemployment insurance laws of all states have provisions under which a worker may be disqualified from receiving benefits. Having been disqualified, the worker loses the benefits for some specified number of weeks (often three to eight) or for the duration of the unemployment, or suffers a reduction in benefit, depending on the nature of the disqualification.

Major reasons for disqualification are voluntarily quitting a job without good cause; discharge for misconduct connected with the work; refusal, without good cause, to apply for or accept suitable work; and unemployment due to a labor dispute. If a worker leaves a job for good cause, such as illness or accepting a better job, there may not be disqualification. Usually (but not in all states), disqualification is terminated by subsequent bona fide employment. Thus, if a worker quits a job without good cause, takes another job, and then is laid off from this second job, benefits may usually be drawn based on the employment with the first employer as well as with the second employer. In most states the definition of good cause is general, permitting a worker to leave a job for personal as well as employment-related reasons. Certain penalties may or may not be attached to leaving work voluntarily without good cause (as determined in each jurisdiction). Different penalties may be attached for being discharged for minor misconduct or gross misconduct.

Refusing suitable work is another major reason for disqualification from receiving unemployment insurance benefits. Suitability is defined either by specific provision in the law or by administrative rulings. If a worker refuses a job offer because the wages, hours, or other conditions of work are substantially less favorable than those prevailing for similar work in the locality, there would be no general disqualification. There is an increasing tendency to view fringe benefits as a condition which should be considered in the definition of suitable work. Other factors considerd are distance from the worker's home; the worker's experience and training; the extent of hazards in the new job affecting the claimant's health, safety, and morals; and any restraining activity engaged in by the claimant.

Under certain conditions in many states, workers who are unemployed because of a labor dispute with their employer are disqualified from receiving benefits. A labor dispute is defined under the laws in different ways. Nine states, for example, exclude lockouts from these provisions on the grounds that a worker should not be denied benefits because the employer refused to permit the workers to enter the premises. A few states do not deny benefits to workers who are unemployed because a labor dispute has closed a plant when the dispute does not involve them directly. There are similar escape clauses that permit benefits to be paid to certain classes of workers during strikes.

Claimants are disqualified for fraudulent misrepresentations in order to obtain benefits and, furthermore, must repay the amounts paid to them as a result of such misrepresentations. Usually the recipient is allowed to make restitution in cash or have the overpayments offset against future benefits. Only four states (California, Minnesota, Tennessee, and Virginia) provide punishment under criminal statutes for this offense.

Supplemental Unemployment Benefits (SUB). A supplemental unemployment benefit plan is a system under which a worker may receive an income during layoffs in addition to unemployment insurance benefits. SUB plans are usually created through collective bargaining. SUB is financed by the employer through a trust fund. The question has arisen as to whether the worker is really unemployed when receiving income from an employer indirectly through this SUB trust fund. All jurisdictions except New Hampshire, New Mexico, South Carolina, South Dakota, and Puerto Rico have taken action on this question; in all cases except Virginia the worker is permitted to receive SUB in addition to unemployment insurance.

Financing. All states receive grants from the federal government to administer unemployment insurance systems. Federal law provides that the state law must meet certain requirements to receive this grant or to receive what is called a tax offset. A federal tax of 6.2 percent is levied on payrolls up to $7,000 annual wages, but employers receive up to a 5.4 percent credit (offset) against this tax to the extent they pay the states under the existing state law. All tax collections must be deposited with the United States

Treasury. Each state has an account and may borrow additional sums to pay benefits.

The effective tax paid by employers depends critically upon the employer's record of employment stability, under a system termed **experience rating.** Most states have a standard tax rate of 5.4 percent of payroll, but employers with favorable benefit cost experience pay less, while some other employers pay more. The average in 1983 was 2.8 percent of taxable payroll, or 1.4 percent of total payroll.[11]

Criticisms of Unemployment Insurance

How well does unemployment insurance work? Labor groups criticize it because of the tight administrative standards which, they claim, are unduly restrictive. Management groups complain that the taxes are too high, benefits are too loosely administered, and financing is unstable. While no attempt will be made to resolve the various issues raised by these criticisms, a listing of the major arguments surrounding the operation of the unemployment compensation system may be helpful in pointing out the main areas that deserve further study.[12]

1. A realistic and comprehensive set of objectives, priorities, and goals for unemployment insurance has never been established. For example, is unemployment insurance supposed to cover only those who are permanently attached to the labor force? Is it supposed to cover longer term unemployment? (and how long is longer term?) What should disqualify a worker for benefits? Until some guiding philosophy is agreed upon, it seems doubtful that unemployment insurance can ever satisfy its critics.
2. Benefits average around 40 percent of earnings, well below the often-stated 50 percent objective.
3. It has been urged that unemployment insurance could afford to pay larger benefits if eligibility standards were tightened. Currently, individuals who are secondary wage earners and are not really permanently attached to the labor force (temporary workers such as seasonal help and students) may draw benefits even though they may not actually wish to obtain another job. At the same time, many groups of workers permanently attached to the labor force are not covered.
4. Because of flat dollar minimum and maximum benefits in many states, higher paid workers may be undercompensated and lower paid workers may be overcompensated during their unemployment.[13]
5. The experience-rating system is subject to many criticisms.
6. Many inequities arise because the worker is treated differently in each state, even though the conditions preceding unemployment may have been identical. It has been suggested that a federal program would help eliminate many of these difficulties and, in addition, would help equalize the tax burden among states. Under present conditions, employers in states with unstable employment due to the nature of their industry are penalized in relation to competing employers in other states.

7. In most unemployment insurance laws no provision is made for a worker who is unemployed because of physical disability. Such a worker is not able or available to work and is therefore usually disqualified. The worker generally has no disability protection under OASDHI unless the disability is expected to last longer than one year. Unless the disability was caused by accident, the worker receives nothing under workers' compensation.

8. It has been claimed that unemployment benefits fail to stabilize income during recessions and recoveries, and employer taxes are actually destabilizing because they increase during recessions and are reduced during recoveries. However, George E. Rejda showed in an extensive study that unemployment benefits have reacted quickly to downswings. During three out of four post-World War II downswings, 24 to 28 percent of the decline in national income was offset by an increase in unemployment benefits. Benefits were relatively ineffective as offsets to rising incomes during upswings, however, due chiefly to high unemployment levels that prevailed after each downswing in the period under study. Employer taxes actually tended to increase during prosperities and to decline during recessions, and thus were behaving desirably in a contracyclic manner.[14] Therefore, it cannot be concluded that unemployment insurance exerts an undesirable effect in destabilizing the business cycle—unemployment insurance has demonstrated its effectiveness in offsetting increases and decreases in national income during the cycle.

TEMPORARY DISABILITY LAWS

Temporary disability laws, sometimes called nonoccupational disability laws, grew out of the fact that unemployment compensation statutes usually deny benefits to employees who are not able and available for work; in other words, the statutes cover only healthy unemployed persons. Eleven states[15] amended their unemployment insurance laws so that unemployed workers would not be denied benefits simply because they became disabled. Five states and Puerto Rico went further than this and passed separate temporary disability laws under which employees could draw income benefits if they became disabled, regardless of whether they were employed or unemployed at the time their disabilities began. Railroad workers also have a program. In California, Puerto Rico, and Rhode Island there is one program of benefits to workers without regard to whether they are employed, unemployed, or in noncovered employment when their disability begins. In Hawaii, New Jersey, and New York there are two separate systems of benefits, one for persons who become disabled during their employment or shortly thereafter, and another for those who become disabled while unemployed. Provisions in the six jurisdictions attempt to restrict benefits to those who have had some permanent attachment to the labor force in the past.

Temporary disability laws provide for benefits regardless of whether the disability is caused by illness or accident. As workers' compensation is intended to cover most job-connected injuries and occupational illnesses, temporary disability laws may be properly described as essentially *nonoccupational*, although, in a strict sense of the word, this distinction is not always made. In Rhode Island, for example, under certain conditions a worker may receive both workers' compensation and temporary disability benefits.

In all jurisdictions except New York, temporary disability laws were generally patterned after unemployment insurance laws and provide very similar benefits. The laws are administered by the employment security agency. The financing of the laws in these states comes from employee contributions formerly made to unemployment insurance funds.

In New York it was felt that payment of disability income was more logically a function of the state's workers' compensation board, which was more experienced in the problems of disability insurance than an employment security agency. Furthermore, in New York separate financing was necessary, because employees made no contribution to unemployment insurance. A state fund was established to operate on a fully competitive basis with private insurers.

In California, New Jersey, and Puerto Rico employers are automatically covered by a state fund unless they elect private coverage that has met the standards established under the law. Approved self-insurance is also permitted in these jurisdictions. In Rhode Island, however, all employers must cover their workers in an exclusive state fund.

To be eligible for benefits, a worker must generally show inability to perform regular or customary work because of physical or mental disability. Disabilities due to pregnancy and intentionally self-inflicted injuries are limited or excluded. However, two states and the railroad program do provide maternity benefits. A claimant must have been attached to the labor force at one time or another, earning some minimum amount of wages, in order to qualify. The amount of the benefit is low, conforming to the floor-of-protection concept, and the duration is limited generally to 26 weeks. If a worker is disqualified from receiving unemployment benefits, there will usually also be disqualification from receiving disability benefits. The benefit formulas are similar to those for unemployment insurance, except in New York. The laws are all compulsory except that individuals who depend on prayer or spiritual means for healing may elect to be out of the coverage.

Temporary disability plans are financed mainly from employee contributions. For example, in California the employee pays 0.6 percent of wages. Employers may also be required to contribute to the plan in New York, Hawaii, Puerto Rico, and New Jersey.

In conclusion, it appears that temporary disability legislation is aimed at a real need, one that may be filled by either public or private insurance methods. Unlike unemployment insurance, however, there seems to be no real reason why private insurers could not handle this particular need without assistance; the peril is fully insurable and there are no insurmountable administrative problems. The growth of private insurance plans (see Chapter 12) has probably been a factor in the failure of any further successful action by states to follow the example of those states that have adopted temporary disability laws. It is also likely that extensive discussion of these laws in many state legislatures has stimulated private insurers to promote appropriate disability income policies.

GOVERNMENT PROPERTY-LIABILITY INSURANCE PROGRAMS

In the field of property-liability insurance, the main federal insurance programs include crime, crop, fire, and flood insurance. At the state level are the following types of property-liability insurance: workers' compensation (18 states); automobile insurance of different types (Maryland, New Jersey, North Dakota); property and liability insurance for state-owned property (22 states); hail insurance (3 states); land title insurance (4 states); and in all states, in cooperation with the federal government, unemployment insurance (already discussed). About half the states also operate Fair Access to Insurance Requirements (FAIR) plans, a joint federal-state program for hard-to-place property insurance on buildings in hazardous areas.

Space does not permit a full description of all the various government insurance programs—federal, state, and local—in the United States.[16] Emphasis in what follows will center on the federal property-liability programs of most current interest: FAIR plans, and flood, crime, and crop insurance.

Rationale for Government Insurance

Why has the government participated directly in the insurance field in an economy dedicated to free enterprise? For example, why has it apparently been necessary to establish OASDHI when private plans are available? At least five basic factors seem to explain governmental activity in insurance: (1) incomplete or absent offerings by private insurance in areas of social need for coverage, (2) the need to supply the element of compulsion for certain types of coverage, (3) greater operating efficiency, (4) the need to achieve some collateral social purpose, and (5) convenience.

The OASDHI program may be used to illustrate these factors. Before Social Security was established in 1935, it became clear that private life insurance had been unable to fill all of the public need for survivors' and retirement security. OASDHI could be made compulsory, thus covering most people, a condition not possible for private insurers to meet. Because OASDHI is compulsory, no sales commissions need be paid. Also, operating expenses could be reduced because other governmental agencies could cooperate in collecting premiums. Thus, direct operating costs of OASDHI are far less than would be possible if private insurers operated the program. Because the program is compulsory, many would object to private agencies operating it except on a nonprofit basis, which is not feasible for most private insurers. OASDHI achieved the collateral social purpose of helping to prevent poverty among dependent persons, such as widows, children, and the aged. Finally, the factor of convenience helped explain the use of a governmental agency to handle the Social Security program: private insurers are not sufficiently well organized to act cooperatively to meet the extensive operations of this program on a permanent and continuing basis.

Types of Competition

Governments tend to occupy one or more of three basic types of relationships with private insurers: as a partner, as a competitor, and as an exclusive agent. Illustrative of the partnership role is the FAIR program under which private insurers offer certain coverage, but the federal government provides reinsurance of losses above a specified level. Examples of the competitor relationship are the federally operated crime and flood insurance programs and the state-operated workers' compensation funds. In each of these cases, the government competes directly with private enterprise in offering similar insurance to the public. Finally, as an exclusive agent, the federal government operates loan guaranty programs, unemployment insurance, war risk insurance for aviation and marine vessels, and all-risk crop insurance. (Private crop insurance is available, but not on an all-risk basis.)

FAIR Plans

Fair Access to Insurance Requirements (FAIR) plans originated as a riot reinsurance plan established under the U.S. Housing and Urban Development Act of 1968, after riots and high losses from arson in major cities made property insurance difficult to obtain through normal channels in certain urban areas. In affected areas property insurance, if it was available at all, was priced several times higher than had been true before the riots. In a survey of 3,000 urban core homeowners and business persons in six cities, it was disclosed that 40 percent of the business people and 30 percent of homeowners had serious difficulties in obtaining property insurance.[17]

FAIR plans are operated in each state by private insurers who cooperate as a pool or syndicate to make property insurance available to customers who are unable to obtain coverage in the regular manner. As of 1985, FAIR plans existed in 26 states, Puerto Rico, and the District of Columbia. Beach and windstorm plans existed in 7 states. Agents and brokers assist property owners by applying for coverage, delivering policies, collecting premiums, and submitting claims. Insurers licensed in a state participate in the pooled experience of losses and expenses in proportion to their share of certain property insurance premiums collected in their state. To induce private insurers to participate, the federal government provides reinsurance against excessive losses resulting from riots or civil disorders.

Insurers participating in the riot reinsurance program are required to reinsure losses stemming from fire or extended-coverage perils, burglary and theft, and certain multiple-peril contract perils. Optionally, insurers may obtain coverage for riot losses under inland and ocean marine, boiler and machinery, glass, and aircraft policies.

Under a FAIR plan, the insured pays the standard premium for insurance unless the insured property falls below certain minimum underwriting standards, in which case an excess premium may be levied. The insured is entitled to have the property inspected and to receive a statement of what is necessary to bring it up to given standards. In some cases the insured may receive a grant from the federal government to make the necessary repairs. The insured's application may not be turned down because the property is located in riot-prone areas or for other environmental hazards.

Over 700,000 FAIR policies and another 100,000 plans covering beach properties were in force in 1984. The largest volume existed in the states of California, New York, Massachusetts, New Jersey, Michigan, and Pennsylvania, which together accounted for over half of the total FAIR plan business in force. The program has shown a steady increase in total volume.

In effect, FAIR plans operate in a manner very similar to automobile assigned-risk plans, with losses of the so-called "bad" risks being borne by other customers of property-liability insurers. To some extent, the stockholders or other owners of insurers also indirectly bear some of the loss.

Since the risks at which FAIR plans are directed stem mainly from social unrest, it appears that the FAIR plan philosophy of shifting the costs of this extra risk to society as a whole (i.e., to taxpayers as a group) is a sound one. In practice, however, FAIR plan legislation is not substantially transferring the environmental risk to society as a whole, but rather transferring it to other private parties who purchase fire insurance.

Flood Insurance

Flood insurance on properties in fixed locations has not generally been available from private insurers. The only source of income to insurers would be those most likely to suffer the loss, making it difficult for insurers to get a sufficient spread of risk and to avoid catastrophic claims. Furthermore, it would be difficult to solve the problem of adverse selection by providing flood coverage in package policies, because the loading necessary for the additional coverage might be substantial.

A national flood insurance program enacted in 1968 established (1) land management and other control measures to help prevent losses due to flood, and (2) federal subsidies to enable the sale of flood insurance to those most likely to be affected.[18] Originally, flood insurance was planned as a partnership with private enterprise. Policies would be distributed by private insurers, and rates would be subsidized by the federal government. Eventually, it was believed, private insurers would be able to operate the program entirely, as a self-supporting actuarial rate level was established gradually. However, difficulties with the partnership developed and the federal government took over the program in 1978, operating it under the supervision of the Federal Insurance Administration.[19]

For a community to become eligible for flood insurance, it must agree to adopt loss-prevention measures and individual property owners must certify the existence of certain loss-preventive devices. Political subdivisions within states may apply for flood-coverage eligibility by establishing certain programs. Some of these programs include measures such as adopting land-use regulations that reserve areas subject to frequent flooding for open-space types of use (playgrounds, parks, agriculture); requiring that new building in areas subject to occasional flooding have minimum first-floor elevations; and requiring that certain minimum floodproofing treatment be administered to existing buildings. Eligible properties include one- to four-family dwellings, properties principally occupied by small business firms, and their contents.[20] Coverage is available with limits of $245,000 for residences and $550,000 for non-residential properties. The policy is written with a deductible amount.

The policy covers flood and mudslide. **Flood** is defined as the inundation of normally dry land areas from the overflow of inland or tidal water, or unusual and rapid accumulation or runoff of surface waters from any source. It does not cover water damage from causes within the insured's control or from conditions that do not cause general flooding in the area.

At first, relatively few persons purchased flood insurance, even though it was available. Business increased, however, following a major $3 billion flood loss in 1972 on the eastern seaboard of the United States. In 1973 Congress imposed an element of compulsion with the requirement that those who are eligible for flood insurance may not receive federal flood disaster assistance unless they had purchased flood insurance. Sales of flood insurance increased very substantially after this action, and by 1984 coverage of $106 billion had been written on 1.7 million dwellings and other properties. Of about 20,000 communities considered to be flood prone, over 17,000 had qualified for flood insurance by 1984. Coverage is now available in every state and in Puerto Rico and the Virgin Islands.

In 1983 Congress opened the flood insurance program to private insurers with federal government backing. During 1984 private companies wrote about 174,000 policies with a face amount totalling $13.1 billion. In this way, the flood insurance program took on some aspects of a partnership program, with the federal government no longer being an exclusive underwriter of the flood risk.

Flood insurance is a good illustration of a type of coverage needed by people, but in which the risk is difficult to handle by private enterprise. The federal government, however, can shift the risk of flood loss to society as a whole through the insurance mechanism, which gradually can be so structured that those living in flood areas will pay for their own losses through paying actuarially sound rates. In the meantime, effective loss-control measures can be developed to minimize total loss. The element of compulsion can only be introduced by governmental action. Without this element, it is doubtful that needed loss-control measures would be employed. It is also doubtful that without compulsion enough eligible people would purchase coverage to enable sufficiently accurate prediction of losses in the aggregate, a necessary element for the insurance mechanism to operate successfully. Thus, federal flood insurance is justified on the grounds of the residual market philosophy, the need for compulsion, and achieving a collateral social purpose (flood control). The elements of convenience and efficiency also play a role in justifying government flood insurance.

Crime Insurance

Urban blight and other factors similar to those that caused the creation of the FAIR plans also resulted in federally sponsored crime insurance. This program, authorized under the Housing and Urban Development Act of 1970, permits the federal government to offer crime coverage (mainly burglary, robbery, and theft other than fidelity or auto theft) directly or through private insurers in any state in which it is determined that there is a critical shortage of crime insurance offered at affordable rates. A Federal Insurance Administration (FIA) survey determined that in 1971 there were 18 states and territories in which such a critical shortage existed. (The federal coverage was actually offered to 11 of these states when the program was started in 1971. Nine other states were listed as likely to require the sale of federal crime insurance.) The list of states affected is amended periodically to reflect changes in the private insurance market or creation of state crime insurance programs. As of 1984, about 32,000 residential and 70,000 commercial policies were in force in 23 states and jurisdictions. In general, the crime insurance program has been shrinking: the number of policies in force declined by about half over the period 1980–1984. Some reasons for this emerge in the following discussion.

Crime policies are sold through private insurers who are service agencies for the federal government. The risk, however, is assumed by the FIA as the insurer. Regular agents or brokers distribute the coverage along with other lines. The federal act provides that the new program will be exempt from any form of federal or state taxation or regulation.[21] Furthermore, no agent or broker will be subjected to any state tax or insurance law or regulation with respect to actions that the agent or broker takes under the law establishing the new coverage. Agents and brokers are not authorized to offer insurance on any terms other than those established by the FIA for the program. Thus, the program establishes the precedent of taking certain taxation authority and other authority over the operation of insurance away from the states, which have traditionally enjoyed freedom in this regard.

Federal crime insurance has not achieved the market acceptance hoped for by its proponents. The reasons are as follows: (1) The high moral hazard surrounding crime insurance requires an imposition of strict safety and loss-prevention measures as a condition of eligibility. These measures are often expensive to install. When they are installed, an insured may discover that private insurance can be obtained at lower cost. (2) Crime policies have strict coverage limits, a 5 percent deductible, and relatively high rates. (3) There has been some difficulty in promoting crime insurance and its availability among those whom it was supposed to benefit the most. Robert J. Hunter, formerly an administrator in the FIA, testified on this point, noting that steps had been taken such as initiating advertising campaigns, installing toll-free lines to inner-city areas to help potential users of crime insurance reach the FIA office directly, offering agents a finder's fee for new customers rather than relying on commissions alone, relaxing requirements for protective devices, and commissioning studies to learn more about the crime insurance market.[22]

Of the $342 billion of federal crime insurance in force in 1984, over 62 percent existed in New York State alone.[23] Most purchasers obtain coverage in the private market. It appears that this coverage represents an area of competition in insurance that private insurers are better equipped to handle than the government. In 1986, Congress ended authority for issuance of all new federal crime policies.

Crop Insurance

Crop insurance is of two basic types: crop-hail contracts and federal all-risk crop insurance. The former plan is written by private insurers, and coverage is generally confined to the perils of fire and hail that cause damage in excess of 5 percent of the value of the crop. Crop-hail insurance has been written since the early 1930s and has expanded steadily. The major types of crops insured are wheat, corn, tobacco, soybeans, and cotton. Coverage is based on an estimate of the value of the harvested crop, and indemnities are intended to reimburse the farmer for the costs and anticipated profit.

Federal all-risk crop insurance differs from private crop-hail coverage in the following ways:

1. All-risk crop insurance is intended to reimburse the farmer only for loss of the actual investment in the crop, not anticipated profit.
2. All-risk crop insurance must be purchased at planting time, while crop-hail insurance may be purchased anytime up through harvest.
3. All-risk crop insurance must cover the entire crop, while crop-hail insurance can be placed on selected acres.
4. In all-risk crop insurance, indemnities are based on the differences between a guaranteed crop size and the size of the actual crop. If the latter falls below a minimum level, the farmer is reimbursed for the production expenses. The coverage cannot exceed 75 percent of the farm's average yield.

Federal all-risk crop insurance was first made available in 1938. By 1985 about $6.6 billion of federal crop insurance was in force with annual premiums of $337 million, compared to $509 million of premiums in private crop-hail insurance. However, farmers are subsidized to the extent that the ratio of losses paid to them in 1985 exceeded premiums collected by 46 percent, because expenses exceeded revenues by about $313 million in the federal program. Thus, the federal crop insurance program, with $650 million in premiums and subsidies, is larger than private crop-hail programs, with $509 million worth of premiums. Federal crop insurance is sold in over 3,000 counties on 60 million acres, on over 37 different crops.

Federal crop insurance is generally delivered to farmers by private agencies operating under contracts with the Federal Crop Insurance Corporation.[24] Like flood insurance, in this sense the program is a partnership between the government and private insurance.

The federal crop insurance program was expanded under the provisions of the Crop Insurance Act of 1980. Insured acres increased about 60 percent in 1981, following a poor crop year in 1980. The new program increased the federal subsidy, allowed more flexibility in coverage, and increased quality control. In 1982 the program was available for 28 different crops in 49 states.[25]

The sale of private crop-hail insurance has expanded along with federal crop insurance. For example, premiums in crop-hail increased 3.3 times over the period 1970–1980.[26] Thus, federal and private crop insurance seem to be needed; farmers apparently desire to transfer to others some of the risks of farming.

SUMMARY

1. Social insurance, which includes government insurance plans providing financial security, is to be distinguished from public assistance plans under which governments make gratuitous payments to individuals in need who have no resources of their own. The chief types of social insurance are (a) old-age, survivors, and disability insurance, and Medicare; (b) workers' compensation insurance; (c) unemployment insurance; and (d) temporary disability insurance.

2. Social insurance is generally introduced when it is impossible or impractical for private insurers to solve a social problem that lends itself to solution by the insurance method. Social insurance in the United States has grown from a negligible amount in 1935, when the Social Security Act was passed, to a point where, in 1985, over 13 percent of personal income was devoted to it. Trends suggest that the insurance method is gaining fast as the preferred way to meet social problems that cause an interruption of income.

3. Social insurance, in contrast to private contracts (a) is compulsory, (b) does not allow individual choice in selecting the amount of benefit, (c) provides only a minimum level of benefit, (d) is subsidized by groups other than the insured group, (e) has a total cost which is basically unpredictable, and (f) covers only individuals who have been attached to the labor force and meet certain minimum requirements.

4. As measured by benefit payments, OASDHI and public retirement plans are 14 times as large as unemployment insurance, and about 13 times as large as workers' compensation and temporary disability insurance combined. OASDHI, which is operated by the federal government, provides three

basic types of income payments to qualified beneficiaries: (a) retirement income to the worker and dependents, (b) income to dependents in case of the worker's death, and (c) income to the worker and dependents in case of permanent disability. The size of these benefits depends on the amount of earnings and the length of time the worker has contributed taxes.

5. In common with all plans of social insurance, OASDHI benefits are conditional on many factors. One of the basic reasons why the size of the promised pension can be relatively large in relation to the total taxes paid is that a certain proportion of those who pay taxes will not qualify for benefits.

6. Unemployment insurance was designed to relieve only certain types of losses, namely those arising from short-term, involuntary unemployment. Long-term, voluntary unemployment is not covered. Unemployment insurance, administered by the states, had its origin in 1935 with passage of the Social Security Act. All states have these acts, which must meet certain minimum federal standards.

7. Benefits under unemployment insurance depend on the amount of wages an employee is able to accumulate during a given base period. Benefits generally may not continue longer than six months and may restore up to one-half of the worker's wages during the benefit period. The worker must be able to work and must be available for work at all times. Refusing suitable work, as defined, is a cause for stopping the payments.

8. In 1956 disability benefits were introduced under OASDHI. Even though at present they are a relatively small part of the total benefits, they represent the first attempt to meet the problem of long-term disability through social insurance and will undoubtedly become more important as time goes on and as qualification standards for benefits are liberalized.

9. Under temporary disability laws existing in five states and Puerto Rico, a disabled worker may draw benefits if he or she would have generally qualified for unemployment benefits had there been no disability. In some states the same is true, regardless of whether it was an accident or sickness that caused the disability, and regardless of whether the disability was suffered on or off the job.

10. In addition to social insurance, governments engage in a number of other insurance programs. In the field of property and liability insurance, four major programs are FAIR programs and flood, crime, and crop insurance. Various reasons exist for government insurance, with perhaps the dominant one being the residual market philosophy—to cover fields not adequately insured through private enterprise.

QUESTIONS FOR REVIEW

1. Suppose Congress passed a law that said that the OASDHI trust fund should be increased immediately to meet the standards of actuarial solvency required of a private insurer. Assess the economic implications of such a law for the coming year.

2. Life insurance agents sometimes object that their sales are hampered by the fact that individuals feel that their life insurance needs are fully cared for by OASDHI. Do you think this fear has any justification? Discuss.

3. What basic types of protection are offered under Medicare?

4. What exclusions and limitations are there in Medicare? Should any of these be eliminated? Why?

5. Why is unemployment generally considered uninsurable for a private insurer?

6. One of the dangers of unemployment insurance is that it will fail to provide incentives for the employee to return to work. What measures have been taken to combat this tendency?

7. What is the difference between crop-hail insurance and all-risk crop insurance? Which is larger in terms of premium volume? In your opinion, should the government be involved in crop insurance? Why?

8. Explain briefly each of the main differences between private and social insurance.

9. What percentage of preretirement income does OASDHI restore? For which income level? Explain.

10. What is the OASDHI "retirement test"? Explain.

QUESTIONS FOR DISCUSSION

1. If a social problem is subject to solution by the insurance method, why have not private insurers supplied the insurance facilities to meet certain problems? In other words, why has it been necessary for government to insure?

2. What evidence (see Table 25–1) do you find for the position that (a) welfare expenditures are increasing at an alarming rate and should be curtailed, or (b) welfare expenditures, particularly social insurance expenditures, are not an unreasonable burden and could be expanded?

3. It has been argued that it is not fair for some workers to receive OASDHI benefits and for others who have paid in an equal amount of taxes to be denied benefits because they failed to meet the retirement test. Rather, it is claimed, all workers should be paid as a matter of right. Analyze this argument, and state what results would follow if the situation were "corrected."

4. Those who have urged the adoption of socialized medicine point out that a system of national compulsory health insurance would not provide coverage for everyone needing it, but would meet only some part of the need for coverage. Referring to the basic differences between social insurance and private insurance outlined in the text, comment on the correctness or incorrectness of this position.

5. Offer at least one reason for the fact that one plan under Medicare is compulsory and the other is voluntary. Why should not both plans be compulsory if Medicare is to be classified as social insurance?

6. Should unemployment insurance be abolished? Discuss pros and cons.

NEW TERMS AND CONCEPTS

Social Insurance
Floor-of-Protection Concept
Old-Age, Survivors,
    Disability, and Health
    Insurance (OASDHI)
Supplemental Security
    Income (SSI)
Retirement Test
Medicare
Supplemental
    Unemployment Benefits (SUB)

Temporary Disability Laws
Flood Insurance Program
Crime Insurance Program
Federal Crop Insurance
    Program
Fully Insured
Currently Insured
Fair Access to Insurance
    Requirements (FAIR Plan)

NOTES

1 For example, Germany passed the first modern workers' compensation statute in 1884 under the sponsorship of Bismarck. It was viewed as a method of counteracting the growing strength of the Socialist Party in Germany. Britain followed suit in 1897. It is interesting that today in the United States many observers look upon social insurance legislation as the forerunner, not a countermeasure, to socialism. Most Western nations of the world have adopted various forms of social insurance, many of which are more complete than those in the United States.

2 *Social Security Bulletin* (March, 1986), p. 24. Latest data are published monthly.

3 *Social Security Bulletin* (January, 1986), p. 16.

4 Unemployment insurance is financed through the federal government in part, but is state-administered. Workers' compensation and temporary disability insurance are both state-financed and -administered plans. Health insurance for the aged is administered by private insurers under government contract.

5 Based on the rate at age 60, $4.65 per $1,000 of proceeds, and 20-year certain and life, from Table D-5. Using this rate, it would take about $53,760 to provide $250 per month for life. However, if the husband dies when the widow is age 40, a 20-year present value factor of 0.3118 (Table D-2) would be applied, providing the sum of $16,760 as the amount of life insurance needed. As the widow gets older, this sum gradually increases.

6 *Life Insurance Fact Book 1985* (Washington, D.C.: American Council of Life Insurance, 1985), p. 17. Payments in 1984 were made up of $16.8 billion in death benefits, $0.7 billion in matured endowments, $17.9 billion in annuities, $14.7 billion in surrender values, $0.6 billion in disability benefits, and $9.7 billion in dividends.

7 U.S. Social Security Administration, *The Financial Status of Social Security after the Social Security Amendments of 1977*, SSA Program Circular No. 414 (February 13, 1978), p. 2.

8 See current issues of *Labor Market and Employment Security* for up-to-date data on insured employment.

9 *Monthly Labor Review* (March, 1986), p. 71.

10 U.S. Department of Labor, *Unemployment Insurance: State Laws and Experience* (Washington, D.C.: U.S. Government Printing Office, 1978), p. 17, and *Social Security Bulletin* (January, 1986), pp. 22–28.

11 *Social Security Bulletin* (January, 1986), p. 28.

12 There have been many studies of unemployment compensation systems, both on a state and a national level. See William Haber and M. G. Murray, *Unemployment Insurance in the American Economy* (Homewood, Ill.: Richard D. Irwin, 1966); George E. Rejda, "Unemployment Insurance as an Automatic Stabilizer," *Journal of Risk and Insurance* (June, 1966), pp. 195–208; and Steven P. Zell, *Unemployment Insurance: Programs, Procedures, and Problems* (Federal Reserve Bank of Kansas City, 1977).

13 Willaim Papier, "What's Wrong with Unemployment Insurance?," *Journal of Risk and Insurance* (March, 1970), pp. 65–74.

14 Rejda, op. cit., p. 208.

15 Alaska, Delaware, Hawaii, Idaho, Maryland, Massachusetts, Montana, Nevada, North Dakota, Tennessee, and Vermont.

16 For a description and analysis of these programs, see Mark R. Greene, "The Government as an Insurer," *Journal of Risk and Insurance*, Vol. XLIII, No. 3 (September, 1976), pp. 393–406; "A Review and Evaluation of Selected Government Programs to Handle Risk," *The Annals of the American Academy of Political and Social Science* (May, 1979), pp. 129–144; and "Government Insurers," *Issues in Insurance*, Vol. 1, John D. Long, Editor (Malvern, Pa.: American Institute for Property and Liability Underwriters, 1978), pp. 303–384.

17 Staford G. Ross, "Federal Reinsurance," *Best's Review* (July, 1968), p. 25.

18 Public Law 90-448, August 1, 1968, 42 USC 4001–4127. An earlier law was passed in 1956 but was never funded by Congress.

19 Samuel H. Weese and J. W. Doms, "The National Flood Insurance Program—Did the Insurance Industry Drop Out?" *CPCU Journal*, Vol. 31, No. 4 (December, 1978), pp. 186–204.

20 A small business is defined as one that does not have assets in excess of $5 million, does not have a net worth in excess of $2.5 million, and does not have a net income after federal income taxes for the preceding two fiscal years in excess of $250,000.

21 Section 1250 of the Act (12 UDC 174bbb-20).

22 Robert J. Hunter, in *Hearings Before a Subcommittee on Housing and Community Development of the Committee on Banking, Finance, and Urban Affairs, House of Representatives, 95th Congress, First Session, February 16, 1977* (Washington, D.C.: U.S. Government Printing Office, 1977), p. 16.

23 *Insurance Facts 1985–86* (New York: Insurance Information Institute, 1985), p. 48.

24 *Appendix Budget of the United States Government, Fiscal Year 1987*, I-E31—E-36.

25 "Federal Crop Insurance," *U.S. Government Manual, 1982-1983* (Washington, D.C.: Office of the Federal Register, 1982), pp. 100–103.

26 *Insurance Facts 1981-82*, p. 26.

26 GOVERNMENT REGULATION OF INSURANCE

After studying this chapter, you should be able to:

1. Explain why insurance needs to be regulated.
2. Identify what aspects of insurance are regulated.
3. Cite three examples of abuse in insurance.
4. State pros and cons of state vs. federal regulation.
5. Indicate how regulation affects insurance rates.

Government has commonly laid down rules governing the conduct of business; insurance is no exception. In the case of insurance, however, special attention has been given by the government, which has actively engaged itself in the business directly. The insurance industry has been significantly influenced by the government in its operations. Some of the ways in which this has taken place, together with some of the reasons, will be discussed in this chapter.

WHY INSURANCE IS REGULATED

There are characteristics of insurance that set it apart from tangible-goods industries and that account for the special interest in government regulation. First, insurance is a commodity people pay for in advance and whose benefits are reaped in the future (sometimes in the far distant

639

future), often by someone entirely different from the insured and who is not present to protect his or her self-interest when the contract is made. Second, insurance is effected by a complex agreement that few lay people understand and by which the insurer could achieve a great and unfair advantage if disposed to do so. Third, insurance costs are unknown at the time the premium is agreed upon, and there exists a temptation for unregulated insurers to charge too little or too much. Charging too little results in the long run in removing the very security the insured thought was being purchased; charging too much results in unwarranted profits to the insurer. Finally, insurance is regulated to control abuses in the industry.

Future Performance

The insurer is, in effect, the manager of policyholders' funds. The management of other people's money, particularly when it has grown to be one of the largest industries in the nation, immediately becomes a candidate for regulation because of the temptation for the unscrupulous to use these funds for their own ends instead of for those to whom the funds belong. One party to the contract (the insurer) receives payment currently, but the ultimate performance is contingent upon the occurrence of some event that may not happen for many years. Two questions arise: How can the insured obtain a guarantee that the insurer's performance will be forthcoming? and How can justice be obtained in case of failure by the insurer?

Complexity

We know that the insurance contract is not simple. There are many instances in which, even if the lay person understands the implications of every legal clause in a contract, the rights of that person are vitally affected by the operation of certain legal principles or industry customs to which no reference exists in the written contract. The legal battles that have been fought over the interpretation of the contractual wording of a policy bear testimony to the fact that misunderstandings arise over the meaning of provisions even after the best legal minds have attempted to make the intent of the insurer clear. If misunderstandings can arise when they are unintended, it is easy to see that in the absence of any restraint an insurer would find no difficulty in framing a contract that looked appealing on the surface, but under which it would be possible for the insurer to avoid any payment at all. (See Chapter 7 for a discussion of the insurance contract.)

Unknown Future Costs

The price the insurer must charge for service must be set far in advance of the actual performance of this service. The cost of the service depends on many unknown factors, such as random fluctuations in loss frequency and unexpected changes in the cost of repairing property. In order to increase business, an insurer may consciously underestimate future costs in order to justify a lower premium and thus attract customers. If the insurer refuses to accept business except at a very high premium, consciously or unconsciously overestimating future costs, those who pay may be over-charged, and those who cannot pay will go without a vital service. Inability to obtain insurance may even prevent potential insureds from engaging in business because of inability to obtain credit or offer surety. Some outside control over pricing in insurance is desirable for both the insured and the insurer.

Abuses

As in any line of business, abuses of power and violations of public trust occur in insurance. These include failure by the insurer to live up to contract provisions, drawing up contracts that are misleading and that seem to offer benefits they really do not cover, refusal to pay legitimate claims, improper investments of policyholders' funds, false advertising, and many others.

Some state insurance departments maintain offices to handle customer complaints against insurers and their agents and to effect settlements of disputes without formal legal or court actions. In a case in Maryland,[1] an insurer was fined $50,000 for having engaged in a general plan to compel insurance claimants either to accept less than the amounts due them under their policies or to sue the insurer. Most insureds do not find it practical to sue under insurance contracts unless the sums involved are relatively large. In this case the insurer's instructions to its claims adjustors prohibited them from using the customary practice of settling an automobile damage claim by a conference between a repair shop and the insurer's appraiser. Instead, the appraiser would lower the estimate presented by the insured by 10 or 15 percent and send a check for the reduced amount without explanation. The insured could either accept the reduced amount, attempt to find a garage that would accept that reduced amount, or bring legal action against the insurer.

Abuses in insurance have been such that major investigations of the insurance business have taken place, many of which resulted in reform legislation that is currently reflected in the regulatory environment. For example, in 1906 the Armstrong investigation in New York uncovered many abuses in life insurance and resulted in the mutualization of many stock insurers. An investigation of health insurance in 1910 in New York resulted in the adoption of uniform standard health insurance provisions. The Meritt Committee Investigation in New York in 1910 resulted in outlawing combinations to fix rates in insurance and also resulted in antirebating laws. In 1939 the Temporary National Economic Committee investigated insurance and uncovered abuses in industrial insurance, but the occurrence of World War II interrupted any significant reform legislation that might have resulted. The Federal Trade Commission investigated false advertising practices in insurance after 1950, resulting in reforms in the field of mail-order health insurance.

The United States Senate Committee on the Judiciary has continued to investigate practices in insurance since 1958 and has been critical of state regulation of the business. Finally, a massive investigation into auto insurance sponsored by the U.S. Department of Transportation in 1970 resulted in pressure on states to pass reforms in the field of automobile insurance, establishing the no-fault principle in about half the states.

**THE LEGAL
BACKGROUND
OF REGULATION**

Insurance traditionally has been regulated by the states. In each state there is an insurance department and an insurance commissioner or superintendent who has several specific duties. Prior to 1850 insurance was operated as a private business, with no more regulation than any other business enterprise. There was a lack of any financial guarantee that losses would be paid when due, and little control was exercised over the investment of funds collected as premiums. In general, the doctrine of *caveat emptor* was the rule.

As a result of the early abuses of insurance, with their resulting ill effects on the consuming public and insurers alike, the need for regulation became apparent. Although many states by 1850 had passed statutes affecting insurance, no state established special enforcement agencies until 1850, when New Hampshire appointed an insurance commissioner. Massachusetts, California, Connecticut, Indiana, Missouri, New York, and Vermont followed this early example shortly afterward, and by 1871 nearly all states had some type of control or supervision.

In 1868 an important United States Supreme Court decision, *Paul* v. *Virginia*,[2] established the right of states to regulate insurance by holding that insurance was *not commerce*, but was in the nature of a personal contract between two local parties. As insurance was held not to be commerce, the federal government would have no direct regulatory power through its right to govern interstate commerce as given under the commerce clause of the Constitution. This decision was upheld repeatedly until reversed in 1944 by the famous decision, the *South-Eastern Underwriters Association* case.[3]

In 1871 an organization that has had a far-reaching effect on regulation was formed. This organization, later named the National Association of Insurance Commissioners, was a group of state insurance commissioners through whose efforts a considerable measure of uniformity in regulation has been achieved. One of its first tasks was to introduce some uniformity into regulations governing the type of reports that insurance companies were required to make. Another task was to agree on a system of exchange of information as to the solvency of insurers, so that an insurer did not have to prove solvency to the satisfaction of each state in which it operated. Still another job was to agree on uniform systems for valuation of legal reserves of life insurers.

The *South-Eastern Underwriters Association* (S.E.U.A.) case overturned by a vote of four to three the *Paul* v. *Virginia* ruling that insurance was not commerce. The court held that insurance was commerce and that, when conducted across state lines, it was interstate commerce. The impact of this decision was to make insurance subject to federal regulation and, of course, to all federal laws regulating trade practices in interstate commerce. Laws that were to apply included the Sherman Act, the Clayton Act, and the Robinson-Patman Act, dealing with the control of business activities in restraint of fair trade, particularly price-fixing, unfair trade practices, false advertising, and the like. The S.E.U.A. case overruled many Supreme Court decisions that exempted the insurance industry and caused great uncertainty as to the future status of regulation.

THE MCCARRAN-FERGUSON ACT

The S.E.U.A. decision made it clear that some insurance associations had influence extending considerably beyond that of cooperative rate making. Certainly it was not the intent of state regulatory laws that boycotts and coercion should be a result of permission to form cooperative rates. Yet the complete abandonment of state regulation of insurance in favor of federal regulation was not desired by either the insurance industry or state insurance commissioners. Accordingly, the National Association of Insurance Commissioners proposed a bill which later became known as the McCarran-Ferguson Act. This bill, also known as Public Law 15, became law on March 9, 1945. It declared that:

1. It was the intent of Congress that state regulation of insurance should continue, and that no state law relating to insurance should be affected by any federal law unless such law is directed specifically at the business of insurance.
2. The Sherman Act, Clayton Act, Robinson-Patman Act, and the Federal Trade Commission Act would, after a three-year delay, be fully applicable to insurance, but only "to the extent that the individual states do not regulate insurance."
3. That part of the Sherman Act relating to boycotts, coercion, and intimidation would henceforth remain fully applicable to insurance.

Except to the extent indicated by the provisions of the McCarran-Ferguson Act, the insurance business continues to be regulated by the states. However, the law does not exempt the insurance business from federal regulation and in fact provides for a limited applicability of certain federal laws to insurance.

Federal regulation of insurance is carried out by many different federal agencies. For example, the Federal Insurance Administration (FIA), which administers several government insurance programs, was involved in an extensive federal investigation of workers' compensation and no-fault automobile insurance. The FIA is involved in the administration of the Price Anderson Act, which regulates nuclear energy liability insurance. The Exim-Bank, a federal agency, administers the export credit insurance program. The Interstate Commerce Commission specifies coverages required of interstate transportation carriers. The Federal Trade Commission regulates insurance company mergers, mail-order advertising, and other trade practices affecting competition.[4] Regulations of the Security and Exchange Commission govern the issuance of variable annuities and some aspects of insurer accounting practices. The U.S. Department of Labor influences coverage for coal miners for black lung disease. It also operates the Occupational Safety and Health Act, which importantly affects risk management practices of industry. The Department of Labor, together with the Internal Revenue Service, administers the Employees Retirement Income Security Act (ERISA) under which the operations of private pension plans, many of them insured, are carefully regulated. A subsidiary agency, the Pension Benefits Guaranty Corporation, regulates and insures financial operations of private pension plans. It seems clear that federal regulation of insurance activity is a continuing force.

Following the passage of the McCarran-Ferguson Act, the National Association of Insurance Commissioners formed a model bill that was designed to accomplish at the state level what the Sherman, Clayton, FTC, and Robinson-Patman Acts accomplish as applied to business generally. This model bill (known as the All-Industry Rating Bill), was adopted in whole or in part by most states and contains many recommendations. In general, the philosophy of the legislation emerging from these recommendations is that rate-making cooperation is *neither required nor prohibited*, except to the extent necessary to meet the general requirement that rates be adequate, not excessive, and nondiscriminatory. Machinery is provided whereby an insurer may file a lower or "deviated" rate upon showing that the rate meets these requirements. Membership in a rate-making organization is not required. Currently, rate competition is relatively unrestricted in about half the states.

In recent years, legislation has been considered by Congress to repeal the McCarran-Ferguson Act. For example, in 1986 bills were introduced in both the Senate and the House of Representatives to remove, wholly or partially, the immunity from federal antitrust legislation now extended to insurance companies under the McCarran-Ferguson Act. The insurance industry generally opposes these changes, and so far no such bills have been enacted.

In summary, both states and the federal government are currently exercising regulatory control over the insurance industry. States still have basic regulatory functions, while the federal government exercises regulation in specified areas only. However, the list of areas over which federal regulation exists appears to be growing steadily.

FEDERAL VERSUS STATE REGULATION

For many years the argument as to whether or not federal regulation would be superior to the present system of state regulation of the insurance industry has been of considerable concern to parties both within and outside of the insurance business. Federal regulation is a continuing possibility since the S.E.U.A. case opened the door, a door that was not entirely closed by the McCarran-Ferguson Act. The chief arguments for federal regulation, many of which amount to criticisms of state control, are as follows:

1. State regulation is not uniform and, in spite of certain accomplishments toward uniformity by the National Association of Insurance Commissioners, is not likely to become so. Insurers are subjected to different requirements in each state.

2. State regulation is relatively ineffective. It is not a suitable mechanism to regulate or control the activities of an insurer that is nationwide in its operation. If a given state prohibits a certain activity as being dangerous or unlawful, this of course does not affect the operation in another state, and so the objectionable practice continues elsewhere. If the particular practice is really dangerous, its continuation may affect the insurer's operation in the particular state, even though the practice is not carried on in that state.

   This complaint gave rise in the state of New York to a law known as the Appleton Rule, whereby an insurer admitted to do business in New York must adhere to New York's requirements not only in New York, but in *all other states* where the insurer is doing business.[5] Thus, if New York prohibits an insurer from issuing a certain type of policy in that state, the insurer, as a condition of continued operation there, will have to forego its right to issue the policy in any other state where it is doing business. The Appleton Rule has had the effect of greatly extending the influence of New York's insurance underwriting requirements in other states because of the great size of the insurance market and the desire of insurers to operate there. However, many insurers do not operate in New York and are not subject to the Appleton Rule.

3. Federal regulation would be more effective and less costly for insurers than state regulation. Many ill-advised statutes have been enacted by various states which presumably would be avoided under federal control because of the greater political insulation from local pressures enjoyed by national legislators. Federal legislators are full-time representatives, whereas state legislators usually work only part time. Federal legislators would therefore, it is argued, have more time to devote to the specialized problems of the insurance industry and could give them more thorough attention. The result should be a higher quality of administration and regulation.

Opposing these arguments are those who favor continued state regulation. In general, state insurance commissioners and representatives of the insurance industry, particularly those representatives engaged in the marketing of insurance, are opposed to federal regulation. Major arguments in favor of state regulation are the following:

1. State supervision and regulation of insurance is reasonably satisfactory, and there is no overpowering reason why federal regulation should be

necessary. The burden of proof that a change is necessary should fall upon those who seek the change, and such proof has not yet been produced.

2. Most of the arguments of those who favor federal control rest on dubious claims of inefficiency and on unproved claims that federal control would necessarily be more efficient. There is reason to believe that federal control would actually be less efficient because of isolation from local conditions and inability to deal with problems from afar.

3. While lack of uniformity is admitted, the really important needs for uniformity have been achieved, or are being achieved through the voluntary cooperation of state insurance commissioners.

4. State regulation is much more flexible than federal regulation would be. State regulation can relate to local needs. It can encourage experimentation and development in insurance procedures and contracts.

5. Those who favor continued state regulation point out that if federal regulation were imposed, the result might be two systems of regulation instead of one. The operations of a very large number of insurance companies are confined entirely within the boundaries of a single state. Presumably, the states would continue to regulate these activities as intrastate commerce. Hence, state insurance departments would have to continue their existence, and the federal system would be superimposed on a state system. This would result in more wasteful overlapping, confusion, and duplication than now exist.

6. The experience of other industries subjected to federal regulation suggests that once begun, federal regulation tends to develop into greater and greater control, leading to direct participation in management decisions, such as in pricing. This is inconsistent with the free-enterprise philosophy of the U.S. economy.

We will probably continue to have some forms of federal influence on state regulation, but outright federal control seems unlikely, at least in the foreseeable future. Increasing federal influence in insurance will likely be felt both in the form of regulation and by means of direct government competition in insurance. This competition has already been established in the field of life insurance for many years, to a lesser extent in the field of property insurance through crop, crime, and flood insurance, and in Fair Access to Insurance Requirements (FAIR) plans.

RESPONSIBILITIES OF THE STATE INSURANCE DEPARTMENT

We can classify the responsibilities of the state insurance department into four categories:

1. Enforcement of minimum standards of financial solvency
2. Regulation of rates and expenses
3. Agents' activities
4. Control over contractual provisions and their effects on the consumer

Financial Solvency

It is the primary responsibility of the state insurance department to see that insurers operating within the boundaries of the state are financially responsible. In order to accomplish this task, the insurance commissioner enforces the state's laws regarding the admission of an insurer to do business, the formation of new insurers, and the liquidation of insurers who become insolvent. The commissioner must see that adequate reserves are maintained for each line of insurance written and that the investments of the insurer are sound and comply with the state requirements.

Minimum Capital. To do business in a state, an insurer must first be licensed. Licenses are granted according to the type of insurance business to be conducted. Different capital standards are applied to each type. Minimum financial standards are set forth in each state, and they vary considerably from state to state and by type of insurer. For example, in New York a new stock life insurer must now have at least an initial minimum paid-in capital of $2,000,000 and a paid-in surplus of $4,000,000, or 200 percent of the initial capital. For stock insurers writing accident and health insurance, the law requires only $300,000 of minimum initial paid-in capital and $150,000 of paid-in surplus, or at least 50 percent of the initial capital.[6]

In many states no distinction is made in capital requirements according to the type of insurance written, but a blanket amount is required for insurers writing any of a long list of contracts. No consistent pattern emerges as to financial standards among the different states regarding the financial requirements for life insurance in relation to property-liability insurance, or in minimum dollar levels.

There is evidence that minimum legal capital requirements for some types of insurers have not always been set at adequate levels. The turnover among insurers has been substantial. One of the important reasons for termination of an insurer is financial difficulties that might well have been avoided with greater financial resources. For example, one of the important reasons for termination of a newly organized life insurer is lack of adequate capital to meet heavy initial expenses and to write new insurance.

Investments. The assets of an insurer may not be invested in just any type of securities. If no regulation were imposed on the investment of assets, it is clear that there would be little point in requiring the existence of so much capital as a condition of doing business. Accordingly, all states impose investment limitations. In general, the philosophy behind these limitations is to require that funds that have been paid in as an advance payment of premiums be invested conservatively in bonds, mortgages, and other fixed-income securities. The objective is to maintain safety and to give sufficient liquidity to enable insurers to pay claims when due, if necessary, by selling assets. Often the law will specify that each bond or mortgage meet certain minimum standards of asset protection, interest coverage, etc. The law also specifies the manner in which each asset is to be valued; bonds are valued on an amortized basis and stocks at cost or market, whichever is lower.

Furthermore, certain types of assets are not recognized or admitted for purposes of state regulation. Nonadmitted assets typically include office furniture, overdue balances from agents, and other assets not normally subject to liquidation for meeting obligations due to policyholders.

Liquidation. The insurance commissioner is charged with the responsibility of liquidating an insolvent insurer. When this happens, an equitable treatment of policyholders and other creditors is essential. Some types of insurers subject their policyholders to additional assessments in the event of financial inability to pay claims, and the insurance commissioner must see that these obligations are paid.

Security Deposits. Most states require that each insurer licensed to do business within state boundaries make a deposit of securities with the insurance commissioner to guarantee that policyholders will be paid claims due them. These laws have been unpopular for several reasons. The size of the deposit is generally too small in proportion to the volume of business carried on to be of any real protection to the insured. The state should logically depend upon the quality of its examinations and other procedures to see that the insurer is solvent. The size of the deposit required generally bears little or no relationship to the size of required amounts of capital and surplus or reserves. It is common for one state to waive the requirements for insurers operating within its boundaries if other states do likewise for insurers chartered in that state. Thus, the security deposits may give little added protection to policyholders while complicating insurance regulation.

Insolvency Funds. All 50 states, Puerto Rico, and the District of Columbia have enacted some type of legislation covering the insolvency of property-liability insurers. Much of this legislation is patterned after, but not identical to, the model bill proposed by the National Association of Insurance Commissioners (NAIC) in 1969. The purpose of the bills, as phrased by the NAIC model, is

> to provide a mechanism for the payment of covered claims under certain insurance policies, to avoid excessive delay in payment, to avoid financial loss to claimants or policyholders because of the insolvency of an insurer, to assist in the detection and prevention of insurer insolvencies, and to provide an association to assess the cost of such protection among insurers.

The success of insurance insolvency funds may be judged by the fact that from their beginning in 1969 through 1984, assessments of nearly $527 million have been made against insurer members, covering insolvencies of 104 property-liability insurers. Assessments have occurred in all states, indicating the pervasive nature of the insolvency problem. The greatest assessments (not counting New York, which has a separate fund) have occurred in four states—Florida, California, Pennsylvania, and Illinois—and Puerto Rico, which together accounted for about 66 percent of the $527 million total.[7]

The guaranty associations represent another example of private action to forestall the creation of any new federal government control over insurance. The associations are controlled by the private insurance industry under state supervision. The programs are consistent with state laws governing insolvency procedures and certainly appear to strengthen these procedures.

Regulation of Rates and Expenses

The state insurance department is responsible for regulating the rates and expenses of insurance companies. If inadequate rates are charged, insolvency becomes a threat. If excessive or discriminatory rates are allowed, the insurance department must handle public complaints.

Property-Liability Rates. The typical rating law in about 32 states permits insurers to form rating bureaus and to pool statistical information with these bureaus. Member insurers may be asked to adhere to rates developed by the rating bureau, but may request permission to deviate from these rates. Insurers are not required to belong to the rating bureau, but may operate independently. In all states, rates that are used must meet three basic requirements:

1. The rate shall be reasonable.
2. The rate shall be adequate to cover expected losses and expenses.
3. The rate shall not be unfairly discriminatory between different insured groups.

In these states, a rate must first be filed with the insurance commissioner before it can be used. The laws are thus termed **prior approval.** Within a period of 10 or 20 days the commissioner must respond, giving permission to use the rate or not. Insurers are supposed to provide statistical evidence that filed rates meet the requirements of reasonableness, adequacy, and nondiscrimination.

The remaining states have what is called **open competition laws.**[8] Under these laws, rating bureaus are not allowed to establish rates that insurers must follow, but can publish advisory rates only. In some cases, insurers are not required to file rates with the commissioner at all, and in others insurers must file rates but are permitted to use these rates immediately. The latter are called **file-and-use** states. Open competition is relied upon to see that the rates meet the three requirements listed. No strong evidence exists that either open competition laws or prior approval laws are more effective in achieving the three objectives of rating legislation.

Prior Approval versus Open Competition Laws. One advantage of open competition laws is their relative flexibility, especially in regard to eliminating the delays in getting approval for rating changes that exist under prior approval laws. Open competition laws also help increase the availability of insurance. Under prior approval laws, if a rate is turned down, the insurer may refuse to issue coverage at all, thus restricting the supply of insurance. Under open competition laws, coverage usually is available, even though the rate may be high.

Prior approval laws are also said to discourage innovation. If an insurer develops a new insurance policy, permission must first be obtained to sell it at an approved price. Prior approval laws subject the insurance commissioner to political pressures to refuse approval of rate increases, even though the increases may be justified. Thus, rates are subject to negotiation between the commissioner and the insurers, and are not determined scientifically. Finally, prior approval laws place the insurance commissioner under a considerable burden to determine the proper rate level. Resources and time to accomplish studies to determine proper rates may be lacking. For example, in one study it was found that among 17 states, only 6 had done actuarial or other statistical reviews to see whether loss data submitted by insurers justified existing territorial boundaries in which rates applied.[9]

Life Insurance Rates. Life insurance rates are essentially unregulated by states, except indirectly through regulation of expenses and reserves. For example, insurers chartered in New York are subject to a limitation on agents' commissions. Commissions must not exceed 55 percent of the first year's premium of an ordinary life insurance policy. This limitation applies to some of the country's largest life insurers, and it affects their business all over the United States. Recall that under New York's "Appleton Rule" insurers operating in New York must adhere to New York's laws wherever they sell insurance. The commission limitation helps keep life insurance rates lower than they might otherwise be. Many insurers not operating in New York are allowed to pay much larger commissions, sometimes as much as 200 percent or more of the first year's premium of an ordinary life insurance policy.

Life insurance rates are also affected by reserve and mortality assumptions. Life insurance reserves represent an insurer's obligations to the policyholder for the savings element in the life insurance policy. In calculating the reserve, an insurer assumes that it will earn some minimum interest rate and will experience a certain mortality rate. The higher the interest assumption and the lower the mortality rate assumed, the lower the reserve can be, and the lower the associated premium rate can be. States generally regulate the maximum interest assumption and the minimum mortality table in order to be assured that the life insurer will not charge so little that it cannot meet its obligations to the policyholder. Thus, the effect of state regulation of reserves is to set a floor on life insurance rates.

It is assumed that competition among insurers will operate to keep life insurance rates from becoming excessive. As shown in Chapter 10, however, there are wide variations in life insurance premiums among insurers in the open market. A considerably active movement exists to require life insurers to disclose more information about costs to the policyholder so that a more intelligent buying decision can be made. It may be presumed that as additional cost information is made available, open competition in life insurance will become more efficient and will result in less variation in premium rates than now exists.

A recent study by *Consumer Reports* on life insurance rates in 1986[10] illustrates the degree of competition which exists among life insurers. Declining mortality rates, increasing interest assumptions, and reduced expenses have also contributed to rate competition and have caused life insurers to reduce the effective rates for life insurance in recent years. The *Consumer Reports* study, which covered about 35 policies issued in 1986, revealed the following variations in 10-year, interest-adjusted costs per $1,000 of nonparticipating (nondividend-paying) term policies:

Age 25	Male	Female
Lowest	1.49	1.45
Median	2.59	2.34
Highest	3.62	3.34
Index		
Lowest	100	100
Median	174	161
Highest	243	479

The variations, which are quite large, were similar for ages 35 and 45. Note that the highest-rated policy was nearly 4.8 times as great for a female age 25, and 2.4 times as great for a male age 25, as the lowest-rated policy. The survey demonstrates another point, frequently overlooked by life insurance buyers, that it pays to shop for life insurance.

Agents' Activities

The agent has been a dominant figure in the insurance industry almost from the beginning, and for most consumers the agent is the only contact with the insurer. Since insurance is a complex business, it is vital that the agent be well trained and possess a requisite degree of business responsibility. Most states require any insurance representative to be licensed and, as a condition of licensing, to pass an examination covering insurance and the details of the state's insurance law.

Part of the reason for the failure of insurers to insist on higher standards is traceable to the fact that agents are generally paid on a commission basis and the insurer assumes that since nothing is paid out unless the agent produces business, the easiest way to obtain more business is to hire more agents. In such an atmosphere, of course, the insurer is not likely to insist that its agents be exceptionally well trained. However, standards of licensing and training are steadily improving. It is being recognized that a poor agent may cost the insurer dearly in terms of public ill will and lawsuits, not to mention the cost of furnishing the agent with service, training materials, and the like.

Most state laws prohibit such practices as twisting, rebating, and misrepresentation in the sale of insurance. **Twisting** occurs when an agent persuades an insured to drop an existing insurance policy by misrepresenting the facts for the purpose of obtaining an insured's new business. **Rebating** occurs when an agent agrees to return part of the commission to an insured as an inducement to secure business. (A recent supreme court decision in Flordia specifically allows rebating, making Florida the first state to amend its law this way.)

An example of **misrepresentation** is making misleading statements about the cost of life insurance. For example, New York has specifically prohibited the use of the traditional net cost method of determining the cost of life insurance by representing that this cost equals the difference between the premiums paid and the sum of dividends and ending cash values.[11] An agent's license can be revoked for any one of these offenses.

The insurance industry has in recent years expanded its offerings to include various types of equity products such as variable life insurance and mutual funds. Since variable annuities are subject to federal as well as state regulation, the Securities Act of 1933, the Securities Exchange Act of 1934, and the Investment Company Act of 1940 affect the insurance business directly. Both the product itself and its distribution are carefully regulated. The 1933 Act requires full disclosure to the buyer of all pertinent data regarding an issue of common stock. The 1934 Act regulates trading and the operations of the securities markets to prevent fraud and manipulation. The 1940 Act gave the Securities and Exchange Commission, which has the responsibility of administering the various securities laws, the power to regulate the type of sales literature, selling behavior, and sales compensation for selling variable annuities and other equity products of insurers.

As a result of these laws, an insurance sales agent of equity products must pass an examination covering the securities market and variable annuities before selling equity products. These examinations are prepared by such agencies as the National Association of Securities Dealers (NASD), the Securities and Exchange Commission (SEC), and the National Association of Insurance Commissioners (NAIC). In addition, the agent must satisfy any state licensing and education requirements.

Regulation of Contract Provisions

We have seen that the provisions of many insurance contracts are determined by statute. New policy forms must be approved in most states before they are offered to the public.

The insurance department of the state handles complaints of the insuring public which arise over the interpretation of policy provisions. Misunderstandings often arise, even over provisions that are considered standard. For example, the insurance department in New York State processes nearly 30,000 complaints involving loss settlements or policy provisions.[12] About two-thirds of these involve automobile insurance, and almost 3,200 involve accident and health insurance. It is interesting but not surprising that only half of these complaints were upheld or adjusted, indicating the extent of misunderstanding by members of the insurance-buying public as well as the considerable necessity of exerting some regulatory control over the insurance product.

MISCELLANEOUS INSURANCE LAWS

A description of some other government regulations regarding insurance will illustrate the extent of government interest in this field.

Service-of-Process Statutes

When a legal action is brought against an insurer, it is necessary to deliver a court summons to the insurer's representative. For insurers admitted to do business within a given state, the insurance commissioner is generally the individual who is authorized to receive such a summons, under what is called a **service-of-process statute.** Formerly a problem arose as to how best to serve an insurer that did not operate within a given state. An insured may have obtained a policy by dealing with the insurer by mail, or the insured may have obtained a policy in one state but subsequently moved to another state wherein the insurer was not admitted to do business. Through the National Association of Insurance Commissioners, most states have now passed statutes known as the **unauthorized insurers service-of-process acts.** Under these statutes, it is no longer necessary for an insured to resort to distant courts in order to bring suit on contracts written by such unauthorized insurers. It is only necessary to serve summons on the insurance commissioner or upon someone representing the out-of-state insurer.

Retaliatory Laws

Most states have laws requiring that if an insurer chartered in one state is subjected to some burden such as an increased tax or license fee on business it does in another state, then the one state will automatically impose a like burden on all of the insurers of the second state that are operating in the first state. Such laws are known as **retaliatory laws,** and about three-fourths of all states have them. The effect of these laws is to discourage each state from passing any unusual taxes on foreign insurers operating within its borders for fear that the same burden will immediately apply to its own insurers operating in other states. Only those states without any domestic companies can ignore retaliatory laws. There is a tendency, therefore, for states with the most domestic insurers to have the lowest insurance taxes. The constitutionality of these laws has been attacked on the ground that they cause one state to surrender its taxing authority to another state, but it has been established that the laws are constitutional.[13]

Anticancellation Laws

A majority of states have passed laws restricting the right of insurers of automobiles to cancel policies without good reason. Laws are not uniform as to the type of vehicles covered, but in general only private passenger autos are subject to the restrictions. A few states limit the application of the laws to liability coverages, but in a majority of states the laws apply to all coverages, including both liability and physical damage. Insurers are also required under these laws to give ample advance notice of intent not to renew when the policy is approaching its expiration date.

Most of the laws state that unless an insurer cancels a newly issued policy within 60 days after its effective date, it may cancel after that only for certain specified reasons. These may include nonpayment of premiums, insurance obtained through fraudulent misrepresentation, violation by the insured of any term or condition of the policy, suspension of the driver's operator's license, existence of heart attacks or epilepsy of the insured, existence of an accident or conviction record, and habitual use of alcoholic beverages or narcotics to excess. The list of permissible reasons for cancellation is so long and is phrased so broadly that it appears to give the insurer broad discretion in the matter of cancellation, but it actually imposes few limitations and gives much protection to an insured whose policy is cancelled capriciously.

Reciprocal Laws

In contrast to a retaliatory law, a **reciprocal law** provides that if one state does something for another, that state shall do the same thing for the first. For example, it is common for state financial responsibility laws to provide that if under the laws of another state an insured motorist would be disqualified from driving, the motorist shall also be prohibited from driving in the first state. Under uniform insurers liquidation acts, it is possible for a claimant of an insolvent insurer in another state to make a claim locally and have it honored, avoiding the necessity of traveling to the other state. In workers' compensation insurance, if an employee is temporarily employed outside a state, and if the other state will excuse the employer from complying with that state's compensation law, the first state will do likewise. In this way, state legislation is made to work much more smoothly than it otherwise would.

Anticoercion Laws

Anticoercion statutes are aimed against the former practice of some lending agencies to require, as a condition of granting a loan, the placing of insurance with the agency. Thus, the purchaser of a home might be prevented from placing property insurance with a personally chosen insurer. The borrower had to pay premiums that were not necessarily the lowest obtainable. Such tie-in practices were held to be in restraint of trade and illegal under one or more federal antimonopoly laws.[14] As a result, anticoercion laws were passed in many states.

TORT REFORM

Because of rising liability awards in the nation's courts, public pressure for reform of tort liability rules has existed for several years. Many states have enacted new laws affecting the liability of a manufacturer for defective products. It was reported that in 1985 alone, 208 bills affecting tort law were enacted in 16 states.[15] One law in the state of Washington placed a limit on jury awards for noneconomic damages and altered several other rules, resulting in a reduction in the cost of liability awards and associated insurance.

A federal law, the Product Liability Risk Retention Act of 1981, permits industry groups to form insurance plans to self-insure product liability. In 1986, this law was expanded to include all forms of commercial liability.

TORT REFORM LAWS

In 1976 Colorado joined several other states in reforming its tort liability laws. The liability reforms reshape laws in four major ways. The new laws (1) repeal the concept of joint and several liability in negligence suits, (2) limit punitive damages to the amount of the actual loss, (3) limit the liability of government agencies and employees to their percentage of fault, and (4) cap all noneconomic damages arising from negligence suits to a maximum of $250,000.

These new laws are designed to reverse the "liberalization" of the tort laws that has occurred in the U.S. for many years.

Source: "Municipal Liability," *Business Insurance* (October 6, 1986), p. 18.

TAXATION OF INSURANCE

Insurance companies represent a relatively substantial source of revenue to states. In 1980, for example, insurance premium taxes amounted to $4 billion, about 2 percent of total state tax collections.[16] Insurance company taxes are greater than tax collections from public utilities, from death and gift taxes, and from corporate licenses. They are almost as large as taxes on alcoholic beverages.

In each state these revenues are raised mainly from a tax on gross premiums. Premium taxes vary from 1 to 4 percent, with the most typical amount being 2 percent, plus an additional 0.25 or 0.50 percent for the support of the state fire marshal's office. Many states have, in addition, special taxes or assessments in connection with different lines of insurance, such as workers' compensation.

Insurance companies are also subject to federal income taxation. Stock property insurers pay taxes on underwriting and investment income at regular corporate rates. Mutual property insurers are treated differently. If a mutual or a reciprocal insurer has a net income of less than $75,000, it is exempt from taxation.[17] It is estimated that about 3 percent of the total mutual premium volume is written by tax-exempt companies. For larger mutuals, the tax is the larger of 1 percent of gross income (net premiums written less policyholder dividends, plus net investment income) or that tax which would be collected by applying regular corporate rates to investment income only, as defined.[18]

Life insurers are subject to federal income taxation under the Deficit Reduction Act of 1984 (DEFRA). The law replaced legislation previously enacted in 1959. In contrast to the 1959 rules, the new law does not distinguish between underwriting and investment income of life insurers, but instead subjects all income to the same taxation rules. DEFRA attempted to simplify life insurance taxation and make it more responsive to changing levels of general interest rates.

Taxable income is defined as gross income less special deductions. These deductions include claims for losses, increases in reserves (as defined), policyholder dividends, and the company's share of tax-exempt interest and dividends.[19] Regular corporate income tax rates apply to the balance. One result of the new tax law was to treat stock and mutual insurers on a more nearly equal basis than had existed before, so that the total tax burden paid by life insurers would be in proportion to the share of total assets controlled by each type of insurer. The new law also standardized the reserve computation for tax purposes, so that reserve laws of individual states no longer affected federal taxes on life insurers. Excess deductions that existed in some states were not allowed, with the result that amounts that could be deducted for reserves were somewhat lower than before.

Two special deductions for life insurers were incorporated. One deduction applied to small life insurers, i.e., those with assets of less than $500 million. Another special deduction was enacted to prevent a dramatic increase in taxes as compared to taxes under the 1959 law. The net effect of these two special deductions was to lower the effective tax rates on taxable income (as defined) of life insurers from 46 percent to about 37 percent.

SUMMARY

1. Insurance is regulated because of several characteristics that set it apart from tangible-goods industries. These include the complexity of insurance, its importance to the financial security of millions of people, the public nature of its many activities,

and the necessity for some control over its pricing policies.

2. Insurance is regulated by states, but the federal government, by virtue of both the 1944 decision in the case of the *South-Eastern Underwriters Association* and the McCarran-Ferguson Act, also has considerable regulatory authority in several areas of insurance.

3. For many years a debate has existed over the relative merits of federal versus state regulation of insurance. In spite of some possible advantages of federal regulation, it appears unlikely that the present system of state rule will give way completely unless more convincing proof of the superiority of federal regulation is forthcoming. However, it seems likely that increased federal regulation in specific areas of insurance will occur.

4. The chief areas of state regulation have to do mainly with rate supervision, standards of financial condition, business acquisition methods, and policy provisions. An insurer must be formally admitted to do business in a given state, must give evidence of its financial ability to meet all claims, and must subject almost every phase of its operations to the supervision of the insurance commissioner.

5. In general, regulation of insurance has had a beneficial effect upon the institution by maintaining public confidence, securing desirable uniformity, and preventing destructive practices arising from unrestricted competition within the industry.

QUESTIONS FOR REVIEW

1. Does the experience so far with state insurer insolvency funds suggest that these funds are needed? In every state? Discuss.

2. What is the difference between a "prior approval" and an "open competition" rating law? Which type do you prefer? Why?

3. In your opinion, does real competition exist in the field of insurance? If so, give specific examples.

4. You are approached by an insurance agent who promises to return 20 percent of the commission to you if you will give this agent your business. Is this approach an acceptable business practice? Comment.

5. *H* buys an insurance policy from a mail-order insurer and, following a loss, is unable to secure payment. In fact, the insurer does not even answer *H*'s letter in which the loss was reported. A local agent informs *H* that this particular insurer is not "admitted" in *H*'s state and has no representatives there. Is it necessary for *H* to go to the state in which this insurer is chartered in order to bring forth legal action? Why?

6. A legislator in your state urges that a good way to raise additional state revenue would be to increase the premium tax on all insurers operating within the state. What point should you investigate first, before recommending that this tax be passed?

7. Differentiate between a retaliatory law and a reciprocal law.

8. In 1984, DEFRA amended life insurance company federal tax rules. Did this change increase or decrease life insurance taxes? How do you think this might affect the policyholder? Explain.

9. What criteria are usually specified in state laws regarding insurance rates?

10. If states were doing a good job in regulating insurer solvency, would insolvency funds be needed? Why or why not?

QUESTIONS FOR DISCUSSION

1. A representative of an association of insurance agencies stated, "The very nature

of our business requires the most rigid adherence to sound methods of operation and therefore there are few who will argue its need for regulation. . . ." Why is it concluded that insurance requires regulation when such an argument would usually be opposed in tangible-goods industries as an interference with the right of free enterprise? Comment.

2. A representative of a group of agents stated, "Because we are small, we do fear federal regulation; while it is difficult enough for the average insurance agent to participate in regulatory problems at the state level, it would be a virtual impossibility for most of us to take our problems to Washington. . . ." What relationship does this argument have to the general case against federal regulation of insurance? Do you agree with it? Explain.

3. An insurance commissioner of a large state wrote, "The commissioner's position is not a particularly happy one today. He is . . . criticized for increases in rates, for a lack of insurance markets, for the insolvency of some companies, for maintaining too high a degree of uniformity in rates or coverage, or for being much too soft in the regulation of the industry. On the other hand, the commissioner is sometimes criticized by people in the insurance industry for a lack of uniformity and for regulating too severely . . . strangulation of the business instead of . . . regulation." In your opinion, is it the task of the insurance commissioner to deal with each of the questions listed above? If so, give an example of the type of activity falling under each category.

4. It has been suggested that under federal regulation of insurance local conditions could be handled through a system of district offices similar to that which exists in the case of the Federal Reserve System. Each of these offices could be given certain degrees of autonomy to adjust to localized conditions. In this way, all the advantages of national uniformity could be achieved without any of the disadvantages of rigid supervision by distant authorities. Evaluate this plan, pointing out advantages and disadvantages.

5. Many professional insurance agents object strongly to the use of part-time agents and are generally in favor of much stricter licensing requirements than most states presently have. Why are part-time agents objected to more than full-time agents?

NEW TERMS AND CONCEPTS

McCarran-Ferguson Act
Insolvency Funds
Prior Approval Rating
Open Competition Rating
File and Use Rating
Twisting
Rebating
DEFRA (Deficit Reduction Act of 1984)

SEUA case (South-Eastern Underwriters Association)
Misrepresentation
Service-of-Process Statute
Unauthorized Insurers Service-of-Process Acts
Retaliatory Laws
Reciprocal Laws
Anticoercion Statutes

NOTES

1 *Maryland Insurance Commissioner* v. *Libery Mutual Insurance Company*, Hearing 804. Closed January 8, 1985.

2 8 Wall. 168, 183 (1868).

3 322 U.S. 533.

4 Roland W. Johnson, "Section of the Clayton Act as a Tool to Curtail Conglomerate Acquisitions of Insurance Companies," *Washington Law Review*, Vol. 46 (May, 1971), pp. 497–539.

5 The Appleton Rule has been upheld by the courts. See *Fireman's Insurance Co. of Newark, N.J.* v. *Beha*, 30 F.2d 539 (1928).

6 *McKinney's Consolidated Laws of New York*, Vol. 27, 1966, paragraphs 191 and 192 (effective 1981–1982).

7 *Insurance Facts 1985-86* (New York: Insurance Information Institute, 1985), p. 41.

8 Open competition states include California, Colorado, Connecticut, Florida, Georgia, Illinois, Massachusetts, Minnesota, Missouri, Montana, Nevada, New Mexico, New York, Oregon, Utah, Virginia, and Wisconsin.

9 U.S. Comptroller General, *Issues and Needed Improvements in State Regulation of the Insurance Business (Executive Summary)*, Report to the Congress, October 9, 1979 (Washington, D.C.: U.S. General Accounting Office, 1979), p. 33.

10 *Consumer Reports* (June, 1986), p. 385.

11 Regulation 74, New York Insurance Department, effective January 1, 1975.

12 New York Insurance Department, *The 1979 Annual Report of the Superintendent of Insurance* (New York, 1979), pp. 61–62.

13 *American Indemnity Company* v. *Hobbs*, 328 U.S. 822 (1946).

14 *United States* v. *Investors Diversified Services*, Civil No. 3713 DC, Minn. (1954).

15 Charles Waselewski, "Tort Reform Courting Public Opinion," *Best's Review*, Property Casualty Edition (June, 1986), p. 15.

16 *Insurance Facts 1985–86*, p. 40.

17 Section 501(15) Internal Revenue Code (1954).

18 Sections 821, 822, 823 Internal Revenue Code (1954).

19 Section 805(a) Internal Revenue Code (1954).

PART 8

INTERNATIONAL INSURANCE

CHAPTER 27   INTERNATIONAL ISSUES IN RISK MANAGEMENT

27 INTERNATIONAL ISSUES IN RISK MANAGEMENT

After studying this chapter, you should be able to:

1. Contrast international risk and insurance conditions with domestic risk and insurance conditions.
2. Explain how world trade and investment growth have made international insurance more important than before.
3. Describe the organization of international insurance companies and associations.
4. Identify the leading insurance countries of the world.
5. Indicate how risks are diffused in the world through reinsurance.
6. Define "nonadmitted" insurance.
7. Describe how global insurance coverages are arranged.
8. Explain how political risk is managed.

In recent years it has become increasingly important for the student of risk and insurance to recognize the importance of the international dimension. Although basic principles of risk and insurance are applicable without reference to international boundaries, the application of these principles abroad is often quite different from at home. This chapter is devoted to a consideration of some of these differences. Emphasis is on the contrasts between United States and foreign insurance practices and environments. The treatment here should be considered illustrative rather than comprehensive in nature.

For risk managers, operating in foreign countries is generally perceived to be more risky than operating domestically. Many factors contribute to this. Language, customs, monetary conditions, government, consumer preferences, inflation rates, geography, climate, and legal environment abroad are often relatively unfamiliar to the risk manager. This lack of knowledge of the operating environment tends to increase perceived risk. Furthermore, statistics of loss records, loss prevention facilities, and other underwriting information are typically lacking.

In addition, insurance contract language is not uniform across various countries, giving rise to gaps in coverage that may not be anticipated. Distances from foreign areas are such that time lapse prevents or discourages close contact with the foreign corporation and hinders fast decision making. For example, in one large multinational corporation with construction operations in several countries, the risk manager reported that it took a full year of negotiation and preparation to finalize the property insurance program for the company. These factors all tend to make the job of the risk manager in large companies quite complex.

In spite of the difficulties, and perhaps because of them, the risk manager's task in foreign operations is increasingly recognized as essential to the development of international business. Without means to handle the risk, foreign operations would be severely handicapped, if not stopped entirely. Foreign opportunities, however, are too large and too important to be ignored by most firms of substance. It is doubtful that most modern nations as we know them could survive without international trade and investment. Hence, ways must be found to handle international risk efficiently and effectively.

GROWTH OF WORLD TRADE

Tables 27-1 and 27-2 confirm the tremendous growth of world trade and international investments in the period 1976–1984. With this expansion, an enlarged world market for insurance was created. Insurance is especially significant because operations outside one's own country are usually considered riskier than domestic operations, and if insurance had not been available it is unlikely that the pace of expansion could have been as great as it has. Over the period the compound annual rate of growth in exports approximated 9 percent annually.

From Table 27-1, it is clear that imports of the United States have exceeded exports to the degree that the United States has incurred a large trade deficit that has grown from about $10 billion in 1976 to $114 billion in 1984, a tenfold increase in eight years. Much of the trade deficit has occurred with industrial nations such as Japan and Western European countries. The failure of U.S. suppliers to sell more goods and services abroad has caused great national concern. At least part of the reason for

Table 27-1   U.S. Exports and Imports of Merchandise, 1976–1984 (in millions of dollars)

	Exports		Percent Increase	Imports		Percent Increase
	1976	1984		1976	1984	
A. Industrial Countries	$72,335	$141,021	95%	$67,665	$207,127	206%
Canada	$26,336	$53,067	101%	$26,652	$69,229	160%
Japan	$10,196	$23,240	128%	$15,531	$60,221	288%
Western Europe	$31,883	$56,886	78%	$23,003	$72,504	215%
Australia, New Zealand, and South Africa	$3,920	$7,849	100%	$2,479	$5,663	128%
B. Other Countries except Eastern Europe	$38,287	$74,214	94%	$55,379	$124,679	125%
OPEC Countries	$11,561	$13,771	19%	$27,409	$26,852	−2%
Other	$26,726	$60,443	126%	$27,970	$97,827	250%
C. Eastern Europe	$4,123	$4,290	4%	$875	$2,217	153%
Total	$114,745	$219,916	92%	$124,228	$334,023	169%

Source: *Economic Report of the President, 1986* (Washington: U.S. Government Printing Office), page 369.

this failure is the greater risks of doing business abroad and the difficulties in managing these risks.

Table 27-2 reveals the extent of U.S. direct investment abroad. Over the period 1975–1984, these investments have increased 88 percent to the level of $233 billion. Much of the increase has occurred in Canada and the United Kingdom, nations whose cultural background is similar to that of the United States, and in which it is likely that perceived risks are

**Table 27-2
U.S. Direct Investment Position Abroad, 1975–1984 (in millions of dollars)**

	1975	1984	Increase
Canada	$90,695	$174,057	92%
France	$5,743	$6,478	13%
Germany	$8,726	$9,362	7%
Italy	$2,679	$4,998	87%
Netherlands	$3,097	$8,262	167%
United Kingdom	$13,927	$32,145	131%
Other Western Europe	$10,532	$24,796	135%
Switzerland	$5,132	$15,983	211%
Japan	$3,339	$8,374	151%
Australia, S. Africa, New Zealand	$7,013	$11,554	65%
Latin America	$16,934	$30,879	82%
Middle East	($4,070)	$3,435	184%
Asia and Pacific	$5,747	$16,156	181%
Total, All Areas	$124,050	$233,412	88%

Source: *Statistical Abstract of the U.S., 1986* (Washington: U.S. Government Printing Office), p. 800.

relatively low. The growth of direct investments abroad has been similar to the growth of exports, 88 percent vs. 92 percent.

Table 27–3 displays the extent to which foreign investors have established positions in the United States. Note that the growth of investments in this country has exceeded the growth of U.S. investments abroad by a factor of about four to one over the period 1977–1984. A factor accounting for at least part of this phenomenon is the fact that the United States has been considered a relatively safe and stable (as well as profitable) environment in which to invest. In other words, risks perceived by foreign investors have apparently been quite low.

The implications for insurance of this growth in world commerce are significant. For example, there has been the development of the multinational corporation, which views the world as its market and attempts to locate its manufacturing operations in the country with the greatest economic advantages. The multinational corporation also seeks insurance coverage on a worldwide basis and has presented a challenge to the world's insurance industry. Ways must be found to protect investments in foreign locations against insurable hazards on some basis acceptable to investors; otherwise, an important deterrent to increased trade and investments exists. The insurance industry must expand its financial ability and create administrative arrangements for protecting increased values exposed to loss abroad. Worldwide networks of agents and claims service offices are being developed. Reinsurance facilities must be continually expanded.

INSURANCE AND ECONOMIC DEVELOPMENT

Analysis of the world markets and economic development reveals the consistent link between economic development and the growth of insurance. Without answering the question of whether or not insurance is indispensable to economic development, it would appear that the two are highly correlated.

Studies by the Economics Department of the Swiss Reinsurance Co. have traced the growth of insurance and compared it to economic growth

Table 27–3
Foreign Direct Investment in U.S., 1977–1984 (in millions of dollars)

	1977	1984	Increase
Canada	$5,650	$14,001	148%
United Kingdom	$6,937	$38,099	449%
Netherlands	$7,830	$32,643	317%
Switzerland	$2,651	$8,349	215%
Germany, F. R.	$2,529	$11,956	373%
Other Europe	$4,347	$15,520	257%
Japan	$1,755	$14,817	744%
Other Areas	$3,436	$24,187	604%
Total of All Areas	$34,595	$159,571	361%

Source: *Statistical Abstract of the U.S., 1986* (Washington: U.S. Government Printing Office), p. 798.

in various nations over the period 1950-1980. Adjusted for inflation, insurance has tended to exceed growth in national output in each of the three decades of the post–World War II period. The growth of insurance has been slightly under 5 percent annually, with almost no fluctuation, in real (price-adjusted) terms, from year to year.[1] The growth of GNP over the period has averaged 3.8 percent annually. Significantly, the real growth of insurance in the period 1980–83 has leveled off or declined, corresponding to worldwide economic slowdown during that period.

The division of insurance among nations and among lines of insurance is shown in Figures 27–1 and 27–2. Figure 27–1 shows that the market share of insurance premiums accounted for by North America (essentially, the United States and Canada) has declined from 88 percent to 55 percent over the period 1950–1983. The North American share has been absorbed mainly by European countries and Japan. Still, the United States is the world's largest insurance country, enjoying 56 percent of the world's nonlife insurance business and 43 percent of the world's life insurance business. The relative growth of automobile insurance (called motor) has increased, and the share enjoyed by life insurance has declined over the period. Otherwise, the division of insurance among various lines has remained quite stable. It is significant that life insurance is the largest single line of insurance worldwide from the standpoint of premiums, followed by automobile insurance.

Figure 27–1
World Premium Volume, 1950 and 1983 by Region

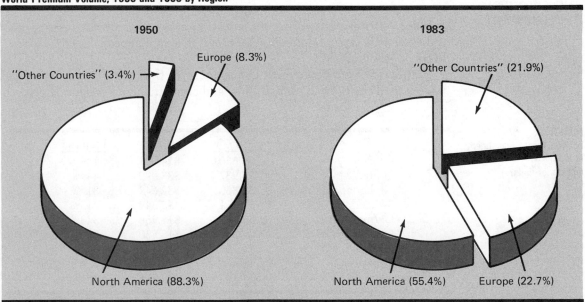

Source: *Sigma* (March, 1986), p. 6

Figure 27–2
World Branch Structure, 1950 and 1983

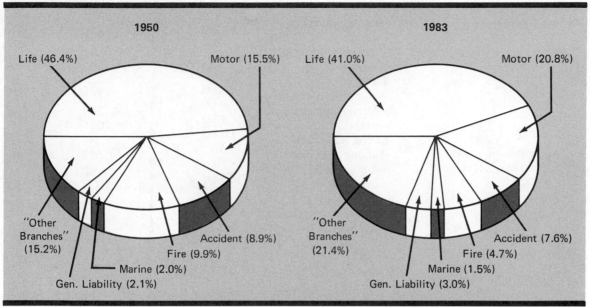

Source: *Sigma* (March, 1986), p. 7

The stable economic position enjoyed by the insurance industry worldwide may be better understood by a review of the contributions of insurance to economic and social welfare. Insurance tends to increase the supply of investable capital through creation of reserves for losses, both present and future. This tends to create a more favorable investment climate and reduces the drain on government resources. Through insurance, credit is expanded by reducing the subjective risk experienced by lenders. Insurance contributes to the incentives to preserve and improve property through loss-prevention efforts.

The problem of insuring personnel, including expatriates, against personal risk must be solved, since investment activity necessarily involves extensive use of many types of trained people for foreign assignments. Loss-prevention engineering is often difficult in strange settings. Countless other problems must be solved by insurers in meeting the demands of worldwide trade and business expansion.

INTERNATIONAL INSURANCE INSTITUTIONS

It is estimated that in 1984 13,484 insurance companies existed worldwide in 72 countries. Table 27–4 shows the distribution of these insurers and the proportion of total insurers represented by foreign companies in each nation. For example, in the United States and Canada foreign insurers constitute 5 percent of the total, while in Europe foreign companies

	Total Number of Companies	Percent of Companies
North America		
—domestic companies	5,791	95.0
—foreign companies	302	5.0
—overall	6,093	100
Europe		
—domestic companies	3,419	75.9
—foreign companies	1,086	24.1
—overall	4,505	100
Latin America		
—domestic companies	768	70.8
—foreign companies	317	29.2
—overall	1,085	100
Australia		
—domestic companies	289	66.6
—foreign companies	145	33.4
—overall	434	100
Asia		
—domestic companies	543	59.7
—foreign companies	367	40.3
—overall	910	100
Africa		
—domestic companies	342	74.8
—foreign companies	115	25.2
—overall	457	100
World total		
—domestic companies	11,152	
—foreign companies	2,332	
—overall	13,484	

Source: *Sigma* (November–December, 1985), p. 9.

constitute 24 percent, and in Latin America 29 percent of the total companies operating. Foreign insurers have not yet penetrated the North American market nearly to the extent that they have penetrated other markets. North America accounted for 45 percent of the total number of insurers operating in the world. Europe and North America together accounted for 79 percent of the total number of insurers in the world.

Figure 27-3 displays the extent to which insurers in one country operate in another. For example, U.S. insurers operate in 48 countries and have 579 agencies of one kind or another representing them abroad. Insurers chartered in Great Britain operate in 43 other countries and employ 608 agencies representing them abroad. The graphic representation in the figure demonstrates again the truly international nature of insurance.

Figure 27–3
Foreign Activity (Countries and Representations)

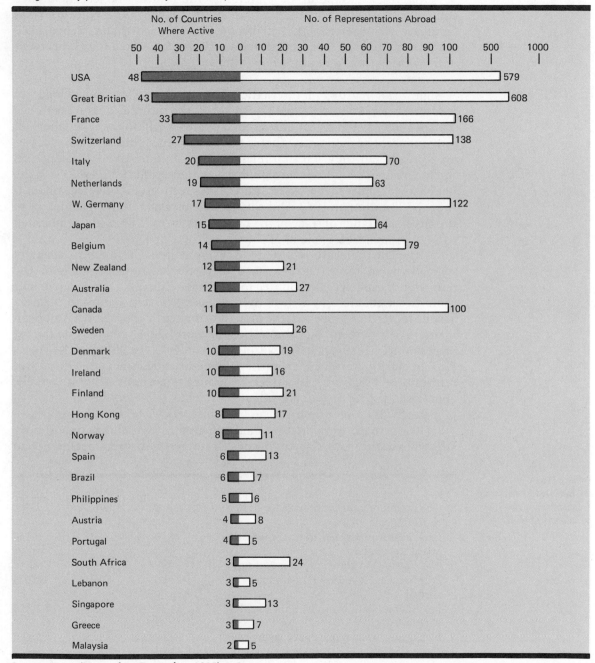

Source: *Sigma* (November–December, 1985), p. 8

From the standpoint of premiums, the world's largest insurance countries in 1984 were the U.S. (50.88 percent), Japan (14.78 percent), West Germany (6.53 percent), Great Britain (5.32 percent), and France (3.83 percent), in that order. Together, these nations accounted for 81.3 percent of the world's total premiums for all lines.[2]

REINSURANCE

A significant feature of international insurance is the dependence of insurers on reinsurance. Table 27-5 displays the international reinsurance "balance of payments" of the United States with foreign suppliers of reinsurance. The data reveal that U.S. insurers cede (purchase) more coverage abroad than they sell to foreign insurers. In fact, the dependence on foreign insurers has more than doubled over the period 1976-1983, with the net balance, adjusted for losses paid and loss recoveries collected, amounting to $788 million in 1983. This adverse balance is small when compared to the adverse balance of trade of the United States in 1984, which amounted to $114 billion. (See Table 27-1.)

Although there are reportedly 376 professional reinsurers (insurers specializing in reinsurance instead of direct insurance), much of the reinsurance capacity is accounted for by primary insurers who supplement their direct business by writing reinsurance. Western European insurers accounted for 46.5 percent of the total reinsurance in 1985, North American insurers 31.1 percent, and the rest of the world 22.4 percent. The largest professional reinsurers in the world are (in order of size) Munich Re, Swiss Re, General Re, Gerling, Mercantile & General, and Employers. The ratio of reinsurance premiums to direct insurance premiums is quite stable, approximating 15–16 percent since 1976.[3] Thus, for every seven dollars of premium written by primary insurers, reinsurers write one.

The fluctuations in international reinsurance availability importantly affect domestic insurance conditions. If foreign reinsurers decide not to

Table 27–5
International Reinsurance Transactions of the U.S. (in millions of dollars)

	1976	1980	1983
1. Net premium paid for foreign reinsurance	1,118	1,896.7	2,299.7
2. Less: Losses recovered from abroad on ceded insurance	619	1037	1322
3. Net outflow on reinsurance premiums	499	859.7	977.7
4. Premiums received on reinsurance sold abroad	729.3	896.5	1007.8
5. Less: Losses paid on reinsurance sold abroad	536.7	660.6	818
6. Net inflow from reinsurance premiums	192.6	235.9	189.8
7. Net balance on U.S. reinsurance transactions abroad ((3) − (6))	−306.4	−623.8	−787.9

Source: *National Underwriter, Property/Casualty Edition*, August 24, 1984, section 2, page 36. Original source of data is the U.S. Dept. of Commerce, Bureau of Economic Analysis.

accept certain risks (e.g., medical malpractice liability or products liability insurance), domestic primary companies will also find it difficult, if not impossible, to accept these risks. If foreign reinsurers raise insurance rates, a rise in domestic primary rates is likely to follow. Insurance tends to be an international business and is very dependent on worldwide economic and social conditions.

Several nations have attempted to restrict reinsurance markets in various ways. These restrictions generally have a goal of conserving foreign currencies which are needed for importing commodities or services other than insurance. For example, in South America, legislation exists in Colombia and Venezuela to limit the freedom local insurers have in purchasing foreign reinsurance. In Brazil local insurers must cede all reinsurance to the national reinsurance company (Instituto de Resseguros do Brasil), which is half-owned by the government and half-owned by private industry. A similar law exists in Argentina. It is doubtful that localized restrictions on the free flow of funds for risk transfer will be in the long-run best economic interests of the nation, since insurance is a substitute for capital and frees up funds for productive use elsewhere. Stated differently, if a nation attempts to prevent its industry from spending money on reinsurance abroad, and instead supplies reinsurance locally, capital that might otherwise be used to develop a nation industrially is tied up for reinsurance purposes. Such a policy can be counterproductive to the economy.

INTERNATIONAL BROKERS AND INSURERS

Multinational corporations usually deal with two major classes of international insurers: American-based insurers operating at home and in foreign countries, and foreign-based insurers operating both in the United States and abroad. Brokers and agents are often necessary as intermediaries.

The largest international brokerage offices and their revenues are given in Table 27–6, according to estimates by *Business Insurance.* Most brokers operating in international markets establish local offices in foreign countries to service the needs of the corporations operating there. In many cases these offices take the form of foreign correspondents, local insurance agencies given a license to represent the international broker in its dealings

Table 27–6
International Insurance Brokers

Company	Gross Revenues		Percentage Change
	1974	1984	
Marsh & McLennan	$204.9	$1,120.9	447%
Alexander & Alexander	$100.5	$576.0	473%
Johnson & Higgins	$125.0	$390.5	212%
Frank B. Hall	$85.8	$372.8	334%
Fred S. James	$63.3	$292.8	363%

Source: *Business Insurance* (July 28, 1975), p. 7; (June 24, 1985), p. 3.
Percentage change calculated.

with local clients. In other cases the international broker actually sets up a subsidiary office for handling local business.

As shown in the table, Marsh & McLennan is the world's largest insurance brokerage firm by a margin of two to one over its nearest competitor, Alexander & Alexander. The top two firms have grown significantly faster than the other major brokers.

American Insurers

United States insurers have organized in different ways to offer coverage for multinational companies operating abroad. Some companies operate individually, and others operate through associations. Current examples of major international insurers operating individually are CIGNA, Commercial Union, Royal, and Continental National America. In the life insurance field, John Hancock, American International Life, Combined Insurance Companies, and Aetna Insurance Company are overseas leaders.

Some U.S. insurers prefer to operate through groups or pools. There are three major examples of these pools: AFIA (American Foreign Insurance Association), AIG (American International Group), and the factory mutuals.

AFIA

Currently operating in about 80 foreign countries, AFIA began business in 1917 in China. A number of insurers had been operating independently in China and maintained separate offices. The idea for a central organization rose out of the need for coordinating these operations, maintaining some degree of uniformity, and obtaining some reduction in expenses. Currently there are about nine United States insurers who are members of the AFIA, which operates as a management pool. AFIA members are entered individually into the countries in which AFIA operates. AFIA is an unincorporated association. Each member submits to AFIA a book of limits stating maximum amounts for which AFIA may bind them in each country. Each year a profit is distributed to local members or each member is asked to make up a deficit, which last happened in 1928 following a major fire in Ecuador.

More than 50 percent of the total premium income of AFIA stems from indigenous business; that is, from customers operating entirely within a foreign country. The remaining premium income is from firms operating as foreign subsidiaries of United States parent corporations.

American International Group

American International Group, in contrast to AFIA, is an incorporated company. AIG is a holding company whose subsidiaries engage in property, liability, and life insurance business in more than 135 countries. Its principal subsidiaries include American Home Assurance, National Union Fire Insurance, New Hampshire Group, American International Underwriters Corporation, American International Life Insurance, and American International Underwriters Overseas. AIG operates as a pool similar to AFIA, except that AIG has greater control over the insurers whose capacity it commits on foreign risks. There is a predetermined percentage of premiums and losses applicable to each of the member companies. As with AFIA, approximately two-thirds of AIG's business is indigenous in nature.

Factory Mutuals

Factory mutuals are also engaged in writing international insurance. Two major systems exist, the Factory Insurance Association (FIA), made up of 81 stock companies which share in a pool, and the Factory Mutual Association (FMA). The FIA as an entity does the underwriting, and its members get a predetermined share of each premium and pay a predetermined share of all losses. The FMA, on the other hand, is composed of four companies which compete until one is awarded the business. The winning company is the sponsoring company and must convince the others to go along with the risk.

Factory mutuals offer engineering services to clients. Actually, both FIA and FMA usually accept only risks which stress loss-prevention activities, i.e., the high-protection risk (HPR) business.

PRIVATE INTERNATIONAL INSURANCE ORGANIZATIONS

In addition to private companies or associations of companies, there exist many international organizations which affect insurance practices abroad. A few of these organizations are described here.

Bureau International de Producteurs d'Assurances et de Reassurances (BIPAR)

BIPAR is an organization of insurance agents and brokers in 12 countries. Over 16 professional associations are represented. In general, the organization attempts to advance the interests of agents and brokers. Under its auspices, the European Center for Insurance Education and Training in St. Gall, Switzerland, was established.

Foreign Credit Insurance Association

Made up of about 50 insurers, this association offers export credit insurance facilities for U.S. exporters, in cooperation with the Export-Import Bank of Washington, D.C.

Insurance Hall of Fame

The Insurance Hall of Fame, sponsored by the International Insurance Society, honors outstanding individuals who have made exceptional contributions to insurance. Approximately 70 persons have been selected for membership, and each year two to four additional individuals are so honored.

International Insurance Advisory Council

The Council speaks for and coordinates the international noncommercial activities of U.S. insurance and reinsurance companies.

International Insurance Society, Inc.

Founded in 1964 by Professor John S. Bickley of the University of Alabama, the International Insurance Society, Inc., sponsors an annual management conference for insurance executives in different countries around the world.

International Credit Insurance Association (ICIA)

The ICIA, founded in 1946, consists of about 18 insurance companies in 17 nations. Its major function is to study domestic and export credit insurance and to promote uniformity of coverage in the field of export credit insurance.

International Union of Aviation Insurance (IUAI)

Founded in 1934, the IUAI comprises over 500 private aviation insurers operating in 25 countries. This organization generally performs for the field of aviation insurance what the IUMI (see next) does for the field of marine insurance.

International Union of Marine Insurance (IUMI)

The IUMI, founded in 1874, is one of the oldest existing international insurance organizations. It comprises 48 marine associations from 46 countries. Its major activities involve annual conferences on marine insurance, promotion of the interests of world marine insurance markets, adoption of uniform policy provisions in marine policies throughout the world, exchange of information, and loss prevention.

Le Comité d'Action pour la Productivité dans l'Assurance (CAPA)

CAPA, an organization to encourage management efficiency in the field of insurance, operates in all of Europe from its headquarters in Paris. Its members are 125 insurance companies and associations in France and 105 similar organizations in 15 other nations in Western Europe. CAPA carries on research which assists its member groups and distributes publications based on this work. Typical of its activities are the coordination of insurance with government administrative agencies, development of uniform insurance accounting practices, and sponsorship of international conferences. Its work is carried out by about 15 standing committees whose leaders are European insurance executives. CAPA works closely with groups such as the Life Insurance Agency Management Association and the Institute of Life Insurance in the United States, and with the British Insurance Association.

Overseas Private Investment Corporation

This organization is a self-sustaining government agency providing political risk insurance and financial services for U.S. investment in developing countries.

The Permanent Committee of International Congresses of Actuaries

This committee, established in 1889, aims to link actuaries and actuarial associations of various countries. It helped organize the International Congress of Actuaries, which sponsors an annual conference for the advancement of actuarial science. Thirty-four nations are represented in the permanent committee.

Reinsurance Association of America

As a trade association of property and casualty reinsurers, this organization provides legislative services for members.

One of the important problems facing the international business person is that of adjusting to the different legal climate which characterizes overseas operations. Some of the legal variations which affect insurance operations are in the rules governing unadmitted versus admitted insurance, the Napoleonic code, the Treaty of Rome provisions, and the operation of tax laws.

**Unadmitted
Versus
Admitted
Insurance**

A problem which must be faced by a business firm seeking insurance on international risks concerns the use of domestic insurers who issue so-called unadmitted insurance. **Unadmitted insurance** is that coverage on risks within a given country by insurers not admitted to do business in that country. Some countries permit unadmitted insurance, but others impose penalties for it ranging from fines to confiscation and imprisonment. Yet, use of the unadmitted market may be necessary in order to obtain adequate coverage, and it is used in apparent violation of the spirit, if not the letter, of the law in some countries.

Admitted insurance is that insurance which is written by insurance companies or branches admitted to do business in the country where the exposure is located and which is governed by the laws of the country concerned. Usually, the policy is written in the local language, and rates and indemnities are payable in local currency. Unadmitted insurance usually is written outside the country concerned, with premiums and losses payable in dollars. The unadmitted contract is normally written in English, with terms similar to those in the United States market.

Admitted insurance has several advantages: (1) It complies with local government insurance regulations and is entirely legal. (2) Premiums are deductible for income tax purposes, and payments of premiums in local currency allows a foreign firm to use up available currency balances for insurance instead of a "hard" currency which may be difficult to obtain. (3) Loss settlements are usually less complex than would be the case with unadmitted coverage, because the firm deals with local insurers for payment of losses in local currency. This also avoids problems associated with foreign exchange fluctuations. (4) Since a corporate branch pays its own premiums and uninsured losses, problems of cost allocation of risk financing costs by corporate headquarters are avoided.

In countries which do not prohibit unadmitted insurance, the insured may still have to use admitted coverage for compulsory insurance such as workers' compensation or automobile liability. There are several advantages in the use of unadmitted coverage: it is easier to control, it usually carries lower rates, it is exempt from foreign sales taxes, and it generally offers more flexibility. Unadmitted coverage also facilitates a standardized approach to risk management whenever the corporation has exposure throughout the world. By using it, the risk manager may avoid the need for using domestic insurers for part of the risk, ceding the excess to reinsurers or to captives. Paying premiums in one currency (usually dollars) and using one international language (English) simplifies the administration of unadmitted coverage.

Still, because many countries require the use of local insurers, most multinational firms employ a combination of admitted and unadmitted insurance. Countries which prohibit unadmitted insurance or severely restrict its use include most South American countries, Portugal, Spain, Italy, Mexico, France, Ireland, and Japan. Unadmitted insurance is generally allowed (except for compulsory coverages) in the United Kingdom, Australia, New Zealand, Belgium, Denmark, West Germany, The Netherlands, Switzerland, Malaysia, Thailand, Korea, Hong Kong, and the Philippines.

If a multinational firm is operating in a country which prohibits unadmitted insurance, and yet it cannot secure the coverage it desires, it may often employ what is called a **difference in conditions (DIC) policy** to fill in the gaps left by the policy issued in the country. Under this policy, which is unadmitted, the home office of the firm pays the premiums and collects any losses, usually in dollars, if there is a loss under the policy.

Unadmitted insurance is often used in such areas as general liability or products liability. A product may be assembled in one country, use parts manufactured in another, and be sold in several countries. Products liability which is insured locally in one country may not be available to meet claims which arise in another country. Hence, a general worldwide policy is needed. Unadmitted insurance is also used to cover machinery in some cases because replacing machinery often requires importing it and paying for replacement in dollars. Local policies may not respond in dollars and may not be suitable.

Tax Laws

Tax legislation abroad affects insurance in many ways. For example, taxes on insurance premiums in foreign countries are often much higher than in the United States, making insurance costs considerably higher in some countries. Premium taxes can be as high as 30 to 40 percent (in Argentina) compared to between 2 and 3 percent in the United States. The existence of wide variations in tax rates obviously favors the use of unadmitted insurance, where possible, in countries with high premium taxes.

Because of the operation of income tax laws abroad, the foreign subsidiary of a firm headquartered in another country may not be allowed to deduct the cost of unadmitted insurance for income taxes. This is true even if the subsidiary purchases admitted insurance to the fullest extent possible and then seeks unadmitted insurance to fill in some of the coverage gaps unavailable on the local market. Obviously, some care is required in arranging foreign coverage most advantageously with respect to tax legislation.

It is common in several foreign countries to allow income tax deductions for the purchase of life insurance, a condition not yet applicable to United States residents. In Great Britain, a direct credit against the income tax is allowed. The tax relief is equal to one-half the income tax rate times the premium. Tax relief is not applicable to premiums greater than one-sixth of one's income. Thus, in Britain, the government subsidizes the life insurance industry directly.

Contrasts in Insurance Conditions Abroad

There are many variations in insurance policy provisions, insurer practices, and government regulations in foreign countries. Some examples of these are as follows:

1. Insurance policies are usually written in the language of the country, not necessarily English. In many cases official translations are not available, but must be made individually. This requires special effort to achieve effective communications between headquarters and foreign branches on insurance programs.
2. In the field of fire insurance, United States firms are accustomed to coverage which does not restrict the definition of fire. Abroad, fire following explosion, windstorm, volcanic eruption, strikes or riot, earthquake, etc., is often not covered in primary policies. Coverage may be provided by endorsement.
3. In foreign countries it is not uncommon for the customer to be appointed as the licensed insurance agent to whom a commission is due. In this role as agent, the customer then receives a "kickback" in the premium equal to the amount of the commission. Known as rebates, these kickbacks are illegal in almost all states of the United States. In some countries, however, the agent is in a more secure position than would be true in the United States. In Argentina, for example, insurance law prohibits circumventing the agent and dealing directly with the insured. Thus, a place for the intermediary has been formally established by law. Agency commissions are also considerably higher in many lines than is true in the United States. For example, workers' compensation commissions in Brazil are 25 percent, auto liability commissions are between 20 and 30 percent, and fire insurance commissions are 35 percent. Typical commissions in the United States are between 10 and 15 percent.
4. Insurance policies generally are stricter regarding the duties of an insured to disclose essential information, including notice of loss and filing a proof of loss, and advising the company of changes which affect the risk.
5. Blanket insurance covering buildings, machinery, and stock in one undivided amount, and blanket insurance for covering a number of separate risks, whether at the same location or not, are usually not permitted abroad.
6. Insurance on inventory based on the selling price value of the inventory calls for special approval and is not readily available from foreign insurers.

7. Fire insurance in other countries is usually written subject to 100 percent coinsurance requirements. In some areas subject to rampant inflation, such as South America, reduced coinsurance percentages are sometimes available.

8. Policy periods vary considerably. For example, in the United Kingdom the standard fire policy is written for one year with no cancellation provision. Sometimes it may be extended for three years upon the exchange of letters of agreement. In the case of fire insurance on commercial properties, the contract period may be as long as 10 years, with premiums payable annually and cancellation allowed only under specific conditions, such as fire loss, transfer of the property, and disposal of stock, or by mutual agreement.

9. Policies which are usually compulsory in the United States are not compulsory in many foreign countries. On the other hand, many policies that are not compulsory in the United States are compulsory elsewhere. For example, workers' compensation insurance is not required in Argentina, Hong Kong, or Jamaica, and applies only to employers with 200 or more employees in Korea. Life insurance is required on employees in Peru who have had four years of service with an employer.

   As a further complication, some insurance which is not legally required in a foreign country may be, in a sense, required by virtue of custom, breach of which may not be advisable for American companies operating abroad. It is not uncommon that a joint venture agreement, for example, will provide that insurance shall be purchased "in accordance with the customs" of the country. Under these customs, some coverages would not be purchased in a foreign country whereas they would be required in the United States. An example is fidelity bonds, which might offend a foreign partner. Some coverages which the United States partner might think of as required or highly indicated, such as earthquake insurance in Japan, are not usually purchased as part of the customary protection.

10. Occasionally, standard coverages available from foreign insurers vary markedly from their United States equivalents.[4] For example, in Japan the automobile insurance policy covers only three-fourths of the insured's liability and the insured must adjust any claims. Underinsurance is not unusual in the field of fire insurance, where buildings might be insured for only 50 percent of their value.

    Most policies in Western Europe cannot be cancelled by the insurer or the insured during their term. Furthermore, in many countries (excluding the United Kingdom) 90 or 180 days' notice must be given by either party if renewal is not desired.

11. Under United States policies, negligence of the insured is generally not a bar to recovery. In other countries, however, the law may alter this result. In Japan, for example, the law requires that if there is heavy

negligence on the part of a tenant or the employees of the tenant, the tenant must pay fire damages.

12. Special hazards often exist in foreign countries. Some areas are particularly subject to earthquakes, tidal waves, or typhoons. Because incomes are often lower in foreign countries than in the United States, the problem of embezzlement is compounded. Many insurance experts feel that fidelity coverage is mandatory because of this problem.

13. The financial strength of foreign insurers is often far below the norms expected in the United States. For example, Spanish insurers tend to write about twice as much business for each dollar of surplus as is true of the typical insurer in the United States. Some insurers in Spain, writing restricted lines of business in a small territory, may be organized under the law for a minimal amount of capital.[5] Also, under the laws of many foreign countries it is legal and common for insurers to invest rather heavily in equities such as real estate, which may further restrict the insurer's liquidity and can hamper the payment of claims under some conditions.

14. There is a tendency for greater secrecy in private business abroad than exists in the United States. Premiums and terms of insurance coverage are most often negotiated and usually are not subject to the degree of governmental regulation that exists in the United States. As a result, some common United States insurance practices, such as a year-end audit to determine the premium due in workers' compensation, liability, and physical damage coverages on inventories, are not practical. The deposit premium tends to become final.

15. In some countries insurance premiums are determined in advance, often at a high level, by a government agency comparable to a state insurance commissioner's office. The premium is called a **tariff** and may be applied strictly, or may be avoided by various means. One method of avoiding the strict application of a tariff is to purchase coverage from a worldwide insurer and obtain concessions in the rates charged by this insurer in countries where the tariff does not exist.

Global Insurance Programs

Because of wide variations in insurance contracts, available limits of coverage, and types of perils that can be insured throughout the world, the multinational firm seeking uniform protection of properties in different locations faces problems that are more complex than when only domestic risk management is involved. Two basic approaches are commonly followed: (1) the use of gap policies to supplement admitted insurance written in various countries, and (2) the use of master policies.

Gap Policies. **Gap policies,** as the name suggests, attempt to unify various individual policies written under different conditions in various countries, and to fill in the "gaps" in coverage that normally exist. A typical gap policy, for example, may try to bring all fire policies held by the multinational corporation up to the broadest possible definition of fire, so as to eliminate the narrower definitions of fire or exclusions that apply to the fire policies in different areas of the world.

Examples of gap policies are Difference in Conditions (DIC), Difference in Perils (DIP), Difference in Limits (DIL), and umbrella policies. DIC policies amend the conditions governing insurance in force in different parts of the world so as to amend policies written under such conditions to conform to the broad and uniform set of conditions specified in the DIC contract. DIP policies are intended to establish a uniform set of covered perils, even if policies in one country may not cover a stated peril. DIL policies attempt to increase limits of coverage so that the same limit applies throughout all regions in which the multinational corporation operates. Umbrella policies, usually associated with liability insurance, are basically excess policies, supplementing primary liability policies and increasing their limits of coverage under the same set of conditions established by the primary policies.

Master Policies. Master policies represent a system under which foreign premiums and losses can be paid locally under a master contract. The master policy is a single policy issued to the corporation and is usually controlled at corporation headquarters. The master policy may be under-written by a panel of co-insurers who participate in the premiums and losses in the same proportion on all scheduled underlying policies. The advantage of the master policy is that of coordination of the corporate insurance program in one central controlling contract, with adjustments in the premium taking into account the premiums paid to underlying local insurers. Accounting systems can be set up to monitor local insurance contracts for their expiration dates, values, costs, losses, and other data needed for effective insurance management. Using the master policy also facilitates keeping track of changes in inflation in each country, asset values, and changes in taxation and other government regulations affecting coverage, as well as in establishing a flowchart of activities needed to manage the insurance program.[6]

EMPLOYEE BENEFIT PLANNING ABROAD

A significant problem facing multinational corporations is the development of suitable programs of benefits for employees working abroad on a more or less permanent basis, including foreign nationals employed abroad. Basic decisions must be made concerning (1) how coverage should be arranged, including whether identical coverage should be provided in all nations or whether coverage should be tailored to the conditions of each country, (2) how employee benefits should be integrated with social insurance systems existing abroad, (3) how much of the management should be controlled from the corporate home office and how much should be decentralized to the local branch in various countries in which the firm

> ## LLOYD'S OF
> ## LONDON
>
> Lloyd's is a unique world insurance institution in that it is a collection of individual traders and underwriters who dominate many aspects of world insurance. The number of members of Lloyd's, or "names," is expected to rise to 31,000 in 1987. Lloyd's controls 25 percent of the world's marine insurance market. Lloyd's is also known for taking unusual risks that are rejected by other insurers. Its largest losses currently stem from asbestos-related claims, estimated to be as high as $10 billion.

Source: Gordon T. Sanders, "World Insurance Forum, London," *Best's Review* (October, 1986), Volume 87, No. 6, p. 100.

operates, and (4) how benefit costs should be effectively controlled and appropriately allocated among corporate divisions.

The risk manager must also give attention to the problem of obtaining a continuous flow of reliable information as to changing economic, social, and political changes abroad that affect employee benefit planning in the countries of operation.

Information Sources

Basic information about foreign environments is widely available from several sources, such as the United States Office of Foreign and Domestic Commerce, and Social Security Administration, and various private international organizations. Specialized sources of benefit information are available from international insurance brokerage firms, public accounting firms, and risk-management consulting firms. For example, Charles D. Spencer & Associates, of Chicago, Illinois, publishes the *International Benefits Information Service,* a loose-leaf publication covering many countries of the world and reporting the changes in economic, political, and regulatory environments that affect employee benefits. This service makes available detailed reference manuals for several foreign countries covering examples of typical benefits, compensation methods, financing, social security, taxes, and legal requirements affecting pensions and other employee benefits.

Arrangement of Coverage

A typical method of providing employee benefits abroad is through arrangements termed "networks." A **network** is an organization of insurers operating as a sort of joint venture to provide needed benefits for employees in different countries. A master contract between the multinational company and the insurer network is formed, and another contract is formed between the corporation and one or more local insurers in each country who are members of the network. Under the local contract, the local insurer charges the local subsidiary corporation a premium for coverage. The local insurer also receives a portion of the premium paid to the network. If losses at the local level are less than the income received by the local insurer, the local insurer derives a dividend from the network organization. If losses exceed local premiums, the local insurer absorbs them, having set its premium originally at a level designed to cover catastrophic coverage, cancellation costs, and other expenses. Through the network organization, pooling of all local contracts takes place; the dividend depends on worldwide experience, so that poor experience in one country can be offset by favorable experience in other countries. Network coverage is available for firms with as few as 25 employees overseas.

Network coverage is available in the form of plans in which the network provides administrative services only and the corporation bears the risk of loss. "Cash flow" programs are used which allow the corporation both to pay premiums only at specified times and to reinsure benefits through captive insurers. In this way, costs, including premium taxes in different nations, may be minimized.

Networks have developed pension plans with benefits expressed in units reflecting a composite of international currencies, such as ECUs (European currency units). In this way, risks produced by fluctuating values of national currencies can be effectively managed. An employee moving from one country to another can be paid in a currency that is both stable and easily convertible to the currency of the country in which he or she retires.[7] Such a situation often pertains to "third-country nationals," employees who are citizens of one country but who work in a second country for a corporation headquartered in a third country.

Self-insurance

Increasingly, international corporations are employing self-insurance methods to the managing of employee benefit risks abroad rather than using commercial insurance networks. In one survey covering the period 1972–1982, it was shown that the use of conventional insurance declined from about 65 percent of the firms to 37 percent.[8] Part of the reason for increasing use of self-insurance is to avoid the high premium taxes levied in some countries. Self-insurance plans can still utilize the services of insurance companies to administer the plans (called ASO, administrative service-only, plans) and to obtain the advantages of risk spreading across nations. Reinsurance of these plans is also common, sometimes through captives.

POLITICAL RISK

Many factors have increased the possibilities of loss of foreign investments due to what has been called political risk. Risk of loss due to actions by foreign governments, terrorist groups, war, rebellion, and other sources are all included in the general term **political risk.** The United States has been especially subject to political risk because of factors such as strained relations with the Soviet Union, increased involvement in problems of the Middle East, a more militant attitude toward countries in Latin America (e.g., Nicaragua), establishment of a missile program in Western Europe, and a combative attitude toward terrorists (e.g., the April, 1986 air raid on Libya). Indeed, the world has become a more dangerous place in which to live and do business. In some countries (Libya and Iran), the government itself has sponsored terrorists who prey on property and individuals wherever they are located in the world. Much political upheaval is traceable to worldwide economic crises brought on by wide fluctuations in the price of oil, interest rates, inflation, and currency exchange rates. Shifts of economic power to Asian Pacific countries have also contributed to world economic instability and change.

Losses stemming from political risk are many: property may be bombed or burned, executives kidnapped and held for ransom, sums extracted from companies through extortion, employees illegally detained, employees evacuated, criminal violence perpetrated on company employees, property confiscated without proper reimbursement, currency exchange blocked, currencies devalued, import or export licenses improperly cancelled, and debtors unable to pay because of any of a number of reasons, including commercial failure.

Managing Political Risk

The methods used to handle domestic risk—avoidance, assumption, noninsurance transfer, diversification, and insurance—are equally applicable to managing political risk in foreign areas. Thus, firms may simply decide not to engage in foreign commerce or not to make foreign investments, thereby utilizing the method of avoidance. Or they may decide to assume the risk of loss and charge more for their goods and services to compensate them for the increased risk of dealing abroad.

Examples of noninsurance transfers include leasing foreign plants instead of owning them outright, selling on terms that do not involve much granting of credit, and requiring foreign customers to bear part of the risk. For example, some countries, such as Mexico, require the use of a domestic partner who bears part of the risk and is entitled to part of the reward as well.

Another example of noninsurance transfer is hedging in foreign currencies. Hedging involves the purchase and sale of futures contracts in currencies in an amount that is equal and opposite to the value of a current transaction. For example, if goods are sold now on credit for 100,000 British pounds (worth $150,000) payable in 180 days, the international risk manager may decide to sell 100,000 British pounds in the futures market so that if the value of the pound falls before the 180 days is up, what is lost on the previous credit sale is made up in the futures market transaction. Thus, if the pound falls in such a way that 100,000 pounds is worth only $125,000 instead of $150,000, the futures contract can be sold in an amount so that a profit of $25,000 is made up on the futures contract, thereby keeping the seller's total expected sales revenue at a stable level of $150,000. The success of hedging depends on futures transaction fees. If these fees are too high, hedging may not be feasible.

Still another example of noninsurance transfer involves managing cash balances in a foreign country in such manner as to minimize the risk of holding currencies. In 1985–1986, the dollar began to fall, precipating actions to minimize losses from holding dollars. A cheaper dollar increases the price of imports, suggesting the need for advancing the timing of purchases of foreign goods. On the other hand, just the opposite action should be taken if the dollar is rising and the foreign currency is falling. For example, if a U.S. firm operates in the United Kingdom and fears a devaluation of the pound, the finance manager may decide to minimize holdings of pounds and maximize holdings of dollars. Payment to creditors to whom the firm owes pounds would be delayed as long as possible, so as to permit repayment of debts in cheaper pounds. Purchases payable in pounds would be sought with longer credit terms, and sales would be made with shorter credit terms. The opposite of these decisions would be taken if the fear was that the dollar might be devalued instead of the pound. In these examples the transfer of risk of loss due to fluctuation in the value of the currency is being placed on the firm's customers and suppliers.

An example of diversification is having plants in many parts of the world, so that the loss of any one will not disrupt the operations of the multinational corporation to any considerable degree. Another example is buying and selling in terms of a "market basket" of currencies (e.g., the European currency unit or ECU), so that fluctuations in any one currency will not unduly affect the value of the transaction.

The use of insurance in managing political risk is illustrated in the next section. Two main types of insurance are described: export credit insurance and insurance of foreign investments.

Export Credit Insurance

Export credit insurance was initiated in the United States in 1961 by the Trade Expansion Act, which directed the Export-Import Bank of the United States (Eximbank) to offer insurance against losses from credit and political risks. The purpose of this program was to place United States exporters on an equal basis with foreign competitors and to promote exporting among private financial institutions. Export credit insurance is also used in most leading countries of Europe and elsewhere.

In the United States, most export credit insurance is underwritten by the U.S. Eximbank and administered by the FCIA (Foreign Credit Insurance Association), an association of about 50 major stock and mutual insurance companies. Some coverage is sold independently by private insurers.

In 1984 the Eximbank provided $8.6 billion of guaranty, loan, and insurance support for U.S. exports.[9] FCIA insures credit term sales by United States exporters to responsible buyers in all free-world markets. The risks covered are (1) commercial credit, i.e., insolvency or deliberate payment default, and (2) political, i.e., exchange transfer delay, war, revolution, expropriation, and other causes of loss arising principally from government action and beyond the control of the buyer or seller.

According to a recent study, it was estimated that less than 8 percent of all U.S. merchandise exports were being insured under export credit insurance policies.[10] Even if adjustments are made for the fact that not all exports require insurance, being sold either on terms such that payment is guaranteed by the government or on terms which are either cash or near cash, less than 10 percent of eligible exports were being insured in most years. Furthermore, the proportion of exports being insured shows no upward trend, suggesting that a plateau of sales of this type of insurance exists under present economic conditions. Some of the reasons for this will be discussed shortly. In the meantime, note that most export credit insurance is issued on five major types of products, listed in order of importance as follows: machinery, food and kindred products, electrical and electronic equipment and supplies, chemicals, and transportation equipment.

Costs. Costs of short-term commercial export credit insurance policies vary according to the country of designation, terms of payment, exporter's credit loss record, and other factors. Costs vary from about 0.1 to 2 percent of gross invoice value. These rates are not annual interest, but rather flat rates applying to the full term of the insurance or guarantee. Charges for preshipment coverage and advance commitments are additional.

An Evaluation. A study of exporters' attitudes toward and experience with export credit insurance in Georgia in 1982 revealed considerable dissatisfaction with the export credit insurance system as it is now administered.[11] The study surveyed 80 exporters, 22 of which were users and 58 nonusers of export credit insurance. The features that exporters liked about the coverage included increased ease of obtaining bank credit, increased ability to sell on unsecured terms in countries where letters of credit are needed to cover political risks, and increased credit protection in case of buyer default. Negative views of exporters centered about the procedural methods required, the amount of paperwork and length of time required to obtain coverage, and the requirement of supplying too much detailed information as a precondition of obtaining insurance. The exporters also criticized the high price of insurance, considering the amount of protection actually granted. An interesting finding of the survey was that about a third of the exporters were unaware of the availability of export credit insurance, even though they had several years of experience in exporting. Apparently, export credit insurance is not widely known or understood among its potential market. In its present form, the coverage is not particularly profitable for sellers either, since the FCIA, formerly an underwriter of part of the risk, is now engaged solely as a servicing agent for Eximbank, having withdrawn from underwriting this insurance in 1983 as being essentially unprofitable.[12]

Since 1948 the United States government has sought to increase direct investment by United States private enterprises in the economies of friendly, less developed countries by protecting investors against certain risks. Under provisions of the Foreign Assistance Act of 1961, as amended, Congress has authorized three investment guarantee programs:

1. Specific political risk guarantees against inconvertibility of foreign currency, loss by expropriation or confiscation, and loss due to war, revolution, insurrection, and civil strife.
2. Extended risk guarantees covering up to 75 percent of political and general business risks.
3. Extended business guarantees covering up to 100 percent of losses on certain housing projects.

Definition of Perils. Expropriation and war are defined in the guarantee contract as follows:

Expropriation occurs when the foreign enterprise is prohibited from exercising (1) effective control over a substantial portion of its property, (2) fundamental rights acquired by reason of ownership, or (3) the receipt of declared dividends. The definition of expropriation may in some circumstances include a breach by the foreign government of a concession agreement which it has made with the foreign enterprise.

In practice, actual expropriation of property by a foreign government is relatively uncommon. Most problems involve repudiation of contracts as a result, directly or indirectly, of actions taken by a foreign government. For example, the foreign government may cancel an import or export license, impose an embargo, or interrupt the supply of crucial parts or raw materials. A government may refuse to abide by an agreement to submit to binding arbitration of disagreements between private companies.

The definition of **war, revolution, insurrection** and **civil strife** does not require that there be a formal declaration of war. Hostile acts of any national or international organized force are covered, as are hostile acts of organized revolutionary or insurrectionary forces, including acts of sabotage. The guarantee does not cover injury to the physical property of the enterprise that is caused directly by civil strife of a lesser degree than revolution or insurrection. In 1983 coverage against civil strife, including terrorism, sabotage, and politically motivated violent acts, was authorized as a rider to war, revolution, and insurrection coverage.

Specific Risk Investment Guarantees. Before guarantees can be issued for investments in a particular country, the government of that country must have agreed to institute a guarantee program. Under the agreement, the project in which the investment is being made must be approved by the foreign government. Guarantees are issued to the investor in the form of a contract between the investor and the Overseas Private Investor Corporation (OPIC), a United States government agency formed in 1970.

This guarantee is backed by the full faith and credit of the United States government. Eligible entries include corporations, partnerships, and other associations created under the laws of the United States and substantially owned by citizens of the United States. The investor may be a foreign entity, such as a branch of a United States company wholly owned or substantially owned by the United States company.

The form of the investment may be buildings, plants, cash, materials or equipment, patents, processes or techniques, engineering or management services, loan guarantees made to foreign banks or corporations, or money advanced to long-term suppliers under certain conditions. The investment must further the economic development or productivity of an economically less developed country. Contracts may be written for a maximum term of 20 years for equity investments, or for the term of a loan in the case of debt investments.

Only new investments are eligible for OPIC coverage, because the purpose of the program is to encourage U.S. investment in friendly third-world nations. OPIC declines coverage for already outstanding transactions, including certain properties such as casinos or other activities which might be harmful to U.S. interests, such as projects that displace U.S. employment. Coverage is available to expand existing facilities. OPIC insures perils that face construction contractors or exporters who perform under a contract with a foreign buyer.[13]

OPIC makes an effort to assist small-business investment in third-world countries. Approximately one-third of its clients in 1984 qualified as small businesses or cooperatives. Special financial assistance, including legal and accounting advice, is extended to small businesses wishing to start up foreign investment operations.

OPIC requires investor participation in any losses to the extent of being a 10 percent coinsurer. An exception is made for financial institutions making project loans, where 100 percent coverage is authorized. Generally, there is a limit of no more than $100 million of coverage for any one project. Insurance is also available for retained earnings and interest which may accrue on the insured investment to a maximum amount of 270 percent of the initial investment.

Cost. Annual premiums for coverage on debt investments are as follows, expressed as a percent of the value of the investment: 0.3 percent for the lack-of-convertibility peril; 0.6 percent for expropriation peril; and 0.6 percent for war, revolution, or insurrection perils. These premiums are the same in all countries. Premiums for coverage on equity investments may be varied somewhat from the premiums applicable to debt investments. The civil strife rider costs 0.15 percent, making total annual costs equal to 1.65 percent of the investment. Premiums must be paid annually in advance. Rates vary according to the type of project being insured and the amount of "standby" coverage (coverage which can be issued to cover potentially increased investments during the contract year).

Effectiveness and Acceptance. Increasing nationalism, exchange controls, foreign takeovers, and worldwide inflation and unrest have increased the need for some type of protection for foreign investors. It is estimated that about a third of all new United States investment (two-thirds if oil investments are excluded from the total) in less developed nations is now insured by OPIC against political risk. As of 1986, estimated investment guarantees in force totalled $11.6 billion.[14]

OPIC's underwriting results have been quite favorable. For example, in 1984 losses totalled only $3.9 million, compared to net premiums and investment guarantee fees of $31.9 million. The use of OPIC's insurance coverage increased to $4.3 billion in the period 1982–1984, up from a level of only $1.5 billion in 1981.

Private Insurance. Insurance on foreign investments is available in the private marketplace on terms that are somewhat more flexible than those offered by OPIC. For example, coverage from insurers such as AFIA, AIG, Chubb, and CIGNA is available on all types of commercial transactions, not just specified investments. In contrast to OPIC coverage, investments in any country, not just friendly third-world nations, are eligible. Also, both new and existing investments are eligible, not just new investments. However, private insurance is usually available for periods up to only three years, and the dollar limits of coverage per project are less than is available from OPIC. Potential investors should investigate both OPIC and private coverage and costs before making a decision on which insurance to purchase.

SUMMARY

1. The rapid increase in world trade and investments in recent years has brought about a new world environment for insurance: increased risk, enlarged markets, new drains on financial capacity to underwrite business, and the necessity for developing new techniques to meet the needs of the multinational corporation.

2. The insurance institution will probably continue to expand to meet the challenges of rising world economic development. United States-based insurers and brokers

are attempting improved coordination and cooperation to increase their international effectiveness.

3. In many respects, the legal environment for international insurance differs considerably from the domestic United States environment. Among the differences are laws regulating admitted versus unadmitted insurance, the operation of the Napoleonic code, and the effect of tax laws applying to insurance.

4. There are many interesting contrasts in

insurance conditions throughout the world which require special attention by multinational business firms. These include differences in policy conditions, differences in unwritten customs affecting the interpretation of policies, and differences in regulations, insurer financial strength, agency practices, and claims settlement practices. In many countries certain types of insurance are compulsory, and special policy provisions, such as 100 percent coinsurance on fire coverage, prevail. One way the insurance industry has responded to these variations is in the development of the difference in conditions (DIC) policy, which offers the multinational corporation relatively uniform protection throughout its worldwide operations.

5. Among the important problems in insurance facing the multinational firm is that of coordinating an employee benefit structure in different countries. Special attention must be given to differences in social insurance benefits, union organization and influence, community standards, and creating a benefit structure that is fair for all employees.

6. Export credit insurance and investment guarantees have been developed as a partnership between business and government in many countries to facilitate export credit and investment in fixed plants and equipment abroad, particularly in developing countries. These programs have not been used extensively in the United States, but their potential appears substantial.

QUESTIONS FOR REVIEW

1. Among the factors which increase international risk levels, as compared to domestic risk levels, which are most significant at the current time? Why?

2. Suggest possible reasons related to insurance for why investments of foreign countries in the United States are increasing faster than U.S. investments abroad.

3. Which are the leading insurance countries in the world? By what measure?

4. Does the United States collect more from foreign reinsurers than foreign reinsurers collect from the U.S.? Suggest reasons for the current negative "international balance of payments" related to reinsurance.

5. A writer stated, "Avoid unadmitted insurance" at all costs. Do you agree? Why, or why not? In your answer, give the advantages of unadmitted insurance.

6. What are gap policies? What need do these contracts serve?

7. What special problems exist in the field of planning employee benefits for overseas personnel? Explain.

8. What is political risk? How may one obtain protection against political risks?

9. Explain why export credit insurance is not more widely used.

10. Are investment guarantees advisable for foreign investors? Why or why not?

QUESTIONS FOR DISCUSSION

1. How can unadmitted insurance lawfully exist in countries which have laws prohibiting it?

2. A United States firm was exporting its products to a Latin American nation. A products liability suit was initiated in that country against the firm. The firm's product liability insurance provided that the insurer was only obligated to defend legal actions brought in the United States. The Latin American plaintiff could not afford to come to the United States to prosecute the case, and complained to his government. As a result, the firm's foreign assets were confiscated and an embargo was

placed on further imports of its product line. How might the problem have been handled to avoid the disastrous consequences which resulted?

3. What value is there in studying differences in foreign insurance conditions as they might affect conditions in other countries, such as the United States? Give examples.

4. The Foster Wheeler Corporation carried an investment guarantee plan for its investment in Turkey. It suffered a loss of $183,947 due to inconvertibility. The government paid the loss and then salvaged practically the entire amount. Explain what an inconvertibility loss is. Why was the government able to recover its loss later through salvage?

5. A service of the FCIA is a computerized credit rating system enabling quick references to the credit ratings of 88,000 foreign buyers and permitting faster service to the clients. Credit ratings may be updated as quickly as every 24 hours. Why is such a service of importance to the users of credit insurance?

NEW TERMS AND CONCEPTS

Admitted Insurance
DIC Policy
DIL Policy
DIP Policy
Eximbank
Export Credit Insurance
FCIA

Gap Policy
Network Coverage
OPIC Coverage
Political Risk
Tariff
Unadmitted Insurance

NOTES

1 Swiss Reinsurance Company, "The International Insurance Industry of the Post-War Period," *Sigma* (March, 1986), p. 3.

2 *Sigma,* (April, 1986), p. 11.

3 *Sigma* (October, 1985), p. 12

4 Some interesting examples of the results of these differences are reported by Philip J. Brown, Jr., "The Role of the U.S. Broker in Europe," *International Insurance and Employee Benefit and Pension Management* (New York: American Management Association, 1966), pp. 6–11. For example, many foreign automobile insurance policies exclude coverage when the driver is drunk, under the influence of drugs, or without a proper license. Sometimes policies exclude damage caused by bad repairs or negligent operation.

5 Mark R. Greene, "The Spanish Insurance Industry—An Analysis," *Journal of Risk and Insurance,* Vol. 39, No. 2 (June, 1972), pp. 221–243.

6 Andrew Coplestone, *International Insurance Report* (London, England: Risk Research Group Ltd., January, 1986).

7 Dianne L. Kastiel, "Benefit Networks Offer Variety of New Products," *Business Insurance,* (October 21, 1985), p. 3.

8 C. C. Gamwell III, "Maximizing Cash Flow in Multinational Benefit Plans," *Risk Management* (October, 1984), p. 52.

9 Eximbank, *Annual Report,* 1984.

10 Sandra M. Huszagh and Mark R. Greene, "How Exporters View Credit Risk and FCIA Insurance—The Georgia Experience," *Journal of Risk and Insurance,* Vol. 52, No. 1 (March, 1985), pp. 119–120.

11 Ibid.

12 "U.S. to Assume Entire Risk on Insurance of Exporters," *Wall Street Journal,* Vol. CCII, No. 1 (July 1, 1985), p. 34.

13 Felton McL. Johnston, "Political Risk Market Expansion Broadens OPIC's Role," *Risk Management* (February, 1984), pp. 18–24.

14 *Budget of the U.S. Government, Appendix, Fiscal Year 1987* (Washington, D.C.: U.S. Government Printing Office, 1986), p. I-D29.

APPENDIX A
GLOSSARY

Actual cash value The replacement cost of property less allowance for depreciation

Actuary A mathematically trained individual in charge of developing appropriate prices and other statistical and financial calculations for insurance

Additional-living-expense insurance Consequential property insurance that offers coverage of additional living expenses when insured property is untenantable because of an insured peril

Adhesion A legal principle stating that any ambiguities or uncertainties in the wording of an insurance agreement will be construed against the insurer

Adjusted gross estate The total value of an estate at the death of the owner less an allowance for settling the estate (funeral expenses, administrative costs, etc.)

Administrative cost ratio (ACR) A formula to measure the cost of administering a savings program

Admitted insurance Insurance authorized by insurers chartered to do business in a given state or country

Aleatory contract A legal contract in which the outcome depends upon an uncertain event

Alien insurer An insurer, incorporated in a foreign country, doing business in a given state

All-line insurer An insurer whose underwriting authority includes the right to issue contracts on all types of insurance, including life

All-risk contract A property or liability insurance contract in which all risks of loss are covered except those specifically excluded

All-risk crop insurance A government program to insure crops of specific types, on an all-risk basis, against loss from unavoidable causes

Allocated benefit plan A type of pension funding in which specific employees are identified and benefits allocated to them

American agency system A distribution system for insurance in which the agent, called a local agent, is an independent retailer representing several different insurers

American Lloyds A form of insurance organization authorized in some states in which owners assume risk as individuals, generally limiting their liability

Annual premium annuity An annuity whose purchase price is paid in annual installments

Annuitant An individual receiving benefits under an annuity

Annuity rent The payments made to an annuitant under an annuity

Anticancellation laws State laws that restrict the right of insurers to cancel insurance policies except for specific reasons

Anticoercion laws The laws that prohibit

lending agencies from requiring the placing of insurance with the agency as a condition of granting a loan

Assessable policy A policy subject to additional charges, or assessments on all policyholders in the company

Assigned-risk plan A plan for sharing specific types of risks in which all insurers operating in the state are required to participate, each accepting its fair share of the risks assigned to the pool

Assignment A clause that allows the transfer of rights under a policy from one person to another, usually by means of a written document

Attorney-in-fact The chief executive officer of a reciprocal insurer, using a power of attorney to bind the members of the group to mutually enforceable contracts of insurance

Attractive-nuisance doctrine A legal doctrine that increases the degree of care owed to a child; greater than ordinary care is required of a child who is a trespasser

Automatic premium-loan clause A life insurance clause under which cash values are automatically borrowed to pay premiums if regular premiums are not paid when due

Average adjuster A name applied to a claims adjuster in the field of marine insurance

Bailee A person in charge of property belonging to others

Beneficiary A person named in a life insurance policy to receive the death proceeds

Best's reports Financial reports of insurance companies; published annually, and include ratings of insurers, financial data, and underwriting results

Binder A written notation evidencing an oral contract of insurance

Binomial distribution A mathematical probability distribution in which an event either occurs or does not occur, as in a distribution of "heads" in a coin-flipping experiment

Blanket bond A fidelity bond that offers a uniform amount of coverage on all employees

Block policies A type of inland marine insurance usually offering all-risk coverage to "floating" property, i.e., property subject to being moved from one location to another

Blue Cross-Blue Shield plans Hospital and surgical insurance plans sponsored by hospital associations called Blue Cross and Blue Shield

Bond Penalty The amount by which a surety must respond for loss under the terms of the given bond, i.e., the face amount of the bond

Bottomry contract An ancient version of an ocean marine insurance contract

Branch office system A distribution system for insurance in which the insurer deals with its agents through a branch or regional office

Broad-form peril An endorsement to the basic fire policy including extended-coverage perils; coverage also offers broader definitions of perils than more limited forms of coverage

Broker A sales agent who is the legal representative of the client for the purpose of securing insurance or other services

Burglary The unlawful taking of property from within premises, entry to which has been obtained by force, leaving visible marks of entry

Business continuation insurance Life insurance designed to permit a business firm to be continued even though the insured owner dies

Business-interruption insurance Consequential insurance covering fixed expenses and the loss of profits in the event physical property is damaged by a named peril; requires that the business be shut down in whole or in part as a direct result of the named peril

Buy-and-sell agreement A legal contract requiring the estate of a deceased business owner to sell his/her interest in a business to others and requiring the other parties to purchase this interest. The agreement is usually funded with life insurance

Buy-term-and-invest-the-difference strategy A way of life insurance planning in which one substitutes term insurance and separate savings program for ordinary life insurance

Cancellation clause A clause that gives the parties the right to terminate coverage offered in a contract under specified conditions

Capitalization of income An approach to determining the need for life insurance by calculating the present value of a stream of income that would be lost if the insured dies

Captive insurer An insurance corporation designed to handle the specific insurance needs of a parent company

Care, custody, or control exclusion A clause in liability insurance that eliminates liability for property in the insured's care, custody, or control

Cargo certificate An insurance contract in which ocean-going cargo is insured

Cash refund annuity An annuity guaranteeing to pay in cash to beneficiaries an amount equal to the difference between the original premium and the sum of the rent payments made at the time of an annuitant's death

Cash value option Option in life insurance policy permitting insured to take the cash value of the policy upon surrender

Ceding company An insurer, also called a primary insurer, which passes on to other insurers some part of its risk under insurance policies it has accepted

Cession A reinsurance term meaning that portion of a risk which is passed on to reinsurers by ceding companies

Class rating A rating system in which all exposure units are grouped into a single category, or class, for pricing purposes

CLU (Chartered Life Underwriter) A professional designation issued by the American Society of Chartered Life Underwriters to life insurance agents and others

meeting specific examination and experience requirements

Coefficient of variation The ratio of the standard deviation to the mean of a probability distribution

Coinsurance A clause that requires the insured to bear part of the loss

Combined ratio The sum of the loss ratio and expense ratio

Common disaster clause A life insurance clause stating what happens to life insurance proceeds if named beneficiaries die in a common accident

Common-law defenses The defenses that are available to defeat liability actions by employees against an employer in negligence cases; three commonly recognized common-law defenses are contributory negligence, assumed risk, and fellow servant

Community rating A rating system under which all health insurance rates in a given community are the same

Comparative negligence The legal principle that requires parties in a negligence action to share the loss in accordance with the degree of negligence

Comprehensive general liability (CGL) A business liability policy designed for a wide variety of business uses, covering premises operations, product liability, completed operations, and operations of independent contractors

Concealment The failure of an applicant to reveal, before the insurance contract is made, a fact that is material to the risk

Concurrent causation Legal doctrine that says if two perils occur and cause a loss, one excluded and the other one is not, coverage applies

Contemplation of death rule Federal tax ruling resulting in the estate taxation of property given away before death, under specific conditions

Contingent beneficiary A person named in a life insurance contract to receive the benefits of the policy if other named beneficiaries are not living

Contractual liability The liability assumed under contract

Conversion clause Clause in a group life or health insurance contract allowing the employee leaving a group to convert group coverage to an individual policy regardless of the status of the employee's health

Coordination of benefits (COB) A clause in a health insurance policy requiring consideration of other sources of benefits in determining the amount of benefits due under an existing contract

Corridor deductible A type of deductible in health insurance

Cost to repair basis Cost to replace but may not be with like materials and labor

Credibility A measurement that shows the degree to which an insurer may rely upon statistical observations in making rates or rate revisions

Credit insurance The insurance that responds to losses caused by failure of debtors to pay accounts when due; sometimes called bad-debt insurance.

Credit life insurance Life insurance arranged in an amount needed to pay a debt in the event of death of the borrower

Currently insured Status under OASDHI in which one may qualify for limited benefits for only short-time coverage under the law

Debit agent A life insurance agent selling the servicing industrial, or home service, life insurance

Decreasing term Term life insurance in which the amount of coverage declines during the period for which it is issued

Deductible An amount subtracted from a full loss settlement under an insurance contract; deductibles may be on a per-occurrence basis or applicable for aggregate losses during an entire year, or both

Deferred annuity An annuity of which the rent begins at some future time

Defined benefit plan Pension plan in which the formula which specifies the pension benefit payable is set forth

Defined contribution plan Pension plan in which the benefits due are specified in terms of the funds being paid in to the plan, such as a percentage of payroll

Dental insurance A health insurance contract providing reimbursement for specified dental expenses

Deposit administration A type of unallocated insured pension funding in which the size of the required fund to pay promised benefits is determined periodically

Deviating insurer An insurer offering rates at a discount, below the rates offered by competitors or promulgated by rate-making organizations

Diagnosis related group (DRG) A system limiting the amounts reimbursible to hospitals for care provided for specified types of illnesses

Difference in conditions (DIC) policy General insurance policy designed to cover risks not covered by other contracts. Used to standardize world-wide coverage of companies operating world-wide

Difference in Limits (DIL) policy General insurance policy designed to standardize policy limits of coverage wherever the insured firm operates

Difference in Perils (DIP) policy General insurance policy designed to standardize coverage of perils insured under other contracts wherever the insured firm operates

Direct loss A loss that stems directly from an unbroken chain of events leading from an insured peril to the loss

Direct writer An insurer using a distribution system in which independent agents are bypassed and coverage is offered to the public through salaried or commissioned employees who serve as company-controlled agents, sometimes referred to as exclusive agents or captive agents

Disability-income insurance Health insurance that provides periodic payments if the insured becomes disabled as a result of illness or accident

Dividend options The clauses in a life insurance contract that give the insured alternative ways of using dividends payable under participating policies

Dollar cost averaging A method of investing in the stock market in which equal amounts of money are paid in regularly, with the goal of reducing the average cost of shares below their average price

Domestic insurer An insurer incorporated to do business in a given state

Double-indemnity rider An endorsement to a life insurance policy giving the insured's beneficiary twice the face amount of the policy in the event of accidental death

Dramshop exclusion An exclusion in liability insurance policies for liability resulting from distribution of alcoholic beverages

Elimination period The period that must elapse before disability income is payable under a health insurance policy covering disability income loss

Employee benefits Term describing non-salary compensation to employees, usually on a tax-free basis, including retirement, life and health insurance, and other benefits

Endowment insurance Life insurance that builds up a large cash value within a stated period of years; the face amount is payable in the event of death before the policy expires

Entire contract clause A life insurance contract stating that the policy and the application form constitute the entire contract between the parties

Errors and ommissions insurance (E&O) Insurance responding to liability of professional persons for malpractice

Estate planning A process under which plans are made to accumulate and manage property during one's lifetime and to dispose of it at one's death

Estate shrinkage The expenses such as debts, taxes, and administrative costs that reduce the value of an estate at the death of the owner

Estoppel A legal doctrine in which a person may be required to do something or prevented from doing something that is inconsistent with previous behavior; may prevent an insurer from denying liability after a loss

Exclusive agent An individual employed to represent an insurer and who serves only that insurer

Expected value A number obtained by multiplying the value of each item in a probability distribution by the probability of its occurrence and adding

Expense ratio The ratio of expenses incurred to premiums written

Experience rating The system of rating or pricing insurance in which the future premium reflects past loss experience of the insured

Extended-coverage endorsement An endorsement to the basic fire insurance policy that adds coverage of losses from the perils windstorm, hail, explosion, riot, riot attending strike, civil commotion, aircraft, vehicles, and smoke

Extended term option One of the non-forfeiture options in life insurance, allowing the insured to take the cash value in the form of term insurance upon the surrender of the contract

Extra-expense insurance The consequential property insurance that covers the extra expense incurred by the interruption of a business; the policy pays if the business does not close down but continues in alternative facilities, with higher-than-normal costs

Factory mutual A mutual insurer specializing in large risks, with special emphasis on loss prevention

Facultative reinsurance Reinsurance in which specific coverage is arranged individually for each exposure, as contrasted with treaty reinsurance, under which each member of the group agrees in advance to cover risks on some predetermined basis

FAIR plans Fair Access to Insurance Requirement plans, operating in about one-half of the states, designed to ensure the availability of property insurance in central cities and elsewhere; operate as a type of assigned-risk pool for substandard property

Family-income policy A life insurance policy combining decreasing term with ordinary life insurance

Farm mutual A mutual insurer organized to insure farm property

Federal crime insurance The burglary and theft insurance offered by the federal government

Federal crop insurance program Federal program to provide all-risk crop insurance to farmers

Federal estate tax The tax levied by the federal government on the value of an estate upon the death of the owner

Federal flood insurance Insurance against flood and mudslide, operated by the federal government in communities meeting specified building codes to protect property against flooding

Fidelity bonding Bonds that protect a principal against loss from dishonesty by employees

File and use rating System under which states allow insurers to file new property-liability rates with state insurance commissioners and use them subject to later approval

Financial responsibility laws State laws that require automobile drivers to carry stated minimum limits of liability insurance, or meet other conditions to assure their financial ability to respond to losses for which they may be held liable as a result of driving automobiles

First surplus treaty A reinsurance agreement under which the ceding company accepts a certain amount of risk in a given line of coverage, and the other members of the treaty accept amounts that depend on the size of the risk retained by the ceding company

Fixed amount option A life insurance option allowing the beneficiary to take the proceeds in the form of a fixed periodic payment

Fixed annuity An annuity whose rent is expressed in a fixed number of dollars

Floater An inland marine insurance policy that covers property subject to movement from one location to another

Floor of protection concept Underlying principle of social insurance specifying that the goal of social insurance is to provide only limited protection, not one's entire need

Foreign Credit Insurance Association (FCIA) An association of about 50 large U.S. property-liability insurers to administer (in cooperation with the Eximbank) the federal program of export credit insurance

Foreign insurer An insurer authorized to do business in a given state although incorporated in a different state

Foute lourde French term referring to negligence

Franchise A deductible under which there is no liability on the part of the insurer unless the loss exceeds a certain stated amount, and full liability after that amount

Fraternal A life insurer organized by a fraternal benefit society to offer coverage on members

Free-of-capture-and-seizure (FC&S) A clause in ocean marine insurance that excludes war as a covered peril

Free-of-particular-average clause (FPA) An ocean marine insurance clause that excludes payment for a partial loss, except under certain conditions such as stranding, sinking, burning, or collision

Freight Money paid for the transportation of goods. Freight insurance is a common coverage in marine insurance, purchased by the owners of transporting vessels

Friendly fire A fire confined to the area of a boiler, stove, or other place designed to contain it

Fully insured Status to be met by those qualifying for most of the benefits of OASDHI

Funding Process of providing money to pay for benefits promised under a plan

Gambling A transaction in which new risk is created where none existed before; it is distinguished from insurance, where a risk already exists

Gap policy Policy, used mainly in international business, to unify various individual policies written under different conditions in various countries of the world

General agent An individual serving an insurer in the channel of distribution of insurance who hires, trains, and supervises other agents at a lower level in the organization

General average clause A clause in ocean marine insurance that requires ship and freight interests other than the insured to respond to losses suffered by the insured interest when those losses result from voluntary, necessary, and successful sacrifice of the insured's freight because of shipping peril

General insurance Another term for property insurance

General-writing mutual A mutual insurer not specializing in any class of risk

Gift tax A federal tax levied on property given away during one's lifetime in excess of $10,000 per year per donee

Grace period A clause in life insurance giving the insured an extra 30 days to pay a premium due, before lapse takes place

Gross-earnings form Business-interruption insurance in which the coverage is based on the gross earnings reported by the business

Gross premium The premium charge for insurance that includes anticipated cost of losses, overhead, and profit

Group accidental death and dismemberment (AD&D) insurance Group health insurance plan paying specified sums in case of accidental death or dismemberment of covered workers

Group annuity An annuity that covers all members of a specified group, as in a private pension plan

Group credit insurance Credit insurance provided under a group plan

Group disability insurance Disability insurance provided income benefits due to disability under a group plan

Group life insurance Term life insurance issued on a master contract for members of a group

Group survivor income benefit insurance Group insurance plan providing death benefits only to specified classes of survivors, usually payable on an income basis

Group term life insurance Term life insurance offered on a group plan basis

Guaranteed insurability rider A life insurance endorsement permitting the insured to purchase more life insurance without evidence of insurability, under given conditions

Guaranteed investment contract (GIC) A type of insured pension plan in which the insurer guarantees principal and a stated interest return

Guest/host statute State laws that reduce the standard of care owed by the driver to a guest riding in a car as a passenger

Harmonization of insurance Term referring to a program of unifying insurance laws, regulations, and operating conditions across members of the EEC

Hazard A condition that introduces or increases the probability of loss stemming from the existence of a given peril

Health Maintenance Organization (HMO) An organization that offers group health care to member families or individuals on a prearranged service basis

Hedging A transferal of risk from one party to another; similar to speculation and may be used to handle risks not subject to insurance, such as price-change risks

Highly protected risk (HPR) A physical property in which management has devoted special attention to loss prevention, usually to qualify for special types of insurance written by factory mutuals

Homeowners' forms The forms within a multiple-line property insurance contract that offer comprehensive package of protection to the homeowner; include fire and other named-perils coverage on property, medical payments, liability, and theft insurance, under one contract

Hospitalization insurance An insurance contract designed to pay hospital room and board, laboratory fees, nursing care, use of the operating room and medicines, and similar expenses

Hostile fire A fire that occurs outside of its normal confines

Immediate annuity An annuity whose rent begins at the time the contract is purchased

Incontestability clause A life insurance clause that prevents the insurer, after two years, from denying liability under the policy for misrepresentations or concealments by the insured

Indirect loss A loss that occurs indirectly as a consequence of a given peril; also referred to as consequential loss

Individual or merit rating A rating system in which rates are developed or modified for specific members of the insured group to reflect the degree of risk

Individual policy pension trust A type of insured pension plan in which a special policy is issued for each employee as benefits accrue

Individual retirement account (IRA) Individual retirement plan allowing tax deductibility of contributions and tax deferral of accumulating interest, under specific conditions and up to specified amounts

Industrial insurance Life insurance sold door-to-door, for which premiums are collected or quoted on a weekly or monthly basis

Inland marine insurance Insurance that covers imports, exports, domestic shipments, instrumentalities of transportation and communication, and various types of floaters

Inpatient coverages Health insurance benefits relating to services provided while the patient is in the hospital

Insolvency funds Funds that have been created by state law to guarantee the payment of bills of insolvent insurers

Installment refund annuity An annuity guaranteeing to pay to beneficiaries the rent of the annuity in installments in a total amount at least equal to the total original premium paid by the annuitant upon the annuitant's death

Insurable risk Uncertainty that is susceptible to being handled by the medium of insurance

Insurance An economic institution that reduces risk by combining under one management a group of objects so situated that the aggregate accidental losses to which the group is subject become predictable within narrow limits; includes certain legal contracts under which the insurer for consideration promises to reimburse the insured or to render services in case of certain described accidental losses

Insurance exchange An insurance organization to facilitate the distribution of special classes of insurance and to effect reinsurance arrangements for specific types of risks. The best known is the New York Insurance Exchange, formed in 1978

Insurance rate The price of insurance, expressed as a price per unit of coverage

Insurance Services Office (ISO) A major national rate-making organization for property and liability insurers; promulgates rates that serve as the basis for individual rates quoted by its members

Insured plan An employee benefit plan managed by an insurance company

Inter vivos trust Trust set up during the lifetime of the estate owner, usually with the purpose of facilitating the transfer of property at death

Interest-adjusted method A method of expressing the costs of life insurance by giving consideration to the time value of money used for premiums

Interest option A life insurance option allowing the beneficiary to leave the proceeds with the insurer and receive only interest income

Interinsurance exchange Another name for a reciprocal

Intestate Without a valid will

Involuntary coverage Insurance contracts required to be purchased by those affected under force of law or contract

Irrevocable beneficiary A beneficiary designation which may not be changed without the written consent of the named beneficiary

Joint-and-last-survivor annuity An annuity issued on two lives that guarantees that the annuity in whole or in part will be paid as long as either party shall live

Joint and several liability Legal doctrine that allows plaintiff to collect in full from one negligent party in an accident where there are two or more negligent parties

Joint ownership A form of legal ownership in which two or more persons are co-owners and in which the property passes to the survivor automatically if one should die; property held jointly does not enter into a decedent's estate for probate purposes and does not pass under will

Keogh (HR 10) plan A retirement plan designed for the self-employed

Key-employee life insurance Life insurance designed to indemnify a business for the loss of a key person within the firm

Law of large numbers A mathematical principle showing that as the number of exposure units increases, the more certain it becomes that actual loss experience will equal probable loss experience

Leasehold interest insurance Consequential property insurance in which the value of a lease is lost because of the occurrence of an insured-peril loss

Life and health insurance That type of insurance covering the risks of losing one's life or health

Life annuity A series of equal payments made by an insurer to an annuitant for life

Life income option A life insurance option allowing the beneficiary to receive the proceeds in the form of a life annuity

Life insurance policy reserve An insurer's financial liability for future benefits payable under the policy; the reserve is measured approximately by the cash value of the policy

Life insurance programming A process under which the proceeds of life insurance are integrated with other assets and resources of the estate planner to accomplish desired objectives

Lloyds association An insurer organized under state law in which individuals accept risks on a cooperative basis

Loading The overhead or administrative expenses of an insurer that is included in the cost of a policy

Loan value provision A life insurance provision allowing the owner to borrow the cash value at a stated interest rate

Local agent An independent middleman in the distribution channel of property-liability insurance. The local agent usually represents more than one insurer at a time

London Lloyd's An organization of individuals offering insurance mainly in the surplus-line market; the members, or "names" of Lloyd's offer coverage as individuals and without limit of liability

Loss assessment Covers assessment against an association of property members that the insured belongs to

Loss ratio The ratio of losses incurred to premiums earned

Lump sum option A life insurance option in which the death beneficiary may elect to take the policy proceeds in a lump sum rather than in installments

Major medical insurance A health insurance contract, usually with a large face value, designed to cover catastrophic expenses that result from loss of health

Manual rate making A method of quoting uniform rates for certain categories of exposure by reference to a rate manual

A

Marital deduction An amount allowed under federal estate tax laws that can be deducted from the gross estate for tax purposes if this amount is given to a spouse

Mass merchandising The sale of group property insurance through payroll deduction; most mass merchandising plans specialize in automobile and homeowners' coverage

Master comprehensive combined risk policy A type of export credit insurance policy

Mean A number obtained by adding a list of numbers of values and dividing by the number of items in the list

Median That point in a range of measurements at which there is an equal number of items above and below

Medicare A federal program under OASDHI to provide insurance coverage for hospitalization and physician's expense to older workers and to certain other persons

Misstatement-of-age clause A clause in life insurance requiring an adjustment of the amount of insurance payable in the event the age of the insured has been misrepresented

Mode The value of the variable that occurs most often in a group of numbers

Moral hazard A hazard resulting from the indifferent or dishonest attitude of an individual in relation to insured property

Morale hazard A hazard resulting from a subconscious desire for loss, as in the accident-prone person

Mortality table A table that shows the number of deaths per thousand and expectation of life at various ages; mortality table in current use in the United States is the Commissioner's Standard Ordinary (CSO) Table of 1980

Mortgage clause A clause in insurance contracts that gives first right of recovery to the mortgagor of property that is covered

Multiple-line insurer An insurer whose underwriting authority includes all different kinds of insurance except life

Multiple-peril policy An insurance policy covering several perils under one policy form, usually in the field of property-liability insurance

Multiple-protection contract A life insurance policy using term insurance to grant extra protection in the form of some multiple of the primary amount of coverage

Mutual insurer A nonprofit insurance company owned by policyholders; there are no stockholders

Named insured An individual in whose name the insurance contract is issued and who is specifically identified as the person being covered

Named-peril contract An insurance contract that lists perils to be insured; perils not listed are not covered

Napoleonic Code A legal code underlying European insurance law

Needs approach A way of determining the need for life insurance by adding up the cost of various uses to which life insurance proceeds would be put if the insured dies.

Negligence The failure to exercise the degree of care required by law

Net level premium The premium required in life insurance which covers the cost of the policy, but which is expressed as an equal periodic amount over the life of the policy

Net single premium The premium designed to cover the present value of future claims under a life insurance policy

Network coverage Insurance coverage arranged through a network, or joint venture, of insurers for specific types of risks, usually employee benefits offered to employees working in foreign countries

No-fault law An automobile-insurance state law that requires an insured to collect for bodily injury claims from his or her own insurer, rather than bring legal action for negligence against third parties

No-fault threshold A dollar limit (often $500) below which one may not bring tort liability action against those responsible for automobile accidents

Nonforfeiture option A provision in life insurance that names ways in which the insured may receive the cash value element; there are generally three such options: lump sum, extended term insurance, or paid-up insurance of a reduced amount

Nonownership liability The legal liability incurred even though the insured does not own the property whose use has caused a loss to another

Normal distribution A mathematical distribution, bell-shaped in nature, in which approximately 68 percent of all observations fall within one standard deviation of the mean, approximately 95 percent fall within two standard deviations of the mean, and approximately 99 percent of all observations fall within three standard deviations of the mean

Notice of loss A provision requiring an insured to notify the insurer in the event of loss, usually within a specified time

Objective risk The relative variation of actual from probable loss

Occurrence basis A clause in liability insurance policies under which covered acts must satisfy certain conditions; the results must be accidental and unintended, but the occurrence itself can be a deliberate act of an insured

Old-Age, Survivors, Disability and Health Insurance (OASDHI) Term describing the U.S. social security system

One-year term purchase option A life insurance option allowing the use of dividends to purchase one-year term protection at the owner's attained age

Open competition rating System under which states allow insurers in property-liability insurance to charge competitive rates without prior approval

Outage insurance Consequential loss insurance applicable to losses incurred during the time a piece of machinery has been put out of commission by a described accident

Outpatient coverages Health insurance benefits provided for services rendered when the insured is not in the hospital

Overseas Private Investment Corporation (OPIC) A federally sponsored corporation to offer insurance against specified political risks affecting given types of foreign investments

Paid-up insurance Life insurance on which all of the required premiums have been paid; the policy remains in force until the death of the insured

Parol evidence rule A legal doctrine making oral testimony to change the terms of the written contract ineffective

Participating plan Employee benefit plan in which the employee pays a portion of the cost of the benefit

Participating policy A life insurance policy in which a dividend (considered a return of an overcharge of a premium) is payable to the insured

Paul vs. Virginia The U.S. Supreme Court decision (1868) that held that insurance is not commerce; this established the authority of states to regulate insurance

Payor clause A clause in life insurance issued on a juvenile under which all future premiums are waived if the parent dies before the child reaches maturity

PBGC Term standing for the Pension Benefits Guaranty Corporation, a federal agency which insures pension benefits of defined benefit pension plans

Peril An exposure that causes a loss

Period certain life income annuity An annuity arranged to distribute the rent over a specified number of months or years

Personal auto policy (PAP) A widely used form for personal automobile insurance that generally replaces the older family auto policy (FAP)

Personal coverages Those lines of insurance designed to cover risks of individuals, as opposed to business firms

Poisson probability distribution A mathematical probability distribution in which more than one event can occur in a given time period and in which the mean is also equal to its variance

Policyholders' surplus The assets minus

A

liabilities as revealed by an insurer's balance sheet; net worth

Policy loan A loan made by a life insurer to an insured under the terms of cash value life insurance contracts

Policy writing The function of creating a specific insurance policy for a client, usually by the agent

Political risk Uncertainty of loss stemming from political events such as war, expropriation, currency blockage, or devaluation of currency

Preferred risk An insured unit receiving a lower insurance rate to reflect the reduced rate applicable to the group in which the unit is placed

Premium The total cost of insurance, found by multiplying the rate by the number of units covered

Premium/surplus ratio The ratio of premiums written to policyholders' surplus; normally this ratio falls between 2-to-1 and 3-to-1

Present value of an annuity due The present value, at some stated interest rate, of the rent of an annuity, with the first installment due immediately

Preshipment coverage A type of export credit insurance covering loss due to cancellation of order before the goods are shipped

Primary loss A dollar deductible, employed in domestic credit insurance on bad debts, intended to reflect normal credit losses of the insured firm

Primary rating factor An index number that reflects the additional risk of various classes of insureds, under rate-making plans in personal automobile insurance

Principle of group selection Principle under which insurers control costs by underwriting entire groups rather than individuals

Principle of indemnity Places limits on the amount that an insured may collect to the actual cash value of the property insured

Principle of insurable interest A legal principle in which an insured must demonstrate a financial interest in the subject of insurance as a precondition to recovery in event of loss; prevents the insurance from becoming a gambling contract

Prior approval rating System under which states must approve property-liability rates before they are used

Private insurance Insurance contracts written by firms in the private sector of the economy (as opposed to governmental insurers)

Probability The long-run chance or frequency of an occurrence

Probability distribution A mutually exclusive and collectively exhaustive list of all possible events that may result from a chance process

Probate A court process under which property is distributed and the terms of wills are carried out at the owner's death

Proof-of-loss clause A clause that requires an insured to prove the amount and type of loss suffered as a condition of collecting the claim

Property coverages Those lines of insurance designed to cover perils that may destroy property

Pro rata liability clause A clause that requires each insurer covering a risk to share pro rata any losses, in the proportion that its particular coverage bears to the total coverage on the risk

Pro rata treaty A reinsurance agreement under which premiums and losses are shared in some stated proportion

Proximate cause The direct cause of loss; exists if there is an unbroken chain of events leading from one act to a resulting injury or loss

Public insurance Insurance coverage written by governmental bodies, or operated by private agencies under governmental supervision and control

Pure premium The portion of an insurance premium that reflects the basic costs of loss, not including overhead or profit

Pure risk The uncertainty of a peril that

can produce only a loss, should the event occur

Quota-share treaty A reinsurance arrangement in which each insurer accepts a certain percentage of premiums and losses in a given line of insurance

Rate-making The process of developing pricing structures for insurance

Rating bureau An organization developing insurance rates on behalf of member insurers. Members of rating bureaus, or rating associations, may deviate from the rates that are promulgated by the bureau

Rebating A practice, usually prohibited under state law, in which a sales agent in insurance returns part of the commission to the purchaser

Reciprocal A form of insurer owned by policyholders who exchange coverage with each other; commonly found in the field of automobile insurance

Recour des voisins doctrine French legal doctrine underlying the Napoleonic Code making one party liable for loss to neighboring property caused by negligence of the first party

Refund annuity A life annuity that provides some amounts (the original cost of the annuity less any payments already made to the annuitant) to the named beneficiaries when the annuitant dies

Regular medical insurance Health insurance that covers physicians' services other than surgical procedures, such as doctor calls

Reinstatement clause A contract in life insurance that allows a policy that has lapsed to be reinstated

Reinsurance The shifting of risk by a primary insurer (known as the ceding company) to another insurer (known as the reinsurer)

Reinsurance pool or exchange A reinsurance arrangement in which several insurers join together to cover risks to which each is subject

Rent of an annuity The income paid under an annuity

Rental-value insurance Consequential coverage that insures the loss of rents in the event of the destruction of the insured property

Replacement-cost insurance Property insurance that pays for the current replacement cost of property without deducting for depreciation

Reporting form A type of fire insurance that requires the insured to make periodic reports showing the amount and location of insured property

Representation A statement made by an applicant for insurance, before the contract is made, which affects the willingness of the insurer to accept the risk

Res ipsa loquitur "The thing speaks for itself"—a level doctrine that enables a plaintiff to collect for losses without proving negligence on the part of the defendant

Respondeat superior A legal doctrine under which a principle is responsible for acts of his or her agent

Retaliatory law A law under which one state automatically imposes an equal burden (e.g., taxes) on insurers operating within its boundaries if another state imposes such burdens on insurers chartered in the first state

Retention The portion of a risk kept by an insurer for its own account while ceding the balance to a reinsurer; also refers to that portion of a risk retained by a corporation for its own account, the balance being transferred to a commercial insurer

Retirement test A set of conditions under OASDHI regulations determining how much, if any, retirement benefits may be paid under OASDHI if the worker is still in covered employment

Retrocession A process under which a reinsurer purchases insurance from another insurer, usually under the terms of a treaty in which each member of the reinsuring pool participates in the risk

Retrospective rating A method of pricing insurance in which the premium depends on the actual loss experience of the insured; the premium is adjusted for past periods according to this loss experience

Revocable beneficiary A beneficiary designation in a life insurance contract which may be changed by the owner

Risk Uncertainty as to economic loss

Risk handling methods Five general methods to manage risk are recognized: assumption, transfer, combination (includes insurance) avoidance, and hazard (loss) control

Risk management The executive function of dealing with specified risks facing the business enterprise or the individual; may incorporate the use of insurance, loss control, avoidance, risk retention, and other techniques

Risk retention Handling risk by bearing the results of risk, rather than employing other methods of handling it, such as transfer or avoidance

Robbery Unlawful taking of property from another person by force, threat of force, or violence

Rollover A procedure by which one may change the trustee or the type of funding of an IRA or other tax-favored retirement plan without federal income tax consequences

Safe-driver plan A method of adjusting rates in automobile insurance to reflect driving safety of the insured, in accordance with his or her record of traffic accidents or citations

Schedule bond A fidelity bond in which employees are listed by name, with the amounts for which they are bonded

Schedule rating A rating system in property-liability insurance in which the final rate is determined by applying a system of charges and credits, depending on the risk features

Second surgical expense opinion insurance Provision in group health plans under which a physician may be reimbursed for rendering a second opinion as to whether a given surgical procedure is needed

Section 401(k) plan Tax-deferred retirement plan allowed under federal tax law for employees of profit-making organizations

Section 403 (b) plan Tax-deferred retirement plan designed for employees of nonprofit organizations

Separate accounts A type of funding in which an insurer maintains accounting and funding on a basis other than its regular accounting. Usually applied to life insurers wishing to invest employer pension funds in common stocks

SEP-IRA plan An IRA plan sponsored by an employer, and usually subject to joint funding by the employer and the employee

Service basis A health insurance plan which promises benefits in the form of services rather than dollar indemnification

Service-of-process statute A state law enabling a person to bring a suit against any insurer doing business in a given state without traveling to the state in which the insurer is incorporated

Settlement options Provisions in the life insurance policy that offer alternatives to the insured in accepting the cash values or the death proceeds of a life insurance contract

Simplified Commercial Lines Portfolio Policy New policy offered by insurance industry; covers most types of property-liability losses

Single premium annuity An annuity whose purchase price is paid in one lump sum

Social insurance Insurance plans operated by public agencies, usually on a compulsory basis

Social Security Social insurance offered in the United States under the Old-Age, Survivors, Disability, and Health Insurance Program (OASDHI)

South-Eastern Underwriters Association (SEUA) Case Famous 1941 case in which insurers were held to be engaged in interstate commerce and were thus subject to federal regulation

Special multiple-peril policy (SMP) A multiple-peril coverage for business that offers a variety of coverages similar to those which are offered to individual homeowners under the homeowners' program

Speculative risk The uncertainty of an event that could produce either a profit or a loss, such as a business venture or a gambling transaction

Spendthrift trust clause A clause in life insurance that prevents the beneficiary's creditors from making legal attachment of proceeds of the life insurance

Standard deviation A measure of how close individual measurements are to their average value or a measure of the "spread" of a probability distribution, obtained by (1) subtracting each item in a distribution from its arithmetic mean, (2) squaring the resulting figures, (3) taking the mean of the sum of squares, and (4) obtaining the square root of this sum

Stock insurer A corporation organized as a profit-making venture in the field of insurance

Straight life annuity A life annuity in which there is no refund to any beneficiary at the death of the annuitant

Strict liability A legal doctrine that increases the degree of care required by a manufacturer of products; it is not necessary to prove negligence on the part of the manufacturer, it need be shown only that there was a defect in the product and that the defect caused harm

Subjective risk The risk based on the mental state of an individual who experiences uncertainty or doubt as to the outcome of a given event

Subrogation A doctrine that allows an insurer to "step into the shoes" of an insured to pursue the insured's rights to proceed against liable third parties for a loss

Substandard risk An insured unit receiving a higher insurance rate because of the greater risk of that group in which the unit is placed

Sue and labor clause A clause, usually in marine insurance, that requires the insured to attempt to protect the property from further loss, and to recover or attempt to recover from other parties

Suicide clause A clause in life insurance that requires payment by the insured, even in the event of suicide, if the suicide occurs after a two-year period

Supplemental Security Income (SSI) A federally sponsored welfare program for the aged, blind, and dependent, administered by the OASDHI program

Supplemental unemployment benefits (SUB) Privately sponsored program to provide unemployment benefits in addition to federally sponsored unemployment insurance

Supplementary payments The provisions in the liability policy that require an insurer to cover defense costs, interest on judgment, and costs of court bonds, in addition to paying judgments handed down by the court

Surety bond A financial guarantee bond that requires one party to respond to another for losses caused by incapacity, inability, or dishonesty, e.g., to guarantee work by a contractor

Surgical insurance Health insurance that provides coverage for various surgical operations

Surplus-line market Suppliers of insurance coverage in areas rejected by domestic insurers; Lloyd's of London offers most of its coverage in this manner, through special agents or brokers

Surplus treaty A reinsurance treaty in which the exposures cover individuals or business firms, as opposed to those treaties covering all kinds of insurance

Tariff European (British) term for a rate promulgated by a rating bureau

Tax sheltered annuity (TSA) An individual retirement plan under which the employee does not pay federal income taxes of the premiums or upon accumulating interest paid under the plan

Temporary disability laws The laws in some states (Hawaii, New Jersey, New York, California, Rhode Island, and Puerto Rico) that offer disability income for workers who are disabled either on or off the job, for a limited period, such as six months

Temporary life annuity An annuity whose rent stops at the death of a person named in the contract

Term life insurance A contract of life insurance of which the face value is payable if death of the insured should occur within a stated period

Terminable interest property Property qualifying under federal estate tax law for exemption from taxation in the estate of a spouse, if certain conditions are met

Testamentary trust A trust set up through a will

Testator A person making a will

Theft Any act of stealing

Third parties Individuals who have certain rights under the terms of insurance policies in which they may not be specifically indentified

3-D policy (dishonesty, destruction, and disappearance) An insurance contract that covers fidelity loss, loss of money and securities, loss from counterfeiting, and depositors' forgery

Title insurance Insurance against losses resulting when title to real estate is not marketable because of a title defect

Tort A civil wrong other than breach of contract

Treaty A contract or arrangement under which risks are shared by agreement between insurers, usually through a process of reinsurance

Treaty of Rome provisions 1957 treaty establishing the goal of harmonization of insurance laws in EEC nations

Trusteed plan An employee benefit plan managed by a private trustee, such as a bank, as opposed to an insurance company

Twisting The acts of a life insurance agent to persuade a client to drop one life policy and accept another, by misrepresenting the terms of either the present policy or the new policy, or both, to the detriment of the insured

Unadmitted insurance Insurance written to cover risks by insurers not chartered to do business in a given country. Practice is prohibited in most South-American and several other countries

Unallocated benefit plan A type of pension funding in which benefits are allocated to employees as a group and specific employees are not identified

Umbrella policy A liability policy designed to supplement basic liability contracts as excess coverage

Underinsured motorist provision The coverage that applies when the motorist meets the state law requirements for liability insurance but a judgment is in excess of these limits

Underwriter An individual accepting risk under specified terms

Underwriting All activities carried out to select risks acceptable to insurers in order that general company objectives are met

Underwriting gain A gain equal to 100 minus the sum of the loss and expense ratios

Unearned premium reserve An item of liability appearing on insurer's balance sheet reflecting liability for funds held by the insurer for premiums paid in advance

Unemployment insurance Insurance that pays an income to qualified individuals who are unemployed; recipients must usually demonstrate their ability, availability, and willingness to work as a condition of receiving benefits

Uninsured motorist provision The coverage in automobile insurance that provides bodily injury liability protection for the named insured for losses caused by motorists who are uninsured or have coverage less than that required by state law

Unsatisfied judgment fund A fund set up by a state to pay automobile accident awards that cannot be collected by any other means

Utility The subjective value given by an individual to monetary results; large losses generally cause greater relative loss of utility than small losses, for most individuals

Utmost good faith (Uberrimae fidei) A legal doctrine in which the highest standard of honesty is imposed upon the parties to an insurance contract

Valued policy law A state law that requires an insurer to pay the entire face amount of the insurance policy in the event of total loss of a covered object from an insured peril

Variable annuity An annuity of which the value may fluctuate according to the value of underlying securities into which the funds are invested

Variable life insurance Life insurance in which the face amount may fluctuate during the term of the policy in accordance with some variable, such as a cost-of-living index or with a value of common stocks into which the reserve assets are invested

Variance The square of the standard deviation

Vesting Term describing conditions under which employer provided benefits become the property of the employees on an unconditional basis

Volcanic eruption A peril insured against to homeowners policy; covers volcanic eruption other than loss by earthquake, land shock waves or tremor

Voluntary coverage Insurance contracts purchased at the discretion of the buyer

Waiver The voluntary relinquishing of a known right

Waiver-of-premium rider A clause in life insurance that waives the premium due in the event of disability of the insured for a period of six months or longer

Warranty A clause in an insurance contract that requires certain conditions, facts, or circumstances to be true before or after the contract is in force

Whole life insurance Life insurance offering protection as long as the insured lives, at a level premium

Will trust A trust set up under will; also called *testamentary trust*

Workers' compensation insurance Insurance that pays medical costs and disability income for persons injured on the job or who suffer from occupational illness

APPENDIX B

BEST'S RATINGS OF PROPERTY AND LIABILITY INSURERS

The following explanation of Best's Ratings of property and liability insurers is based on *Best's Insurance Reports,* published annually.

Companies and associations are assigned two ratings: a Policyholders' Rating and a Financial Rating. If an insurer is not rated, it may be for one of the following reasons: necessary information was refused or furnished too late for use; a company disputes the application of the rating system or disputes the construction of items appearing in the annual statements; the insurer writes primarily life insurance; or four years operating experience is not available. About 25 percent of the 1700 companies covered by Best in 1986 were not rated.

POLICYHOLDERS' RATINGS

Six policyholders' rating classifications are used: A+ and A (Excellent), B+ (Very good), B (Good), C+ (Fairly Good), and C (Fair), to reflect Best's opinion of the relative position of each institution in comparison with others, based upon averages within the insurance industry. Companies classified as Excellent are considered outstanding on a comparative basis, whether rated A or A+. Only nominal variances from industry standards generally exist among A companies, with the most common difference being in underwriting results. For other ratings, the variances or median points widen at each level.

Three quantitative factors and three qualitative factors determine Best's ratings. The quantitative factors are (1) profitability, (2) leverage, and (3) liquidity. The measures of these factors are compared to norms based on the property-liability industry as a whole.

The qualitative factors are (1) the amount and soundness of reinsurance, (2) the adequacy of reserves, and (3) management experience and competence.

Best has introduced modifiers to its basic ratings to further refine them. For example, an insurer may receive an "A_c," instead of "A." The "c" subscript means "contingent." The "c" may reflect temporary factors causing a decline in profitability, leverage, or liquidity. The subscript "w" means that the company is on Best's "watch" list because it experienced a decline in profitability or liquidity, or an increase in the amount of leverage employed, but the changes are not considered serious enough to warrant a reduced rating. About 20 different modifiers are used.

Profitability

Satisfactory profits are deemed essential by Best for a strongly rated insurer. Profits reflect a competent management and are measured by different financial ratios, such as the ratio of premiums earned to policyholders' surplus for the previous five years. Stability of profits is also considered, as are loss reserves, expense ratios, and yields on investments. The combined ratio (sum of the loss and expense ratios) and return on surplus are among the measures used.

Leverage

Leverage, or the use of debt, may increase the return on capital, but also may increase financial risk. Leverage is measured by Best in different ways, such as the ratio of net premiums written to policyholders' surplus and net liabilities to policyholders' surplus.

Liquidity

Sufficient liquidity is required to enable an insurer to pay losses and other obligations to policyholders. It enables an insurer to meet current needs without untimely sale of investments. It is measured by the quick ratio (cash and near cash items divided by current liabilities) and by cash flow.

In judging liquidity, the diversification and quality of assets are considered, such as proportion of bonds in the portfolio and adequacy of loss reserves.

Reinsurance

Best examines the quantity and quality of reinsurance used by the insurer in order to judge the adequacy of loss-spreading efforts. Reinsurance is necessary for such a purpose, especially for small insurers. The financial ratings of reinsurers are examined as a part of this procedure.

Reserves

Reserves significantly affect profitability and liquidity of an insurer. If reserves are deemed deficient, both solvency and profitability may be threatened. Both loss and unearned premium reserves are examined and compared to industry averages.

Management

The competence, experience, and integrity of management are judged by Best based on all of the above factors and by the experience of Best's officers in dealing with insurers over the past 80 years.

Effect of Size of Insurer

A small insurer can be just as safe as a large insurer. Many small insurers writing specialized lines are carefully and efficiently managed, and are sound in proportion to liabilities assumed. The policy of a small specialty fire insurance company that writes only moderate lines and conscientiously avoids writing in any congested area more than it could afford to pay in the event of a conflagration or a catastrophe may be more desirable than that of a much larger concern operating in less conservative lines.

FINANCIAL RATINGS

The financial rating indicates Best's estimate of the net safety factor of each company and is based upon the surplus to policyholders, plus equities, less indicated shortages in reserves, if any. Policyholders' surplus is the sum of capital and surplus funds in stock companies, and surplus funds as regards mutual companies, Lloyd's organizations, and reciprocal exchanges, including guaranty or permanent funds, if any; contingent resources are not considered.

Ratings of foreign companies are based upon their home office balance sheets that include the assets and liabilities of the United States branches.

Foreign companies keep in trust, for the exclusive benefit of U.S. branch policyholders and creditors as required by law, funds to cover all liabilities and statutory deposit requirements. Furthermore, all assets, whether trusteed or not, are subject to withdrawal only with the consent of the State Insurance Department of qualified entry. In addition to resources in this country, all of a company's free funds, capital and surplus, are liable for losses wherever they are incurred.

To prevent confusion of these size categories with the Best's Policyholders' Ratings the category is represented by Roman numerals ranging from Class I (the smallest) to Class XV (the largest) as designated below:

**Adjusted Policyholders
Surplus (000,000's)**

Class I	0	to	$1
Class II	$1	to	2
Class III	2	to	5
Class IV	5	to	10
Class V	10	to	25
Class VI	25	to	50
Class VII	50	to	100
Class VIII	100	to	250
Class IX	250	to	500
Class X	500	to	750
Class XI	750	to	1,000
Class XII	1,000	to	1,250
Class XIII	1,250	to	1,500
Class XIV	1,500	to	2,000
Class XV	2,000 or more		

APPENDIX C
BEST'S RATINGS OF LIFE INSURERS

Best's reports on life insurers cover such items as the history of a company, a description of the management and operations, a list of officers and directors, territory of operations, investment data and yields, quality of assets, and efficiency of operations.

Of special interest are Best's comments on an insurer's operations. Reports are not made on all life insurers—only those which are large enough and which have been in business a sufficient length of time for reasonable evaluation. The following criteria are used:

1. Net yield on investments
2. Required interest earnings to cover the interest assumed in rate calculations
3. Renewal expenses
4. Mortality experience
5. Lapse rate
6. Reserves
7. Reserve for dividends to policyholders

Each of these items is studied and compared to those typical of other insurers, and a ranking is made of the insurer over seven to ten categories, ranging from "good" to "poor" or "high" to "low." The ranking for renewal expenses, for example, is one of the following: remarkably low, very low, low, fairly low, moderate, fairly moderate, fairly high, high, and very high. Similar terms are employed for the other criteria.

As in property liability insurance, Best rates life insurers on profitability, leverage, and liquidity. Best also uses rating modifiers.

Rating classifications of life insurers are the same as those used for property and liability insurers, i.e., A+ and A (excellent), B+ (very good), B (good), C+ (fairly good), and C (fair). These ratings are assigned depending on Best's analysis of the quality of underwriting, management efficiency and cost control, adequacy of reserves for undischarged liabilities of all types, net resources to absorb unusual shock, and soundness of investments.

All life insurers are classed according to financial size in the same 15 groups shown for property liability insurers.

APPENDIX D
INTEREST TABLES

Problems in the use of life insurance and annuities may often be solved more easily by the use of interest tables than by laborious hand calculations or even by use of a computer. Examples of the use of these tables follow.

COMPOUND INTEREST

If $1,000 is left with an insurance company at interest as savings and the insurer pays 3 percent compound interest, what will the value of the savings be in 20 years?

Referring to Table D-1, we see that $1 left at 3 percent compound interest for 20 years amounts to $1.806. Therefore, the value of the savings would be $1,806.

PRESENT VALUE

If an insured wishes to have the sum of $1,000 in a savings account 20 years from now, how much must be deposited at compound interest if the insured receives interest at the rate of 3 percent? At 6 percent?

Referring to Table D-2, we see that at 3 percent interest, the present value of $1 is $0.55367. Therefore, the sum of $553.67 must be deposited at 3 percent in order to accumulate $1,000 in 20 years. At 6 percent, we see that $311.80 must be deposited.

AMOUNT OF AN ANNUITY

If an estate planner saves $1,000 a year, to what sum will this savings accumulate if it is earning 6 percent interest? If it is earning 7 percent interest? How much more will this savings be if it earns 7 percent instead of 6 percent after 20 years? After 40 years?

According to Table D-3, $1 per year accumulates to $36.785 in 20 years at 6 percent interest. Therefore, the saver would have an account worth $36,785. At 7 percent, the saver would have $40,995. Due to the operation of compound interest, after 20 years the saver has about 11 percent more money in the account at 7 percent than with 6 percent. After 40 years, the saver would have about 28 percent more in the account at 7 percent than at 6 percent ($199,635 ÷ $154,761 = 1.28).

PRESENT VALUE OF AN ANNUITY

1. If a person wishes to be paid the sum of $1,000 annually over a period of 20

years, how much money must the person pay, assuming the funds earn 6 percent interest? How much must be paid if the person wishes to receive $1,000 a year for 15 years?

From Table D-4 we see that at 6 percent interest the present value of $1 annually for 20 years is $11.469. Therefore, the annuitant must pay $11,469 in order to receive $1,000 a year for 20 years. For 15 years, the annuitant must pay $9,712.

2. If an insured has $25,000 of insurance proceeds available, how much of an annual income will be paid by the insurer in an equal amount over 20 years if the insurer earns 6 percent interest?

According to Table D-4, the present value of $1 a year for 20 years is $11,469.

Dividing this amount into $25,000, we obtain an annual equal payment of $2,107.97.

LIFE ANNUITIES

If a male insured, age 65, has $25,000 of proceeds, how much guaranteed life income per month can he leave his wife, who is the same age, under a 10-year certain, 20-year certain, and joint and last survivorship option?

Referring to Table D-5, we see that for each $1,000 of proceeds, the insured wife age 65 may obtain $5.63 monthly under the 10-year certain, $5.02 under the 20-year certain, and $5.23 under the joint and last survivorship option. Multiplying these sums by 25, we obtain $140.75, $125.50, and $130.75 respectively.

Table D–1

AMOUNT AT COMPOUND INTEREST $(1 + i)^n$

Periods			RATE i		
n	.03 (3%)	.06 (6%)	.07 (7%)	.08 (8%)	.10 (10%)
1	1.0300 0000	1.0600 0000	1.0700 0000	1.0800 0000	1.1000 0000
2	1.0609 0000	1.1236 0000	1.1449 0000	1.1664 0000	1.2100 0000
3	1.0927 2700	1.1910 1600	1.2250 4300	1.2597 1200	1.3310 0000
4	1.1255 0881	1.2624 7696	1.3107 9601	1.3604 8896	1.4641 0000
5	1.1592 7407	1.3382 2558	1.4025 5173	1.4693 2808	1.6105 1000
6	1.1940 5230	1.4185 1911	1.5007 3035	1.5868 7432	1.7715 6100
7	1.2298 7387	1.5036 3026	1.6057 8148	1.7138 2427	1.9487 1710
8	1.2667 7008	1.5938 4807	1.7181 8618	1.8509 3021	2.1435 8881
9	1.3047 7318	1.6894 7896	1.8384 5921	1.9990 0463	2.3579 4769
10	1.3439 1638	1.7908 4770	1.9671 5136	2.1589 2500	2.5937 4246
11	1.3842 3387	1.8982 9856	2.1048 5195	2.3316 3900	2.8531 1671
12	1.4257 6089	2.0121 9647	2.2521 9159	2.5181 7012	3.1384 2838
13	1.4685 3371	2.1329 2826	2.4098 4500	2.7196 2373	3.4522 7121
14	1.5125 8972	2.2609 0396	2.5785 3415	2.9371 9362	3.7974 9834
15	1.5579 6742	2.3965 5819	2.7590 3154	3.1721 6911	4.1772 4817
16	1.6047 0644	2.5403 5168	2.9521 6375	3.4259 4264	4.5949 7299
17	1.6528 4763	2.6927 7279	3.1588 1521	3.7000 1805	5.0544 7029
18	1.7024 3306	2.8543 3915	3.3799 3228	3.9960 1950	5.5599 1731
19	1.7535 0605	3.0255 9950	3.6165 2754	4.3157 0106	6.1159 0904
20	1.8061 1123	3.2071 3547	3.8696 8446	4.6609 5714	6.7274 9995
21	1.8602 9457	3.3995 6360	4.1405 6237	5.0338 3372	7.4002 4994
22	1.9161 0341	3.6035 3742	4.4304 0174	5.4365 4041	8.1402 7494
23	1.9735 8651	3.8197 4966	4.7405 2986	5.8714 6365	8.9543 0243
24	2.0327 9411	4.0489 3464	5.0723 6695	6.3411 8074	9.8497 3268
25	2.0937 7793	4.2918 7072	5.4274 3264	6.8484 7520	10.8347 0594
26	2.1565 9127	4.5493 8296	5.8073 5292	7.3963 5321	11.9181 7654
27	2.2212 8901	4.8223 4594	6.2138 6763	7.9880 6147	13.1099 9419
28	2.2879 2768	5.1116 8670	6.6488 3836	8.6271 0639	14.4209 9361
29	2.3565 6551	5.4183 8790	7.1142 5705	9.3172 7490	15.8630 9297
30	2.4272 6247	5.7434 9117	7.6122 5504	10.0626 5689	17.4494 0227
31	2.5000 8035	6.0881 0064	8.1451 1290	10.8676 6944	19.1943 4250
32	2.5750 8276	6.4533 8668	8.7152 7080	11.7370 8300	21.1137 7675
33	2.6523 3524	6.8405 8988	9.3253 3975	12.6760 4964	23.2251 5442
34	2.7319 0530	7.2510 2528	9.9781 1354	13.6901 3361	25.5476 6986
35	2.8138 6245	7.6860 8679	10.6765 8148	14.7853 4429	28.1024 3685
36	2.8982 7833	8.1472 5200	11.4239 4219	15.9681 7184	30.9126 8053
37	2.9852 2668	8.6360 8712	12.2236 1814	17.2456 2558	34.0039 4859
38	3.0747 8348	9.1542 5235	13.0792 7141	18.6252 7563	37.4043 4344
39	3.1670 2698	9.7035 0749	13.9948 2041	20.1152 9768	41.1447 7779
40	3.2620 3779	10.2857 1794	14.9744 5784	21.7245 2150	45.2592 5557
41	3.3598 9893	10.9028 6101	16.0226 6989	23.4624 8322	49.7851 8113
42	3.4606 9589	11.5570 3267	17.1442 5678	25.3394 8187	54.7636 9924
43	3.5645 1677	12.2504 5463	18.3443 5475	27.3666 4042	60.2400 6916
44	3.6714 5227	12.9854 8191	19.6284 5959	29.5559 7166	66.2640 7608
45	3.7815 9584	13.7646 1083	21.0024 5176	31.9204 4939	72.8904 8369
46	3.8950 4372	14.5904 8748	22.4726 2338	34.4740 8534	80.1795 3205
47	4.0118 9503	15.4659 1673	24.0457 0702	37.2320 1217	88.1974 8526
48	4.1322 5188	16.3938 7173	25.7289 0651	40.2105 7314	97.0172 3378
49	4.2562 1944	17.3775 0403	27.5299 2997	43.4274 1899	106.7189 5716
50	4.3839 0602	18.4201 5428	29.4570 2506	46.9016 1251	117.3908 5288

714

Table D–2

PRESENT VALUE OF $1/(1 + i)^n$

Periods			RATE i		
n	.03 (3%)	.06 (6%)	.07 (7%)	.08 (8%)	.10 (10%)
1	0.9708 7379	0.9433 9623	0.9345 7944	0.9259 2593	0.9090 9091
2	0.9425 9591	0.8899 9644	0.8734 3873	0.8573 3882	0.8264 4628
3	0.9151 4166	0.8396 1928	0.8162 9788	0.7938 3224	0.7513 1480
4	0.8884 8705	0.7920 9366	0.7628 9521	0.7350 2985	0.6830 1346
5	0.8626 0878	0.7472 5817	0.7129 8618	0.6805 8320	0.6209 2132
6	0.8374 8426	0.7049 6054	0.6663 4222	0.6301 6963	0.5644 7393
7	0.8130 9151	0.6650 5711	0.6227 4974	0.5834 9040	0.5131 5812
8	0.7894 0923	0.6274 1237	0.5820 0910	0.5402 6888	0.4665 0738
9	0.7664 1673	0.5918 9846	0.5439 3374	0.5002 4897	0.4240 9762
10	0.7440 9391	0.5583 9478	0.5083 4929	0.4631 9349	0.3855 4329
11	0.7224 2128	0.5267 8753	0.4750 9280	0.4288 8286	0.3504 9390
12	0.7013 7988	0.4969 6936	0.4440 1196	0.3971 1376	0.3186 3082
13	0.6809 5134	0.4688 3902	0.4149 6445	0.3676 9792	0.2896 6438
14	0.6611 1781	0.4423 0096	0.3878 1724	0.3404 6104	0.2633 3125
15	0.6418 6195	0.4172 6506	0.3624 4602	0.3152 4170	0.2393 9205
16	0.6231 6694	0.3936 4628	0.3387 3460	0.2918 9047	0.2176 2914
17	0.6050 1645	0.3713 6442	0.3165 7439	0.2702 6895	0.1978 4467
18	0.5873 9461	0.3503 4379	0.2958 6392	0.2502 4903	0.1798 5879
19	0.5702 8603	0.3305 1301	0.2765 0833	0.2317 1206	0.1635 0799
20	0.5536 7575	0.3118 0473	0.2584 1900	0.2145 4821	0.1486 4363
21	0.5375 4928	0.2941 5540	0.2415 1309	0.1986 5575	0.1351 3057
22	0.5218 9250	0.2775 0510	0.2257 1317	0.1839 4051	0.1228 4597
23	0.5066 9175	0.2617 9726	0.2109 4688	0.1703 1528	0.1116 7816
24	0.4919 3374	0.2469 7855	0.1971 4662	0.1576 9934	0.1015 2560
25	0.4776 0557	0.2329 9863	0.1842 4918	0.1460 1790	0.0922 9600
26	0.4636 9473	0.2198 1003	0.1721 9549	0.1352 0176	0.0839 0545
27	0.4501 8906	0.2073 6795	0.1609 3037	0.1251 8682	0.0762 7768
28	0.4370 7675	0.1956 3014	0.1504 0221	0.1159 1372	0.0693 4335
29	0.4243 4636	0.1845 5674	0.1405 6282	0.1073 2752	0.0630 3941
30	0.4119 8676	0.1741 1013	0.1313 6712	0.0993 7733	0.0573 0855
31	0.3999 8715	0.1642 5484	0.1227 7301	0.0920 1605	0.0520 9868
32	0.3883 3703	0.1549 5740	0.1147 4113	0.0852 0005	0.0473 6244
33	0.3770 2625	0.1461 8622	0.1072 3470	0.0788 8893	0.0430 5676
34	0.3660 4490	0.1379 1153	0.1002 1934	0.0730 4531	0.0391 4251
35	0.3553 8340	0.1301 0522	0.0936 6294	0.0676 3454	0.0355 8410
36	0.3450 3243	0.1227 4077	0.0875 3546	0.0626 2458	0.0323 4918
37	0.3349 8294	0.1157 9318	0.0818 0884	0.0579 8572	0.0294 0835
38	0.3252 2615	0.1092 3885	0.0764 5686	0.0536 9048	0.0267 3486
39	0.3157 5355	0.1030 5552	0.0714 5501	0.0497 1341	0.0243 0442
40	0.3065 5684	0.0972 2219	0.0667 8038	0.0460 3093	0.0220 9493
41	0.2976 2800	0.0917 1904	0.0624 1157	0.0426 2123	0.0200 8630
42	0.2889 5922	0.0865 2740	0.0583 2857	0.0394 6411	0.0182 6027
43	0.2805 4294	0.0816 2962	0.0545 1268	0.0365 4084	0.0166 0025
44	0.2723 7178	0.0770 0908	0.0509 4643	0.0338 3411	0.0150 9113
45	0.2644 3862	0.0726 5007	0.0476 1349	0.0313 2788	0.0137 1921
46	0.2567 3653	0.0685 3781	0.0444 9859	0.0290 0730	0.0124 7201
47	0.2492 5876	0.0646 5831	0.0415 8746	0.0268 5861	0.0113 3819
48	0.2419 9880	0.0609 9840	0.0388 6679	0.0248 6908	0.0103 0745
49	0.2349 5029	0.0575 4566	0.0363 2410	0.0230 2693	0.0093 7041
50	0.2281 0708	0.0542 8836	0.0339 4776	0.0213 2123	0.0085 1855

Table D-3

AMOUNT OF ANNUITY $[(1 + i)^n - 1]/i$

Periods			RATE i		
n	.03 (3%)	.06 (6%)	.07 (7%)	.08 (8%)	.10 (10%)
1	1.0000 0000	1.0000 0000	1.0000 0000	1.0000 0000	1.0000 0000
2	2.0300 0000	2.0600 0000	2.0700 0000	2.0800 0000	2.1000 0000
3	3.0909 0000	3.1836 0000	3.2149 0000	3.2464 0000	3.3100 0000
4	4.1836 2700	4.3746 1600	4.4399 4300	4.5061 1200	4.6410 0000
5	5.3091 3581	5.6370 9296	5.7507 3901	5.8666 0096	6.1051 0000
6	6.4684 0988	6.9753 1854	7.1532 9074	7.3359 2904	7.7156 1000
7	7.6624 6218	8.3938 3765	8.6540 2109	8.9228 0336	9.4871 7100
8	8.8923 3605	9.8974 6791	10.2598 0257	10.6366 2763	11.4358 8810
9	10.1591 0613	11.4913 1598	11.9779 8875	12.4875 5784	13.5794 7691
10	11.4638 7931	13.1807 9494	13.8164 4796	14.4865 6247	15.9374 2460
11	12.8077 9569	14.9716 4264	15.7835 9932	16.6454 8746	18.5311 6706
12	14.1920 2956	16.8699 4120	17.8884 5127	18.9771 2646	21.3842 8377
13	15.6177 9045	18.8821 3767	20.1406 4286	21.4952 9658	24.5227 1214
14	17.0863 2416	21.0150 6593	22.5504 8786	24.2149 2030	27.9749 8336
15	18.5989 1389	23.2759 6988	25.1290 2201	27.1521 1393	31.7724 8169
16	20.1568 8130	25.6725 2808	27.8880 5355	30.3242 8304	35.9497 2986
17	21.7615 8774	28.2128 7976	30.8402 1730	33.7502 2568	40.5447 0285
18	23.4144 3537	30.9056 5255	33.9990 3251	37.4502 4374	45.5991 7313
19	25.1168 6844	33.7599 9170	37.3789 6479	41.4462 6324	51.1590 9045
20	26.8703 7449	36.7855 9120	40.9954 9232	45.7619 6430	57.2749 9949
21	28.6764 8572	39.9927 2668	44.8651 7678	50.4229 2144	64.0024 9944
22	30.5367 8030	43.3922 9028	49.0057 3916	55.4567 5516	71.4027 4939
23	32.4528 8370	46.9958 2769	53.4361 4090	60.8932 9557	79.5430 2433
24	34.4264 7022	50.8155 7735	58.1766 7076	66.7647 5922	88.4973 2676
25	36.4592 6432	54.8645 1200	63.2490 3772	73.1059 3995	98.3470 5943
26	38.5530 4225	59.1563 8272	68.6764 7036	79.9544 1515	109.1817 6538
27	40.7096 3352	63.7057 6568	74.4838 2328	87.3507 6836	121.0999 4192
28	42.9309 2252	68.5281 1162	80.6976 9091	95.3388 2983	134.2099 3611
29	45.2188 5020	73.6397 9832	87.3465 2927	103.9659 3622	148.6309 2972
30	47.5754 1571	79.0581 8622	94.4607 8632	113.2832 1111	164.4940 2269
31	50.0026 7818	84.8016 7739	102.0730 4137	123.3458 6800	181.9434 2496
32	52.5027 5852	90.8897 7803	110.2181 5426	134.2135 3744	201.1377 6745
33	55.0778 4128	97.3431 6471	118.9334 2506	145.9506 2044	222.2515 4420
34	57.7301 7652	104.1837 5460	128.2587 6481	158.6266 7007	245.4766 9862
35	60.4620 8181	111.4347 7987	138.2368 7835	172.3168 0368	271.0243 6848
36	63.2759 4427	119.1208 6666	148.9134 5984	187.1021 4797	299.1268 0533
37	66.1742 2259	127.2681 1866	160.3374 0202	203.0703 1981	330.0394 8586
38	69.1594 4927	135.9042 0578	172.5610 2017	220.3159 4540	364.0434 3445
39	72.2342 3275	145.0584 5813	185.6402 9158	238.9412 2103	401.4477 7789
40	75.4012 5973	154.7619 6562	199.6351 1199	259.0565 1871	442.5925 5568
41	78.6632 9753	165.0476 8356	214.6095 6983	280.7810 4021	487.8518 1125
42	82.0231 9645	175.9505 4457	230.6322 3972	304.2435 2342	537.6369 9237
43	85.4838 9234	187.5075 7724	247.7764 9650	329.5830 0530	592.4006 9161
44	89.0484 0911	199.7580 3188	266.1208 5125	356.9496 4572	652.6407 6077
45	92.7198 6139	212.7435 1379	285.7493 1084	386.5056 1738	718.9048 3685
46	96.5014 5723	226.5081 2462	306.7517 6260	418.4260 6677	791.7953 2054
47	100.3965 0095	241.0986 1210	329.2243 8598	452.9001 5211	871.9748 5259
48	104.4083 9598	256.5645 2882	353.2700 9300	490.1321 6428	960.1723 3785
49	108.5406 4785	272.9584 0055	378.9989 9951	530.3427 3742	1057.1895 7163
50	112.7968 6729	290.3359 0458	406.5289 2947	573.7701 5642	1163.9085 2880

716

Table D-4

PRESENT VALUE OF ANNUITY $[1 - (1 + i)^{-n}]/i$

Periods	RATE i				
n	.03 (3%)	.06 (6%)	.07 (7%)	.08 (8%)	.10 (10%)
1	0.9708 7379	0.9433 9623	0.9345 7944	0.9259 2593	0.9090 9091
2	1.9134 6970	1.8333 9267	1.8080 1817	1.7832 6475	1.7355 3719
3	2.8286 1135	2.6730 1195	2.6243 1604	2.5770 9699	2.4868 5199
4	3.7170 9840	3.4651 0561	3.3872 1126	3.3121 2684	3.1698 6545
5	4.5797 0719	4.2123 6379	4.1001 9744	3.9927 1004	3.7907 8677
6	5.4171 9144	4.9173 2433	4.7665 3966	4.6228 7966	4.3552 6070
7	6.2302 8296	5.5823 8144	5.3892 8940	5.2063 7006	4.8684 1882
8	7.0196 9219	6.2097 9381	5.9712 9851	5.7466 3894	5.3349 2620
9	7.7861 0892	6.8016 9227	6.5152 3225	6.2468 8791	5.7590 2382
10	8.5302 0284	7.3600 8705	7.0235 8154	6.7100 8140	6.1445 6711
11	9.2526 2411	7.8868 7458	7.4986 7434	7.1389 6426	6.4950 6101
12	9.9540 0399	8.3838 4394	7.9426 8630	7.5360 7802	6.8136 9182
13	10.6349 5533	8.8526 8296	8.3576 5074	7.9037 7594	7.1033 5620
14	11.2960 7314	9.2949 8393	8.7454 6799	8.2442 3698	7.3666 8746
15	11.9379 3509	9.7122 4899	9.1079 1401	8.5594 7869	7.6060 7951
16	12.5611 0203	10.1058 9527	9.4466 4860	8.8513 6916	7.8237 0864
17	13.1661 1847	10.4772 5969	9.7632 2299	9.1216 3811	8.0215 5331
18	13.7535 1308	10.8276 0348	10.0590 8691	9.3718 8714	8.2014 1210
19	14.3237 9911	11.1581 1649	10.3355 9524	9.6035 9920	8.3649 2009
20	14.8774 7486	11.4699 2122	10.5940 1425	9.8181 4741	8.5135 6372
21	15.4150 2414	11.7640 7662	10.8355 2733	10.0168 0316	8.6486 9429
22	15.9369 1664	12.0415 8172	11.0612 4050	10.2007 4366	8.7715 4026
23	16.4436 0839	12.3033 7898	11.2721 8738	10.3710 5895	8.8832 1842
24	16.9355 4212	12.5503 5753	11.4693 3400	10.5287 5828	8.9847 4402
25	17.4131 4769	12.7833 5616	11.6535 8318	10.6747 7619	9.0770 4002
26	17.8768 4242	13.0031 6619	11.8257 7867	10.8099 7795	9.1609 4547
27	18.3270 3147	13.2105 3414	11.9867 0904	10.9351 6477	9.2372 2316
28	18.7641 0823	13.4061 6428	12.1371 1125	11.0510 7849	9.3065 6651
29	19.1884 5459	13.5907 2102	12.2776 7407	11.1584 0601	9.3696 0591
30	19.6004 4135	13.7648 3115	12.4090 4118	11.2577 8334	9.4269 1447
31	20.0004 2849	13.9290 8599	12.5318 1419	11.3497 9939	9.4790 1315
32	20.3887 6553	14.0840 4339	12.6465 5532	11.4349 9944	9.5263 7559
33	20.7657 9178	14.2302 2961	12.7537 9002	11.5138 8837	9.5694 3236
34	21.1318 3668	14.3681 4114	12.8540 0936	11.5869 3367	9.6085 7487
35	21.4872 2007	14.4982 4636	12.9476 7230	11.6545 6822	9.6441 5897
36	21.8322 5250	14.6209 8713	13.0352 0776	11.7171 9279	9.6765 0816
37	22.1672 3544	14.7367 8031	13.1170 1660	11.7751 7851	9.7059 1651
38	22.4924 6159	14.8460 1916	13.1934 7345	11.8288 6899	9.7326 5137
39	22.8082 1513	14.9490 7468	13.2649 2846	11.8785 8240	9.7569 5579
40	23.1147 7197	15.0462 9687	13.3317 0884	11.9246 1333	9.7790 5072
41	23.4123 9998	15.1380 1592	13.3941 2041	11.9672 3457	9.7991 3702
42	23.7013 5920	15.2245 4332	13.4524 4898	12.0066 9867	9.8173 9729
43	23.9819 0213	15.3061 7294	13.5069 6167	12.0432 3951	9.8339 9753
44	24.2542 7392	15.3831 8202	13.5579 0810	12.0770 7362	9.8490 8867
45	24.5187 1254	15.4558 3209	13.6055 2159	12.1084 0150	9.8628 0788
46	24.7754 4907	15.5243 6990	13.6500 2018	12.1374 0880	9.8752 7989
47	25.0247 0783	15.5890 2821	13.6916 0764	12.1642 6741	9.8866 1808
48	25.2667 0664	15.6500 2661	13.7304 7443	12.1891 3649	9.8969 2553
49	25.5016 5693	15.7075 7227	13.7667 9853	12.2121 6341	9.9062 9594
50	25.7297 6401	15.7618 6064	13.8007 4629	12.2334 8464	9.9148 1449

D

Table D-5

MONTHLY LIFE INCOME PER $1000 PROCEEDS
(3% INTEREST ASSUMPTION)[1]

Age	10 Years Cert. Men	20 Years Cert. Men	10 Years Cert. Women	20 Years Cert. Women	Joint and Last Survivor[2]
15	2.96	2.96	2.88	2.88	——
20	3.05	3.05	2.96	2.96	——
25	3.17	3.16	3.06	3.05	——
30	3.31	3.30	3.17	3.17	——
35	3.49	3.46	3.32	3.31	3.20
40	3.72	3.67	3.50	3.48	3.35
45	4.00	3.91	3.73	3.69	3.55
46	4.07	3.97	3.78	3.74	3.59
47	4.14	4.02	3.84	3.79	3.64
48	4.21	4.08	3.90	3.85	3.69
49	4.28	4.14	3.96	3.90	3.75
50	4.36	4.20	4.03	3.96	3.80
51	4.44	4.26	4.10	4.02	3.86
52	4.53	4.32	4.17	4.08	3.93
53	4.62	4.39	4.25	4.14	3.99
54	4.71	4.46	4.33	4.21	4.06
55	4.81	4.52	4.42	4.28	4.14
56	4.92	4.59	4.51	4.35	4.22
57	5.03	4.66	4.61	4.42	4.30
58	5.15	4.73	4.71	4.50	4.39
59	5.27	4.80	4.82	4.57	4.49
60	5.40	4.87	4.94	4.65	4.59
61	5.53	4.94	5.06	4.72	4.70
62	5.68	5.00	5.19	4.80	4.82
63	5.83	5.07	5.33	4.88	4.95
64	5.98	5.13	5.47	4.95	5.08
65	6.15	5.18	5.63	5.02	5.23
66	6.32	5.24	5.79	5.09	5.39
67	6.50	5.28	5.96	5.15	5.56
68	6.68	5.33	6.14	5.21	5.74
69	6.88	5.36	6.33	5.27	5.94
70	7.07	5.40	6.53	5.32	6.15
71	7.27	5.42	6.73	5.36	6.38
72	7.48	5.45	6.94	5.40	6.63
73	7.68	5.46	7.16	5.43	6.91
74	7.88	5.48	7.38	5.45	7.21
75	8.08	5.49	7.60	5.47	7.53
80	8.94	5.51	8.64	5.51	——
85	9.42	5.51	9.32	5.51	——

[1]Participating during period certain. Since cost assumptions vary among insurers, these data should be considered as illustrative only.

[2]Man and woman of equal age, life only.

Table D-6

MONTHLY LIFE INCOME PER $1000 PROCEEDS
(5.75% INTEREST ASSUMPTION)
MALE LIVES*

Age	Without Refund	Ten Years Certain and Life	Installment Refund	Joint Life Income, ⅔ to Survivor, 120 Months Certain	
				Female Age	Amount Paid if Male is Age 65 at Death
45	$ 6.03	$5.81	$ 5.90	---	---
46	6.12	5.87	5.98	---	---
47	6.22	5.94	6.06	---	---
48	6.32	6.01	6.15	---	---
49	6.42	6.08	6.24	---	---
50	6.53	6.15	6.33	50	$4.59
51	6.64	6.23	6.42	51	4.65
52	6.76	6.30	6.52	52	4.71
53	6.88	6.38	6.62	53	4.77
54	7.00	6.45	6.73	54	4.83
55	7.14	6.53	6.84	55	4.90
56	7.27	6.61	6.96	56	4.96
57	7.42	6.69	7.08	57	5.02
58	7.57	6.77	7.21	58	5.08
59	7.73	6.85	7.35	59	5.15
60	7.90	6.93	7.49	60	5.22
61	8.06	6.99	7.61	61	5.29
62	8.22	7.05	7.74	62	5.36
63	8.40	7.10	7.88	63	5.43
64	8.59	7.16	8.03	64	5.51
65	8.79	7.21	8.18	65	5.59
66	8.99	7.25	8.33	66	5.67
67	9.20	7.28	8.48	67	5.75
68	9.42	7.31	8.64	68	5.83
69	9.66	7.34	8.81	69	5.91
70	9.92	7.37	8.99	70	5.99
71	10.20	7.39	9.19	71	6.07
72	10.50	7.41	9.39	72	6.14
73	10.82	7.42	9.61	73	6.22
74	11.16	7.44	9.83	74	6.29
75	11.52	7.45	10.07	75	6.37
76	11.91	7.46	10.33	---	---
77	12.32	7.46	10.60	---	---
78	12.76	7.46	10.89	---	---
79	13.23	7.47	11.19	---	---
80	13.72	7.47	11.51	---	---

*Monthly life income on a female life is approximately equal to that shown for a male life five years younger.

D

APPENDIX E
STANDARD FIRE POLICY

IN CONSIDERATION OF THE PROVISIONS AND STIPULATIONS HEREIN OR ADDED HERETO and of the premium above specified, this Company, for the term of *years specified above* from *inception date shown above* at Noon (Standard Time) to *expiration date shown above* at Noon (Standard Time) at location of property involved, to an amount not exceeding the amount(s) above specified, does insure *the insured named above* and legal representatives, to the extent of the actual cash value of the property at the time of loss, but not exceeding the amount which it would cost to repair or replace the property with material of like kind and quality within a reasonable time after such loss, without allowance for any increased cost of repair or reconstruction by reason of any ordinance or law regulating construction or repair, and without compensation for loss resulting from interruption of business or manufacture, nor in any event for more than the interest of the insured, against all **DIRECT LOSS BY FIRE, LIGHTNING AND BY REMOVAL FROM PREMISES ENDANGERED BY THE PERILS INSURED AGAINST IN THIS POLICY, EXCEPT AS HEREINAFTER PROVIDED,** to the property described herein while located or contained as described in this policy, or pro rata for five days at each proper place to which any of the property shall necessarily be removed for preservation from the perils insured against in this policy, but not elsewhere.

Assignment of this policy shall not be valid except with the written consent of this Company.

This policy is made and accepted subject to the foregoing provisions and stipulations and those hereinafter stated, which are hereby made a part of this policy, together with such other provisions, stipulations, and agreements as may be added hereto, as provided in this policy.

1 **Concealment,** This entire policy shall be void if, whether
2 **fraud.** before or after a loss, the insured has will-
3 fully concealed or misrepresented any ma-
4 terial fact or circumstance concerning this insurance or the
5 subject thereof, or the interest of the insured therein, or in case
6 of any fraud or false swearing by the insured relating thereto.
7 **Uninsurable** This policy shall not cover accounts, bills,
8 **and** currency, deeds, evidence of debt, money or
9 **excepted property.** securities; nor, unless specifically named
10 hereon in writing, bullion or manuscripts.
11 **Perils not** This Company shall not be liable for loss by
12 **included.** fire or other perils insured against in this
13 policy caused, directly or indirectly, by: (a)
14 enemy attack by armed forces, including action taken by mili-
15 tary, naval or air forces in resisting an actual or an immediately
16 impending enemy attack; (b) invasion; (c) insurrection; (d)
17 rebellion; (e) revolution; (f) civil war; (g) usurped power; (h)
18 order of any civil authority except acts of destruction at the time
19 of and for the purpose of preventing the spread of fire, provided
20 that such fire did not originate from any of the perils excluded
21 by this policy; (i) neglect of the insured to use all reasonable
22 means to save and preserve the property at and after a loss, or
23 when the property is endangered by fire in neighboring prem-
24 ises; (j) nor shall this Company be liable for loss by theft.
25 **Other insurance.** Other insurance may be prohibited or the
26 amount of insurance may be limited by en-
27 dorsement attached hereto.
28 **Conditions suspending or restricting insurance. Unless other-**
29 **wise provided in writing hereto this Company shall not**
30 **be liable for loss occurring**
31 (a) while the hazard is increased by any means within the con-
32 trol or knowledge of the insured; or
33 (b) while a described building, whether intended for occupancy
34 by owner or tenant, is vacant or unoccupied beyond a period of
35 sixty consecutive days; or
36 (c) **as a result of explosion or riot, unless fire ensues, and in**
37 that event for loss by fire only.
38 **Other perils** Any other peril to be insured against or sub-
39 **or subjects.** ject of insurance to be covered in this policy
40 shall be by endorsement in writing hereon or
41 added hereto.

86 **Pro rata liability.** This Company shall not be liable for a greater
87 proportion of any loss than the amount
88 hereby insured shall bear to the whole insurance covering the
89 property against the peril involved, whether collectible or not.
90 **Requirements in** The insured shall give immediate written
91 **case loss occurs.** notice to this Company of any loss, protect
92 the property from further damage, forthwith
93 separate the damaged and undamaged personal property, put
94 it in the best possible order, furnish a complete inventory of
95 the destroyed, damaged and undamaged property, showing in
96 detail quantities, costs, actual cash value and amount of loss
97 claimed; **and within sixty days after the loss, unless such time**
98 **is extended in writing by this Company, the insured shall render**
99 **to this Company a proof of loss,** signed and sworn to by the
100 insured, stating the knowledge and belief of the insured as to
101 the following: the time and origin of the loss, the interest of the
102 insured and of all others in the property, the actual cash value of
103 each item thereof and the amount of loss thereto, all encum-
104 brances thereon, all other contracts of insurance, whether valid
105 or not, covering any of said property, any changes in the title,
106 use, occupation, location, possession or exposures of said prop-
107 erty since the issuing of this policy, by whom and for what
108 purpose any building herein described and the several parts
109 thereof were occupied at the time of loss and whether or not it
110 then stood on leased ground, and shall furnish a copy of all the
111 descriptions and schedules in all policies and, if required, verified
112 plans and specifications of any building, fixtures or machinery
113 destroyed or damaged. The insured, as often as may be reason-
114 ably required, shall exhibit to any person designated by this
115 Company all that remains of any property herein described, and
116 submit to examinations under oath by any person named by this
117 Company, and subscribe the same; and, as often as may be
118 reasonably required, shall produce for examination all books of
119 account, bills, invoices and other vouchers, or certified copies
120 thereof if originals be lost, at such reasonable time and place as
121 may be designated by this Company or its representative, and
122 shall permit extracts and copies therof to be made.
123 **Appraisal.** In case the insured and this Company shall
124 fail to agree as to the actual cash value or
125 the amount of loss, then, on the written demand of either, each
126 shall select a competent and disinterested appraiser and notify

Appendix E   Standard Fire Policy

42 **Added provisions.**   The extent of the application of insurance
43   under this policy and of the contribution to
44 be made by this Company in case of loss, and any other pro-
45 vision or agreement not inconsistent with the provisions of this
46 policy, may be provided for in writing added hereto, but no pro-
47 vision may be waived except such as by the terms of this policy
48 is subject to change.

49 **Waiver**   No permission affecting this insurance shall
50 **provisions.**   exist, or waiver of any provision be valid,
51   unless granted herein or expressed in writing
52 added hereto. **No provision, stipulation or forfeiture shall be**
53 held to be waived by any requirement or proceeding on the part
54 of this Company relating to appraisal or to any examination
55 provided for herein.

56 **Cancellation**   This policy shall be canceled at any time
57 **of policy.**   at the request of the insured, in which case
58   this Company shall, upon sur-
59 render of this policy, refund the excess of paid premium above
60 the customary short rates for the expired time. This pol-
61 icy may be canceled at any time by this Company by giving
62 to the insured a five days' written notice of cancellation with
63 or without tender of the excess of paid premium above the pro
64 rata premium for the expired time, which excess, if not ten-
65 dered, shall be refunded. Notice of cancellation shall
66 state that said excess premium (if not tendered) will be re-
67 funded on demand.

68 **Mortgagee**   If loss hereunder is made payable, in whole
69 **interests and**   or in part, to a designated mortgagee not
70 **obligations.**   named herein as the insured, such interest in
71   this policy may be canceled by giving to such
72   mortgagee a ten days' written notice of can-
73 cellation.

74 If the insured fails to render proof of loss such mortgagee, upon
75 notice, shall render proof of loss in the form herein specified
76 within sixty (60) days thereafter and shall be subject to the pro-
77 visions hereof relating to appraisal and time of payment and of
78 bringing suit. If this Company shall claim that no liability ex-
79 isted as to the mortgagor or owner, it shall, to the extent of pay-
80 ment of loss to the mortgagee, be subrogated to all the mort-
81 gagee's rights of recovery, but without impairing mortgagee's
82 right to sue; or it may pay off the mortgage debt and require
83 an assignment thereof and of the mortgage. Other provisions
84 relating to the interests and obligations of such mortgage may
85 **be added hereto by agreement in writing.**

127 the other of the appraiser selected within twenty days of such
128 demand. The appraisers shall first select a competent and dis-
129 interested umpire; and failing for fifteen days to agree upon
130 such umpire, then, on request of the insured or this Company,
131 such umpire shall be selected by a judge of a court of record in
132 the state in which the property covered is located. The ap-
133 praisers shall then appraise the loss, stating separately actual
134 cash value and loss to each item; and, failing to agree, shall
135 submit their differences, only, to the umpire. An award in writ-
136 ing, so itemized, of any two when filed with this Company shall
137 determine the amount of actual cash value and loss. Each
138 appraiser shall be paid by the party selecting him and the ex-
139 penses of appraisal and umpire shall be paid by the parties
140 equally.

141 **Company's**   It shall be optional with this Company to
142 **options.**   take all, or any part, of the property at the
143   agreed or appraised value, and also to re-
144 pair, rebuild or replace the property destroyed or damaged with
145 other of like kind and quality within a reasonable time, on giv-
146 ing notice of its intention so to do within thirty days after the
147 receipt of the proof of loss herein required.

148 **Abandonment.**   There can be no abandonment to this Com-
149   pany of any property.

150 **When loss**   The amount of loss for which this Company
151 **payable.**   may be liable shall be payable sixty days
152   after proof of loss, as herein provided, is
153 received by this Company and ascertainment of the loss is made
154 either by agreement between the insured and this Company ex-
155 pressed in writing or by the filing with this Company of an
156 award as herein provided.

157 **Suit.**   No suit or action on this policy for the recov-
158   ery of any claim shall be sustainable in any
159 court of law or equity unless all the requirements of this policy
160 shall have been complied with, and unless commenced within
161 twelve months next after inception of the loss.

162 **Subrogation.**   This Company may require from the insured
163   an assignment of all right of recovery against
164 any part for loss to the extent that payment therefor is made
165 by this Company.

In Witness Whereof, this Company has executed and attested
these presents; but this policy shall not be valid unless countersigned
by the duly authorized Agent of this Company at the agency herein-
before mentioned.

APPENDIX F
PERSONAL AUTOMOBILE POLICY

AGREEMENT

In return for payment of the premium and subject to all the terms of this policy, we agree with you as follows:

DEFINITIONS

A. Throughout this policy, "you" and "your" refer to:
1. The "named insured" shown in the Declarations; and
2. The spouse if a resident of the same household.

B. "We", "us" and "our" refer to the Company providing this insurance.

C. For purposes of this policy, a private passenger type auto shall be deemed to be owned by a person if leased:
1. Under a written agreement to that person; and
2. For a continuous period of at least 6 months.

Other words and phrases are defined. They are in quotation marks when used.

D. "Bodily injury" means bodily harm, sickness or disease, including death that results.

E. "Business" includes trade, profession or occupation.

F. "Family member" means a person related to you by blood, marriage or adoption who is a resident of your household. This includes a ward or foster child.

G. "Occupying" means in, upon, getting in, on, out or off.

H. "Property damage" means physical injury to, destruction of or loss of use of tangible property.

I. "Trailer" means a vehicle designed to be pulled by a:
1. Private passenger auto; or
2. Pickup or van.
It also means a farm wagon or farm implement while towed by a vehicle listed in 1. or 2. above.

J. "Your covered auto" means:
1. Any vehicle shown in the Declarations.

2. Any of the following types of vehicles on the date you become the owner:
   a. a private passenger auto; or
   b. a pickup or van.

   This provision (J.2.) applies only if:
   a. you acquire the vehicle during the policy period;
   b. you ask us to insure it within 30 days after you become the owner; and
   c. with respect to a pickup or van, no other insurance policy provides coverage for that vehicle.

   If the vehicle you acquire replaces one shown in the Declarations, it will have the same coverage as the vehicle it replaced. You must ask us to insure a replacement vehicle within 30 days only if:
   a. you wish to add or continue Coverage for Damage to Your Auto; or
   b. it is a pickup or van used in any "business" other than farming or ranching.

   If the vehicle you acquire is in addition to any shown in the Declarations, it will have the broadest coverage we now provide for any vehicle shown in the Declarations.

3. Any "trailer" you own.

4. Any auto or "trailer" you do not own while used as a temporary substitute for any other vehicle described in this definition which is out of normal use because of its:
   a. breakdown;   d. loss; or
   b. repair;   e. destruction.
   c. servicing;

PP 00 01 04 86   Copyright, Insurance Services Office, Inc., 1985

723

PART A—LIABILITY COVERAGE

INSURING AGREEMENT

A. We will pay damages for "bodily injury" or "property damage" for which any "insured" becomes legally responsible because of an auto accident. Damages include pre-judgment interest awarded against the "insured." We will settle or defend, as we consider appropriate, any claim or suit asking for these damages. In addition to our limit of liability, we will pay all defense costs we incur. Our duty to settle or defend ends when our limit of liability for this coverage has been exhausted. We have no duty to defend any suit or settle any claim for "bodily injury" or "property damage" not covered under this policy.

B. "Insured" as used in this Part means:

1. You or any "family member" for the ownership, maintenance or use of any auto or "trailer."

2. Any person using "your covered auto."

3. For "your covered auto," any person or organization but only with respect to legal responsibility for acts or omissions of a person for whom coverage is afforded under this Part.

4. For any auto or "trailer," other than "your covered auto," any other person or organization but only with respect to legal responsibility for acts or omissions of you or any "family member" for whom coverage is afforded under this Part. This provision (B.4.) applies only if the person or organization does not own or hire the auto or "trailer."

SUPPLEMENTARY PAYMENTS

In addition to our limit of liability, we will pay on behalf of an "insured:"

1. Up to $250 for the cost of bail bonds required because of an accident, including related traffic law violations. The accident must result in "bodily injury" or "property damage" covered under this policy.

2. Premiums on appeal bonds and bonds to release attachments in any suit we defend.

3. Interest accruing after a judgment is entered in any suit we defend. Our duty to pay interest ends when we offer to pay that part of the judgment which does not exceed our limit of liability for this coverage.

4. Up to $50 a day for loss of earnings, but not other income, because of attendance at hearings or trials at our request.

5. Other reasonable expenses incurred at our request.

EXCLUSIONS

A. We do not provide Liability Coverage for any person:

1. Who intentionally causes "bodily injury" or "property damage."

2. For damage to property owned or being transported by that person.

3. For damage to property:

   a. rented to;

   b. used by; or

   c. in the care of;

   that person.

   This exclusion (A.3.) does not apply to damage to a residence or private garage.

4. For "bodily injury" to an employee of that person during the course of employment. This exclusion (A.4.) does not apply to "bodily injury" to a domestic employee unless workers' compensation benefits are required or available for that domestic employee.

5. For that person's liability arising out of the ownership or operation of a vehicle while it is being used to carry persons or property for a fee. This exclusion (A.5.) does not apply to a share-the-expense car pool.

6. While employed or otherwise engaged in the "business" of:

a. selling;	d. storing; or
b. repairing;	e. parking;
c. servicing;	

   vehicles designed for use mainly on public highways. This includes road testing and delivery. This exclusion (A.6.) does not apply to the ownership, maintenance or use of "your covered auto" by:

   a. you;

   b. any "family member;" or

   c. any partner, agent or employee of you or any "family member."

7. Maintaining or using any vehicle while that person is employed or otherwise engaged in any "business" (other than farming or ranching) not described in Exclusion A.6. This exclusion (A.7.) does not apply to the maintenance or use of a:

PP 00 01 04 86   Copyright, Insurance Services Office, Inc., 1985

EXCLUSIONS (Continued)

    a.   private passenger auto;

    b.   pickup or van that you own; or

    c.   "trailer" used with a vehicle described in a. or b. above.

8. Using a vehicle without a reasonable belief that that person is entitled to do so.

9. For "bodily injury" or "property damage" for which that person:

    a.   is an insured under a nuclear energy liability policy; or

    b.   would be an insured under a nuclear energy liability policy but for its termination upon exhaustion of its limit of liability.

A nuclear energy liability policy is a policy issued by any of the following or their successors:

    a.   American Nuclear Insurers;

    b.   Mutual Atomic Energy Liability Underwriters; or

    c.   Nuclear Insurance Association of Canada.

B. We do not provide Liability Coverage for the ownership, maintenance or use of:

1. Any motorized vehicle having fewer than four wheels.

2. Any vehicle, other than "your covered auto," which is:

    a.   owned by you; or

    b.   furnished or available for your regular use.

3. Any vehicle, other than "your covered auto," which is:

    a.   owned by any "family member;" or

    b.   furnished or available for the regular use of any "family member."

However, this exclusion (B.3.) does not apply to your maintenance or use of any vehicle which is:

    a.   owned by a "family member;" or

    b.   furnished or available for the regular use of a "family member."

LIMIT OF LIABILITY

A. The limit of liability shown in the Declarations for this coverage is our maximum limit of liability for all damages resulting from any one auto accident. This is the most we will pay regardless of the number of:

1. "Insureds;"

2. Claims made;

3. Vehicles or premiums shown in the Declarations; or

4. Vehicles involved in the auto accident.

B. We will apply the limit of liability to provide any separate limits required by law for bodily injury and property damage liability. However, this provision (B.) will not change our total limit of liability.

OUT OF STATE COVERAGE

If an auto accident to which this policy applies occurs in any state or province other than the one in which "your covered auto" is principally garaged, we will interpret your policy for that accident as follows:

A. If the state or province has:

1. A financial responsibility or similar law specifying limits of liability for "bodily injury" or "property damage" higher than the limit shown in the Declarations, your policy will provide the higher specified limit.

2. A compulsory insurance or similar law requiring a nonresident to maintain insurance whenever the nonresident uses a vehicle in that state or province, your policy will provide at least the required minimum amounts and types of coverage.

B. No one will be entitled to duplicate payments for the same elements of loss.

FINANCIAL RESPONSIBILITY

When this policy is certified as future proof of financial responsibility, this policy shall comply with the law to the extent required.

OTHER INSURANCE

If there is other applicable liability insurance we will pay only our share of the loss. Our share is the proportion that our limit of liability bears to the total of all applicable limits. However, any insurance we provide for a vehicle you do not own shall be excess over any other collectible insurance.

F

PP 00 01 04 86   Copyright, Insurance Services Office, Inc., 1985

PART B—MEDICAL PAYMENTS COVERAGE

INSURING AGREEMENT

A. We will pay reasonable expenses incurred for necessary medical and funeral services because of "bodily injury:"

1. Caused by accident; and

2. Sustained by an "insured."

We will pay only those expenses incurred within 3 years from the date of the accident.

B. "Insured" as used in this Part means:

1. You or any "family member:"

   a. while "occupying;" or

   b. as a pedestrian when struck by;

   a motor vehicle designed for use mainly on public roads or a trailer of any type.

2. Any other person while "occupying" "your covered auto."

EXCLUSIONS

We do not provide Medical Payments Coverage for any person for "bodily injury:"

1. Sustained while "occupying" any motorized vehicle having fewer than four wheels.

2. Sustained while "occupying" "your covered auto" when it is being used to carry persons or property for a fee. This exclusion (2.) does not apply to a share-the-expense car pool.

3. Sustained while "occupying" any vehicle located for use as a residence or premises.

4. Occurring during the course of employment if workers' compensation benefits are required or available for the "bodily injury."

5. Sustained while "occupying," or when struck by, any vehicle (other than "your covered auto") which is:

   a. owned by you; or

   b. furnished or available for your regular use.

6. Sustained while "occupying," or when struck by, any vehicle (other than "your covered auto") which is:

   a. owned by any "family member;" or

   b. furnished or available for the regular use of any "family member."

   However, this exclusion (6.) does not apply to you.

7. Sustained while "occupying" a vehicle without a reasonable belief that that person is entitled to do so.

8. Sustained while "occupying" a vehicle when it is being used in the "business" of an "insured." This exclusion (8.) does not apply to "bodily injury" sustained while "occupying" a:

   a. private passenger auto;

   b. pickup or van that you own; or

   c. "trailer" used with a vehicle described in a. or b. above.

9. Caused by or as a consequence of:

   a. discharge of a nuclear weapon (even if accidental);

   b. war (declared or undeclared);

   c. civil war;

   d. insurrection; or

   e. rebellion or revolution.

10. From or as a consequence of the following, whether controlled or uncontrolled or however caused:

   a. nuclear reaction;

   b. radiation; or

   c. radioactive contamination.

LIMIT OF LIABILITY

A. The limit of liability shown in the Declarations for this coverage is our maximum limit of liability for each person injured in any one accident. This is the most we will pay regardless of the number of:

1. "Insureds;"

2. Claims made;

3. Vehicles or premiums shown in the Declarations; or

4. Vehicles involved in the accident.

B. Any amounts otherwise payable for expenses under this coverage shall be reduced by any amounts paid or payable for the same expenses under Part A or Part C.

C. No payment will be made unless the injured person or that person's legal representative agrees in writing that any payment shall be applied toward any settlement or judgment that person receives under Part A or Part C.

OTHER INSURANCE

If there is other applicable auto medical payments insurance we will pay only our share of the loss. Our share is the proportion that our limit of liability bears to the total of all applicable limits. However, any insurance we provide with respect to a vehicle you do not own shall be excess over any other collectible auto insurance providing payments for medical or funeral expenses.

PP 00 01 04 86   Copyright, Insurance Services Office, Inc., 1985

PART C—UNINSURED MOTORISTS COVERAGE

INSURING AGREEMENT

A. We will pay damages which an "insured" is legally entitled to recover from the owner or operator of an "uninsured motor vehicle" because of "bodily injury:"

1. Sustained by an "insured;" and
2. Caused by an accident.

The owner's or operator's liability for these damages must arise out of the ownership, maintenance or use of the "uninsured motor vehicle."

Any judgment for damages arising out of a suit brought without our written consent is not binding on us.

B. "Insured" as used in this Part means:

1. You or any "family member."
2. Any other person "occupying" "your covered auto."
3. Any person for damages that person is entitled to recover because of "bodily injury" to which this coverage applies sustained by a person described in 1. or 2. above.

C. "Uninsured motor vehicle" means a land motor vehicle or trailer of any type:

1. To which no bodily injury liability bond or policy applies at the time of the accident.
2. To which a bodily injury liability bond or policy applies at the time of the accident. In this case its limit for bodily injury liability must be less than the minimum limit for bodily injury liability specified by the financial responsibility law of the state in which "your covered auto" is principally garaged.
3. Which is a hit and run vehicle whose operator or owner cannot be identified and which hits:
   a. you or any "family member;"
   b. a vehicle which you or any "family member" are "occupying;" or
   c. "your covered auto."
4. To which a bodily injury liability bond or policy applies at the time of the accident but the bonding or insuring company;
   a. denies coverage; or
   b. is or becomes insolvent.

However, "uninsured motor vehicle" does not include any vehicle or equipment:

1. Owned by or furnished or available for the regular use of you or any "family member."
2. Owned or operated by a self-insurer under any applicable motor vehicle law.
3. Owned by any governmental unit or agency.
4. Operated on rails or crawler treads.
5. Designed mainly for use off public roads while not on public roads.
6. While located for use as a residence or premises.

EXCLUSIONS

A. We do not provide Uninsured Motorists Coverage for "bodily injury" sustained by any person:

1. While "occupying," or when struck by, any motor vehicle owned by you or any "family member" which is not insured for this coverage under this policy. This includes a trailer of any type used with that vehicle.
2. If that person or the legal representative settles the "bodily injury" claim without our consent.
3. While "occupying" "your covered auto" when it is being used to carry persons or property for a fee. This exclusion (A.3.) does not apply to a share-the-expense car pool.
4. Using a vehicle without a reasonable belief that that person is entitled to do so.

B. This coverage shall not apply directly or indirectly to benefit any insurer or self-insurer under any of the following or similar law:

1. workers' compensation law; or
2. disability benefits law.

LIMIT OF LIABILITY

A. The limit of liability shown in the Declarations for this coverage is our maximum limit of liability for all damages resulting from any one accident. This is the most we will pay regardless of the number of:

1. "Insureds;"
2. Claims made;
3. Vehicles or premiums shown in the Declarations; or
4. Vehicles involved in the accident.

B. Any amounts otherwise payable for damages under this coverage shall be reduced by all sums:

1. Paid because of the "bodily injury" by or on behalf of persons or organizations who may be legally responsible. This includes all sums paid under Part A; and
2. Paid or payable because of the "bodily injury" under any of the following or similar law:
   a. workers' compensation law; or
   b. disability benefits law.

C. Any payment under this coverage will reduce any amount that person is entitled to recover for the same damages under Part A.

F

OTHER INSURANCE

If there is other applicable similar insurance we will pay only our share of the loss. Our share is the proportion that our limit of liability bears to the total of all applicable limits. However, any insurance we provide with respect to a vehicle you do not own shall be excess over any other collectible insurance.

ARBITRATION

A. If we and an "insured" do not agree:

1. Whether that person is legally entitled to recover damages under this Part; or

2. As to the amount of damages;

either party may make a written demand for arbitration. In this event, each party will select an arbitrator. The two arbitrators will select a third. If they cannot agree within 30 days, either may request that selection be made by a judge of a court having jurisdiction.

B. Each party will:

1. Pay the expenses it incurs; and

2. Bear the expenses of the third arbitrator equally.

C. Unless both parties agree otherwise, arbitration will take place in the county in which the "insured" lives. Local rules of law as to procedure and evidence will apply. A decision agreed to by two of the arbitrators will be binding as to:

1. Whether the "insured" is legally entitled to recover damages; and

2. The amount of damages. This applies only if the amount does not exceed the minimum limit for bodily injury liability specified by the financial responsibility law of the state in which "your covered auto" is principally garaged. If the amount exceeds that limit, either party may demand the right to a trial. This demand must be made within 60 days of the arbitrators' decision. If this demand is not made, the amount of damages agreed to by the arbitrators will be binding.

PART D—COVERAGE FOR DAMAGE TO YOUR AUTO

INSURING AGREEMENT

A. We will pay for direct and accidental loss to "your covered auto" or any "non-owned auto," including their equipment, minus any applicable deductible shown in the Declarations. We will pay for loss to "your covered auto" caused by:

1. Other than "collision" only if the Declarations indicate that Other Than Collision Coverage is provided for that auto.

2. "Collision" only if the Declarations indicate that Collision Coverage is provided for that auto.

If there is a loss to a "non-owned auto," we will provide the broadest coverage applicable to any "your covered auto" shown in the Declarations.

B. "Collision" means the upset of "your covered auto" or its impact with another vehicle or object.

Loss caused by the following is considered other than "collision:"

1. Missiles or falling objects;
2. Fire;
3. Theft or larceny;
4. Explosion or earthquake;
5. Windstorm;
6. Hail, water or flood;
7. Malicious mischief or vandalism;
8. Riot or civil commotion;
9. Contact with bird or animal; or
10. Breakage of glass.

If breakage of glass is caused by a "collision," you may elect to have it considered a loss caused by "collision."

C. "Non-owned auto" means any private passenger auto, pickup, van or "trailer" not owned by or furnished or available for the regular use of you or any "family member" while in the custody of or being operated by you or any "family member." However, "non-owned auto" does not include any vehicle used as a temporary substitute for a vehicle you own which is out of normal use because of its:

1. Breakdown;
2. Repair;
3. Servicing;
4. Loss; or
5. Destruction.

TRANSPORTATION EXPENSES

In addition, we will pay up to $10 per day, to a maximum of $300, for transportation expenses incurred by you. This applies only in the event of the total theft of "your covered auto." We will pay only transportation expenses incurred during the period:

1. Beginning 48 hours after the theft; and

2. Ending when "your covered auto" is returned to use or we pay for its loss.

PP 00 01 04 86   Copyright, Insurance Services Office, Inc., 1985

EXCLUSIONS

We will not pay for:

1. Loss to "your covered auto" which occurs while it is used to carry persons or property for a fee. This exclusion (1.) does not apply to a share-the-expense car pool.

2. Damage due and confined to:

    a. wear and tear;

    b. freezing;

    c. mechanical or electrical breakdown or failure; or

    d. road damage to tires.

    This exclusion (2.) does not apply if the damage results from the total theft of "your covered auto."

3. Loss due to or as a consequence of:

    a. radioactive contamination;

    b. discharge of any nuclear weapon (even if accidental);

    c. war (declared or undeclared);

    d. civil war;

    e. insurrection; or

    f. rebellion or revolution.

4. Loss to equipment designed for the reproduction of sound. This exclusion (4.) does not apply if the equipment is permanently installed in "your covered auto " or any "non-owned auto".

5. Loss to tapes, records or other devices for use with equipment designed for the reproduction of sound.

6. Loss to a camper body or "trailer" you own which is not shown in the Declarations. This exclusion (6.) does not apply to a camper body or "trailer" you:

    a. acquire during the policy period; and

    b. ask us to insure within 30 days after you become the owner.

7. Loss to any "non-owned auto" or any vehicle used as a temporary substitute for a vehicle you own, when used by you or any "family member" without a reasonable belief that you or that "family member" are entitled to do so.

8. Loss to:

    a. TV antennas;

    b. awnings or cabanas; or

    c. equipment designed to create additional living facilities.

9. Loss to any of the following or their accessories:

    a. citizens band radio;

    b. two-way mobile radio;

    c. telephone; or

    d. scanning monitor receiver.

    This exclusion (9.) does not apply if the equipment is permanently installed in the opening of the dash or console of "your covered auto" or any "non-owned auto". This opening must be normally used by the auto manufacturer for the installation of a radio.

10. Loss to any custom furnishings or equipment in or upon any pickup or van. Custom furnishings or equipment include but are not limited to:

    a. special carpeting and insulation, furniture, bars or television receivers;

    b. facilities for cooking and sleeping;

    c. height-extending roofs; or

    d. custom murals, paintings or other decals or graphics.

11. Loss to equipment designed or used for the detection or location of radar.

12. Loss to any "non-owned auto" being maintained or used by any person while employed or otherwise engaged in the "business" of:

    a. selling;   d. storing; or

    b. repairing;   e. parking;

    c. servicing;

    vehicles designed for use on public highways. This includes road testing and delivery.

13. Loss to any "non-owned auto" being maintained or used by any person while employed or otherwise engaged in any "business" not described in exclusion 12. This exclusion (13.) does not apply to the maintenance or use by you or any "family member" of a "non-owned auto" which is a private passenger auto or "trailer".

LIMIT OF LIABILITY

A. Our limit of liability for loss will be the lesser of the:

    1. Actual cash value of the stolen or damaged property; or

    2. Amount necessary to repair or replace the property.

    However, the most we will pay for loss to any "non-owned auto" which is a "trailer" is $500.

B. An adjustment for depreciation and physical condition will be made in determining actual cash value at the time of loss.

PAYMENT OF LOSS

We may pay for loss in money or repair or replace the damaged or stolen property. We may, at our expense, return any stolen property to:

1. You; or

2. The address shown in this policy.

If we return stolen property we will pay for any damage resulting from the theft. We may keep all or part of the property at an agreed or appraised value.

NO BENEFIT TO BAILEE

This insurance shall not directly or indirectly benefit any carrier or other bailee for hire.

OTHER INSURANCE

If other insurance also covers the loss we will pay only our share of the loss. Our share is the proportion that our limit of liability bears to the total of all applicable limits. However, any insurance we provide with respect to a "non-owned auto" or any vehicle used as a temporary substitute for a vehicle you own shall be excess over any other collectible insurance.

APPRAISAL

A. If we and you do not agree on the amount of loss, either may demand an appraisal of the loss. In this event, each party will select a competent appraiser. The two appraisers will select an umpire. The appraisers will state separately the actual cash value and the amount of loss. If they fail to agree, they will submit their differences to the umpire. A decision agreed to by any two will be binding. Each party will:

1. Pay its chosen appraiser; and

2. Bear the expenses of the appraisal and umpire equally.

B. We do not waive any of our rights under this policy by agreeing to an appraisal.

PART E—DUTIES AFTER AN ACCIDENT OR LOSS

A. We must be notified promptly of how, when and where the accident or loss happened. Notice should also include the names and addresses of any injured persons and of any witnesses.

B. A person seeking any coverage must:

1. Cooperate with us in the investigation, settlement or defense of any claim or suit.

2. Promptly send us copies of any notices or legal papers received in connection with the accident or loss.

3. Submit, as often as we reasonably require:

    a. to physical exams by physicians we select. We will pay for these exams.

    b. to examination under oath and subscribe the same.

4. Authorize us to obtain:

    a. medical reports; and

    b. other pertinent records.

5. Submit a proof of loss when required by us.

C. A person seeking Uninsured Motorists Coverage must also:

1. Promptly notify the police if a hit and run driver is involved.

2. Promptly send us copies of the legal papers if a suit is brought.

D. A person seeking Coverage for Damage to Your Auto must also:

1. Take reasonable steps after loss to protect "your covered auto" and its equipment from further loss. We will pay reasonable expenses incurred to do this.

2. Promptly notify the police if "your covered auto" is stolen.

3. Permit us to inspect and appraise the damaged property before its repair or disposal.

PART F—GENERAL PROVISIONS

BANKRUPTCY

Bankruptcy or insolvency of the "insured" shall not relieve us of any obligations under this policy.

CHANGES

This policy contains all the agreements between you and us. Its terms may not be changed or waived except by endorsement issued by us. If a change requires a premium adjustment, we will adjust the premium as of the effective date of change.

We may revise this policy form to provide more coverage without additional premium charge. If we do this your policy will automatically provide the additional coverage as of the date the revision is effective in your state.

FRAUD

We do not provide coverage for any "insured" who has made fraudulent statements or engaged in fraudulent conduct in connection with any accident or loss for which coverage is sought under this policy.

LEGAL ACTION AGAINST US

A. No legal action may be brought against us until there has been full compliance with all the terms of this policy. In addition, under Part A, no legal action may be brought against us until:

1. We agree in writing that the "insured" has an obligation to pay; or

2. The amount of that obligation has been finally determined by judgment after trial.

B. No person or organization has any right under this policy to bring us into any action to determine the liability of an "insured."

OUR RIGHT TO RECOVER PAYMENT

A. If we make a payment under this policy and the person to or for whom payment was made has a right to recover damages from another we shall be subrogated to that right. That person shall do:

1. Whatever is necessary to enable us to exercise our rights; and

2. Nothing after loss to prejudice them.

However, our rights in this paragraph (A.) do not apply under Part D, against any person using "your covered auto" with a reasonable belief that that person is entitled to do so.

B. If we make a payment under this policy and the person to or for whom payment is made recovers damages from another, that person shall:

1. Hold in trust for us the proceeds of the recovery, and

2. Reimburse us to the extent of our payment.

POLICY PERIOD AND TERRITORY

A. This policy applies only to accidents and losses which occur:

1. During the policy period as shown in the Declarations; and

2. Within the policy territory.

B. The policy territory is:

1. The United States of America, its territories or possessions;

2. Puerto Rico; or

3. Canada.

This policy also applies to loss to, or accidents involving, "your covered auto" while being transported between their ports.

TERMINATION

A. **Cancellation.** This policy may be cancelled during the policy period as follows:

1. The named insured shown in the Declarations may cancel by:

   a. returning this policy to us; or

   b. giving us advance written notice of the date cancellation is to take effect.

2. We may cancel by mailing to the named insured shown in the Declarations at the address shown in this policy:

   a. at least 10 days notice:

      (1) if cancellation is for nonpayment of premium; or

      (2) if notice is mailed during the first 60 days this policy is in effect and this is not a renewal or continuation policy; or

   b. at least 20 days notice in all other cases.

3. After this policy is in effect for 60 days, or if this is a renewal or continuation policy, we will cancel only:

   a. for nonpayment of premium; or

   b. if your driver's license or that of:

      (1) any driver who lives with you; or

      (2) any driver who customarily uses "your covered auto;"

      has been suspended or revoked. This must have occurred:

      (1) during the policy period; or

      (2) since the last anniversary of the original effective date if the policy period is other than 1 year; or

   c. if the policy was obtained through material misrepresentation.

B. **Nonrenewal.** If we decide not to renew or continue this policy, we will mail notice to the named insured shown in the Declarations at the address shown in this policy. Notice will be mailed at least 20 days before the end of the policy period. If the policy period is other than 1 year, we will have the right not to renew or continue it only at each anniversary of its original effective date.

C. **Automatic Termination.** If we offer to renew or continue and you or your representative do not accept, this policy will automatically terminate at the end of the current policy period. Failure to pay the required renewal or continuation premium when due shall mean that you have not accepted our offer.

If you obtain other insurance on "your covered auto," any similar insurance provided by this policy will terminate as to that auto on the effective date of the other insurance.

D. **Other Termination Provisions.**

1. If the law in effect in your state at the time this policy is issued, renewed or continued:

   a. requires a longer notice period;

   b. requires a special form of or procedure for giving notice; or

   c. modifies any of the stated termination reasons;

   we will comply with those requirements.

2. We may deliver any notice instead of mailing it. Proof of mailing of any notice shall be sufficient proof of notice.

3. If this policy is cancelled, you may be entitled to a premium refund. If so, we will send you the refund. The premium refund, if any, will be computed according to our manuals. However, making or offering to make the refund is not a condition of cancellation.

4. The effective date of cancellation stated in the notice shall become the end of the policy period.

TRANSFER OF YOUR INTEREST IN THIS POLICY

A. Your rights and duties under this policy may not be assigned without our written consent. However, if a named insured shown in the Declarations dies, coverage will be provided for:

1. The surviving spouse if resident in the same household at the time of death. Coverage applies to the spouse as if a named insured shown in the Declarations; and

2. The legal representative of the deceased person as if a named insured shown in the Declarations. This applies only with respect to the representative's legal responsibility to maintain or use "your covered auto."

B. Coverage will only be provided until the end of the policy period.

TWO OR MORE AUTO POLICIES

If this policy and any other auto insurance policy issued to you by us apply to the same accident, the maximum limit of our liability under all the policies shall not exceed the highest applicable limit of liability under any one policy.

F

APPENDIX G
WHOLE LIFE POLICY

THE COUNCIL LIFE INSURANCE COMPANY

The Council Life Insurance Company agrees to pay the benefits
provided in this policy, subject to its terms and conditions.
Executed at New York, New York on the Date of Issue.

David Olson

Secretary

Barbara Sloan

President

Life Policy — Participating

Amount payable at death of Insured $10,000.

Premiums payable to age 90.

Schedule of benefits and premiums page 2.

Right to Examine Policy—Please examine this policy carefully. The Owner may return
the policy for any reason within ten days after receiving it. If returned, the policy will be
considered void from the beginning and any premium paid will be refunded.

TO THE STUDENT:

There are no "standard" life insurance policies, and the contracts
vary in wording and appearance from company to company.
Sometimes there are also significant differences in policy
provisions. This policy is generally representative of contracts
issued in the United States.

A GUIDE TO THE PROVISIONS OF THIS POLICY

Accidental Death Benefit	Dividends
Beneficiaries	Loans
Cash Value, Extended Term,	Ownership
and Paid-up Insurance	Premiums and Reinstatement
Change of Policy	Specifications
Contract	Waiver of Premium Right

Endorsements Made At Issue Appear After "General Provisions." Additional Benefits, If Any, Are Provided By Rider.

Specifications

Plan and Additional Benefits	Amount	Premium	Years Payable
Whole Life (Premiums payable to age 90)	$10,000	$229.50	55
Waiver of Premium (To age 65)		4.30	30
Accidental Death (To age 70)	10,000	7.80	35

A premium is payable on the policy date and every 12 policy months thereafter. The first premium is $241.60.

TABLE OF GUARANTEED VALUES

END OF POLICY YEAR	CASH OR LOAN VALUE	PAID-UP INSURANCE	EXTENDED TERM INSURANCE	
			YEARS	DAYS
1	$ 14	$ 30	0	152
2	174	450	4	182
3	338	860	8	65
4	506	1,250	10	344
5	676	1,640	12	360
6	879	2,070	14	335
7	1,084	2,500	16	147
8	1,293	2,910	17	207
9	1,504	3,300	18	177
10	1,719	3,690	19	78
11	1,908	4,000	19	209
12	2,099	4,300	19	306
13	2,294	4,590	20	8
14	2,490	4,870	20	47
15	2,690	5,140	20	65
16	2,891	5,410	20	66
17	3,095	5,660	20	52
18	3,301	5,910	20	27
19	3,508	6,150	19	358
20	3,718	6,390	19	317
AGE 60	4,620	7,200	18	111
AGE 65	5,504	7,860	16	147

Paid-up additions and dividend accumulations increase the cash values; indebtedness decreases them.
The percentage referred to in section 5.6 is 83.000%.

Direct Beneficiary   Helen M. Benson, wife of the insured

Owner   Thomas A. Benson, the insured

Insured	Thomas A. Benson	**Age and Sex**	35 Male
Policy Date	May 1, 1978	**Policy Number**	000/00
Date of Issue	May 1, 1978		

SECTION 1. THE CONTRACT

1.1 LIFE INSURANCE BENEFIT

The Council Life Insurance Company agrees, subject to the terms and conditions of this policy, to pay the Amount shown on page 2 to the beneficiary upon receipt at its Home Office of proof of the death of the Insured.

1.2 INCONTESTABILITY

This policy shall be incontestable after it has been in force during the lifetime of the Insured for two years from the Date of Issue.

1.3 SUICIDE

If within two years from the Date of Issue the Insured dies by suicide, the amount payable by the Company shall be limited to the premiums paid.

1.4 DATES

The contestable and suicide periods commence with the Date of Issue. Policy months, years and anniversaries are computed from the Policy Date. Both dates are shown on page 2 of this policy.

1.5 MISSTATEMENT OF AGE

If the age of the Insured has been misstated, the amount payable shall be the amount which the premiums paid would have purchased at the correct age.

1.6 GENERAL

This policy and the application, a copy of which is attached when the policy is issued, constitute the entire contract. All statements in the application are representations and not warranties. No statement shall void this policy or be used in defense of a claim under it unless contained in the application.

Only an officer of the Company is authorized to alter this policy or to waive any of the Company's rights or requirements.

All payments by the Company under this policy are payable at its Home Office.

SECTION 2. OWNERSHIP

2.1 THE OWNER

The Owner is as shown on page 2, or his successor or transferee. All policy rights and privileges may be exercised by the Owner without the consent of any beneficiary. Such rights and privileges may be exercised only during the lifetime of the Insured and thereafter to the extent permitted by Sections 8 and 9.

2.2 TRANSFER OF OWNERSHIP

The Owner may transfer the ownership of this policy by filing written evidence of transfer satisfactory to the Company at its Home Office and, unless waived by the Company, submitting the policy for endorsement to show the transfer.

2.3 COLLATERAL ASSIGNMENT

The Owner may assign this policy as collateral security. The Company assumes no responsibility for the validity or effect of any collateral assignment of this policy. The Company shall not be charged with notice of any assignment unless the assignment is in writing and filed at its Home Office before payment is made.

The interest of any beneficiary shall be subordinate to any collateral assignment made either before or after the beneficiary designation.

A collateral assignee is not an Owner and a collateral assignment is not a transfer of ownership.

G

SECTION 3. PREMIUMS AND REINSTATEMENT

3.1 PREMIUMS

(a) Payment. All premiums after the first are payable at the Home Office or to an authorized agent. A receipt signed by an officer of the Company will be provided upon request.

(b) Frequency. Premiums may be paid annually, semiannually, or quarterly at the published rates for this policy. A change to any such frequency shall be effective upon acceptance by the Company of the premium for the changed frequency. Premiums may be paid on any other frequency approved by the Company.

(c) Default. If a premium is not paid on or before its due date, this policy shall terminate on the due date except as provided in Sections 3.1(d), 5.3 and 5.4.

(d) Grace Period. A grace period of 31 days shall be allowed for payment of a premium not paid on its due date. The policy shall continue in full force during this period. If the Insured dies during the grace period, the overdue premium shall be paid from the proceeds of the policy.

(e) Premium Refund at Death. The portion of any premium paid which applies to a period beyond the policy month in which the Insured died shall be refunded as part of the proceeds of this policy.

3.2 REINSTATEMENT

If the policy has not been surrendered for its cash value, it may be reinstated within five years after the due date of the unpaid premium provided the following conditions are satisfied:

(a) Within 31 days following expiration of the grace period, reinstatement may be made without evidence of insurability during the lifetime of the Insured by payment of the overdue premium.

(b) After 31 days following expiration of the grace period, reinstatement is subject to:

(i) receipt of evidence of insurability of the Insured satisfactory to the Company;

(ii) payment of all overdue premiums with interest from the due date of each at the rate of 6% compounded annually; or any lower rate established by the Company.

Any policy indebtedness existing on the due date of the unpaid premium, together with interest from that date, must be repaid or reinstated.

SECTION 4. DIVIDENDS

4.1 ANNUAL DIVIDENDS

This policy shall share in the divisible surplus, if any, of the Company. This policy's share shall be determined annually and credited as a dividend. Payment of the first dividend is contingent upon payment of the premium or premiums for the second policy year and shall be credited proportionately as each premium is paid. Thereafter, each dividend shall be payable on the policy anniversary.

4.2 USE OF DIVIDENDS

As directed by the Owner, dividends may be paid in cash or applied under one of the following:

(a) Paid-Up Additions. Dividends may be applied to purchase fully paid-up additional insurance. Paid-up additions will also share in the divisible surplus.

(b) Dividend Accumulations. Dividends may be left to accumulate at interest. Interest is credited at a rate of 3% compounded annually, or any higher rate established by the Company.

(c) Premium Payment. Dividends may be applied toward payment of any premium due within one year, if the balance of the premium is paid. If the balance is not paid, or if this policy is in force as paid-up insurance, the dividend will be applied to purchase paid-up additions.

If no direction is given by the Owner, dividends will be applied to purchase paid-up additions.

4.3 USE OF ADDITIONS AND ACCUMULATIONS

Paid-up additions and dividend accumulations increase the policy's cash value and loan value and are payable as part of the policy proceeds. Additions may be surrendered and accumulations withdrawn unless required under the Loan, Extended Term Insurance, or Paid-up Insurance provisions.

4.4 DIVIDEND AT DEATH

A dividend for the period from the beginning of the policy year to the end of the policy month in which the Insured dies shall be paid as part of the policy proceeds.

SECTION 5. CASH VALUE, EXTENDED TERM AND PAID-UP INSURANCE

5.1 CASH VALUE

The cash value, when all premiums due have been paid, shall be the reserve on this policy less the deduction described in Section 5.5, plus the reserve for any paid-up additions and the amount of any dividend accumulations.

The cash value within three months after the due date of any unpaid premium shall be the cash value on the due date reduced by any subsequent surrender of paid-up additions or withdrawal of dividend accumulations. The cash value at any time after such three months shall be the reserve on the form of insurance then in force, plus the reserve for any paid-up additions and the amount of any dividend accumulations.

If this policy is surrendered within 31 days after a policy anniversary, the cash value shall be not less than the cash value on that anniversary.

5.2 CASH SURRENDER

The Owner may surrender this policy for its cash value less any indebtedness. The policy shall terminate upon receipt at the Home Office of this policy and a written surrender of all claims. Receipt of the policy may be waived by the Company.

The Company may defer paying the cash value for a period not exceeding six months from the date of surrender. If payment is deferred 30 days or more, interest shall be paid on the cash value less any indebtedness at the rate of 3% compounded annually from the date of surrender to the date of payment.

5.3 EXTENDED TERM INSURANCE

If any premium remains unpaid at the end of the grace period, this policy shall continue in force as nonparticipating extended term insurance. The amount of insurance shall be the amount of this policy, plus any paid-up additions and dividend accumulations, less any indebtedness. The term insurance shall begin as of the due date of the unpaid premium and its duration shall be determined by applying the cash value less any indebtedness as a net single premium at the attained age of the Insured. If the term insurance would extend to or beyond attained age 100, paid-up insurance under Section 5.4 below will be provided instead.

5.4 PAID-UP INSURANCE

In lieu of extended term insurance this policy may be continued in force as participating paid-up life insurance.

Paid-up insurance may be requested by written notice filed at the Home Office before, or within three months after, the due date of the unpaid premium. The insurance will be for the amount that the cash value will purchase as a net single premium at the attained age of the Insured. Any indebtedness shall remain outstanding.

5.5 TABLE OF GUARANTEED VALUES

The cash values, paid-up insurance, and extended term insurance shown on page 2 are for the end of the policy year indicated. These values are based on the assumption that premiums have been paid for the number of years stated and are exclusive of any paid-up additions, dividend accumulations, or indebtedness. During the policy year allowance shall be made for any portion of a year's premium paid and for the time elapsed in that year. Values for policy years not shown are calculated on the same basis as this table and will be furnished on request. All values are equal to or greater than those required by the State in which this policy is delivered.

In determining cash values a deduction is made from the reserve. During the first five policy years, the deduction for each \$1,000 of Amount is \$9 plus \$.15 for each year of the Insured's issue age. After the fifth policy year, the deduction decreases yearly by one-fifth of the initial deduction until there is no deduction in the tenth and subsequent policy years. If the premium paying period is less than ten years, there is no deduction in the last two policy years of the premium paying period or thereafter.

5.6 RESERVES AND NET PREMIUMS

Reserves, net premiums and present values are determined in accordance with the Commissioners 1958 Standard Ordinary Mortality Table and 3% interest, except that for the first five years of any extended term insurance, the Commissioners 1958 Extended Term Insurance Table is used. All reserves are based on continuous payment of premiums and immediate payment of claims. Net annual premiums are the same in each policy year, except that if premiums are payable for more than 20 years, the net annual premium in the 21st and subsequent policy years is determined by applying the percentage shown on page 2 to the net annual premium for the 20th policy year. On the Policy Date, the present value of all future guaranteed benefits equals the present value of all future net annual premiums. The reserve at the end of any policy year is the excess of the present value of all future guaranteed benefits over the present value of all future net annual premiums. The reserve is exclusive of any additional benefits.

G

SECTION 6. LOANS

6.1 POLICY LOAN

The Owner may obtain a policy loan by assignment of this policy to the Company. The amount of the loan, plus any existing indebtedness, shall not exceed the loan value. No loan shall be granted if the policy is in force as extended term insurance. The Company may defer making a loan for six months unless the loan is to be used to pay premiums on policies issued by the Company.

6.2 PREMIUM LOAN

A premium loan shall be granted to pay an overdue premium if the premium loan option is in effect. If the loan value, less any indebtedness, is insufficient to pay the overdue premium, a premium will be paid for any other frequency permitted by this policy for which the loan value less any indebtedness is sufficient. The premium loan option may be elected or revoked by written notice filed at the Home Office.

6.3 LOAN VALUE

The loan value is the largest amount which, with accrued interest, does not exceed the cash value either on the next premium due date or at the end of one year from the date of the loan.

6.4 LOAN INTEREST

Interest is payable at the rate of 8% compounded annually, or at any lower rate established by the Company for any period during which the loan is outstanding.

The Company shall provide at least 30 days written notice to the Owner (or any other party designated by the Owner to receive notice under this policy) and any assignee recorded at the Home Office of any increase in interest rate on loans outstanding 40 or more days prior to the effective date of the increase.

Interest accrues on a daily basis from the date of the loan on policy loans and from the premium due date on premium loans, and is compounded annually. Interest unpaid on a loan anniversary is added to and becomes part of the loan principal and bears interest on the same terms.

6.5 INDEBTEDNESS

Indebtedness consists of unpaid policy and premium loans on the policy including accrued interest. Indebtedness may be repaid at any time. Any unpaid indebtedness will be deducted from the policy proceeds.

If indebtedness equals or exceeds the cash value, this policy shall terminate. Termination shall occur 31 days after a notice has been mailed to the address of record of the Owner and of any assignee recorded at the Home Office.

SECTION 7. CHANGE OF POLICY

7 CHANGE OF PLAN

The Owner may change this policy to any permanent life or endowment plan offered by the Company on the Date of Issue of this policy. The change may be made upon payment of any cost and subject to the conditions determined by the Company. For a change made after the first year to a plan having a higher reserve, the cost shall not exceed the difference in cash values or the difference in reserves, whichever is greater, plus 3½% of such difference.

SECTION 8. BENEFICIARIES

8.1 DESIGNATION AND CHANGE OF BENEFICIARIES

(a) By Owner. The Owner may designate and change direct and contingent beneficiaries and further payees of death proceeds:

(1) during the lifetime of the Insured.

(2) during the 60 days following the date of death of the Insured, if the Insured immediately before his death was not the Owner. Any such designation of direct beneficiary may not be changed. If the Owner is the direct beneficiary and elects a payment plan, any such designation of contingent beneficiaries and further payees may be changed.

(b) By Direct Beneficiary. The direct beneficiary may designate and change contingent beneficiaries and further payees if:

(1) the direct beneficiary is the Owner.

(2) at any time after the death of the Insured, no contingent beneficiary or further payee is living, and no designation is made by the Owner under Section 8.1 (a) (2).

(3) the direct beneficiary elects a payment plan after the death of the Insured, in which case the interest in the share of such direct beneficiary or any other payee designated by the Owner shall terminate.

(c) By Spouse (Marital Deduction Provision). Notwithstanding any provision of Section 8 or 9 of this policy to the contrary, if the Insured immediately before death was the Owner and if the direct beneficiary is the spouse of the Insured and survives the Insured, such direct beneficiary shall have the power to appoint all amounts payable under the policy either to the executors or administrators of the direct beneficiary's estate or to such other contingent beneficiaries and further payees as he may designate. The exercise of that power shall revoke any then existing designation of contingent beneficiaries and further payees and any election of a payment plan applying to them.

(d) Effective Date. Any designation or change of beneficiary shall be made by the filing and recording at the Home Office of a written request satisfactory to the Company. Unless waived by the Company, the request must be endorsed on the policy. Upon the recording, the request will take effect as of the date it was signed. The Company will not be held responsible for any payment or other action taken by it before the recording of the request.

8.2 SUCCESSION IN INTEREST OF BENEFICIARIES

(a) Direct Beneficiaries. The proceeds of this policy shall be payable in equal shares to the direct beneficiaries who survive to receive payment. The unpaid share of any direct beneficiary who dies while receiving payment shall be payable in equal shares to the direct beneficiaries who survive to receive payment.

(b) Contingent Beneficiaries. At the death of the last surviving direct beneficiary, payments due or to become due shall be payable in equal shares to the contingent beneficiaries who survive to receive payment. The unpaid share of any contingent beneficiary who dies while receiving payment shall be payable in equal shares to the contingent beneficiaries who survive to receive payment.

(c) Further Payees. At the death of the last to survive of the direct and contingent beneficiaries, the proceeds, or the withdrawal value of any payments due or to become due if a payment plan is in effect, shall be paid in one sum:

(1) in equal shares to the further payees who survive to receive payment; or
(2) if no further payees survive to receive payment, to the executors or administrators of the last to survive of the direct and contingent beneficiaries.

(d) Estate of Owner. If no direct or contingent beneficiaries or further payees survive the Insured, the proceeds shall be paid to the Owner or the executors or administrators of the Owner.

8.3 GENERAL

(a) Transfer of Ownership. A transfer of ownership will not change the interest of any beneficiary.

(b) Claims of Creditors. So far as permitted by law, no amount payable under this policy shall be subject to the claims of creditors of the payee.

(c) Succession under Payment Plans. A direct or contingent beneficiary succeeding to an interest in a payment plan shall continue under such plan subject to its terms, with the rights of transfer between plans and of withdrawal under plans as provided in this policy.

SECTION 9. PAYMENT OF POLICY BENEFITS

9.1 PAYMENT

Payment of policy benefits upon surrender or maturity will be made in cash or under one of the payment plans described in Section 9.2, if elected.

If policy benefits become payable by reason of the Insured's death, payment will be made under any payment plan then in effect. If no election of a payment plan is in effect, the proceeds will be held under the Interest Income Plan (Option A) with interest accumulating from the date of death until an election or cash withdrawal is made.

9.2 PAYMENT PLANS

(a) Interest Income Plan (Option A). The proceeds will earn interest which may be received in monthly payments or accumulated. The first interest payment is due one month after the plan becomes effective. Withdrawal of accumulated interest as well as full or partial proceeds may be made at any time.

(b) Installment Income Plans. Monthly installment income payments will be made as provided by the plan elected. The first payment is due on the date the plan becomes effective.

(1) Specified Period (Option B). Monthly installment income payments will be made providing for payment of the proceeds with interest over a specified period of one to 30 years. Withdrawal of the present value of any unpaid installments may be made at any time.

(2) Specified Amount (Option D). Monthly installment income payments will be made for a specified amount of not less than $5 per $1,000 of proceeds. Payments will continue until the entire proceeds with interest are paid, with the final payment not exceeding the unpaid balance. Withdrawal of the unpaid balance may be made at any time.

(c) Life Income Plans. Monthly life income payments will be made as provided by the plan elected. The first payment is due on the date the plan becomes effective. Proof of date of birth satisfactory to the Company must be furnished for any individual upon whose life income payments depend.

(1) Single Life Income (Option C). Monthly payments will be made for the selected certain period, if any, and thereafter during the remaining lifetime of the individual upon whose life income payments depend. The selections available are:

    (i) no certain period,
    (ii) a certain period of 10 or 20 years, or
    (iii) a refund certain period such that the sum of the income payments during the certain period will be equal to the proceeds applied under the plan, with the final payment not exceeding the unpaid balance.

(2) Joint and Survivor Life Income (Option E). Monthly payments will be made for a 10 year certain period and thereafter during the joint lifetime of the two individuals upon whose lives income payments depend and continuing during the remaining lifetime of the survivor.

(3) Withdrawal. Withdrawal of the present value of any unpaid income payments which were to be made during a certain period may be made at any time after the death of all individuals upon whose lives income payments depend.

(d) Payment Frequency. In lieu of monthly payments a quarterly, semiannual or annual frequency may be selected.

9.3 PAYMENT PLAN RATES

(a) Interest Income and Installment Income Plans. Proceeds under the Interest Income and Installment Income plans will earn interest at rates declared annually by the Company, but not less than a rate of 3% compounded annually. Interest in excess of 3% will increase payments, except that for the Installment Income Specified Amount Plan (Option D), excess interest will be applied to lengthen the period during which payments are made.

The present value for withdrawal purposes will be based on a rate of 3% compounded annually.

The Company may from time to time also make available higher guaranteed interest rates under the Interest Income and Installment Income plans, with certain conditions on withdrawal as then published by the Company for those plans.

(b) Life Income Plans. Life Income Plan payments will be based on rates declared by the Company. These rates will provide not less than 104% of the income provided by the Company's Immediate Annuities being offered on the date the plan becomes effective. The rates are based on the sex and age nearest birthday of any individual upon whose life income payments depend, and adjusted for any certain period and the immediate payment of the first income payment. In no event will payments under these rates be less than the minimums described in Section 9.3(c).

(c) Minimum Income Payments. Minimum monthly income payments for the Installment Income Plans (Options B and D) and the Life Income Plans (Options C and E) are shown in the Minimum Income Table. The minimum Life Income payments are determined as of the date the payment plan becomes effective and depend on the age nearest birthday adjusted for policy duration.

The adjusted age is equal to the age nearest birthday decreased by one year if more than 25 years have elapsed since the Policy Date, two years if more than 35 years have elapsed, three years if more than 40 years have elapsed, four years if more than 45 years have elapsed or five years if more than 50 years have elapsed.

9.4 ELECTION OF PAYMENT PLANS

(a) Effective Date. Election of payment plans for death proceeds made by the Owner and filed at the Home Office during the Insured's lifetime will be effective on the date of death of the Insured. All other elections of payment plans will be effective when filed at the Home Office, or later if specified.

(b) Death Proceeds. Payment plans for death proceeds may be elected:

(1) by the Owner during the lifetime of the Insured.

(2) by the Owner during the 60 days following the date of death of the Insured, if the Insured immediately before his death was not the Owner. Any such election may not be changed by the Owner.

(3) by a direct or contingent beneficiary to whom such proceeds become payable, if no election is then in effect and no election is made by the Owner under Section 9.4(b) (2).

(c) Surrender or Maturity Proceeds. Payment plans for surrender or maturity proceeds may be elected by the Owner for himself as direct beneficiary.

(d) Transfers Between Payment Plans. A direct or contingent beneficiary receiving payment under a payment plan with the right to withdraw may elect to transfer the withdrawal value to any other payment plan then available.

(e) Life Income Plan Limitations. An individual beneficiary may receive payments under a Life Income Plan only if the payments depend upon his life. A corporation may receive payments under a Life Income Plan only if the payments depend upon the life of the Insured, or a surviving spouse or dependent of the Insured.

(f) Minimum Amounts. Proceeds of less than $5,000 may not be applied without the Company's approval under any payment plan except the Interest Income Plan (Option A) with interest accumulated. The Company retains the right to change the payment frequency or pay the withdrawal value if payments under a payment plan are or become less than $25.

9.5 INCREASE OF MONTHLY INCOME

The direct beneficiary who is to receive the proceeds of this policy under a payment plan may increase the total monthly income by payment of an annuity premium to the Company. The premium, after deduction of charges not exceeding 2% and any applicable premium tax, shall be applied under the payment plan at the same rates as the policy proceeds. The net amount so applied may not exceed twice the proceeds payable under this policy.

MINIMUM INCOME TABLE

Minimum Monthly Income Payments Per $1,000 Proceeds

INSTALLMENT INCOME PLANS (Options B and D)

PERIOD (YEARS)	MONTHLY PAYMENT	PERIOD (YEARS)	MONTHLY PAYMENT	PERIOD (YEARS)	MONTHLY PAYMENT
1	$84.50	11	$8.86	21	$5.32
2	42.87	12	8.24	22	5.15
3	29.00	13	7.71	23	4.99
4	22.07	14	7.26	24	4.84
5	17.91	15	6.87	25	4.71
6	15.14	16	6.53	26	4.59
7	13.17	17	6.23	27	4.48
8	11.69	18	5.96	28	4.37
9	10.54	19	5.73	29	4.27
10	9.62	20	5.51	30	4.18

MINIMUM INCOME TABLE

Minimum Monthly Income Payments Per $1,000 Proceeds

LIFE INCOME PLANS

SINGLE LIFE MONTHLY PAYMENTS (Option C)					
ADJUSTED AGE		CERTAIN PERIOD			
MALE	FEMALE	NONE	10 YEARS	20 YEARS	REFUND
50	55	$ 4.62	$4.56	$4.34	$4.36
51	56	4.72	4.65	4.40	4.44
52	57	4.83	4.75	4.46	4.52
53	58	4.94	4.85	4.53	4.61
54	59	5.07	4.96	4.59	4.69
55	60	5.20	5.07	4.66	4.79
56	61	5.33	5.19	4.72	4.88
57	62	5.48	5.31	4.78	4.99
58	63	5.64	5.43	4.84	5.09
59	64	5.80	5.57	4.90	5.20
60	65	5.98	5.70	4.96	5.32
61	66	6.16	5.85	5.02	5.44
62	67	6.36	5.99	5.07	5.57
63	68	6.57	6.14	5.13	5.71
64	69	6.79	6.30	5.17	5.85
65	70	7.03	6.45	5.22	6.00
66	71	7.28	6.62	5.26	6.15
67	72	7.54	6.78	5.30	6.31
68	73	7.83	6.95	5.33	6.48
69	74	8.13	7.11	5.36	6.66
70	75	8.45	7.28	5.39	6.85
71	76	8.79	7.45	5.41	7.05
72	77	9.16	7.62	5.43	7.26
73	78	9.55	7.79	5.45	7.48
74	79	9.96	7.95	5.46	7.71
75	80	10.41	8.11	5.48	7.95

JOINT AND SURVIVOR MONTHLY PAYMENTS (Option E)

ADJUSTED AGE   **JOINT PAYEE ADJUSTED AGE**

MALE		45	50	55	60	65	70	75
	FEMALE	50	55	60	65	70	75	80
45	50	$3.68	$3.80	$3.90	$3.97	$4.02	$4.06	$4.10
50	55	3.80	3.97	4.13	4.25	4.34	4.41	4.46
55	60	3.90	4.13	4.35	4.56	4.72	4.84	4.92
60	65	3.97	4.25	4.56	4.86	5.13	5.33	5.48
65	70	4.02	4.34	4.72	5.13	5.51	5.85	6.10
70	75	4.06	4.41	4.84	5.33	5.85	6.33	6.73
75	80	4.10	4.46	4.92	5.48	6.10	6.73	7.28

G

WAIVER OF PREMIUM BENEFIT

1. THE BENEFIT

If total disability of the Insured commences before the policy anniversary nearest his 60th birthday, the Company will waive the payment of premiums becoming due during total disability of the Insured.

If total disability of the Insured commences on or after the policy anniversary nearest his 60th birthday but before the policy anniversary nearest his 65th birthday, the Company will waive the payment of premiums becoming due during total disability of the Insured and before the policy anniversary nearest his 65th birthday.

The Company will refund that portion of any premium paid which applies to a period of total disability beyond the policy month in which the disability began.

The premium for this benefit is shown on page 2.

2. DEFINITION OF TOTAL DISABILITY

Total disability means disability which:

(a) resulted from bodily injury or disease;
(b) began after the Date of Issue of this policy and before the policy anniversary nearest the Insured's 65th birthday;
(c) has existed continuously for at least six months; and
(d) prevents the Insured from engaging in an occupation. During the first 24 months of disability, occupation means the occupation of the Insured at the time such disability began; thereafter it means any occupation for which he is reasonably fitted by education, training or experience, with due regard to his vocation and earnings prior to disability.

The total and irrecoverable loss of the sight of both eyes, or of speech or hearing, or of the use of both hands, or of both feet, or of one hand and one foot, shall be considered total disability, even if the Insured shall engage in an occupation.

3. PROOF OF DISABILITY

Before any premium is waived, proof of total disability must be received by the Company at its Home Office:

(a) during the lifetime of the Insured;
(b) during the continuance of total disability; and
(c) not later than one year after the policy anniversary nearest the Insured's 65th birthday.

Premiums will be waived although proof of total disability was not given within the time specified, if it is shown that it was given as soon as reasonably possible, but not later than one year after recovery.

4. PROOF OF CONTINUANCE OF DISABILITY

Proof of the continuance of total disability may be required once a year. If such proof is not furnished, no further premiums shall be waived. Further proof of continuance of disability will no longer be required if, on the policy anniversary nearest the Insured's 65th birthday, the Insured is then and has been totally and continuously disabled for five or more years.

5. PREMIUMS

Any premium becoming due during disability and before receipt of proof of total disability is payable and should be paid. Any such premiums paid shall be refunded by the Company upon acceptance of proof of total disability. If such premiums are not paid, this benefit shall be allowed if total disability is shown to have begun before the end of the grace period of the first unpaid premium.

If on any policy anniversary following the date of disablement the Insured continues to be disabled and this benefit has not terminated, an annual premium will be waived.

6. TERMINATION

This benefit shall be in effect while this policy is in force, but shall terminate on the policy anniversary nearest the Insured's 65th birthday unless the Insured is then totally disabled and such disability occurred prior to the policy anniversary nearest the Insured's 60th birthday. It may also be terminated within 31 days of a premium due date upon receipt at the Home Office of the Owner's written request.

G

ACCIDENTAL DEATH BENEFIT

1. THE BENEFIT

The Company agrees to pay an Accidental Death Benefit upon receipt at its Home Office of proof that the death of the Insured resulted, directly and independently of all other causes, from accidental bodily injury, provided that death occurred while this benefit was in effect.

2. PREMIUM AND AMOUNT OF BENEFIT

The premium for and the amount of this benefit are shown on page 2. This benefit shall be payable as part of the policy proceeds.

3. RISKS NOT ASSUMED

This benefit shall not be payable for death of the Insured resulting from suicide, for death resulting from or contributed to by bodily or mental infirmity or disease, or for any other death which did not result, directly and independently of all other causes, from accidental bodily injury.

Even though death resulted directly and independently of all other causes from accidental bodily injury, this benefit shall not be payable if the death of the Insured resulted from:

(a) Any act or incident of war. The word "war" includes any war, declared or undeclared, and armed aggression resisted by the armed forces of any country or combination of countries.

(b) Riding in any kind of aircraft, unless the Insured was riding solely as a passenger in an aircraft not operated by or for the Armed Forces, or descent from any kind of aircraft while in flight. An Insured who had any duties whatsoever at any time on the flight or any leg of the flight with respect to any purpose of the flight or to the aircraft or who was participating in training shall not be considered a passenger.

4. TERMINATION

This benefit shall be in effect while this policy is in force other than under the Extended Term Insurance or Paid-up Insurance provisions, but shall terminate on the policy anniversary nearest the Insured's 70th birthday. It may also be terminated within 31 days of a premium due date upon receipt at the Home Office of the Owner's written request.

David Olson
Secretary
THE COUNCIL LIFE INSURANCE COMPANY

RECEIPT FOR PAYMENT AND CONDITIONAL LIFE INSURANCE AGREEMENT

When premium is paid at the time of application, complete this Agreement and give to the Applicant. No other Agreement will be recognized by the Company. If premium is not paid—do not detach.

THOMAS A. BENSON $10,000   LIFE POLICY - PARTICIPATING
Name of Proposed Insured   Face Amount   Plan
Received of ___THOMAS A. BENSON___
the sum of $ _241.60_ for the policy applied for in the application to THE COUNCIL INSURANCE COMPANY (CL) with the same date and number as this receipt. Checks, drafts, and money orders are accepted subject to collection.

NEW YORK, NEW YORK MAY 1 19 78.   J.R. WASHINGTON _____ Agent.
Place and Date

CONDITIONAL LIFE INSURANCE AGREEMENT

I. **No Insurance Ever in Force.** No insurance shall be in force at any time if the proposed insured is not an acceptable risk on the Underwriting Date for the policy applied for according to CL's rules and standards. No insurance shall be in force under an Additional Benefit for which the proposed insured is not an acceptable risk.

II. **Conditional Life Insurance.** If the proposed insured is an acceptable risk on the Underwriting Date, the insurance shall be in force subject to the following maximum amounts if the proposed insured dies before the policy is issued:

Life Insurance			Accidental Death Benefit	
Age at Issue	Policies Issued at Standard Premiums	Policies Issued at Higher Premiums	Age at Issue	Maximum Amount
0-24	$ 500,000	$250,000	0-14	$ 25,000
25-45	1,000,000	500,000	15-19	50,000
46-55	800,000	400,000	20-24	75,000
56-65	400,000	200,000	25-60	150,000
66-70	200,000	100,000	Over 60	-0-
Over 70	-0-	-0-		

Reduction in Maximum Amounts. The maximum amounts set forth in the preceding table shall be reduced by any existing CL insurance on the life of the proposed insured with an Issue Date within 90 days of the date of this Agreement or by any pending prepaid applications for CL insurance on the life of the proposed insured with an Underwriting Date within 90 days of the date of this Agreement.

Termination of Conditional Life Insurance. If the proposed insured is an acceptable risk for the policy applied for according to CL's rules and standards only at a premium higher than the premium paid, any insurance under this Agreement shall terminate on the date stated in a notice mailed by CL to the applicant unless by such date the applicant accepts delivery of the policy and pays the additional premium required.

Underwriting Date. The Underwriting Date is the date of page 2 (90-2) of the application or the date of the medical examination [if required, otherwise the date of the nonmedical, page 4 (90-4)], whichever is later.

III. **Premium Adjustment.** If the proposed insured is an acceptable risk for the policy applied for only at a premium higher than the premium paid and dies before paying the additional premium required, that additional premium shall be subtracted from the insurance benefit payable to the beneficiary.

IV. **Premium Refund.** Any premium paid for any insurance or Additional Benefit not issued or issued at a higher premium but not accepted by the applicant shall be returned to the applicant.

NOT A "BINDER"—NO INSURANCE WHERE SECTION I APPLIES—NO AGENT MAY MODIFY.

PART I   Life Insurance Application To *The COUNCIL Life Insurance Company*

IMPORTANT NOTICE—This application is subject to approval by the Company's Home Office. Be sure all questions in all parts of the application are answered completely and accurately, since the application is the basis of the insurance contract and will become part of any policy issued.

1. Insured's Full Name (Please Print-Give title as Mr., Dr., Rev., etc.)

	Mo., Day, Yr. of Birth	Ins. Age	Sex	Place of Birth	Social Security No.
MR. THOMAS A. BENSON	APRIL 6, 1943	35	M	BOSTON, MASS.	000-00-0000

Single ☐   Married ☑   Widowed ☐   Divorced ☐   Separated ☐

2. Addresses last 5 yrs.

		Number	Street	City	State	Zip Code	County	Yrs.
Mail to ☐ Home:	Present	217	E. 62 STREET	NEW YORK, N.Y.		10017	NEW YORK	6
	Former							
☑ Business:	Present	PEPPER, GRINSTEAD, ₤ CROUCH	55 E. 49TH ST			10017	NEW YORK	7
	Former							

3. Occupation

	Title	Describe Exact Duties	Yrs.
Present	ATTORNEY	REPRESENTS CLIENTS IN LEGAL MATTERS	7
Former			

4. a) Employer
   b) Any change contemplated? Yes ☐ (Explain in Remarks)   No ☑

5. Have you ever   Yes   No

   a) been rejected, deferred or discharged by the Armed Forces for medical reasons or applied for a government disability rating?   ☐   ☑

   b) applied for insurance or for reinstatement which was declined, postponed, modified or rated?   ☐   ☑

   c) used LSD, heroin, cocaine or methadone?   ☐   ☑

6. a) In the past 3 years have you

   (i) had your driver's license suspended or revoked or been convicted of more than one speeding violation?   ☐   ☑

   (ii) operated, been a crew member of, or had any duties aboard any kind of aircraft?   ☐   ☑

   (iii) engaged in underwater diving below 40 feet, parachuting, or motor vehicle racing?   ☐   ☑

   b) In the future, do you intend to engage in any activities mentioned in (ii) and (iii) of a) above?   ☐   ☑
   (If "Yes" to 5a or any of 6, complete Supplemental Form 3375)

7. Have you smoked one or more cigarettes within the past 12 months?   ☑   ☐

8. Are other insurance applications pending or contemplated?   ☐   ☑

9. Do you intend to go to any foreign country?   ☑   ☐

10. Will coverage applied for replace or change any life insurance or annuities? (If "Yes", submit Replacement Form)   ☐   ☑

11. Total Life Insurance in force $ 35,000   None ☐

12. Face Amount $ 10,000   Plan WL

   Accidental Death ☑   Waiver of Premium ☐
   Purchase Option—Regular ☐   Preferred ☐   PEP ☐   GOR ☐
   _____ units of Wife's Term—name: _____
   $_____ initial amount Decreasing Term, _____ Years
   (Joint ☐)   (Mot. Pro. ☐)   (Straight Line ☐)
   Children's Term ☐   Other: _____

13. Auto. Prem. Loan provision operative if available? Yes ☐   No ☑

14. Dividend Option
   Additions (for other than Term policies) ☐   Deposits ☐
   Reduce premium, if applicable, otherwise cash ☑
   Supplemental Protection (Keyman only) ☐
   1 Year Term—any balance to
   Deposits ☐   Additions ☐   Reduce prem. (cash if mo.) ☐

15. Beneficiary—for children's, wife's or joint insurance as provided in contract; for other insurance as follows, subject to policy's beneficiary provisions:

	(Name)	(Relationship to Insured)	
1st	HELEN M. BENSON	WIFE	if living, if not
2nd	DAVID A. BENSON	SON	if living, if not
3rd			if living, if not

   the executors or administrators of: Insured ☑   Other (use Remarks) ☐
   (Joint beneficiaries will receive equally or survivor, unless otherwise specified.)

16. Flexible Plan settlement (personal beneficiary only) ☐

17. Rights—During Insured's lifetime all rights belong to
   Insured ☑   Other: _____
   Trustee ☐ (attach Trust)
   (After Insured's death as provided in contract on wife's insurance.)

18. Premium—Frequency ANNUAL Amt. Paid $ 241.60   None ☐
   Have you received a Conditional Receipt? Yes ☑   No ☐

REMARKS [Include details (company, date, amt., etc.) for all "Yes" answers to questions 4b, 5b, 5c, 8, 9 and 10]

Q9: PLANS VACATION IN SWITZERLAND

I agree that: (1) No one but the Company's President, a Vice-President or Secretary has authority to accept information not contained in the application, to modify or enlarge any contract, or to waive any requirement. (2) Except as otherwise provided in any conditional receipt issued, any policy issued shall take effect upon its delivery and payment of the first premium during the lifetime of each person to be insured. Due dates of later premiums shall be as specified in the policy.

Dated at NEW YORK, N.Y. on MAY 1 19 78   Signature of Insured   Thomas A. Benson

Signature of Applicant (if other than Insured) who agrees to be bound by the representations and agreements in this and any other part of this application _____

(Name)   (Relationship)   (Complete address of Applicant)

Countersigned by Ed Hatey _____

Field Underwriter (Licensed Resident Agent)

G

Statements Forming Part Of Application To *The COUNCIL Life Insurance Company*
[Complete this Part if any Non-Medical or Family Insurance is Applied For]

1. Name of Insured **THOMAS A. BENSON**   Ins. Age **35**   Height **6** ft. **1** in.   Weight **185** lbs.

2. If Family, Children's, Wife's or Joint Insurance desired, other family members proposed for insurance:

Wife (include maiden name)	Ins. Age	Mo., Day, Yr. of Birth	Height ft. in.	Weight lbs.	Life in Force $	Place of Birth

Children	Sex	Ins. Age	Mo., Day, Yr. of Birth	Children	Sex	Ins. Age	Mo., Day, Yr. of Birth

3. Has any eligible dependent (a) been omitted from 2? Yes ☐ No ☐   (b) applied for insurance or for reinstatement which was declined, postponed, modified or rated or had a policy cancelled or renewal refused? Yes ☐ No ☐ (Give name, date, company in 8)

4. Have you or anyone else proposed for insurance, so far as you know, ever been treated for or had indication of (underline applicable item)   Yes   No
   a) high blood pressure? (If "Yes", list drugs prescribed and dates taken.)   ☐ ☑
   b) chest pain, heart attack, rheumatic fever, heart murmur, irregular pulse or other disorder of the heart or blood vessels?   ☐ ☑
   c) cancer, tumor, cyst, or any disorder of the thyroid, skin, or lymph glands?   ☐ ☑
   d) diabetes or anemia or other blood disorder?   ☐ ☑
   e) sugar, albumin, blood or pus in the urine, or venereal disease?   ☐ ☑
   f) any disorder of the kidney, bladder, prostate, breast or reproductive organs?   ☐ ☑
   g) ulcer, intestinal bleeding, hepatitis, colitis, or other disorder of the stomach, intestine, spleen, pancreas, liver or gall bladder?   ☐ ☑
   h) asthma, tuberculosis, bronchitis, emphysema or other disorder of the lungs?   ☐ ☑
   i) fainting, convulsions, migraine headache, paralysis, epilepsy or any mental or nervous disorder?   ☐ ☑
   j) arthritis, gout, amputation, sciatica, back pain or other disorder of the muscles, bones or joints?   ☐ ☑
   k) disorder of the eyes, ears, nose, throat or sinuses?   ☐ ☑
   l) varicose veins, hemorrhoids, hernia or rectal disorder?   ☐ ☑
   m) alcoholism or drug habit?   ☐ ☑

5. Have you or anyone else proposed for insurance, so far as you know, (underline applicable item)   Yes   No
   a) consulted or been examined or treated by any physician or practitioner in the past 5 years?   ☑ ☐
   b) had, or been advised to have, an x-ray, cardiogram, blood or other diagnostic test in the past 5 years?   ☑ ☐
   c) been a patient in a hospital, clinic, or other medical facility in the past 5 years?   ☐ ☑
   d) ever had a surgical operation performed or advised?   ☑ ☐
   e) ever made claim for disability or applied for compensation or retirement based on accident or sickness?   ☐ ☑

6. Are you or any other person proposed for insurance, so far as you know, in impaired physical or mental health, or under any kind of medication?   ☐ ☑

7. Weight change in last 6 months of adults proposed for insurance: **N.A.**

Name	Gain	Loss	Cause

8. Details of all "Yes" answers. For any checkup or routine examination, indicate what symptoms, if any, prompted it and include results of the examination and any special tests. Include clinic number if applicable.

Question No.	Name of Person	Illness & Treatment	No. of Attacks	Dates: Onset-Recovery	Doctor, Clinic or Hospital and Complete Address
5a	THOMAS A. BENSON	ANNUAL CHECKUP	—	—	LIFE EXTENSION INSTITUTE
5b	THOMAS A. BENSON	ROUTINE OF ANNUAL CHECKUP	—	—	"
5d	THOMAS A. BENSON	TONSILLECTOMY-AGE 5	1	JUNE 1949	BOSTON HOSPITAL 2 PITTS STREET, BOSTON, MASS.

So far as may be lawful, I waive for myself and all persons claiming an interest in any insurance issued on this application, all provisions of law forbidding any physician or other person who has attended or examined, or who may attend or examine, me or any other person covered by such insurance, from disclosing any knowledge or information which he thereby acquired.

I represent the statements and answers in this and in any other part of this application to be true and complete to the best of my knowledge and belief, and offer them to the Company for the purpose of inducing it to issue the policy or policies and to accept the payment of premiums thereunder. I also agree that payment of the first premium (if after this date) shall be a representation by me that such statements and answers would be the same if made at the time of such payment.

Dated at **NEW YORK, N.Y.** on **MAY 1** 19 **78**   Signature of Insured **Thomas A. Benson**

Witnessed by **Ed Hatley**   Signature of Wife (if insured) _____
Field Underwriter (Licensed Resident Agent)

AUTHORIZATION

For purposes of determining my eligibility for insurance, I hereby authorize any physician, practitioner, hospital, clinic, institution, insurance company, Medical Information Bureau, or other organization or person that has records or knowledge of me or my health to give any such information to the Council Life Insurance Company.
If application is made to The Council Life Insurance Company for insurance on any member of my family, this authorization also applies to such member. A photostatic copy of this authorization shall be as valid as the original.

Signed on **MAY 1** , 19 **78**   **Thomas A. Benson**
Signature of Insured

APPENDIX H
HOMEOWNERS' 84 PROGRAM POLICY

AGREEMENT

We will provide the insurance described in this policy in return for the premium and compliance with all applicable provisions of this policy.

DEFINITIONS

In this policy, "you" and "your" refer to the "named insured" shown in the Declarations and the spouse if a resident of the same household. "We," "us" and "our" refer to the Company providing this insurance. In addition, certain words and phrases are defined as follows:

1. **"bodily injury"** means bodily harm, sickness or disease, including required care, loss of services and death that results.

2. **"business"** includes trade, profession or occupation.

3. **"insured"** means you and residents of your household who are:

    a. your relatives; or

    b. other persons under the age of 21 and in the care of any person named above.

    Under Section II, **"insured"** also means:

    c. with respect to animals or watercraft to which this policy applies, any person or organization legally responsible for these animals or watercraft which are owned by you or any person included in 3a or 3b above. A person or organization using or having custody of these animals or watercraft in the course of any **business** or without consent of the owner is not an **insured;**

    d. with respect to any vehicle to which this policy applies:

        (1) persons while engaged in your employ or that of any person included in 3a or 3b above; or

        (2) other persons using the vehicle on an **insured location** with your consent.

4. **"insured location"** means:

    a. the **residence premises;**

    b. the part of other premises, other structures and grounds used by you as a residence and:

        (1) which is shown in the Declarations; or

        (2) which is acquired by you during the policy period for your use as a residence;

    c. any premises used by you in connection with a premises in 4a or 4b above;

    d. any part of a premises:

        (1) not owned by an **insured;** and

        (2) where an **insured** is temporarily residing;

    e. vacant land, other than farm land, owned by or rented to an **insured;**

    f. land owned by or rented to an **insured** on which a one or two family dwelling is being built as a residence for an **insured;**

    g. individual or family cemetery plots or burial vaults of an **insured;** or

    h. any part of a premises occasionally rented to an **insured** for other than **business** use.

5. **"occurrence"** means an accident, including exposure to conditions, which results, during the policy period, in:

    a. **bodily injury;** or

    b. **property damage.**

6. **"property damage"** means physical injury to, destruction of, or loss of use of tangible property.

7. **"residence employee"** means:

    a. an employee of an **insured** whose duties are related to the maintenance or use of the **residence premises,** including household or domestic services; or

    b. one who performs similar duties elsewhere not related to the **business** of an **insured.**

8. **"residence premises"** means:

   a. the one family dwelling, other structures, and grounds; or

   b. that part of any other building;

   where you reside and which is shown as the **"residence premises"** in the Declarations.

"Residence premises" also means a two family dwelling where you reside in at least one of the family units and which is shown as the **"residence premises"** in the Declarations.

SECTION I—PROPERTY COVERAGES

COVERAGE A—Dwelling

We cover:

1. the dwelling on the **residence premises** shown in the Declarations, including structures attached to the dwelling; and

2. materials and supplies located on or next to the **residence premises** used to construct, alter or repair the dwelling or other structures on the **residence premises.**

This coverage does not apply to land, including land on which the dwelling is located.

COVERAGE B—Other Structures

We cover other structures on the **residence premises** set apart from the dwelling by clear space. This includes structures connected to the dwelling by only a fence, utility line, or similar connection.

This coverage does not apply to land, including land on which the other structures are located.

We do not cover other structures:

1. used in whole or in part for **business;** or

2. rented or held for rental to any person not a tenant of the dwelling, unless used solely as a private garage.

The limit of liability for this coverage will not be more than 10% of the limit of liability that applies to Coverage A. Use of this coverage does not reduce the Coverage A limit of liability.

COVERAGE C—Personal Property

We cover personal property owned or used by an **insured** while it is anywhere in the world. At your request, we will cover personal property owned by:

1. others while the property is on the part of the **residence premises** occupied by an **insured;**

2. a guest or a **residence employee,** while the property is in any residence occupied by an **insured.**

Our limit of liability for personal property usually located at an **insured's** residence, other than the **residence premises,** is 10% of the limit of liability for Coverage C, or $1000, whichever is greater. Personal property in a newly acquired principal residence is not subject to this limitation for the 30 days from the time you begin to move the property there.

Special Limits of Liability. These limits do not increase the Coverage C limit of liability. The special limit for each numbered category below is the total limit for each loss for all property in that category.

1. $200 on money, bank notes, bullion, gold other than goldware, silver other than silverware, platinum, coins and medals.

2. $1000 on securities, accounts, deeds, evidences of debt, letters of credit, notes other than bank notes, manuscripts, passports, tickets and stamps.

3. $1000 on watercraft, including their trailers, furnishings, equipment and outboard motors.

4. $1000 on trailers not used with watercraft.

5. $1000 on grave markers.

6. $1000 for loss by theft of jewelry, watches, furs, precious and semi-precious stones.

7. $2000 for loss by theft of firearms.

8. $2500 for loss by theft of silverware, silver-plated ware, goldware, gold-plated ware and pewterware. This includes flatware, holloware, tea sets, trays and trophies made of or including silver, gold or pewter.

9. $2500 on property, on the **residence premises,** used at any time or in any manner for any **business** purpose.

10. $250 on property, away from the **residence premises,** used at any time or in any manner for any **business** purpose.

HO-3 Ed. 4-84

Property Not Covered. We do not cover:

1. articles separately described and specifically insured in this or other insurance;

2. animals, birds or fish;

3. motor vehicles or all other motorized land conveyances. This includes:

   a. equipment and accessories; or

   b. any device or instrument for the transmitting, recording, receiving or reproduction of sound or pictures which is operated by power from the electrical system of motor vehicles or all other motorized land conveyances, including:

      (1) accessories or antennas; or

      (2) tapes, wires, records, discs or other media for use with any such device or instrument;

   while in or upon the vehicle or conveyance.

   We do cover vehicles or conveyances not subject to motor vehicle registration which are:

   a. used to service an **insured's** residence; or

   b. designed for assisting the handicapped;

4. aircraft and parts. Aircraft means any contrivance used or designed for flight, except model or hobby aircraft not used or designed to carry people or cargo;

5. property of roomers, boarders and other tenants, except property of roomers and boarders related to an **insured;**

6. property in an apartment regularly rented or held for rental to others by an **insured;**

7. property rented or held for rental to others off the **residence premises;**

8. a. books of account, drawings or other paper records; or

   b. electronic data processing tapes, wires, records, discs or other software media;

   containing **business** data. But, we do cover the cost of blank or unexposed records and media;

9. credit cards or fund transfer cards except as provided in Additional Coverages 6.

COVERAGE D—Loss Of Use

The limit of liability for Coverage D is the total limit for all the coverages that follow.

1. If a loss covered under this Section makes that part of the **residence premises** where you reside not fit to live in, we cover, at your choice, either of the following. However, if the **residence premises** is not your principal place of residence, we will not provide the option under paragraph b. below.

   a. **Additional Living Expense,** meaning any necessary increase in living expenses incurred by you so that your household can maintain its normal standard of living; or

   b. **Fair Rental Value,** meaning the fair rental value of that part of the **residence premises** where you reside less any expenses that do not continue while the premises is not fit to live in.

   Payment under a. or b. will be for the shortest time required to repair or replace the damage or, if you permanently relocate, the shortest time required for your household to settle elsewhere.

2. If a loss covered under this Section makes that part of the **residence premises** rented to others or held for rental by you not fit to live in, we cover the:

   Fair Rental Value, meaning the fair rental value of that part of the **residence premises** rented to others or held for rental by you less any expenses that do not continue while the premises is not fit to live in.

   Payment will be for the shortest time required to repair or replace that part of the premises rented or held for rental.

3. If a civil authority prohibits you from use of the **residence premises** as a result of direct damage to neighboring premises by a Peril Insured Against in this policy, we cover the Additional Living Expense or Fair Rental Value loss as provided under 1 and 2 above for no more than two weeks.

The periods of time under 1, 2 and 3 above are not limited by expiration of this policy.

We do not cover loss or expense due to cancellation of a lease or agreement.

ADDITIONAL COVERAGES

1. **Debris Removal.** We will pay your reasonable expense for the removal of:

   a. debris of covered property if a Peril Insured Against causes the loss; or

   b. ash, dust or particles from a volcanic eruption that has caused direct loss to a building or property contained in a building.

   This expense is included in the limit of liability that applies to the damaged property. If the amount to be paid for the actual damage to the property plus the debris removal expense is more than the limit of liability for the damaged property, an additional 5% of that limit of liability is available for debris removal expense.

HO-3 Ed. 4-84   Copyright, Insurance Services Office, Inc., 1984

We will also pay your reasonable expense for the removal of fallen trees from the **residence premises** if:

a. coverage is not afforded under Additional Coverages 3. Trees, Shrubs and Other Plants for the peril causing the loss; or

b. the tree is not covered by this policy;

provided the tree damages covered property and a Peril Insured Against under Coverage C causes the tree to fall. Our limit of liability for this coverage will not be more than $500 in the aggregate for any one loss.

2. **Reasonable Repairs.** We will pay the reasonable cost incurred by you for necessary repairs made solely to protect covered property from further damage if a Peril Insured Against causes the loss. This coverage does not increase the limit of liability that applies to the property being repaired.

3. **Trees, Shrubs and Other Plants.** We cover trees, shrubs, plants or lawns, on the **residence premises,** for loss caused by the following Perils Insured Against: Fire or lightning, Explosion, Riot or civil commotion, Aircraft, Vehicles not owned or operated by a resident of the **residence premises,** Vandalism or malicious mischief or Theft.

The limit of liability for this coverage will not be more than 5% of the limit of liability that applies to the dwelling, or more than $500 for any one tree, shrub or plant. We do not cover property grown for **business** purposes.

This coverage is additional insurance.

4. **Fire Department Service Charge.** We will pay up to $500 for your liability assumed by contract or agreement for fire department charges incurred when the fire department is called to save or protect covered property from a Peril Insured Against. We do not cover fire department service charges if the property is located within the limits of the city, municipality or protection district furnishing the fire department response.

This coverage is additional insurance. No deductible applies to this coverage.

5. **Property Removed.** We insure covered property against direct loss from any cause while being removed from a premises endangered by a Peril Insured Against and for no more than 30 days while removed. This coverage does not change the limit of liability that applies to the property being removed.

6. **Credit Card, Fund Transfer Card, Forgery and Counterfeit Money.**

We will pay up to $500 for:

a. the legal obligation of an **insured** to pay because of the theft or unauthorized use of credit cards issued to or registered in an **insured's** name;

b. loss resulting from theft or unauthorized use of a fund transfer card used for deposit, withdrawal or transfer of funds, issued to or registered in an **insured's** name;

c. loss to an **insured** caused by forgery or alteration of any check or negotiable instrument; and

d. loss to an **insured** through acceptance in good faith of counterfeit United States or Canadian paper currency.

We do not cover use of a credit card or fund transfer card:

a. by a resident of your household;

b. by a person who has been entrusted with either type of card; or

c. if an **insured** has not complied with all terms and conditions under which the cards are issued.

All loss resulting from a series of acts committed by any one person or in which any one person is concerned or implicated is considered to be one loss.

We do not cover loss arising out of **business** use or dishonesty of an **insured.**

This coverage is additional insurance. No deductible applies to this coverage.

Defense:

a. We may investigate and settle any claim or suit that we decide is appropriate. Our duty to defend a claim or suit ends when the amount we pay for the loss equals our limit of liability.

b. If a suit is brought against an **insured** for liability under the Credit Card or Fund Transfer Card coverage, we will provide a defense at our expense by counsel of our choice.

c. We have the option to defend at our expense an **insured** or an **insured's** bank against any suit for the enforcement of payment under the Forgery coverage.

7. **Loss Assessment.** We will pay up to $1000 for your share of any loss assessment charged during the policy period against you by a corporation or association of property owners. This only applies when the assessment is made as a result of each direct loss to the property, owned by all members collectively, caused by a Peril Insured Against under Coverage A—Dwelling, other than earthquake or land shock waves or tremors before, during or after a volcanic eruption.

This coverage applies only to loss assessments charged against you as owner or tenant of the **residence premises.**

We do not cover loss assessments charged against you or a corporation or association of property owners by any governmental body.

HO-3 Ed. 4-84

8. Collapse. We insure for direct physical loss to covered property involving collapse of a building or any part of a building caused only by one or more of the following:

a. Perils Insured Against in Coverage C—Personal Property. These perils apply to covered building and personal property for loss insured by this additional coverage;

b. hidden decay;

c. hidden insect or vermin damage;

d. weight of contents, equipment, animals or people;

e. weight of rain which collects on a roof; or

f. use of defective material or methods in construction, remodeling or renovation if the collapse occurs during the course of the construction, remodeling or renovation.

Loss to an awning, fence, patio, pavement, swimming pool, underground pipe, flue, drain, cesspool, septic tank, foundation, retaining wall, bulkhead, pier, wharf or dock is not included under items b, c, d, e, and f unless the loss is a direct result of the collapse of a building.

Collapse does not include settling, cracking, shrinking, bulging or expansion.

This coverage does not increase the limit of liability applying to the damaged covered property.

SECTION I—PERILS INSURED AGAINST

COVERAGE A—DWELLING and
COVERAGE B—OTHER STRUCTURES

We insure against risks of direct loss to property described in Coverages A and B only if that loss is a physical loss to property; however, we do not insure loss:

1. involving collapse, other than as provided in Additional Coverage 8;

2. caused by:

a. freezing of a plumbing, heating, air conditioning or automatic fire protective sprinkler system or of a household appliance, or by discharge, leakage or overflow from within the system or appliance caused by freezing. This exclusion applies only while the dwelling is vacant, unoccupied or being constructed unless you have used reasonable care to:

   (1) maintain heat in the building; or

   (2) shut off the water supply and drain the system and appliances of water;

b. freezing, thawing, pressure or weight of water or ice, whether driven by wind or not, to a:

   (1) fence, pavement, patio or swimming pool;

   (2) foundation, retaining wall or bulkhead; or

   (3) pier, wharf or dock;

c. theft in or to a dwelling under construction, or of materials and supplies for use in the construction until the dwelling is finished and occupied;

d. vandalism and malicious mischief or breakage of glass and safety glazing materials if the dwelling has been vacant for more than 30 consecutive days immediately before the loss. A dwelling being constructed is not considered vacant;

e. constant or repeated seepage or leakage of water or steam over a period of weeks, months or years from within a plumbing, heating, air conditioning or automatic fire protective sprinkler system or from within a household appliance;

f. (1) wear and tear, marring, deterioration;

   (2) inherent vice, latent defect, mechanical breakdown;

   (3) smog, rust, mold, wet or dry rot;

   (4) smoke from agricultural smudging or industrial operations;

   (5) release, discharge or dispersal of contaminants or pollutants;

   (6) settling, cracking, shrinking, bulging or expansion of pavements, patios, foundations, walls, floors, roofs or ceilings; or

   (7) birds, vermin, rodents, insects or domestic animals.

If any of these cause water damage not otherwise excluded, from a plumbing, heating, air conditioning or automatic fire protective sprinkler system or household appliance, we cover loss caused by the water including the cost of tearing out and replacing any part of a building necessary to repair the system or appliance. We do not cover loss to the system or appliance from which this water escaped.

3. excluded under Section I—Exclusions.

Under items 1 and 2, any ensuing loss to property described in Coverages A and B not excluded or excepted in this policy is covered.

COVERAGE C—PERSONAL PROPERTY

We insure for direct physical loss to the property described in Coverage C caused by a peril listed below unless the loss is excluded in Section I—Exclusions.

1. **Fire or lightning.**

2. **Windstorm or hail.**

    This peril does not include loss to the property contained in a building caused by rain, snow, sleet, sand or dust unless the direct force of wind or hail damages the building causing an opening in a roof or wall and the rain, snow, sleet, sand or dust enters through this opening.

    This peril includes loss to watercraft and their trailers, furnishings, equipment, and outboard motors, only while inside a fully enclosed building.

3. **Explosion.**

4. **Riot or civil commotion.**

5. **Aircraft,** including self-propelled missiles and spacecraft.

6. **Vehicles.**

7. **Smoke,** meaning sudden and accidental damage from smoke.

    This peril does not include loss caused by smoke from agricultural smudging or industrial operations.

8. **Vandalism or malicious mischief.**

9. **Theft,** including attempted theft and loss of property from a known place when it is likely that the property has been stolen.

    This peril does not include loss caused by theft:

    a. committed by an **insured;**

    b. in or to a dwelling under construction, or of materials and supplies for use in the construction until the dwelling is finished and occupied; or

    c. from that part of a **residence premises** rented by an **insured** to other than an **insured.**

    This peril does not include loss caused by theft that occurs off the **residence premises** of:

    a. property while at any other residence owned by, rented to, or occupied by an **insured,** except while an **insured** is temporarily living there. Property of a student who is an **insured** is covered while at a residence away from home if the student has been there at any time during the 45 days immediately before the loss;

    b. watercraft, including their furnishings, equipment and outboard motors; or

    c. trailers and campers.

10. **Falling objects.**

    This peril does not include loss to property contained in a building unless the roof or an outside wall of the building is first damaged by a falling object. Damage to the falling object itself is not included.

11. **Weight of ice, snow or sleet** which causes damage to property contained in a building.

12. **Accidental discharge or overflow of water or steam** from within a plumbing, heating, air conditioning or automatic fire protective sprinkler system or from within a household appliance.

    This peril does not include loss:

    a. to the system or appliance from which the water or steam escaped;

    b. caused by or resulting from freezing except as provided in the peril of freezing below; or

    c. on the **residence premises** caused by accidental discharge or overflow which occurs off the **residence premises.**

13. **Sudden and accidental tearing apart, cracking, burning or bulging** of a steam or hot water heating system, an air conditioning or automatic fire protective sprinkler system, or an appliance for heating water.

    We do not cover loss caused by or resulting from freezing under this peril.

14. **Freezing** of a plumbing, heating, air conditioning or automatic fire protective sprinkler system or of a household appliance.

    This peril does not include loss on the **residence premises** while the dwelling is unoccupied, unless you have used reasonable care to:

    a. maintain heat in the building; or

    b. shut off the water supply and drain the system and appliances of water.

15. **Sudden and accidental damage from artificially generated electrical current.**

    This peril does not include loss to a tube, transistor or similar electronic component.

16. **Damage by glass or safety glazing material** which is part of a building, storm door or storm window.

    This peril does not include loss on the **residence premises** if the dwelling has been vacant for more than 30 consecutive days immediately before the loss. A dwelling being constructed is not considered vacant.

17. **Volcanic Eruption** other than loss caused by earthquake, land shock waves or tremors.

HO-3 Ed. 4-84

SECTION I—EXCLUSIONS

1. We do not insure for loss caused directly or indirectly by any of the following. Such loss is excluded regardless of any other cause or event contributing concurrently or in any sequence to the loss.

   a. **Ordinance or Law,** meaning enforcement of any ordinance or law regulating the construction, repair, or demolition of a building or other structure, unless specifically provided under this policy.

   b. **Earth Movement,** meaning earthquake including land shock waves or tremors before, during or after a volcanic eruption; landslide; mudflow; earth sinking, rising or shifting; unless direct loss by:

      (1) fire;

      (2) explosion; or

      (3) breakage of glass or safety glazing material which is part of a building, storm door or storm window;

      ensues and then we will pay only for the ensuing loss.

      This exclusion does not apply to loss by theft.

   c. **Water Damage,** meaning:

      (1) flood, surface water, waves, tidal water, overflow of a body of water, or spray from any of these, whether or not driven by wind;

      (2) water which backs up through sewers or drains; or

      (3) water below the surface of the ground, including water which exerts pressure on or seeps or leaks through a building, sidewalk, driveway, foundation, swimming pool or other structure.

      Direct loss by fire, explosion or theft resulting from water damage is covered.

   d. **Power Failure,** meaning the failure of power or other utility service if the failure takes place off the **residence premises.** But, if a Peril Insured Against ensues on the **residence premises,** we will pay only for that ensuing loss.

   e. **Neglect,** meaning neglect of the **insured** to use all reasonable means to save and preserve property at and after the time of a loss.

   f. **War,** including undeclared war, civil war, insurrection, rebellion, revolution, warlike act by a military force or military personnel, destruction or seizure or use for a military purpose, and including any consequence of any of these. Discharge of a nuclear weapon will be deemed a warlike act even if accidental.

   g. **Nuclear Hazard,** to the extent set forth in the Nuclear Hazard Clause of Section I—Conditions.

   h. **Intentional Loss,** meaning any loss arising out of any act committed:

      (1) by or at the direction of an **insured;** and

      (2) with the intent to cause a loss.

2. We do not insure for loss to property described in Coverages A and B caused by any of the following. However, any ensuing loss to property described in Coverages A and B not excluded or excepted in this policy is covered.

   a. **Weather conditions.** However, this exclusion only applies if weather conditions contribute in any way with a cause or event excluded in paragraph 1. above to produce the loss;

   b. **Acts or decisions,** including the failure to act or decide, of any person, group, organization or governmental body;

   c. **Faulty, inadequate or defective:**

      (1) planning, zoning, development, surveying, siting;

      (2) design, specifications, workmanship, repair, construction, renovation, remodeling, grading, compaction;

      (3) materials used in repair, construction, renovation or remodeling; or

      (4) maintenance;

      of part or all of any property whether on or off the **residence premises.**

SECTION I—CONDITIONS

1. Insurable Interest and Limit of Liability. Even if more than one person has an insurable interest in the property covered, we will not be liable in any one loss:

a. to the **insured** for more than the amount of the **insured's** interest at the time of loss; or

b. for more than the applicable limit of liability.

2. Your Duties After Loss. In case of a loss to covered property, you must see that the following are done:

a. give prompt notice to us or our agent;

b. notify the police in case of loss by theft;

c. notify the credit card or fund transfer card company in case of loss under Credit Card or Fund Transfer Card coverage;

d. (1) protect the property from further damage;

    (2) make reasonable and necessary repairs to protect the property; and

    (3) keep an accurate record of repair expenses;

e. prepare an inventory of damaged personal property showing the quantity, description, actual cash value and amount of loss. Attach all bills, receipts and related documents that justify the figures in the inventory;

f. as often as we reasonably require:

    (1) show the damaged property;

    (2) provide us with records and documents we request and permit us to make copies; and

    (3) submit to questions under oath and sign and swear to them;

g. send to us, within 60 days after our request, your signed, sworn proof of loss which sets forth, to the best of your knowledge and belief:

    (1) the time and cause of loss;

    (2) the interest of the **insured** and all others in the property involved and all liens on the property;

    (3) other insurance which may cover the loss;

(4) changes in title or occupancy of the property during the term of the policy;

(5) specifications of damaged buildings and detailed repair estimates;

(6) the inventory of damaged personal property described in 2e above;

(7) receipts for additional living expenses incurred and records that support the fair rental value loss; and

(8) evidence or affidavit that supports a claim under the Credit Card, Fund Transfer Card, Forgery and Counterfeit Money coverage, stating the amount and cause of loss.

3. Loss Settlement. Covered property losses are settled as follows:

a. (1) Personal property;

    (2) Awnings, carpeting, household appliances, outdoor antennas and outdoor equipment, whether or not attached to buildings; and

    (3) Structures that are not buildings;

at actual cash value at the time of loss but not more than the amount required to repair or replace.

b. Buildings under Coverage A or B at replacement cost without deduction for depreciation, subject to the following:

    (1) If, at the time of loss, the amount of insurance in this policy on the damaged building is 80% or more of the full replacement cost of the building immediately before the loss, we will pay the cost to repair or replace, after application of deductible and without deduction for depreciation, but not more than the least of the following amounts:

        (a) the limit of liability under this policy that applies to the building;

        (b) the replacement cost of that part of the building damaged for like construction and use on the same premises; or

        (c) the necessary amount actually spent to repair or replace the damaged building.

HO-3 Ed. 4-84

(2) If, at the time of loss, the amount of insurance in this policy on the damaged building is less than 80% of the full replacement cost of the building immediately before the loss, we will pay the greater of the following amounts, but not more than the limit of liability under this policy that applies to the building:

    (a) the actual cash value of that part of the building damaged; or

    (b) that proportion of the cost to repair or replace, after application of deductible and without deduction for depreciation, that part of the building damaged, which the total amount of insurance in this policy on the damaged building bears to 80% of the replacement cost of the building.

(3) To determine the amount of insurance required to equal 80% of the full replacement cost of the building immediately before the loss, do not include the value of:

    (a) excavations, foundations, piers or any supports which are below the undersurface of the lowest basement floor;

    (b) those supports in (a) above which are below the surface of the ground inside the foundation walls, if there is no basement; and

    (c) underground flues, pipes, wiring and drains.

(4) We will pay no more than the actual cash value of the damage unless:

    (a) actual repair or replacement is complete; or

    (b) the cost to repair or replace the damage is both:

       (i) less than 5% of the amount of insurance in this policy on the building; and

       (ii) less than $1000.

(5) You may disregard the replacement cost loss settlement provisions and make claim under this policy for loss or damage to buildings on an actual cash value basis. You may then make claim within 180 days after loss for any additional liability on a replacement cost basis.

4. **Loss to a Pair or Set.** In case of loss to a pair or set we may elect to:

    a. repair or replace any part to restore the pair or set to its value before the loss; or

    b. pay the difference between actual cash value of the property before and after the loss.

5. **Glass Replacement.** Loss for damage to glass caused by a Peril Insured Against will be settled on the basis of replacement with safety glazing materials when required by ordinance or law.

6. **Appraisal.** If you and we fail to agree on the amount of loss, either may demand an appraisal of the loss. In this event, each party will choose a competent appraiser within 20 days after receiving a written request from the other. The two appraisers will choose an umpire. If they cannot agree upon an umpire within 15 days, you or we may request that the choice be made by a judge of a court of record in the state where the **residence premises** is located. The appraisers will separately set the amount of loss. If the appraisers submit a written report of an agreement to us, the amount agreed upon will be the amount of loss. If they fail to agree, they will submit their differences to the umpire. A decision agreed to by any two will set the amount of loss.

Each party will:

    a. pay its own appraiser; and

    b. bear the other expenses of the appraisal and umpire equally.

7. **Other Insurance.** If a loss covered by this policy is also covered by other insurance, we will pay only the proportion of the loss that the limit of liability that applies under this policy bears to the total amount of insurance covering the loss.

8. **Suit Against Us.** No action can be brought unless the policy provisions have been complied with and the action is started within one year after the date of loss.

9. **Our Option.** If we give you written notice within 30 days after we receive your signed, sworn proof of loss, we may repair or replace any part of the damaged property with like property.

10. **Loss Payment.** We will adjust all losses with you. We will pay you unless some other person is named in the policy or is legally entitled to receive payment. Loss will be payable 60 days after we receive your proof of loss and:

    a. reach an agreement with you;

    b. there is an entry of a final judgment; or

    c. there is a filing of an appraisal award with us.

11. **Abandonment of Property.** We need not accept any property abandoned by an **insured.**

HO-3 Ed. 4-84   Copyright, Insurance Services Office, Inc., 1984

12. Mortgage Clause.

The word "mortgagee" includes trustee.

If a mortgagee is named in this policy, any loss payable under Coverage A or B will be paid to the mortgagee and you, as interests appear. If more than one mortgagee is named, the order of payment will be the same as the order of precedence of the mortgages.

If we deny your claim, that denial will not apply to a valid claim of the mortgagee, if the mortgagee:

a. notifies us of any change in ownership, occupancy or substantial change in risk of which the mortgagee is aware;

b. pays any premium due under this policy on demand if you have neglected to pay the premium; and

c. submits a signed, sworn statement of loss within 60 days after receiving notice from us of your failure to do so. Policy conditions relating to Appraisal, Suit Against Us and Loss Payment apply to the mortgagee.

If the policy is cancelled or not renewed by us, the mortgagee will be notified at least 10 days before the date cancellation or nonrenewal takes effect.

If we pay the mortgagee for any loss and deny payment to you:

a. we are subrogated to all the rights of the mortgagee granted under the mortgage on the property; or

b. at our option, we may pay to the mortgagee the whole principal on the mortgage plus any accrued interest. In this event, we will receive a full assignment and transfer of the mortgage and all securities held as collateral to the mortgage debt.

Subrogation will not impair the right of the mortgagee to recover the full amount of the mortgagee's claim.

13. No Benefit to Bailee.
We will not recognize any assignment or grant any coverage that benefits a person or organization holding, storing or moving property for a fee regardless of any other provision of this policy.

14. Nuclear Hazard Clause.

a. "Nuclear Hazard" means any nuclear reaction, radiation, or radioactive contamination, all whether controlled or uncontrolled or however caused, or any consequence of any of these.

b. Loss caused by the nuclear hazard will not be considered loss caused by fire, explosion, or smoke, whether these perils are specifically named in or otherwise included within the Perils Insured Against in Section I.

c. This policy does not apply under Section I to loss caused directly or indirectly by nuclear hazard, except that direct loss by fire resulting from the nuclear hazard is covered.

15. Recovered Property.
If you or we recover any property for which we have made payment under this policy, you or we will notify the other of the recovery. At your option, the property will be returned to or retained by you or it will become our property. If the recovered property is returned to or retained by you, the loss payment will be adjusted based on the amount you received for the recovered property.

16. Volcanic Eruption Period.
One or more volcanic eruptions that occur within a 72-hour period will be considered as one volcanic eruption.

SECTION II—LIABILITY COVERAGES

COVERAGE E — Personal Liability

If a claim is made or a suit is brought against an **insured** for damages because of **bodily injury** or **property damage** caused by an **occurrence** to which this coverage applies, we will:

1. pay up to our limit of liability for the damages for which the **insured** is legally liable; and

2. provide a defense at our expense by counsel of our choice, even if the suit is groundless, false or fraudulent. We may investigate and settle any claim or suit that we decide is appropriate. Our duty to settle or defend ends when the amount we pay for damages resulting from the **occurrence** equals our limit of liability.

COVERAGE F — Medical Payments To Others

We will pay the necessary medical expenses that are incurred or medically ascertained within three years from the date of an accident causing **bodily injury.** Medical expenses means reasonable charges for medical, surgical, x-ray, dental, ambulance, hospital, professional nursing, prosthetic devices and funeral services. This coverage does not apply to you or regular residents of your household except **residence employees.** As to others, this coverage applies only:

1. to a person on the **insured location** with the permission of an **insured;** or

HO-3 Ed. 4-84

2. to a person off the **insured location,** if the **bodily injury:**

   a. arises out of a condition on the **insured location** or the ways immediately adjoining;

   b. is caused by the activities of an **insured;**

c. is caused by a **residence employee** in the course of the **residence employee's** employment by an **insured;** or

d. is caused by an animal owned by or in the care of an **insured.**

SECTION II—EXCLUSIONS

1. **Coverage E — Personal Liability and Coverage F — Medical Payments to Others** do not apply to **bodily injury** or **property damage:**

   a. which is expected or intended by the **insured;**

   b. arising out of **business** pursuits of an **insured** or the rental or holding for rental of any part of any premises by an **insured.**

      This exclusion does not apply to:

      (1) activities which are usual to non-**business** pursuits; or

      (2) the rental or holding for rental of an **insured location:**

         (a) on an occasional basis if used only as a residence;

         (b) in part for use only as a residence, unless a single family unit is intended for use by the occupying family to lodge more than two roomers or boarders; or

         (c) in part, as an office, school, studio or private garage;

   c. arising out of the rendering of or failure to render professional services;

   d. arising out of a premises:

      (1) owned by an **insured;**

      (2) rented to an **insured;** or

      (3) rented to others by an **insured;**

      that is not an **insured location;**

   e. arising out of:

      (1) the ownership, maintenance, use, loading or unloading of motor vehicles or all other motorized land conveyances, including trailers, owned or operated by or rented or loaned to an **insured;**

      (2) the entrustment by an **insured** of a motor vehicle or any other motorized land conveyance to any person; or

(3) statutorily imposed vicarious parental liability for the actions of a child or minor using a conveyance excluded in paragraph (1) or (2) above.

This exclusion does not apply to:

(1) a trailer not towed by or carried on a motorized land conveyance.

(2) a motorized land conveyance designed for recreational use off public roads, not subject to motor vehicle registration and:

   (a) not owned by an **insured;** or

   (b) owned by an **insured** and on an **insured location.**

(3) a motorized golf cart when used to play golf on a golf course.

(4) a vehicle or conveyance not subject to motor vehicle registration which is:

   (a) used to service an **insured's** residence;

   (b) designed for assisting the handicapped; or

   (c) in dead storage on an **insured location.**

   f. arising out of:

      (1) the ownership, maintenance, use, loading or unloading of a watercraft described below;

      (2) the entrustment by an **insured** of a watercraft described below to any person; or

      (3) statutorily imposed vicarious parental liability for the actions of a child or minor using a watercraft described below.

      Watercraft:

      (1) with inboard or inboard-outdrive motor power owned by an **insured;**

      (2) with inboard or inboard-outdrive motor power of more than 50 horsepower rented to an **insured;**

(3) that is a sailing vessel, with or without auxiliary power, 26 feet or more in length owned by or rented to an **insured**; or

(4) powered by one or more outboard motors with more than 25 total horsepower if the outboard motor is owned by an **insured.** But, outboard motors of more than 25 total horsepower are covered for the policy period if:

(a) you acquire them prior to the policy period and:

(i) you declare them at policy inception; or

(ii) your intention to insure is reported to us in writing within 45 days after you acquire the outboard motors.

(b) you acquire them during the policy period.

This exclusion does not apply while the watercraft is stored.

g. arising out of:

(1) the ownership, maintenance, use, loading or unloading of an aircraft;

(2) the entrustment by an **insured** of an aircraft to any person; or

(3) statutorily imposed vicarious parental liability for the actions of a child or minor using an aircraft.

An aircraft means any contrivance used or designed for flight, except model or hobby aircraft not used or designed to carry people or cargo.

h. caused directly or indirectly by war, including undeclared war, civil war, insurrection, rebellion, revolution, warlike act by a military force or military personnel, destruction or seizure or use for a military purpose, and including any consequence of any of these. Discharge of a nuclear weapon will be deemed a warlike act even if accidental.

Exclusions d., e., f., and g. do not apply to **bodily injury** to a **residence employee** arising out of and in the course of the **residence employee's** employment by an **insured.**

2. **Coverage E — Personal Liability,** does not apply to:

a. liability:

(1) for your share of any loss assessment charged against all members of an association, corporation or community of property owners;

(2) under any contract or agreement. However, this exclusion does not apply to written contracts:

(a) that directly relate to the ownership, maintenance or use of an **insured location;** or

(b) where the liability of others is assumed by the **insured** prior to an **occurrence;**

unless excluded in (1) above or elsewhere in this policy;

b. **property damage** to property owned by the **insured;**

c. **property damage** to property rented to, occupied or used by or in the care of the **insured.** This exclusion does not apply to **property damage** caused by fire, smoke or explosion;

d. **bodily injury** to any person eligible to receive any benefits:

(1) voluntarily provided; or

(2) required to be provided;

by the **insured** under any:

(1) workers' compensation law;

(2) non-occupational disability law; or

(3) occupational disease law;

e. **bodily injury** or **property damage** for which an **insured** under this policy:

(1) is also an insured under a nuclear energy liability policy; or

(2) would be an insured under that policy but for the exhaustion of its limit of liability.

A nuclear energy liability policy is one issued by:

(1) American Nuclear Insurers;

(2) Mutual Atomic Energy Liability Underwriters;

(3) Nuclear Insurance Association of Canada;

or any of their successors; or

f. **bodily injury** to you or an **insured** within the meaning of part a. or b. of "**insured**" as defined.

HO-3 Ed. 4-84

3. **Coverage F—Medical Payments to Others,** does not apply to **bodily injury:**

   a. to a **residence employee** if the **bodily injury:**

      (1) occurs off the **insured location;** and

      (2) does not arise out of or in the course of the **residence employee's** employment by an **insured;**

   b. to any person eligible to receive benefits:

      (1) voluntarily provided; or

      (2) required to be provided;

      under any:

      (1) workers' compensation law;

      (2) non-occupational disability law; or

      (3) occupational disease law;

   c. from any:

      (1) nuclear reaction;

      (2) nuclear radiation; or

      (3) radioactive contamination;

      all whether controlled or uncontrolled or however caused; or

      (4) any consequence of any of these.

   d. to any person, other than a **residence employee** of an **insured,** regularly residing on any part of the **insured location.**

SECTION II—ADDITIONAL COVERAGES

We cover the following in addition to the limits of liability:

1. **Claim Expenses.** We pay:

   a. expenses we incur and costs taxed against an **insured** in any suit we defend;

   b. premiums on bonds required in a suit we defend, but not for bond amounts more than the limit of liability for Coverage E. We need not apply for or furnish any bond;

   c. reasonable expenses incurred by an **insured** at our request, including actual loss of earnings (but not loss of other income) up to $50 per day, for assisting us in the investigation or defense of a claim or suit;

   d. interest on the entire judgment which accrues after entry of the judgment and before we pay or tender, or deposit in court that part of the judgment which does not exceed the limit of liability that applies;

   e. prejudgment interest awarded against the **insured** on that part of the judgment we pay. If we make an offer to pay the applicable limit of liability, we will not pay any prejudgment interest based on that period of time after the offer.

2. **First Aid Expenses.** We will pay expenses for first aid to others incurred by an **insured** for **bodily injury** covered under this policy. We will not pay for first aid to you or any other **insured.**

3. **Damage to Property of Others.** We will pay, at replacement cost, up to $500 per **occurrence** for **property damage** to property of others caused by an **insured.**

   We will not pay for **property damage:**

   a. to the extent of any amount recoverable under Section I of this policy;

   b. caused intentionally by an **insured** who is 13 years of age or older;

   c. to property owned by an **insured;**

   d. to property owned by or rented to a tenant of an **insured** or a resident in your household; or

   e. arising out of:

      (1) **business** pursuits;

      (2) any act or omission in connection with a premises owned, rented or controlled by an **insured,** other than the **insured location;** or

      (3) the ownership, maintenance, or use of aircraft, watercraft or motor vehicles or all other motorized land conveyances.

      This exclusion does not apply to a motorized land conveyance designed for recreational use off public roads, not subject to motor vehicle registration and not owned by an **insured.**

4. **Loss Assessment.** We will pay up to $1000 for your share of any loss assessment charged during the policy period against you by a corporation or association of property owners, when the assessment is made as a result of:

   a. each **occurrence** to which Section II of this policy would apply;

b. liability for each act of a director, officer or trustee in the capacity as a director, officer or trustee, provided:

    (1) the director, officer or trustee is elected by the members of a corporation or association of property owners; and

    (2) the director, officer or trustee serves without deriving any income from the exercise of duties which are solely on behalf of a corporation or association of property owners.

This coverage applies only to loss assessments charged against you as owner or tenant of the **residence premises.**

We do not cover loss assessments charged against you or a corporation or association of property owners by any governmental body.

Section II — Coverage E — Personal Liability Exclusion 2.a.(1) does not apply to this coverage.

SECTION II—CONDITIONS

1. **Limit of Liability.** Our total liability under Coverage E for all damages resulting from any one **occurrence** will not be more than the limit of liability for Coverage E as shown in the Declarations. This limit is the same regardless of the number of **insureds,** claims made or persons injured.

    Our total liability under Coverage F for all medical expense payable for **bodily injury** to one person as the result of one accident will not be more than the limit of liability for Coverage F as shown in the Declarations.

2. **Severability of Insurance.** This insurance applies separately to each **insured.** This condition will not increase our limit of liability for any one **occurrence.**

3. **Duties After Loss.** In case of an accident or **occurrence,** the **insured** will perform the following duties that apply. You will help us by seeing that these duties are performed:

    a. give written notice to us or our agent as soon as is practical, which sets forth:

        (1) the identity of the policy and **insured;**

        (2) reasonably available information on the time, place and circumstances of the accident or **occurrence;** and

        (3) names and addresses of any claimants and witnesses;

    b. promptly forward to us every notice, demand, summons or other process relating to the accident or **occurrence;**

    c. at our request, help us:

        (1) to make settlement;

        (2) to enforce any right of contribution or indemnity against any person or organization who may be liable to an **insured;**

        (3) with the conduct of suits and attend hearings and trials;

        (4) to secure and give evidence and obtain the attendance of witnesses;

    d. under the coverage — Damage to Property of Others — submit to us within 60 days after the loss, a sworn statement of loss and show the damaged property, if in the **insured's** control;

    e. the **insured** will not, except at the **insured's** own cost, voluntarily make payment, assume obligation or incur expense other than for first aid to others at the time of the **bodily injury.**

4. **Duties of an Injured Person—Coverage F—Medical Payments to Others.**

    The injured person or someone acting for the injured person will:

    a. give us written proof of claim, under oath if required, as soon as is practical; and

    b. authorize us to obtain copies of medical reports and records.

    The injured person will submit to a physical exam by a doctor of our choice when and as often as we reasonably require.

5. **Payment of Claim—Coverage F—Medical Payments to Others.** Payment under this coverage is not an admission of liability by an **insured** or us.

6. **Suit Against Us.** No action can be brought against us unless there has been compliance with the policy provisions.

    No one will have the right to join us as a party to any action against an **insured.** Also, no action with respect to Coverage E can be brought against us until the obligation of the **insured** has been determined by final judgment or agreement signed by us.

7. **Bankruptcy of an Insured.** Bankruptcy or insolvency of an **insured** will not relieve us of our obligations under this policy.

8. **Other Insurance — Coverage E — Personal Liability.** This insurance is excess over other valid and collectible insurance except insurance written specifically to cover as excess over the limits of liability that apply in this policy.

HO-3 Ed. 4-84

SECTIONS I AND II—CONDITIONS

1. **Policy Period.** This policy applies only to loss in Section I or **bodily injury** or **property damage** in Section II, which occurs during the policy period.

2. **Concealment or Fraud.** We do not provide coverage for an **insured** who has:

   a. intentionally concealed or misrepresented any material fact or circumstance; or

   b. made false statements or engaged in fraudulent conduct;

   relating to this insurance.

3. **Liberalization Clause.** If we adopt a revision which would broaden the coverage under this policy without additional premium within 60 days prior to or during the policy period, the broadened coverage will immediately apply to this policy.

4. **Waiver or Change of Policy Provisions.**

   A waiver or change of a provision of this policy must be in writing by us to be valid. Our request for an appraisal or examination will not waive any of our rights.

5. **Cancellation.**

   a. You may cancel this policy at any time by returning it to us or by letting us know in writing of the date cancellation is to take effect.

   b. We may cancel this policy only for the reasons stated below by letting you know in writing of the date cancellation takes effect. This cancellation notice may be delivered to you, or mailed to you at your mailing address shown in the Declarations.

   Proof of mailing will be sufficient proof of notice.

   (1) When you have not paid the premium, we may cancel at any time by letting you know at least 10 days before the date cancellation takes effect.

   (2) When this policy has been in effect for less than 60 days and is not a renewal with us, we may cancel for any reason by letting you know at least 10 days before the date cancellation takes effect.

   (3) When this policy has been in effect for 60 days or more, or at any time if it is a renewal with us, we may cancel:

      (a) if there has been a material misrepresentation of fact which if known to us would have caused us not to issue the policy; or

      (b) if the risk has changed substantially since the policy was issued.

   This can be done by letting you know at least 30 days before the date cancellation takes effect.

   (4) When this policy is written for a period of more than one year, we may cancel for any reason at anniversary by letting you know at least 30 days before the date cancellation takes effect.

   c. When this policy is cancelled, the premium for the period from the date of cancellation to the expiration date will be refunded pro rata.

   d. If the return premium is not refunded with the notice of cancellation or when this policy is returned to us, we will refund it within a reasonable time after the date cancellation takes effect.

6. **Non-Renewal.** We may elect not to renew this policy. We may do so by delivering to you, or mailing to you at your mailing address shown in the Declarations, written notice at least 30 days before the expiration date of this policy. Proof of mailing will be sufficient proof of notice.

7. **Assignment.** Assignment of this policy will not be valid unless we give our written consent.

8. **Subrogation.** An **insured** may waive in writing before a loss all rights of recovery against any person. If not waived, we may require an assignment of rights of recovery for a loss to the extent that payment is made by us.

   If an assignment is sought, an **insured** must sign and deliver all related papers and cooperate with us.

   Subrogation does not apply under Section II to Medical Payments to Others or Damage to Property of Others.

9. **Death.** If any person named in the Declarations or the spouse, if a resident of the same household, dies:

   a. we insure the legal representative of the deceased but only with respect to the premises and property of the deceased covered under the policy at the time of death;

   b. **insured** includes:

      (1) any member of your household who is an **insured** at the time of your death, but only while a resident of the **residence premises;** and

      (2) with respect to your property, the person having proper temporary custody of the property until appointment and qualification of a legal representative.

HO-3 Ed. 4-84

APPENDIX I
BIBLIOGRAPHY

PART 1 NATURE OF RISK AND RISK MANAGEMENT

Allen, T.C., and R.M. Duvall. *A Theoretical and Practical Approach to Risk Management.* New York: The American Society of Insurance Management, Inc., 1971.

Arrow, K.J. *Essays in the Theory of Risk Bearing.* Chicago: Markham Publishing Company, Inc., 1971.

Athearn, James L., and S. Travis Pritchett, *Risk and Insurance.* St. Paul: West Publishing Co., 1984.

Baglini, Norman A. *Risk Management in International Corporation.* New York: Risk Studies Foundation, 1976.

Barrett, Francis D. *Professional's Guide to Insurance and Risk Management.* Sausalito, Cal.: Compton and Rowe, Pubs., 1978.

Beard, Robert E., T. Pentikainen, and E. Pesonen. *Risk Theory: The Stochastic Basis of Insurance,* 3d ed. New York: Chapman and Hall, 1984.

Binford, Charles, Cecil Fleming, and Z.A. Prust. *Loss Control in the OSHA Era.* New York: McGraw-Hill Book Company, 1975.

Borch, Karl Henrik. *The Economics of Uncertainty.* Princeton: Princeton University Press, 1968.

Cox, Donald F. (ed.). *Risk Taking and Information Handling in Consumer Behavior.* Cambridge, Mass.: Harvard University Press, 1967.

Daenzer, Bernard J. *Fact-Finding Questionnaire for Risk Managers.* New York: Risk and Insurance Management Society, Inc., 1978.

Edelstein, Robert H. *The Theory of Insurance Reconsidered for Urban Analysis: An Expected Utility Approach.* Philadelphia: The Wharton School of Finance and Commerce, University of Pennsylvania, 1975.

Faulkner, E.J. (ed.). *Man's Quest for Security.* Freeport, N.Y.: Books for Libraries, Inc., 1966.

Goshay, Robert C. *Corporate Self-Insurance and Risk Retention Plans.* Homewood, Ill.: Richard D. Irwin, Inc., 1964.

Greene, Mark R. *A Primer on Quantitative Methods.* New York: Risk and Insurance Management Society, Inc., 1977.

——. *Risk Aversion, Insurance, and the Future.* Bloomington: Indiana Press, 1971.

——, for the Small Business Administration. *Risk and Insurance Management,* 2d ed. SBMS No. 30. Washington: U.S. Government Printing Office, 1970.

Greene, Mark R., and Oscar N. Serbein. *Risk Management: Test and Cases,* 2d ed. Reston, Va.: Reston Publishing Company, 1983.

Hammes, Carol J., Peter R. Kensicki, E. J. Leverett, and Ronald T. Anderson. *Agency Operation and Sales Management,* 2d ed., Vols. I and II. Malvern, Pa.: Insurance Institute of America, 1986.

Hammond, J.D. *Essays in the Theory of Risk and Insurance.* Glenview, Ill.: Scott, Foresman and Company, 1968.

Hardy, C.O. *Readings in Risk and Risk Bearing.* Chicago: University of Chicago Press, 1924.

_____. *Risk and Risk Bearing.* Chicago: University of Chicago Press, 1931.

Head, George L. *The Risk Management Process.* New York: Risk and Insurance Management Society, Inc., 1984.

Head, George L., and Stephen Horn II. *Essentials of the Risk Management Process,* Vols. I and II. Malvern, Pa.: Insurance Institute of America, 1985.

Hoffman, Fredrick Ludwig. *Insurance Science and Economics.* Chicago: The Spectator Co., 1911.

Long, John D., and Everett D. Randall (eds.). *Issues in Insurance,* 3d. ed. Vols. I and II. Malvern, Pa.: American Institute for Property and Liability Underwriters, 1984.

Lalley, Edward P. *Corporate Uncertainty & Risk Management.* New York: Risk Management Society Publishing Co., 1982.

MacCrimmon, Kenneth R., and Donald A. Wehrung. *Taking Risks.* New York: The Free Press, 1986.

MacDonald, Donald L. *Corporate Risk Control.* New York: The Ronald Press Company, 1966.

Mehr, Robert I., and Robert A. Hedges. *Risk Management—Concepts and Applications.* Homewood, Ill.: Richard D. Irwin, Inc., 1974.

Municipal Risk Management: A Risk Management and Insurance Handbook. Cincinnati: Society of Chartered Property and Casualty Underwriters, 1971.

Petersen, Daniel C. *Techniques of Safety Management.* New York: McGraw-Hill Book Company, 1971.

Pfeffer, Irving. *Insurance and Economic Theory.* Homewood, Ill.: Richard D. Irwin, Inc., 1956.

Risk Analysis Questionnaire. New York: American Management Assn., Inc.

Snider, H.W. (ed.). *Risk Management.* Homewood, Ill.: Richard D. Irwin, Inc., 1964.

Vaughan, Emmett J. *Fundamentals of Risk and Insurance,* 4th ed. New York: John Wiley & Sons, Inc., 1985.

Watson, Donald, and D. Homan for Small Business Administration. *Insurance and Risk Management for Small Business.* Washington: U.S. Government Printing Office, 1963.

Werbel, B.G. *General Insurance Guide.* New York: Werbel Publishing Company, annually, and supplements.

Willett, A.H. *Economic Theory of Risk and Insurance.* Homewood, Ill.: Richard D. Irwin, Inc., 1951.

Williams, C. Arthur, Jr., and Richard M. Heins. *Risk Management and Insurance,* 5th ed. New York: McGraw-Hill Book Company, 1985.

PART 2
THE INSURANCE INSTITUTION

Athearn, James L., and S. Travis Pritchett. *Risk and Insurance.* St. Paul: West Publishing Company, 1984.

Bachman, James E. *Capitalization Requirements for Multiple-Line Property/Liability Companies.* Philadelphia: S.S. Huebner Foundation for Insurance Education, 1978.

Best, A.M. *Fire and Casualty Aggregates and Averages.* New York: A.M. Best Company, annually.

Bickelhaupt, David L. *General Insurance,* 11th ed. Homewood, Ill.: Richard D. Irwin, Inc., 1983.

Black, Kenneth, Jr., and Harold Skipper, Jr. *Life Insurance,* 11th ed. Englewood Cliffs, N.J.: Prentice-Hall, 1987.

Casey, Barbara, Jacques Peazier, and Carl Spetzler. *The Role of Risk Classifications in Property and Casualty Insurance: A Study of the Risk Assessment Process,* 3 vols. Menlo Park, Cal.: Stanford Research Institute, 1976.

Cummins, J. David, and Steven Weisbart. *The Impact of Consumer Services on Independent Insurance Agency Performance.* Glenmont, N.Y.: IMA Education and Research Foundation, 1977.

Denenberg, H.S., *et al. Risk and Insurance*, 2d ed. Englewood Cliffs, N.J.: Prentice-Hall, Inc., 1974.

Factory Mutaul Engineering Division. *Handbook of Industrial Loss Prevention.* New York: McGraw-Hill Book Company, Inc., 1959.

Gart, Alan, and David J. Nye. *Insurance Company Finance.* Malvern, Pa.: Insurance Institute of America, 1986.

Goshay, Robert C. *Corporate Self-Insurance and Risk Retention Plans.* Homewood, Ill.: Richard D. Irwin, Inc., 1964.

Greene, Mark R., and Paul Swadener. *Insurance Insights.* Cincinnati: South-Western Publishing Co., 1974.

Gregg, Davis W., and Vane B. Lucas (eds.). *Life and Health Insurance Handbook,* 3d ed. Homewood, Ill.: Dow Jones-Irwin, 1973.

Head, George L. *Insurance to Value.* Homewood, Ill.: Richard D. Irwin, Inc., 1971.

Heinrich, H.W. *Industrial Accident Prevention,* 4th ed. New York: McGraw-Hill Book Company, 1959.

Kenney, Roger. *Fundamentals of Fire and Casualty Strength.* Dedham, Mass.: Roger Kenney, 1957.

Long, John D. *Ethics, Morality, and Insurance.* Bloomington: Indiana University Press, 1971.

Loss and Expense Ratios—Insurance Expense Exhibits. Albany: New York Insurance Department, annually.

Marshall, Robert A. *Life Insurance Company Mergers and Consolidations.* Homewood, Ill.: Richard D. Irwin, Inc., 1972.

Mehr Robert I., *Fundamentals of Insurance.* Homewood, Ill.: Richard D. Irwin, Inc., 1983.

Mehr, Robert I., and Seev Neumann. *Inflation, Technology and Growth: Possible Long Range Implications for Insurance.* Bloomington: Division of Research, Graduate School of Business, Indiana University, 1972.

Michelbacher, G.F., and Nestor Roos. *Multiple-Line Insurers: Their Nature and Operation,* 2d ed. New York: McGraw-Hill Book Company, 1970.

Reed, Prentiss B. *Adjustment of Property Losses,* 2d ed. New York: McGraw-Hill Book Company, 1953.

Strain, Robert (ed.). *Property-Liability Insurance Accounting.* Strain Publishing, Inc., 1986.

Troxel, Terrie, and Cormick L. Breslin. *Property-Liability Accounting and Finance,* 2d ed. Malvern, Pa.: Insurance Institute of America, 1983

U.S. Department of Justice. *The Pricing and Marketing of Insurance: A Report of the U.S. Department of Justice to the Task Group on Antitrust Immunities.* Washington: U.S. Government Printing Office, 1977.

U.S. Senate, Committee on Banking, Housing, and Urban Affairs. *Problems of Property Insurance in Urban America.* Washington: U.S. Government Printing Office, 1978.

Webb, Bernard L., J.J. Launie, Willis P. Rokes, and Norman A. Baglini. *Insurance Company Operations,* 3d ed. Malvern, Pa.: American Institute for Property and Liability Underwriters, 1984.

Weese, Samuel H. *Nonadmitted Insurance in the United States.* Homewood, Ill.: Richard D. Irwin, Inc., 1971.

PART 3
THE LEGAL ENVIRONMENT

Freedman, Warren. *Richards on the Law of Insurance.* New York: Baker Voorhis and Company, 1952.

Greider, Janice E., and William T. Beadles. *Law and the Life Insurance Contract,* 5th ed. Homewood, Ill.: Richard D. Irwin, Inc., 1984.

Head, George L. *Insurance to Value.* Homewood, Ill.: Richard D. Irwin, Inc., 1971.

The Hold Harmless Agreement. Cincinnati: The National Underwriter Co., 1968.

Horn, Harold M., and D. Bruce Mansfield. *The Life Insurance Contract.* New York: Life Office Management Association, 1948.

Horn, Ronald C. *Subrogation in Insurance Theory and Practice.* Homewood, Ill.: Richard D. Irwin, Inc., 1964.

Keeton, Robert E. *Insurance Law: Basic Text.* St. Paul: West Publishing Company, 1971.

Lorimer, James J., Harry F. Perlet, Frederick G. Kempin, Jr., and Frederick R. Hodosh. *The Legal Environment of Insurance*, 2d ed., Vols. I and II. Malvern, Pa.: Insurance Institute of America, 1981.

McGill, Dan M. *Legal Aspects of Life Insurance*. Homewood, Ill.: Richard D. Irwin, Inc., 1959.

Patterson, Edwin W. *Essentials of Insurance Law*. New York: McGraw-Hill Book Company, 1957.

Rejda, George E. *Principles of Insurance*, 2d ed. Glenview, Ill.: Scott, Foresman, and Company, 1986.

Schwartzschild, Stuart. *Rights of Creditors in Life Insurance Policies*. Homewood, Ill.: Richard D. Irwin, Inc., 1963.

Vance, William R. *Handbook on the Law of Insurance*, 3d ed., edited by Buist M. Anderson. St. Paul: West Publishing Company, 1951.

PART 4 PERSONAL RISK MANAGEMENT: LIFE, HEALTH, AND INCOME

Athearn, James L., and S. Travis Pritchett. *Risk and Insurance*. St. Paul: West Publishing Company, 1984.

Belth, Joseph M. *Life Insurance: A Consumer's Handbook*. Bloomington: Indiana University Press, 1973.

Black, Kenneth. *Group Annuities*. Philadelphia: University of Pennsylvania Press, 1955.

Black, Kenneth, Jr., and Harold D. Skipper, Jr. *Life Insurance*, 11th ed. Englewood Cliffs, NJ.: Prentice-Hall, 1987.

Braverman, Jordan. *Crisis in Health Care*. Washington: Acropolis Books, 1978.

Consumer's Union, *The Consumer Union Report on Life Insurance: A Guide to Planning the Protection You Need*, 4th ed. Mt. Vernon, New York, 1980.

Cummins, J. David. *Development of Life Insurance Surrender Values in the United States*, Monograph No. 2. Philadelphia: S.S. Huebner Foundation for Insurance Education, 1973.

Eilers, Robert D., and Robert M. Crowe (eds.). *Group Insurance Handbook*. Homewood, Ill.: Dow Jones-Irwin, Inc., 1965.

Eilers, Robert D., and Sue S. Moyerman (eds.). *National Health Insurance*. Homewood, Ill.: Richard D. Irwin, Inc., 1971.

Employee Benefits 1981. Washington: Chamber of Commerce of the United States, 1981.

Flitcraft Compend. Morristown: A.M. Best Co., annually.

Fuchs, Victor. *Essays in the Economics of Health and Medical Care*. New York: National Bureau of Economic Research, 1972.

Greene, Mark R. *Preretirement Counseling, Retirement Adjustment, and the Older Employee*. Eugene: University of Oregon, 1969.

——. *The Role of Employee Benefit Structures in Manufacturing Industry*. Eugene: University of Oregon, 1964.

Greene, Mark R., Charles Pyron, U. Vincent Manion, and Howard Winklevoss. *Early Retirement: A Survey of Company Policies and Retirees' Experiences*. Eugene: University of Oregon, 1969.

Greenough, William C., and F.P. King. *Pension Plans and Public Policy*. New York: Columbia University Press, 1976.

Gregg, Davis W., and Vane B. Lucas (eds.). *Life and Health Insurance Handbook*, 3d ed. Homewood, Ill.: Dow Jones-Irwin, Inc., 1973.

Life Insurance Fact Book. New York: Institute of Life Insurance, annually.

Longest, Beaufort B., Jr. *Management Practices for the Health Professional*, 3d ed. Reston, Va.: Reston Publishing Co., Inc., 1984.

Marshall, Robert A. *Life Insurance Company Mergers and Consolidations*. Homewood, Ill.: Richard D. Irwin, Inc., 1972.

McGill, Dan M. *Fulfilling Pension Expectations*. Homewood, Ill.: Richard D. Irwin, Inc., 1962.

——. *Fundamentals of Private Pensions*, 4th ed. Homewood, Ill.: Richard D. Irwin, Inc., 1979.

———. *Guaranty Fund for Private Pension Obligations.* Homewood, Ill.: Richard D. Irwin, Inc., 1970.

———. *Life Insurance,* rev. ed. Homewood, Ill.: Richard D. Irwin, Inc., 1967.

———. (ed.). *Social Security and Private Pension Plans: Competitive or Complementary?* Homewood, Ill.: Richard D. Irwin, Inc., 1977.

Mehr, Robert I., and Sandra G. Gustavson. *Life Insurance: Theory and Practice,* 3d ed. Plano, Tex.: Business Publications, Inc., 1984.

Myers, Robert J. *Indexation of Pensions and Other Benefits.* Homewood, Ill.: Richard D. Irwin, Inc., 1978.

———. *Social Security,* 2d ed. Homewood, Ill.: Richard D. Irwin, Inc., 1981.

Reed, Louis S., Evelyn S. Myers, and Patricia L. Scheidemandel. *Health Insurance and Psychiatric Care: Utilization and Cost.* Washington: The American Psychiatric Association, 1972.

Rejda, George E. *Social Insurance and Economic Security,* 2d ed. Englewood Cliffs, N.J.: Prentice-Hall, Inc., 1984.

Report on Life Insurance: A Guide to Planning and Buying the Protection You Need, rev. ed. Mt. Vernon, N.Y.: The Consumer's Union, 1977.

Rosenbloom, Jerry S. *Handbook of Employee Benefits.* Homewood, Ill.: Dow Jones-Irwin, 1984.

Rosenbloom, Jerry S., and G. Victor Hallman. *Employee Benefit Planning,* 2d ed. Homewood, Ill.: Richard D. Irwin, Inc., 1986.

Rotman Zelizer, Vivina A. *Morals and Markets—The Development of Life Insurance in the United States.* Irvington, N.Y.: Columbia University Press, 1979.

Social Security Administration. *Social Security Programs Throughout the World, 1977.* Research Report No. 44. Washington: U.S. Government Printing Office, 1977.

Source Book of Health Insurance Data. New York: Health Insurance Institute, annually.

Stephenson, Gilbert T., and Norman A. Wiggins. *Estates and Trusts,* 5th ed. New York: Appleton-Century-Crofts, 1973.

Stone, Gary K., and Jerry S. Rosenbloom (eds.). *Personal and Business Estate Planning—Selected Readings.* East Lansing, Mich.: MSU Graduate School of Business Administration, 1976.

1975 Study of Industrial Retirement Plans, Including Analysis of Complete Programs Recently Adopted or Revised. New York: Bankers Trust Company, 1975.

White, E.H. (ed.). *Fundamentals of Federal Income Estate and Gift Taxes.* Indianapolis: The Research and Review Service of America, Inc. (most recent edition).

White, Edwin H., and Herbert Chasman. *Business Insurance,* 5th ed. Englewood Cliffs, N.J.: Prentice-Hall, Inc., 1980.

Wilhaus, C. Arthur, Jr., John G. Turnbull, Jr., and Earl Cheit. *Economic and Social Security,* 5th ed. New York: The Ronald Press Company, 1982.

Winkelvoss, Howard E. *Pension Mathematics.* Homewood, Ill.: Richard D. Irwin, Inc., 1977.

Wood, Glenn L., Claude C. Lilly, Donald S. Malecki, and Jerry S. Rosenbloom. *Personal Risk Management and Insurance,* 3d ed., Vol. 1. Malvern, Pa.: Insurance Institute of America, 1984.

PART 5 PERSONAL RISK MANAGEMENT—PROPERTY LIABILITY

Analysis of Automobile No-Fault Statutes. New York: General Adjustment Bureau, 1979.

Bickelhaupt, David L. *General Insurance,* 11th ed., Homewood, Ill.: Richard D. Irwin, Inc., 1983.

Fire, Casualty, and Surety Bulletins, 3 vols. Cincinnati: The National Underwriter Company.

Gordis, Philip. *Property and Casualty Insurance.* Indianapolis: Rough Notes Co., Inc., annually.

House of Representatives, Hearings before the Subcommittee on Commerce and Finance of the Committee on Interstate and Foreign Commerce. *No-Fault Motor Vehicle In-*

surance. Washington: U.S. Government Printing Office, 1976.

Keeton, Robert E., and Jeffrey O'Connell. *Basic Protection for the Traffic Victim.* Boston: Little, Brown and Co., 1965.

Lee, J. Finley. *Servicing the Shared Automobile Insurance Market.* New York: National Industry Committee on Automobile Insurance Plans, Mutual Insurance Rating Bureau, 1977.

Mehr, Robert I. *Fundamentals of Insurance.* Homewood, Ill.: Richard D. Irwin, Inc., 1983.

O'Connell, Jeffrey. *The Injury Industry and the Remedy of No-Fault Insurance.* Urbana, Ill.: University of Illinois Press, 1971.

O'Connell, Jeffrey, and Rita James Simon. *Payment for Pain and Suffering: Who Wants What, When and Why?* Santa Monica: Insurors Press, Inc., 1972.

Riegel, Robert, J.S. Miller, and C. Arthur Williams, Jr. *Insurance Principles and Practices: Property and Liability,* 6th ed. Englewood Cliffs, N.J.: Prentice-Hall, Inc. 1976.

Rokes, Willis Park. *No-Fault Insurance.* Santa Monica: Insurors Press, Inc., 1971.

Shopper's Guide to Pennsylvania Automobile Insurance: Some Key Premium Comparisons for Beginning Your Search for the Best Automobile Insurance Bargain, rev. ed. Harrisburg, Pa.: Pennsylvania Insurance Department, 1972.

Tuan, Kalin (ed.). *Modern Insurance Theory and Education.* Orange, N.J.: Varsity Press, 1972.

Vaughan, Emmett J. *Fundamentals of Risk and Insurance,* 4th ed. New York: John Wiley & Sons, Inc., 1985.

Williams, C. Arthur, Jr., George L. Head, Ronald C. Horn, and G. William Glendenning. *Principles of Risk Management and Insurance,* Vols. I and II. Malvern, Pa.: American Institute for Property and Liability Underwriters, 1981.

Wood, Glenn L., Claude C. Lilly, Donald S. Malecki, and Jerry S. Rosenbloom. *Personal Risk Management and Insurance,* Vols. I and II, 3d ed. Malvern, Pa.: American Insti-

tute for Property and Liability Underwriters, 1984.

PART 6 BUSINESS RISK MANAGEMENT

Bickelhaupt, David L. *General Insurance,* 11th ed. Homewood, Ill.: Richard D. Irwin, Inc., 1983.

Building Codes, Their Scope and Aims. New York: National Board of Fire Underwriters.

Construction Default: The Contractor's Bond. New York: Practicing Law Institute, 1976.

Fire, Casualty, and Surety Bulletins, 3 vols. Cincinnati: The National Underwriter Company.

Gordis, Philip. *Property and Casualty Insurance.* Indianapolis: Rough Notes Co., Inc., annually.

Hollingsworth, E.P., and J.J. Launie. *Commercial Property and Multiple Lines Underwriting.* 2d ed. Malvern, Pa.: Insurance Institute of America, 1984.

Huebner, S.S., Kenneth Black, Jr., and Robert S. Cline. *Property and Liability Insurance.* 3d ed. Englewood Cliffs, N.J.: Prentice-Hall, Inc., 1982.

Knepper, William E. *Liability of Corporate Officers and Directors.* Indianapolis: The Allen Smith Co., Pubs., (1985 Supplement).

Malecki, Donald S., James H. Donaldson, and Ronald C. Horn. *Commercial Liability Risk Management and Insurance,* Vols. I and II, 2d ed. Malvern, Pa.: American Institute for Property and Liability Underwriters, 1986.

Mehr, Robert I. *Fundamentals of Insurance.* Homewood, Ill.: Richard D. Irwin, Inc., 1983.

Millus, Albert J., and Willard J. Gentile. *Workers' Compensation Law and Insurance,* 2d ed. New York: Roberts Publishing Corp., 1980.

Porter, David. *Fundamentals of Bonding,* 7th ed. Indianapolis: Rough Notes Co., Inc., 1983.

Rheingold, Paul D., and Sheila L. Birnbaum. *Product Liability: Law Practices Science,* 2d ed. New York: Practicing Law Institute, 1975.

Riegel, Robert, J.S. Miller, and C. Arthur Williams, Jr. *Insurance Principles and Practices: Property and Liability*, 6th ed. Englewood Cliffs, N.J.: Prentice-Hall, Inc. 1976.

Rodda, William H., James S. Trieschmann, Eric A. Wrening, and Bob A. Hedges. *Commercial Property Risk Management and Insurance,* Vols. I and II. Malvern, Pa.: American Institute for Property and Liability Underwriters, 1983.

Tuan, Kalin (ed.). *Modern Insurance Theory and Education.* Orange, N.J.: Varsity Press, 1972.

Vaughan, Emmett J. *Fundamentals of Risk and Insurance,* 4th ed. New York: John Wiley & Sons, Inc., 1985.

Williams, C. Arthur, Jr., George L. Head, Ronald C. Horn, and G. William Glendenning. *Principles of Risk Management and Insurance,* Vols. I and II. Malvern, Pa.: American Institute for Property and Liability Underwriters, 1981.

Youd, James D. *A Practical Approach to Inland Marine Insurance.* Boston: Standard Publishing Company, 1979.

PART 7 GOVERNMENT AND INSURANCE

Blair, Franklin B. *Interpreting Life Insurance Company Annual Reports.* Bryn Mawr, Pa.: American College of Life Underwriters, 1960.

Center, Charles C., and Richard M. Heins (eds.). *Insurance and Government.* New York: McGraw-Hill Book Company, 1962.

Chamber of Commerce of the U.S. *Analysis of Workers' Compensation Laws,* 1982 ed., annually.

Cooper, Robert W. *Investment Return and Property-Liability Insurance Ratemaking.* Homewood, Ill.: Richard D. Irwin, Inc., 1974.

Greene, Mark R. *Government and Private Insurance.* Des Plaines, Ill.: National Association of Independent Insurers, 1975.

Hensley, Roy J. *Competition, Regulation, and the Public Interest in Non-Life Insurance.*
Berkeley: University of California Press, 1962.

Kimball, Spencer L., and Herbert S. Denenberg. *Insurance, Government, and Social Policy.* Homewood, Ill.: Richard D. Irwin, Inc., 1973.

Kunreuther, Howard. *Disaster Insurance Protection: Public Policy Lessons.* New York: John Wiley & Sons, Inc., 1978.

National Commission on Social Security. *Social Security in America's Future.* Washington, 1981.

Nelson, Daniel. *Unemployment Insurance: The American Experience, 1915–1935.* Madison: University of Wisconsin Press, 1969.

O'Connell, Jeffrey. *The Injury Industry and the Remedy of No-Fault Insurance.* Urbana, Ill.: University Illinois Press, 1971.

Orren, Karen. *Corporate Power and Social Change: The Politics of the Life Insurance Industry.* Baltimore: The Johns Hopkins University Press, 1973.

Pension Facts, 1982. Washington: American Council on Life Insurance, annually.

The Regulation of Mass Marketing in Property and Liability Insurance. Milwaukee: National Association of Insurance Commissioners, 1971.

Skipper, Harold D. *Privacy and the Insurance Industry.* Atlanta: Georgia State University, Publishing Services Division, 1979.

Spiegelman, M. *Significant Mortality and Morbidity Trends in the United States Since 1900.* Bryn Mawr, Pa.: American College of Life Underwriters, 1962.

Stalson, J.O. *Marketing Life Insurance.* Homewood, Ill.: Richard D. Irwin, Inc., 1971.

Williams, C.A. *Price Discrimination in Property and Liability Insurance.* Studies in Economics and Business No. 19. Minneapolis: University of Minnesota Press, 1959.

PART 8 INTERNATIONAL INSURANCE

Bawcutt, P.A. *Captive Insurance Companies— Establishment. Operation and Management.* Homewood, Ill.: Dow Jones-Irwin, 1982.

Bickelhaupt, David L. *International Insurance.* New York: Insurance Information Institute, 1983.

Carter, Robert L., and G. N. Crockford (eds.). *Handbook of Risk Management.* London, England: Kluwer-Harrap Handbooks, 1985.

Crowe, Robert M. (ed.). *Insurance in the World's Economies.* Philadelphia, Pa.: Corporation for the Philadelphia World Insurance Congress, 1982.

Greene, Mark R., and Oscar N. Serbein. *Risk Management: Text and Cases.* Reston, Va.: Reston Publishing Co., Inc., 1983. See, especially, Chapter 18.

Hogue, Michael E., and Douglas G. Olson (eds.). *World Insurance Outlook—Summary Proceedings of the Philadelphia World Insurance Congress.* Philadelphia, Pa: Corporation for the Philadelphia World Insurance Congress, 1982.

INDEX

Note: Page numbers in italics indicate glossary pages; page numbers followed by *n* indicate notes.

A

Accidental death, 282–283
Accidental death and dismemberment insurance (AD&D), 296
Accident-prone person, 13
Accident rates, and age, 420
Accounting
  in insurance companies, 121
  and risk manager, 69–70
Accounts receivable insurance, 501, 518, 551
Accumulation unit, 339*n*
Acquisition costs, 278, 289*n*
Acts of God, 508
Acts or negligence of the shipper, 508
Actual cash value, 176–177, *691*
  of personal property, 396
Actuary(ies), 109, *691*
Additional insureds, 166
Additional interests, 166
Additional-living-expense insurance, 415, *691*
Adhesion, *691*
  contract of, 156–157, 160
Adjustable life policy, 254
Adjusted gross estate, 343, *691*
Adjuster(s)
  independent, 119
  public, 119
Adjustment bureau, 119
Administrative cost ratio, 328, *691*
Admitted insurance, 675–676, *691*
Adverse selection, 13, 100, 174
AFIA, 672–673
Aged. *See* Elderly
Age Discrimination in Employment Act of 1978 (ADEA), 293
Agency agreement, 158
Agency system, 85
Agent. *See* Insurance agent

Aggregate deductible, 596–598
Aggregate limits, 526–527
Agricultural society, and insurance, 25
Aiding in saving human life, 515
AIG, 672–673
Air-conditioning system, coverage, 402
Aircraft, 409
Aircraft damage, coverage, in homeowners' insurance, 399
Airline insurance, 192
Aleatory contract, 32–33, 155–156, *691*
Alien insurer, *691*
All-Industry Rating Bill, 644
All-line insurer, 125, *691*
Allocated benefit plan, 319–320, *691*
All-risk contract, 67, 166, 188, *691*
All-risk crop insurance, 634–635, *691*
American Agency System, 95–99, *691*
  advantages of
    for consumer, 98
    for insurer, 98–99
  definition, 96
  outlook for, 98–99
American Credit Indemnity Company, 551–552
American Foreign Insurance Association. *See* AFIA
American International Group. *See* AIG
American Lloyds, 89, *691*
American Municipal Bond Assurance Corporation, 551
American Society of Insurance Management (ASIM), 45
Annual-premium annuity, 261, *691*
Annual transit floater, 516
Annuitant, 259, *691*

Annuity, 259, 267. *See also specific annuity type*
  amount of, interest table for, 712, 716
  method of purchase, 261
  number of lives insured, 261–262
  period payment starts at, 261
  present value of, interest table for, 712–713, 717
  price of, 260
Annuity rent, *691*
Annuity unit, 339*n*
Anticancellation laws, 654, *691*
Anticoercion laws, 654–655, *691–692*
Antiselection, 13
Appleton Rule, 645, 659*n*
Appraisal, of loss, 51–53, 173
Arithmetic mean, 581–582
Assessable policy, 85, *692*
Assigned-risk plan, *692*
Assignee, 175
Assignment, 170, 175, 176, 283, *692*
Assignor, 175
Assumed risk, 196, 211
Assumption of risk. *See* Risk retention
Assured, 16
Attorney. *See also* Lawyers' professional liability
  liability for negligence, 208
Attorney-in-fact, 87, *692*
Attractive-nuisance doctrine, 203, *692*
Automatic premium-loan clause, 278–279, *692*
Automobile
  liability, 212
    of employers, 210
    of operator, 208–209
    of owner-nonoperator, 209–210